Introduction to Conservation Genetics

The biological diversity of the planet is being rapidly depleted due to the direct and indirect consequences of human activity. As the size of animal and plant populations decreases, loss of genetic diversity reduces their ability to adapt to changes in the environment, with inbreeding and reduced fitness inevitable consequences for most species. This textbook provides a clear and comprehensive introduction to genetic principles and practices involved in conservation. Topics covered include:

- evolutionary genetics of natural populations
- loss of genetic diversity in small populations
- inbreeding and loss of fitness
- population fragmentation
- resolving taxonomic uncertainties
- genetic management of threatened species
- contributions of molecular genetics to conservation.

The text is presented in an easy-to-follow format, with main points and terms clearly highlighted. Each chapter concludes with a concise summary, which, together with worked examples and problems and answers, illuminates the key principles covered. Text boxes containing interesting case studies and other additional information enrich the content throughout, and over 100 beautiful pen-and-ink drawings help bring the material to life.

Written for advanced undergraduate and graduate students studying conservation, this book will be equally useful to practising conservation biologists and wildlife managers needing an accessible introduction to this important field.

The authors comprise a team with a range of skills and experience that make them uniquely qualified to put together the first teaching text on conservation genetics:

DICK FRANKHAM is Professor of Biology at Macquarie University, Sydney, Australia. He began his career in quantitative genetics, achieving international recognition for his work on *Drosophila* before turning to conservation genetics in the early 1990s. He has made a significant contribution to the establishment and advancement of the field and has become one of the major figures in the discipline.

JON BALLOU is Population Manager at the Smithsonian Institution's National Zoological Park in Washington DC, USA and an adjunct member of the faculty at the University of Maryland. His career has focused on developing the science underlying the practical management of small populations of endangered or threatened species, both captive and wild. The results of his studies have been instrumental in highlighting the key role played by genetics in wildlife conservation and management.

DAVID BRISCOE is Associate Professor of Biology at Macquarie University, Sydney, Australia where he has been a close collaborator with Dick Frankham on *Drosophila* research, as well as working with others on rock wallabies, velvet worms and slime molds. An outstanding communicator, his inspirational teaching enthuses students at all levels and reaches beyond the academic sphere through television appearances and popular books such as *Biodiversity: Australia's Living Wealth* to which he contributed.

Introduction to Conservation Genetics

Richard Frankham,
Macquarie University, Sydney

Jonathan D. Ballou
Smithsonian Institution, Washington, DC

and David A. Briscoe
Macquarie University, Sydney

Line drawings by
Karina H. McInness
Inkbyte, Melbourne

PUBLISHED BY THE PRESS SYNDICATE OF THE UNIVERSITY OF CAMBRIDGE

The Pitt Building, Trumpington Street, Cambridge, United Kingdom

CAMBRIDGE UNIVERSITY PRESS
The Edinburgh Building, Cambridge CB2 2RU, UK
40 West 20th Street, New York, NY 1011–4211, USA
477 Williamstown Road, Port Melbourne, VIC 3207, Australia
Ruiz de Alarcón 13, 28014 Madrid, Spain
Dock House, The Waterfront, Cape Town 8001, South Africa

http://www.cambridge.org

First published 2002

Printed in the United Kingdom at the University Press, Cambridge

Typeface 9.5/12pt Swift   *System* QuarkXPress® [SE]

A catalogue record for this book is available from the British Library

Library of Congress Cataloguing in Publication data

Frankham, Richard, 1942–
    Introduction to conservation genetics/Richard Frankham, Jonathan D. Ballou,
and David A. Briscoe; line drawings by Karina H. McInness.
        p.   cm.
    Includes bibliographical references and index.
     ISBN 0 521 63014 2 – ISBN 0 521 63985 9 (pb.)
       1. Germplasm resources.   I. Briscoe, David A. (David Anthony), 1947–
II. Ballou, J. D. (Jonathan D.)   III. Title.

QH75.A1 F73 2002
333.95′34–dc21   2001035028

ISBN 0 521 63014 2 hardback
ISBN 0 521 63985 9 paperback

Contents

Chapter 4 | Characterizing genetic diversity: single loci   72

Chapter 5 | Characterizing genetic diversity: quantitative variation   96

Chapter 6 | Evolution in large populations. I. Natural selection and adaptation   126

Chapter 13 | Population fragmentation

Chapter 14 | Genetically viable populations

SECTION III | FROM THEORY TO PRACTICE

Chapter 15 | Resolving taxonomic uncertainties and defining management units

Chapter 16 | Genetics and the management of wild populations 395

Chapter 17 | Genetic management of captive populations 419

Chapter 18 | Genetic management for reintroduction 448

Preface

The World Conservation Union (IUCN), the primary international conservation body, recognizes the crucial need to conserve genetic diversity as one of the three fundamental levels of biodiversity. This book provides the conceptual background for understanding the importance of genetic diversity in avoidance of species extinctions.

Conservation genetics encompasses the following activities:

- genetic management of small populations to maximize retention of genetic diversity and minimize inbreeding,
- resolution of taxonomic uncertainties and delineation of management units, and
- the use of molecular genetic analyses in forensics and to understand species' biology.

> Conservation genetics is the theory and practice of genetics in the preservation of species as dynamic entities capable of evolving to cope with environmental change to minimize their risk of extinction

Purpose of the book

We have endeavoured to make this book appealing to a wide readership. However it is primarily directed towards those encountering the discipline for the first time, either through formal coursework or by self-instruction.

> This book is intended to provide an accessible introduction to conservation genetics with an emphasis on general principles

Conservation genetics is a relatively young discipline. While it is founded on more than a century of advances in evolutionary theory, including population genetics, quantitative genetics and plant and animal breeding, it has developed its own unique attributes, specialist journals, etc. In particular, conservation genetics focuses on processes within small and fragmented populations and on practical approaches to minimize deleterious effects within them. It has implications for organizations and individuals with very different immediate concerns. These include zoo staff undertaking captive breeding programs, wildlife biologists and ecologists, planners and managers of National Parks, water catchments and local government areas, foresters and farmers. Perhaps of most importance to the future, conservation genetics is of concern to a growing body of undergraduate and postgraduate students, to whom will fall much of the onus of implementing practical measures. Their enthusiasm was a major stimulus to our preparing this volume.

We have endeavoured to make *Introduction to Conservation Genetics* as accessible as possible to this broad array of readers. At the time we began, there were a number of excellent and scholarly texts on population, quantitative and evolutionary genetics and conservation biology, but no introductory textbook on conservation genetics. We have placed emphasis on general principles, rather than on detailed experimental procedures which can be found in specialist books, journals and conference proceedings. We have assumed a basic knowledge of Mendelian genetics and simple statistics. Conservation genetics is a quantitative discipline as its strength lies in its predictions. We have restricted most use of mathematics to simple algebra to make it accessible to a wide audience.

We trust that colleagues will find this material suitable for a full tertiary course on conservation genetics. At the same time, we hope that it will satisfy the needs of evolutionary geneticists and evolutionary ecologists seeking conservation examples to enthuse their students. Finally, we have endeavoured to create an easily accessible and formalized reference book for both professional conservation geneticists and a wider readership.

Précis of contents

This book provides a broad coverage of all strands of conservation genetics

We have encompassed all of the major facets that comprise conservation genetics, from the impacts of inbreeding and loss of genetic diversity, through taxonomic uncertainties and genetic management of threatened species, to the use of molecular genetic analysis in forensics and resolution of critical aspects of species' biology. We conclude by exploring connections between conservation genetics and the wider field of conservation biology.

Chapter 1 provides an overview of the contemporary conservation context and the reasons why genetic theory and information are crucial in management of endangered species. **Chapter 2** explores the central issues in the application of genetics to conservation biology. Inbreeding reduces reproductive potential and survival and, thereby, increases extinction risk in the short term, while loss of genetic diversity reduces the long-term capacity of species to evolve in response to environmental changes.

We have divided the book into three subsequent sections; **Section I** describes the evolutionary genetics of natural populations, **Section II** explores the genetic consequences of reduced population size, and **Section III** focuses on applications of genetic principles to management of threatened and endangered species in wild, semi-wild and captive situations. The relationships of genetics with broader issues in conservation biology conclude this section.

Section I (Chapters 3–9) covers essential background material in evolutionary genetics. **Chapter 3** deals with the extent of genetic diversity and methods for measuring it. Special attention is paid to comparisons of genetic diversity in endangered versus non-endangered species. **Chapters 4** and **5** describe methods and parameters used to characterize genetic diversity. As major genetic concerns in conservation biology are centred on reproduction and survival in the short term (the effects of inbreeding) and the long term (evolutionary potential and speciation), we have placed considerable emphasis on quantitative (continuously varying) characters, as reproductive fitness is such a character (**Chapter 5**). Molecular measures of genetic diversity, for which vast data sets have accumulated, have a disturbingly limited ability to predict quantitative genetic variation. The paramount importance placed on the functional significance of genetic diversity distinguishes conservation genetics from the related field of molecular ecology, where selectively neutral variation is frequently favoured. **Chapters 6** and **7** introduce factors affecting the amount and evolution of genetic diversity in large populations. The same processes in small populations, including species of conservation concern, are detailed in **Chapter 8**. Chance (stochastic) effects have a much greater impact on the fate of genetic diversity in small, endangered populations than in very large populations, where natural selection has far greater influence. Since conservation genetics focuses on retention of evolutionary potential, **Chapter 9** examines the maintenance of genetic diversity.

Having established the basic principles, Section II concentrates on the genetic implications of population size reduction, loss of genetic diversity (**Chapter 10**), the deleterious consequences of inbreeding on reproduction and survival (inbreeding depression) (**Chapters 11** and **12**), and the genetic effects of population fragmentation (**Chapter 13**). The section concludes with consideration of the population size required to maintain the genetic viability of a population (**Chapter 14**).

Section III explores practical issues, genetic resolution of taxonomic uncertainties and delineation of management units (**Chapter 15**), the genetic management of wild (**Chapter 16**) and captive (**Chapter 17**) populations, and reintroduction (**Chapter 18**). **Chapter 19** addresses the developing use of molecular genetic analyses in forensics and resolution of cryptic aspects of species biology. **Chapter 20** expands to a broader picture, the integration of genetic, ecological and demographic factors in conservation biology. In particular, we explore the concepts of population viability analysis (PVA) using computer simulations. The final component, **Take home messages** presents a brief summary of the contents of the book, followed by a **Glossary**.

Introduction to Conservation Genetics concentrates on naturally outbreeding species of plants and animals, with lesser attention to self-fertilizing plants. Microbes have not been included, as little conservation effort has been directed towards them.

We have used examples from threatened species wherever possible. However, most conceptual issues in conservation genetics have been resolved using laboratory and domesticated species, non-threatened but related species, or by combined analyses of data sets (typically small) from many species (meta-analyses). Endangered species are clearly unsuitable for experimentation.

Format

The book is profusely illustrated to make it visually attractive and to tap the emotional commitment that many feel to conservation. To highlight significant points and make it easy to revise, the **main points** of each chapter are given in a box at the start of the chapter along with **Terms** used in the chapter and a **Summary** is given at the end of each chapter. Within chapters, the **main points** of each section are highlighted in small boxes. Much of the information is presented in figures, as we find that biology students respond better to those than to information in text or tables. In many figures, the message is highlighted in italics. Numerous examples and case studies have been used to illustrate the application of theory to real world conservation applications. These have been chosen to be motivating and informative to our audience. Case studies are given in **Boxes** throughout the book. Boxes are also used

Extensive effort has been made to motivate readers by making the book attractive, interesting, informative and easy to follow to provide additional or more difficult information in a way that does not impede the flow of information for those who wish to skip such detail.

We are deeply indebted to Karina McInnes, whose elegant drawings add immeasurably to our words.

The text and format have been trialled on four cohorts of final-year undergraduate students at Macquarie University and extensively refined in response to their comments, and those from many colleagues.

The order of topics both within and across chapters has been designed to motivate students

The order of topics throughout the book, and within chapters, is based on our teaching experience. We have chosen to introduce practical conservation issues as early as possible, with the details of parameter estimation etc. provided later. We hope that readers will find it more stimulating to appreciate *why* a parameter is important, before understanding *how* it is logically or mathematically derived. As an example, Chapter 2 directly addresses the relationship between genetics and extinction, and provides an overview of much of the later material, prior to a detailed treatment of inbreeding (Chapters 11 and 12).

In presenting material, we have aimed for a balance between that necessary for student lectures, and a comprehensive coverage for advanced students and conservation professionals. The material in each chapter is more than adequate for a single lecture, allowing instructors to choose what they wish to emphasize in their course. However the material in each chapter should not prove overwhelming to their students. Some topics are too extensive for a single lecture. We have therefore divided 'Evolution in large populations' into two chapters. We have also allowed some repetition of material, as this is inevitable if different chapters are to be comprehensible on a 'stand-alone' basis.

Each chapter has been designed to provide instructors with material suitable for one lecture, with additional information for independent study

Worked examples and problems with solutions are provided

Everyone who has taught genetics recognizes that mastery of the discipline comes through active participation in problem-solving, rather than passive absorption of facts. Worked **Examples** are given within the text for most equations presented. **Problem** questions are posed at the end of each chapter, together with **Problem answers** and **Revision problems** at the end of the book.

Named species are used in many problem questions, to make them more realistic. These are usually fictitious problems, but reflect situations similar to those that have, or reasonably might have, occurred in the named species. Real data are referenced where used.

Practical exercises are suggested for many chapters

Practical exercises are suggested at the end of chapters covering topics where laboratory exercises are relevant. Most of these have been trialled in our own teaching and are frequently computer exercises, using readily available software. These have proved to be particularly valuable in illuminating the relationship between inbreeding and extinction (Chapter 2), evolutionary genetics of large and small populations (Chapters 6 and 8), maintenance of genetic diversity (Chapter 9), loss of genetic diversity in small populations (Chapter 10) and the use of population viability analysis in management of threatened species

(Chapter 20). Suggestions for molecular genetics practicals are given for Chapters 3, 15 and 19.

Referencing is not intended to be exhaustive, nor to quote primary papers. The references given to reviews and recent papers are sufficient to gain access to the most significant literature. Space does not permit direct reference to many other excellent studies by our colleagues. An annotated list of **General references**, relevant to many chapters, is given at the end of Chapter 1. Readers seeking further detail on specific topics will find an annotated list of suggested **Further reading** at the end of each chapter. We have also included a sprinkling of related books written for popular audiences. These may serve as an introduction to some of the, often controversial, characters involved in conservation biology, and the passions that motivate their work. In the interests of balance, referencing and data presentation are more extensive for contentious topics.

As most of the principles of conservation genetics apply equally to different eukaryotic species, we primarily use common names in the text. Genus and species names in the **Index** are cross-referenced to common names.

For clarity and brevity, referencing is mainly restricted to reviews and recent papers

Controversies

The development of conservation genetics has been driven by what many consider to be a global environmental crisis – 'the sixth extinction'. As a consequence, many other dimensions, economic, political, social, ethical and emotional, impact upon the field. The fate of species, populations and habitats are in the balance. We have flagged these controversies and attempted to provide a balanced, up-to-date view, based upon information available in mid-2000. Where feasible, we have consulted experts to corroborate facts and interpretations. Inevitably, some readers will disagree with some of our views, but we trust that they will accept that alternative interpretations are honestly given. New data will alter perspectives in some cases. For example, the controversial red wolf and northern spotted owl scenarios have changed during the time we were writing the book. We hope that readers find the book as stimulating to read as we found it to write, but not as tiring! Feedback, constructive criticism and suggestions will be deeply appreciated (email: rfrankha@Rna.bio.mq.edu.au).

We will maintain a web site to post updated information, corrections, etc. (http://consgen.mq.edu.au/).

Acknowledgments

Our entries into conservation genetics were initiated by Kathy Ralls of the Smithsonian National Zoo, Washington, DC. Subsequently we have received much-needed support and encouragement from many colleagues, especially from Kathy Ralls, Georgina Mace, Bob Lacy, Rob Fleischer, Stephen O'Brien, Michael Soulé and Ulie Seal. We owe a substantial intellectual debt to Douglas Falconer, author of *Introduction to Quantitative Genetics*. RF and DAB trained using this textbook, and its successive editions have subsequently been major reference sources for us. DAB is particularly appreciative of the mentorship and friendship freely given, over 25 years, by Douglas and his colleagues in The Institute of Animal Genetics, Edinburgh. Not surprisingly, we used Falconer's crisp but scholarly texts as models in our preparation of this book. RF thanks Stuart Barker for his highly influential roles as undergraduate lecturer, PhD supervisor, collaborator and mentor.

Our book could not have been written without the efforts of the students, staff and collaborators in the RF–DAB laboratory. Suzanne Borlase carried out the first experimental modelling of problems in conservation genetics using *Drosophila*. She has been followed by many others, especially Margaret Montgomery and Lynn Woodworth who with Edwin Lowe managed the pedigreed populations for the MVP experiment that have been used in so many studies, including the tests for mutational accumulation done by Dean Gilligan. Roderick Nurthen, in his quiet and efficient way, has supervised all our electrophoretic work, while Phillip England developed microsatellites and supervised their use. Barry Brook and Julian O'Grady conducted computer simulation studies on inbreeding and extinction and on the predictive accuracy of population viability analysis. David Reed completed two important meta-analyses and kept the 'Flyfarm' running while this book was in its final throes. Jennifer Mickelberg took care of business at the Zoo while JDB was in Australia completing the book

The support of our home institutions is gratefully acknowledged. They have made it possible for us to be involved in researching the field and writing this book. The research work by RF and DAB was made possible by Australian Research Council and Macquarie University research grants. RF acknowledges the hospitality of the Smithsonian National Zoological Park during 1997 when the first two drafts were written. JDB also gratefully acknowledges the Smithsonian National Zoological Park for providing a sabbatical to Macquarie University to finalize the preparation of this book. We thank Alan Crowden from Cambridge University Press for his advice and assistance during the writing of the book and to Jayne Aldhouse, Shana Coates, Anna Hodson and Maria Murphy for facilitating the path to publication.

This book could not have been completed without the continued support and forbearance of our wives Annette Lindsay, Vanessa Ballou and Helen Briscoe, and families. Annette and Vanessa (plus Lara and Grace) spent extended periods away from their home countries to facilitate its completion. Vanessa sorted and filed our copious reference collection while Annette corrected the final draft of the book.

We thank the students in the Conservation and Evolutionary Genetics course at Macquarie University in 1998–2001. Their comments, criticisms and suggestions did much to improve the book, especially those from A. Corson, A. Gibberson, H. Ferguson, E. Laxton, H. Macklin and R. Suwito. We are grateful to L. Bingaman-Lackey, D. Cooper, N. Flesness, T. Foose, J. Groombridge, S. Haig, C. Lynch, S. Medina, P. Pearce-Kelly and M. Whalley for supplying information, and to M. Eldridge, R. Fleischer, J. Howard, T. Madsen, B. Pukazhenthi,

I. Saccheri, M. Sun, P. Sunnucks, R. Vrijenhoek, A. Young and G. Zegers for supplying material for illustrations. The book was improved greatly by comments on individual sections and chapters from A. Beattie, L. Beheregaray, M. Burgman, D. Charlesworth, S. Haig, L. Mills (and his class of students at University of Montana), S. O'Brien, K. Ralls, I. Saccheri, P. Sunnucks, A. Taylor, B. Walsh, R. Wayne and A. Young. S. Barker, B. Brook, M. Eldridge, B. Latter, J. O'Grady and D. Reed generously provided detailed comments on the whole text. We apologize to those whose assistance we have omitted to record. We have not followed all of their suggestions and some disagree with our conclusions on controversial issues. Any errors and omissions that remain are ours.

Copyright acknowledgments

We are grateful to the following for kind permission to reproduce copyright material:

The Cambridge University Press for the elephant seal illustrations in Box 8.2 and Ex. 10.5 and the chimpanzee image in Table 3.4 from figures 3–6 and 1–10, respectively, in Austin, C. R. and R. V. Short (1984) *The Evolution of Reproduction* (illustrated by J. R. Fuller); The Kluwer Academic Publishers for: Fig. 19.13 from figure 1 in Lens, L., P. Galbusera, T. Brooks, E. Waiyaki and T. Schenck (1998) Highly skewed sex ratios in the critically endangered Taita thrush as revealed by CHD genes. *Biodiversity and Conservation* 7: 869–873 and Fig. 3.3 from figure 2 page 10 from Avise, J. *Molecular Markers, Natural History and Evolution*; The Oxford University Press for: the figure in Box 3.1 from figure 3 in Gilbert, D. A., C. Packer, A. E. Pusey, J. C. Stephens and S. J. O'Brien (1991) Analytical DNA fingerprinting in lions: parentage, genetic diversity, and kinship. *Journal of Heredity* 82: 378–386; the frontispiece Chapter 19 from figure 1 in Harry, J. L. and D. A. Briscoe. 1988. Multiple paternity in the loggerhead turtle (*Caretta caretta*). *Journal of Heredity* 79: 96–99; the frontispiece Chapter 6 from Plate 8.2 in Kettlewell, B (1973) *The Evolution of Melanism*; Fig. 19.11 from Fritsch, P. and L. H. Rieseberg (1966) The use of random amplified polymorphic DNA in conservation genetics, in *Molecular Genetic Approaches in Conservation*, ed. T. B. Smith and R. K. Wayne, copyright 1996 by Oxford University Press, Inc. Used by permission of Oxford University Press. Inc.; Fig. 7.4 from Map 5 in Mourant, A. E., A. C. Kopéc and Domaniewsha-Sobczak, K. (1976) *The Distribution of the Human Blood Groups and Other Polymorphisms*, Oxford University Press, London; The MIT Press for Fig. 10.2 from figure 2 in Foose, T. J. (1986) Riders of the last ark, in *The Last Extinction*, ed. Kaufman, L. and K. Mallory; The Social Contract Press for Fig. 1.3 from the maps in Tanton, J. H. (1994) End of the migration epoch? *The Social Contract*, 4(3): 162–176 (for critiques of this essay see *The Social Contract* 5(1): 28–47. Note: These texts are available online); The Center for Applied Studies in Forestry for the map in Box 13.1 and the Chapter 16 frontispiece from figure 2 in James, F (1995) The status of the red-cockaded woodpecker and the prospect for recovery, in Kulhavy, D. L., R. G. Hooper and R. Costa, *Red-cockaded Woodpecker: Recovery, Ecology and Management*. Center for Applied Studies, Stephen F. Austin State University, Nacogdoches, TX; CSIRO Publishing for Fig. 15.3 from figure 2 in Johnston, P. G., R. J. Davey and J. H. Seebeck (1984) Chromosome homologies in *Potoroos tridactylus* and *P. longipes* based on G-banding patterns. *Australian Journal of Zoology* 32: 319–324; John Wiley and Sons, Inc. for Fig. 8.6 from figure 1 in Hedrick, P., P. S. Miller, E. Geffen and R. Wayne (1997) Genetic evaluation of the three captive Mexican wolf lineages. *Zoo Biology* 16: 47–69; The Carnegie Institute of Washington for Fig. 5.2 from figures 19, 23 and 25 in Clausen, J., D. D. Keck and W. M. Hiesey (1940) Experimental studies on the nature of species. I. Effect of varied environments on Western North American Plants. *Carnegie Institution of Washington Publications No. 520.* Carnegie Institute, Washington, DC; Blackwell Publishers Ltd, for Fig. 6.4 from figure 1 in Kettlewell, H. B. D. (1958) A survey of the frequencies of *Biston betularia* (L.) (Lep.) and its melanic forms in Great Britain. *Heredity* 12: 551–572; The Evolution Society for the map in Box 12.1 from Vrijenhoek, R. C., Pfeiler, E. and J. Wetherington (1992) Balancing selection in a desert stream-dwelling fish, *Peociliopsis monacha. Evolution* 46: 1642–1657; and the National Academy of Sciences for Fig. 19.9 from Bowen, B. W., F. A. Abreu-Grobois, G. H. Balazs, N. Kamenzaki, C. J. Limpus and R. J. Ferl (1995) Trans-Pacific migrations of the loggerhead turtle (*Caretta caretta*) demonstrated with mitochondrial DNA markers. *Proceedings of the National Academy of Sciences, USA* 92: 3731–3734.

Chapter 1

Introduction

Conservation genetics is the application of genetics to preserve species as dynamic entities capable of coping with environmental change. It encompasses genetic management of small populations, resolution of taxonomic uncertainties, defining management units within species and the use of molecular genetic analyses in forensics and understanding species' biology.

Terms:
Biodiversity,
ecosystem services,
endangered,
evolutionary potential,
forensics,
genetic diversity,
inbreeding depression,
introgression,
meta-analysis,
outbreeding depression,
population viability analysis,
purging,
reproductive fitness,
threatened,
vulnerable

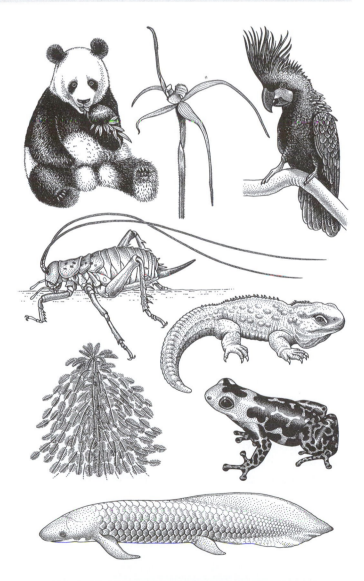

Selection of threatened species: Clockwise: panda (China), an Australian orchid, palm cockatoo (Australia), tuatara (New Zealand), poison arrow frog (South America), lungfish (Australia), Wollemi pine (Australia) and New Zealand weta.

The 'sixth extinction'

The biological diversity of the planet is rapidly being depleted as a direct and indirect consequence of human actions

Biodiversity is the variety of ecosystems, species, populations within species, and genetic diversity within species. The biological diversity of the planet is being rapidly depleted as a direct and indirect consequence of human actions. An unknown but large number of species are already extinct, while many others have reduced population sizes that put them at risk (WCMC 1992). Many species now require benign human intervention to improve their management and ensure their survival. The scale of the problem is enormous, as described below. The current extinction problem has been called the 'sixth extinction', as its magnitude compares with that of the other five mass extinctions revealed in the geological record (Leakey & Lewin 1995). Extinction is a natural part of the evolutionary process. For example, the mass extinction at the end of Cretaceous 65 million years ago eliminated much of the previous flora and fauna, including the dinosaurs. However, this extinction made way for proliferation of the mammals and flowering angiosperm plants. The sixth extinction is different. Species are being lost at a rate that far outruns the origin of new species.

Conservation genetics, like all components of conservation biology, is motivated by the need to reduce current rates of extinction and to preserve biodiversity.

Why conserve biodiversity?

Four justifications for maintaining biodiversity have been advanced; the economic value of bioresources, ecosystem services, aesthetics, and rights of living organisms to exist

Humans derive many direct and indirect benefits from the living world. Thus, we have a stake in conserving biodiversity for the resources we use, for the ecosystem services it provides for us, for the pleasure we derive from living organisms and for ethical reasons.

Bioresources include all of our food, many pharmaceutical drugs, clothing fibres (wool and cotton), rubber and timber for housing and construction, etc. Their value is many billions of dollars annually. For example, about 25% of all pharmaceutical prescriptions in the USA contain active ingredients derived from plants (Primack 1998). Further, the natural world contains many potentially useful novel resources (Beattie 1995). For example, ants contain novel antibiotics that are being investigated for use in human medicine, spider silk may provide the basis for light high-tensile fibres that are stronger weight-for-weight than steel, etc.

Ecosystem services are essential biological functions that are provided free of charge by living organisms and which benefit humankind. They include oxygen production by plants, climate control by forests, nutrient cycling, natural pest control, pollination of crop plants, etc. (Daily 1999). These services have been valued at $US33 trillion ($10^{12}$) per year, almost double the $US18 trillion yearly global national product (Costanza *et al.* 1997).

Humans derive pleasure from living organisms (aesthetics), as expressed in growing ornamental plants, keeping pets, visits to zoos and nature reserves, and ecotourism. This translates into direct economic value. For example, koalas are estimated to contribute $US750 million annually to the Australian tourism industry (Australia Institute 1997).

The ethical justifications for conserving biodiversity are simply that one species on Earth does not have the right to drive others to extinction, analogous to abhorrence of genocide among human populations.

The peak international conservation body, IUCN (the World Conservation Union), recognizes the need to conserve the biological diversity on Earth for the reasons above (McNeely *et al.* 1990). IUCN recognizes the need for conservation at the levels of genetic diversity, species diversity and ecosystem diversity. Genetics is involved directly in the first of these and is a crucial factor in species conservation.

> IUCN recognizes the need to conserve biodiversity at three levels; genetic diversity, species diversity, and ecosystem diversity

Endangered and extinct species

Extent of endangerment

Threatened species of animals fall into the categories of critically endangered, endangered, and vulnerable, as defined below. IUCN (1996) classified more than 50% of species in every one of the vertebrate classes into one of the threatened categories, as shown in Fig. 1.1.

> Over 50% of vertebrate animal species and 12.5% of plant species are classified as threatened

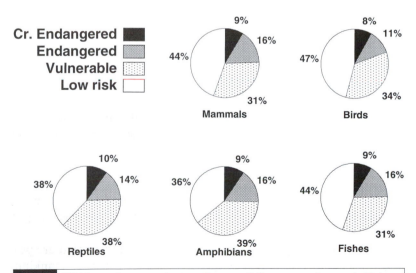

Fig. 1.1 Which vertebrates are the most threatened? Percentages of mammals, birds, reptiles, amphibians and fishes categorized as critically endangered, endangered, vulnerable and at lower risk (after IUCN 1996).

Table 1.1 Recorded extinctions, 1600 to present

Taxa	Number of extinctions on				Percentage of extinctions on islands	Percentage of taxon extinct
	Island	Mainland	Ocean	Total		
Mammals[a]	51	30	4	85	60	2.1
Birds[a]	92	21	0	113	81	1.3
Reptiles[a]	20	1	0	21	95	0.3
Amphibians[a]	0	2	0	2	0	0.05
Fish[a]	1	22	0	23	4	0.1
Molluscs[b]	151	40	0	191	79	
Invertebrates[a]	48	49	1	98	49	0.01
Flowering plants[a]	139	245	0	384	36	0.2

Notes:
[a] From Primack (1998).
[b] From WCMC (1992).

The situation in plants is similarly alarming. IUCN (1997) classified 12.5% of vascular plants as threatened, with a much higher proportion of gymnosperms (32%) than angiosperms (9%) being threatened. Estimates for invertebrates and microbes are not available as the number of extant species in these groups is not known.

Recorded extinctions

Over 800 extinctions have been documented since records began in 1600, the majority being of island species

Recorded extinctions since 1600 for different groups of animal and plants on islands and mainlands are given in Table 1.1. The proportions of species in different groups that have gone extinct are small, being only 1%–2% in mammals and birds. However, the pattern of extinctions is a matter for concern as the rate of extinction has generally increased with time (Fig. 1.2) and many species are threatened. Further, many extinctions must have occurred without being recorded; habitat loss must have resulted in many extinctions of undescribed species of invertebrates and plants (Gentry 1986).

Fig. 1.2 Changes in extinction rates over time in mammals and birds (after Primack 1998, based on Smith *et al.* 1995). *Extinction rates have generally increased for successive 50-year periods.*

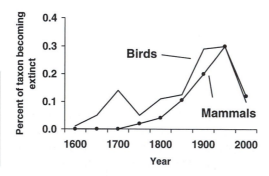

Table 1.2	Projected extinction rates for different groups based on a variety of arguments	
Estimated extinction rate	Percent global loss per decade	Method of estimation
1 million species between 1975 and 2000	4	Extrapolation of past exponential trend
15%–20% of species between 1980 and 2000	8–11	Species–area curves and projected forest loss
12% of plant species in neotropics		Species–area curves
15% bird species in Amazon basin		As above
2000 plant species per year in tropics and subtropics	8	Loss of half the species in areas likely to be deforested by 2015
25% of species between 1985 and 2015	9	As above
At least 7% of plant species	7	Half of species lost in next decade in 10 'hotspots' covering 3.5% of forest area
0.2%–0.3% per year	2–3	Half of rainforest species lost in tropical rainforests are local endemics and becoming extinct with forest loss
5%–15% of forest species by 2020	2–5	Species–area curve; forest loss assumed twice rate projected by FAO for 1980–85
2%–8% loss between 1980 and 2015	1–5	Species–area curve; range includes current rate of forest loss and 50% increase

Source: WCMC (1992).

The majority of recorded extinctions, and a substantial proportion of currently threatened species, are on islands. For example, 81% of all recorded bird extinctions are insular, yet only about 20% of bird species have existed on islands (Myers 1979). We will return to vulnerability and significance of insular populations many times throughout this book.

Projected extinction rates

Several projections of extinction levels into the future are given in Table 1.2. While these estimates are crude and vary widely, there is a consensus that extinction rates are destined to accelerate markedly, typically by 1000-fold or more above 'normal' background extinction rates.

Average lifespans of species provide an alternative way of viewing rates of extinction. The average lifespan of an animal species in the fossil record, from origin to extinction, is around 1–10 million years, with the higher number being more typical. For birds and mammals, rates of documented extinction over the past century correspond to species'

Projections point to greatly elevated extinction rates in the near future

Table 1.3	Defining endangerment (IUCN 1996 criteria)		
Category	Probability of extinction	Time	
Critically endangered	50%	10 yrs or 3 generations	
Endangered	20%	20 yrs or 5 generations	
Vulnerable	10%	100 yrs	

lifespans of around 10 000 years. Three different methods suggest an average lifespan for bird and mammal species of around 200–400 years if current trends continue (Lawton & May 1995) i.e. current extinction rates are 5000–25 000 times those in the fossil record.

What is an endangered species?

Endangered species are those with a high risk of immediate extinction

The IUCN (1996) has defined criteria to classify species into **critically endangered**, **endangered**, **vulnerable** and **lower risk**. These are based on population biology principles developed largely by Mace & Lande (1991). They defined a **threatened** species as one with a high risk of extinction within a short time frame. For example, a critically endangered species has a risk of extinction of 50% within 10 years or three generations, whichever is longer (Table 1.3).

IUCN (1996) set out simple rules to define these categories in terms of the rate of decline in population size, restriction in habitat area, the current population size and/or the probability of extinction. A critically endangered species exhibits any one of the characteristics described under A–E in Table 1.4, i.e. it has either an 80% or greater decline in population size over the last 10 years (or three generations), or an extent of occupancy of less than 100 square kilometres, or a population size of less than 250 mature adults, or a probability of extinction of 50% or more over 10 years (or three generations), or some combination of these. For example, there are only about 65 Javan rhinoceroses surviving in Southeast Asia and the numbers are continuing to decline, so this species falls into the category of critically endangered. Other examples are given in the Problems at the end of the chapter.

There are similar, but less threatening characteristics required to categorize species as endangered, or vulnerable. Species falling outside these categories are designated as lower risk. IUCN has also defined categories of extinct, extinct in the wild, conservation dependent, near threatened and data deficient (IUCN 1996).

While there are many other systems used throughout the world to categorize endangerment, the IUCN categorization system is used as the basis of listing species in the IUCN Red Books of endangered animals (IUCN 1996). In general, we have used the IUCN system throughout this book.

Table 1.4 | Information used to decide whether species fall into the critically endangered, endangered or vulnerable IUCN categories (IUCN 1996).

A species falling within any of the categories A–E in the critically endangered column is defined as critically endangered. Similar rules apply to endangered and vulnerable

Criteria (any one of A–E)	Critically endangered	Endangered	Vulnerable
A. Actual or projected reduction in population's size	80% decline over the last 10 years or 3 generations	50%	20%

B. Extent of occurrence or area of occupancy of	< 100 km^2
	< 10 km^2 and any two of
	  (i) severely fragmented or known
	    to exist at a single location,
	  (ii) continuing declines, and
	  (iii) extreme fluctuations
		5000 km^2
		500 km^2
		5 locations
			20000 km^2
			2000 km^2
			10 locations

C. Population numbering	< 250 mature individuals and an estimated continuing decline	< 2500	< 10000
D. Population estimated to number	< 50 mature individuals	< 250	< 1000
E. Quantitative analysis showing the probability of extinction in the wild	at least 50% within 10 years or 3 generations, whichever is the longer	20% in 20 years or 5 generations	10% in 100 yrs

Importance of listing

It is of great importance to define endangerment, as it is the basis for legal protection for species. For example, most countries have Endangered Species Acts that provide legal protection for threatened species and usually require the formulation of recovery plans. In addition, trade in threatened species is banned by countries that have signed the Convention on International Trade in Endangered Species (CITES; Hutton & Dickson 2000). This provides important protection for threatened parrots, reptiles, cats, fish, whales, etc.

> Listing a species or sub-species as endangered provides a scientific foundation for national and international legal protection from exploitation and trade, and may lead to remedial actions to recover it

What causes extinctions?

Human-associated factors

The primary factors contributing to extinction are directly or indirectly related to human impacts. Since the human population is growing rapidly (Fig. 1.3), the impacts of these factors are continually increasing. The human population reached 6 billion on 12 October 1999, the last billion increase (20%) having occurred in only 12–14 years. The human population will continue to increase. By 2050, the population is projected to rise to 8.9 billion, with a range of projections between 7.3 and 10.7 billion. However, the rate of increase has declined from a peak of just over 2% per year to below 1.5% in the early 1990s (Smil 1999).

> The primary factors contributing to extinction are habitat loss, introduced species, over-exploitation and pollution. These factors are caused by humans, and related to human population growth

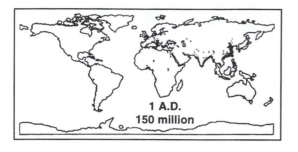

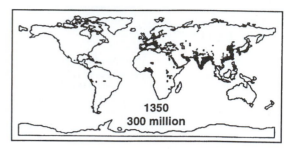

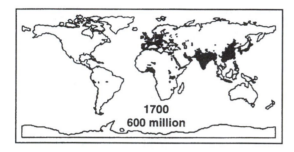

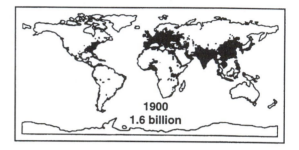

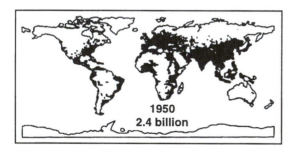

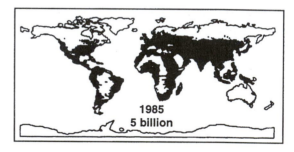

Fig. 1.3 Visual representation of human population growth in different parts of the world (from Tanton 1994).

The total human population is projected to climax at 10–11 billion around 2070 and then begin to decline (Pearce 1999). Even the lower projection of a peak population size of 7.7 billion in 2040 represents a 28% increase above the current population. Consequently, human impacts on wild animals and plants will continue to worsen in the foreseeable future.

Stochastic factors

Additional accidental (stochastic) demographic, environmental, catastrophic and genetic factors increase the risk of extinction in small populations

Human-related factors can reduce species to population sizes where they are susceptible to stochastic effects. These are naturally occurring fluctuations experienced by small populations. These may have environmental, catastrophic, demographic, or genetic (inbreeding depression, and loss of genetic diversity) origins. Stochastic factors are discussed throughout the book. Even if the original cause of population decline is removed, problems associated with small population size will still persist.

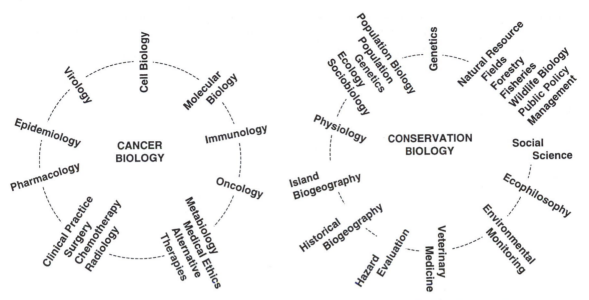

Fig. 1.4 Structure of conservation biology and the position of genetics in it (after Soulé 1985). *Conservation biology is a crisis discipline akin to cancer biology, to which it is compared.*

Recognition of genetic factors in conservation biology

Sir Otto Frankel, an Austrian-born Australian, was largely responsible for recognizing the importance of genetic factors in conservation biology, beginning with papers in the early 1970s (Frankel 1970, 1974; see Soulé & Frankham 2000 for biographical information). Subsequently, Frankel collaborated with Michael Soulé of the USA on the first conservation book that clearly discussed the contribution of genetic factors (Frankel & Soulé 1981). Frankel strongly influenced Soulé's entry into conservation biology. Soulé is the 'father' of modern conservation biology, having been instrumental in founding the Society for Conservation Biology, serving as its first President, and participating in the establishment of *Conservation Biology*, the premier journal in the field. Throughout the 1980s, Michael Soulé had a profound influence on the development of conservation biology as a multidisciplinary crisis field drawing on ecology, genetics, wildlife biology and resource biology (Fig. 1.4).

What is conservation genetics?

Conservation genetics deals with the genetic factors that affect extinction risk and genetic management regimes required to minimise these risks. There are 11 major genetic issues in conservation biology:

Conservation genetics aims to minimize the risk of extinction from genetic factors

• The deleterious effects of **inbreeding** on reproduction and survival (**inbreeding depression**)
• Loss of **genetic diversity** and ability to evolve in response to environmental change

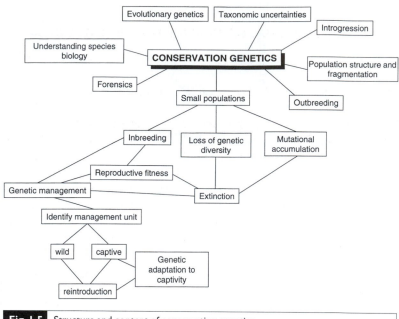

Fig. 1.5 Structure and content of conservation genetics.

- Fragmentation of populations and reduction in gene flow
- Random processes (genetic drift) overriding natural selection as the main evolutionary process
- Accumulation and loss (**purging**) of deleterious mutations
- Genetic adaptation to captivity and its adverse effects on reintroduction success
- Resolving taxonomic uncertainties
- Defining management units within species
- Use of molecular genetic analyses in forensics
- Use of molecular genetic analyses to understand aspects of species biology important to conservation
- Deleterious effects on fitness that sometimes occur as a result of outcrossing (**outbreeding depression**).

The effects of small population size are of major concern in conservation biology, since endangered species have small and/or declining populations. Small populations suffer from inbreeding and loss of genetic diversity resulting in elevated extinction risks. Consequently, a major objective of genetic management is to minimize inbreeding and loss of genetic diversity.

This textbook is concerned with the 11 issues listed above.

The structure and content of conservation genetics is illustrated in Fig. 1.5. Conservation genetics is an applied discipline that draws heavily upon evolutionary, population and quantitative genetics and taxonomy.

How is genetics used to minimize extinctions?

Knowledge of genetics aids conservation in the following ways.

Reducing extinction risk by minimizing inbreeding and loss of genetic diversity

Many small, threatened populations are inbred and have reduced levels of genetic diversity. Inbreeding reduces fecundity and survival and so directly increases extinction risk (Chapters 2, 11 and 12). Reduced genetic diversity compromises the ability of populations to evolve to cope with environmental change and reduces their chances of long-term persistence (Chapters 3, 10 and 13). For example, the endangered Florida panther suffers from genetic problems as evidenced by low genetic diversity, and inbreeding-related defects (poor sperm quality and quantity and morphological abnormalities). To alleviate these effects, individuals from its most closely related sub-species in Texas have been introduced into this population. Captive populations of many endangered species (e.g. golden lion tamarin) are managed to minimize loss of genetic diversity and inbreeding (Chapter 17).

Identifying populations of concern

Genetic markers can identify populations where genetic issues are likely to affect their prospects of long-term survival. Asiatic lions that exist in the wild only in a small population in the Gir Forest in India have very low levels of genetic diversity. Consequently, they have a severely compromised ability to evolve (Chapter 10), as well as being susceptible to demographic and environmental risks (Chapter 20). The recently discovered Wollemi pine, an Australian relict species previously known only from fossils, contains no genetic diversity among individuals at several hundred loci, so its extinction risk is extreme; it is susceptible to a common die-back fungus and all individuals that were tested were similarly susceptible (Woodford 2000).

Resolving population structure

Information regarding the extent of gene flow among populations is critical to determine whether a species requires translocation of individuals to prevent inbreeding and loss of genetic diversity (Chapter 13). Wild populations of the red-cockaded woodpecker are fragmented and genetically differentiated. Further, levels of genetic diversity are correlated with population sizes. Consequently, part of the management of this species involves translocating individuals into small populations to minimize the risks of inbreeding and loss of genetic diversity.

Resolving taxonomic uncertainties

The taxonomic status of many species, especially invertebrates and lower plants, is frequently unknown (Chapter 15). Thus, an apparently widespread and low-risk species may, in reality, comprise a complex of distinct taxa, some rare or endangered. Such is the case for the unique

New Zealand reptile, the tuatara. Genetic marker studies revealed two distinct species, one of which was being neglected in terms of conservation. Similar studies have shown that Australia is home to well over 100 locally distributed species of velvet worms (*Peripatus*) rather than the seven widespread morphological species previously recognized. Equally, genetic markers may reveal that populations of common species are attracting undeserved protection and resources. Molecular genetic analyses have shown that the endangered colonial pocket gopher from Georgia is indistinguishable from the common pocket gopher in that region, so that there was no necessity to preserve the colonial pocket gopher. In a related vein, the threatened northern spotted owl, the subject of great controversy in the Pacific Northwest of the USA, is genetically very similar to the non-endangered California spotted owl (see Box 1.1). This latter case remains controversial and unresolved.

Defining management units within species

Populations within species may be sufficiently differentiated that they deserve management as separate units i.e. they are adapted to somewhat different environments (Chapter 15). Their hybrids may be at a disadvantage, sometimes even displaying partial reproductive isolation. For example, coho salmon (and many other fish species) display genetic differentiation among geographic populations and evidence of adaptation to different conditions (morphology, swimming ability and age at maturation). Thus, they should be managed as separate populations (Small *et al.* 1998).

Detecting hybridization

Many rare species of plants, salmonid fish and canids are threatened with being 'hybridized out of existence' by crossing with common species (Chapter 15). Molecular genetic analyses have shown that the critically endangered Ethiopian wolf (simian jackal) is subject to hybridization with local domestic dogs.

Non-intrusive sampling for genetic analyses

Many species are difficult to capture, or become stressed by the process. DNA can be obtained from hair, feathers, sloughed skin, faeces, etc. in non-intrusive sampling, the DNA amplified and genetic studies completed without disturbing the animals (Chapter 3). For example, the critically endangered northern hairy-nosed wombat is a nocturnal burrowing marsupial that can only be captured with difficulty. They are stressed by trapping and become trap-shy. Sampling has been achieved by placing adhesive tape across their burrows to capture hair when the animals exit their burrows. DNA from non-invasive sampling can be used to identify individuals, determine mating patterns and population structure, and measure levels of genetic diversity (Chapters 10 and 19).

Defining sites for reintroduction

The northern hairy-nosed wombat exists in a single population of approximately 75 animals at Clermont in Queensland, Australia. DNA samples obtained from museum skins identified an extinct wombat population at Deniliquin in NSW as belonging to this species. Thus, Deniliquin is a potential site for reintroduction (Chapter 19). Similarly, information from genotyping DNA from sub-fossil bones has revealed that the endangered Laysan duck previously existed on islands other than its present distribution in the Hawaiian Islands (Chapter 19).

Choosing the best populations for reintroduction

Island populations are considered as an invaluable genetic resource for re-establishing mainland populations, particularly in Australia and New Zealand. However, the black-footed rock wallaby population on Barrow Island, Australia, a potential source of individuals for reintroductions onto the mainland, has extremely low genetic variation and reduced reproductive rate (presumably due to inbreeding). More endangered mainland populations are genetically healthier and may be a more suitable source of animals for reintroductions to other mainland localities (Chapter 18). Alternatively, the pooling of several different island populations of this wallaby should provide a genetically healthy population suitable for reintroduction purposes.

Forensics

Consumption of meat from threatened whales has been detected by analysing whale meat in Japan and South Korea. Mitochondrial DNA sequences showed that about 9% of the whale meat on sale came from protected species of whales, rather than from the minke whales that can be taken legally (Chapter 19). Work is in progress to develop related methods to identify tiger bones in Asian medicines. Many other related forensic applications are deriving from molecular genetics.

Understanding species biology

Many aspects of species biology can be determined using molecular genetic analyses (see Chapter 19). For example, mating patterns and reproduction systems are often difficult to determine in threatened species. Studies using genetic markers established that loggerhead turtle females mate with several males. Mating systems in many plants have been established using genetic makers. Birds are often difficult to sex, resulting in several cases where two birds of the same sex were placed together to breed. Probes for loci on the sex chromosomes are now available so that birds can be sexed without having to resort to surgery. Paternity has been determined in many species, including chimpanzees. Methods to census endangered kit foxes, that are nocturnal and secretive, are being developed, based upon counts of scats (faeces). This is only possible because mitochondrial DNA (mtDNA) can be used to distinguish kit fox scats from those of gray foxes, coyotes, red foxes and domestic dogs in the area.

Dispersal and migration patterns are often critical to species' survival prospects. These are difficult to determine directly, but can be inferred using genetic analyses.

Each of these issues is treated in detail in later chapters.

Box 1.1 | Use of molecular genetic analyses in an attempt to resolve the controversial taxonomic status of the threatened northern spotted owl
(Barrowclough *et al.* 1999; Haig *et al.* 2001)

Efforts to conserve the threatened northern sub-species of spotted owl in the Pacific Northwest of the USA have created enormous controversy. Logging has been suspended in large areas of old growth forest, local communities have complained bitterly about job losses and economic dislocation, and it was an issue in the 1996 presidential election. However, there have been uncertainties about the distinctiveness of the northern spotted owl from related California and Mexican spotted owls. The distributions of the three sub-species of spotted owl are shown below. The northern and California spotted owls have no gap between their distributions and field biologists cannot distinguish them in areas where they meet. Morphological measurements failed to distinguish the northern and Californian sub-species, as did two genetic studies of nuclear loci. However, evidence from sequencing of mitochondrial DNA (mtDNA; maternally inherited) indicated a greater degree of differentiation, as described below.

Studies using electrophoretic separation of proteins (described in Chapter 3) failed to differentiate the northern and California spotted owls, but they differed at one gene locus from the Mexican spotted owl. A further analysis was done using the random amplified polymorphic DNA (RAPD) method (Chapter 3). Blood samples were collected from 276 birds from 21 breeding populations, 16 populations being northern spotted owl, 2 California spotted owl and 3 Mexican spotted owl. DNA from each of the samples was screened for genetic differences following amplification. Data on 11 variable bands (each band probably represented a separate locus) was analysed. No bands differentiated northern from California spotted owls. One band differentiated Mexican spotted owls from northern and Californian.

In contrast, mtDNA sequences from 73 spotted owls detected a considerable difference between the three sub-species (Barrowclough *et al.* 1999). Only one mtDNA sequence from the northern spotted owl was identical to sequences from the California spotted owls and all Mexican spotted owl sequences were distinct

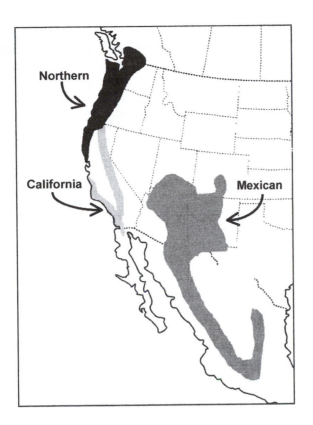

from the other sub-species. More extensive analyses from the region where north-ern and California spotted owl populations meet have revealed considerable gene flow between the sub-species, probably due to secondary contact as a result of habitat destruction (Haig *et al.* 2001). About 13% of northern spotted owls in the region nearest to the California spotted owl have mtDNA that is normally associated with California spotted owls. Consequently, the taxonomic status of the northern spotted owl as a distinct sub-species remains controversial. Listing under the US Endangered Species Act requires that a population be a distinct species, or sub-species, or a distinct population segment. This is interpreted to mean that they should have mtDNA sequences that are not shared and that there should be evidence of some frequency differences in nuclear loci, or evidence of genetically determined morphological, behavioural or life history differences. The ability of the northern spotted owl to satisfy these criteria, as a distinctly different population from the California spotted owl, is open to question.

Additional concerns have arisen recently. First, the California spotted owl is in decline as a result of human encroachment in the south, so the combined northern –California spotted owl may justify listing in the future (Lahaye *et al.* 1994). Second, hybridization of spotted owls to barred owls is becoming common since the habitat was fragmented (Hamer *et al.* 1994). Thus, northern spotted owls may warrant con-servation effort, but not necessarily for the reasons originally envisaged.

Genetic versus demographic and environmental factors in conservation biology

A number of ecologists and wildlife biologists have questioned the significance of genetic factors in conservation (see Chapter 2). Several have suggested that demographic factors, environmental fluctuations (stochasticity) and catastrophes will drive wild populations to extinction before genetic factors take effect. However, there is a clear theoretical basis and a growing body of experimental evidence that genetic factors are involved in extinctions (Chapter 2). Genetic factors may frequently interact with demographic and environmental fluctuations in precipitating species to decline towards extinction.

What do we need to know to genetically manage threatened species?

A flowchart of the information required for the genetic management of threatened populations is given in Fig. 1.6. The first crucial group of questions relate to whether the taxonomy is clearly known. If not, this can often be resolved using genetic marker studies. A related question is whether populations within species differ sufficiently to justify separate management, as would typically be accorded to sub-species. The final question in this area is concerned with whether the species is hybridizing with another species (**introgression**). These issues are addressed in Chapter 15.

The second group of critical questions relates to population size. We have already alluded to the fact that the total species population size and the extent of fragmentation are central to an assessment of extinction risk through genetic factors. These questions are addressed in Section II of the textbook.

The third question relates to whether all the critical aspects of the species' biology are known and whether unknown parameters can be resolved using molecular genetic analyses. The fourth question relates to the existence of illegal hunting or trade, and whether molecular genetic analyses can aid in their detection. These issues are all treated in Section III of the book, 'From theory to practice'.

Conservation genetics relies heavily upon knowledge of population and quantitative genetics to understand the genetic consequences of small population size. Consequently, Section I of the book deals with the required principles of evolutionary genetics. Section II builds upon this background by exploring the genetic consequences of small populations. These sections provide the background for us to deal with practical management issues in conservation genetics in Section III.

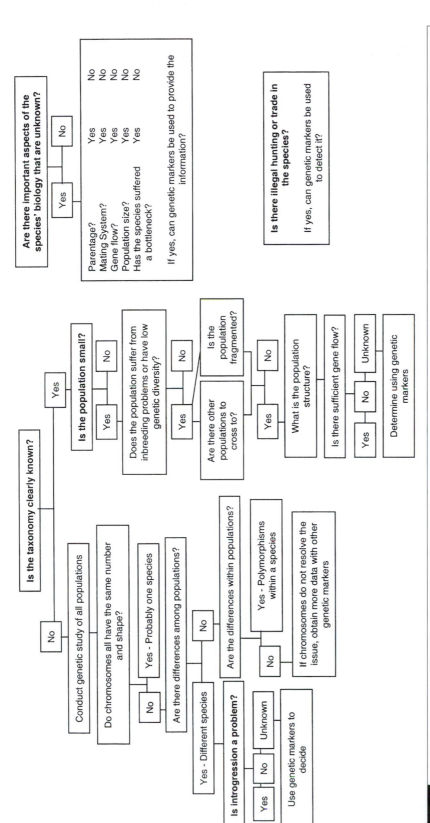

Fig. 1.6 Flowchart of questions that are asked in relation to genetic issues in conservation.

Methodology in conservation genetics

Conceptual issues in conservation genetics are typically resolved using experiments with laboratory species, computer simulations and combined analyses of data from many wildlife species (meta-analyses)

An important feature of conservation genetics is the methodology used for resolving issues and advancing the field. Information on endangered species is often limited and these species are often unsuitable for experimental studies. Advances in the field come from the interplay of theory, computer simulations and experimentation, in a manner analogous to that used in economics or climate modelling. Theory and evaluation must be involved in a feedback loop. The traditional means for testing theory and resolving issues are to use replicated experiments with controls. However, endangered species are unsuitable for doing this, as they are typically slow breeders, expensive to keep and present in low numbers, and experimentation is ruled out by both practical and ethical considerations.

As the genetics of all outbreeding species are similar, laboratory species such as fruit flies, flour beetles, and mice have long been used to investigate parallel problems in the related fields of evolutionary genetics and animal breeding. For example, inbreeding has been found to result in deleterious effects on reproduction and survival (**reproductive fitness**) in essentially all naturally outbreeding populations of laboratory animals, domestic animals, domestic plants and wild species that have been adequately investigated (see Chapter 12). We are aware of no case where studies with laboratory species have yielded qualitative results at variance with those found for other species with similar breeding systems.

Computer simulations provide means for dealing with complex models with many interacting factors. Mathematical models and computer simulation have provided much of the theory that we apply to the biology of small populations. Computer simulation has an extremely important role in **population viability analysis** (PVA) which determines extinction risk due to the combined effects of demographic and environmental factors, catastrophes and genetic factors (Chapters 2 and 20).

Data sets for endangered species are typically small, so conclusions from any one species are usually not convincing. Consequently, statistical analyses frequently combine data from a variety of species or populations (**meta-analyses**). For example, the impact of inbreeding on captive mammals was evaluated by combining data on juvenile survival of inbred versus outbred offspring from 44 populations of mammals (Chapter 11). Relationships between genetic diversity and population size were also resolved in this way (Chapter 10).

Much of the supporting evidence in the book comes from laboratory studies, computer simulations and meta-analyses. However, we have sought to use examples from endangered populations wherever adequate evidence could be found.

Island theme

Parallels between populations of conservation concern and island populations are a recurring theme throughout the book. Endangered species in captivity are akin to island populations. Fragmented populations often have the characteristics of island populations, including small sizes and restricted migration, but have typically been isolated for much shorter periods than oceanic island populations.

Island populations usually experience environments different from those of their mainland counterparts, especially the absence of many predators, parasites and diseases. The evolution of endangered species in captivity has features akin to this. Island populations were frequently founded from a small number of individuals so they have often experienced population size bottlenecks. Further, they are typically smaller than their mainland counterparts. As a consequence of bottlenecks at foundation and small size, island populations usually have less genetic diversity than mainland populations, are often inbred and may have lowered reproductive fitness (Chapters 10–12). A disturbing implication of the island analogy is that island populations have proved to be much more prone to extinction than mainland populations (Table 1.1).

> Island populations share many features with endangered species, including small population size and elevated risks of extinction and so provide a useful analogy to draw upon

Sources of information

An annotated list of widely used references is given at the end of this chapter. References within the text are primarily given to reviews and recent papers that provide an entry into each topic area. The primary research information appears in the specialist journal *Conservation Genetics*, in general conservation biology journals (*Conservation Biology*, *Animal Conservation* and *Biological Conservation*) and in more broadly based evolutionary biology journals including *Molecular Ecology*, *Evolution*, *Journal of Heredity*, *Heredity*, *Genetics* and *Genetical Research*.

Summary

1. The biodiversity of the planet is rapidly being depleted due to direct and indirect human actions.

2. An endangered species is one with a high risk of extinction within a short time.

3. The primary factors contributing to extinction are habitat loss, introduced species, over-exploitation and pollution. Additional accidental (stochastic) demographic, environmental, catastrophic and genetic factors increase the risk of extinction in small populations.

4. Conservation genetics is the use of genetics to preserve species as dynamic entities that can evolve to cope with environmental change and thus minimize their risk of extinction.

5. Genetics is used to minimize extinction probabilities by minimizing inbreeding and loss of genetic diversity, identifying populations of concern, determining population structure, resolving taxonomic uncertainties, defining management units within species, identifying populations and sites for reintroductions, using molecular genetic analyses in forensics and by providing tools to improve our understanding of species biology.

GENERAL BIBLIOGRAPHY
(For full bibliographical details see References.)

Avise (1994) *Molecular Markers, Natural History and Evolution*. Readable textbook concerned with molecular population genetics, determination of life history parameters and taxonomy.

Avise & Hamrick (1996) *Conservation Genetics*. Advanced scientific reviews on the conservation genetics of major groups of animals and plants.

Burgman & Lindenmayer (1998) *Conservation Biology in the Australian Environment*. Excellent textbook in conservation biology with a focus on Australian examples and a solid treatment of genetic issues.

Falconer & Mackay (1996) *Introduction to Quantitative Genetics*. Outstanding textbook on population and quantitative genetics, with applications given for animal and plant breeding. Similar level to this textbook.

Falk & Holsinger (1991) *Genetics and Conservation of Rare Plants*. Monograph on conservation of rare plants. Advanced level, but readable.

Frankel & Soulé (1981) *Conservation and Evolution*. Excellent book on conservation biology, the first with a reasonable genetic component. Quite old, but still worth consulting. Level similar to this textbook.

Futuyma (1998) *Evolutionary Biology*. Excellent textbook covering all aspects of evolutionary biology; chapters 9–16 cover topics of direct relevance to conservation genetics.

Hartl & Clarke (1997) *Principles of Population Genetics*. Basic textbook in population genetics with a strong molecular flavour for advanced undergraduates and graduate students.

Landweber & Dobson (1999) *Genetics and the Extinction of Species*. Edited volume with contributions from different authors on reasons for extinctions, measurement of biodiversity, captive breeding, etc.

Loeschcke *et al.* (1994) *Conservation Genetics*. A collection of scientific review papers on conservation genetics by different authors. Advanced, but fairly readable.

Meffe & Carroll (1997) *Principles of Conservation Biology*. Basic textbook in conservation biology, with a reasonable coverage of genetic issues.

Primack (1998) *Essentials of Conservation Biology*. Basic textbook in conservation biology with a good, but limited coverage of genetic issues.

Quammen (1996) *The Song of the Dodo*. An interesting and stimulating book written for a popular audience; it has a fine coverage of island populations and their relevance to extinctions.

Roff (1997) *Evolutionary Quantitative Genetics*. Textbook on quantitative genetics of non-domestic populations for advanced undergraduates and above.

Schonewald-Cox *et al.* (1983) *Genetics and Conservation*. A collection of scientific review papers by different authors. Written at a level that should be understood by the audience of this book. Excellent science and still worth reading.

Singh & Krimbas (2000) *Evolutionary Genetics*. Recent reviews on all aspects of evolutionary genetics that provide the background to Sections I and II of this book. Advanced.

Smith & Wayne (1996) *Molecular Genetic Approaches in Conservation*. A book containing scientific review chapters on the molecular aspect of conservation. Advanced.

Soulé & Wilcox (1980) *Conservation Biology*. Proceedings of the conference that began the modern era of conservation biology, one that included genetic issues. A classic reference that is generally intelligible to the audience of this book. Still worth consulting.

Soulé (1987) *Viable Populations for Conservation*. An important reference to papers by different authors on the size of population required to avoid extinction. Advanced, but reasonably readable.

PROBLEMS

These problems are designed to review material on Mendelian inheritance, probability and statistics that are assumed knowledge (1.1–1.8), and to evaluate your ability to place species in the IUCN categories of risk (1.9–1.12).

1.1 Mendelian inheritance: If two parents have genotypes of A_1A_2 and A_1A_2 at a locus, what genotypes of progeny do they produce? What are the expected proportions of the different progeny?

1.2 Mendelian inheritance: What progeny genotypes are expected from the cross between $A_1A_2 B_1B_2$ and $A_1A_2 B_1B_2$ parents, assuming independent assortment of the A and B loci? What are the expected proportions of the different progeny?

1.3 Mendelian inheritance: What does independent assortment of two gene loci imply about the location of the two loci?

1.4 Transcription and translation: Given the strand of DNA below, insert the complementary strand, the mRNA, the tRNA anticodon and the amino acids specified.

Complementary DNA
Coding DNA strand   TAC TTT GGG ATT
mRNA
tRNA anticodon
Amino acids

1.5 Statistics: A family of mice produces 50 males and 80 females in their lifetime. Use a χ^2 test to determine whether this differs from a 1:1 ratio.

1.6 Probability: What are the possible ratios of females to males in families of size 4? What are their respective probabilities of occurrence?

1.7 Statistics: The four phenotypes in an F_2 were found in the numbers 100: 20: 35: 5. Use a χ^2 test to determine whether these differ from the 9:3:3:1 expectation.

1.8 Statistics: Nine golden lion tamarin females have litter sizes of 0, 1, 2, 3, 2, 1, 0, 2, and 3. What is the mean litter size? What is the standard deviation?

1.9 IUCN categories: In what IUCN category would you place the northern hairy-nosed wombat? It exists as a relatively stable population of approximately 75 individuals (say 45 adults) in one location in Queensland, Australia.

1.10 IUCN categories: In what IUCN category would you place the southern bluefin tuna? Its population size has declined by almost 90% over the last 30 years, from 3.7 million in 1965 to 423 000 in 1994.

1.11 IUCN categories: In what IUCN category would you place the thylacine, a marsupial carnivore from Tasmania, Australia? It has not been seen in the wild since 1933, and the last animal in captivity died in 1936.

1.12 IUCN categories: In what IUCN category would you place Attwater's prairie chicken? It occurs in Texas, USA and has a total population size of 456 in 1993, distributed over three fragmented populations (populations of 372, 24 and 60) that may have been isolated since 1937. The species once numbered about 1 million, and has recently been declining at a rate of about 5% per year.

PRACTICAL EXERCISES: CATEGORIZING ENDANGERMENT OF SPECIES
Provide students with groups of three species (one abundant, and two falling into different threatened categories) and ask them to categorize them using the IUCN system. Supply students with suitable reference materials. Students can work in groups of three for this. Example of species to use include the following:

Gray wolf, Puerto Rican parrot, northern right whale
Deer mouse, whooping crane, golden lion tamarin
Red kangaroo, orange-bellied parrot, koala
Indian mynah bird, giant panda, Javan rhinoceros
African buffalo, Mauritius pink pigeon, chimpanzee
European starling, Iberian lynx, Mediterranean monk seal

Chapter 2

Genetics and extinction

Inbreeding and loss of genetic diversity are inevitable in small populations of threatened species. They reduce reproduction and survival in the short term and diminish the capacity of populations to evolve in response to environmental change in the long term; they have undoubtedly contributed to previous extinctions and constitute part of the threat to endangered species.

Terms:
Demographic stochasticity, endemic, environmental stochasticity, extinction vortex, genetic diversity, inbreeding, inbreeding coefficient, inbreeding depression, major histocompatibility complex (MHC), outbreeding, self-incompatibility

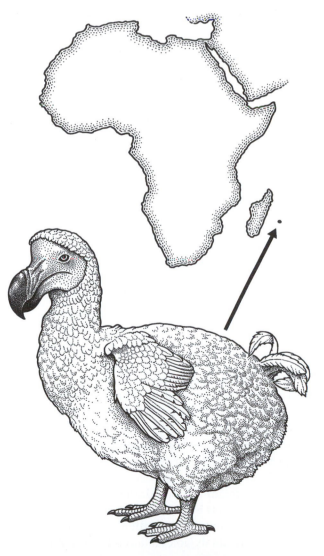

Extinct dodo and its previous distribution on the Island of Mauritius.

Genetics and the fate of endangered species

Little more than a decade ago, the contribution of genetic factors to the fate of endangered species was considered to be minor. Lande (1988) summarized this opinion by suggesting that demographic and environmental fluctuations (stochasticity), and catastrophes, would cause extinction before genetic deterioration became a serious threat to wild populations. A healthy controversy has persisted (see Caro & Laurenson 1994; Frankham 1995a; Hedrick *et al.* 1995; Caughley & Gunn 1996; Frankham & Ralls 1998; Dobson 1999; Frankham 2000). However, there is now a compelling body of both theoretical and empirical evidence supporting the contention that genetic changes in small populations are intimately involved with their fate. Specifically:

- Many surviving populations have now been shown to be genetically compromised (reduced genetic diversity and inbred)
- Inbreeding causes extinctions in deliberately inbred captive populations
- Inbreeding has contributed to extinctions in some natural populations and there is circumstantial evidence to implicate it in many other cases
- Computer projections based on real life histories, including demographic, environmental and catastrophic factors, indicate that inbreeding will cause elevated extinction risks in realistic situations faced by natural populations
- Loss of genetic diversity increases the susceptibility of populations to extinction.

Inbreeding reduces reproduction and survival

Inbreeding is the production of offspring by individuals related by descent, e.g. self-fertilization, brother–sister, parent–offspring, cousin matings, etc. (Box 2.1 and Chapter 11). Inbreeding reduces reproduction and survival (reproductive fitness) – this is referred to as **inbreeding depression**. For example, inbred individuals showed higher juvenile mortality than outbred individuals in 41 of 44 captive mammal populations studied by Ralls & Ballou (1983). On average, brother–sister mating resulted in a 33% reduction in juvenile survival. By extrapolation, it was anticipated that inbreeding would increase the risk of extinction in wild populations. Further, the impact of inbreeding depression was expected to be greater in the wild than in captivity, as natural environments are generally harsher.

There is now clear evidence that inbreeding adversely affects most wild populations. Crnokrak & Roff (1999) reviewed 157 valid data sets, including 34 species, for inbreeding depression in natural situations. In 141 cases (90%) inbred individuals had poorer attributes than comparable outbreds (i.e. they showed inbreeding depression), two were equal and only 14 were in the opposite direction. Results were very similar across birds, mammals, poikilotherms and plants. Significant inbreeding depression has been reported in at least another 15 taxa (Chapter 12). Species exhibiting inbreeding depression in the wild include the following: mammals (golden lion tamarins, lions, native mice, shrews and Soay sheep), birds (greater prairie chicken, Mexican jay, song sparrow, American kestrel and reed warbler), fish (Atlantic salmon, desert topminnow and rainbow trout), a reptile, a snail, an insect (butterfly) and many species of plants (see Bensch *et al.* 1994; Frankham 1995a; Madsen *et al.* 1996; Brown & Brown 1998; Saccheri *et al.* 1998; Westemeier *et al.* 1998; Coltman *et al.* 1999).

In the desert topminnow fish, Vrijenhoek (1994) used a co-occurring and related asexual species, lacking genetic variation, as a natural control. Prior to a drought that eliminated their habitat, the genetically diverse and sexually reproducing topminnows numerically dominated the asexual species. Following the drought, populations of both species were re-established. However, the asexual species now numerically dominated the sexual species. The sexual species had lost much of its genetic variation (and was inbred) as a consequence of small numbers of individuals taking part in the re-establishment (founding) event. After deliberate replacement of 30 of the sexual fish with 30 outbred individuals from elsewhere, to restore genetic diversity, the sexual species regained numerical dominance (details in Box 12.1). In a similar example, the Illinois population of greater prairie chickens declined from millions to only 200 in 1962, and failed to recover following habitat restoration. It showed clear evidence of inbreeding depression by reduced fertility and hatchability. However, when inbreeding effects were removed by crossing to unrelated birds from other states, the population recovered its fertility and hatchability and grew in numbers.

Box 2.1 | Measures of inbreeding

Inbreeding is the production of offspring from related individuals. There are repeated matings of relatives in the pedigree below of the Nigerian giraffe X born in Paris Zoo in 1992 (Bingaman-Lackey 1999). This highly inbred calf died three weeks after birth.

There are several ways to measure the extent of inbreeding in a population. While these measures are detailed in Chapter 11, it is useful to briefly explore the concept in the present context.

THE INBREEDING COEFFICIENT (F)

The inbreeding coefficient of an individual refers to how closely related its parents are. When parents are unrelated, offspring $F = 0$, while when inbreeding is complete $F = 1$. Level of inbreeding for different kinds of relationships among parents are:

Parents	Offspring F
Unrelated	0
Brother–sister, mother–son, or father–daughter	0.25
Half-brother–half-sister (half-sibs)	0.125
First cousins	0.0625
Self-fertilization (or selfing)	0.5

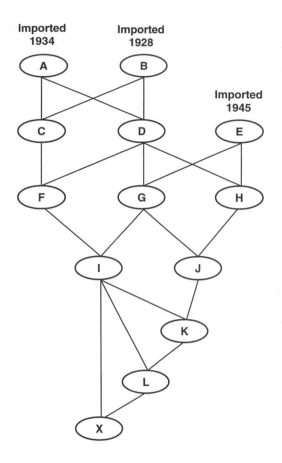

Imported
1934

Imported
1928

Imported
1945

Inbreeding accumulates in closed populations (those without immigration) and complete inbreeding can eventually be reached with repeated inbred matings; an F of 0.999 is reached after 10 generations of self-fertilization, while an F of 0.986 is reached after 20 generations of brother–sister mating. The Nigerian giraffe X above had an inbreeding coefficient of 0.52 (see Problem 11.11).

AVERAGE INBREEDING
A second measure of inbreeding is the average inbreeding coefficient of all individuals in a population. In small closed populations, average F will inevitably rise as mates become increasingly related. Average F increases at a rate of $1/(2N)$ per generation in a randomly breeding population of size N (Chapter 10).

The figure opposite illustrates the increase in average inbreeding coefficient in populations of 10 and 20 randomly breeding individuals. In the population of size 10, average F reaches the level of brother–sister matings ($F = 0.25$) by generation 6, while the population of size 20 reaches this inbreeding level by generation 12.

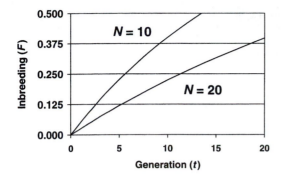

Genetic diversity is the extent of heritable variation in a population, or species, or across a group of species, e.g. heterozygosity, or number of alleles, or heritability (Chapters 3, 4 and 5). Genetic diversity is required for populations to evolve in response to environmental change (Chapters 6, 8 and 10). Such environmental change is a ubiquitous feature of life on Earth. Consequently, if there is no genetic diversity in a population or species, it is likely to go extinct in response to major environmental change. Genetic diversity is lost in small random mating populations at the same time they become inbred, so the two processes are closely related (Chapters 8, 10 and 11).

Genetic diversity is required for populations and species to evolve in response to environmental change

Relationship between inbreeding and extinction

The first line of evidence on the relationship between inbreeding and extinction came from deliberately inbred populations of laboratory and domestic animals and plants. Between 80% and 95% of deliberately inbred populations die out after eight generations of brother–sister mating or three generations of self-fertilization (Frankel & Soulé 1981). For example, 338 populations of Japanese quail, inbred by continued brother–sister mating, were all extinct after four generations. Such extinctions could be due to either inbreeding, or to **demographic stochasticity** (fluctuations in birth and death rates and sex-ratios), or a combination of these effects. However, under circumstances where

Deliberately inbred populations of laboratory and domestic animals and plants show greatly elevated extinction rates

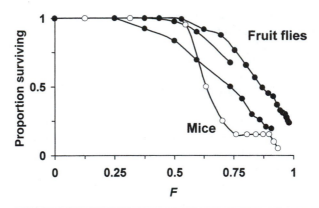

Fig. 2.1 Relationship between inbreeding and extinction. Populations of mice and two species of fruit flies (one with two populations) were inbred using brother sister–matings (Bowman & Falconer 1960; Kosuda 1972; Rumball *et al.* 1994). Demographic stochasticity made very little or no contribution to these extinctions (Frankham 1995b). *The proportions of populations going extinct rises with inbreeding, but extinctions do not begin until intermediate, threshold, levels of inbreeding have been reached.*

demographic stochasticity is excluded, inbreeding clearly increased the risk of extinction in captive populations (Frankham 1995b, 1998). Examples from mice and fruit flies are shown in Fig. 2.1.

Rate of inbreeding and extinction risk

Even slow inbreeding increases the risk of extinction

Rapid inbreeding (brother–sister mating or self-fertilization) was used to inbreed the populations referred to above. Natural populations of **outbreeding** wild animals and plants (those whose mating systems do not include substantial selfing or close inbreeding) are usually subject to slower rates of inbreeding, dependent on their population sizes (Box 2.1). Slower inbreeding allows natural selection more opportunity to remove genetically compromised individuals (and thereby remove deleterious alleles). For fitness components such as survival and fecundity, slower rates of inbreeding generally do lead to less inbreeding depression than fast inbreeding for the same total amount for inbreeding, although the effects are typically small (Chapter 12).

However, even slow rates of inbreeding increase the risk of extinction; it just takes longer for inbreeding to accumulate and extinction to occur. For example, 15 of 60 fruit fly populations, inbred due to sizes of 67 individuals per generation, went extinct within 210 generations (Latter *et al.* 1995). In a similar manner, 5 of 6 replicate housefly populations of size 50 went extinct over 64 generations (Reed & Bryant 2000). Further, a comparison of extinction risks for the same amount of inbreeding, but due to slower double first-cousin versus faster brother–sister inbreeding, revealed no significant difference in extinction risk due to rate of inbreeding (Frankham 1995b). Accordingly, differences in the effects of rate of inbreeding on extinction risk for the same amount of inbreeding are unlikely to be large.

Do taxonomic groups differ in susceptibility to inbreeding depression?

Much information on inbreeding and extinctions comes from species used in laboratory experiments. It is therefore essential to know whether these findings can be extrapolated to other species and taxonomic groups. Most studies find little evidence of difference among major diploid taxa in inbreeding depression for naturally outbreeding species. Inbreeding depression for wild populations of homeotherms, poikilotherms and plants do not differ significantly (Crnokrak & Roff 1999). Nor were there any significant differences in inbreeding depression under captive conditions among mammalian orders (Ralls *et al.* 1988). Further, a comparison of extinction proneness due to inbreeding in 25 captive populations failed to find significant differences among mammals, birds, invertebrates and plants (Frankham unpublished data); extinction rates at $F = 0.85$ (equivalent to nine generations of brother–sister mating) were 68% for mammals, 81% for birds, 60% for invertebrates and 99% for a single plant species.

Inbreeding depression in plants is typically higher for gymnosperms than angiosperms (Husband & Schemske 1996). This could be related to a higher level of polyploidy (more than two doses of each chromosome, e.g., $4n$ vs. $2n$) in the latter than the former. Since the rate of increase in homozygosity is slower in polyploids than in diploids, polyploids are expected to suffer less inbreeding depression (see Chapter 12).

> Differences in susceptibility to inbreeding depression among mammals, birds, invertebrates and plants seem to be small

Inbreeding and extinction in the wild

Since inbreeding leads to elevated extinction risks in captive populations, it is logical to extrapolate this to wild populations. Three lines of evidence point to the susceptibility of wild populations to inbreeding and consequent elevated extinction risk:

- Computer projections have predicted that inbreeding will increase extinction risks for wild populations
- Many small surviving wild populations have now been shown to be genetically compromised
- Direct evidence of inbreeding and loss of genetic variation contributing to the extinction of populations in nature has been presented.

> There is a growing body of evidence showing that inbreeding elevates extinction risks in wild populations

Computer projections

Computer projections incorporating factual life history information are often used to assess the combined impact of all deterministic and stochastic factors on the probability of extinction of populations (see Chapter 20). Information on population size, births and survival rates and their variation over age and years together with measures of

> Computer projections predict that inbreeding elevates extinction risk for most outbreeding wild populations

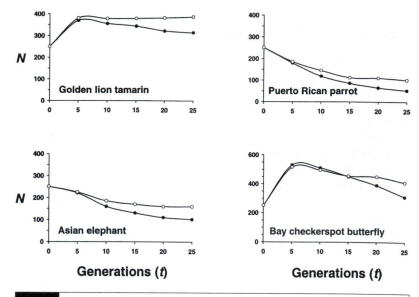

Fig. 2.2 Impact of inbreeding on population size. Computer projections of population sizes for threatened populations of two mammals, a bird and an invertebrate in the wild, when the deleterious effects of inbreeding are included (●), or excluded (○).

inbreeding depression, changes in habitat quality, etc. form the input. Stochastic models are then run through repeated cycles to project the fate of populations into the future.

Mills & Smouse (1994) used computer simulations to show that inbreeding generally increases the risk of extinction, especially in species with low reproductive rates. These simulations encompassed only a 20-year time frame, representing less than five generations for the types of life cycles they simulated. Since the effects of inbreeding continue to accumulate over generations in closed populations, their simulations underestimate the impacts of inbreeding over periods of conservation concern (typically 100–200 years). Computer projections over 100 years, using a range of outbreeding bird, mammal, and invertebrate life cycles, were conducted by Brook and co-workers (unpublished data). Almost all yielded substantial increases in extinction risk when the effects of inbreeding were included, compared to runs with inbreeding effects excluded. Runs for four different species show lower population size for models that include inbreeding depression than for those excluding it (Fig. 2.2). These differences translate into differences in extinction risk over time. A similar computer projection for the rare European plant *Gentiana pneumonanthe* yielded similar conclusions (Oostermeijer 2000).

Direct evidence of extinctions due to inbreeding and loss of genetic diversity

The most compelling single body of evidence for the involvement of inbreeding in extinction of natural populations is for butterfly populations in Finland (Box 2.2). Inbreeding was a significant predictor of extinction risk after the effects of all other ecological and demographic variables had been removed. Further, experimental populations of the evening primrose plant founded with a low level of genetic diversity (and high inbreeding) exhibited 75% extinction rates over three generations in the wild, while populations with lower inbreeding showed only a 21% extinction rate (Newman & Pilson 1997). Differences in inbreeding, as well as differences in genetic diversity, were presumed to be involved.

> There is direct evidence that inbreeding and loss of genetic diversity increase the risk of extinction for populations in nature

Box 2.2	Inbreeding and extinction risk in butterfly populations in Finland (Saccheri *et al.* 1998)

Forty-two butterfly populations in Finland were typed for genetic markers in 1995, and their extinction or survival recorded in the following year. Of these, 35 survived to autumn 1996 and seven went extinct. Extinction rates were higher for populations with lower heterozygosity, an indication of inbreeding, even after accounting for the effects of demographic and environmental variables (population size, time trend in population size and area) known to affect extinction risk, as shown in the figure below. The different curves represent the relationships between extinction probability and proportion of loci heterozygous for populations with different numbers (1–5) of larval groups.

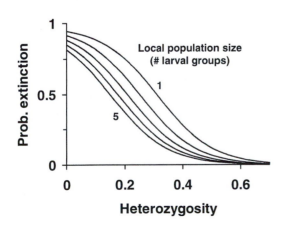

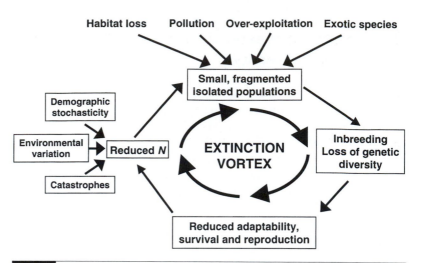

Fig. 2.3 The extinction vortex. This describes the possible interactions between human impacts, inbreeding, loss of genetic diversity and demographic instability in a downward spiral towards extinction.

Circumstantial evidence for extinctions due to inbreeding

The effects of inbreeding depression and loss of genetic diversity can interact with demographic, environmental and catastrophic factors in an 'extinction vortex'

The responses of populations to **environmental stochasticity** (random unpredictable variation in environmental factors), demographic stochasticity and the impact of catastrophes are not independent of inbreeding and genetic diversity. Inbreeding, on average, reduces birth rates and increases death rates and may distort sex-ratios. It therefore interacts with the basic parameters determining population viability, such as population growth rate and variation in population size. Adverse effects of inbreeding on population growth rates probably occur in most naturally outbreeding species.

Experimental populations of mosquito fish founded from brother–sister pairs showed 56% lower growth in numbers than populations founded from unrelated pairs (Leberg 1990a). Strong reductions in population growth were also observed in flour beetle populations inbred due to small numbers (McCauley & Wade 1981). They even detected adverse effects at $F = 0.1$ (equivalent to a level between cousin and half-sib matings).

If populations become small for any reason, they become more inbred and less demographically stable, further reducing population size and increasing inbreeding. This feedback between reduced population size, loss of genetic diversity and inbreeding is referred to as the **extinction vortex** (Fig. 2.3). One very clear message derives from Fig. 2.3. The complicated interactions between genetic, demographic and environmental factors can make it extremely difficult to identify the

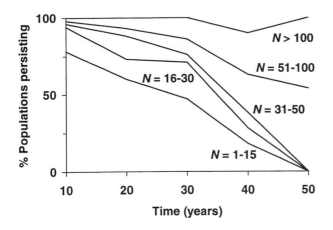

Fig. 2.4 Extinction rates are higher in smaller than larger populations. Relationship between persistence and population size in North American bighorn sheep (after Berger 1990).

immediate cause(s) for any particular extinction event (see Chapters 12 and 20).

Smaller populations are expected to be more extinction prone than larger ones for demographic, ecological and genetic reasons. Berger (1990) found a strong relationship between population size and persistence in North American bighorn sheep (Fig. 2.4). All populations of < 50 became extinct within 50 years. A wide variety of demographic, ecological and genetic factors may have contributed to these extinctions. Inbreeding depression and loss of genetic diversity were among those considered likely to be involved. In a related vein, mammalian extinctions in national parks in western North America were related to park area, and presumably population sizes (Newmark 1995). Extinctions were more frequent for populations with smaller initial population sizes, or large fluctuations in population size, than in those with longer generation times. As we will see later, all of these effects are predicted by genetic considerations (Chapters 10–12), but most are also expected from demographic and environmental considerations.

> Small populations are more likely to suffer from extinctions than large populations for both genetic and ecological reasons

Declines in population size or extinction in the wild have been attributed, at least in part, to inbreeding in many populations including bighorn sheep, Florida panthers, Isle Royale gray wolves, greater prairie chickens, heath hens, middle spotted woodpeckers, adders, and many island species (Frankham 1995a; Westemeier *et al.* 1998; Madsen *et al.* 1999). Further, inbreeding colonial spiders have a higher rate of colony extinction than non-inbreeding species.

> There is circumstantial evidence that inbreeding has contributed to many other wildlife extinctions

Extinction proneness of island populations

Recorded extinctions since 1600 reveal that a majority of extinctions have been of island forms, even though island species represent a minority of total species in all groups (Table 1.1). For example, only 20% of all bird species live on islands, but 80% of bird species driven to extinction have been island dwellers (Myers 1979). Further, substantial proportions

> The majority of extinctions of plants and animals have been of island species, although these represent a minority of all species. Endemic island species are more prone to extinction than non-endemic species

of species listed as endangered and vulnerable species are insular (Chapter 1). In vertebrates, **endemic** island species (species not found elsewhere) are more prone to extinction than non-endemic species. This holds true for birds in general, for New Zealand land birds, and for reptiles (Frankham 1998).

Human factors have been the major recorded causes of extinction on islands over the past 50 000 years. The human impacts have typically driven down population sizes to the point where stochastic factors come into play and the *coup de grâce* is usually delivered by stochastic factors, whether demographic, environmental, catastrophic or genetic.

The mechanisms underlying susceptibility of island populations to extinction are controversial. Ecologists stress the susceptibility of small island populations to demographic and environmental stochasticity. However, this susceptibility is also predicted on genetic grounds (Frankham 1998). Island populations are expected to be inbred due to both low numbers of founders on remote islands (often a single inseminated female animal or a single plant propagule), and subsequent small population sizes. There is essentially little critical evidence to separate the effects of 'non-genetic' factors from the effects of inbreeding and loss of genetic diversity. Inbreeding can certainly diminish the resistance of a population by reducing its reproductive rate and survival such that it is more susceptible to 'non-genetic' factors.

Circumstantial evidence points to inbreeding and loss of genetic diversity contributing to the extinction proneness of island populations of many species

Island populations typically have less genetic diversity and are more inbred than mainland populations (Frankham 1997, 1998). A meta-analysis of data involving 202 island populations revealed that 82% had lower levels of genetic diversity than their mainland counterparts.

Island populations are significantly inbred with endemic island populations more so than non-endemics (Fig. 2.5). Significantly, inbreeding in many island populations is at levels where captive populations show an elevated risk of extinction. The levels of inbreeding in these island populations are not in accord with predictions that demographic and environmental stochasticity and catastrophes will drive populations to extinction before genetic factors become a problem. A particularly telling case is that of black-footed rock wallabies on Barrow Island and other islands off the west coast of Australia (Box 2.3). These populations have very low levels of genetic diversity and the Barrow Island population exhibits evidence of inbreeding depression. In addition, euros (a kangaroo species) on Barrow Island also have reduced genetic diversity and suffer from chronic anaemia and higher parasite loads than their mainland counterparts (Eldridge *et al.* personal communication).

The greater extinction proneness of endemic than non-endemic island species is predicted by genetic, but not by demographic and ecological considerations

Endemic island populations have generally existed on islands at restricted population sizes for longer than non-endemics. They are therefore expected to be more inbred. This is evident in Fig. 2.5. Consequently, endemic island populations are expected to be more prone to extinction than non-endemics for genetic reasons. Conversely, there are no obvious demographic or environmental reasons why endemic and non-endemic island populations should differ in extinction proneness. Consequently, this indicates that genetic factors are, at least partly, responsible for the extinction proneness of island populations.

Endemics

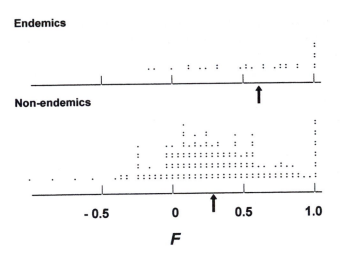

Non-endemics

-0.5   0   0.5   1.0

F

Fig. 2.5 Distributions of inbreeding coefficients in endemic and non-endemic island populations of wildlife (after Frankham 1998). Arrows indicate means. *Island populations are significantly inbred and endemic populations more so than non-endemics. Many populations are inbred to levels where captive populations show elevated extinction risks.*

Box 2.3	Island populations of black-footed rock wallabies have persisted for 1600 or more generations at small sizes, are highly inbred, have low levels of genetic diversity and exhibit inbreeding depression (Eldridge *et al.* 1999)

Rock wallabies are small macropod marsupials (about 1 m tall) that live on rocky out-crops on the Australian mainland and on offshore islands (see map below). The shaded regions on the map show the distribution of black-footed rock wallabies on the mainland and on offshore islands. The Barrow Island population of black-footed rock wallabies (1) has been isolated from the mainland for 8000 years (about 1600 generations) and has a relatively small population size. Genetic diversity in the

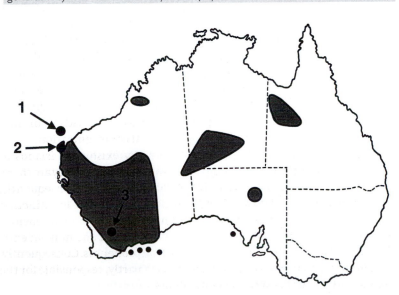

Barrow Island population, and in other island populations, is markedly lower than in mainland sites at Exmouth (2) and Wheatbelt (3).

The Barrow Island population has the lowest recorded genetic diversity in any vertebrate, as assessed by microsatellites (described in Chapter 3). Genetic diversity for two mainland and the Barrow Island populations are shown below. Other island populations (shown as •) also have low genetic diversity, as described in Chapter 13.

Population (location)	Proportion of loci polymorphic	Mean number of alleles/locus	Average heterozygosity
Barrow Island (1)	0.1	1.2	0.05
Mainland			
Exmouth (2)	1.0	3.4	0.62
Wheatbelt (3)	1.0	4.4	0.56

The Barrow Island population has an inbreeding coefficient of 0.91. Further, it displays inbreeding depression compared to the mainland population. The frequency of lactating females is 92% in mainland rock wallabies, but only 52% on Barrow Island. These rock wallaby populations demonstrate that genetics can have an impact before demographic and environmental stochasticity or catastrophes cause extinctions. They have clearly survived stochastic fluctuations and catastrophes, but they are suffering genetic problems that increase their risk of extinction.

Island populations have been viewed as ideal sources for restocking depleted or extinct mainland populations, especially in Australasian species. However, as they often have low genetic diversity and are inbred, they may not be good candidates for translocations, if alternative mainland populations still exist.

Humans are fragmenting mainland populations and creating 'island' populations

Humans are fragmenting habitat throughout the world. This results in 'islands' (remnants, reserves, national parks, etc.) in a 'sea' of now-inhospitable landscape (Chapter 13). Consequently, these population fragments share many characteristics, including susceptibility to extinction, with their island counterparts. This is the case for isolated populations of greater prairie chickens in Illinois and adders in Sweden. Both populations declined due to inbreeding depression and only recovered following introduction of additional genetic diversity (Chapter 12).

Relationship between loss of genetic diversity and extinction

To cope with ever-changing environments, species must evolve, or face extinction

In the section above we have briefly surveyed the relationship between inbreeding, inbreeding depression and extinction risk. We now focus on the intimately related issue of loss of genetic diversity, particularly with respect to loss of potential for future adaptive evolution.

Natural populations face continuous assaults from environmental changes including new diseases, pests, parasites, competitors and predators, pollution, climatic cycles such as the *El Niño–La Niña* cycles, and human-induced global climate change. Species must evolve to cope with these new conditions or face extinction. To evolve, species require genetic diversity (Chapter 6). Naturally outbreeding species with large populations normally possess large stores of genetic diversity that confer differences among individuals in their responses to such environmental changes (Chapters 3 and 6). Evolutionary responses to environmental change have been observed in many species (Chapter 6). For example, over 200 species of moths have evolved black body colours (melanics) to aid in camouflage in response to industrial pollution (Kettlewell 1973).

Small populations typically have lower levels of genetic diversity than large populations. This is due to sampling of alleles in the parental generation in production of offspring. During this random sampling process, some alleles increase in frequency, others decrease and some alleles may be lost entirely. The smaller the population, the more change there will be between the parental and offspring gene pools. Over time genetic diversity will decline, with loss being more rapid in smaller than in larger populations (Chapters 8 and 10).

Genetic diversity is lost in small populations

Genetic variation allows populations to tolerate a wide range of environmental extremes (Hoffmann & Parsons 1997). These include ability to tolerate climatic extremes, heavy metal pollutants, herbicides, pesticides, etc. Humans are generating increasing rates of environmental change. For example, increasing levels of greenhouse gas are causing global climate change. If populations are to cope with these factors they require genetic diversity.

Populations with lower genetic diversity are poorer at coping with environmental extremes and diseases than populations with higher genetic diversity

There are compelling theoretical predictions that loss of genetic diversity will reduce the ability of populations to evolve in response to environmental change. Experimental evidence validates these predictions. Consequently, we expect a similar relationship between loss of genetic diversity and extinction rate due to environmental change. However, there are only a few examples where extinctions of natural populations can be directly attributed to lack of genetic variation.

Relationship between loss of genetic diversity at self-incompatibility loci and extinction in plants

The most direct evidence of a relationship between loss of genetic diversity and increased risk of extinction comes from studies of **self-incompatibility** loci in plants. About half of all flowering plant species have genetic systems that reduce or prevent self-fertilization (Richards 1997). Such self-incompatibility prevents fertilization when the pollen and the egg come from the same plant. Self-incompatibility is regulated by one or more loci that may have 50 or more alleles in large populations. If the same allele is present in a pollen grain and the stigma, fertilization by that pollen grain will not be successful. Self-incompatability is presumed to have evolved to avoid the deleterious effects of inbreeding.

Loss of self-incompatibility alleles in small populations of many plant species leads to reduced reproductive fitness

Self-incompatibility alleles are lost by random sampling in small populations. This leads to a reduction in the number of plants that can potentially fertilize the eggs of any individual and eventually to reduced seed set and extinction. For example, the Lakeside daisy population from Illinois declined to three plants. This population did not reproduce for 15 years despite bee pollination, as it contained only one allele (Demauro 1993), i.e. this population was functionally extinct. Plants did however produce viable seed when fertilized with pollen from large populations in Ohio or Canada. While reduced fitness due to loss of self-incompatibility alleles has only been documented in a few species of plants (Les *et al.* 1991; Demauro 1993; Young *et al.* 2000), it is likely to be a problem, or become so, in most threatened, self-incompatible plants.

Relationship between loss of genetic diversity and susceptibility to disease, pests and parasites

Populations with low genetic diversity are expected to suffer more seriously from diseases, pests and parasites than those with high genetic diversity

Novel pathogens constitute one of the most significant challenges to all species. Indeed it has been argued that the evolutionary origin of sexual reproduction, to generate diverse genetic combinations (genotypes), was in response to pathogen pressure (Hurst & Peck 1996). Loss of genetic diversity severely diminishes the capacity of populations to respond to this pressure (Chapters 6, 8 and 10). For example, the American chestnut was driven to near extinction in the 1950s by the introduced chestnut blight disease, as it had no genetic variation for resistance. Previously, the chestnut had dominated the northeastern forests of the USA, so this event represents one of the largest ecological disasters to strike the USA.

There is circumstantial evidence that loss of genetic diversity in the **major histocompatibility complex** (MHC) is associated with reduced ability to evolve to cope with new and changed diseases. In most vertebrates, there are very high levels of genetic diversity at the major histocompatibility complex, a cluster of loci involved in immune responses. Genetic diversity is maintained by selection that either favours heterozygotes or rare genotypes (Chapter 9). Even though MHC diversity is maintained by selection, it is lost by chance during sampling of gametes in small populations (Seddon & Baverstock 1998; Zegers 2000). With reduced diversity at the MHC in small populations, a pathogen capable of killing one individual becomes capable of killing all. Conversely, individuals within genetically variable populations will differ widely in their abilities to respond to new disease threats. Following sequential assaults by different pathogens, populations with high genetic diversity are more likely to persist than populations with low genetic diversity. Populations with low genetic diversity may survive some assaults, but are likely to succumb to others (Fig. 2.6). For example, Lively *et al.* (1990) found that fish populations with low genetic diversity had higher parasite loads than populations with greater diversity. Mortality due to gastrointestinal nematode parasites, following periods of high population density, is elevated in Soay sheep with low genetic diversity and high inbreeding when compared with sheep with more diversity (Coltman *et al.* 1999). Parasite levels

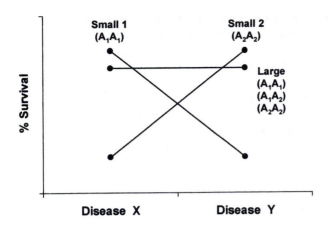

Fig. 2.6 Hypothetical example of the relationship between genetic diversity and disease resistance. Two small inbred populations, each homozygous for different alleles, are resistant to one disease but not to the other. Conversely, a larger population containing both alleles has resistance to both diseases.

are negatively correlated with levels of genetic diversity among populations of deer mice and bumblebees (Meagher 1999).

Summary

1. Inbreeding and loss of genetic diversity are of conservation concern as they increase the risk of extinction.

2. Inbreeding reduces reproductive fitness in essentially all well-studied populations of naturally outbreeding species.

3. Inbreeding increases the risk of extinction in captive populations, and there is growing evidence that it is one of the factors causing extinctions of wild populations.

4. Loss of genetic diversity reduces the ability of species to evolve to cope with environmental change.

FURTHER READING

Demauro (1993) Describes functional extinction in a population of Lakeside daisies due to loss of genetic diversity for self-incompatibility alleles.

Frankham (1995b) Review and analysis of the evidence on the relationship between inbreeding and extinction in laboratory and domestic species.

Frankham & Ralls (1998) A brief news and views describing the Saccheri et al. (1998) article and reviewing evidence that refutes claims that demographic and environmental factors are likely to drive populations to extinction before genetic factors become important.

Hedrick et al. (1995) Response addressing the controversy on the role of genetics in extinction.

Lande (1988) Summarizes the view that demographic and environmental factors are likely to drive populations to extinction before genetic factors become important.

Mills & Smouse (1994) Detailed computer modelling work showing that genetic factors often make important contributions to extinction risk in wild populations.

Saccheri et al. (1998) Describes the first direct evidence that inbreeding contributes to the extinction of wild populations in nature.

Westemeier et al. (1998) Describes decline of a small, isolated greater prairie chicken population in Illinois due to loss of genetic diversity and inbreeding, and its recovery following introduction of unrelated birds from other states.

PROBLEMS

2.1 Inbreeding: What is inbreeding?

2.2 Inbreeding: Why is inbreeding of conservation concern?

2.3 Relationship between population size and extinction: What factors could account for the association of extinction rates and population size in bighorn sheep (Fig. 2.4)?

PRACTICAL EXERCISES: COMPUTER PROJECTIONS

Use the VORTEX simulation package to determine the extinction risk of the following populations when the effects of inbreeding on reproductive fitness are included and when they are ignored. Use the following input files for Mauritius pink pigeon and the Capricorn silvereye, plus that for the golden lion tamarin (Fig. 20.4). Number of individuals in each species are adjusted for this exercise. Look for other data files on the book's web site (Preface).

PIGEON.OUT ***Output Filename***
N ***Graphing Files?***
1000 ***Simulations***
100 ***Years***
1 ***Reporting Interval***
0 ***Definition of Extinction***
1 ***Populations***
Y ***Inbreeding Depression?***
3.14 ***Lethal equivalents***
0.5 ***Prop genetic load as lethals***
N ***EV concordance repro and surv?***
3 ***Types Of Catastrophes***
M ***Monogamous, Polygynous, or
   Hermaphroditic***
1 ***Female Breeding Age***
1 ***Male Breeding Age***
15 ***Maximum Age***
0.55 ***Sex Ratio***
2 ***Maximum Litter Size (0 = normal
   distribution) *****
N ***Density Dependent Breeding?***
40.0 **breeding
4.0 ***EV—Reproduction***
87.5 ***Population 1: Percent Litter Size 1***
25.0 *FMort age 0
5.0 ***EV—FemaleMortality***

15.0 *Adult FMort
2.0 ***EV—AdultFemaleMortality***
25.0 *MMort age 0
5.0 ***EV—MaleMortality***
15.0 *Adult MMort
2.0 ***EV—AdultMaleMortality***
6.0 ***Prob Of Catastrophe 1***
1.0 ***Severity—Reproduction***
0.5 ***Severity—Survival***
3.0 ***Prob Of Catastrophe 2***
1.0 ***Severity—Reproduction***
0.9 ***Severity—Survival***
1.0 ***Prob Of Catastrophe 3***
0.9 ***Severity—Reproduction***
0.5 ***Severity—Survival***
N ***All Males Breeders?***
80.0 ***Percent Males In Breeding Pool***
Y ***Start At Stable Age Distribution?***
16 ***Initial Population Size***
35 ***K***
0.0 ***EV—K***
N ***Trend In K?***
N ***Harvest?***
N ***Supplement?***
N ***AnotherSimulation?***

SILV_EYE.OUT ***Output Filename***
N ***Graphing Files?***
1000 ***Simulations***
100 ***Years***
1 ***Reporting Interval***
0 ***Definition of Extinction***
1 ***Populations***
Y ***Inbreeding Depression?***
3.14 ***Lethal equivalents***
0.5 ***Prop of genetic load as lethals***
Y ***EV concordance repro and surv?***
1 ***Types Of Catastrophes***
M ***Monogamous, Polygynous, or
   Hermaphroditic***
1 ***Female Breeding Age***
1 ***Male Breeding Age***
11 ***Maximum Age***
0.5 ***Sex Ratio***
0 ***Maximum Litter Size (0 = normal distribution) *****
N ***Density Dependent Breeding?***
77.5 **breeding
8.2 ***EV—Reproduction***

1.927 ***Population 1: Mean Litter Size***
1.245 ***Population 1: SD in Litter Size***
42.3 *FMort age 0
8.93 ***EV—FemaleMortality***
37.6 *Adult FMort
9.31 ***EV—AdultFemaleMortality***
42.3 *MMort age 0
8.93 ***EV—MaleMortality***
37.6 *Adult MMort
9.31 ***EV—AdultMaleMortality***
10.0 ***Probability Of Catastrophe 1***
1.0 ***Severity—Reproduction***
0.645 ***Severity—Survival***
Y ***All Males Breeders?***
Y ***Start At Stable Age Distribution?***
342 ***Initial Population Size***
500 ***K***
50.0 ***EV—K***
N ***Trend In K?***
N ***Harvest?***
N ***Supplement?***
N ***AnotherSimulation?***

Section I

Evolutionary genetics of natural populations

Since our objective in conservation genetics is to preserve species as dynamic entities, capable of evolving to adapt with environmental change, it is essential to understand the natural forces determining evolutionary change. Such information is indispensable if we are to understand how to genetically manage threatened and endangered populations. Since evolution at its most basic level is a change in the genetic composition of a population, it only occurs when there is genetic diversity. Consequently, we need to appreciate how genetic diversity arises, how it is lost, and what forms of genetic diversity exist.

Extent of genetic diversity

Chapter 3 introduces methods for measuring genetic diversity for DNA, proteins, deleterious alleles and quantitative characters, and documents levels of genetic diversity for them. Most large populations of animals and plants contain extensive genetic diversity. However, levels of genetic diversity are often reduced in small populations, island populations and endangered species.

Genetic constitution of populations

To evaluate changes in genetic diversity, we must have means for quantifying it. **Chapter 4** covers the estimation of allele (gene) frequencies and heterozygosity that are used to describe diversity at single loci. **Chapter 5** describes the measures used to characterize genetic diversity for quantitative characters, especially the concept of heritability. Quantitative characters are centrally involved in the major areas of conservation concern, evolutionary potential, the deleterious effects of inbreeding and the deleterious effects that sometimes occur when different populations are mixed.

Changes in genetic diversity

Genetic diversity is generated by mutation, and the frequency of different alleles change due to migration, selection and chance. The roles of these forces in natural evolutionary changes for large populations are discussed in Chapters 6–9. Since environment change is ubiquitous, species must adapt to better cope with these changes. Selection is the only agent leading to adaptive evolutionary changes (**Chapter 6**). Deleterious mutations exist in populations due to a balance between input of deleterious alleles through mutation and their removal by natural selection (**Chapter 7**). Deleterious mutations have major conservation implications, as they cause the reductions in reproductive fitness associated with inbreeding.

Chapter 8 is concerned with evolution in small populations, the situation for most species of conservation concern. Evolutionary processes in small populations differ in two critical ways from those in large populations:
• Chance has a much greater role
• Selection has a lesser impact.

Chapter 9 considers how genetic diversity is maintained in natural populations, as we are concerned with the mechanisms normally involved in retaining evolutionary potential. This information provides the background for devising genetic management procedures to retain genetic diversity in threatened species. The relative importance of chance, mutation and selection in maintaining genetic diversity varies among different traits (DNA, proteins, visible polymorphisms, gene clusters, and quantitative characters). A proportion of the diversity in populations is selectively neutral. It arises by mutation and its fate is influenced by chance sampling events in finite populations. Other alleles are actively maintained by the action of balancing selection. A substantial proportion of the genetic diversity for fitness characters results from mutation–selection balance. In small populations, the influence of the various forces changes, with chance assuming a greater role. Even alleles subject to selection are lost by chance.

Chapter 3

Genetic diversity

Genetic diversity is required for populations to adapt to environmental change. It is measured using an array of molecular and quantitative methods. Large populations of naturally outbreeding species usually have extensive genetic diversity, but it is usually reduced in populations and species of conservation concern

Terms:
Allelic diversity, allozyme, chloroplast DNA (cpDNA), DNA fingerprint, electrophoresis, exon, genetic distance, genetic load, genome, heterozygosity, intron, inversion, locus, microsatellite, mitochondrial DNA (mtDNA), monomorphic, polymerase chain reaction (PCR), polymorphism, quantitative character, quantitative genetic variation, randomly amplified polymorphic DNA (RAPD), restriction fragment length polymorphism (RFLP), silent substitution, single nucleotide polymorphism (SNP)

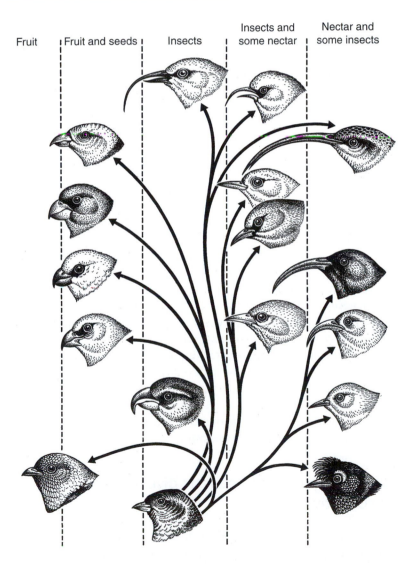

Fruit | Fruit and seeds | Insects | Insects and some nectar | Nectar and some insects

Diversification in endangered Hawaiian honeycreepers. All were derived from one finch-like ancestral species about 5 million years ago. Diets of different forms are indicated (after Whitfield *et al.* 1987).

Importance of genetic diversity

Genetic diversity is required for populations to evolve to cope with environmental change, and loss of genetic diversity is often associated with reduced reproductive fitness

Maintenance of genetic diversity is a major focus in conservation biology. First, environmental change is a continuous process and genetic diversity is required for populations to evolve to adapt to such change. Second, loss of genetic diversity is often associated with inbreeding and reduction in reproductive fitness. Consequently, IUCN recognizes the need to conserve genetic diversity as one of three global conservation priorities (McNeely *et al.* 1990).

This chapter addresses the basis of these two concerns about genetic diversity, defines what it is, describes methods for measuring it, and reviews the evidence on its extent in non-endangered and endangered species.

Genetic diversity is required for evolutionary change

Genetic diversity is the raw material for adaptive evolutionary change

Species face ever-changing environments, be they climatic changes due to global warming, pollution, introduction of novel competitors, or changes in diseases, pests or parasites (Chapter 6). To cope with these changes species must evolve or become extinct. Genetic diversity in a population reflects its evolutionary potential. There is no short-term evolution in populations lacking genetic diversity, while populations with genetic diversity can respond to environmental change.

Numerous species have been observed to evolve in response to environmental change as a result of genetic diversity (Chapter 6). For example, industrial melanism has evolved in about 200 species of moths in areas subject to industrial pollution (Kettlewell 1973; Majerus 1998). Similarly, numerous 'pest' species have evolved resistance to insecticides, herbicides, antibiotics and other biocontrol agents (Georghiou 1986; McKenzie 1996).

The necessity of genetic diversity for evolution to occur is illustrated by two plant examples. Plants with genetic diversity for ability to tolerate heavy metal pollution (*Agrostis tennuis* and bunch grass) were able to colonize the polluted soils (containing Cu, Zn and Cd) on slagheaps from mines in Wales, UK. They achieved this by evolving heavy-metal-tolerant forms. Conversely, those plant species without the appropriate genetic diversity failed (Bradshaw 1991). Similarly, the American chestnut was almost driven to extinction by an introduced disease to which it had no genetic diversity for resistance.

Relationship between genetic diversity and reproductive fitness

Loss of genetic diversity is related to reduction in reproductive fitness in naturally outbreeding species

A second concern is that low genetic diversity in many species is related to reduced reproduction and survival (reproductive fitness). Such a correlation is expected as loss of genetic diversity is related directly to the level of inbreeding and inbreeding leads to reductions in reproductive fitness (Chapters 2, and 10–12). Data from a meta-analysis indicate that there is a significant overall relationship between population mean heterozygosity and population fitness (Reed & Frankham 2001). These relationships are discussed in detail in Chapters 9–12.

The importance of genetic diversity over the long term (mainte-nance of adaptive evolutionary potential) as well as the short term (maintenance of reproductive fitness) makes it a primary focus for con-servation genetics. Captive breeding and wildlife management pro-grams typically recognize the importance of avoiding inbreeding and loss of genetic diversity. Pedigrees are maintained for captive popula-tions and management action includes consulting pedigrees when establishing matings or choosing individuals to reintroduce into the wild (Chapters 17 and 18). Levels of genetic diversity are analysed and monitored in wild populations of endangered species, and gene flow between isolated wild populations may be instigated (Chapter 16).

> Maintenance of genetic diversity is a primary objective in the management of wild and captive populations of threatened species.

The remainder of this chapter deals with means for measuring genetic diversity, and the extent and distribution of genetic diversity. Many of the issues introduced here are considered in more detail later.

What is genetic diversity?

Genetic diversity is reflected in the differences among individuals for many characters, including eye, skin and hair colour in humans, colour and banding patterns of snail shells, flower colours in plants, and pro-tein and DNA sequences. For example, diversity among Hawaiian honey-creepers (chapter frontispiece) reflects genetic diversity in their finch-like ancestor. Similarly, the vast variety of dog breeds have all been derived from the gray wolf (Vila *et al.* 1997). Starting with the wolf, selec-tion based on phenotypes has produced breeds of different size (St. Bernard versus chihuahua), behaviour (German shepherd guard dogs, fox terriers, hunting dogs such as pointers, water hunting dogs such as labradors, sheep dogs, cattle dogs, etc.), shape (bulldogs, dachshunds), etc. These differences reflect both genetic diversity within the ancestral wolf and new mutations that arose during selection.

> Genetic diversity is the variety of alleles and genotypes present in the group under study (population, species or group of species)

Genes are sequences of nucleotides in a particular segment (locus) of a DNA molecule. Genetic diversity represents slightly different sequences. In turn, DNA sequence variants may result in amino acid sequence differences in the protein coded for by the locus. Such protein variation may result in functional biochemical or morphological dis-similarities that cause differences in reproductive rate, survival or beha-viour of individuals.

The terminology used to describe genetic diversity is defined in Table 3.1. Genetic diversity is typically described using **polymorphism**, average **heterozygosity**, and **allelic diversity**. Example 3.1 illustrates different measures of genetic diversity in African lions, as assessed by allozyme electrophoresis; 23% of loci were variable (polymorphic), 7.1% of loci were heterozygous in an average individual, and there was an

| Table 3.1 | Terminology used to describe genetic diversity |

Locus: A segment of DNA, or an individual gene, e.g. the segment of DNA coding for the alcohol dehydrogenase enzyme is a separate locus from that coding for haemoglobin (they are located in different positions on chromosomes). Molecular loci, such as microsatellites (see below), are simply segments of DNA that may have no functional products.

Genotypes: The combination of alleles present at a locus in an individual, e.g. A_1A_1, A_1A_2, or A_2A_2. Genotypes are heterozygous (A_1A_2) or homozygous (A_1A_1, A_2A_2). Sometimes compound genotypes, including two or more loci, are specified ($A_1A_1B_1B_2$).

Genome: The complete genetic material of a species, or individual. All of the DNA, all of the loci, or all of the chromosomes.

Homozygote: An individual with two copies of the same allele at a locus e.g. A_1A_1.

Heterozygote: An individual with two different alleles at a locus, e.g. A_1A_2.

Alleles: Different forms of the same locus that differ in DNA base sequence, e.g. A_1, A_2, A_3, A_4, etc.

Allele frequency: The frequency of an allele in a population (often referred to as gene frequency). For example, if a population has 8 A_1A_1 individuals and 2 A_1A_2 individuals, then there are 18 copies of the A_1 allele and 2 of the A_2 allele. Thus, the A_1 allele has a frequency of 0.9 and the A_2 allele a frequency of 0.1.

Polymorphic: Having genetic diversity; a locus in a population is polymorphic if it has more than one allele, e.g. A_1 and A_2. Polymorphic loci are usually defined as having the most frequent allele at a frequency of less than 0.99, or less than 0.95 (to minimize problems with different sample sizes).

Monomorphic: Lacking genetic diversity; a locus in a population is monomorphic if it has only one allele present in the population, e.g. A_1. All individuals are homozygous for the same allele.

Proportion of loci polymorphic (P): Number of polymorphic loci / total number of loci sampled. For example, if three loci are polymorphic, and seven are monomorphic,

$$P = 3 / 10 = 0.3$$

Average heterozygosity (H): Sum of the proportions of heterozygotes at all loci / total number of loci sampled. For example, if the proportions of individuals heterozygous at five loci in a population are 0, 0.10, 0.20, 0.05 and 0, then

$$H = (0 + 0.10 + 0.20 + 0.05 + 0) / 5 = 0.07$$

Typically, expected heterozygosities (Chapter 4) are reported, as they are less sensitive to sample size than observed heterozygosities. In random mating populations, observed and expected heterozygosities are similar (Chapter 4).

Allelic diversity (A): average number of alleles per locus. For example, if the number of alleles at 6 loci are 1, 2, 3, 2, 1, 1

$$A = (1 + 2 + 3 + 2 + 1 + 1) / 6 = 1.67$$

Co-dominance: Situation where all genotypes can be distinguished from phenotypes, i.e. A_1A_1, A_1A_2 and A_2A_2 can be distinguished. This contrasts with dominance where the phenotypes of some genotypes are indistinguishable.

Genetic distance: A measure of the genetic difference between allele frequencies in two populations or species, e.g. Nei's genetic distance (Chapter 15). These are usually based on many loci.

average of 1.27 alleles per locus. These levels of genetic diversity are typical of electrophoretic variation for non-threatened mammals. By contrast, endangered Asiatic lions have low genetic diversity (Box 3.1). Further details on measures of genetic diversity are given in Chapter 4.

Example 3.1 | Genetic diversity in African lions (Newman *et al.* 1985)

Genetic diversity (as measured by allozyme electrophoresis) was surveyed at 26 loci in African lions. Of the 26 loci, 20 showed no variation (monomorphic), while six loci showed variation (polymorphic). Five of the six loci had two alleles, while one had three. Frequencies of alleles at the polymorphic loci are shown, along with the proportions of individuals in the population that were heterozygous (*H*) for each of the six loci. The computations of proportion of loci polymorphic and average heterozygosity are given below.

Enzyme locus	Allele			Heterozygosity
	1	2	3	
ADA	0.56	0.33	0.11	0.564
DIAB	0.61	0.39		0.476
ES1	0.88	0.12		0.211
GPI	0.85	0.15		0.255
GPT	0.89	0.11		0.196
MPI	0.92	0.08		0.147
20 other loci monomorphic	1.00			0

Since six of 26 loci were variable, the proportion of loci polymorphic (*P*) is

$$P = 6 / 26 = 0.23$$

Thus, 23% of loci are estimated to be polymorphic in African lions.
   The proportion of loci heterozygous in an average individual (*H*) is computed as follows:

$$H = [0.564 + 0.476 + 0.211 + 0.255 + 0.196 + 0.147 + (20 \times 0)] / 26$$
$$= 0.071$$

Thus, 7.1% of loci are heterozygous in an average lion. The levels of polymorphism and heterozygosity in the lions are fairly typical of large populations of non-endangered mammals. By contrast, endangered Asiatic lions show no allozyme genetic diversity, as shown in Box 3.1.
   The allelic diversity (*A*) is computed as follows:

$$A = [3 + 5 \times 2 + (20 \times 1)] / 26 = 1.27$$

Thus, there is an average of 1.27 alleles per locus.

Box 3.1 | Very low genetic diversity in endangered Asiatic lions from Gir Forest, India (O'Brien 1994)

Asiatic lions occur in the wild only in the Gir Forest of northwest India in a relict group of fewer than 250 individuals. They experienced a severe reduction in population size (to less than 20 individuals) in the early 1900s. O'Brien and coworkers measured genetic diversity for 50 allozyme loci (more than used in the study described in Example 3.1), and for DNA fingerprints. Levels of genetic diversity for Gir lions and for several populations of non-endangered African lions with much larger population sizes are given below.

| | Allozymes | | DNA fingerprints |
	P	H	H
Gir lions	0	0	0.038
African lions	0.04–0.11	0.015–0.038	0.45

For both measures, Gir lions had far less genetic diversity than African lions. For DNA fingerprints, Gir lions are almost as similar as identical twins in humans.

Why is there so little genetic diversity in Asiatic lions? The most probable explanation is that the population has been small (bottlenecked) for an extensive period (Chapter 10).

Surprisingly, captive populations of 'Asiatic' lions were found to have genetic diversity for allozymes. However, this proved to be due to inadvertent crossing with African lions.

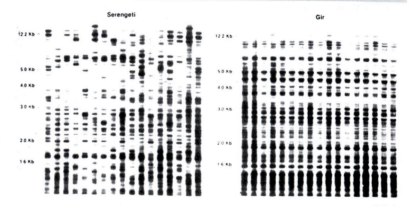

Low genetic diversity in DNA fingerprints from Gir lions compared to African lions (from the Serengeti, Tanzania). (From Gilbert *et al.* 1991.)

Measuring genetic diversity

Genetic diversity has been measured for many different traits, including continuously varying (quantitative) characters, deleterious alleles, proteins, nuclear DNA loci, mitochondrial DNA (mtDNA), chloroplast DNA (cpDNA) and for chromosomes. The most extensive data exist for proteins, but an increasing body of data is being generated for variation at the DNA level, as methods improve and costs decease.

Quantitative characters

The most important form of genetic variation is that for reproductive fitness as this determines the ability to evolve. Individuals vary in reproduction and survival (e.g. age at first reproduction, litter size, seed set, lifetime reproductive output, longevity). These traits and other measurable characters, such as height, weight, etc., are referred to as **quantitative characters**.

The existence of variation in quantitative characters is obvious in humans; we differ in height, weight and shape. However, this variation is due to both genetic and environmental causes. Consequently, methods are required to determine how much of this variation is due to heritable genetic differences among individuals and how much to environment. Artificial selection or statistical analyses of resemblances among relatives have been used to demonstrate genetic contributions to differences among individuals for these kinds of characters (Chapter 5). While genetic variation for quantitative characters (**quantitative genetic variation**) is the genetic diversity of most importance in conservation biology, it is difficult and time-consuming to measure (Chapter 5).

Variation for quantitative characters is due to both genetic and environmental causes. A genetic component is demonstrated by response to artificial selection, or by significant resemblance between relatives that is not due to a common environment

Deleterious alleles

As the majority of mutations are from a functional allele to a less functional state, part of the genetic diversity present in populations is due to deleterious alleles, such as those causing genetic diseases in humans and other species. Detection of this type of genetic diversity requires identification of genetically based deformities and malfunctions. However, deleterious alleles are usually rare and mostly recessive and so are often hidden in heterozygotes. Consequently, deliberate inbreeding has been used to measure the level of deleterious alleles in some species, especially fruit flies. Inbreeding increases the frequency of homozygotes and so increases the probability of exposing deleterious recessive alleles (Chapter 11). Special techniques are also available in fruit flies to make chromosomal homozygotes (instant complete inbreeding) (Lewontin 1974). Using these techniques, the number of lethal, sublethal and deleterious alleles can be estimated. Consequently, much of the most precise data on deleterious alleles come from fruit fly species. In endangered species, inbreeding is deleterious, so deliberate inbreeding cannot be justified as a management practice. Thus, the limited available data come from inadvertent inbreeding.

Recessive deleterious alleles are exposed by matings among relatives (inbreeding)

Proteins

The first measures of genetic diversity using molecular methods were provided in 1966 using electrophoresis. This technique separates proteins according to their net charge and molecular weights (Box 3.2). Electrophoresis allows us to distinguish among different forms of proteins and

Extensive information on genetic diversity has been obtained using electrophoretic separation of proteins

measure the level of genetic variation for a particular protein locus. About 30% of DNA base changes result in charge changes, so electrophoresis appreciably underestimates the full extent of genetic diversity.

Protein electrophoresis is typically done using blood, liver or kidney in animals, or leaves and root tips in plants as these contain ample amounts and varieties of soluble proteins. Consequently, animals must be captured to obtain blood samples, or killed to obtain liver or kidney samples. These are unsuitable practices for endangered species.

Box 3.2	Measuring genetic diversity in proteins using allozyme electrophoresis (see Lewontin 1974; Leberg 1996)

Genes consist of segments of DNA. If there is a base change in the DNA, this results in a change in the base composition of the messenger RNA (mRNA). Some of these base changes result in amino acid changes in the resulting protein. Five of the 20 naturally occurring amino acids are charged (lysine, arginine and histidine [+], glutamic acid and aspartic acid [−]), so about 30% of the base substitutions result in charge changes in the protein. These charge changes, as well as differences in molecular weights caused by base changes, can be detected by electrophoresis, as illustrated below.

DNA	DNA with base substitution
....ATG CTT GAC GTT.... ....TAC GAA CTG CAA....	....ATG CTT G**G**C GTT.... ....TAC GAA C**C**G CAA....

mRNA
....AUG CUU GAC GUU....   ....AUG CUU G**G**C GUU....
amino acid composition of the two proteins
.... met − leu − asp − val .... met − leu − **gly** − val ....

The DNA base substitution results in the substitution of uncharged glycine (gly) for negatively charged aspartic acid (asp) and is detectable by electrophoresis, as described below. The protein on the right will migrate more slowly through the gel.

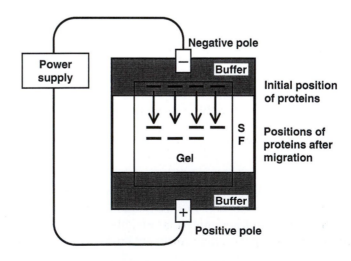

A gel electrophoresis apparatus is shown above (after Hedrick 1983). Tissue samples that have been homogenized to release soluble proteins are placed in spaced positions across the top of the gel. An electrical potential gradient applied to the gel causes the proteins to migrate through the gel. Proteins coded for by the same genetic locus but with different charges migrate to different positions (F–fast vs. S–slow). Proteins from specific loci are usually detected by their unique enzymatic activity, using a histochemical stain.

DNA

There are several means for directly, or indirectly, measuring DNA base sequence variation, and new methods are regularly being devised (Box 3.3). DNA sequencing for nuclear and especially mitochondrial genes is now done routinely, especially for taxonomic purposes. Microsatellites (variable number short tandem repeats; Box 3.3) are rapidly becoming the marker of choice for population studies. DNA fingerprints and restriction fragment length polymorphisms (RFLP), once commonly used, are losing popularity as more sensitive and convenient methods are developed.

The characteristics of different molecular techniques for measuring genetic diversity are compared in Table 3.2. The mode of inheritance is an important determinant of the utility of a technique. Co-dominant inheritance is most desirable as this allows all genotypes to be distinguished. Methods that reveal higher levels of genetic diversity provide greater precision for most uses in conservation biology. For example, they provide more powerful comparisons of threatened and non-threatened species, better discrimination in parentage, etc. Microsatellites reveal much higher levels of genetic diversity per locus than allozymes, while RAPDs, AFLPs and DNA fingerprints allow many more loci to be surveyed than is usually possible for allozymes.

A wide array of methods are available for measuring genetic diversity in the DNA, with microsatellites being the method currently favoured

Box 3.3	Techniques for measuring genetic diversity in DNA (Avise 1994; Smith & Wayne 1996; Hoelzel 1998)

MICROSATELLITES (SIMPLE SEQUENCE REPEATS [SSR], OR SHORT TANDEM REPEATS [STR])

Microsatellite loci are tandem repeats of short DNA segments, typically 1–5 bases in length. For example, CA sequences with 7 and 9 repeats are shown. CA repeats are found in many species. The number of microsatellite repeats is highly variable due to 'slippage' during DNA replication. Three genotypes, two different homozygotes and a heterozygote, are illustrated below, along with their banding patterns on a sequencing gel. **X** and **Y** are invariant (conserved) DNA sequences (primer sites) flanking the microsatellite repeat.

A_1A_1	A_1A_2	A_2A_2
XCACACACACACACA**Y**	**X**CACACACACACACACACA**Y**	**X**CACACACACACACACACA**Y**
XGTGTGTGTGTGTGT**Y**	**X**GTGTGTGTGTGTGTGTGT**Y**	**X**GTGTGTGTGTGTGTGTGT**Y**
XACACACACACACAC**Y**	**X**ACACACACACAC**Y**	**X**ACACACACACACACAC**Y**
XTGTGTGTGTGTGTG**Y**	**X**TGTGTGTGTGTG**Y**	**X**TGTGTGTGTGTGTGTG**Y**

Fragment sizes on a gel (the samples loaded at top, migration is down the page, with smaller fragments coded for by the A_1 allele migrating furthest)

———   ———

———   ———

Microsatellite diversity is detected by amplifying DNA using PCR. Unique conserved sequences (primers) flanking microsatellites are used to define the DNA segment that is to be amplified. The resulting DNA fragments are separated according to size using eletrophoresis on acrylamide or agarose gels. After separation the fragments are detected by (1) staining gels with ethidium bromide (a DNA stain), (2) use of radioactively labelled primers and autoradiography of gels, or (3) use of fluorescently labelled primers and running the PCR products on a DNA sequencing machine. If an individual is heterozygous for two microsatellite alleles with different numbers of repeats, then two different sized bands will be detected, as shown above.

Microsatellites have advantages over other DNA markers as they combine high variability with nuclear co-dominant inheritance and they can be typed following non-invasive sampling. They have the disadvantage that they must be developed anew for each species, though primers from closely related species, such as humans and chimpanzees, will often work in both species. Methods for detecting microsatellites are detailed in Avise (1994) and Smith & Wayne (1996).

DNA FINGERPRINTS (MINISATELLITES, OR VARIABLE NUMBER TANDEM REPEATS [VNTR])

Alex Jeffreys in England made the serendipitous discovery that there are variable number tandem repeat sequences throughout the genome of humans and other eukaryotes. These minisatellite sequences have core repeat sequences with lengths in the range of 10 to 100 bases (i.e. they are larger than microsatellites). Variability in repeat number is generated by unequal crossing-over. To identify minisatellites DNA is purified, cut with a restriction enzyme that cleaves outside the repeat, releasing the minisatellite DNA fragment, and the fragmented DNA separated according to size on an agarose gel. The two strands of the DNA fragments are separated (denatured) and transferred to a membrane (Southern blotting). The membrane with attached DNA is placed in a solution containing many copies of single stranded radioactively labelled DNA of the core repeat sequence (probed). Radioactively labelled core sequences attach (hybridize) to minisatellite fragments on the membrane by complementary base pairing. Single stranded unhybridized probe DNA is washed away, the membrane is dried and a photographic film is placed over it (autoradiography). The resulting autoradiograph reveals a pattern of bands akin to a barcode (see Box 3.1).

The number of repeats is highly variable, such that each individual in outbreeding species normally has a unique DNA fingerprint (apart from identical twins). Three genotypes for a single minisatellite locus are shown below, along with their banding patterns on a gel. 'o' represents a single repeat of the core sequence. Many such loci are typed simultaneously.

-----OOOOO-----   -----OOOOOO-----   -----OOOOOO-----
-----OOOOO-----   -----OOOOO-----   -----OOOOOO-----

DNA fragments on a gel

The advantages of DNA fingerprints are that they are highly variable, assess nuclear DNA variation over a wide range of loci, and do not require a prior knowledge of DNA sequence in the species being typed. The disadvantages are that individual loci are not normally identifiable, as the fragments derive from many different places in the genome. The inheritance of bands is not defined and they cannot be typed following non-invasive sampling as they require considerable amounts of DNA. DNA fingerprints are now being replaced by methods that allow non-invasive sampling following PCR. For example, PCR-based fingerprints are produced using AFLP or RAPDs, as described below.

RAPD: RANDOM AMPLIFIED POLYMORPHIC DNA

For this technique, random primer sequences (rather than specific ones, as used in microsatellites), usually 10–20 base pairs in length, are used for PCR reactions on nuclear DNA samples. These yield a series of DNA fragments, which are separated on agarose or sequencing gels. Typically, several fragments in the 100–200 base size range amplify, so that several bands are detected for each primer. If there is variation in the priming sites in the DNA, then some bands will reveal a presence–absence pattern. Inheritance is dominant (presence) / recessive (absence). RAPDs assay many loci without the need to sequence the genome and design specific primers and they can be typed following non-invasive sampling. Their disadvantages are the dominant mode of inheritance and the considerable care required to obtain repeatable results. Longer primer sequences generally provide higher repeatability. RAPDs have been widely used in plants, but less so in animals. A single RAPD locus is illustrated below, along with the pattern observed for the three genotypes on a gel. 'o' represents a site in the DNA that has a sequence homologous to the random primer and the solid line the fragment of DNA amplified by PCR. **A** is dominant and **a** recessive (absence of primer sites). Several such loci are usually typed simultaneously.

AA	**Aa**	**aa**
-------o————o---------	-------o————o---------	-------o----------------------
-------o————o---------	-------o-----------------------	-------o----------------------
DNA fragments on a gel		
———	———	(no band)

AFLP: AMPLIFIED FRAGMENT LENGTH POLYMORPHISM

This method is closely related to RAPDs. Genomic DNA is cut with a restriction enzyme and short synthetic DNA fragments (adapters) of known sequence are attached to the cut ends. PCR is carried out using primers that match the known adapter sequence plus additional 'selective' nucleotides. The method produces a multilocus DNA fingerprint apparent as either band presence (dominant) or absence (recessive) as for RAPDs. This method is more repeatable than RAPDs.

RFLP: RESTRICTION FRAGMENT LENGTH POLYMORPHISM

For this method, DNA is purified, cut with a restriction enzyme and run on a gel to separate fragments of different size. The DNA strands are separated and transferred to a membrane, and the membrane dried. The membrane is placed in a solution containing many copies of single stranded, radioactively labelled (often ^{32}P) segments of DNA (probe) for the locus in question. After complementary base pairing, unhybridized single stranded probe molecules are washed off, the membrane is dried and autoradiographed. If there is variation in the DNA sequence at the restriction enzyme cutting site, then different sized fragments will be evident on the autoradiograph. A RFLP locus is shown below. 'o' represents sequences cut by the particular restriction enzyme used (a dash in the corresponding position indicates absence of the cut site) and the region recognized by the probe is shown as a solid line.

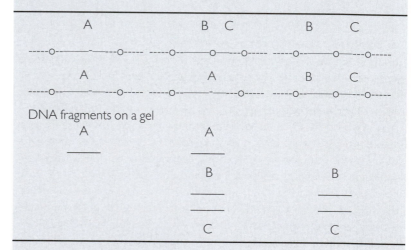

The advantages of RFLP are that they show co-dominant inheritance, they track variation in known genes and are moderately variable. They have several disadvantages: they require large amounts of DNA so they cannot be typed following non-invasive sampling, known locus probes must be available and they are not as variable as microsatellites. RFLP are being replaced by more convenient PCR-based methods.

SNP: SINGLE NUCLEOTIDE POLYMORPHISM

A position in the DNA of a species at which two or more alternative bases occur at appreciable frequency ($>1\%$) is referred to as a single nucleotide polymorphism. These are detected by sequencing, or using DNA chips (Wang et al. 1998). Their utility in conservation genetics has yet to be established.

SSCP: SINGLE STRAND CONFORMATIONAL POLYMORPHISMS

Genetic diversity among PCR products from different individuals can be detected without sequencing by using SSCP. In this procedure, the two complementary stands of the DNA from the PCR product are separated at high temperatures (denatured), immediately cooled, and the single stranded products subjected to electrophoresis in a polyacrylamide gel, at low temperature. Under these conditions, the single DNA strands fold upon themselves in a sequence-specific manner. These molecules migrate in the gel according to both their size and their conformation. This method has been applied to detection of genetic diversity in mtDNA, and a few nuclear loci (especially MHC loci). Examples of two mtDNA sequences and their mobilities following SSCP are shown (after Smith & Wayne 1996). Note that there is a band for each of the single DNA strands.

GATTAGGATCCGAT**C**CGATCG**T**AGCTGAT   GATTAGGATCCGAT**T**CGATCG**C**AGCTGAT
CTAATCCTAGGCTA**G**GCTAGC**A**TCGACTA   CTAATCCTAGGCTA**A**GCTAGC**G**TCGACTA

Single stranded DNA fragments on a gel

DNA SEQUENCING

The most direct means for measuring genetic diversity is to determine the sequences of bases in the DNA. This is usually done using DNA sequencing machines (Avise 1994). This is still relatively time-consuming and expensive, and has primarily been used for taxonomic purposes, where mtDNA (or sometimes nuclear loci) are sequenced for a restricted number of individuals. However, technical improvements have markedly reduced the cost and time taken to sequence DNA, as is evident from the Human Genome Project and similar endeavours to sequence the complete genomes of other species.

Table 3.2 | Characteristics of different molecular methods for assessing genetic diversity

Method	Source	Non-invasive sampling	Cost	Development time[a]	Inheritance
Electrophoresis	Blood, kidney, liver, leaves	No	Low	None	Co-dominant
Microsatellites	DNA	Yes	Moderate	Considerable	Co-dominant
DNA fingerprints	DNA	No	Moderate	Limited	Dominant
RAPD[b]	DNA	Yes	Low–moderate	Limited	Dominant
AFLP	DNA	Yes	Moderate–high	Limited	Dominant
RFLP	DNA	No	Moderate	Limited	Co-dominant
SSCP	DNA	Yes	Moderate	Moderate	Co-dominant
DNA sequencing	DNA	Yes	High	None	Co-dominant
SNP	DNA	Yes	Moderate–high	Considerable	Co-dominant

Notes:
[a]Indication of time taken to develop the technique so that genotyping can be done for threatened species.
[b]There are sometimes problems of repeatability with RAPDs. All other methods are highly repeatable.

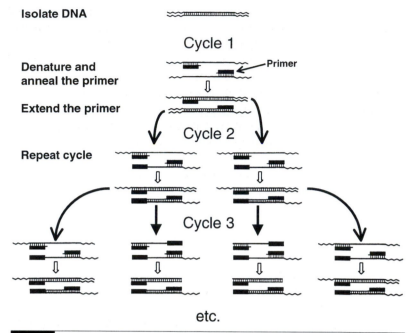

Isolate DNA

Cycle 1

Denature and anneal the primer — Primer

Extend the primer

Cycle 2

Repeat cycle

Cycle 3

etc.

Fig. 3.1 Non-invasive sampling of DNA and use of the polymerase chain reaction (PCR) to amplify DNA (after Avise 1994). PCR is used to amplify (generate multiple copies of) DNA from tiny samples (as little as a single molecule). PCR is essentially an *in vitro* version of natural DNA replication, except that it only replicates the region of DNA of interest. DNA is extracted and purified from the biological sample and added to a reaction mix containing all the necessary reagents. These include DNA oligonucleotide primers, a heat-resistant DNA replicating enzyme (*Taq* polymerase), magnesium, the four DNA nucleotides and buffer. The primers are homologous to DNA sequences on either side of (flanking) the DNA sequence to be amplified (i.e. the locus of interest). The *Taq* polymerase enzyme replicates DNA, the nucleotides are the building blocks of the new DNA and magnesium and buffer are required for the enzyme to work.

Repeated temperature cycles are used to denature the DNA (separate the strands), allow the DNA primers to attach to the flanking sequences (anneal), and to replicate the DNA sequence between the two primers (extend). Each cycle doubles the quantity of DNA of interest. All other DNA in the sample becomes so relatively rare that is it irrelevant in subsequent analyses.

Genotyping of individuals can be done following non-invasive or 'remote' sampling and PCR amplification of DNA

A major advantage of measuring DNA variation is that sampling can often be done non-invasively, and genotyping done following DNA amplification using the **polymerase chain reaction** (PCR) (Fig. 3.1). Since extremely small samples of DNA can be amplified by around a million times by PCR, only small biological samples are now needed to conduct molecular genetic analyses. This contrasts with electrophoresis where animals must be caught or killed to take the samples required to genotype them. Consequently, the development of 'remote' sampling methods involving extraction of DNA from shed hair, skin, feathers, faeces, urine, egg shell, fish scales, museum specimens and even fossils has been a major advance for species of conservation concern (see Smith & Wayne 1996; Hoelzel 1998).

To amplify a DNA segment of interest, specific invariant (conserved) sequences on either side of the segment of interest must be identified to design primers for the PCR reaction. The two primers will define the segment to be amplified. Copies of these sequences are synthesized (oligonucleotides) and used in the PCR reaction. Primer sequences can often be obtained from published sequence information for mtDNA, but must usually be developed anew for nuclear loci, especially for microsatellites (see Smith & Wayne 1996 for technical details). Primers developed for one species may also work in a closely related species. For example, human primers usually work in chimpanzees, and some of the primers from domestic ruminants work in the endangered Arabian oryx (Marshall *et al.* 1999).

Mitochondrial DNA (mtDNA)

Mitochondria contain circular DNA molecules that are maternally inherited (mother to offspring) in most species. Genetic diversity in their DNA can be detected by a range of methods, including cutting with restriction enzymes (RFLP), SSCP and sequencing (Box 3.3). DNA primers that work for most species are now available for the control region (also known as the D-loop), for the cytochrome *b* locus and the 12S rRNA locus. These regions can be amplified by PCR and the products sequenced. Sequencing of mtDNA has the advantages over other techniques that it can be done following non-invasive sampling, that mtDNA has a high mutation rate and is highly variable, and that it can be used to specifically trace female lines of descent, or migration patterns. Its disadvantages are that it is relatively expensive, it traces only a single maternally inherited unit, and mtDNA can only be considered a single 'locus'. We will defer further consideration of mtDNA variation to Chapters 15 and 19, as its main conservation uses are in resolving taxonomic uncertainties and defining management units, and in helping understand important aspects of species biology.

> Mitochondrial DNA is maternally inherited in most species. It is used widely to assess taxonomic relationships and differences among populations within species

Chromosomes

The primary use of chromosomal diversity is to differentiate species (Benirschke & Kumamoto 1991). Species usually differ in the number, shape and/or banding patterns of their chromosomes. For example, the Chinese and Indian muntjac (barking deer) appear so similar that some authorities considered them to belong to the same species. However, they are dramatically dissimilar in chromosome number, the Chinese muntjac having 46 chromosomes and the Indian muntjac 6 in males and 7 in females (Ryder & Fleischer 1996).

Chromosomes are characterized from rapidly dividing tissues. Animal somatic cells may be cultured from blood or skin biopsies, and germ line cells from testis biopsies. In plants, root tips provide somatic

> The number, size and shape of chromosomes within species are usually constant, but chromosomes often differ between species

cells while flower buds provide germ line material. In many species, more precise characterization of chromosomes can be achieved by differential staining methods that reveal chromosomal bands. This may reveal variation among individuals within species. For example, variants with different gene orders (inversions) are common in fruit flies, but are not common in other species. However, individuals heterozygous for some types of chromosome rearrangements have reduced fertility. Animals with reproductive difficulties in captive breeding programs may be examined cytologically. Populations of plants may differ in ploidy level (the number of sets of chromosomes – 2n diploid, 4n tetraploid, etc). Further information on chromosomes is provided in Chapter 15.

Extent of genetic diversity

Quantitative variation

Large populations of naturally outbreeding species usually have sizeable amounts of genetic diversity as detected for quantitative character, deleterious alleles, proteins or DNA

Virtually all quantitative characters in outbreeding species show genetic diversity. Quantitative genetic variation has been found for reproductive characters (egg production in chickens, number of offspring in sheep, mice, pigs and fruit flies, and seed yield in plants, etc.), for growth rate (in cattle, pigs, mice, chickens, fruit flies and plants), for chemical composition (fat in animals, protein and oil in maize), for behaviour (in insects and mammals), and for disease resistance in plants and animals (Lewontin 1974). A familiar example is the diversity of breeds in domestic dogs that all belong to the same species. Extensive genetic diversity is also found within plant species. For example, the cabbage species has diversified to give cabbages (edible leaves), kohlrabi (edible roots), Brussels sprouts (edible buds), broccoli (edible flowers), etc. (Diamond 1997). These examples serve to illustrate the vast potential that could be produced in species with high levels of genetic diversity for quantitative characters (Chapters 5 and 6).

Deleterious alleles

All outbred populations contain a load of rare deleterious alleles that can be exposed by inbreeding

The extent of diversity in populations attributable to deleterious alleles is important in conservation because these alleles reduce reproductive fitness when they are made homozygous by inbreeding (Chapter 12). Deleterious alleles are constantly generated by mutation and removed by selection. Consequently, all outbred populations contain deleterious rare alleles ('mutation load') (Chapter 7). Typically, these occur at frequencies of less than 1%. Rare human genetic syndromes, such as phenylketonuria, albinism and Huntington's chorea are examples. Equivalent syndromes are found in wild populations of plants and animals. For example, mutations leading to a lack of chlorophyll are found in many species of plants. Further, a range of genetically based defects has been described in endangered animals (dwarfism in California condors, vitamin E malabsorption in Przewalski's horse, undescended testes and fatal heart defects in Florida panthers and hairlessness in red-ruffed lemurs; Ryder 1988; Roelke *et al.* 1993; Ralls *et al.* 2000).

Most deleterious alleles probably make no useful contribution to evolutionary potential. However, some are advantageous in different environments and a few show heterozygote advantage. For example, in humans heterozygotes for sickle cell anaemia possess higher resistance to malaria than the normal homozygote, while most sickle cell homozygotes die (semi-lethal) due to defective haemoglobin (Chapter 9).

Protein variation

Until recently, it was impractical to survey DNA sequence diversity directly, so most of the available data on genetic diversity are for protein variation. It was the primary molecular tool for measuring genetic diversity from the late 1960s until the 1980s. Electrophoresis has been used to estimate level of genetic diversity in well over 1000 species (see Ward *et al.* 1992), but is rapidly being replaced by microsatellite analyses.

> There is extensive genetic diversity at protein-coding loci in most large populations of outbred species. On average 28% of loci are polymorphic and 7% of loci are heterozygous in an average individual, as assessed by electrophoresis

The first analyses of electrophoretic variation, in humans and fruit flies, revealed surprisingly high levels of genetic diversity. Similar results are found for most non-threatened species with large population sizes. For example, in African lions 23% of 26 loci were variable (polymorphic) and the average individual was heterozygous for 7.1% of the loci (Example 3.1 above). The corresponding figures from humans (based on 104 loci) are 32% of loci polymorphic and an average heterozygosity of 6% (Harris *et al.* 1977). Table 3.3 summarizes allozyme heterozygosities for several major taxa. Average heterozygosity within species (*H*) is lower in vertebrates (6.4%) than in invertebrates (11.2%) or plants (23%), possibly due to lower population sizes in the former (Chapters 9 and 10).

The abundant genetic diversity found in large populations contrasts with that found in many small or bottlenecked populations. The northern elephant seal was the first species of conservation interest studied using electrophoresis. It had been hunted almost to extinction, but has subsequently recovered from its population size bottleneck. Allozymes revealed no variation (Bonnell & Selander 1974). Similarly, no allozyme diversity has been found in a range of threatened or endangered species (or sub-species) including the cheetah, Asiatic lion, eastern barred bandicoot, northern spotted owl, Torrey pine, Furbish's lousewort, *Howellia aquatilis* and King's lomatia (Ledig & Conkle 1983; Waller *et al.* 1987; Lesica *et al.* 1988; Barrowclough & Gutierrez 1990; Sherwin *et al.* 1991; O'Brien 1994; Lynch *et al.* 1998). Most endangered species have lower genetic diversity than related, non-endangered species (see below).

> Smaller or bottlenecked populations often have reduced genetic diversity

	H	G_{ST}
Vertebrates		
Total	0.064	0.202
Mammals	0.054	0.242
Birds	0.054	0.076
Reptiles	0.090	0.258
Amphibians	0.094	0.315
Fish	0.054	0.135
Invertebrates		
Total	0.113	0.171
Insects	0.122	0.097
Crustaceans	0.063	0.169
Molluscs	0.121	0.263
Plants		
Total	0.230	0.224
Gymnosperms	0.271	0.068
Monocotyledons	0.238	0.231
Dicotyledons	0.214	0.273

Table 3.3 | Allozyme genetic diversity in different taxa. H is the average heterozygosity within populations and G_{ST} is the proportion of the variation in allele frequencies that is attributable to variation among populations

Source: Hamrick & Godt (1989); Ward *et al.* (1992).

Nuclear DNA

There is extensive genetic diversity in DNA sequences among individuals within outbreeding species, the most extensive diversity usually being found in sites with little functional significance

The first extensive study of DNA sequence variation at a locus within a population was by Kreitman for the alcohol dehydrogenase (*Adh*) locus in fruit flies (Fig. 3.2). Among 11 samples, there were 43 variable (polymorphic) sites across 2379 base pairs. The majority of base changes (42/43) do not result in amino acid substitutions (i.e. they are **silent substitutions**) as they were in non-coding regions of the locus (**introns**), or involved the third position in triplets coding for amino acids. Such variation is not detectable by protein electrophoresis. Most **exons** (regions coding for amino acids) showed low variation. However, polymorphism was highest around the one polymorphic site causing an amino acid polymorphism in the Adh protein, a site where selection favours genetic diversity (Chapter 9). Sequence variation at the *Adh* locus in two outbreeding plant species from the Brassica family was, if anything, even higher than that found in the fruit fly (Liu *et al.* 1998).

Most of the polymorphisms at the DNA level have little functional significance, as they occur in non-coding regions of the genome, or do not alter the amino acid sequence of a protein

The highest levels of genetic diversity in DNA are typically found for bases with little functional significance; ones that either do not code for functional products, or where substitutions do not change the function of the molecule. Conversely, the lowest genetic diversity is found for functionally important regions of molecules, such as the active sites of

```
           5'    Exon          Intron              Exon Intron        Exon        Intron    Exon          Untranslated          3'
                                                                                                          region
Consensus  CCG  CAATATGGG     C   G C   T   A C   C   CCC GGAATCTCCACTA G   A   C   A G C       C       T
   1-S     ...  .....AT..     .   . .   .   . .   T   T.A CA.TAAC......     .   . .   . . .       .       .
   2-S     ..C  .........     .   . .   .   . .   T   T.A CA.TAAC......     .   . .   . . .       .       .
   3-S     ...  .........     .   . .   .   . .   .   ... ............A     .   . .   . . T       .       A
   4-S     ...  .........     .   . .   .   G T   .   ... ............A     .   . .   T A .       .       .
   5-S     ...  AG...A.TC     .   . A   G   G T   .   ... .............     C   . .   . . .       .       .
   6-S     ..C  .........     .   . .   G   . .   .   ... .......T.T.C A     C   . .   . . .       T       .
   7-F     ..C  .........     .   . .   G   . .   .   ... .......GTCTCC .     C   . .   . . .       .       .
   8-F     TGC  AG...A.TC     G   . .   G   . .   .   ... .......GTCTCC .     C   G   . . .       .       .
   9-F     TGC  AG...A.TC     G   . .   G   . .   .   ... .......GTCTCC .     C   G   . . .       .       .
  10-F     TGC  AG...A.TC     G   . .   G   . .   .   ... ........GTCTCC .     C   G   . . .       .       .
  11-F     TGC  AGGGGA...     .   T .   G   . .   .   .A. ..G....GTCTCC .     C   . .   . . .       .       .
                                                                    *
```

Fig. 3.2 DNA sequence variation found among 11 samples of the alcohol dehydrogenase locus from wild populations of fruit flies (after Li & Graur 1991 from data of Kreitman). Only polymorphic sites are illustrated and only differences from the most common (consensus) sequence in the top row are shown. Dots indicate identity with the consensus sequence. The asterisk in exon 4 indicates the site of the lysine for threonine replacement that is responsible for the polymorphism in electrophoretic mobility, a site whose variation is subject to balancing natural selection.

enzymes (Hartl & Clarke 1997). Much of the DNA in an organism does not code for functional products. Changes in the base composition in these regions are unlikely to have selective significance. They include regions between loci as well as regions within loci (introns) that are transcribed, but not translated. Further, about 70% of base substitutions within loci are silent so they are likely to be subjected, at most, to only very weak natural selection. Some regions of polypeptide chains are cleaved off before a functional protein is produced. These regions, and many regions outside the active sites of enzymes and proteins, are constrained by limited functional demands.

There are two major exceptions to the generalization that polymorphism is lowest in regions with important functions, the major histocompatibility complex (a large family of genes that play an important role in the vertebrate immune system and in fighting disease) and self-incompatibility loci in plants. Both regions have very high levels of genetic diversity due to natural selection that favours genetic diversity (Chapters 2 and 9).

Microsatellites have recently been used to measure genetic diversity in a wide variety of species, many of them endangered. They typically show very high levels of polymorphism and many alleles per locus. For example, CA repeats are common and often vary in repeat number within populations; alleles with 10 repeats vs. 12 vs. 15 may segregate in the same population. Such diversity has been found in all species so far examined. For example, data from a survey of microsatellite variation at eight loci in 35 wild chimpanzees detected an average of 5.75 alleles per locus and an average heterozygosity of 0.65 (Table 3.4). Genetic diversity in large populations of a variety of non-endangered species is given in Table 3.5. All show remarkably high levels of genetic diversity.

Genetic diversity detected by microsatellites is typically much greater than that detected by electrophoresis (compare Example 3.1 and

Microsatellites show high levels of genetic diversity. They provide one of the most powerful and practical means currently available for surveying genetic diversity in threatened species

Table 3.4 Microsatellite variation at eight loci in 35 wild chimpanzees from Gombe National Park, Tanzania. Allele frequencies at each of the eight loci are given, along with the proportions of individuals heterozygous (*H*) for each locus and the average number of alleles (*A*)

Allele	Locus							
	Mfd3	Mfd18	Mfd23	Mfd32	FABP	Pla2a	Rena4	LL
1	0.026	0.066	0.042	0.014	0.237	0.176	0.618	0.041
2	0.316	0.211	0.194	0.527	0.066	0.014	0.382	0.027
3	0.026	0.013	0.264	0.122	0.053	0.662		0.027
4	0.079	0.132	0.056	0.270	0.513	0.122		0.014
5	0.553	0.026	0.083	0.054	0.132	0.027		0.216
6		0.303	0.014	0.014				0.014
7		0.250	0.181					0.324
8		0.167						0.338
H	0.587	0.779	0.820	0.631	0.656	0.515	0.472	0.731

Av. *H* = 0.649
A = 5.75

Source: Morin *et al.* (1994). Illustration from Austin & Short (1984).

Table 3.5). The number of microsatellite alleles per locus is typically 5–10 for large outbreeding populations, while most polymorphic loci detected by electrophoresis have only two alleles. Heterozygosities for polymorphic microsatellite loci are often 0.6–0.8, while polymorphic allozyme loci typically have average heterozygosities of 0.2–0.4. Similarly, the proportion of microsatellite loci polymorphic in large outbred populations is around 0.8, while that for allozyme loci average around 0.3. Fewer species have been surveyed for microsatellites than for allozymes, and there are no wide-ranging comparative surveys for microsatellites.

Comparisons of genetic diversity for microsatellites are not as straightforward as for allozymes. Microsatellite mutation rates differ among species and microsatellites with more repeats have more variation than smaller ones. Further, the use of primers developed in other species can lead to lower levels of variation being detected when the species are not closely related (Primmer *et al.* 1996).

DNA fingerprints (minisatellites), RAPD and AFLP

Extensive genetic diversity for DNA fingerprints, RAPDs and AFLP is typically found in large populations of non-threatened species

Large, non-threatened populations of outbreeding species contain extensive levels of genetic diversity for DNA fingerprints (Avise 1994). For example, the African lion shows extensive DNA fingerprint variation (Box 3.1). In most species, individuals can be distinguished from each other with an extremely high probability. This has led to widespread use of DNA fingerprints in human forensics to detect criminals, as well as to its use to identify paternity.

RAPDs and AFLP have been used more extensively in plants than animals. However, they are less convenient for population genetic analyses as they show dominance, rather than co-dominance, as is found for

Table 3.5 Levels of microsatellite genetic diversity in a range of non-endangered and related, threatened taxa. Average number of alleles per locus (A) and heterozygosity (H) are given for polymorphic loci. Globally threatened, or previously threatened, species (or sub-species) are placed adjacent to the nearest one or more related, but non-endangered species (or sub-species) for which data are available (n = sample size)

Non-endangered species				Threatened species			
	A	H	n		A	H	n	Reference
Human	8.9	0.81	28	Chimpanzee	7.8	0.65	35	1
Polar bear	5.4	0.62	30					2
Grey seal	8.0	0.74	805					3
African buffalo	8.6	0.73	34	Black rhinoceros	4.2	0.69	7	4,5
Gray wolf	4.5	0.62	18	Mexican wolf	2.7	0.42	38	1
Coyote	5.9	0.68	17	Ethiopian wolf	2.4	0.21	20	1
Domestic dog	6.4	0.73	26	African wild dog	3.5	0.56	78	1
African lion	4.3	0.66	8	Cheetah	3.4	0.39	10	1
Puma	4.9	0.61	10					1
American crow	6.0	0.68	14	Mariana crow	1.8	0.16	16	1
Northern raven	4.3	0.68	21					1
European kestrel	5.5	0.68	10	Mauritius kestrel	1.4	0.10	75	1
Greater kestrel	4.5	0.59	10	Seychelles kestrel	1.3	0.12	4	1
Lesser kestrel	5.4	0.70	8	Peregrine falcon	4.1	0.48	28	1,6
Loggerhead shrike (mainland)	5.6	0.58	20	San Clemente Island loggerhead shrike	2.1	0.34	26	7
Swallow	19.3	0.78	46					1
				Laysan finch	3.1	0.52	44	1
Koala	8.0	0.81	25					8
Southern hairy-nosed wombat	5.9	0.71	3–90	Northern hairy-nosed wombat	2.1	0.32	7–65	1
Allied rock wallaby	12.0	0.86	153	Long-footed potoroo	3.7	0.56	9	1
				Bridled nail-tail wallaby	11.6	0.83	73	1
American alligator	8.3	0.67	28	Komodo dragon	4.0	0.31	78	1
Northern water snake	9.1	0.72	50					9
Sleepy lizard	11.5	0.71	38					10
Atlantic salmon	9.3	0.82	25					11
Fruit fly	7.3	0.61	72					12
Wild soybeans	13.8	0.87	32					13
Royal mahogany	9.3	0.67	32	Mahogany tree	9.7	0.55	79	1

References: 1. Frankham (2001a); 2. Paetkau *et al.* (1995); 3. Allen *et al.* (1995); 4. O'Ryan *et al.* (1998); 5. Brown & Houlden (1999); 6. Nesje *et al.* (2000); 7. Mundy *et al.* (1997); 8. Houlden *et al.* (1996); 9. Prosser *et al.* (1999); 10. Cooper *et al.* (1997); 11. Nielsen *et al.* (1999); 12. England *et al.* (1996); 13. Maughan *et al.* (1995).

microsatellites. It is more difficult to compare results across species, especially if they are not closely related. The typical measure of genetic diversity is percentage of band sharing between individuals. Populations with high levels of band sharing have low genetic diversity, since band sharing increases with relatedness. For example, band

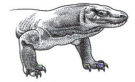

sharing was 91% for the endangered burying beetle species in the USA and only 77% in a related non-endangered species (Kozol *et al.* 1994), indicating that the endangered species had lower genetic diversity than the non-endangered one.

Low genetic diversity in endangered species

Endangered species usually have lower levels of genetic diversity than non-endangered species

Most endangered species and populations have lower genetic diversity than related, non-endangered species with large population sizes. Of 38 endangered mammals, birds, fish, insects and plants, 32 had lower genetic diversity (mainly for allozymes) than related non-endangered species, five had similar genetic diversity and one greater (Frankham 1995a). In endangered birds, 11 of 13 species had lower allozyme genetic diversity than the average of 70 non-endangered species (Haig & Avise 1996). Further, all 17 endangered taxa listed in Table 3.5 have lower genetic diversity than related, non-endangered species for microsatellites. For example, endangered species such as the northern hairy-nosed wombat and the Ethiopian wolf have greatly reduced microsatellite variation compared to related non-endangered species. Endangered species have about half the genetic diversity of non-endangered species (Table 3.5).

A similar conclusion applies to almost all comparisons involving DNA fingerprints, RAPD and AFLP. Low DNA fingerprint genetic diversity, compared to non-endangered species (or sub-species) has been reported in Arabian oryx, Asiatic lion, Florida panther, Isle Royale gray wolf, St. Lawrence beluga whales, Mariana crow, nene, Chatham Island black robin, palila, Puerto Rican plain pigeon, Puerto Rican parrot, Seychelles warbler and whooping crane (Wayne *et al.* 1991; Brock & White 1992; Longmire *et al.* 1992; Roelke *et al.* 1993; Fleischer *et al.* 1994; Miyamoto *et al.* 1994; O'Brien 1994; Patenaude *et al.* 1994; Rave *et al.* 1994; Wayne *et al.* 1994; Ardern & Lambert 1997; Komdeur *et al.* 1998; Tarr & Fleischer 1999). For example, Komdeur *et al.* (1998) reported an average band sharing of 0.57 in four endangered bird species compared to only 0.21 in natural outbred non-endangered birds. Conversely, the humpback whale has levels of fingerprint diversity that are equal to, or greater than, those found in non-endangered mammals (Baker *et al.* 1993).

Low genetic diversity compared to non-endangered species has been reported for RAPD or AFLP in endangered light-footed clapper rail from California, and in endangered plants *Cerastium fischerianum* var. *molle*, *Lysimachia minoricensis* from Minorca and Wollemi pine from Australia, in addition to the burying beetle described above (Kozol *et al.* 1994; Nusser *et al.* 1996; Calero *et al.* 1998; Maki & Horie 1999; Hogbin *et al.* 2000).

There can be no doubt that most endangered species have lower genetic diversity than related non-endangered species. The reasons for low genetic diversity in endangered species will be considered in Chapter 10.

What genetic diversity determines evolutionary potential?

It is important to define what genetic diversity we are seeking to conserve to maintain evolutionary potential, as we can assess genetic diversity by the wide array of methods just described. Evolutionary potential is most directly measured by quantitative genetic variation (Franklin 1980). Most important is quantitative genetic variation for reproductive fitness. Unfortunately, this is the most difficult to measure and the aspect of genetic diversity for which we have least information in threatened species (Chapter 5). Other measures such as DNA and allozymes are only of conservation value if they reflect evolutionary potential (Chapter 5).

> Quantitative genetic variation for life history traits is the major determinant of evolutionary potential. Unfortunately, we have least information on this form of genetic diversity and it is the most difficult to measure

Variation over space and time

As an approximation, the magnitude of genetic differentiation among animal populations is inversely correlated with dispersal ability (Chapter 13). The relationship between genetic differentiation and dispersal ability can be gauged from the G_{ST} values in Table 3.3. G_{ST} measures the proportion of the total variation that occurs among populations; zero represents populations that show no genetic differentiation, while values above zero indicate species where populations are partially genetically subdivided. Birds with high dispersal ability show the lowest G_{ST} values of all vertebrate groups. Similarly, insects, which disperse easily, show the lowest G_{ST} amongst invertebrates. For example, highly mobile fruit flies in the Hunter Valley region of southeastern Australia showed no significant differences among populations from 10 different wineries. Conversely, the critically endangered sentry milk-vetch plant species that lives on the rim of the Grand Canyon in Arizona has very limited dispersal; 63% of its variation is among populations, 11% among sub-populations and only 27% within populations (Travis *et al.* 1996).

> Spatial variation in genetic composition depends critically on rates of gene flow, population sizes and selection

Plants typically have locally adapted races for quantitative genetic variation, and often show allozyme differences among populations, especially for self-fertilizing species.

Most allele frequencies in large populations are relatively stable for molecular genetic markers over tens of years. For example, there were no consistent changes in allozyme frequencies in wild fruit fly populations over five years and frequencies were still indistinguishable over 20 years (over 200 generations) later (Frankham & Loebel 1992). In the same populations, microsatellite allele frequencies were similar over four years (England 1997).

> Large populations typically show negligible change in genetic diversity over tens of years. Conversely, small populations typically lose genetic diversity rapidly over time

In contrast, small populations of threatened species typically lose genetic diversity over time. For example, analyses based upon museum specimens have documented loss of genetic diversity in the whooping crane, Arabian oryx, Mauritius kestrel and nene (Glenn *et al.* 1999;

Marshall *et al.* 1999; Groombridge *et al.* 2000; Paxinos *et al.* in press); all four species have suffered severe population bottlenecks (Chapters 8 and 10).

What explains differences in levels of genetic diversity?

In brief, the following factors affect levels of genetic diversity:
- Historical and current population sizes (Chapters 6 and 10)
- Population bottlenecks (Chapter 8)
- Breeding system (Chapters 4 and 11)
- Natural selection (Chapters 6 and 9)
- Different mutation rates (Chapter 7)
- Immigration and emigration among populations (Chapters 7, 9 and 13)
- Interactions among the above factors (Chapter 9).

Genetic differences among species

The genetic differences among species roughly reflect their taxonomic divergence

Genetic divergence among species roughly reflects their phylogeny. Trees of relationship among higher taxonomic ranks derived from DNA or proteins are often similar to those based upon morphology. However, the genetic divergence among species within different genera varies widely (Fig. 3.3), reflecting the somewhat arbitrary nature of taxonomic classifications. Genetic differentiation among bird species is on average less than that among species of other vertebrate groups (Johns & Avise 1998). Species of fruit flies in the genus *Drosophila* typically show much greater genetic differentiation than primates currently placed in different taxonomic families (Avise & Johns 1999). Use of genetic diversity among taxa to resolve taxonomic uncertainties is considered in Chapter 15.

Summary

1. Genetic diversity represents the essential evolutionary potential for species to respond to changing environments.

2. Genetic diversity can be measured for quantitative characters, for deleterious alleles, for proteins and for DNA.

3. Microsatellites are currently the most practical and informative of the molecular techniques for measuring DNA variation within populations.

4. Large populations of non-endangered species typically have extensive genetic diversity.

5. Most endangered species have reduced genetic diversity when compared to related non-endangered species.

6. Genetic diversity among taxa roughly reflects their taxonomic divergence.

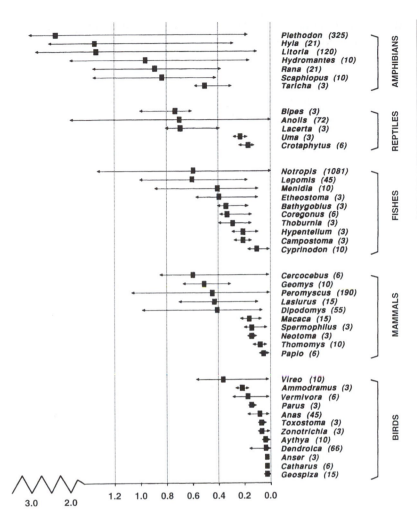

Fig. 3.3 Genetic differences among species in selected vertebrate genera (from Avise 1994). Means and ranges of genetic distances among species, based upon multilocus protein electrophoresis. This is an indirect measure of the amount of DNA sequence divergence among species. *Genetic distances among species within genera vary considerably among vertebrate classes.*

FURTHER READING

Avise (1994) *Molecular Markers, Natural History and Evolution.* Clear descriptions of the molecular methods for measuring genetic diversity and results achieved with them.

Avise & Hamrick (1996) *Conservation Genetics.* Advanced scientific reviews on the conservation of major groups of animals and plants. Contains considerable information on genetic diversity.

Goldstein & Schlotterer (1999) *Microsatellites.* An edited volume covering a range of topics on microsatellites.

Hamrick & Godt (1989) Compilation of data on electrophoretic variation in plants and factors affecting it.

Hartl & Clarke (1997) *Principles of Populations Genetics.* Provides an easy-to-follow coverage of genetic diversity and its importance.

Hoelzel (1998) *Molecular Genetic Analysis.* Advanced information on molecular methods used to measure genetic diversity.

Smith & Wayne (1996) *Molecular Genetic Approaches in Conservation.* Contains information on genetic diversity in threatened species and the diverse molecular methods for measuring it. Advanced.

Ward *et al.* (1992) Compilation of data on electrophoretic variation for more than 1000 species, with analyses testing for differences relating to taxa and protein size and structure. See also the earlier paper by Nevo *et al.* (1984) on the same topic.

Wright (1978) *Evolution and the Genetics of Populations*, vol. 4. Review of much of the earlier literature on genetic diversity.

PROBLEMS

3.1 Genetic diversity: Why is genetic diversity of importance in conservation biology?

3.2 Measurement of genetic diversity: What is the basis for using electrophoretic separation of proteins to measure the extent of genetic diversity?

3.3 Measuring genetic diversity: What are microsatellites?

3.4 Measuring genetic diversity: What is a RFLP?

3.5 Measuring genetic diversity: What is a RAPD?

3.6 Measuring genetic diversity: What is an AFLP?

3.7 Measuring genetic diversity: What is a DNA fingerprint?

3.8 Measuring genetic diversity: What genetic markers can be typed following non-invasive sampling?

3.9 Genetic diversity: What form of genetic diversity is most important for retaining evolutionary potential?

3.10 Levels of genetic diversity: How do major taxonomic groups compare in genetic diversity?

3.11 Levels of genetic diversity: How do endangered and non-endangered species compare in genetic diversity?

PRACTICAL EXERCISE: MEASURING GENETIC DIVERSITY USING MICROSATELLITES

A practical that is suitable for illustrating genetic diversity involves non-invasive sampling, PCR amplification and microsatellite typing. Choose a species where microsatellites have been developed. Beware of cross-contamination during all stages of the procedure. This practical can conveniently be spread over two weeks, the first involving preparing hair, DNA extraction and DNA amplification. Microsatellite typing can be done on a sequencing machine during the intervening period and genotypes illustrated on a computer screen in the second week, when allele frequencies and heterozygosities can be estimated from the data.

Use of hair as a source of DNA   Hair from an interesting species (we used tammar wallabies) can be collected from live animals, or frozen samples. Hairs with good roots are chosen. These are cut at a point about 3 mm above the bulb with a razor blade.

DNA extraction   DNA can be extracted by a simple boiling method, such as that of Sloane *et al.* (2000).

DNA amplification   It is necessary to get microsatellite primers made with fluorochromes added (thus avoiding use of radioactive isotopes)

that are suitable for running in a DNA sequencing machine. Two loci, labelled with different fluorochromes provide suitable material, though a single locus will suffice. Add microsatellite DNA primers, *Taq* polymerase, nucleotides and buffer, and amplify the DNA.

Separate the amplified microsatellite fragments on a DNA sequencing machine
The use of a sequencing machine allows the microsatellite typing to be done and the results stored in electronic form. These can be viewed and the data analysed to obtain allele frequencies and heterozygosities.

Chapter 4

Characterizing genetic diversity: single loci

Terms:

Allotetraploid,
autotetraploid,
effective number of alleles,
equilibrium,
expected heterozygosity,
gene diversity,
haplotype,
Hardy–Weinberg equilibrium,
hermaphrodite,
linkage disequilibrium,
observed heterozygosity,
polyploid,
selfing,
sex-linked,
tetraploid

Frequencies of alleles at individual loci and heterozygosities are used to characterize genetic diversity in populations. Allele and genotype frequencies are in equilibrium under random mating when there are no other perturbing forces operating

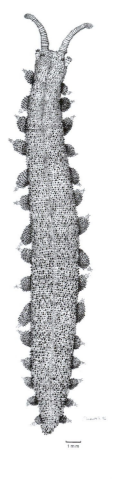

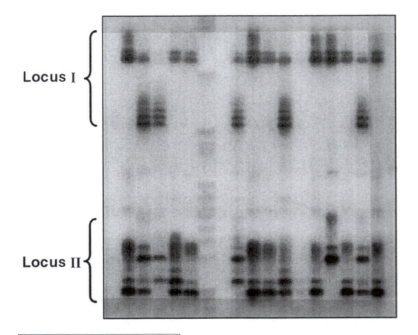

Locus I {

Locus II {

An Australian velvet worm and an autoradiograph illustrating genetic diversity at microsatellite loci in this species.

Describing genetic diversity

In the previous chapter, we examined techniques for ascertaining the genotype of each individual from a sample of organisms from a population or species. We now describe the parameters that allow us to extrapolate from samples to the entire population. These values are essential for comparisons among populations and species, and for predicting changes in the genetic composition of populations. Parameters are required for both single loci, and for more complex, multilocus, quantitative characters. This chapter is concerned with simple one or two loci situations. Chapter 5 addresses quantitative traits.

> Measures of genetic diversity are required if we are to document loss of genetic diversity or adaptive evolutionary changes

Frequencies of alleles and genotypes

The information we collect provides the numbers of each genotype at a locus. This is illustrated for an egg-white protein locus in Scottish eider ducks (Table 4.1). This species was severely reduced due to harvest for feathers for pillows and eiderdowns. Genotype frequencies are simply calculated from the proportion of the total sample of that type (e.g. genotype frequency of FF = 37/67 = 0.552).

> The genetic composition of a population is usually described in terms of allele frequencies, number of alleles and heterozygosity

For comparative and predictive use, the information is usually reported in the form of allele frequencies (often referred to as gene frequencies), rather than genotype frequencies. We will use the letters p and q to represent the allele frequencies for two alleles at a locus. The frequency of the F allele (p) in the eider duck population is simply the proportion of all alleles examined which are F. Note that we double the number of each homozygote, and the total, as the ducks are diploid (each bird has inherited one copy of the locus from each of its parents).

$$p = \frac{(2 \times FF) + FS}{2 \times Total} \tag{4.1}$$

The calculation in Example 4.1 shows that the F allele has a frequency of 0.73.

Table 4.1 | Numbers and frequencies for each of the genotypes at an egg-white protein locus in eider ducks from Scotland. Individuals were genotyped by protein electrophoresis. F refers to the faster migrating allele and S to the slower

| | Genotypes | | | |
	FF	FS	SS	Total
Numbers	37	24	6	67
Genotype frequencies	0.552	0.358	0.090	1.00

Source: Milne & Robertson (1965).

| Example 4.1 | Calculation of F and S allele frequencies at an egg-white protein locus in eider ducks |

The frequency for the F allele p is obtained as follows:

$$p = [(2 \times 37) + (1 \times 24)] / [2 \times 67] = 0.73$$

and that for S q as

$$q = [(2 \times 6) + (1 \times 24)] / [2 \times 67] = 0.27$$

q can also be obtained as $1 - p$ when there are only two alleles, as the sum of relative frequencies is 1.00, i.e.

$$p + q = 0.73 + 0.27 = 1.00.$$

Allele frequencies may also be reported as percentages.

Similar procedures are applied to obtain allele frequencies when there are more than two alleles at a locus, as found for many microsatellite loci. Numbers of each genotype at a microsatellite locus with three alleles in the endangered Hawaiian Laysan finch are given in Table 4.2. The method for estimating the frequency of one of the alleles is shown in Example 4.2.

| Table 4.2 | Numbers of each genotype at a microsatellite locus with three alleles in the endangered Hawaiian Laysan finch. The allelic designations 91, 95 and 97 are the sizes, in base pairs, of the amplified PCR fragments |

| | Genotypes | | | | | | |
	91/91	91/95	91/97	95/95	95/97	97/97	Total
Numbers	7	10	8	5	11	3	44

Source: Tarr et al. (1998).

| Example 4.2 | Estimating allele frequencies at a locus with three alleles in the endangered Laysan finch |

The frequency of the 91 allele p is obtained by counting the number of 91 alleles (twice the number of the 91/91 genotype, plus the numbers of the 91/95 and 91/97 genotypes) and dividing by twice the total number of individuals, as follows:

$$p = [(2 \times 7) + 10 + 8] / [2 \times 44] = 0.364$$

The frequencies of the 95 and 97 alleles, calculated in a similar manner, are 0.352 and 0.284, respectively. The frequencies of the three alleles sum to 1.000.

The extent of genetic diversity at a locus is expressed as heterozygosity. **Observed heterozygosity** (H_0) is simply the number of heterozygotes at a locus divided by the total number of individuals sampled. For example, the observed frequency of heterozygotes at the egg-white protein locus in eider ducks (Table 4.1) is $24 / 67 = 0.36$. A similar procedure is followed when there are more than two alleles at a locus. For the Laysan finch microsatellites (Table 4.2), the observed heterozygosity is $[10 + 8 + 11]/44 = 0.659$. Generally, expected heterozygosity (H_e), described later, is reported for outbreeding species, as it is less sensitive to sample size than observed heterozygosity.

> Heterozygosity is the measure most commonly used to characterize genetic diversity for single loci

Having described the parameters used to characterize the genetic composition of populations, we will now deal with factors that influence the frequencies of alleles and genotypes. The remainder of this chapter covers the consequences of different mating systems. Chapters 6 and 7 deal with mutation, migration and selection and Chapter 8 with the consequences of small population size.

We now address the questions, what determines the frequencies of genotypes in a population? What is the relationship between allele and genotype frequencies under random mating?

Hardy–Weinberg equilibrium

In dealing with the factors influencing the frequencies of alleles and genotypes in populations, we begin with the simplest case – that of a large population where mating is random and there is no mutation, migration or selection. Allele and genotype frequencies under random mating attain an equilibrium referred to as the **Hardy–Weinberg equilibrium**, after its discoverers Godfrey Hardy, an English mathematician, and Wilhelm Weinberg, a German physician. While the Hardy–Weinberg equilibrium is very simple, it is crucial in conservation and evolutionary genetics. It provides a basis for detecting deviations from random mating, testing for selection, modelling the effects of inbreeding and selection, and estimating the allele frequencies at loci showing dominance.

> Allele and genotype frequencies at an autosomal locus attain equilibrium after one generation in large, random mating populations when there are no perturbing forces (no mutation, migration or selection)

Assume that we are dealing with an autosomal locus with two alleles A_1 and A_2 at relative frequencies of p and q in a large random mating population ($p + q = 1$). Imagine **hermaphroditic** (both sperm and eggs released by each individual) marine organisms shedding their gametes into the water, where sperm and eggs unite by chance (Table 4.3). Since the allele frequency of A_1 in the population is p, the frequency of sperm or eggs carrying that allele is also p. The probability of a sperm carrying A_1 uniting with an egg bearing the same allele, to produce an A_1A_1 zygote, is therefore $p \times p = p^2$ and the probability of an A_2 sperm fertilizing an A_2 egg, to produce an A_2A_2 zygote is, likewise, $q \times q = q^2$. Heterozygous zygotes can be produced in two ways, it does not matter which gamete contributes which allele, and their expected frequency is therefore $2 \times p \times q = 2pq$. Consequently, the expected frequencies of A_1A_1, A_1A_2 and A_2A_2 zygotes are p^2, $2pq$ and q^2, respectively. These are the *Hardy–Weinberg equilibrium* genotype frequencies.

Table 4.3 | Genotype frequencies resulting from random union of gametes at an autosomal locus

			Ova	
			A_1	A_2
	frequencies		p	q
	A_1	p	p^2 A_1A_1	pq A_1A_2
Sperm				
	A_2	q	pq A_2A_1	q^2 A_2A_2

The resulting genotype frequencies in progeny are:

A_1A_1	A_1A_2	A_2A_2
p^2	$2pq$	q^2

These are the Hardy–Weinberg equilibrium genotype frequencies.

Note that the genotype frequencies sum to 1, i.e. $p^2 + 2pq + q^2 = (p + q)^2 = 1$. If the frequencies of the alleles A_1 and A_2 are 0.9 and 0.1, then the Hardy–Weinberg equilibrium genotype frequencies are:

A_1A_1	A_1A_2	A_2A_2	Total
0.9^2	$2 \times 0.9 \times 0.1$	0.1^2	1.0
0.81	0.18	0.01	1.0

In example 4.1, we calculated allele frequencies by taking the values of $(2 \times \text{number of homozygotes}) + \text{number of heterozygotes} / 2 \times \text{total number of individuals}$. Now that we are using simple algebraic terms, this equates to $[(2 \times p^2) + 2pq] / [2(p^2 + 2pq + q^2)]$. As the denominator equals 2, the frequency of the A_1 allele in the progeny (p_1) is

$$p_1 = p^2 + pq = p(p + q),$$

and, as $p + q = 1$, $p_1 = p$

Likewise the frequency of A_2 is $q_1 = q$

Thus, the frequencies of the two alleles have not changed, indicating that allele frequencies are in **equilibrium**. As further generations of random mating yield the same genotype frequencies, genotype frequencies do not change over generations. Consequently, *allele and genotype frequencies are at equilibrium after one generation of random mating and remain so in perpetuity in the absence of other influences.*

The relationships between allele and genotype frequencies according to the Hardy–Weinberg equilibrium are shown in Fig. 4.1. This illustrates two points. First, the frequency of heterozygotes cannot be greater than 50% for a locus with two alleles; this occurs when the alleles both have frequencies of 0.5. Second, when an allele is rare, most of its alleles are in heterozygotes, while most are in homozygotes when it is at a high frequency. This is important in the context of the effectiveness of selection (Chapter 6). For example, when the A_1 allele is

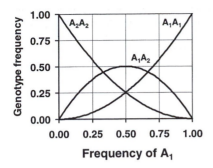

Fig. 4.1 Relationship between genotype frequencies and allele frequencies in a population in Hardy–Weinberg equilibrium.

at a frequency of 0.1, the frequency of A_1A_1 homozygotes is 0.01, that of heterozygotes 0.18, while A_2A_2 homozygotes have a frequency of 0.81 (Table 4.3). In this case, 90% of the A_1 alleles are in heterozygotes. Conversely, at a frequency of 0.5, the three genotypes have frequencies of 0.25, 0.50 and 0.25. Here half the alleles are in heterozygotes and half in homozygotes.

Do genotypes in real populations obey the Hardy–Weinberg equilibrium frequencies? It may seem that we have considered an unrealistically simple situation. To obtain the Hardy–Weinberg equilibrium we assumed:

- Random mating
- Normal Mendelian segregation of alleles
- Equal fertility of parent genotypes
- Equal fertilizing capacity of gametes
- Equal survival of all genotypes
- A closed population (no migration)
- No mutation
- A large population size.

The genotype frequencies for the eider duck egg-white protein locus are tested for agreement with the Hardy–Weinberg equilibrium in Table 4.4. Values of p and q, calculated previously, are used to calculate p^2, $2pq$ and q^2. These frequencies are then multiplied by the total number (67) to obtain expected numbers for the three genotypes.

The observed genotype frequencies are very close to the values expected from the Hardy–Weinberg equilibrium at this locus. In general, agreement with expectations is found for most loci in large naturally outbreeding populations. This does not mean that the loci are not subject to mutation, migration, selection and sampling effects, only that these effects are often small.

> Genotype frequencies for most loci usually agree with Hardy–Weinberg genotype frequency expectations in large naturally outbreeding populations

Chi-square (χ^2) test to assess agreement between observed and expected numbers

Differences between observed and expected numbers will occur by chance. To determine if the differences are of statistical significance (i.e.

Table 4.4 | Test for agreement of genotype frequencies with Hardy–Weinberg equilibrium genotype frequencies for the eider duck egg-white protein locus

	Genotypes			
	FF	FS	SS	Total
Observed numbers (O)	37	24	6	67
Expected frequencies	p^2	$2pq$	q^2	1.0
	0.73^2	$2 \times 0.73 \times 0.27$	0.27^2	1.0
	0.5329	0.3942	0.0729	1.0
Expected numbers (E)	35.7	26.4	4.9	67
(expected frequency $\times$ 67)				

unlikely to be due to chance alone), the deviation between observed numbers (O) and expected numbers (E) is tested using a χ^2 test, computed as follows:

$$\chi^2 = \Sigma \, (O - E)^2 / E$$

The larger the difference between observed and expected, the larger the χ^2 value. The χ^2 value is computed as follows:

$$\Sigma \, (O - E)^2 / E = \frac{(37 - 35.7)^2}{35.7} + \frac{(24 - 26.4)^2}{26.4} + \frac{(6 - 4.9)^2}{4.9}$$

$$\chi^2 = \quad 0.047 \quad + \quad 0.218 \quad + \quad 0.247 \quad = 0.512$$

To assess the probability of obtaining a χ^2 value as great as this by chance, we need to determine the number of degrees of freedom (df). This is the number of genotypes (3) minus 1 (for using the total number) minus the number of alleles (1 in this case). Thus

$$\mathrm{df} = 3 - 1 - 1 = 1$$

The probability is obtained by looking up the χ^2 value in statistical tables under the appropriate degrees of freedom, or by using statistical software, yielding

$$\mathrm{Probability} = 0.47$$

Thus, we conclude that the observed genotype frequencies do not differ significantly from the expectations. If the probability had been < 0.05, we would have concluded that there was a significant deviation from expectations.

Expected heterozygosity

The Hardy–Weinberg expected heterozygosity is usually reported when describing genetic diversity as it is less sensitive to sample size than observed heterozygosity

Genetic diversity at single loci is characterized by expected heterozygosity, observed heterozygosity and allelic diversity. For a single locus with two alleles with frequencies of p and q, the **expected heterozygosity** $H_e = 2pq$ (also called **gene diversity**). When there are more than two alleles, there are related expressions as shown below. However, in these cases it is simpler to calculate expected heterozygosity as 1 minus the sum of the squared allele frequencies:

$$H_e = 1 - \sum_{i=1}^{\substack{\text{No. of}\\\text{alleles}}} p_i^2 \tag{4.2}$$

where p_i is the frequency of the ith allele. The reasoning behind this can be appreciated for the case of two alleles at a locus where the expected genotype frequencies are p^2, $2pq$ and q^2. Since $p^2 + 2pq + q^2 = 1$, $2pq = 1 - p^2 - q^2$, an expression that corresponds to equation 4.2. H_e is usually reported in preference to observed heterozygosity as it is less affected by sampling.

Example 4.3 illustrates the calculation of expected heterozygosity for the microsatellite locus in Laysan finches. The Hardy–Weinberg expected heterozygosity is 0.663, based upon the allele frequencies at this locus.

Example 4.3 | Calculating expected heterozygosity for a microsatellite locus in the Laysan finch

The allele frequencies for the 91, 95 and 97 alleles are 0.364, 0.352 and 0.284, respectively, based on the data in Table 4.2. Consequently, the Hardy–Weinberg expected heterozygosity is

$$H_e = 1 - (0.364^2 + 0.352^2 + 0.284^2) = 1 - (0.1325 + 0.1239 + 0.0807)$$
$$= 0.663$$

The observed and expected heterozygosities of 0.659 and 0.663 at this locus are very similar.

To assess the evolutionary potential of a species, information is required about genome-wide genetic diversity. Information on a single locus is unlikely to accurately depict genetic diversity for all loci in a species. For example, mammals have around 35 000 loci. Consequently, genetic diversity measures (H_O, H_e) are averaged over several loci (hopefully a random sample) to characterize genetic diversity for a population or species. These measures are demonstrated in Box 4.1, where comparisons are made between levels of genetic diversity in endangered Ethiopian wolves, domestic dogs, gray wolves and coyotes, based on nine microsatellite loci.

Average heterozgyosity over several loci is used to characterize genetic diversity in a species

Conservation biologists are often concerned with changes in levels of genetic diversity over time, as loss of genetic diversity is one indication that the population is undergoing inbreeding and losing its evolutionary potential. Heterozygosity is often expressed as the proportion of heterozygosity retained over time, i.e. H_t/H_0 where H_t is the level of heterozygosity at generation t and H_0 the level at some earlier time, referred to as time 0. For example, H_0 may be the heterozygosity before a population crash, and H_t after the crash. Then $1 - H_t/H_0$ reflects the proportion of heterozygosity lost as a result of the crash. The Mauritius kestrel passed through a single-pair bottleneck in 1974 and recovered to

Box 4.1 | Characterizing genetic diversity in the endangered Ethiopian wolf and its conservation implications (after Gottelli *et al.* 1994))

The Ethiopian wolf is one of the most endangered canids. It exists in only six isolated areas of Ethiopia and has a total population of no more than 500 individuals. Numbers are decreasing due to habitat destruction associated with agriculture, over-grazing and increasing human population pressure. Further, in at least one population, the wolves coexist with domestic dogs and may hybridize with them. Several phenotypically abnormal wolves were suspected of being hybrids. Dogs also compete for prey with wolves and may act as disease vectors.

Data were obtained for nine microsatellite loci on two populations of Ethiopian wolves, one on the Sanetti Plateau, where there were very few dogs, and the other in Web Valley where dogs were abundant. These results were compared with globally non-endangered canids, gray wolves, coyotes and domestic dogs. Allele frequencies at the nine loci in the Sanetti population are shown in the table below (slightly modified from the original data), with summary statistics for the Web population, domestic dogs, gray wolf and coyotes.

| Locus | Allele | | | | | A | H_0 | H_e | n_e | Sample size |
	1	2	3	4	5					
225	0.933	0.067				2	0.133	0.125	1.14	15
109	0.133	0.867				2	0.267	0.231	1.30	15
204	1.000					1	0.000	0.000	1	15
123	1.000					1	0.000	0.000	1	16
377	0.889	0.028	0.028	0.028	0.028	5	0.222	0.207	1.26	18
250	0.933	0.067				2	0.133	0.125	1.14	15
213	0.031	0.969				2	0.063	0.060	1.06	16
173	0.533	0.467				2	0.533	0.498	1.99	15
344	1.000					1	0.000	0.000	1	18
Means										
Ethiopian wolf										
Sanetti						2.0	0.150	0.138	1.21	16
Web						2.8	0.313	0.271	1.37	23
Domestic dogs						6.4	0.516	0.679	3.11	35
Gray wolf						4.5		0.620	2.63	18
Coyote						5.9		0.675	3.08	17

To characterize the genetic diversity, we use observed heterozygosity (H_o), Hardy–Weinberg expected heterozygosity (H_e), allelic diversity (A) and effective number of alleles (n_e). These are averaged over the nine loci, as shown at the bottom. Observed heterozygosity is calculated for each locus as the total number of heterozygotes divided by the sample size. We calculate the Hardy–Weinberg expected heterozygosity for each locus (using equation 4.2), and average them. The number of alleles per locus are also averaged, as shown. Finally the effective number of alleles is calculated for each locus and averaged.

Several pieces of information of conservation relevance can be gleaned from this information. First, the Ethiopian wolf populations have lower genetic diversity than the related globally non-endangered gray wolf, coyote and domestic dog, as gauged by allelic diversity, effective number of alleles and average heterozygosity. Consequently, the Ethiopian wolf has less evolutionary potential than non-endangered canids.

Second, the relatively 'pure' Sanetti population has less genetic diversity than the Web Valley population that coexists with domestic dogs, suggesting that there may be hybridization with dogs. This was verified when seven phenotypically abnormal Ethiopian wolves were found to contain alleles present in domestic dogs, but absent from 'pure' Ethiopian wolves.

Third, observed and expected heterozygosities are similar (they do not differ significantly in either of the Ethiopian wolf populations). Consequently, mating in the wolves is approximately random within populations.

The study also established that Ethiopian wolves are distinctly different from other canids, but related to gray wolves and coyotes (data not shown here).

The management recommendations that arose from this study were:

- that feral domestic dogs be controlled to eliminate hybridization and disease spread
- that a captive breeding program be instituted immediately with genetically 'pure' Ethiopian wolf founders
- that the other Ethiopian wolf populations be surveyed
- that the Ethiopian wolf be recognized as a distinct species deserving conservation.

a population size of 400–500 by 1997. Its average heterozygosity for microsatellites prior to the bottleneck (based on genotyping of museum skins) was 0.23, but heterozygosity had dropped to 0.10 by 1997 (Groombridge *et al.* 2000). Hence, $H_t/H_0 = 0.1 / 0.23 = 0.43$. Thus, the Mauritius kestrel has lost 57% of the genetic diversity it possessed before the bottleneck.

Allelic diversity

Allelic diversity, the average number of alleles per locus, is also used to characterize the extent of genetic diversity. For example, there are two alleles at the locus determining egg-white protein differences in eider ducks and three alleles at the microsatellite locus in Laysan finches. When there is more than one locus, allelic diversity (A) is the number of alleles averaged across loci:

Allelic diversity is also used to characterize genetic diversity

$$A = \text{total number of alleles over all loci} / \text{number of loci} \qquad (4.3)$$

For example, the Sanetti population of the endangered Ethiopian wolf (Box 4.1) has a total of 18 alleles over the nine microsatellite loci surveyed, so $A = 18 / 9 = 2.0$.

A second measure reflecting the number of alleles is the **effective number of alleles**. This is the number of alleles there would be to provide the same heterozygosity if all were equally frequent, and is less influenced by rare alleles. This measure is used as it is less sensitive to sample sizes and it ties in with theory we consider in Chapter 9. The effective number of alleles (n_e) is calculated as follows:

$$n_e = 1 / \Sigma p_i^2 \qquad (4.4)$$

where p_i is the frequency of each allele, and the values are summed for all alleles. For example, the Mdg3 microsatellite locus in chimpanzees has five alleles, but the effective number of alleles is 2.42 (Example 4.4). By contrast, the microsatellite locus in Laysan finch above with three alleles has a n_e of 2.96, very close to the actual value, as the allele frequencies are almost equal. The effective number of alleles only equals the actual number when all alleles are equally frequent, and in most cases, n_e is much less than A.

Example 4.4 | Effective number of alleles at the Mfd3 microsatellite locus in chimpanzees

The frequencies of the five alleles at the Mfd3 microsatellite locus are 0.026, 0.316, 0.026, 0.079 and 0.553 (Table 3.4). Consequently, the effective number of alleles is

$$n_e = 1 / \Sigma p_i^2 = 1 / (0.026^2 + 0.316^2 + 0.026^2 + 0.079^2 + 0.553^2) = 2.42$$

Thus, the effective number of alleles at this locus is 2.42.

Estimating the allele frequency for a recessive allele

The Hardy–Weinberg equilibrium provides a means for estimating the frequencies of recessive alleles in random mating populations

It is not possible to determine the frequency of an allele at a locus showing dominance using the allele counting method outlined above. This is because dominant homozygotes cannot be distinguished, phenotypically, from heterozygotes. However, the Hardy–Weinberg equilibrium provides a means for estimating the frequencies of such alleles. Homozygous recessives are phenotypically detectable and have an expected frequency of q^2 for loci in Hardy–Weinberg equilibrium. Thus, the observed frequency of homozygous recessive phenotypes can be equated to q^2, and the recessive allele frequency obtained as the square root of this frequency. The calculation is illustrated for chondrodystrophic dwarfism in the endangered California condor in Example 4.5. This allele has an estimated frequency of 0.17, a surprisingly high frequency for a recessive lethal allele.

Since there are several assumptions underlying this method of estimating q (random mating, no selection or migration), it should never be used for loci where all genotypes can be distinguished.

Relatively high frequencies of particular recessive inherited defects have also been found in other populations derived from few founders, including other endangered species and human isolates, such as the Amish (Chapter 7).

Example 4.5 | Estimating the allele frequency for the recessive chondrodystrophy allele in California condors using the Hardy–Weinberg equilibrium frequencies

Chondrodystrophy in California condors is a condition that results in severe malformations (dwarfing) in the long bones and death around hatching. It is thought to be due to homozygosity for a recessive allele, as are similar conditions in domestic turkeys. Of 169 hatched eggs in the condors, 5 exhibited chondrodystrophy (4 from the one family and another from a related individual), a frequency of 0.0296 (Ralls *et al.* 2000). If we use + and *dw* as the symbol for the normal and chondrodystrophic alleles, and *p* and *q* for their frequencies, the phenotypes, corresponding genotypes, and their expected Hardy–Weinberg equilibrium frequencies are as follows:

Phenotypes	Normal	Chondrodystrophic
Genotypes	(++ and + *dw*)	*dwdw*
Observed frequency	0.9704	0.0296
H–W equilibrium expected frequency	$p^2 + 2pq$	q^2

As the homozygous normal and the heterozygotes cannot be distinguished, it is not possible to obtain the allele frequencies by direct counting. However, if the assumptions of the Hardy–Weinberg equilibrium are upheld, we can estimate the frequency of the *dw* allele by equating the observed frequency of affected individuals to q^2 and solving, as follows:

$$q^2 = 0.0296$$

Taking the square root of both sides of the equation

$$q = \sqrt{0.0296} = 0.17$$

The chondrodystrophy allele has a frequency of about 17% at hatching. This is a very high level for a deleterious allele, but is not surprising given that the condors have been reduced to very low numbers (minimum of 14 individuals).

Frequency of carriers (heterozygotes)

The frequency of carriers of recessive mutations is of interest in conservation genetics, as well as in human and veterinary medicine. However, carriers of deleterious recessives (Aa) cannot be distinguished from non-carriers. Nevertheless, we can predict the frequency of carriers amongst those with normal phenotypes from the Hardy–Weinberg equilibrium. It is the ratio of the frequency of heterozygotes (Aa = 2pq) to that of all individuals with normal phenotypes (AA + Aa = $p^2 + 2pq$), as follows:

The Hardy–Weinberg equilibrium allows us to predict the frequency of carriers for genetic diseases

$$\text{frequency (carriers)} = 2q / (1+q) \qquad (4.5)$$

In the case of chondrodystrophy, the frequency of carriers among individuals with normal phenotypes is expected to be $2 \times 0.17 / (1 + 0.17) = 0.29$. Thus, about 30% of the condor population are carriers, almost 10 times the frequency of affected homozygotes (if we can assume random mating).

Deviations from Hardy–Weinberg equilibrium

Deviations from Hardy–Weinberg equilibrium genotype frequencies are highly informative, allowing us to detect inbreeding, population fragmentation, migration and selection

When any of the assumptions underlying the Hardy–Weinberg equilibrium are violated, then deviations from the equilibrium genotype frequencies will occur. Immigration, selection and non-random mating will all lead to deviations from the equilibrium. Thus, the Hardy–Weinberg equilibrium provides a null hypothesis that allows us to detect if the population has non-random mating, migration or selection.

There are two types of non-random mating, those where mate choice is based on ancestry (inbreeding and crossbreeding), and those where choice is based on genotypes at a particular locus (assortive and dissortive mating).

Inbreeding

Inbreeding is the production of offspring from mating of relatives. It reduces the frequency of heterozygotes compared to random mating

The mating of relatives is called inbreeding (Chapter 2). It is of major importance in conservation genetics as it leads to reduced reproductive fitness (Chapters 2 and 12). When related individuals mate at a rate greater than expected by random mating, the frequency of heterozygotes is reduced relative to Hardy–Weinberg expectations, and homozygote frequencies correspondingly increased. We can see how this arises in the case of self-fertilization (the most extreme form of inbreeding) by following the genotype frequencies expected under Mendelian inheritance (Fig. 4.2). If an A_1A_2 individual is self-fertilized, heterozygosity is halved in the progeny. By generation 2, the frequency of heterozygotes is 25%, compared to the Hardy–Weinberg equilibrium expectation of 50%, and it continues to halve in each subsequent generation.

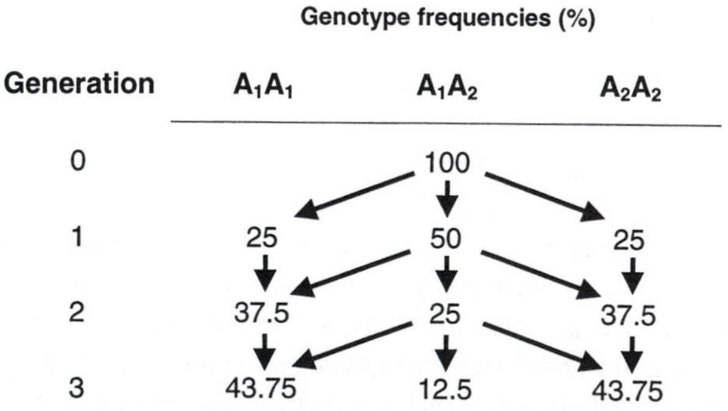

Fig. 4.2 Effect of self-fertilization on genotype frequencies. *The frequency of heterozygotes halves with each generation of selfing.*

Genotype frequencies (%)

Generation	A_1A_1	A_1A_2	A_2A_2
0		100	
1	25	50	25
2	37.5	25	37.5
3	43.75	12.5	43.75

Table 4.5 | Heterozygote deficiency in an inbreeding plant population. Observed numbers for the three genotypes at the phosphoglucomutase-2 locus in a phlox population are given, along with expected numbers for a random mating population in Hardy–Weinberg equilibrium. In this species, 78% of the seeds are estimated to result from self-fertilization

	Genotypes		
	FF	FS	SS
Observed numbers	15	6	14
Hardy–Weinberg expectations	9.3	17.5	8.3

Source: Data from Hartl & Clark (1997) after Levin.

Consequently, deficiencies of heterozygotes in populations, compared to Hardy–Weinberg equilibrium expectations, indicate that they are not mating randomly. There is a deficiency of heterozygotes in phlox plants (Table 4.5). This species shows a high level of self-fertilization. Note that there are only six heterozygotes, while 17 are expected with random mating under the Hardy–Weinberg equilibrium. While inbreeding leads to lower than expected heterozygosity, avoidance of inbreeding and outcrossing can lead to higher than expected heterozygosity. Inbreeding is treated in detail in Chapter 11.

Assortive and dissortive mating

The preferential mating of like-with-like genotypes is called assortive (or assortative) mating, while the mating of unlike genotypes is referred to as dissortive (or disassortative) mating. In general, assortive mating leads to increased homozygosity, while dissortive mating increases heterozygosity compared to Hardy–Weinberg equilibrium frequencies.

Assortive mating based on phenotypic resemblance has been documented in humans for stature, intelligence and other quantitative characters. Genotypic dissortive mating is common in the self-sterility systems found in many plant species. In these systems, pollen must carry a different allele to the female parent (or ovum) for fertilization to succeed. For example, if the female parent is S_1S_2, then pollen that succeeds in fertilization carries alleles S_3, S_4, etc., i.e. not S_1 or S_2. This type of mating serves to avoid inbreeding and its deleterious consequences.

Fragmented populations

Allele frequencies diverge in isolated populations due to chance and selection (Chapter 13). This results in an overall deficiency of heterozygotes, even when individual populations are themselves in Hardy–Weinberg equilibrium. In the extreme case, where one population only has allele A_1 and the other only has allele A_2, there are no heterozygotes.

Fragmented populations with restricted gene flow show deficiencies of heterozygotes compared to Hardy–Weinberg expectations

This is much less than the overall expectation of 50% heterozygosity with two alleles, both at frequencies of 0.5. For example, two isolated populations of black-footed rock wallabies on Barrow and Mondrain Islands off the Western Australian coast are fixed for alleles 136 and 124 respectively at the Pa297 microsatellite locus (Table 13.1). A similar situation also exists at several other loci.

An extreme case of isolation exists when two undescribed species are mistakenly considered as one population. For example, when velvet worms (see chapter frontispiece) from a single log in the Blue Mountains near Sydney were genotyped using electrophoresis, genetic diversity was detected at several loci, but there were no heterozygotes. Two forms that differed slightly in body colour were both found to be homozygous at all loci, but they were homozygous for different alleles at 86% of the sampled loci. This was a clear indication that the two forms (previously considered to belong to a single species) were not exchanging alleles, even though they shared the same habitat. Consequently, this led to them being designated as separate species (Briscoe & Tait 1995). Genetic markers can be used to determine whether there is gene flow between populations, and so assist in resolving taxonomic uncertainties (Chapter 15).

Extensions of the Hardy–Weinberg equilibrium

Three alleles

Hardy–Weinberg equilibrium occurs for autosomal loci with any number of alleles in random mating populations

Expressions for the Hardy–Weinberg equilibrium can be obtained for more than two alleles at a locus. If there are three alleles A_1, A_2 and A_3 at a locus with frequencies p, q and r, then the Hardy–Weinberg equilibrium genotype frequencies are given by the terms of the binomial expansion $(p + q + r)^2$ (Example 4.6). This expression can be derived in a similar manner to that for a diallelic locus (Table 4.3). Related expressions can easily be derived for any number of alleles at a locus. Example 4.6 illustrates calculation of expected genotype frequencies for a locus with three alleles in the endangered Laysan finch.

| **Example 4.6** | Calculating the expected Hardy–Weinberg equilibrium frequencies at a locus with three alleles |

For the Laysan finches in Table 4.2, the frequencies of the 91, 95 and 97 microsatellite alleles are 0.364 (p), 0.352 (q) and 0.284 (r), respectively. Consequently, the expected genotype frequencies are:

	Genotypes						
	91/91	91/95	91/97	95/95	95/97	97/97	Total
Expected frequencies	p^2	$2pq$	$2pr$	q^2	$2qr$	r^2	1
	0.364^2	$2 \times 0.364 \times 0.352$	$2 \times 0.364 \times 0.284$	0.352^2	$2 \times 0.352 \times 0.284$	0.284^2	1
	0.132	0.256	0.207	0.124	0.200	0.081	1

Sex-linked loci

Sex-linked loci occur in different doses in females and males. In mammals and fruit flies, sex-linked loci are located on the X chromosome. Females have XX sex chromosomes and males XY. The Y chromosome lacks the loci present on the X, and females have two copies of each locus and males have only one. Conversely, birds and Lepidoptera have ZZ males and ZW females. Here the Z chromosome has the sex-linked loci, while the W chromosome is devoid of these loci. Fish have species with both these forms of sex chromosomes, while plants are most often hermaphroditic (both sexes in each individual). When dealing with sex-linked loci we will display alleles as superscripts on the X or Z chromosomes (e.g. X^A, or Z^A) and the Y or W as devoid of sex-linked alleles, to avoid confusion with autosomal loci.

It is important to distinguish sex-linked loci as they have Hardy–Weinberg equilibrium genotype frequencies that differ from those for autosomal loci. Consequently, these differences could be confused with the effects of inbreeding, assortative mating or population fragmentation.

The procedure for calculating allele frequencies for a sex-linked locus is similar to the allele counting method used in Example 4.1, except that we must take account of the different number of copies of loci in the two sexes. Table 4.6 illustrates genotype frequencies for the sex-linked 6-pgd locus in a *Heliconius* butterfly from Trinidad, and Example 4.7 illustrates the estimation of allele frequencies. In mammals 2/3 of the sex-linked alleles are found in females and 1/3 in males when there is an equal sex ratio, while these proportions in the two sexes are reversed in birds and Lepidoptera.

> As sex-linked loci exist in different numbers of copies in females and males, they have different genotype frequencies in the two sexes

---

Table 4.6 | Numbers of each genotype in females and males at the sex-linked 6-phosphogluconate dehydrogenase enzyme (6-pgd) locus in a *Heliconius* butterfly from Trinidad, and the numbers expected with Hardy–Weinberg equilibrium. Note that males have ZZ and females ZW chromosomes

	Males				Females		
	$Z^F Z^F$	$Z^F Z^S$	$Z^S Z^S$	Total	$Z^F W$	$Z^S W$	Total
Numbers	39	46	27	112	29	33	62
Expected	32.1	55.7	24.2	112	33.2	28.8	62

Source: Simplified from Johnson & Turner (1979).

Example 4.7 | Estimation of allele frequencies at the sex-linked 6-pgd locus in *Heliconius* butterflies from Trinidad

The frequency of the Z^F allele is obtained by counting the number of copies of the *F* allele in all the females and males, as done previously. However, for a sex-linked locus we must take account of the different number of copies of the locus in females (1) and males (2). Thus, the number of F alleles is $2 \times 39 = 78$ from the $Z^F Z^F$ males, 46 from the $Z^F Z^S$ males and 29 from the $Z^F W$ females, totalling 153 F alleles.

We divide this by the total number of allele copies in the sample, counting two for each male (2×112) and one for each female 62, totalling 286.

Thus, the frequency of the sex-linked Z^F allele (p) is

$$p = [(2 \times 39) + 46 + 29] / [2 \times 112 + 62] = 153/286$$
$$= 0.535$$

Similarly, the frequency of the sex-linked Z^S allele (q) is

$$q = [(2 \times 27) + 46 + 33)] / [2 \times 112 + 62] = 133/286$$
$$= 0.465$$

and checking $p + q = 0.535 + 0.465 = 1$

Thus, the frequency of the sex-linked F allele is 53.5% and that of S is 46.5%.

Hardy–Weinberg equilibrium for sex-linked loci

Sex-linked loci reach Hardy–Weinberg equilibrium under random mating with different genotype frequencies in females and males

If the allele frequencies in males and females are equal, then the population reaches equilibrium allele and genotype frequencies in one generation with random mating (and no other perturbing forces), as for autosomal loci (Table 4.7). Female genotype frequencies for the three genotypes in mammals are the same as those for autosomal loci, while male genotype frequencies are p and q, the allele frequencies.

For birds and Lepidoptera with ZZ males ZW females, the males and females are reversed from those in Table 4.7. Observed and Hardy–Weinberg expected numbers for the sex-linked 6-pgd locus in the *Heliconius* butterfly population are compared in Table 4.6. Neither the male nor the female numbers deviate significantly from Hardy–Weinberg expectations. There is, however, a suspicious deficiency of heterozygotes in males that could be due to combining individuals from partially isolated populations.

Populations with different allelic frequencies in the two sexes, do not attain equilibrium genotype frequencies in one generation, but approach it asymptotically over generations. Equilibrium is attained only when allele frequencies are equal in females and males (Falconer & Mackay 1996).

Table 4.7 Hardy–Weinberg equilibrium genotype frequencies in females and males for a sex-linked locus following random mating in a species with XX females and XY males

Females			Males	
$X^{A1}X^{A1}$	$X^{A1}X^{A2}$	$X^{A2}X^{A2}$	$X^{A1}Y$	$X^{A2}Y$
p^2	$2pq$	q^2	p	q

Polyploids

Many plants and a small number of animals are **polyploids**. They have more than two doses of each chromosome. For example, some populations of the endangered grassland daisy in Australia are tetraploid (Young & Murray 2000). They have four doses of each chromosome rather than two, as in diploids. We refer to the chromosome number in **tetraploids** as 4n, as compared to 2n in diploids. If all chromosomes come from the same species, it is referred to as an **autotetraploid**, while it is an **allotetraploid** if the chromosomes come from two different species because of hybridization and chromosome doubling. For example, a form of cord grass *Spartina × townsendii* is an allotetraploid that formed spontaneously on the coast of England following the accidental introduction of *Spartina alterniflora* into the range of *S. maritima* (Jones & Wilkins 1971).

In what follows, we consider only tetraploids, but the same principles apply to other even-number ploidies (6n hexaploid, 8n octoploid, etc). Triploids (3n) usually have abnormal meiosis and are highly sterile.

Allele frequencies in tetraploids are calculated by the same allele counting method used in diploids. However, remember that there are four copies of each locus in each individual, and five genotypes for a locus with two alleles (Table 4.8). Hardy–Weinberg equilibrium occurs in tetraploids, but the genotype frequencies are different from those in diploids (Table 4.8). The genotype frequencies at a locus with two alleles in an autotetraploid are given as the terms of the binomial expansion ($p + q$)^4. Recall that the genotype frequencies for a diploid are given by the expansion of $(p + q)^2$.

At a polymorphic locus with two alleles in a tetraploid, there are three heterozygous genotypes, rather than one as found in an equivalent diploid. The three heterozygotes ($A_1A_1A_1A_2$, $A_1A_1A_2A_2$ and $A_1A_2A_2A_2$) have a total frequency of

$$H_e = 4p^3q + 6p^2q^2 + 4pq^3 = 2pq \,(2p^2 + 3pq + 2q^2)$$
$$= 2pq \,(2 - pq) \tag{4.6}$$

Thus, the frequency of heterozygotes of $2pq \,(2 - pq)$ is considerably greater than the $2pq$ frequency for an equivalent diploid. This is strictly correct only for loci close to the centromere in autotetraploids. Expected heterozygosities for loci distant from the centromere are

> Hardy–Weinberg equilibrium occurs in tetraploids, but results in a higher frequency of heterozygotes than found in diploids when allele frequencies are the same

Table 4.8 | Hardy–Weinberg equilibrium genotype frequencies in a random mating autotetraploid

| | Genotypes | | | | | |
	$A_1A_1A_1A_1$	$A_1A_1A_1A_2$	$A_1A_1A_2A_2$	$A_1A_2A_2A_2$	$A_2A_2A_2A_2$	Total
Frequency	p^4	$4p^3q$	$6p^2q^2$	$4pq^3$	q^4	1
Example: $p = 0.6$ and $q = 0.4$						
Frequency	0.1296	0.3456	0.3456	0.1536	0.0256	1

slightly lower than indicated above, but the difference is likely to be small (Bever & Felber 1994).

For example, if we have two alleles with frequencies of 0.6 and 0.4, the frequency of heterozygotes in an autotetraploid is 0.84, compared to 0.48 in an equivalent diploid. This has important implications when we consider loss of genetic diversity and inbreeding in small populations (Chapters 10–12), as well as for genetic management of polyploids (Chapter 16).

More than one locus–linkage disequilibrium

Alleles at different loci are expected to be randomly associated in a large random breeding population at equilibrium, i.e. to show linkage equilibrium

In large randomly breeding populations at equilibrium, alleles at different loci are expected to be randomly associated. Consider two loci, A and B with alleles A_1, A_2 and B_1, B_2, and frequencies p_A, q_A, p_B, q_B respectively. These loci and alleles form gametes A_1B_1, A_1B_2, A_2B_1 and A_2B_2. Under random mating and independent assortment, these gametes will have frequencies that are the product of their allele frequencies. For example, gamete A_1B_2 will have frequency of p_Aq_B. Random association of alleles at different loci is referred to as **linkage equilibrium**. Alleles at most loci in large random mating populations are in linkage equilibrium (Huttley *et al.* 1999).

If there is a deviation from random combinations of allele frequencies at different loci (linkage disequilibrium), the fate of an allele will be correlated with that of neighbouring loci

Non-random association of alleles among loci is referred to as **linkage disequilibrium**. Chance events in small populations, population bottlenecks, recent mixing of different populations and selection all may cause non-random associations among loci. Loci that show deviations from linkage equilibrium (linkage disequilibrium) in large random mating populations are often subject to strong forces of natural selection. For example, important functional clusters of loci, such as the major histocompatibility complex (MHC) that is involved in immune response and disease resistance, show linkage disequilibrium due to natural selection (see Box 4.2 below).

In small populations, neutral alleles that have no selective difference between genotypes may behave as if they are under selection, due to non-random association with alleles at nearby loci that are being strongly selected.

Linkage disequilibrium is of importance in populations of conservation concern, as:

- Linkage disequilibrium will be common in threatened species as their population sizes are small
- Population bottlenecks frequently cause linkage disequilibrium
- Evolutionary processes are altered when there is linkage disequilibrium
- Functionally important gene clusters exhibiting linkage disequilibrium (such as the MHC) are of major importance to the persistence of threatened species
- Linkage disequilibrium is one of the signals that can be used to detect admixture of differentiated populations
- Linkage disequilibrium can be used to estimate genetically effective population sizes (Chapter 10).

Table 4.9 | Measuring linkage disequilibrium among alleles at two loci, A and B. Each locus has two alleles A_1, A_2 and B_1, B_2 at frequencies p_A, q_A and p_B, q_B, respectively

	Gametic types (haplotypes)				
	A_1B_1	A_1B_2	A_2B_1	A_2B_2	
Actual frequencies	r	s	t	u	1.0
Equilibrium frequencies	p_Ap_B	p_Aq_B	q_Ap_B	q_Aq_B	1.0

Disequilibrium $D = ru - st$

Numerical example $p_A = 0.7$, $q_A = 0.3$, $p_B = 0.7$, $q_B = 0.3$

Actual frequencies	0.7	0.0	0.0	0.3
Equilibrium frequencies	0.7×0.7	0.7×0.3	0.3×0.7	0.3×0.3
	0.49	0.21	0.21	0.09

Disequilibrium $D = 0.7 \times 0.3 - 0.0 \times 0.0 = 0.21$

To demonstrate the effects of linkage disequilibrium, let us consider an example where two different monomorphic populations with genotypes $A_1A_1B_1B_1$ and $A_2A_2B_2B_2$, are combined and allowed to mate at random. Each autosomal locus is expected to attain individual Hardy–Weinberg equilibrium with one generation of random mating (see above). However, alleles at different loci do not attain linkage equilibrium frequencies in one generation, they only approach it asymptotically at a rate dependent on the recombination frequency between the two loci. In the above pooled population, let 70% of the pooled population have genotype $A_1A_1B_1B_1$ and 30% have genotype $A_2A_2B_2B_2$. There are equal numbers of males and females for each of the two genotypes. Only two gametic types (**haplotypes**) are produced, A_1B_1 and A_2B_2, so progeny in the next generation will consist of only three genotypes $A_1A_1B_1B_1$, $A_1A_2B_1B_2$ and $A_2A_2B_2B_2$, and none of the other six possible genotypes. These loci are clearly in linkage disequilibrium.

In subsequent generations, the two other possible gametic types A_1B_2 and A_2B_1 are generated by recombination in the multiply heterozygous genotype. For example, A_1B_1/A_2B_2 heterozygotes produce recombinant gametes A_1B_2 and A_2B_1 at frequencies of $\frac{1}{2}c$, where c is the rate of recombination, as well as non-recombinant A_1B_1, A_2B_2 gametes in frequencies of $\frac{1}{2}(1-c)$. Eventually all nine possible genotypes will be formed and attain an equilibrium frequency, i.e. linkage equilibrium.

As in the above example, until equilibrium is reached, genotypes will deviate from their expected frequencies. Linkage disequilibrium is the deviation of gametic frequencies from their equilibrium frequencies (Table 4.9).

The measure of linkage disequilibrium D is the difference between the product of the frequencies of the A_1B_1 and A_2B_2 gametes (referred to as r and u) and the product of the frequencies of the A_1B_2 and A_2B_1 gametes (s and t):

Linkage disequilibrium is measured as the deviation of haplotype frequencies from linkage equilibrium

$$D = ru - st \qquad\qquad (4.7)$$

Note that under equilibrium $ru = st$, since both ru and st are equal to $p_A q_A p_B q_B$, and $D = 0$. In our example, the four gametic types had frequencies of 0.7, 0, 0, and 0.3 in the first generation, so $D = 0.7 \times 0.3 - 0 \times 0 = 0.21$. The maximum value of D is 0.25, and the minimum -0.25. The maximum value of D occurs when the frequencies of the four gametic types are 0.5, 0, 0, and 0.5.

Linkage disequilibrium is found in the MHC, a cluster of loci involved in immune response, transplant rejection and fighting disease organisms (Box 4.2). In general, loci further apart than 1 centimorgan (1% crossing-over) in large random mating populations do not show linkage disequilibrium unless they involve a cluster of loci that are subject to balancing selection (Chapter 9). Linkage disequilibrium between pairs of loci in the MHC is generally greater for more closely linked loci (Hedrick *et al.* 1991). Linkage disequilibrium at the MHC is a feature of all well-studied vertebrates.

| Box 4.2 | Linkage disequilibrium at the major histocompatibility complex (MHC) in humans |

The MHC is a cluster of linked loci involved in immune response that is found in all vertebrates (Edwards & Hedrick 1998). These loci have a major role in fighting pathogens. There are consistent non-random associations of alleles at different loci (linkage disequilibrium) in the MHC. The data below show the associations between alleles at the HLA-A and HLA-B loci in Caucasians based on 2106 haplotypes (data after Spiess 1989). The data have been simplified to show only four alleles at one locus and three at the other. There are actually many more alleles (for this reason, the total of allele frequencies for each locus in our example do not add to unity).

Note the non-random association between alleles at the two loci, as shown by the sign of the deviation from expectation. All of these are statistically significant deviations. For example, the frequency of the A1–B7 haplotype was 0.0074. At linkage equilibrium it would be expected to have a frequency of $0.1439 \times 0.1143 = 0.0164$, so that it shows a deficiency of -0.0090. This deficiency is the linkage disequilibrium associated with this haplotype and is 55% of the maximum value that D could have for alleles with these frequencies.

Haplotype frequencies for HLA-A and HLA-B loci. The sign after each figure indicates a deficiency $(-)$, or excess of $(+)$ of the haplotype

		HLA-A alleles			Overall HLA-B
		A1	A2	A3	allele frequencies
HLA-B allele	B7	0.0074(−)	0.0260(−)	0.0477(+)	0.1143
	B8	0.0672(+)	0.0110(−)	0.0019(−)	0.0971
	B35	0.0029(−)	0.0178(−)	0.0257(+)	0.1052
	B44	0.0089(−)	0.0503(+)	0.0068(−)	0.1242
Overall HLA-A allele frequencies					
		0.1439	0.2855	0.1335	

Linkage disequilibrium decays as recombination produces under-represented gametes. Recombination results from independent segregation of unlinked loci and crossing-over between linked loci. In our first example above, linkage disequilibrium decayed with random mating as A_1B_2 and A_2B_1 gametes were produced by recombination in multiply heterozygous genotypes $A_1B_1A_2B_2$ and $A_1B_2A_2B_1$. The rate of decay of disequilibrium depends on the recombination frequency as shown below. After t generations, the remaining disequilibrium is (Falconer & Mackay 1996):

$$D_t = D_0(1-c)^t \qquad (4.8)$$

where c is the recombination frequency. The amount of recombination between two loci depends on their positions on a chromosome. It generally increases with the distance between loci, reaching a maximum value of 0.5 for independently assorting loci on different chromosomes. Loci do not have to be linked to show disequilibrium. With unlinked loci, $c = 0.5$, meaning that the disequilibrium halves each generation and is rapidly lost. Conversely, with tightly linked loci, disequilibrium decays very slowly. For example, in the case in Table 4.9, D_0 was 0.21, so for loci on separate chromosomes it would drop to 0.21 $(1-0.5) = 0.105$ in a single generation. For linked loci showing only 10% recombination, it would drop much less – to 0.21 $(1-0.1) = 0.189$. Fig. 4.3 illustrates the decline in linkage disequilibrium over 10 generations for loci with different recombination rates. Linkage disequilibrium declines rapidly for unlinked loci, with approximate linkage equilibrium reached in five generations. Conversely, decay of disequilibrium is slow for closely linked loci.

> Linkage disequilibrium decays at a rate dependent on the recombination rate between the loci

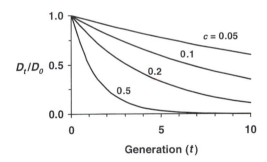

Fig. 4.3 Decay in linkage disequilibrium between two loci under random mating, with recombination frequencies of 0.05, 0.1, 0.2 and 0.5 (unlinked loci). The proportion of linkage disequilibrium remaining (D_t / D_0) is plotted against generations (t).

Summary

1. Genetic diversity within a population is characterized by the frequencies of each of the genotypes. This is normally simplified by reporting the allele (gene) frequencies at each locus.

2. In large random mating populations with no perturbing factors, the allele and genotype frequencies at autosomal loci are in equilibrium after one generation (Hardy–Weinberg equilibrium).

3. Deviations from Hardy–Weinberg equilibrium genotype frequencies allow us to detect inbreeding, population fragmentation, migration and selection.

4. Inbreeding reduces the frequency of heterozygotes compared to random mating.

5. If there is linkage disequilibrium between allele frequencies at different loci, the fate of an allele will be affected by that of neighbouring loci. Linkage disequilibrium decays towards equilibrium at a rate dependent on recombination frequency between the loci.

FURTHER READING

Falconer & Mackay (1996) *Introduction to Quantitative Genetics*. Contains a very clear introduction to population genetics, with a focus on animal and plant breeding.

Hartl & Clark (1997) *Principles of Population Genetics*. Clear introduction to population genetics with a molecular evolutionary focus.

Hedrick (2000) *Genetics of Populations*. Clearly written coverage of population genetics with an evolutionary slant.

PROBLEMS

4.1 Allele frequency: Estimate the frequencies for the M and N alleles in the following sample of humans from Greenland (after Falconer & Mackay 1996).

	Blood group genotype			
	MM	MN	NN	Total
Numbers	475	89	5	569

4.2 Hardy–Weinberg equilibrium: What are the expected Hardy–Weinberg equilibrium frequencies and numbers at the MN blood group locus in the human population described in Problem 4.1? Do the observed numbers differ from those expected according to the Hardy–Weinberg equilibrium?

4.3 Allele frequencies for a locus with four alleles: What are the frequencies of the 85, 91, 93 and 95 alleles at the 11B4E microsatellite locus in the endangered Laysan finch of Hawaii (data of Tarr *et al.* 1998)? (The allele designations are sizes of PCR fragments.) Check that the allele frequencies add to unity.

	Genotypes									
	85/85	85/91	85/93	85/95	91/91	91/93	91/95	93/93	93/95	95/95
Numbers	2	13	0	0	15	2	12	0	0	0

4.4 Observed heterozygosity: What is the observed heterozygosity for the microsatellite locus in Laysan finches in Problem 4.3?

4.5 Hardy–Weinberg equilibrium for a triallelic locus: What are the expected genotypic frequencies for the microsatellite locus in Laysan finches from Table 4.2? What are the expected numbers? Do the observed numbers agree with Hardy–Weinberg expectations?

4.6 Hardy–Weinberg equilibrium in trisomics: If the frequencies of the F and S alleles at an electrophoretic locus situated on chromosome 21 in humans are 0.6 and 0.4, what are the Hardy–Weinberg equilibrium genotype frequencies in a population of Down's Syndrome sufferers (they have three doses of chromosome 21)?

4.7 Random mating: The three alleles at the human ABO blood group have frequencies of about 0.3 A, 0.1 B and 0.6 O in Caucasians. What is the expected frequency of AA × OO matings?

4.8 Random mating: Is the human population in Ashibetsu, Japan, mating at random with respect to the MN blood group locus? The number of people with each of the blood group genotypes were (from Strickberger 1985 after Matsunaga & Itoh):

MM	MN	NN	Total
406	744	332	1482

and the 741 mating couples had the following distribution of genotypes:

MM × MM	58
MM × MN	202
MM × NN	88
MN × MN	190
MN × NN	162
NN × NN	41

4.9 Effective number of alleles: What is the effective number of alleles for the eider duck egg-white protein locus described in Table 4.1?

4.10 Allele frequency for a recessive: Assume that hernias in golden lion tamarins are inherited as an autosomal recessive and that 96 individuals have the normal phenotype and 4 have hernias. What is the frequency of the recessive allele causing hernias?

4.11 Linkage disequilibrium: What is the linkage disequilibrium D in a population with the following gametic frequencies? What will be the gametic frequencies at equilibrium?

	A_1B_1	A_1B_2	A_2B_1	A_2B_2
Frequency	0.2	0.5	0.2	0.1

4.12 Decay of linkage disequilibrium: If the linkage disequilibrium between two loci D is 0.20 initially, and the two loci show 5% recombination, what will be the value of D after 20 generations?

Chapter 5

Characterizing genetic diversity: quantitative variation

Terms:
Additive,
additive variance,
dominance variance,
epistatic variance,
genotype × environment interaction,
heritability,
heterosis,
interaction variance,
normal distribution,
overdominant,
quantitative genetic variation,
quantitative trait locus (QTL),
realized heritability,
reproductive fitness,
selection differential

Characters of interest in conservation biology are primarily quantitative. Variation for these traits is due to both genetic and environmental factors. Components of quantitative genetic variation determine the ability to undergo adaptive evolution, the effects of inbreeding on reproductive fitness, and the effects of outcrossing on fitness

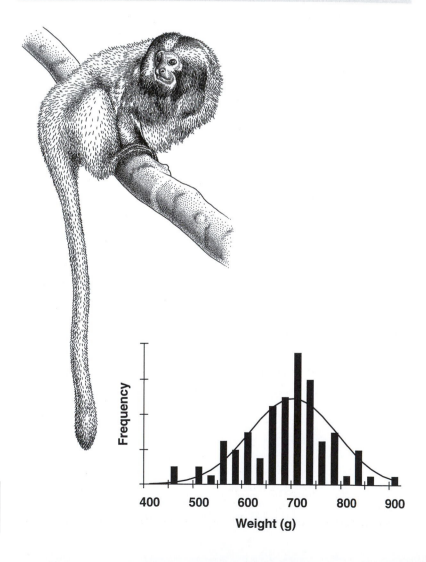

Distribution of adult body weights in golden lion tamarins, a quantitative character.

Importance of quantitative characters

In the previous chapter, we considered variation due to segregation of alleles at single loci. However, the characteristics of most importance in evolution, and in the conservation of evolutionary potential, do not show such simple inheritance. The quantitative (or metric, or polygenic) characters of most concern to conservation biologists are those related to **reproductive fitness**. This is number of fertile offspring contributed by an individual that survive to reproductive age. Such characters include all components of individual survival, reproductive rate, mating ability, longevity, etc. In endangered species quantitative variation for reproductive fitness is involved in the major genetic concerns in conservation biology, namely:

- Reduction in reproductive fitness due to inbreeding (inbreeding depression)
- Loss of evolutionary potential due to small population sizes
- Impact of crossing between different populations on fitness, whether beneficial (heterosis), or deleterious (outbreeding depression)
- Effects of translocating individuals from one environment to another.

Study of this kind of variation is termed 'quantitative' genetics. For example, Box 5.1 illustrates quantitative genetic variation for resistance to an introduced root rot fungus in an Australian tree, and its conservation implications.

The four issues defined above are explored in detail in Chapters 10–14. Here we introduce the concepts underlying quantitative genetics, its terminology, and its modes of analysis and prediction.

It may be thought that molecular measures of genetic diversity answer the questions we wish to know in conservation genetics. However, correlations between molecular and quantitative measures of genetic diversity are low (see below). Consequently, molecular measures of genetic variation provide, at best, only a very imprecise indication of evolutionary potential.

> The characters of greatest concern in conservation biology show quantitative variation among individuals

Box 5.1	Quantitative genetic variation in resistance to an introduced root rot fungus in a Western Australian eucalypt tree and its conservation implications (Stukely & Crane 1994)

The introduced 'dieback' root rot fungus is known to attack 90 Western Australian native plant species, many rare or endangered. It has caused serious degradation to many highly diverse plant communities in the southwest of Western Australia, where tourism to view the wildflowers is a major industry. One victim of this dieback is jarrah, a hardwood eucalypt tree of economic importance, and the ecosystem it supports. Areas of jarrah forest that suffered dieback have previously been replanted with exotics, such as pines and eastern Australian eucalypts (that are

relatively resistant to dieback) with subsequent loss, or alteration of habitat for birds, mammals and invertebrates. To avoid such habitat loss, the objective now is to revegetate with native species.

Occasional healthy jarrah trees persist in dieback affected sites, but it was not known whether these had fortuitously escaped infection, or whether they were genetically resistant to the disease. Seedlings of 16 families were either inoculated with the fungus, or kept as uninfected controls in an adjacent, disease-free site. There were clear and significant differences among families in mortality rates at six years of age in inoculated treatments, as shown in the figure below. Mortality rates ranged from below 30% in family 5 to over 90% in family 11. Conversely, uninfected controls did not differ significantly in mortality. This demonstrates that there is genetic variation in resistance to the fungus. Since the families showed a continuous range of mortality, quantitative genetic variation is present, rather than single locus variation.

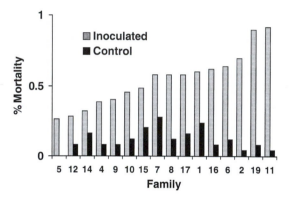

Heritable factors were responsible for 85% of the variation in resistance among families. In a short-term experiment where stems were inoculated with the fungus, 43% of the variation in resistance among individuals was attributable to heritable factors (a heritability of 43%).

The finding of heritable resistance indicates that replanting can be done with dieback-resistant jarrah, rather than with introduced species, such as pines, that suppress other species. Consequently, forest habitat will be maintained for other threatened species. Further, other affected species (some of them rare or endangered) may also show genetic variation for resistance.

Properties of quantitative characters

Quantitative characters typically show continuous rather than discrete distributions, are influenced by many loci and are strongly affected by the environment

Properties of quantitative characters are contrasted with those of qualitative (usually single locus) traits in Table 5.1. Quantitative characters typically have continuous, approximately normal distributions, rather than discrete distributions (Fig. 5.1). They include characters such as reproductive fitness, longevity, height, weight, disease resistance, etc.

Table 5.1	Comparison of the characteristics of quantitative and qualitative characters	
	Quantitative	Qualitative
Distributions	Unimodal and continuous	Multimodal and discrete
Genotype–phenotype relationship	Incomplete	Close
Loci	Many	Few
Environmental effects	Often large	Usually small
Parameters for describing	Means, variances, h^2, V_A	p, q
Examples	Reproductive fitness, weight, height	Brown vs. yellow snail shells, Adh Fast vs. Slow electrophoretic mobility, DNA sequence differences at the haemoglobin locus

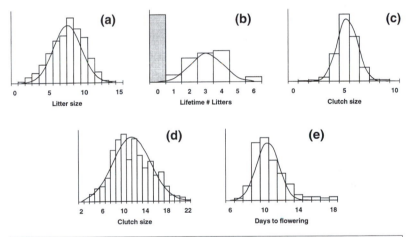

Fig. 5.1 Distributions of phenotypes for five quantitative characters that are components of reproductive fitness: (a) litter size in mice, (b) lifetime production of litters per female in endangered black-footed ferrets, (c) clutch size in starlings, (d) clutch size in a rattlesnake and (e) time to flowering in thale cress plants. Normal distributions are fitted to the distributions. The large number of non-breeding individuals in black-footed ferrets is probably due to poor adaptation to captive conditions. Data from (a) Falconer & Mackay (1996), (b) Russell (1999), (c) and (d) Wright (1968) and (e) Jones & Wilkins (1971).

As we shall see, quantitative characters are influenced by many loci plus environmental influences, such as nutritional state. We are thus concerned with the inheritance of differences between individuals that are of degree rather than of kind.

It is not possible to directly infer genotype from observed phenotype for quantitative characters. Individuals with the same genotype may

The association between genotype and phenotype is typically weaker for quantitative than qualitative characters

have different phenotypic values. Conversely, individuals with the same phenotypic value may have very different genotypes. For example, black-footed ferrets producing six litters (Fig. 5.1b) will, on average, carry more alleles for large numbers of litters than those ferrets producing only one litter. However, both high and low groups will contain some animals whose reproductive performance is heavily influenced by positive or negative environmental influences during their development.

Environmental variation

A proportion of the observed variation among individuals for quantitative characters is attributable to environmental, rather than genetic, causes

Environmental differences affecting phenotype may arise from many influences, including food supply, living conditions, disease status, etc. in animals, and differences in soil fertility, temperature, light, crowding, etc. in plants. The endangered Seychelles warbler elegantly illustrates the impact of environmental factors on a quantitative trait closely associated with reproductive fitness. On Cousin Island, annual production of offspring surviving to one year of age averaged 0.28 young per pair. Within this island, offspring production was 7.3 times higher in high-quality than in low-quality territories. When birds were translocated to Aride Island, where the insect food supply was over three times greater than Cousin Island, production of young for the same birds rose by a factor of 44 (Komdeur *et al.* 1998).

Basis of quantitative genetic variation

Quantitative characters are typically influenced by genetic variation at many loci

The underlying genetic basis to quantitative characters is that they are affected by a number of loci, each possessing alleles that add to, or detract from, the magnitude of the character. Genetic diversity for quantitative characters in outbred populations is due to the segregation of multiple polymorphic Mendelian loci, referred to as **quantitative trait loci** (QTL). The loci affecting quantitative characters, individually, show the usual Mendelian properties of segregation and linkage (see Frankham & Weber 2000).

Quantitative characters are analysed using statistical parameters including means, variances, covariances, etc.

A major challenge in the study of quantitative genetics is to determine how much of the observed variation is due to genetics, and how much to the environment (i.e. to partition the variation into genetic and environmental components). This is typically accomplished by studying the resemblances among relatives who share a proportion of their genetic constitution. Consequently, the parameters used to describe quantitative traits, and to partition variation, are statistical values: means, variances, covariances, regressions and correlations in groups of organisms. These statistics are described in Box 5.2, using data from a species of endangered Tahitian land snail.

Box 5.2 | **Statistics used to describe and analyse quantitative characters, illustrated using data for shell width in an endangered Tahitian snail**

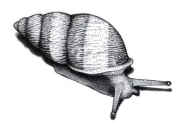

The following data describe the shell width for parents and offspring of 40 families of an endangered *Partula* snail originating from the island of Moorea in Tahiti (data from Murray & Clarke 1968). This and several other endangered species have been depleted due to predation by an introduced carnivorous snail. Each pair of data points represents the mean shell width of a female and male parent (P) together with the mean shell width (mm) in their offspring (O).

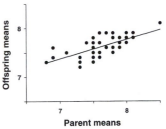

Parent means P	Offspring means O	Parent means P	Offspring means O	Parent means P	Offspring means O
6.8	7.3	7.5	7.3	7.8	7.5
6.9	7.4	7.6	7.7	7.9	7.6
6.9	7.6	7.6	7.7	7.9	7.7
7.1	7.5	7.6	7.9	7.9	7.7
7.3	7.3	7.6	7.4	7.9	7.7
7.3	7.2	7.6	7.5	7.9	7.8
7.3	7.4	7.6	7.4	8.0	7.7
7.4	7.7	7.7	7.6	8.0	7.9
7.5	7.6	7.7	7.9	8.0	7.8
7.5	7.5	7.8	7.5	8.1	7.8
7.5	7.7	7.8	7.8	8.1	7.8
7.5	7.4	7.8	7.9	8.1	7.9
7.5	7.8	7.8	7.6	8.5	8.1
7.5	7.6				

The **mean** shell length of parents $\bar{P}$ is:

$$\bar{P} = \sum_{i=1}^{n} P_i / n = [6.8 + 6.9 + \dots + 8.5] / 40 = 7.65 \text{ mm}$$

Similarly the mean for the offspring $\bar{O}$ is

$$\bar{O} = \sum_{i=1}^{n} O_i / n = 7.63 \text{ mm}$$

The **variance** is a measure of the spread of the data around the mean. The phenotypic variance for the parents, V_P, is

$$V_P = \sum_{i=1}^{n} (P_i - \bar{P})^2 / (n-1) = [(6.8 - 7.65)^2 + \dots + (8.5 - 7.65)^2] / (40 - 1)$$
$$= 0.125$$

The variance for the offspring V_O is

$$V_O = \sum_{i=1}^{n} (O_i - \bar{O})^2 / (n-1) = [(7.3 - 7.63)^2 + \dots + (8.1 - 7.63)^2] / (40 - 1)$$
$$= 0.043$$

The **standard deviations** for parents and offspring, SD_P and SD_O, are the square roots of the respective variances. Standard deviations are usually presented as a measure of spread around the mean, as they have the same units of measurement as the data (e.g. mm), while the unit for variance is squared (mm²).

$$SD_P = \sqrt{0.125} = 0.354$$

$$SD_O = \sqrt{0.043} = 0.207$$

Often a data set is described as mean ± SD, so for parents shell width is 7.65 ± 0.35.

The **covariance** between offspring and parents (Cov_{PO}) measures the extent to which they vary in concert (+), vary independently (0), or in opposition (−). It is defined as

$$Cov_{PO} = \sum_{i=1}^{n} (P_i - \bar{P})(O_i - \bar{O})/(n-1)$$

$$= [(6.8 - 7.65)(7.3 - 7.63) + \dots + (8.5 - 7.65)(8.1 - 7.63)]/(40 - 1)$$

$$= 0.050$$

The **correlation** between offspring and parents (r_{PO}) is a standardized measure of the extent to which they vary in concert. Correlations range from −1 to +1. It is defined as

$$r_{PO} = Cov_{PO}/\sqrt{(V_P . V_O)} = 0.050/\sqrt{(0.125 \times 0.043)} = 0.679$$

Thus, there is a positive correlation between offspring and parents; parents with wider shells have offspring with wider than average shells, while parents with narrower shells have offspring with narrower than average shells.

The **regression** of offspring on parent (b_{OP}) is the slope of the line of best fit relating offspring and parents, as shown in the figure above. It is defined as

$$b_{OP} = Cov_{PO}/V_P = 0.050/0.125 = 0.40$$

This regression is of major importance as it measures the degree to which variation is due to additive genetic causes (heritability) – it is the measure of genetic diversity for quantitative characters. The heritability is 40% for *Partula* shell width, meaning that 40% of the observed variation is due to additively inherited differences and 60% to minor differences in the environment experienced by different individuals. Heritability is discussed in detail below.

Further details about the above measures are given in statistics textbooks. They are easily calculated using scientific calculators, or statistical or spreadsheet software.

The heritability (h^2) is used to measure genetic diversity for quantitative characters

One of the central concepts of quantitative genetics is that of **heritability**. In its simplest form, this is the proportion of the total phenotypic variance in a population due to genetic differences among individuals. More specifically, heritability is the proportion of phenotypic variance attributable to genetic variation that parents can pass on to their offspring.

Thus, it is the heritability of a character in a population that determines its evolutionary potential. Two examples illustrate this concept. The Wollemi pine lacks genetic variation at hundreds of DNA marker loci (Hogbin *et al.* 2000), and all individuals tested were susceptible to dieback fungus (Woodford 2000). Variation among trees is of entirely environmental origin and the capacity of this species to evolve is close to zero. In contrast, resistance to root rot fungus in jarrah trees has a significant heritability (Box 5.1), so jarrahs can evolve to resist the introduced dieback fungus.

Methods for detecting quantitative genetic variation

Three methods are used to determine whether a portion of phenotypic variance for quantitative characters derives from genetic variation among individuals:

- Resemblances among relatives
- Variation within and among populations
- Comparisons of inbred with outbred populations.

Because of the major impact that environment can have on quantitative characters, it is critical that all comparisons, whether of families, or populations, be carried out contemporaneously in standardized environments.

Genetic variation for quantitative characters can be detected using data from different genotypes or families compared under the same environmental conditions

By definition, the more closely related two individuals are, the more similar will be their genetic makeup, being greatest between identical twins (or clones), lower among full-sibs or between parents and offspring, and least among unrelated individuals. A correlation in phenotypic resemblance for relatives is an indication of heritable variation, as seen for shell width in endangered *Partula* snails (Box 5.2). Similarly, a higher correlation for closer than more distant relatives demonstrates genetic variation for a character. Such resemblances among relatives have been demonstrated for innumerable characters in many outbreeding species of animals and plants. Perhaps the best known are analyses of personality traits, mental abilities, disease risk, etc. by comparisons of monozygotic (genetically identical) with dizygotic (50% genetic identity) twins in humans.

A very similar rationale can be applied to comparisons of individuals derived from different populations, when they are compared under the same environmental conditions (i.e. a 'common garden' experiment). Members of the same population will, on average, have greater genetic similarity with each other than with members of other populations. If analysis of the total phenotypic variation, assessed across all individuals, reveals that a part is attributable to population of origin, then there is genetic variation among populations and, hence, a genetic basis underlying the trait. For example, two populations of tobacco differed in corolla length when grown in the same conditions (Box 5.3).

Genetic variation among individuals within highly inbred (homozygous) populations is reduced in comparison with that in outbred populations of the same species. In highly inbred populations, all phenotypic variation is due solely to environmental causes. Thus, if phenotypic variation within inbred populations is less than that in outbred populations, raised under the same environmental conditions, then a genetic component underlying the trait is clearly present. This is illustrated for corolla length in tobacco in Box 5.3. Variation was greatest in the F_2 generation. This generation displays both environmental and genetic heterogeneity among individuals. The extent to which the outbred variation exceeds that within the genetically invariant genotypes (both parents and the F_1) is the genetic variation (see Example 5.1).

Box 5.3	**Quantitative genetic variation for corolla length in tobacco** (after Strickberger 1985, based on East 1916)

In a classical study on inheritance of a quantitative character, East crossed two highly inbred (homozygous) parental populations (P_1 and P_2) of tobacco that differed in corolla length. He grew them and their F_1 and F_2 (created by self-pollination of F_1 individuals) crosses contemporaneously in the same field. Quantitative genetic variation in corolla length was shown by the difference in mean between the two parental populations and their non-overlapping distributions (under the same environmental conditions).

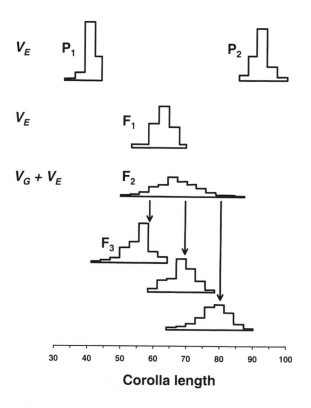

The study demonstrated genetic variation for corolla length by a second means, as variation was greater in the F_2 than in the parents or the F_1. If the loci affecting corolla length show normal Mendelian segregation, we expect the F_1 to show similar variation to the parental populations, while the F_2 should show increased variation due to allelic segregation. For example, if the parental populations are A_1A_1 and A_2A_2, the F_1 will be A_1A_2, while the F_2 will show segregation with $\frac{1}{4}A_1A_1$, $\frac{1}{2}A_1A_2$ and $\frac{1}{4}A_2A_2$. East observed this type of segregation in his experiments. The variation among individuals within the parental populations, and within the F_1 is due to environmental variation, while the variation in the F_2 is due to environmental variation plus genetic variation due to the segregation of multiple Mendelian loci, each of relatively small effect.

East verified that there were genetic differences among individuals in the F_2 by breeding F_2 individuals with different corolla lengths and showing that their offspring differed on average in the same directions as the parents. The increase in variance in the F_2 over that within the parent and F_1 populations measures the extent of genetic variation (Example 5.1).

Partitioning genetic and environmental variation

So far we have simply stated that the phenotypic value of an individual is the consequence of the alleles it inherits together with the environmental influences it has encountered during its development. Algebraically, the above statement can be expressed:

$$P = G + E \tag{5.1}$$

where P = phenotype, G = genotype and E = environment. We now describe how the genetic component can be partitioned from the environmental component.

Phenotypic variance (V_P) within a population represents the sum total of all contributions from genetic diversity (V_G), the environment (V_E) and interactions between genotypes and environment (often termed $G \times E$ interactions):

$$V_P = V_G + V_E + 2\,Cov_{GE} \tag{5.2}$$

where Cov_{GE} is the covariance between genetic and environmental effects. A numerical example is given in Example 5.1 (note that in this example the covariance term is negligible as the plants were raised under the same conditions). Of the variation in corolla length in the F_2, 68% was due to segregation of polymorphic loci (V_G) and 32% to environmental variation (V_E).

> Genetic and environmental variation can be partitioned using data from different genotypes or families compared under the same environmental conditions

---

Example 5.1 | Partitioning genetic and environmental variation

The variances for corolla length in tobacco for the data in Box 5.3 are 48 and 32 for the two homozygous parent populations, 46 in the F_1 population and 130.5 in the F_2. The variances in both parents and the F_1 are due only to environmental variance V_E. Consequently, we have three separate estimates of V_E and average them.

$$V_E = (V_{P_1} + V_{P_2} + V_{F_1}) / 3 = (48 + 32 + 46) / 3 = 42$$

Variation in the F_2 is due to both genetic diversity and environmental variation

$$V_{F_2} = V_G + V_E = 130.5$$

Since we have an estimate of V_E, we can rearrange this equation to estimate V_G, as follows:

$$V_G = V_{F_2} - V_E = 130.5 - 42 = 88.5$$

Thus, of the total F_2 variance in corolla length, $88.5/130.5 = 68\%$ is due to segregation of polymorphic loci and the remaining 32% due to environmental variation.

The covariance term in Equation 5.2 is expected to be zero if conditions for different genotypes are equalized by randomly allocating individuals across the range of environments. This is routinely done with quantitative genetic experiments in domestic animals and plants, where cultivation or rearing conditions can be standardized, but is difficult to achieve in wild populations. For example, in territorial species of birds and mammals, the genetically fittest parents may obtain the best territories (and the least fit, the poorest territories). Offspring inheriting the best fitness genotypes also 'inherit' the best environments (and the least fit offspring genotypes are reared in the worst environments). This results in a genotype × environment correlation that increases the phenotypic resemblance among relatives.

Genotype × environment interaction

Genotypes may show different performances in different environments, termed genotype × environment interactions

Differences in performance of genotypes in different environments are referred to as **genotype × environment interactions**. They typically develop when populations adapt to particular environmental conditions, and survive and reproduce better in their native conditions than in other environments. Genotype × environment interactions may take the form of altered rankings of performance in different environments or magnitudes of differences that vary in diverse environments. A classical example is provided by the growth and survival of transplanted individuals of the sticky cinquefoil plant from high, medium and low elevations in California (Fig. 5.2). When grown in each of the three environments, strains generally grew best in the environment from which they originated and poorest in the most dissimilar environment.

Genotype × environment interactions are of major significance to the genetic management of endangered species, as follows:
- The reproductive fitness of translocated individuals cannot be predicted if there are significant genotype × environment interactions
- Success of reintroduced populations may be compromised by genetic adaptation to captivity – superior genotypes under captive conditions may perform relatively poorly when released to the wild

Grown at sea level	Grown at 1400m	Grown at 3050m

Potentilla g. nevadensis **from 3050m**

Potentilla g. hanseni **from 1400m**

No survivors

Potentilla g. typica **from sea level**

Fig. 5.2 Genotype × environment interaction in the sticky cinquefoil plant. Strains of cinquefoil derived from high, medium and low altitudes were transplanted into their native and different locations in California and their growth and survival monitored (after Clausen *et al.* 1940). *Populations generally grow best in their own environment and poorest in the environment most dissimilar from their own.*

- Mixing of genetic material from fragmented populations may generate genotypes that do not perform well under some, or all, conditions
- Knowledge of genotype × environment interaction can strongly influence the choice of populations for return to the wild.

These issues are discussed in Chapters 15–18.

Genotype × environment interactions must be distinguished from the genotype × environment covariances and correlations described above. Genotype × environment correlations occur when genotypes are non-randomly distributed over environments. By contrast, genotype × environment interactions are detected by comparing all genotypes in several common garden environments; if their relative performances differ in the different environments there is genotype × environment interaction.

The likelihood of genotype × environment interactions increases with the magnitude of both genetic and environmental differences. Thus, it is most likely to be detected in species with wide geographic, ecological or altitudinal ranges (Fig. 5.2; Frankham & Weber 2000). Further, quantitative traits closely associated with reproductive fitness appear to be more prone to genotype × environment interactions than characters more peripheral to fitness (**peripheral characters**). As plants are immobile, they often exhibit local genetic adaptation to their immediate environment (soil chemical composition, grazing pressure, wind, etc.), sometimes over remarkably short distances (Briggs & Walters 1997). Thus, genotype × environment interactions are more likely in plants than animals.

> Genotype × environment interactions are most common when genotypic differences and environmental differences are large. Reproductive fitness characters are usually more prone to genotype × environment interactions than other characters

The need for contemporary comparisons and control populations

Considerable care must be taken to discern whether change in a quantitative trait in a population results from genetic or environmental causes. Changes in captive populations may derive from inbreeding depression, outcrossing, or from unwitting improvement in husbandry of the population. Juvenile survival increased with year of birth in both the endangered Mexican wolf and the red wolf, presumably as a result of improved husbandry in spite of increased inbreeding and lack of outcrossing (Kalinowski *et al.* 1999). Thus, it is imperative to compare genotypes contemporaneously under the same conditions. For example, the deleterious effects of inbreeding on captive mammals were studied by comparing the juvenile survival of inbred and non-inbred offspring matched for zoo, enclosure in zoo, year of birth and density of population (Ballou & Ralls 1982).

> Comparisons of genotypes must be carried out contemporaneously under identical conditions, so that environmental differences are not confused with genetic ones

To detect genetic changes over time (e.g. inbreeding depression, or change due to selection) genetically stable populations must be maintained for comparison with the population of interest. Uncontrolled environmental fluctuations from generation to generation can then be detected by phenotypic changes in the genetically stable control populations. Control populations include randomly mated outbred populations, related species, or samples derived from stored seed or cryopreserved embryos.

> Detection of genetic changes over time requires that comparisons be made with a genetically stable control population

Partitioning of quantitative genetic variation

In the previous sections we discussed how total phenotypic variation can be partitioned into its genetic and environmental components. In a similar manner, the genetic variance, V_G, can be partitioned into components with critical importance in conservation.

Quantitative genetic variation has contributions from the average

> Genetic diversity for quantitative characters is partitioned into components reflecting adaptive evolutionary potential (V_A), susceptibility to inbreeding depression (V_D) and effects of outbreeding (V_I)

effects of loci V_A, from their dominance deviations V_D, and from interaction (epistatic) deviations among gene loci, V_I.

$$V_G = V_A + V_D + V_I \qquad (5.3)$$

These are referred to as **additive genetic variance** (V_A), **dominance variance** (V_D) and **interaction** variance (V_I). Each of these components has major conservation implications, as follows:

- V_A and especially the ratio V_A/V_P (the heritability) reflect the adaptive evolutionary potential of the population for the character under study
- V_D reflects susceptibility to inbreeding depression
- V_I influences the effects of outbreeding, whether beneficial or deleterious.

In what follows, we indicate the genetic basis of these components of genetic variation and how they are measured (see also Chapters 8, 12 and 15).

A single locus model illustrating partitioning of variance

To understand the meaning of V_A and V_D, consider a single locus model with two alleles per locus. The three genotypes A_1A_1, A_1A_2 and A_2A_2 are assigned genotypic values of a, d and $-a$ (Fig. 5.3). Homozygotes differ in genotypic value by $2a$, and the heterozygotes differ from the mean of the two homozygotes by d.

Genotypic values for **additive, dominant** and **overdominant** loci are illustrated in Fig. 5.4. For an additive locus, heterozygotes are intermediate between homozygotes, so the three genotypes have values of a ,0 and $-a$, with d being zero. If the A_1 allele is dominant (A_2 recessive) the

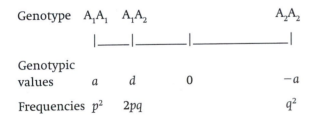

Genotype A_1A_1 A_1A_2 A_2A_2

Genotypic
values a d 0 $-a$

Frequencies p^2 $2pq$ q^2

Fig. 5.3   Genotypic values assigned to the three genotypes at a locus along with their frequencies with random mating.

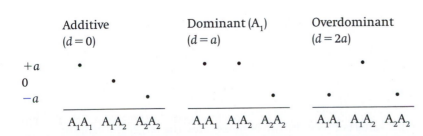

Fig. 5.4   Genotypic values for additive, dominant and overdominant loci.

genotypes have values, a, a and $-a$, respectively, so $d = a$. Conversely, if A_1 is recessive, the genotypes have values a, $-a$ and $-a$, and $d = -a$. For an overdominant (heterozygote advantage) locus, the genotypic values are $-a$, a and $-a$, so $d = 2a$. Example 5.2 illustrates the computation of a and d for litter sizes at the Booroola locus (B) in Merino sheep. The B allele is partially dominant in this case.

Example 5.2 | Calculating a and d for mean litter sizes for genotypes at the Booroola locus in Merino sheep (after Lynch & Walsh 1998)

The Booroola (B) allele increases litter size in Merino sheep. Mean litter sizes for the three genotypes at the Booroola locus are:

	Genotypes		
	BB	Bb	bb
Litter size	2.66	2.17	1.48

These are mean litter sizes under normal environmental conditions and are therefore equivalent to genotypic values. The mid-point of the genotypic value between the two homozygotes is $(1.48 + 2.66)/2 = 2.07$. This is the zero point on the scale in Fig. 5.4. Consequently, the value of a is computed as:

$$a = \text{BB value} - \text{mid-point} = 2.66 - 2.07 = 0.59$$

The dominance deviation, d, is

$$d = \text{Bb value} - \text{mid-point} = 2.17 - 2.07 = 0.10.$$

Thus, each copy of the Booroola allele increases litter size by an average of 0.59 lambs, and there is partially dominance with the heterozygote having 0.10 lambs above the average for the two homozygotes.

Additive genetic variance (V_A)

Additive genetic variation depends on the level of heterozygosity in the population and the average effects of alleles

If we have a polymorphic locus with additive effects ($d = 0$) and frequencies and genotypic values as given in Fig. 5.3, additive genetic variation is defined as:

$$V_A = 2pqa^2 \tag{5.4}$$

This relationship contains two essential elements. First, additive genetic variation depends on the heterozygosity ($2pq$) in the population, there being no additive genetic variation (and no potential for immediate adaptive evolutionary change) in a homozygous population. V_A is highest when the heterozygosity is maximum, i.e. when $p = q = 0.5$ (for two alleles at a locus). Second, V_A depends on a, half the difference in mean between the homozygous genotypes. The larger the difference in genotypic value between the two homozygotes, the larger the value of V_A.

When dominance exists ($d \neq 0$), the additive genetic variation is:

$$V_A = 2pq \, [a + d \, (q - p)]^2 \tag{5.5}$$

Thus, V_A also depends on the dominance deviation, d. Even when there is overdominance ($a = 0$), there may still be additive genetic variation, due to the remaining $2pq \, [d \, (q - p)]^2$ term. However, this term is zero when $p = q = 0.5$.

V_A in a population is due to the combined impacts of all segregating loci with effects on the character.

Dominance variance (V_D)

For a locus with effects and frequencies defined in Fig. 5.3, dominance variance is defined as:

$$V_D = (2pqd)^2 \tag{5.6}$$

> Dominance variance depends on the heterozygosity and the dominance deviation **d**

Dominance variance is present at a segregating locus if alleles show some degree of dominance ($d \neq 0$). Clearly, it is zero if d is zero, or the population is homozygous. The response of a character to inbreeding depends on $2pqd$ and the extent of inbreeding (Chapter 12). Consequently, characters and populations with higher levels of dominance variation will be more susceptible to the deleterious effects of inbreeding than those with low V_D.

V_D in a population is due to the combined impacts of all segregating loci exhibiting dominance effects on the character.

Interaction variance (V_I)

The interaction variance V_I arises from variation in the deviations of the effects of multilocus genotypes from the sum of the average effects of each component locus. It is similar to the concept applied to determine the dominance deviation and its variance, but applied between loci, rather than within them (Falconer & Mackay 1996). V_I is one of the components determining whether crossing of populations has deleterious or beneficial effects (Chapter 15).

In practice, the partitioning of genetic variance is difficult and imprecise. Partitioning is generally into additive (V_A) and non-additive ($V_D + V_I$) components, as it is very difficult to separate V_D and V_I. Readers are referred to Falconer & Mackay (1996) and Lynch & Walsh (1998) for more detail.

Evolutionary potential and heritability

Conservation genetics is concerned with the evolution of quantitative traits, and how their ability to adapt is affected by reduced population size, fragmentation, and changes in the environment. The immediate

> The immediate evolutionary potential of a population is determined by the heritability

evolutionary potential of a population is determined by the heritability. We now explore this parameter in more detail.

Heritability (h^2) is defined as the proportion of total phenotypic variation due to additive genetic variation:

$$h^2 = V_A / V_P \tag{5.7}$$

Heritabilities range from 0 to 1. The former is found in highly inbred populations with no genetic variation, while the latter is expected for a character with no environmental variance in an outbred population, if all the genetic variation is additive.

A heritability estimate is specific to a particular population in a particular environment

Heritabilities are specific to particular populations living under specific environmental conditions. Different populations may have different levels of genetic variation; those with greater additive variation will have greater heritabilities in the same environment. For example, populations of fruit flies lost allozyme genetic diversity over time, and their heritabilities for sternopleural bristle number decreased correspondingly (Briscoe *et al.* 1992). For outbred populations measured in different environments, the one in the least variable environment should have the greatest heritability as higher environmental variances increase total phenotypic variance, and thus decrease heritability. Despite these provisos, heritability estimates show relatively consistent patterns in magnitude for similar characters among populations within species, and across species (see below).

The slope of the relationship between offspring means and parent means is a direct measure of the heritability (h^2) of a trait

Heritability and V_A are fundamentally measures of how well quantitative traits are transmitted from one generation to the next. Figure 5.5 illustrates three contrasting strengths of relationship between parents and offspring. Figure 5.5a shows an example of complete inheritance. Parents with larger than average values for the trait produce offspring with similar, larger, values, while smaller than average parents produce smaller than average offspring. This population will have a high V_A. In this case, the slope defining the relationship of parent mean to offspring mean (the regression) is 1. In this example, it is clear that environmental differences among parents, and among offspring, have negligible influence on the phenotype for the trait (a heritability of 1). An example that approaches this level of relationship is fingerprint ridge count in humans.

Inheritance is less complete in Fig. 5.5b. Parents with high phenotypic values produce, on average, offspring closer to the population mean than they are and low value parents produce offspring not as low as themselves. The slope of the relationship between offspring mean and parent mean is <1. Some of the superiority or inferiority of the parents is not due to additive variation and cannot be inherited by their offspring (in this example, heritability has an intermediate value). Many quantitative characters have relationships of this kind, including shell width in *Partula* snails (Box 5.2) and body size in many species, including endangered cotton-top tamarins (Cheverud *et al.* 1994).

There is no relationship between parent and offspring values in Fig. 5.5c. The slope of the relationship is 0 ($h^2 = 0$). Parents with high and low values of the trait have similar offspring with values randomly distrib-

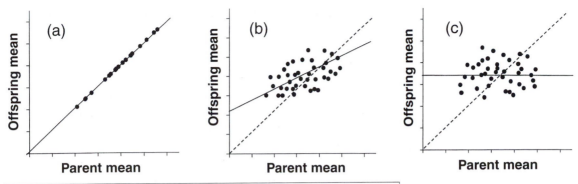

Fig. 5.5 Hypothetical relationships between mean values of parents and mean values of offspring for three cases, representing (a) complete, (b) incomplete and (c) zero relationships between parents and offspring.

uted around the mean. In this case V_A and h^2 are zero, so there will be no evolutionary change. Such relationships are found in homozygous populations, such as the Wollemi pine, where all differences among parents are of environmental origin. Further, some reproductive characters in outbred populations, such as conception rate in cattle, approach this value.

The relationship between parent mean (termed mid-parent value, P) and offspring mean (O) is described by the following equation (provided that environmental conditions are the same for parents and offspring):

$$\overline{O} = (1 - h^2)\,M + h^2\,\overline{P} \tag{5.8}$$

where M = population mean for the trait and h^2 is its heritability in the population. The heritability is the slope of the line relating offspring and parents (regression). As the heritability approaches zero, the offspring values cluster closer around the population mean, M, and all parents, regardless of their own values, produce similar offspring. Box 5.2 illustrates the relationship between offspring and mid-parent values for shell width in endangered *Partula* snails from the Tahitian Islands and Example 5.3 estimates the heritability of shell width from these data.

Example 5.3	Estimating the heritability of shell size in endangered *Partula* snails from offspring–parent regression

The relationship between the shell width for parents and their offspring for 40 families of *Partula* snail is illustrated in Box 5.2. The fitted line is the linear regression of offspring mean on mid-parent mean and has a slope of 0.40 ± 0.07. This slope estimates the heritability. This means that 40% of the variation in shell length for this population, under these environmental conditions, is due to additive genetic causes.

Predicting response to selection

Evolutionary potential is a measure of how rapidly and how much a population can adapt in response to a selective force. The genetic change (response) produced by **directional selection** (selection favouring one extreme) can be predicted from the intensity of selection, and the heritability. This is illustrated graphically in Fig. 5.6, where directional selection corresponds to selecting individuals with the highest value to be parents. These parents have a mean S units above the mean of all individuals in the parent generation. S is termed the **selection differential**. Some of this superiority is due to environmental effects and some to genotypic differences, the heritability being the proportion due to additive genetic effects. Consequently, response to selection R (the difference in the offspring of selected parents compared to that of offspring of unselected parents) is

$$R = Sh^2 \tag{5.9}$$

Thus, selection response (evolutionary change) will occur if selection is applied ($S > 0$, or $S < 0$), and there is additive genetic variation for the character ($h^2 > 0$). There can be no selection response in highly inbred (homozygous) populations lacking genetic variation ($h^2 = 0$).

Where parents have a higher value than the mean of their generation, the offspring mean will increase over that of offspring from randomly selected parents. Conversely, when selected parents have a lower value than the mean of their generation, the offspring mean will decrease.

Example 5.4 illustrates prediction of response to selection for Darwin's medium ground finch from the Galapagos Islands. The predicted change in bill width (response to selection) was 0.19 mm.

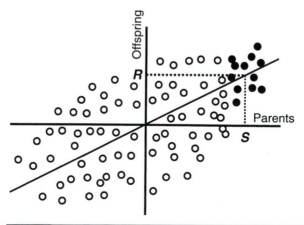

Fig. 5.6 Predicting response to directional selection (after Falconer & Mackay 1996). The plot of values for a quantitative character in offspring is given against the mean of their parents for a quantitative character. The line is the linear regression of offspring mean on mid-parent mean (slope of h^2). A perpendicular is taken from the mean of selected parents S (filled circles), on the x axis to the regression line, and then a perpendicular is dropped from this point to the y axis (at R). R is the superiority of the offspring of selected parents compared to that of unselected parents. R *is predicted to be S* $\times$ *slope of the line* (h^2).

Example 5.4 | Predicting response to directional selection for bill width in Darwin's medium ground finch on the Galapagos Islands (after Grant & Grant 1995, 2000)

Over an 18-month period of drought and no breeding from the middle of 1976 to the end of 1978, the finches suffered 85% mortality. Survivors had beaks that were 0.25 mm wider than the original population (S). The heritability for bill width in this population is 74.5%. Hence, we predict a genetic change (R), as follows:

$$R = S\,h^2 = 0.25 \times 0.745 = 0.19 \text{ mm}$$

Thus, bill width in offspring is expected to increase by 0.19 mm. An increase of 0.25 mm was observed in the average bill width in the offspring.

If selection is applied to reduce the value of a character, S is negative and the mean is expected to drop. Natural selection in the finches favoured small bill width in 1984–86, resulting in a selection differential of −0.10 mm. The predicted change in mean is:

$$R = S\,h^2 = -0.10 \times 0.745 = -0.07 \text{ mm}$$

Thus, we predict a reduction in bill width of 0.07 mm. The observed change in mean was a reduction of 0.16 mm. This change is in the predicted direction, but the magnitude is not as well predicted. (The analysis for the finches is more complicated than this due to selection operating on several characters, but that does not affect the conclusions we have reached.)

The accuracy of predictions

In general, Equation 5.9 provides reasonable predictions of short-term selection response, especially for peripheral characters (Falconer & Mackay 1996; Roff 1997). For example, Fig. 5.7 illustrates the relationship between observed and predicted selection response for Darwin's medium ground finch in the Galapagos where the forces of natural selection vary across years largely as a result of *El Niño* climatic cycles. Observed changes showed relatively good agreement with predictions.

Equation 5.9 gives only an average prediction. If just single pairs of parents were used, then there would be a wide variation in the outcome. In some cases selected parents would have higher means for genetic reasons, in others for environmental reasons and, in most cases, it would result from a combination of both factors. Replicate selected populations from the same source population typically vary somewhat in selection response. Further, predictions from Equation 5.9 are strictly valid for only one generation, as the genetic makeup of the population will change as a consequence of selection. In practice, it provides reasonable predictions for at least five generations (Falconer & Mackay 1996). Importantly, the prediction applies only to the particular population under the environmental conditions where the heritability was measured.

> The agreement between predicted and observed selection response for quantitative characters is usually good

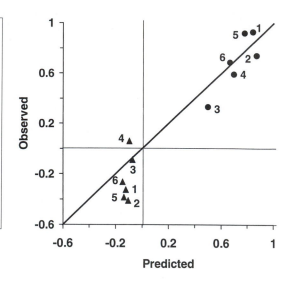

Fig. 5.7 Comparison of observed and predicted response (in standard deviation units) to natural selection in Darwin's medium ground finch on the Galapagos Islands (after Roff 1997, based on Grant & Grant 1992). The straight line represents perfect agreement between observed and predicted selection response. 1 = weight, 2 = wing length, 3 = tarsus length, 4 = bill length, 5 = bill depth and 6 = bill width. Circles = 1976–77, triangles = 1984–86.

Response to selection for fitness characters is usually asymmetrical with poorer response for increased than reduced fitness

Equation 5.9 predicts symmetrical response to selection in both the high and low directions, provided equal selection is applied to each. An important exception to the usual agreement between predicted and observed selection response occurs for reproductive fitness characters. These show a consistent pattern of asymmetry in response to selection, with less response to selection for increased than reduced fitness (Frankham 1990a).

While this is not predicted, asymmetrical response to selection for fitness traits is not biologically surprising. Reproductive fitness is continuously subject to directional natural selection. Thus, we would expect less response for improved than reduced fitness.

Magnitudes of heritabilities

Most quantitative characters in naturally outbreeding species show heritable variation ($h^2 > 0$)

Since we wish to understand the potential for evolutionary change in quantitative traits in natural populations, it is important that we have estimates of the magnitude of their heritabilities. Not surprisingly, data from natural populations are limited. Estimates of heritabilities for a range of fitness, size and beak characters in natural populations of birds are given in Table 5.2. Most characters in most species have $h^2 > 0$. A similar conclusion applies for essentially all outbred populations.

Heritabilities are consistently lower for characters related to reproductive fitness than for more peripheral characters

Heritabilities are typically lower for reproductive fitness characters than for size or for peripheral characters (Table 5.3). Averages of heritabilities for wild bird species were 24% for fitness characters, 57% for size and 67% for peripheral (beak size) characters. The average of estimates from humans, domestic and laboratory species also indicated lower heritabilities for fitness characters than for size, or peripheral characters. This finding is supported by meta-analyses. Heritabilities

Table 5.2 Heritabilities of fitness, body size (or tarsus length) and bill size for birds in nature. Values greater than 100% or less than 0 can arise due to sampling variation in small experiments. Parent–offspring environmental correlations and biases due to maternal effects can also lead to values of greater than 100%

Species	h^2 (%)		
	Fitness	Body size	Bill size
Barnacle goose		35, 54, 76	
Blue tit		62, 70[a]	
Canada goose		11	46
Collared flycatcher	−5, 0, 29, 32	47, 59	35, 48, 56, 40, 44
Darwin's medium ground finch	−17	42, 61, 95	75, 102, 103, 108
Darwin's cactus finch		37, 110, 126	2, 13, 44, 129
Darwin's large cactus finch		54, 95	67, 69, 104, 137
European bee-eater		28	
European starling	34	49[a]	
Great tit	37, 48	59, 59, 61, 64, 76	49, 71, 68
Indigo bunting		38	
Lesser snow goose	20, 61		
Penguin		92	76
Pied flycatcher		50[a]	
Pigeon		28, 50	50, 58
Red grouse	30	35, 50	
Song sparrow		27, 36[a], 71, 101[a]	40[a], 123, 71, 59
Tree swallow		−4, 54	
Willow tit		60	
Means	**24.5**	**57.2**	**67.4**

Note:
[a]Progeny cross-fostered to minimize postnatal maternal effects.
Sources: After Smith (1993); Weigensberg & Roff (1996); Lynch & Walsh (1998).

across 1120 estimates from animals (excluding fruit flies) tended to be lower for life history characters (related to reproductive fitness), than for behavioural, physiological, or morphological characters (Table 5.3). A similar conclusion applied to fruit fly species.

Lower heritabilities for fitness than for peripheral characters were thought to be due to directional natural selection depleting additive genetic variation for reproductive fitness and its components (Roff 1997). However, differences seem to be due to higher environmental variances or higher non-additive genetic variation ($V_D + V_I$), rather than to lower additive genetic variation for fitness characters (Merila & Sheldon 2000).

Individual heritability estimates for different characters in different species vary widely (Table 5.2). Much of this variation is due to the large standard errors on individual estimates. Some estimates fall outside the expected range of 0 to 100%. Values greater than 100% or less than zero can arise due to sampling variation in small experiments.

Table 5.3 Mean heritabilities for different characters in (1) humans, domestic and laboratory animals, (2) animals excluding fruit flies and (3) fruit flies

Species group	h^2 (%)		
	Fitness	Size	Peripheral/Sundry
(1) Mean of humans, domestic and laboratory animals[a]	11	50	48

	Life history	Behaviour	Physiology	Morphology
(2) Animals (excluding fruit flies)[b]	26	30	33	46
(3) Fruit flies[b]	12	18	—	32

Notes:
[a]After Strickberger (1985); Falconer & Mackay (1996); Morris (1998).
[b]From Roff (1997).

Parent–offspring environmental correlations and biases due to maternal effects can also lead to values of greater than 100%.

Heritabilities in endangered species

Very few heritability estimates exist for endangered species (Table 5.4). Since molecular measures of genetic diversity are generally lower in endangered than in related endangered species (Chapter 3), we might expect heritabilities to differ in the same direction. In fact, four of the five estimates are lower than estimates for comparable characters in non-endangered species, but there are insufficient data to decide the issue. There is clearly a need for many more estimates of heritabilities to be made in threatened species.

Table 5.4 Heritabilities in endangered and in comparable non-endangered species

Endangered species	Character	h^2	Non-endangered species	Characters	h^2
Cotton-top tamarin	Body weight	35	Laboratory and domestic animals	Body size	50
Snails					
Partula taeniata	Shell length	36	*Arianta arbustorum*	Shell width	70
	Shell width	40			
Partula suturalis	Shell length	81			
	Shell width	53			

Sources: Cook (1965); Murray & Clarke (1968); Cheverud *et al.* (1994).

Estimating heritabilities

We saw above how heritabilities could be estimated from the regression of offspring means on parental means. In addition, they are estimated using regression of offspring mean on that of one parent, and from full-sib correlations, and half-sib correlations. In each case, the degree of genetic relationship between the relatives must be taken into account. For example, the heritability equals the regression of offspring on mid-parent, is twice the regression of offspring on one parent, twice the full-sib correlation and four times the half-sib correlation. In Example 5.5 the heritability for clutch size in lesser snow geese is estimated from twice the regression of daughter's mean on mother's mean. Falconer & Mackay (1996) and Lynch & Walsh (1998) give further details of these methods.

Heritability estimates may be biased by genotype × environmental correlations. Similarity between relatives due to exposure to similar environments may be interpreted as similarity due to shared genotypes. Maternal effects are a particularly important cause of bias. A maternal effect is indicated if heritability estimates are different between mother–offspring (contains maternal effects) and father–offspring regression (no maternal effects), or between a full-sib estimate (maternal effects) and a half-sib estimate (no maternal effects) (see Falconer & Mackay 1996; Lynch & Walsh 1998). Cross-fostering can be used to eliminate the contribution of maternal effects to heritability estimates and has been used in a number of bird studies in the field (Roff 1997).

> Heritabilities are estimated from phenotypic resemblances between relatives for quantitative characters

---

Example 5.5 | Estimating the heritability for clutch size in lesser snow geese from regression of daughter's mean on mother's mean

Findlay & Cooke (1983) recorded clutch sizes of 132 mother–daughter pairs in lesser snow geese in Manitoba, Canada. Mean clutch sizes of daughters are plotted against those of their mothers in the figure below. Points indicate single observations, larger circles multiple observations (more than one daughter per mother, and more than one clutch recorded per female).

The regression of daughter's mean clutch size (D) on mother's mean clutch size (M) is

$$D = 2.538 + 0.306\,M$$

The slope of this line, given on the figure, is equal to half the heritability, so we estimate heritability as:

$$h^2 = 2 \times 0.306 = 0.612$$

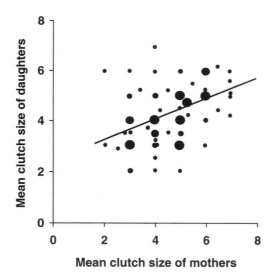

Thus, the heritability of clutch size in the lesser snow goose is 61%, indicating that mean clutch size can be rapidly adjusted towards its optimum value in any given environment.

Precision

Estimates of heritabilities are imprecise unless they are based on hundreds to thousands of individuals

The precision of heritability estimates depends on the number of families, total number of individuals studied and on the magnitude of the heritability itself. In general, several hundred to a few thousand progeny from 30 or more parental groups need to be measured to obtain precise estimates of heritabilities (Falconer & Mackay 1996). For example, the standard error with 100 offspring–mid-parent groups is ± 0.15 and that for a half-sib correlation based on 1000 offspring would be ± 0.06 when the heritability is about 0.10. Consequently, estimating heritabilities with precision is very difficult for endangered species.

Susceptibility to inbreeding depression

V_D reflects the susceptibility of characters and populations to inbreeding depression

The impact of inbreeding on a trait in a particular population depends upon $2pqdF$, where F is the inbreeding coefficient (Chapter 12). Since $V_D = (2pqd)^2$, its magnitude reflects the susceptibility of characters to inbreeding depression. Since this is one of the most important issues in conservation genetics, we need to understand how to estimate V_D, and to review information on its magnitude for different characters.

Estimating V_D

To estimate V_D, data need to be collected on many groups of full-sibs and many groups of paternal half-sibs. The covariances between full-sibs depends both on both V_A and V_D, while the covariance between half-sibs is dependent only on V_A (Table 5.5). We can obtain an estimate of V_D by subtracting 8 times the half-sib covariance from 4 times the full-sib covariance. In doing so, it is assumed that there are no common environmental effects (V_{E_c}) contributing to similarities among full-sibs.

V_D is typically estimated from the differences between full-sib and half-sib covariances

Table 5.5 Covariances between full-sibs and half-sibs and their composition in terms of V_A, V_D and V_{E_c}. Estimation of V_D is shown in the bottom part of the table

Relatives	Covariance
Full-sibs	$Cov_{FS} = \frac{1}{2} V_A + \frac{1}{4} V_D + V_{E_c}$
Half-sibs	$Cov_{HS} = \frac{1}{4} V_A$

$$4\,Cov_{FS} = 2 V_A + V_D + 4 V_{E_c}$$
$$-8\,Cov_{HS} = 2 V_A$$
$$= V_D + 4 V_{E_c}$$

Source: After Falconer & Mackay (1996).

Magnitude of V_D

Non-additive genetic variation is highest for the fitness character and lowest for peripheral characters (Table 5.6). Consequently, we expect that fitness characters will be more susceptible to inbreeding depression than peripheral characters. This prediction is borne out in practice (Chapter 12).

Reproductive fitness characters typically show greater dominance variance than peripheral characters

Table 5.6 Dominance variance for life history, behavioural, physiological and morphological characters, expressed as a percentage of genetic variance (V_D/V_G) and as a percentage of phenotypic variance (V_D/V_P), based upon a meta-analysis. Values for life-history characters are higher on average than for other characters

Measure	Life history	Behaviour	Physiology	Morphology
V_D/V_G	54	24	27	17
V_D/V_P	31	4	21	13

Source: Crnokrak & Roff (1995).

Correlations between molecular and quantitative genetic variation

Correlations between quantitative genetic variation and molecular measures of genetic diversity are low and are zero for life history traits

Since additive genetic variation determines the ability of a population to evolve (as we shall see below), its dependence on heterozygosity provides the connection between heterozygosity and evolutionary potential. If single locus heterozygosities for DNA and allozyme loci are correlated with heterozygosity at loci influencing quantitative characters, then they will reflect the evolutionary potential of populations. This correlation, although intuitively appealing, is controversial.

A meta-analysis based on 71 data sets found an average correlation of only 0.22 between molecular diversity and quantitative genetic variation (Reed & Frankham, 2001). Further, the correlation did not differ significantly from zero for life history traits (-0.11), but was higher and significant for morphological traits (0.30). The most probable explanation for the lack of correlation for life history traits is that selection operates on reproductive fitness (life history) characters, but has little impact on molecular genetic markers. Consequently, molecular measures of genetic variation provide, at best, only a very imprecise indication of evolutionary potential.

Organization of quantitative genetic variation

Reproductive fitness and peripheral characters differ in average dominance of alleles, in symmetry of allelic frequencies and in the importance of interactions among loci

The basic parameters underlying quantitative genetic variation, the number of loci involved, alleles per locus, dominance and effects of alleles are still poorly known. This is especially true for reproductive fitness characters. Current information about QTL indicates (Falconer & Mackay 1996; Frankham & Weber 2000):

- There are no clear differences between the loci affecting qualitative and quantitative characters. Alleles affecting quantitative characters are often alleles at loci with known major qualitative effects.
- Fewer than 20 loci account for a substantial proportion of quantitative genetic variation for most characters.
- Quantitative variation is due to a small proportion of loci with large effects and a large proportion with small effects (Fig. 5.8).
- Deleterious alleles are rare and beneficial ones common.

Fig. 5.8 Distribution of effects of quantitative trait loci (QTL) for several traits in maize (after Frankham & Weber 2000 based on data of Tanksley). *A small proportion of QTL have large effects, but most have small effects.*

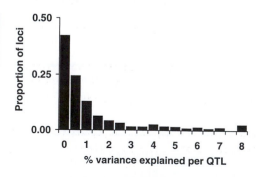

- QTL exhibit the full range of dominance from recessive to dominant, to overdominant, with the majority being in the additive range. For fitness characters, deleterious alleles are partially recessive and favourable alleles partially dominant. For peripheral traits, there is little directional dominance.
- QTL often show interactions among loci, especially for fitness characters.

Importantly, fitness characters differ from peripheral characters in showing directional dominance of effects, asymmetrical allele frequencies, greater levels of interactions and probably have more loci influencing them. These characteristics have important conservation implications, especially in terms of the impact of inbreeding (Chapter 12).

Summary

1. Characters of importance in conservation biology are primarily quantitative. The ability of a population to reproduce and survive (reproductive fitness) is a quantitative character.

2. Variation for quantitative characters among individuals is due to both genetic and environmental effects.

3. Groups of individuals must be studied for quantitative characters, and statistical analyses used to study and partition variation.

4. Genetic diversity for quantitative characters is due to the segregation of multiple Mendelian loci (QTL).

5. The evolutionary potential of a character in a population is determined by its additive genetic variation and heritability (the additive genetic variation as a proportion of the total variation).

6. Heritabilities are typically lower for reproductive fitness characters than for characters peripheral to fitness.

7. Heritabilities are typically estimated from the resemblances between relatives for quantitative characters, e.g. offspring–parent regressions.

8. Variance due to dominance deviations reflects the susceptibility of characters and populations to inbreeding depression. It is greater for fitness than for peripheral characters.

9. The interaction variance is important in the context of crossing different populations.

10. Different genotypes may show altered ranking in different environments (genotype × environment interactions); this is important in the context of translocating individuals.

FURTHER READING
Arnold (1995) A review of monitoring quantitative genetic variation and evolution in captive populations; fairly advanced.
Falconer & Mackay (1996) *Introduction to Quantitative Genetics*. An excellent readable textbook on quantitative genetics with a focus on applications in animal and plant breeding.

Frankham (1999) A review on quantitative genetics in conservation biology.

Lynch (1996) A review of the importance of quantitative genetics in conservation biology; advanced.

Lynch & Walsh (1998) *Genetics and Analysis of Quantitative Traits*. A comprehensive advanced treatment of quantitative genetics.

Roff (1997) *Evolutionary Quantitative Genetics*. A readable textbook on quantitative genetics with an evolutionary focus and many examples from wild populations.

Storfer (1996) A brief intelligible review about assessing quantitative genetic variation in endangered species.

PROBLEMS

5.1 Statistics: Compute the parent and offspring means and variances and the covariance between parent and offspring values for the following data set on shell size in 21 families of *Partula* snails, an endangered species originating from Tahiti (data from Murray & Clarke 1968). Each pair of data represents the mean shell length of the parents (P) and their offspring (O) for a single family.

P	O	P	O	P	O
18.5	17.5	19.8	19.2	20.4	19.3
18.6	18.3	19.8	17.8	20.7	21.3
18.7	19.1	19.9	19.4	20.7	20.7
18.9	19.0	20.0	19.9	20.7	19.1
19.2	18.7	20.1	18.5	21.2	20.3
19.4	17.4	20.3	21.6	21.2	19.3
19.6	18.3	20.3	18.9	21.4	20.2

5.2 Heritability: Compute the regression of offspring on parent for the data on shell length in endangered *Partula* snails in Problem 5.1. Compute the heritability from the regression coefficient. Plot the relationship and insert the regression line.

5.3 Heritability: For the following hypothetical data on lifetime offspring numbers in seven families of endangered California condors, compute the regression of offspring mean on parent mean and calculate the heritability. Plot the relationship between offspring mean and parent mean and insert the regression line.

Family	1	2	3	4	5	6	7
Offspring mean	5.4	5.6	5.8	6.0	6.2	6.4	6.6
Parent mean	3.0	4.0	5.0	6.0	7.0	8.0	9.0

5.4 Heritability: If the slope of the regression of offspring phenotype on father's mean for body size in the Barnacle goose is 0.27 (Weigensberg & Roff 1996), what is the heritability of body size in this population?

5.5 Genotypic values: Specify the genotypic values for a locus with alleles A_1 and A_2 where A_2 is recessive (in terms of the symbols a, d and $-a$), similar to Fig. 5.3.

5.6 Relationship between heterozygosity and quantitative genetic variation: What happens to V_A, V_D and h^2 if the heterozygosity increases by 10%?

5.7 Inbreeding and quantitative genetic variation: What happens to h^2, V_A and V_D if there is inbreeding and heterozygosity drops by 50%?

5.8 Selection differential: If the breeding individuals for an endangered species in captivity have a mean 'wildness' score of 8, and the whole population has a mean of 10, what is the selection differential (S)?

5.9 Response to selection for a quantitative character: What is the expected response to selection for body size in cotton-top tamarins if individuals producing offspring have a mean body size of 490 g, while the population mean body size is 450 g and the heritability of body size is 35%?

5.10 Response to selection: What is the expected response to selection for depth of bill in Darwin's medium ground finch on the Galapagos Islands due to the drought in 1977 (Grant & Grant 1995, 2000)? The heritability of bill depth in this population is 0.73. Bill depth was 9.42 mm before the drought and 9.96 mm in those that survived the drought.

Chapter 6

Evolution in large populations. I. Natural selection and adaptation

Terms:

Adaptive evolution,
convergent evolution,
directional selection,
disruptive selection,
ecotype,
fitness,
fixation,
lethal,
natural selection,
partial dominance,
relative fitness,
reproductive fitness,
selection coefficient,
stabilizing selection

Species must evolve to cope with environmental change. Adaptive evolutionary changes in large natural populations occur through the impact of selection increasing the frequency of beneficial alleles

Industrial melanism in the peppered moth; peppered and melanic (black) moths on trees in polluted (blackened tree trunk) and unpolluted (tree with lichen) areas (Europe). The melanic form is better camouflaged in the polluted area and the peppered moth in the unpolluted area (from Kettlewell 1973).

The need to evolve

Species have to cope with a plethora of environmental changes. There are continual changes over time in pests, parasites, diseases and competitors, as well as changes wrought by human activities. Disease organisms evolve new strains, and new diseases arise, pathogens switch hosts and diseases spread to new locations (Garrett 1994). Adaptations in competitors, pests and parasites are such common events that Van Valen (1973) proposed that species had to evolve continually to avoid falling behind competing organisms (the 'Red Queen' hypothesis). Climatic cycles, such as the *El Niño–La Niña* cycle, result in hot-dry periods with drought and wildfires that alternate with cool-wet periods with floods. On the geological time scale of millions of years, there are major climatic shifts between ice ages and warm periods.

Global warming is occurring as a consequence of the burning of fossil fuels. Impacts of this warming on living organisms are already evident and many more changes are predicted (Hughes 2000). Species have to move, or adapt to the changed climatic conditions. Birds, butterflies and plants have already altered their ranges in response to global warming. Coral reefs are experiencing increased frequencies of bleaching and mass deaths due to warming. Several disease organisms have moved their ranges and many others are predicted to do so (Hughes 2000). An adaptive evolutionary change as a result of climate change has already been observed in a fruit fly population (Rodríguez-Trelles & Rodríguez 1998).

Alterations in disease organisms are probably the most pervasive and frequent environmental change faced by species. For example, 300 plagues affecting humans are recorded in Chinese history between 243 BC and 1911, approximately one every seven years (McNeill 1976). Disease outbreaks may have devastating impacts on species. Plague killed nearly 20 million Europeans in the 14th century, while rinderpest eliminated 95% of the great wildebeest and Cape buffalo herds in East Africa in the 1890s (O'Brien & Evermann 1988). New influenza strains arise every few years and spread throughout the world.

Many diseases have crossed species boundaries, including HIV-1 (a cause of AIDS) from chimpanzees to humans, canine distemper from dogs to lions in Africa and to black-footed ferrets in the USA, and Hendra virus from fruit bats to horses and humans in Australia (Daszak *et al.* 2000).

Human activities are also spreading disease organisms from their original locations. For example, toxoplasmosis has moved with eutherian mammals from Europe to Australia and infected susceptible marsupials, increasing their mortality rates (Daszak *et al.* 2000). Further, avian disease pathogens introduced by European settlers into Hawaii caused extinctions of nearly half of the endemic land birds.

Environmental challenges exert new selective forces, so species must adapt to cope with them. Adaptation may take the form of either physiological or behavioural modifications where individuals change to cope with altered conditions, or genetic adaptation through natural selection altering the genetic composition of the populations.

Environmental change is a ubiquitous feature of the conditions faced by species. Consequently, species need to be able to evolve to avoid extinction due to environmental change

In the face of environmental change, species must adapt, or face extinction

Individuals may adapt physiologically by modification in haemoglobin levels to cope with altitude, immune responses to fight diseases, induction of enzymes to cope with altered diets, etc. There is, however, a limit to physiological adaptation. If environment changes are greater than any individual can cope with then the species becomes extinct.

Adaptive evolutionary changes may allow populations to cope with conditions that no individual could previously survive

Evolutionary change through **natural selection** is the second means for adjusting to environmental change. This is referred to as **adaptive evolution**. Natural selection is differential reproduction and survival of different genotypes. When adaptive evolutionary changes continue over time, they may allow a population to cope with conditions more extreme than any individual could originally tolerate.

Adaptive evolution is observed wherever large genetically variable populations are subjected to altered biotic or physical environments. It is of major importance in five conservation contexts:

• Preservation of the ability of species to evolve in response to new environments
• Loss of adaptive evolutionary potential in small populations
• Most endangered species now exist only on the periphery of their historical range (Channell & Lomollno 2000), so they must adapt to what was previously a marginal environment
• Genetic adaptation to captivity and its deleterious effects on reintroduction success (Chapter 18)
• Adaptation of translocated populations to their new environment.

This chapter provides evidence for the ubiquity of adaptive evolutionary change, considers the factors controlling the evolution of populations and discusses the impact of selection on populations.

Genetic adaptation of species to their environmental conditions is ubiquitous in species with genetic diversity

Species adapt through natural selection to their environmental conditions, provided they have the necessary genetic diversity. Adaptive evolution has been described in a large number of animals and plants (Endler 1986; Briggs & Walters 1997; Thompson 1998). Endler (1986) alone reported adaptive changes in over 139 species. Evolutionary changes have been documented in animals for morphology, behaviour, colour form, host plant resistance, prey size, body size, alcohol tolerance, life history attributes, disease resistance, predator avoidance, tolerance to pollutants, biocide resistance, etc. Adaptive changes in colour and shape to provide better camouflage are widespread (Cott 1940). For example, many land snails are polymorphic for shell colour and banding; natural selection favours better camouflaged forms – yellow banded shells in tall, grassy habitats and unbanded brown or pink shells in woodlands (Futuyma 1998).

Humans in Eurasia have evolved resistance to a range of diseases, including smallpox and measles; other populations that have evolved in the absence of these diseases have been devastated when exposed to them (Diamond 1997). Humans from malarial areas have evolved a variety of different genetic mechanisms of resistance that are very rare or absent elsewhere.

Adaptive evolutionary changes to a wide range of conditions have been reported in plants, including those to soil conditions, water stress, flooding, light regimes, exposure to wind, grazing, air pollution and herbicides (Briggs & Walters 1997). Plants have evolved a wide range of secondary compounds to avoid being eaten by herbivores. For example, white clover and bird's-foot trefoil are polymorphic for the production of cyanogenic glucosides that provide protection from herbivory by slugs and snails (Briggs & Walters 1997). Plant populations adapted to different ecological conditions are so common that they have their own term (**ecotypes**).

Adaptive evolutionary changes have allowed species to inhabit almost every imaginable niche on Earth; species inhabit altitudes from 6500 m on Mount Everest to deep ocean trenches, from arctic saline pools at $-23\,°C$ to hot thermal springs and deep sea vents, from oceans and freshwater to deserts, while plants have adapted to grow in almost every soil on the planet (Dobzhansky *et al.* 1977).

Adaptation to local environments has important implications in conservation. Translocations are likely to be more successful when populations are moved to similar, rather than to different environments (Chapters 16 and 18). Further, crossing of populations adapted to different environments may be deleterious (Chapters 13 and 15).

Convergent evolution of similar forms in equivalent ecological niches, but derived from different progenitors, illustrates the pervasive influence of adaptive evolution. For example, there are morphologically similar forms amongst marsupials in Australia and eutherian mammals from other parts of the world, e.g. the marsupial versus eutherian wolves, moles and mice, etc. (Futuyma 1998).

> Different species evolve similar characteristics when placed in similar environments – convergent evolution

Measurable adaptive evolutionary changes have occurred from year to year in beak and body dimensions in Darwin's medium ground finch in response to environmental changes associated with *El Niño*–Southern Oscillation climate changes (Chapter 5). Rapid evolutionary changes in migration rates have been described in birds and plants. The blackcap bird has established a novel wintering area in Britain in the last 30 years, distinct from its traditional area in the Mediterranean (Berthold *et al.* 1992). Plants of nine species that migrated to 240 islands off the coast of British Columbia in Canada underwent two evolutionary changes in dispersal ability (Cody & Overton 1996). The initial change was in the direction of increased dispersal ability as only seeds with high dispersal ability reach the islands. Within 10 years of reaching the islands, the plants evolved lowered dispersal ability, as seeds with high dispersal ability were more likely to be lost into the ocean.

> Adaptive evolutionary changes may be rapid

Humans have been responsible for many environmental changes due to pollution, translocations of species, species extinctions, etc. In many cases, adaptive evolutionary changes have been recorded in affected species. Rabbits in Australia evolved resistance to the myxoma virus when it was introduced as a control measure (Box 6.1). Over 200 species of moths worldwide have evolved industrial melanism in polluted industrial areas (Kettlewell 1973). Several species of plants have evolved tolerance to heavy metals in the process of colonizing polluted heavy metal mine wastes and plants are progressively evolving resistance to herbi-

> Evolutionary changes have been observed in response to many human caused environmental changes

cides (Briggs & Walters 1997). Increased resistance to toxic cyanobacteria has evolved in water fleas as a consequence of cyanobacterial blooms following eutrophication of Lake Constance in central Europe (Hairston *et al.* 1999). A population of a rare sub-species of checkerspot butterfly in Nevada has altered host preference, now preferring an introduced plant weed to its ancestral diet (Singer *et al.* 1993).

The evolution of resistance to biocontrol agents (insecticides, pesticides, antibiotics, etc.) is a universal phenomenon (Georghiou 1986). For example, hundreds of insect species have evolved resistance to insecticides (McKenzie 1996) and microbes rapidly evolve resistance to each new antibiotic (Garrett 1994). Rats and mice have evolved resistance to warfarin and other anti-coagulant rodenticides (Futuyma 1998).

Even species extinctions can result in evolutionary change. The extinction of its favoured lobeloid host plant caused a Hawaiian honeycreeper (*Vestiaria*) to evolve a shorter beak as alternative host plants had shorter corollas (Smith *et al.* 1995).

Box 6.1	**Rapid adaptive evolutionary changes in rabbits in Australia following the introduction of myxoma virus as a control agent** (Fenner & Ratcliffe 1965)

European settlers introduced rabbits into Australia in the 19th century for sport hunting. Several unsuccessful attempts were made until genuine wild rabbits were introduced in 1859. The wild rabbits rapidly increased in numbers until they reached plague proportions throughout much of the country. Rabbits caused many native plant species to decline and were one of the causes in the decline of native marsupial bilbies (they also burrow).

When myxoma virus was introduced into Australia to control rabbits in 1950, mortality rates of infected rabbits were over 99%. Strong directional selection resulted in rapid increases in genetic resistance of rabbits to the myxoma virus. The myxoma virus also evolved lower virulence, as this increased the probability of being transmitted. The mortality to a less severe virus strain dropped from around 90% to 25% in 1958 (the sixth epizootic), as shown below. The data below reflect only the genetic changes in rabbit resistance as the same virus stain was used throughout the study.

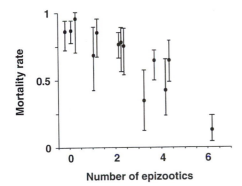

Conservation biology is concerned with preserving species as dynamic entities that can evolve to cope with environmental change. Retaining the ability to evolve requires the preservation of genetic diversity. Consequently, we must understand the factors that influence the evolution of natural populations.

Preserving the ability to evolve in response to environmental change is a major concern in conservation biology

In this chapter and the next we will consider the evolution of large natural populations, while Chapter 8 contrasts this with the evolution of small populations.

Factors controlling the evolution of populations

An evolving population is a complex system influenced by mutation, migration, selection and chance, operating within the context of the breeding system (Fig. 6.1). To understand the interactions of these factors in their full complexity is difficult. Consequently, we seek to understand the components of an evolving population by modelling it with none of the factors operating, then with the factors one at a time, followed by two at a time, etc. By doing this we can see how large an effect each factor has and what role it is likely to play in evolution. Further, we seek to identify circumstances where factors can be ignored, as it is rare for all factors to have important effects simultaneously. For example, mutations occur at very low rates, so we can often ignore them over the short term.

Populations evolve through the action of mutation, migration, selection and chance

In Chapter 4, we showed that allele and genotype frequencies are in equilibrium at an autosomal locus after one generation of random mating (Hardy–Weinberg equilibrium) in populations with no

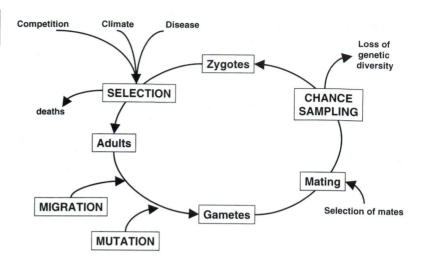

Fig. 6.1 An evolving population as a complex system.

impacts of mutation, migration, selection or chance. In this chapter and the next we consider the independent action of mutation, selection and migration, and then the joint actions of mutation with selection and migration with selection. Chance effects are generally minor in large populations, so we will defer detailed treatment of them until Chapter 8.

Evolution involves a change in the genetic composition of a population. At its simplest level, this involves a change in the frequency of an allele due to mutation, migration, selection or chance.

The impacts of these factors can be summarized as:

- Mutation is the source of all genetic diversity, but is a weak evolutionary force over the short term
- Selection is the only force causing adaptive evolutionary change
- Migration reduces differences between populations generated by mutation, selection and chance
- Chance effects in small populations lead to loss of genetic diversity and reduced adaptive evolutionary change
- Fragmentation and reduced migration lead to random differentiation among sub-populations derived from the same original source population.

These insights have been obtained principally from detailed consideration of population models.

Evolution at its simplest level is a change in the frequency of an allele

Role of mathematical models

Simple mathematical models have a crucial role in illuminating genetics of the evolutionary process

To investigate the evolutionary impacts of selection, mutation, migration and chance we will build simple mathematical models. Wilson (1975) summarized the value of such models. They can:

- Establish quantitative laws to describe underlying processes
- Provide testable predictions
- Provide expressions for estimating parameters that are difficult or impossible to estimate otherwise
- Predict the existence of still undiscovered phenomena and unexpected relations among phenomena.

The models we build are usually simplifications of the real world. To determine whether our models explain that world, we require quantitative predictions that can be evaluated against experimental or observational data. For example, equations to predict the decline in frequency of a recessive lethal allele are evaluated later in this chapter and applied to predict changes in the frequency of chondrodystrophy (a lethal dwarfism) in California condors. In Chapter 10, equations which predict that equalizing family sizes effectively doubles the size of populations (and so maximizes the use of scarce captive breeding spaces) are presented, and their predictions validated in tests using fruit flies.

Often methods for estimating parameters that we wish to know are not obvious. Parameters that have been estimated using models include:

- Mutation rates in humans (from the balance between mutation and selection)
- Magnitude of selection on industrial melanism in moths (from models of the time taken for changes in frequency)
- Migration rates in human populations (from allele frequencies in current, source and immigrant populations)
- Extent of gene flow among populations and species (from allele frequencies in different populations)
- Number and effect of deleterious alleles in populations of endangered species (from the effect of inbreeding on mortality).

By building mathematical models of evolutionary processes, new insights are often revealed. For example, cost–benefit analyses of altruistic behaviour led to the predictions that it would typically involve close relatives, and that it would be more common in haplo-diploid species such as the Hymenoptera than in diploids.

Selection

Selection arises because different genotypes have different rates of reproduction and survival (reproductive fitness). Such selection changes the frequency of alleles. Alleles whose carriers have relatively larger numbers of fertile offspring surviving to reproductive age increase in frequency, while alleles whose carriers have fewer offspring decrease in frequency.

Selection operates at all stages of the life cycle; in animals this involves mating ability and fertility of males and females, fertilizing ability of sperm (sometimes ability of sperm to compete), number of off-

> Selection is the only force that causes adaptive evolution

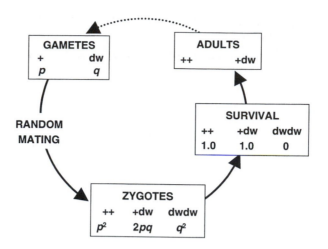

Fig. 6.2 Selection model for a recessive lethal.

spring per female, survival of offspring to reproductive age and longevity. In plants, selection can involve pollen production, ability of pollen to reach the stigma of flowers, germinate, grow down the style and fertilize, number of ova, viability of the fertilized zygotes, their ability to disperse, germinate and grow to sexual maturity, and the fertility of the resulting plant. Selection may also operate via impacts of individual behaviour on relatives (parental care, helpers). For simplicity, we will use models that involve differential survival of individuals from zygote formation to adult. The consequences of selection on other stages of the life cycle are similar.

Recessive lethal

Selection reduces the frequency of deleterious alleles

The most intensive selection that can apply against a recessive allele is when all homozygotes die (**lethal**). For example, all individuals homozygous for chondrodystrophic dwarfism (*dwdw*) in endangered California condors die around hatching time. We consider a simple model with discrete generations, random mating and viability selection (Fig. 6.2).

The effect of selection against chondrodystrophy in California condors is derived in Table 6.1. We begin with a normal allele (+) at a frequency of p and the recessive lethal (*dw*) allele at a frequency of q. With random mating, the genotype frequencies at zygote formation are the Hardy–Weinberg equilibrium frequencies p^2, $2pq$ and q^2. However, the three genotypes have different survival. The important factor in the genetic effects of selection is not the absolute survival, but the relative survival of the three genotypes. For example, if the $+ +$, $+ dw$ and *dwdw* genotypes have 75%, 75% and 0% survival, it is the relative values 1, 1 and 0 that determine the impact of selection; we term these values the **relative fitnesses**.

Table 6.1 | Modelling the impact of selection against chondrodystrophy (a recessive lethal) in California condors

	Phenotype			
	Normal	Normal	Dwarf	
	Genotype			
	$++$	$+dw$	$dwdw$	Total
Zygotic frequencies	p^2	$2pq$	q^2	1.0
Relative fitnesses	1	1	0 (lethal)	
After selection (frequency × fitness)	$p^2 \times 1$	$2pq \times 1$	$q^2 \times 0 = 0$	$1 - q^2$
Adjusted frequencies	$\dfrac{p^2}{1-q^2}$	$\dfrac{2pq}{1-q^2}$	0	1

The frequency of surviving adults is obtained by multiplying the initial frequencies by the relative fitnesses. For example, the frequency of lethal homozygotes goes from q^2 at fertilization to $q^2 \times 0 = 0$ in adults. After selection, we have lost some of the population $(-q^2)$, so the total no longer adds to 1. We must therefore divide by the total $(1 - q^2)$ to obtain relative frequencies, as shown.

The allele frequency in the succeeding generation is then obtained by determining the allele frequency in survivors using the allele counting method described in Chapter 4. The methods for deriving allele frequency changes due to all other forms of selection are similar to that used here.

The frequency of the dw allele in the next generation after selection (q_1) is

$$q_1 = \frac{pq}{1-q^2} = \frac{q(1-q)}{(1-q)(1+q)} = \frac{q}{1+q} \tag{6.1}$$

Note that $1 - q$ can be substituted for p, as $p + q = 1$.

The change in frequency Δq is:

$$\Delta q = q_1 - q = \frac{q}{1+q} - q = \frac{q - q(1+q)}{1+q} \tag{6.2}$$

$$\Delta q = \frac{-q^2}{1+q}$$

Thus, the lethal dw allele always declines in frequency, as the sign of Δq is negative. However, the rate of decline slows markedly at lower frequencies as it depends on the square of the frequency (Fig. 6.3). Example 6.1 uses Equation 6.1 to calculate the change in frequency of the dw alleles in California condors.

Example 6.1 | Change in frequency of the chondrodystrophy allele in endangered California condors

How rapidly does the frequency of the recessive lethal chondrodystrophy allele decline due to selection? The allele had an initial frequency at hatching of about 0.17 (Example 4.5). All homozygotes died, so the frequency was reduced in surviving adults. The expected frequency of the deleterious allele in adults as a result of this natural selection can be predicted by using Equation 6.1 and substituting $q = 0.17$, as follows:

$$q_1 = \frac{q}{1+q} = 0.17 / (1+0.17) = 0.145$$

Thus, the frequency is expected to have dropped from 17% to 14.5% as a result of one generation of natural selection, a drop of about 15%.

Does Equation 6.1 predict the behaviour of lethal alleles in real populations? The observed frequency of a recessive lethal allele in an experimental fruit fly population declined continuously at approximately the predicted rate (Fig. 6.3). The decline in lethal frequency slows down over time as expected from the equation above. An important implication of this relationship is that it becomes progressively harder to reduce the frequency of a deleterious recessive allele as its frequency declines.

The observed decline is slightly faster than predicted. This suggests that heterozygotes have a slightly reduced fitness compared to homozygous normal individuals, i.e. the lethal allele is only partially recessive. 'Recessive' alleles frequently have a small impact in heterozygotes.

Fig. 6.3 Change in frequency of a recessive lethal allele (q) over generations in a fruit fly population. The solid line is the observed change and the dashed line is the decline expected according to Equation 6.1 (after Wallace 1963).

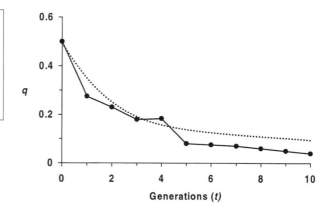

Adaptive evolutionary change

In conservation genetics, we are concerned both with selection against deleterious mutations and with selection favouring alleles that improve the ability of a population to adapt to changing environments. We will use industrial melanism in the peppered moth in the UK as an example illustrating adaptive evolutionary change (Kettlewell 1973; Majerus 1998; Grant 1999). Camouflage is critical to the survival of the peppered moth as it is active at night and rests on trees during the day; if it is not camouflaged it is vulnerable to predation by birds. Prior to the industrial revolution, its peppered wings were well camouflaged as it rested on speckled lichen-covered tree trunks in the midlands of England (chapter frontispiece). However, sulfur pollution during the industrial revolution killed most lichen and soot darkened trees. Consequently, the speckled moth became clearly visible on blackened tree trunks. The previously rare dark variants (melanics) were better camouflaged on the black trunks. This resulted in a higher frequency of the melanic allele (M) in the industrial areas than in relatively unpolluted areas (Fig. 6.4). The melanic form of the peppered moth was first recorded in 1848, but by 1900 they represented about 99% of all moths in the polluted midlands of England.

A model of this selection is developed below. This model shows that the frequency of the M allele always increases until the allele is fixed ($p = 1$), as the sign of Δp is positive. The rate of change depends on the strength of selection against the non-melanic form (s, the **selection coefficient**) and the allele frequencies p and q.

Pollution controls would be expected to reverse the selective forces and to result in a decline in the frequency of industrial melanism. As predicted, the frequency of the melanics (now poorly camouflaged) has been reduced markedly. At one site near Liverpool, the frequency of melanics has dropped from 90% in 1959 to 10% now, and similar declines have been observed in other areas of the UK. Parallel changes have also occurred in the northern American sub-species of the peppered moth (Grant 1999).

The melanic form of the moth is due to a single dominant allele. The impacts of selection on the melanic and typical allele frequencies are given below (the insularia allele is ignored here, but this does not affect our conclusions). We begin with frequencies for melanic (M) and typical (t) alleles of p and q, respectively. We will assume that we are dealing with a large random mating population with no migration or mutation. Selection is assumed to occur on adults, but before reproduction. Since the tt genotype has poorer survival than melanics in polluted areas, but we do not necessarily know the precise value, we give it a relative fitness of $1 - s$, where s is the **selection coefficient**. The value of s represents the reduction in fitness of the tt genotype compared to the fittest genotypes, MM and Mt.

> Selection increases the frequency of advantageous alleles

Fig. 6.4 Adaptive changes in the frequency of industrial melanism due to selection in polluted areas (after Kettlewell 1973; Majerus 1998; Grant 1999). Map of the UK with pie diagrams showing the frequency of the melanic, a milder melanic (insularia) and the non-melanic (typical) forms of the peppered moths (after Kettlewell 1958). The melanic form had high frequencies in industrial areas (Midlands, around London in the southeast and around Glasgow toward the northwest) and low frequencies in less polluted areas.

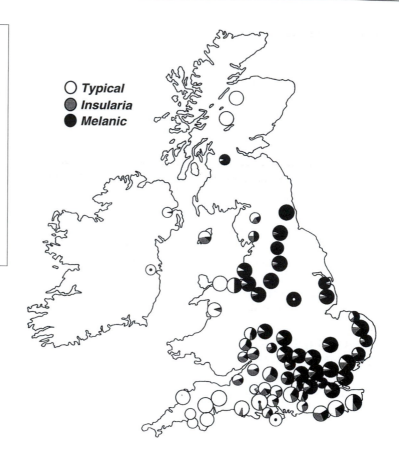

○ *Typical*
◑ *Insularia*
● *Melanic*

	Melanic MM	Melanic Mt	Typical tt	Total
Zygotic frequencies	p^2	$2pq$	q^2	1
Relative fitnesses	1	1	$1-s$	
After selection	p^2	$2pq$	$q^2(1-s)$	$1-sq^2$
Adjusted frequencies	$\dfrac{p^2}{1-sq^2}$	$\dfrac{2pq}{1-sq^2}$	$\dfrac{q^2-sq^2}{1-sq^2}$	1

Frequency of M after selection (p_1) is

$$p_1 = \frac{p^2}{1-sq^2} + (\tfrac{1}{2})\frac{2pq}{1-sq^2}$$

$$= \frac{p^2+pq}{1-sq^2} = \frac{p(p+q)}{1-sq^2}$$

$$= \frac{p}{1-sq^2}$$

The change in frequency of M (Δp) is

$$\Delta p = p_1 - p$$

$$= \frac{p}{1 - sq^2} - p = \frac{p - p(1 - sq^2)}{1 - sq^2}$$

$$= \frac{spq^2}{1 - sq^2}$$

Thus, the melanic allele increases in frequency, as the sign of Δp is positive. The rate of increase depends upon the selection coefficient and upon the allele frequencies. This can be illustrated using a numerical example.

If the melanic allele was at a frequency p of 0.005 in 1848, and typicals had only 70% the survival of melanics ($s = 0.3$) in polluted areas, then the frequency of the melanic allele would change in one generation to

$$p_1 = \frac{p}{1 - sq^2} = 0.005 / [1 - (0.3 \times 0.995^2)] = 0.0071$$

This represents ~40% increase in the frequency of the melanic allele. The change in frequency is

$$\Delta p = p_1 - p = 0.0071 - 0.005 = 0.0021$$

Thus, the melanic allele increased by 0.0021, from 0.005 to 0.0071, in the first generation.

Other selection models

Models with four different degrees of dominance with respect to fitness are illustrated in Fig. 6.5. In each case, the selection coefficient (s) represents the reduction in relative fitness of the genotype compared to that in the most fit genotype (fitness $= 1$). Values of s range from 0 to 1. In the additive case, the heterozygote has a fitness intermediate between the two homozygotes, while in the completely dominant case its fitness is equal to that of the A_1A_1 homozygote. In the **partial dominance** case, the heterozygote has a fitness nearer one homozygote (here A_1A_1) than the other, with its position on the scale depending on the value of h. In the **overdominant** case the heterozygote has a higher fitness than either homozygote.

Selection coefficients are calculated from survivals of the genotypes by first converting the survivals into relative fitnesses by dividing by the highest value of survival for the three genotypes. In the additive example, the percentage survivals of 90, 70 and 50 are all divided by 90 to give relative fitnesses of $90/90 = 1$, $70/90 = 0.778$ and $50/90 = 0.556$, respectively. The relative fitness of A_2A_2 (0.556) is equated to $1 - s$, giving a s value of 0.444.

The changes in allele frequency for different degrees of dominance

> The impact of selection on the frequencies of alleles depends on the strength of the selection, on the dominance of the alleles, and on the frequencies of the alleles

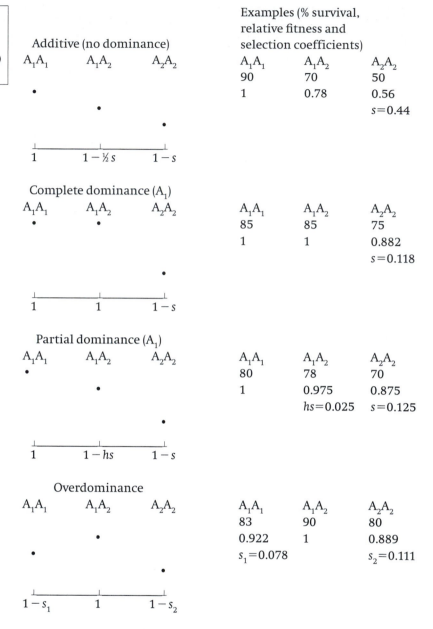

Fig. 6.5 Degrees of dominance with respect to fitness and examples of % survival, relative fitness and selection coefficients (s) for each.

Examples (% survival, relative fitness and selection coefficients)

Additive (no dominance)

A_1A_1	A_1A_2	A_2A_2	A_1A_1	A_1A_2	A_2A_2
			90	70	50
			1	0.78	0.56
					$s=0.44$
1	$1-\frac{1}{2}s$	$1-s$			

Complete dominance (A_1)

A_1A_1	A_1A_2	A_2A_2	A_1A_1	A_1A_2	A_2A_2
			85	85	75
			1	1	0.882
					$s=0.118$
1	1	$1-s$			

Partial dominance (A_1)

A_1A_1	A_1A_2	A_2A_2	A_1A_1	A_1A_2	A_2A_2
			80	78	70
			1	0.975	0.875
				$hs=0.025$	$s=0.125$
1	$1-hs$	$1-s$			

Overdominance

A_1A_1	A_1A_2	A_2A_2	A_1A_1	A_1A_2	A_2A_2
			83	90	80
			0.922	1	0.889
			$s_1=0.078$		$s_2=0.111$
$1-s_1$	1	$1-s_2$			

with autosomal and sex-linked loci are shown in Table 6.2. These are important in both the context of adaptive changes due to selection, and in the context of the deleterious alleles that are exposed by inbreeding. Consequently, we will spend some time on the details of selection.

The change in allele frequency due to one generation of selection against a recessive A_2 allele (Table 6.2 c) is

$$\Delta q = -spq^2 / (1 - sq^2) \tag{6.3}$$

Table 6.2 Changes in allele frequency in one generation, with different dominance relationships for fitness for autosomal and sex-linked loci. Initial frequencies are p and q for A_1 and A_2, respectively

Initial frequencies and fitness of genotypes	Change in frequency

Autosomal

A_1A_1	A_1A_2	A_2A_2	$\Delta q = q_1 - q_0$
p^2	$2pq$	q^2	

(a) Additive: selection against A_2

1	$1 - \frac{1}{2}s$	$1 - s$	$-\frac{1}{2} spq / (1 - sq)$

(b) Partial dominance of A_1, selection against A_2

1	$1 - hs$	$1 - s$	$- spq[q + h(p - q)]/[1 - 2hspq - sq^2]$

(c) Complete dominance of A_1, selection against A_2 ($\equiv A_2$ recessive)

1	1	$1 - s$	$- spq^2 / (1 - sq^2)$

(d) Complete dominance of A_1, selection against A_1 ($\equiv A_2$ recessive)

$1 - s$	$1 - s$	1	$spq^2 / [1 - s(1 - q^2)]$

(e) Overdominance, selection against A_1A_1 and A_2A_2

$1 - s_1$	1	$1 - s_2$	$pq (s_1 p - s_2 q) / [1 - s_1 p^2 - s_2 q^2]$

Sex-linked[a]

Females			Males		Δq
$X^{A1}X^{A1}$	$X^{A1}X^{A2}$	$X^{A2}X^{A2}$	$X^{A1}Y$	$X^{A2}Y$	
p^2	$2pq$	q^2	p	q	

(f) Sex-linked recessive, selection against A_2

1	1	$1 - s$	1	$1 - s$	$- 1/3 spq / (1 - sq)$ (approx)

(g) Additive sex-linked, selection against A_2

1	$1 - \frac{1}{2}s$	$1 - s$	1	$1 - s$	$- 2/3 spq / (1 - sq)$

Note:
[a] For birds and Lepidoptera, the sexes must be reversed.

Three important points are revealed by this equation:
• The negative sign indicates that the deleterious A_2 allele declines in frequency until it is completely eliminated
• The rate of change depends on the amount of selection (s)
• The rate of change depends on the allele frequencies, p and q.

Considering all the models in Table 6.2, the direction of change is always against the allele whose carriers have the lowest fitness. For example, the signs are opposite in direction for selection against A_2 (Table 6.2c), compared to selection against A_1 (Table 6.2d). Over-dominance is slightly more complex, so we will defer treatment of it until Chapter 9.

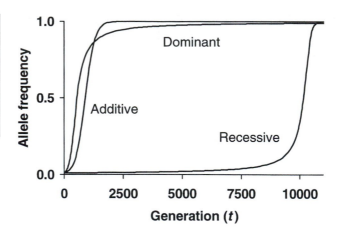

Fig. 6.6 Fate of rare, but favourable alleles over time. Change in frequency over generations for advantageous dominant, recessive and additive alleles. All have selection coefficients of 1% and all begin at a frequency $p = 1\%$ (after Nei 1975).

All expressions for change in allele frequency contain the term spq, so they all depend on the intensity of selection and heterozygosity.

The pattern of change in allele frequencies over time differs for dominant, additive and recessive alleles subject to the same selection coefficient and all beginning with the same frequency of the favoured allele (Fig. 6.6). A favoured dominant allele initially increases more rapidly than additive or recessive alleles. However, its rate of change slows markedly when it reaches a high frequency as the recessive homozygote, against which selection is acting, becomes increasingly rare. Conversely, the favoured recessive initially increases very slowly, and only when its frequency reaches about 10% does it rapidly rises in frequency to **fixation** (the population becomes all homozygotes and $p = 1$). The dominant and recessive patterns are the mirror images of each other. The trajectory for the additive allele is intermediate between these; its initial increase is slightly slower than that for the dominant, but it continues to increase and goes to fixation.

For equivalent circumstances selection has greater impact on haploid loci than on autosomal diploid loci, with sex-linked loci intermediate

Selection of the same intensity has a greater impact on a haploid locus ($\Delta q = spq \mathbin{/} [1 - sq]$) than on an additive autosomal diploid locus, with an additive sex-linked locus intermediate (see Table 6.2); their Δq values for equivalent situations are in the ratios 1: 1/2: 2/3. Further, selection against a recessive is much more effective for a sex-linked than an autosomal locus. These observations become of major importance when we consider the balance between mutation and selection in the next chapter.

Number of generations required for a given change in allele frequency

The number of generations for a given change in frequency depends on the selection coefficient, the mode of inheritance and the dominance of the allele

How long does it take for an allele frequency to change by a given amount under selection? This clearly depends on the intensity of selection, and on the mode of inheritance. We can obtain exact solutions in some cases, and approximate solutions are available in other cases when selection is weak (Crow & Kimura 1970).

For a recessive lethal, an expression for the time taken in generations can be obtained by rearranging Equation 6.1. If we refer to the allele frequencies after 0, 1, 2, t generations as q_0, q_1, q_2, q_t, then

$$q_1 = q_0 / (1 + q_0)$$

and

$$q_2 = q_1 / (1 + q_1)$$

by substituting for q_1, and simplifying,

$$q_2 = q_0 / (1 + 2q_0)$$

by extension:

$$q_t = q_0 / (1 + tq_0) \tag{6.4}$$

By rearranging this expression we obtain the number of generations, t, required to change the allele frequency from q_0 to q_t:

$$t = (q_0 - q_t) / q_0 q_t = 1/q_t - 1/q_0 \tag{6.5}$$

How many generations will it take to reduce the frequency of the chondrodystrophy allele in California condors from 17% to 1%? Using Equation 6.5, we predict that it will take 94 generations (Example 6.2). As we saw earlier, selection is very ineffective in changing the frequency of a rare recessive allele, as a large proportion of the recessive alleles are hidden from selection in heterozygotes. For example, the number of generations required to change the frequency of a recessive lethal allele from 0.1 to 0.01 is 90 generations, while it takes 900 generations to change it from 0.01 to 0.001.

When selection is less intense, the time taken for a given change in allele frequency is longer. It also depends on the dominance relationships at the locus, as is evident from Fig. 6.6.

Example 6.2 | How long will it take to reduce the frequency of the recessive lethal chondrodystrophy allele in California condors to a frequency of 1%?

The current frequency of the recessive lethal chondrodystrophy allele in California condors is approximately 0.17. To determine the number of generations required to reduce its frequency to 0.01, we use Equation 6.5 and substitute 0.17 for q_0 and 0.01 for q_t, as follows:

$$t = 1/q_t - 1/q_0 = (1/0.01) - (1/0.17) = 100 - 5.9 = 94.1 \text{ generations}$$

Consequently, it will take 94 generations to reduce the frequency of the chondrodystrophy allele to 1% as a result of natural selection.

Selection coefficients

Expressions for change in allele frequencies (Δq) can be used (after rearrangement) to estimate selection coefficients. For example, Haldane

(1924) estimated the magnitude of selective differences between melanic and typical phenotypes of peppered moths (Box 6.2). He estimated that typical moths had a relative fitness about 1/3 lower than melanics in polluted environments, a value that led to ridicule at the time. However, subsequent work by Kettlewell (1973) found selection coefficients of about the magnitude predicted by Haldane.

Box 6.2 | **Magnitude of selection involved in industrial melanism in the peppered moth** (after Haldane 1924 and Kettlewell 1973)

The melanic form of peppered moths increased from a frequency of about 1% to about 99% in 52 years in the polluted midlands of England. Haldane (1924) used the following reasoning to derive an approximate expression for the time in generations for a dominant favourable (M) allele to increase in frequency from p_0 to p_t:

	Melanic MM	Melanic Mt	Typical tt	Total
Zygotic frequencies	p^2	$2pq$	q^2	1
Relative fitnesses	1	1	$1-s$	
Frequencies 1848		0.01	0.99	$p_0 = 0.005$
Frequencies 1900		0.99	0.01	$p_t = 0.90$

The value for q_0 is obtained by equating $q_0^2 = 0.99$, taking square roots to obtain $q_0 = 0.995$, and equating $p_0 = 1 - q_0 = 1 - 0.995 = 0.005$.

Similarly, p_t is obtained by equating $q_t^2 = 0.01$, taking square roots to obtain $q_t = 0.1$, and equating $p_t = 1 - q_t = 1 - 0.1 = 0.9$.

The equation for change in frequency of the melanic allele (Fig. 6.4)

$$\Delta p = spq^2 / (1 - sp^2)$$

can be equated to the rate of change in allele frequency with time (dp / dt) and integrated to obtain an expression for number of generations t.

$$t = \frac{1}{s} \left\{ \ln \left[\frac{p_t(1 - p_0)}{p_0(1 - p_t)} \right] + \frac{1}{1 - p_t} - \frac{1}{1 - p_0} \right\}$$

As peppered moths breed annually, $t = 52$ generations. Consequently, the selection coefficient is

$$s = \frac{1}{52} \left\{ \ln \left[\frac{0.90 \times 0.995}{0.005 \times 0.10} \right] + \frac{1}{0.100} - \frac{1}{0.995} \right\}$$

$$\therefore s = 0.32$$

i.e. the survival of typical moths was predicted to be 32% lower in each generation than that of melanic moths in polluted areas.

Thirty years later, experiments done by Kettlewell yielded a selection coefficient of about this magnitude, as shown below. Kettlewell captured melanic and typical moths, marked and re-released them. A second sample of moths was captured shortly afterwards.

	Polluted area		Unpolluted	
	Melanic	Typical	Melanic	Typical
Numbers marked and released	447	137	473	496
Released moths recaptured	27.5%	13.1%	6.34%	12.5%

The recapture rate for melanics was approximately twice as high as that for typicals in the polluted area, yielding a selection coefficient of about 50%. Selection in unpolluted areas was approximately as strong in the opposite direction. The selection coefficient is higher than predicted by Haldane, attributable both to the use of a very heavily polluted area to carry out the experiment, and to migration of moths from unpolluted areas.

Selection coefficients for morphological characters may be strong, especially for morphological polymorphisms involved in camouflage. However, selection on protein and DNA polymorphism is thought to be very much weaker, around 1% or less. For example, selection coefficients are typically only 1% or less at the MHC, where evidence of selection is compelling (Satta *et al.* 1994). Many polymorphisms at the DNA level may involve no selective differences, or very weak selection. The extent of selection on allozyme polymorphisms is a matter of vigorous debate as to whether they are neutral, or subject to weak selection (Chapter 9).

Selection on quantitative characters

So far we have discussed the effects of selection on allele frequencies at single loci. For quantitative characters, this is an oversimplification as variation for quantitative traits is determined by segregation at multiple loci in combination with varying inputs from environmental effects (Chapter 5). Consequently, we will switch from discussing the effects of selection on allele frequencies to the effects of selection on phenotypic means and variances.

> Adaptive evolutionary change results from natural selection on reproductive fitness, a quantitative character

There are three basic forms of selection that operate on quantitative characters: directional, stabilizing and disruptive (Fig. 6.7). **Directional selection** favours phenotypes towards one direction and results in a shift in the mean in this direction (provided there is genetic variation) (Chapter 5). **Stabilizing selection** favours phenotypic intermediates and results in no change in the mean, but may result in reduced variation in future generations. **Disruptive selection** favours both phenotypic extremes and does not alter the mean, but may lead to increased variation in future generations.

> Natural selection on quantitative characters affects the character mean and/or variance

In a constant and relatively uniform environment, reproductive fitness is subject to directional selection, while characters more peripheral to reproduction and survival typically exhibit selection favouring phenotypic intermediates (stabilizing selection). In heterogeneous envi-

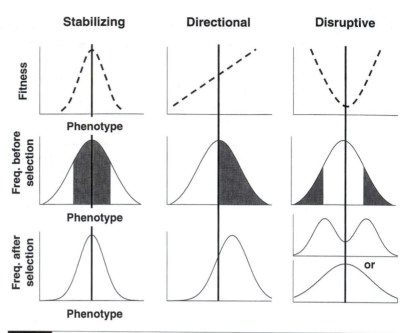

Fig. 6.7 Forms of selection operating on quantitative characters (after Futuyma 1979). Stabilizing, directional and disruptive selection are shown. The upper panels indicate the relationships between phenotype and fitness, the middle panels the phenotypic distributions before selection and the bottom panels the distributions after selection in the subsequent generation. The shaded areas in the middle panels indicate the portions of the distribution favoured by selection.

ronments, selection may vary in different directions in different habitats (disruptive). We elaborate on these three forms of selection below.

Directional selection

> Consistent selection in the one direction (directional selection) results in phenotypic change in the direction of selection, provided there is genetic diversity

Directional selection occurs when the environment is changing in a consistent manner such as global warming, increasing levels of pollutants in air, water, or soil (around cities, mines, or intensive agriculture), or when new diseases affect a population. Directional selection has been shown to produce large changes in outbred populations of many species of wild and domestic animals and plants, for reproductive rate, growth rate in body size, behaviour, chemical composition, tolerance to heavy metals, resistance to disease, etc. (Frankham & Weber 2000). For example, selection for tameness changed silver foxes from extremely hostile aggressive animals to ones approaching the tameness of domestic dogs within 17 generations (Box 6.3).

Reproductive fitness, even in a relatively constant environment, is subject to directional selection; the individuals with the highest fitness have the most offspring surviving to reproductive maturity and make the greatest genetic contributions to the next generation.

One example of adaptive evolutionary change with important conservation implications is worthy of recording in detail. King (1939) brought wild rats into captivity and maintained them under relatively constant conditions for 14 years (25 generations) under 'natural' selection. Over this time their reproductive lifespan increased from about 204 days to 440 days, the number of litters per female increased from 3.7 litters to 10.2, average litter size was relatively unchanged and female sterility decreased (from 37.3% to 5.8% in generations 1–8, to 0% in later generations). In addition, the female rats became better mothers and the adults increased in weight by 17%–20%. Reproductive fitness in the captive environment has increased by about three-fold. Similar adaptive increases in reproductive fitness have also been observed in fruit flies brought into captivity (Gilligan 2001). Captive populations of endangered species are likely to show similar adaptation to captivity. Disturbingly, this will typically result in decreased fitness when they are reintroduced to the wild (see Chapter 18).

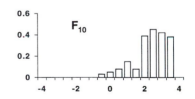

| **Box 6.3** | Response to directional selection for tameness in foxes (after Belyaev 1979) |

Silver foxes are farmed for their fur. They were so hostile towards humans that they could not be handled without special precautions against being bitten. Initially 30% were extremely aggressive towards humans, 20% were fearful, 40% were aggressively fearful and only 10% displayed a quiet exploratory reaction without fear or aggression. Directional selection for tameness resulted in a major genetic shift over 17 generations. The foxes of the selected population were not only unafraid of people, but they now displayed a positive reaction to human contact, and answered to nicknames. Like dogs, these foxes seek contact with familiar persons, tend to get close to them, and lick their hands and faces. These changes were due to genetic changes, not improved handling.

Reproductive functions in the selected foxes also changed. The reproductive season was prolonged with out-of-season oestrus in some females. Selection for tameness brought about a change in the hypothalamic–hypophyseal–adrenal system, in levels of steroid sex hormones and in serotonin levels. The characteristics of these domesticated foxes are similar to those of other domesticated animal species. These changes are instructive in the conservation context, as related changes may be occurring in endangered species in captivity, albeit much more slowly.

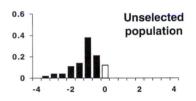

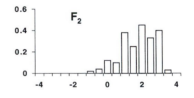

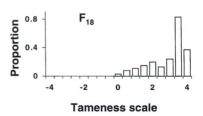

Selection response in the short term operates primarily on pre-existing genetic diversity, rather than on new mutations, as mutation is a rare event

Adaptive evolutionary change may utilize either pre-existing genetic diversity, or that arising due to mutation. Most adaptation in the short to medium term is due to pre-existing genetic diversity, since there may be a long waiting time for beneficial mutations to occur in any but vast populations (Chapter 7). Species that evolved heavy metal tolerance and colonized polluted mine tailings in Great Britain were those with pre-existing genetic variation for heavy metal tolerance. Species without the prerequisite genetic variation did not evolve resistance (Bradshaw 1991). The American chestnut has been driven almost to extinction by the introduced chestnut blight disease, presumably because it did not have genetic diversity for resistance to the disease and no disease-resistant mutations have occurred since (Burdon 1987). Conversely, microbe populations are so vast that new mutations occur at most loci in every generation, and they can adapt rapidly by relying on new mutations.

Long-term adaptive changes

Directional selection for many generations in large populations may produce extremely large genetic changes

Large changes in phenotype over time have been observed in many populations subjected to directional selection, especially of laboratory and domestic species (Fig. 6.8). One of the most rapid and sustained responses to selection was for flying speed in fruit flies from about 2 cm per second to 170 over 100 generations (Fig. 6.8b).

In the fossil record, the height of the molar tooth in the horse lineage increased from ~4.7 mm to 52.5 mm over about 40 million years (Manly 1985). This was presumably an adaptation to a change from browsing on leaves and succulent plants to feeding on grass which contains silica and wears teeth rapidly (Futuyma 1998). It only requires selective deaths of about one individual in a million per generation to account for this evolutionary change. Brain size increased markedly in the human lineage from about 400 cm^3 to 1400 cm^3 in 3 million years (Futuyma 1998). Changes per unit time wrought by artificial selection are typically greater than those found in either the fossil record or in species colonizing new regions within recent history (Futuyma 1998).

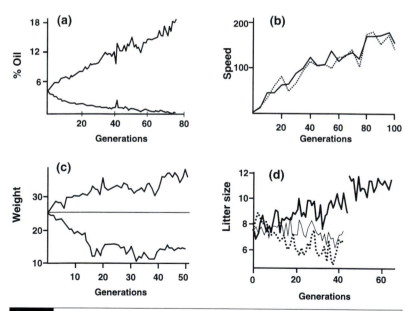

Fig. 6.8 Long-term response to directional selection. (a) Two-way selection for oil content in maize seeds (after Dudley 1977). (b) Selection for increased flying speed in replicate populations of fruit flies (after Weber 1996). (c) Two-way selection for 6-week body weight in mice (after Roberts 1966). (d) Selection for litter size in mice (after Falconer 1977); the bold solid line shows the impacts of selection for increased litter size, the dotted line selection for decreased litter size, while the fine solid line is an unselected control population.

Stabilizing selection

Stabilizing selection is the most frequent form of selection found for quantitative characters in populations in stable habitats. Phenotypic intermediates are favoured with this form of selection. For example, stabilizing selection is found for birth weight in humans (Fig. 6.9). The smallest and largest babies have poorer survival than intermediate weight babies. Large babies are more likely to die from birth complications, while small babies are often insufficiently mature to survive (these effects are now greatly reduced by medical intervention). Similarly, intermediate sized eggs in ducks and domestic fowl hatch best, and higher survival has been found for individuals with intermediate phenotypes for shell size in snails, body size in lizards and body dimensions in female sparrows following a severe storm (Lerner 1954).

As stabilizing selection favours phenotypic intermediates, it is not expected to change the mean of the character. In its simplest form, stabilizing selection is expected to reduce genetic diversity (Roff 1997). However, selection favouring heterozygotes also causes phenotypic stabilizing selection (Robertson 1956), leading to the retention of genetic diversity (Chapter 9).

> For populations that have been in the same relatively stable environment for a long period, most quantitative characters are subject to selection that favours phenotypic intermediates (stabilizing selection)

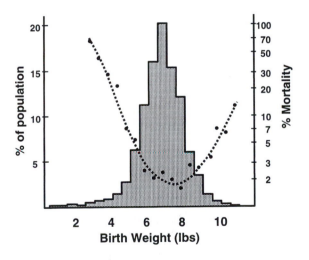

Fig. 6.9 Stabilizing selection for birth weight in humans (after Mather 1973).

Disruptive selection

Populations of conservation concern are often fragmented. Different fragments may have dissimilar environmental conditions, such that natural selection operates in diverse directions across fragments. For example, selection favours genotypes that tolerate heavy metals (Cu, Zn, Cd, etc.) in several grass species on polluted mine tailings in Wales, but operates against them in nearby non-contaminated pastures (Box 7.2; Bradshaw & McNeilly 1981).

> When the environment is heterogeneous in space, selection may act in different directions in dissimilar habitats (disruptive selection)

The overall consequence of disruptive selection in fragmented habitats is generation of local adaptation, i.e. adaptation is to each separate environment, rather than to the average of environments. One possible long-term outcome of disruptive selection is speciation (Chapter 15).

Summary

1. Change is a ubiquitous feature of the environmental conditions faced by species.

2. Species must evolve if they are to survive environmental changes that are more severe than individuals can cope with behaviourally or physiologically.

3. Adaptive evolution occurs through natural selection acting on genetic diversity within populations. At its simplest level it represents the change in frequency of a beneficial allele.

4. The impact of selection on a single locus depends upon selection coefficients, allele frequencies, dominance and the mode of inheritance.

5. The impact of selection on a quantitative character depends on the form of selection, the intensity of selection and the heritability.

FURTHER READING

Briggs & Walters (1997) *Plant Variation and Evolution*. Reviews evidence for adaptive genetic changes in plants.

Crow & Kimura (1970) *Introduction to Population Genetics Theory*. In spite of its age this is still the classic reference for theoretical population genetics. More mathematical and advanced than this text.

Endler (1986) *Natural Selection in the Wild*. An excellent book reviewing evidence and methods for detecting natural selection in the wild.

Falconer & Mackay (1996) *Introduction to Quantitative Genetics*. This textbook provides a very clear treatment of the topics in this chapter with a focus on animal breeding applications

Futuyma (1998) *Evolutionary Biology*. A textbook with a broad readable coverage of evolution, adaptations and the genetic processes underlying them.

Hartl & Clarke (1997) *Principles of Population Genetics*. A widely used textbook on population genetics.

Hedrick (2000) *Genetics of Populations*. A widely respected textbook in population genetics. Has a more extensive treatment of many of the topics in this chapter.

Karieva *et al.* (1993) *Biotic Interactions and Climate Change*. Contains a series of chapters by different authors on the likely biological impacts of global climate change including the potential for evolutionary adaptation.

Mousseau *et al.* (2000) *Adaptive Genetic Variation in the Wild*. Recent reviews on natural selection and adaptation in the wild.

PROBLEMS

6.1 Selection coefficients: If the three genotypes at a locus showing partial dominance have survival rates as shown, determine the relative fitnesses and the value of s and hs.

A_1A_1	A_1A_2	A_2A_2
1	$1 - hs$	$1 - s$
90%	88%	40%

6.2 Selection: What will be the frequency of the chondrodystrophy allele (recessive lethal) in endangered California condors in the next three generations as a result of natural selection, if the initial frequency is 14.5% (Example 6.1)?

6.3 Selection: How many generations will it take for the frequency of chondrodystrophy (recessive lethal) to drop from 17% to 0.1% as a result of natural selection?

6.4 Selection: For a dominant allele (A) with the relative fitnesses below and an initial frequency p of 0.3, follow the genotype frequencies through from the zygotic stage, through selection, to the adjusted frequencies. Compute the new frequency of the allele after selection p_1 and the change in frequency Δp.

	Genotypes			
	AA	Aa	aa	Total
Genotype frequencies at fertilization			1	
Relative fitnesses	1	1	0.9	
After selection				
Adjust so total is 1				
New frequency of A $= p_1 =$				
Change in frequency $\Delta p = p_1 - p_0 =$				

6.5 Selection: Derive the expression for the change in frequency as a result of selection against an additive deleterious allele, given that the initial frequency of the deleterious allele is q and the relative fitnesses are as shown in the table below.

	Genotypes			
	AA	Aa	aa	Total
Genotype frequencies at fertilization				1
Relative fitnesses	1	$1 - \frac{1}{2}s$	$1 - s$	
After selection				
Adjust so total is 1				
New frequency of A $= p_1 =$				
Change in frequency $\Delta p = p_1 - p_0 =$				

6.6 Impact of selection: Assume that we are dealing with an allele that was favoured in the wild, but is deleterious in captivity. By how much would the frequency of the allele change if its initial frequency was 0.9 and was selected against with a selection coefficient of 0.1, as

(a) additive, (b) recessive, (c) dominant and (d) partial recessive with $hs = 0.02$?

PRACTICAL EXERCISES: COMPUTER SIMULATIONS

Use a computer simulation program such as POPGEN to simulate the following:

1. Selection against chondrodystrophy (recessive lethal) in California condors.

The relative fitnesses of the three genotypes at this locus are

++	+dw	dwdw
1	1	0 [need to use 0.000001 in POPGEN]

Commence with a frequency of the dw allele of 0.17 and simulate 100 generations of selection against this condition. What do you observe?

2. Selection for industrial melanism in peppered moths (favoured dominant allele). Industrial melanism increased in frequency from an allele frequency of about 0.005 in 1848 to about 0.90 in 1900 (52 generations). By trial and error, find a value of s that is adequate to explain this evolutionary event (e.g. try a relative fitness for tt of 0.5, and subsequently try other values for W11). The selection model is

tt	Mt	MM
$1-s$	1	1

3. The impact of different selection coefficients on change in frequency of an advantageous additive allele. Compare the allele frequency trajectories with selection coefficients of 0.4, 0.1 and 0.01. Begin all cases with an initial frequency of 0.01. How long does each take to go to fixation? You will need to run the simulations for 1000 generations.

aa	Aa	AA
$1-s$	$1-\frac{1}{2}s$	1

What is the effect of different sized selection coefficients on the rate of allele frequency change?

4. Effect of dominance on allele frequency changes. Compare the allele frequency trajectories for advantageous dominant, additive and recessive alleles for loci with the following relative fitnesses. In each case begin with a frequency of 0.01 for the favoured allele and run for 2000 generations.

	aa	Aa	AA
Dominant	0.9	1	1
Additive	0.9	0.95	1
Recessive	0.9	0.9	1

How do they differ?

What difference does it make to the recessive case if it is partially recessive with a slight effect in the heterozygote (try a heterozygote fitness of 0.902)?

5. Evolution of resistance to a biocide in a pest species. Predation by European red foxes is a major factor threatening small mammals in Australia. Sodium fluoroacetate poison (1080) is widely used to control foxes. If a dominant allele for 1080 resistance exists with an initial frequency of 0.1%, how long will it take for it to rise in frequency to 50% in a region with continuous baiting with 1080 (and no migration)? Assume that the relative fitnesses of RR, RS and SS under baiting are 1, 1 and 0.5, respectively.

Chapter 7

Evolution in large populations. II. Mutation, migration and their interactions with selection

Terms:
Cline,
genetic load,
introgression,
mutation,
mutation load,
mutation–selection balance,
neutral mutation,
silent substitutions,
stable equilibrium,
transposon

Mutation and migration are the only means for regaining lost genetic diversity. The balance between mutation and selection results in a load of rare deleterious alleles in species that result in inbreeding depression

Mutation–selection balance: white mutant chinchilla in South America being taken by a great horned owl, while camouflaged agouti chinchillas survive.

Factors controlling the evolution of populations

An evolving population is a complex system influenced by mutation, migration, selection and chance, operating within the context of the breeding system. In Chapter 6 we dealt with selection and its role in adaptive evolution. In this chapter we consider mutation, and migration, and the joint actions of mutation with selection and migration with selection, again in the context of large populations. These are essentially deterministic forces; responses of large populations are predictable and different replicate populations subject to the same conditions will behave very similarly.

> Populations evolve through the action of mutation, migration, selection and chance

Importance of mutation, migration and their interactions with selection in conservation

Mutation and migration, and their interactions with selection have six important implications in conservation genetics:

- Regeneration of genetic diversity due to mutation. Genetic diversity, lost by chance and selection, regenerates through mutation. We deal with the rate at which this occurs.
- Recovery of genetic diversity by migration. When genetic diversity is lost in small threatened populations, it can be recovered by migration from other genetically distinct populations. This may occur through natural migration, or deliberate translocations. This is an extremely important tool in the genetic management of fragmented populations (Chapters 13 and 16).
- Migration often reverses inbreeding depression.
- The impact of gene flow (migration) from related species (introgression). Many rare species are being 'hybridized out of existence' by crossing with common related species (Chapter 16).
- Maintenance of genetic diversity. Mutation and migration are often important determinants in the maintenance of genetic diversity (Chapter 9).
- The load of deleterious alleles in populations. The balance between deleterious mutation and selection results in an ever-present but changing pool of rare deleterious mutations (**mutation load**) in populations. Inbreeding exposes these mutations (mostly recessive), resulting in reduced reproduction and survival (Chapters 11 and 12). This in turn increases extinction risk in threatened species.

Origin and regeneration of genetic diversity

Genetic diversity is the raw material required for adaptive evolutionary change. Most naturally outbreeding species and large populations carry a substantial store of genetic diversity. However, genetic diversity is lost by chance in small populations and as a result of directional selection. This leads to the questions:

- How is genetic diversity produced?
- How quickly can it be regenerated?

Mutation is the ultimate source of genetic diversity, while recombination can produce new combinations of alleles. If genetic diversity is lost, it can be regenerated by mutation, but this is a very slow process. Alternatively, genetic diversity can be restored by natural or artificial immigration between populations that differ in allelic content.

Mutation

Mutation is the ultimate source of all genetic diversity

A **mutation** is a sudden genetic change in an allele or chromosome. All genetic diversity originates from mutation. Mutations include all changes in DNA sequence at a locus, the order of loci along chromosomes and changes in chromosome number. Most of these arise spontaneously from errors in DNA replication, or other errors during meiosis.

In this chapter we concentrate on single locus mutations. They are generated by base substitutions, additions and deletions in the DNA, by gene duplications and by insertions and excisions of mobile segments of DNA (**transposons**). It has come as a surprise that half or more of spontaneous mutations in fruit flies (and probably all eukaryotes) are due to transposons that can best be viewed as DNA parasites (Finnegan 1989). Chromosomal mutations (duplications, deletions, inversions, translocations and polyploidy) are important in tracing speciation, and in hybrid infertility, so we shall defer consideration of them until Chapter 15.

The patterns of genetic diversity in populations are the result of a variety of forces that act to eliminate or increase and disperse these novel alleles and chromosome arrangements among individuals and populations. In conservation genetics we are concerned with:

- How rapidly do mutations add genetic diversity to populations?
- How do mutations affect the adaptive potential and reproductive fitness of populations?
- How important is the accumulation of deleterious alleles to fitness decline in small populations?

The most important mutations are those at loci affecting fitness traits, most notably lethal or deleterious mutations. Some mutations, such as the melanic allele in moths, actually increase fitness. However, many mutations that occur in non-coding regions of the genome and those that do not result in amino acid substitutions in proteins (**silent substitutions**) probably have little or no impact on fitness (**neutral mutations**). Neutral mutations are, however, important as molecular markers and clocks that provide valuable information on genetic differences among individuals, populations and species.

Mutations typically occur at a very low rate

The rate of mutation is critical to its role in evolution. For a range of loci in eukaryotic species, the typical spontaneous mutation rate of morphological mutations is one new mutation per locus per 100 000 gametes per generation (Table 7.1). Rates of reverse mutation (mutant to

Table 7.1 | Spontaneous mutation rates for different loci and characters in a variety of eukaryote species. Approximate mean rates are given as the frequency of new mutations per locus, per generation, except where specified otherwise

Type of mutation	Rate
Morphological mutations	
Mice, maize and fruit flies (normal → mutant)	$\sim 1 \times 10^{-5}$ / locus
Reverse mutation (mutant → normal)	0.3×10^{-5} / locus
Electrophoretic variants (mobility change)	0.1×10^{-5} / locus
Microsatellites	
Mammals	1×10^{-4} / locus
Fruit flies	0.7×10^{-5} / locus
DNA nucleotides	$10^{-8} - 10^{-9}$ / base
mtDNA nucleotides	
Mammals	$5-10 \times$ nuclear
Quantitative characters	
Fruit flies, mice, maize	$10^{-3} \times V_E$ / trait

Source: Houle *et al.* (1996); Hedrick (2000).

normal) are typically lower. Apart from microsatellites, mutation rates are similar in humans, mice, maize and fruit flies, and are assumed to be similar across all eukaryotes.

Mutation rates for different classes of loci differ. Rates for morphological mutations are higher than for electrophoretic variants, but microsatellite loci in mammals have higher rates. Mutation rates per nucleotide base are clearly lower as there are typically 1000 or more bases per gene locus. Mitochondrial DNA has a much higher mutation rate than nuclear loci, making it a valuable tool in studying short-term evolutionary processes (Chapter 19).

Loci affecting quantitative characters mutate in a similar manner to single loci, the cumulative rate being approximately 10^{-3} times the environmental variance per generation for a range of characters across a range of species (Table 7.1). This relatively high rate, compared to single loci, is due to the fact that a mutation at any of the many loci underlying the character can affect the trait. Quantitative trait loci appear to mutate by the same range of mechanisms known for qualitative gene loci (Frankham 1990b).

Spontaneous mutation rates are considered to be almost constant over time. However, mutation rates may be elevated under stressful conditions (Hoffmann & Parsons 1997). Further, mutation rates are increased by particular environmental agents, such as radiation and chemical mutagens, including mutagenic compounds found in some plants. As these factors are rarely experienced and stress has only a modest effect on mutation rate, they are unlikely to materially influence conclusions we reach about the evolutionary impact of mutation.

Deleterious mutations occur at many loci, so their cumulative rates per haploid genome are much higher than the rates given above for single loci. These cumulative rates are of major importance when we consider the total load of mutations in populations and the impact of inbreeding on them. For example, the total rate of recessive lethal mutation is about 0.01 per haploid genome per generation in fruit flies, nematodes and ferns (Drake *et al.* 1998). We can readily account for this in fruit flies as the product of the mutation rate per locus per generation (10^{-5}), times the number of loci that can produce lethal mutations (3600 out of 12 000; Miklos & Rubin 1996). As there are other deleterious mutations that are not lethal, the cumulative rate of deleterious mutation is considerably higher. This has been estimated to be 0.1–0.4 per haploid genome per generation in fruit flies, 0.1–0.8 in plants, 0.01 for rodents and 0.6–1.6 for humans, chimpanzees and gorillas (Drake *et al.* 1998; Eyre-Walker & Keightley 1999). Other estimates are, if anything, higher than these (Lynch *et al.* 1999). While there are uncertainties and controversies about these estimates, the overall rates of deleterious mutation per genome are relatively high.

Mutation is normally a recurrent process where mutations continue to arise over time. It is in fact a slow chemical reaction. We can model the impact of mutation on a population by considering a single locus with two alleles A_1 and A_2 at frequencies of p and q, with mutations only changing A_1 into A_2 at a rate of u per generation, as follows:

Mutation rate

$$A_1 \xrightarrow{\ u\ } A_2$$

Initial allele frequencies $\quad p_0 \qquad\qquad q_0$

The frequency of the A_1 allele in the next generation p_1 is the frequency of alleles that do not mutate, namely

$$p_1 = p_0 (1 - u) \tag{7.1}$$

Thus, the frequency of the A_1 allele declines.

The change in frequency of the A_1 allele (Δp) is the difference between the frequencies in the two generations

$$\Delta p = p_1 - p_0 = p_0(1 - u) - p_0$$
$$\Delta p = -up_0 \tag{7.2}$$

Consequently, the frequency of A_1 declines by an amount that depends on the mutation rate u and the starting frequency p_0. There is a corresponding increase in the frequency of A_2 ($\Delta q = +up_0$). Since the mutation rate is approximately 10^{-5} for morphological mutations, the maximum change in allele frequency is 10^{-5} when $p = 1$. This is very small and can be ignored in many circumstances.

When genetic diversity is lost from a species, it is only regenerated by mutation. The time taken to regenerate genetic diversity is a major issue in conservation genetics. As can be seen from Box 7.1, regeneration times are very long, typically taking thousands to millions of generations for single locus variation. Regeneration times depend on mutation rates, so they are shorter for quantitative characters and microsatellites (in mammals) and longer for allozymes and single locus morphological variation (Chapter 14).

This discussion assumes no selection. Selection favouring beneficial mutation (alleles increasing fitness) will shorten regeneration times, while selection against deleterious mutations will extend them. Most mutations are deleterious, so the estimates below are likely to be under-estimates.

Box 7.1 | Time to regenerate genetic diversity by mutation

Several endangered species have lost much of their genetic diversity, presumably as a consequence of small population size (Chapters 3, 8 and 10). For example, the cheetah is presumed to have lost its genetic diversity 10 000 years ago (O'Brien 1994). The northern elephant seal has no allozyme genetic diversity, probably as a result of a population size bottleneck due to hunting, while the related southern elephant seal has relatively normal levels of genetic diversity (Bonnell & Selander 1974).

The lost genetic diversity is only regenerated by mutation. How long does this take? We can address this question in a simple manner by asking how long it would take to regenerate a frequency of 0.5 for an allele that had been lost. From Equation 7.1, the change in allele frequency due to mutation is

$$p_1 = p_0(1-u)$$

This equation represents any single generation transition in frequency, so we can write

$$p_2 = p_1(1-u)$$

and by substituting for p_1 from above, we obtain

$$p_2 = p_0(1-u)^2$$

Consequently the expression for the frequency after t generations p_t is:

$$p_t = p_0(1-u)^t \sim p_0 e^{-ut}$$

By taking natural logarithms (ln) and rearranging, we obtain the following expression for the number of generations t for the frequency to change from p_0 to p_t as

$$t = \frac{\ln p_0 - \ln p_t}{u}$$

The conditions we specified translate into $p_0 = 1$ and $p_t = 0.5$. If we consider allozymes with a mutation rate of approximately $u = 10^{-6}$, then

$$t = [\ln 1 - \ln 0.5] / 10^{-6} = 693\,147 \text{ generations}$$

For microsatellites in mammals $u = 10^{-4}$, so the number of generations will be

$$t = [\ln 1 - \ln 0.5] / 10^{-4} = 6931 \text{ generations}$$

Clearly, genetic diversity is only regenerated very slowly by mutation. More detailed consideration of the regeneration of mutation suggests that $10^5 - 10^7$ generations are required to regenerate single locus morphological or allozyme diversity (Lande & Barrowclough 1987) and 10^4 generations to regenerate microsatellite genetic diversity in mammals.

The balance between forward and reverse mutations results in an equilibrium with both alleles present. Other stronger forces often overwhelm this

Mutation typically occurs in both directions. Since there are two opposing forces, this results in an equilibrium. If the mutation rates in the two directions are u and v, the equilibrium occurs when the mutations occurring in each direction are equal ($up = vq$), resulting in an equilibrium frequency:

$$A_1 \underset{v}{\overset{u}{\rightleftarrows}} A_2$$

$$\hat{q} = \frac{u}{(u+v)} \tag{7.3}$$

Thus, the equilibrium frequency for the A_2 allele depends only on u and v, the forward and reverse mutation rates. This is a **stable equilibrium** as the frequencies move back towards the equilibrium point, if perturbed.

To obtain an equilibrium frequency, we can insert numerical values of forward and reverse mutation rates (Example 7.1). It takes a very long time to reach this equilibrium, so we can only observe it in species with short generation times, e.g. bacteria. As the forces generating this equilibrium are very weak, it is easily overwhelmed by other stronger factors, such as natural selection.

Example 7.1 | Equilibrium frequency due to the balance between forward and reverse mutations

Typically reverse mutation rates for morphological mutations are lower than forward rates (Table 7.1), so we consider a case where $u = 10^{-5}$, and $v = 3 \times 10^{-6}$. Substituting these values into Equation 7.2, we obtain:

$$\hat{q} = \frac{u}{(u+v)} = \frac{10^{-5}}{10^{-5} + 3 \times 10^{-6}} = 10/13 = 0.77$$

Thus, the equilibrium frequency of the A_2 allele is 77%, and that of the normal A_1 allele $1 - 0.77 = 0.23$.

Selective value of mutations

The majority of newly arisen mutations are deleterious

New mutations are being continually added to populations, albeit at a slow rate. These consist of
• neutral mutations,
• deleterious mutations,
• favourable mutations, and
• mutations favoured in some circumstances, but not in others.

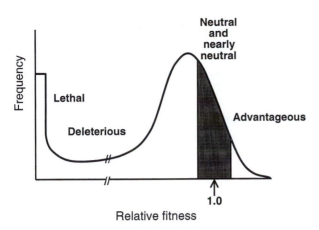

Fig. 7.1 Hypothetical distribution of effects of new mutations in functional loci on reproductive fitness. *Some mutations are lethal, most are deleterious, some are neutral, or near neutral (shaded region) and a small proportion is advantageous.*

Most mutations outside functional loci are expected to be neutral or nearly so. Mutations within functional loci will be predominantly dele-terious as random changes in the DNA sequence of a locus will usually be from a functional allele to an equal, or less-functional state. Some are lethal and a small proportion is advantageous, as shown in the hypo-thetical distribution in Fig. 7.1. For example, mean fitness declines if the mutation rate is increased using mutagenic agents such as γ-rays, chem-ical mutagens or transposons (Mackay 1989). Similarly, if initially homo-zygous populations are allowed to accumulate spontaneous mutations with minimal natural selection, the mean fitness declines with time (Garcia-Dorado *et al.* 1999; Hedrick 2000). Conversely, for quantitative characters that are not closely associated with fitness, such as bristle number in fruit flies, mutation increases the variance, but has little effect on the mean.

The distribution of effects of mutations is a critical issue in two con-servation contexts:
* maintenance of genetic diversity (Chapter 9)
* accumulation of newly arisen mildly deleterious mutations (Chapter 14).

There is limited evidence on the proportions of mutations that fall into the different categories. About 90% of spontaneous mutations in fruit flies are deleterious and only 10% fall in the neutral and near neutral category (Lande 1995a). The proportion of mutations that is favourable is presumed to be no more than 1%–2%.

Some mutations are deleterious in some conditions, but favourable in others (Kondrashov & Houle 1994). However, we are unaware of any estimates of the proportion of mutations falling into this class. It is very difficult to study mutations, especially those of very small effect as they require vast experiments to detect and their effects may be confounded with the impact of other factors.

Selection acts to reduce the frequencies of deleterious mutations. The next section considers the balance between mutation and selec-tion.

Mutation–selection balance and the mutation load

While selection is capable of removing deleterious alleles from populations, in reality the time taken is so long that new mutations usually occur before previous mutations have been eliminated, especially for recessive alleles. A balance (equilibrium) is reached between addition of deleterious alleles by mutation and their removal by selection (**mutation–selection balance**). Consequently, low frequencies of deleterious alleles are found in all naturally outbreeding populations (mutation load). This is illustrated for humans in Table 7.2. We refer to this as the **mutation load**. These mutations are extremely important in understanding the deleterious consequences of inbreeding (Chapters 11 and 12).

Several important points summarize mutation loads:

- Mutational loads are found in essentially all species, including several threatened species (Table 7.3)
- Deleterious alleles are normally found only at low frequencies, typically much less than 1% at any locus
- Deleterious alleles are found at many loci
- There are characteristic differences in frequencies of deleterious alleles according to the mode of inheritance (Table 7.2). For mutations that are equally deleterious, autosomal recessives have the highest frequencies and autosomal dominants the lowest, with sex-linked recessives intermediate. This arises from the differential effectiveness of selection on mutations with different modes of inheritance.

Table 7.2 | Frequencies of deleterious mutations in Caucasian humans, listed according to mode of inheritance

Disease	Frequency
Autosomal dominant	
Achondroplasia	5×10^{-5}
Retinoblastoma	5×10^{-5}
Huntington's chorea	5×10^{-4}
Autosomal recessive	
Albinism	3×10^{-3}
Xeroderma pigmentosum	2×10^{-3}
Phenylketonuria	7×10^{-3}
Cystic fibrosis	2.5×10^{-3}
Tay–Sachs syndrome	1×10^{-3}
Sex-linked recessive	
Haemophilia	1×10^{-4}
Duchenne's muscular dystrophy	2×10^{-4}

Source: Nei (1975).

Table 7.3 Deleterious mutations found segregating in threatened species or populations

Species	Deleterious mutation	Reference
Brown bear	blindness	1
California condor	chondrodystrophy	2
Golden lion tamarin	hernia, liver enzyme defect	3, 4
Gray wolf	blindness	5
Przewalski's horse	vitamin E maladsorption	3
Red-ruffed lemur	hairlessness, funnel chest	3

References: 1, Laikre *et al.* (1996); 2, Ralls *et al.* (2000); 3, Ryder (1988); 4, Schulman *et al.* (1993); 5, Laikre & Ryman (1991).

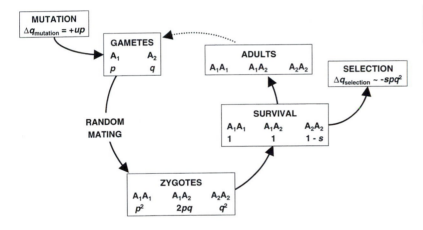

Fig. 7.2 Flow chart for mutation–selection balance.

To understand the different allele frequencies for genetic diseases with different modes of inheritance, we derive expressions for allele frequency equilibria due to mutation–selection balance using the flow chart in Fig. 7.2.

We will begin by deriving the expression for the equilibrium frequency for a deleterious recessive allele. The change in allele frequency is due to the combined impacts of mutation ($\Delta q_{mutation}$) and selection ($\Delta q_{selection}$), as follows:

$$\Delta q = \Delta q_{mutation} + \Delta q_{selection}$$

Deleterious alleles increase due to mutation (up) (Equation 7.2) and are removed by selection $-spq^2/(1 - sq^2)$ (Table 6.2c). Therefore

$$\Delta q = up - \frac{spq^2}{1 - sq^2} \sim up - spq^2$$

(the denominator is essentially 1 as sq^2 is a very small quantity for rare alleles).

> The mutation–selection equilibrium frequency for a given mode of inheritance depends only on the mutation rate and the selection coefficient

At equilibrium, $\Delta q = 0$, so

$$up \sim spq^2$$

and

$$q^2 \sim u/s$$

Thus, the equilibrium frequency $\hat{q}$ is:

$$\hat{q} \sim \sqrt{(u/s)} \qquad (7.4)$$

The equilibrium between mutation and selection depends only upon the mutation rate and the selection coefficient. This equilibrium results in low frequencies of deleterious alleles in random mating populations. The frequency will be highest for mildly deleterious alleles, and least for lethal alleles. For example, if the mutation rate is 10^{-5}, and the mutation is lethal ($s = 1$), the equilibrium frequency is $\sqrt{10^{-5}/1} = 3.2 \times 10^{-3}$, while if the selection coefficient is 0.1, the equilibrium frequency is 10^{-2}.

Equilibrium frequencies for autosomal and sex-linked loci with different degrees of dominance, derived using the same rationale as above, are shown in Table 7.4. While the equilibria differ depending upon degree of dominance and whether the locus is autosomal or sex-linked, all depend only on the mutation rate and the selection coefficient. Equilibrium frequencies are higher for recessive than dominant alleles, with additive alleles intermediate (for alleles with the same selection coefficients and mutation rates). Further, for recessives the equilibrium frequencies are higher for autosomal than for sex-linked loci due to the greater efficiency of selection against recessives in the hemizygous sex. Overall, the equilibrium frequencies accord with the observed patterns of frequencies of deleterious alleles in humans (Table 7.2).

Alleles are rarely completely recessive (Simmons & Crow 1983). This has a substantial effect on their equilibrium frequencies. For example, 'recessive' lethals in fruit flies generally reduce heterozygote fitness by 1%–3%. A 2% reduction in heterozygote survival results in an equilibrium frequency for a lethal of 5×10^{-4}, nearly an order of magnitude lower than that for a completely recessive lethal (Table 7.4).

Mutation–selection balance in polyploids

Mutation–selection equilibrium frequencies for recessives are higher in polyploids than in diploids, but similar for partial recessives

Many species of plants are polyploid (Chapter 4). We will consider mutation–selection equilibria in polyploids as a prelude to considering the impact of inbreeding in polyploids versus diploids (Chapters 11 and 12). In what follows, we will concentrate on tetraploids, as they are sufficient to illustrate the relevant principles.

Equilibrium frequencies for completely recessive alleles are typically higher in tetraploids than for equivalent diploid loci (Table 7.4). For example, a lethal with a mutation rate of 10^{-5} will have an equilibrium frequency of about 0.056 in a tetraploid and 3×10^{-3} in a diploid. There is more opportunity for deleterious recessives alleles to be hidden from

Table 7.4 | Mutation–selection equilibrium frequencies in diploids and tetraploids for alleles with different degrees of dominance. Examples of the expected equilibrium frequencies for lethal alleles ($s = 1$) with mutation rates (u) of 10^{-5} are shown, along with that for a partial recessive ($hs = 0.02$).

Mode of inheritance and dominance	Equilibrium frequency ($\hat{q}$)	Expected equilibrium frequency for lethal
Diploid		
Autosomal		
Recessive	$\sqrt{(u/s)}$	3.16×10^{-3}
Partial recessive	u/hs	5×10^{-4}
Dominant	u/s	10^{-5}
Additive	$2u/s$	2×10^{-5}
Sex-linked		
Recessive	$3u/s$	3×10^{-5}
Haploid	u/s	10^{-5}
Tetraploid		
Recessive		
allotetraploid	$(u/s)^{1/4}$	0.056
autotetraploid		
close to centromere	$(u/s)^{1/4}$	0.056
distant from centromere	$< (u/s)^{1/4}$	<0.056
Partial recessive		
allotetraploid	u/hs	5×10^{-4}

Source: Lande & Schemske (1985); (Falconer & Mackay (1996).

selection as ploidy rises, i.e. selection against deleterious alleles is most effective for haploid loci, followed by sex-linked, diploid and weakest for tetraploid loci. Equilibrium frequencies under mutation–selection balance rise correspondingly. By contrast, partial recessive mutations have similar equilibria in diploids and tetraploids. As most deleterious mutations appear to be partial recessives, the latter situation is more realistic.

Estimating mutation rates from mutation–selection balance

It is extremely difficult to detect recessive mutations in diploid species as the genotypes of heterozygotes and homozygous normals cannot be distinguished phenotypically. For example, haemophilia, the sex-linked bleeding disease, is frequent in the descendants of

Many estimates of mutation rates have been obtained from the balance between mutation and selection

Queen Victoria of the United Kingdom, but it is not possible to determine in which of her ancestors the mutation occurred, or if it occurred in her.

The equations for mutation–selection equilibrium can be used to obtain estimates of mutation rates in species where this cannot be done directly (most species). For example, the first estimate of a mutation rate in humans was obtained for the sex-linked haemophilia allele, based on estimates of the equilibrium frequency and on the selection coefficient derived from hospital records (Example 7.2). The estimate was approximately 3×10^{-5}, in line with estimates from fruit flies and plants, species where mutations rates had been estimated by more direct methods.

| **Example 7.2** | Estimating the mutation rate for haemophilia in humans from mutation–selection equilibrium (after Falconer & Mackay 1996) |

Haldane recognized that the equation for mutation–selection equilibrium could be rearranged to provide an estimate of the mutation rate. Taking the equation for mutation–selection equilibrium for a sex-linked recessive (Table 7.4) and rearranging, we obtain:

$$u = s\hat{q} / 3$$

Using hospital records in Denmark, Haldane estimated that the frequency of haemophilia in males (q) lay between 4×10^{-5} and 17×10^{-5}, so we shall use the mid-point of these values, 10.5×10^{-5}. The survival rate of haemophiliacs relative to normal males ($1 - s$) was 0.25. Thus, the selection coefficient is 0.75. Consequently, the estimate of mutation rate is

$$u = s\hat{q} / 3 = [0.75 \times 10.5 \times 10^{-5}] / 3 = 2.6 \times 10^{-5}$$

Thus, the first estimate of mutation rate in humans was approximately 3×10^{-5}.

Mutation–selection balance and fitness

Outbreeding populations contain a load of rare partially recessive alleles that reduce reproductive fitness when homozygous

Mutation–selection balance affects both single loci and quantitative characters such as reproductive fitness. The impact of these deleterious alleles on fitness can be measured experimentally by making chromosomes homozygous. In fruit flies most chromosomal homozygotes have reduced egg–adult survival (viability) (Fig. 7.3). Similar results have been obtained for autosomes in a range of fruit fly species. The effects on total reproductive fitness are even greater. The mean reproductive fitness of chromosomal homozygotes is reduced by 70%–90%

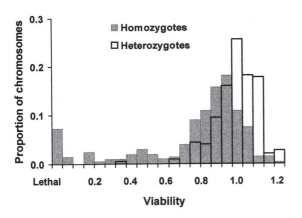

Fig. 7.3 Viabilities of second chromosome homozygotes and heterozygotes in fruit flies (after Hedrick 1983). Only 40% of the genome is being made homozygous in this experiment. *The average effect on fitness of making a chromosome homozygous is deleterious, with some homozygotes being lethal, a majority less deleterious, and a minority relatively normal.*

compared to that of chromosomal heterozygotes in a range of tests (Latter & Sved 1994). Almost all chromosomes sampled from outbreeding species carry alleles that are deleterious when homozygous. However, different samples of the same chromosome carry different complements of deleterious alleles, i.e. individually rare deleterious alleles are found at many separate loci. Inbreeding experiments also provide data on the impact of deleterious alleles on fitness (Chapter 12). These experiments lead to conclusions similar to those described above and extend them to a very wide range of species, including endangered species.

Migration

The gene pools of populations diverge over time as a result of chance and selection. Such differences are reduced by migration (Chapter 13). The impact of migration is illustrated by B blood group allele frequencies in human populations across Eurasia (Fig. 7.4). Prior to about AD 500, the B allele was essentially absent from Western Europe, but it existed in high frequencies in the east. However, between AD 500 and 1500, Mongols and Tartars invaded Europe. As was typical of such military invasions, they left a trail of rape and pillage, and they left some of their alleles behind. Note the gradual decrease in frequency of the B blood group allele from east to west (termed a **cline**).

The effect of migration on allele frequencies is modelled in Fig. 7.5. The change in allele frequency due to migration is

$$\Delta q = m\,(q_m - q_o) \tag{7.5}$$

Thus, the change in allele frequency depends on the proportion of alleles contributed by migrants (m), and on the difference in frequency between the immigrants (q_m) and the native (original) population (q_o).

The introduction of immigrants from one population into another reduces genetic differentiation among populations and may restore lost genetic diversity

The genetic impact of migration depends on the proportion of alleles contributed by migrants and on the difference in frequency between the native population and the immigrants

Fig. 7.4 B blood group allele frequencies across Eurasia, resulting from the Mongol and Tartar invasions between AD 500 and 1500. (© Oxford University Press 1976. Reprinted from *The Distribution of the Human Blood Groups and Other Polymorphisms*, Mourant, A.E., C. Kopé and Kazimiera Domaniewska-Sobczak (1976) 2nd edn, by permission of Oxford University Press.) Prior to this, the B blood group allele was presumed to be absent from Western Europeans as it still is in native Basques in Spain, and in other isolated populations.

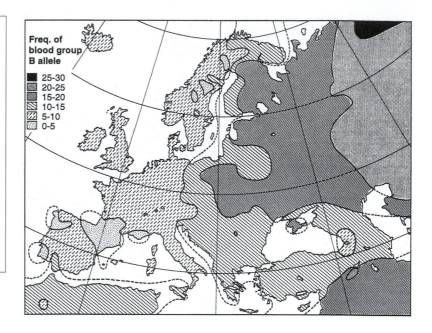

Fig. 7.5 Modelling the impact of migration on the genetic composition of a population.

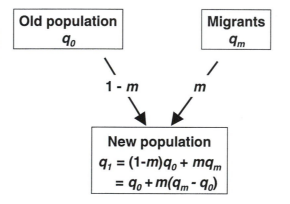

The change in frequency from the original population to the new population after immigration is

$$\Delta q = q_1 - q_0 = q_0 + m\,(q_m - q_0) - q_0 = m\,(q_m - q_0)$$

Thus, the change in frequency depends on the proportion of migrants and the difference in allele frequency between migrants and residents.

Migration may have very large effects on allele frequencies. For example, if immigrants are homozygous for an allele absent from the native population, and 20% of the population in the next generation are immigrants, then the immigrant allele increases in frequency from 0 to 0.2 in a single generation.

Equation 7.5 can be used to estimate the migration rate from allele frequency data. Many species are threatened by gene flow (**introgression**) from related non-endangered species (Chapter 16). The extent of admixture from domestic dog genes in the endangered Ethiopian wolf is determined in Example 7.3. Approximately 22% of the genetic material in the Web Valley population of Ethiopian wolves derives from domestic dogs.

Example 7.3 | Estimating dog introgression in the endangered Ethiopian wolf from microsatellite allele frequencies (data from Gottelli *et al.* 1994)

Ethiopian wolves are genetically distinct from domestic dogs, but hybridization occurs in areas where they co-occur, as in Web Valley, Ethiopia (Box 4.1). The population from the Sanetti Plateau is relatively pure. The extent of admixture from domestic dogs in the Web population of Ethiopian wolves can be estimated using the allele frequencies at microsatellite locus 344. Dogs lack the J allele, while 'pure' Ethiopian wolves are homozygous for it. Frequencies of this allele are:

		J allele frequency
Sanetti population	q_o	1.00 ('old')
Web population	q_1	0.78 ('new' – containing dog admixture)
Domestic dogs	q_m	0.00 ('migrants')

All the non-J alleles in the Web population have come from dogs. The equation from Fig. 7.5 can be rearranged to provide an expression for the migration rate m

$$q_1 = q_o + m(q_m - q_o)$$

$$m = \frac{q_1 - q_0}{q_m - q_0}$$

Upon substituting allele frequencies from above into this expression, we obtain

$$m = \frac{0.78 - 1.0}{0 - 1.0} = 0.22$$

Thus, the Web Valley population of Ethiopian wolves contains about 22% of its genetic composition from domestic dogs. This is the accumulated contribution of alleles from dogs, not a per generation estimate. Phenotypically abnormal individuals, suspected of being hybrid individuals, represent about 17% of the population. Estimates can also be made from other microsatellite loci and the best estimate would come from combining information from all informative loci.

Migration–selection equilibria and clines

Clines can also form when there is a balance between selection for different alleles in different habitats (local adaptation) and there is migration (gene flow) across habitats. For example, there is such a cline in heavy metal tolerance in colonial bent grass plants passing from polluted mine

Migration among populations subject to differential selection may lead to gradation in allele frequencies (clines)

wastes to nearby unpolluted pasture in Wales (Box 7.2). Selection favours heavy-metal-tolerant plants on the mine waste, but acts against them in the unpolluted surrounding pasture. Pollen flow (migration) moves alleles among the populations, such that there is a gradation in frequency of heavy-metal-tolerant plants across the transition zone between the two habitats. Heavy metal tolerance declines with distance in the downwind directions, as less pollen reaches more distant pasture.

Clines are common for morphological and quantitative characters. In fact, they are so common that they are accorded the status of ecogeographic rules (Futuyma 1998). Bergmann's rule states that races from cooler climates are larger than races from warmer climates. Allen's rule states that in warm-blooded animals, protruding parts (e.g. ears, tail) are shorter in races from colder climates than in races from warmer climates. Gloger's rule states that races of warm-blooded vertebrates are more darkly pigmented in warm and humid areas than in cool and dark areas.

While these rules refer to phenotypes, they typically reflect both environmental and genetic differences. Fruit flies in Europe show a latitudinal cline in wing length. This is due, at least partially, to genetic differences, as it is still found when flies from different regions are raised under the same laboratory conditions. This cline is due to natural selection as it evolved again, within 20 years, when this species of fruit fly was introduced into North America (Huey *et al.* 2000). Clines seem to be more frequent in quantitative characters than for allozymes or DNA markers (see Hedrick & Savolainen 1996).

Box 7.2 | Cline in heavy metal tolerance in colonial bent grass due to migration–selection equilibrium (Bradshaw & McNeilly 1981)

Genetically determined heavy metal tolerance is high on the polluted slagheaps from old mines in Wales, but low in the surrounding pastures that are relatively unpolluted by heavy metals. Pollen flows predominantly from plants on mine wastes in the direction of the prevailing wind. This creates a gradient of heavy metal tolerance that declines with distance from the mine. Selection favours heavy metal tolerance on the mine wastes, and acts against tolerant plants on the normal pasture. Heavy metal tol-

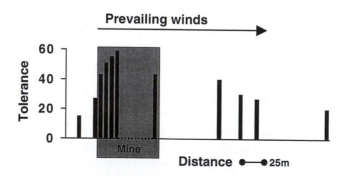

erance has evolved in several different species of grasses (including colonial bent grass, *Anthoxanthum odoratum* and *Festuca ovina*), allowing them to colonize polluted mine tailings (Jones & Wilkins 1971; Briggs & Walters 1997). However, only species with pre-existing genetic variation for heavy metal tolerance succeeded in colonizing mine wastes. Those species without the prerequisite genetic variation failed to colonize.

Clines are expected to be steep (i.e. large changes over short distances) when dispersal rates are low and more gradual when dispersal rates are high. For example, clines in the frequency of industrial melanic versus typical moths from highly polluted to essentially unpolluted regions of Britain are steeper for the weakly dispersing scalloped hazel moth than for the more strongly dispersing peppered moth (Bishop & Cook 1975). Species that disperse readily over long distances show less local differentiation and fewer clines than species with lesser dispersal ability (Chapter 13). Plants show considerable local adaptations to soil and climate (as they cannot escape them), and probably develop clines more frequently than animals.

> The shape of clines is related to dispersal ability of species

Simple models can be constructed to provide expressions for the equilibrium between migration and selection (Fig. 7.6). The equilibrium frequency is derived for this simple case. This equilibrium depends only upon the migration rate (m), the selection coefficient (s) and the allele frequency in the migrants (q_m), i.e. it does not depend on the allele frequency in the initial population. When migration rates are high and selection is weak, migration dominates the process and essentially erases local adaptation ('swamping'). Conversely, when migration rates are low and selection is strong, there will be local adaptation. This is consistent with the effects of dispersal rates on the steepness of clines, as described above. Example 7.4 illustrates the equilibrium achieved for given values of the selection coefficient, migration rate and frequency in the immigrants.

> The migration–selection equilibrium frequency depends on the intensity of selection, the proportion of immigrants and the allele frequency in the immigrants

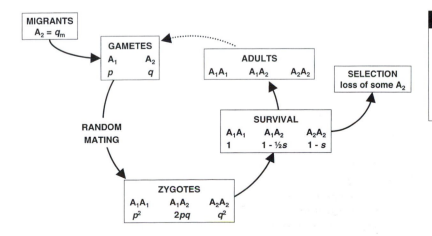

Fig. 7.6 Model of the balance between migration and selection. A large random mating population is subject to additive viability selection that is being balanced by migration from a population with a different allele frequency.

$$\Delta q_{\text{selection}} = \frac{-\frac{1}{2} sq(1-q)}{1-sq} \sim \frac{1}{2} sq^2 - \frac{1}{2} sq \qquad \Delta q_{\text{migration}} = m\,(q_m - q)$$

Overall $\Delta q = \Delta q_{\text{selection}} + \Delta q_{\text{migration}}$

$$= \frac{1}{2} sq^2 - \frac{1}{2} sq + m\,(q_m - q) = \frac{1}{2} sq^2 - q\,(m + \frac{1}{2} s) + m\,q_m$$

(the denominator ~ 1, assuming sq is small).

At equilibrium $\Delta q = 0$, so the equilibrium frequencies are obtained as the solutions of the quadratic equation, yielding (Li 1976):

$$\hat{q} = \frac{(2m + s) \pm \sqrt{\{(2m + s)^2 - 8s\,m\,q_m\}}}{2s}$$

While there are two solutions to the equation, only one of them will be possible (frequency between 0 and 1).

Example 7.4 | Migration–selection equilibrium

If $s = 0.2$, $m = 0.1$ and $q_m = 0.1$, we obtain the equilibrium frequency by substituting into the expression for allele frequency equilibrium due to the opposing forces of selection and migration for an additive locus given above:

$$\hat{q} = \frac{(2m + s) \pm \sqrt{\{(2m + s)^2 - 8s\,m\,q_m\}}}{2s}$$

$$\hat{q} = \frac{(2 \times 0.1 + 0.2) \pm \sqrt{[(2 \times 0.1 + 0.2)^2 - 8 \times 0.1 \times 0.2 \times 0.1]}}{2 \times 0.2}$$

$$= (0.4 \pm \sqrt{[0.16 - 0.016]}) / 0.4$$

$$= 0.0513 \text{ (or 1.95, an impossible solution)}$$

Thus, the equilibrium frequency is 5.1% due to the balance between migration and selection.

Clines may reflect changes in selection across environmental gradients, such as temperature, altitude, etc. They may also occur as the result of short-term historical migration events (Fig. 7.4).

Clines due to migration–selection balance will be disrupted in threatened species if habitat fragmentation eliminates allele flow. This will alter the balance between local adaptation and 'swamping' in the direction of local adaptation.

Migration–selection balance can arise between wild and captive populations of endangered species when there is regular movement of wild individuals into captivity, or vice versa. For example, the wild population of nene (Hawaiian goose) is regularly augmented by captive-bred individuals, as are many fish species. Selective forces are typically different in wild and captive environments. Captive populations adapt to their captive environment and are likely to have reduced reproductive fitness when returned to their natural habitat (Chapter 17).

Summary

1. Mutation is the ultimate source of all genetic diversity.

2. Mutation and migration are the only means for regaining genetic diversity lost through chance or selection.

3. Mutations occur at a very low rate, so mutation is a weak evolutionary force over the short term.

4. All naturally outbreeding populations contain a load of deleterious mutations due to mutation–selection balance. When populations are inbred, these mutations cause reduced reproductive fitness (inbreeding depression).

5. Migration breaks down genetic differentiation caused by natural selection and chance.

6. Migration from an introduced species may compromise the genetic integrity of an endangered species.

7. Migration and selection may result in a balance, or a cline.

FURTHER READING

Crow & Kimura (1970) *Introduction to Population Genetics Theory.* Relatively advanced treatment of topics in this chapter.

Falconer & Mackay (1996) *Introduction to Quantitative Genetics.* Provides a very clear treatment of the topics in this chapter.

Futuyma (1998) *Evolutionary Biology.* Contains a broad readable coverage of evolutionary genetics.

Hartl & Clarke (1997) *Principles of Population Genetics.* This widely used textbook covers many of the topics in this chapter.

PROBLEMS

7.1 Mutation: By how much will the frequency of a microsatellite allele in cheetahs change due to mutation in one generation, if the allele has a current frequency of 0.1 and the mutation rate from other alleles to this allele is 10^{-4}?

7.2 Forward and reverse mutation: What is the equilibrium frequency due to forward and reverse mutation at a locus where the mutation rates are 10^{-5} and 10^{-6}, respectively?

7.3 Regeneration of genetic diversity by mutation: Northern elephant seals lost all of their allozyme variation as a result of a population size bottleneck caused by over-exploitation. How many generations would it take for an allele that had been lost to reach a frequency of 0.4 due to mutation alone, assuming a mutation rate of 4×10^{-6}?

7.4 Mutation–selection equilibrium: What equilibrium frequency would you expect for the recessive lethal chondrodystrophy in California condors as a result of mutation–selection balance, if the mutation rate was 2×10^{-5}?

7.5 Mutation–selection equilibrium: What mutation rate would be needed to explain the current frequency of chondrodystrophy among captive hatchlings of about 17%? Is this a realistic mutation rate? Why do you think the frequency of the lethal allele is so high?

7.6 Mutation–selection equilibrium: Derive the equilibrium frequency for an additive autosomal locus as a result of mutation–selection equilibrium. Use the expressions from Equation 7.2 and Table 6.2 to obtain an expression for the overall change in allele frequency (remember to insert Δq, not Δp).

$$\Delta q = \Delta q_{mutation} + \Delta q_{selection} =$$

(hint: it is reasonable to assume that the denominator of the selection term is approximately unity for a rare allele)

At equilibrium $\Delta q =$

$\therefore$

7.7 Mutation–selection equilibrium: Estimate the mutation rate for a dominant autosomal dwarfism in humans using the appropriate mutation selection equilibrium equation. The phenotypic frequency of affected babies at birth is 10/94 000, and their relative fitness is approximately 20% (after Strickberger 1985).

7.8 Mutation–selection equilibrium: Compute the equilibrium frequencies for loci that are autosomal recessive, additive autosomal, autosomal dominant, sex-linked recessive and haploid, given that the selection coefficient is 0.10 and the mutation rate 10^{-5} per locus per generation. What are the impacts of ploidy (haploid vs. diploid) and dominance on the equilibrium frequencies?

7.9 Migration: Use the migration equation to estimate the extent of racial admixture in US African Americans in Georgia from Fy^a allele frequencies at the Duffy blood group locus (data from Strickberger 1985):

	Fy^a frequency
Africans	0.000
US Caucasians	0.422
US African Americans	0.045

Chapter 8

Evolution in small populations

Populations of conservation concern are small, or declining. Mutation, migration, selection and chance determine evolution in both small and large populations. However, chance has a much greater impact and selection is less effective in small populations than in large populations

Terms:
Binomial distribution,
bottleneck,
effective population size,
evolutionary potential,
fixation,
idealized population,
inbreeding,
Poisson distribution,
random genetic drift,
stochastic

Mauritius kestrel: a species that survived a population size bottleneck of a single pair.

Importance of small populations in conservation biology

Species of conservation concern have, by definition, small or declining population sizes

Small or declining populations of threatened and endangered species are more prone to extinction than large stable populations. Population size is the most influential of the five criteria for listing species as endangered under the IUCN system (J. O'Grady *et al.*, unpublished data). Species whose adult population sizes are less than 50, 250 or 1000 are respectively critically endangered, endangered and vulnerable (Chapter 1). For example, there are only ~75 (adults plus juveniles) critically endangered northern hairy-nosed wombats surviving in Australia, while the Mauna Kea silversword in Hawaii declined to about two dozen plants. Some species have reached such low numbers that they exist, or have existed, only in captivity. These include Arabian oryx, black-footed ferret, European bison, Père David's deer, Przewalski's horse, scimitar-horned oryx, California condor, Socorro dove, Guam rail, four species of fish, eleven species of *Partula* snail, Cooke's kok'io plant, Franklin tree, and Malheur wirelettuce (WCMC 1992; Falk *et al.* 1996).

Over-exploitation has reduced population sizes in many species that were previously present in large numbers. American plains bison once numbered about 30–40 million on the prairies but were reduced to about 500 (Ehrlich & Ehrlich 1981), while European bison were reduced to 13 from, presumably, millions. Elephants, rhinoceroses and many fish have similarly experienced major reductions through over-exploitation. Harvesting has depleted many tree species, cacti and American ginseng. The numbers of many frog species have recently crashed, perhaps due to a fungal disease (Daszak *et al.* 2000). Numerous species with once large population sizes and continuous distributions have been fragmented by habitat clearance causing reductions in overall numbers, and separation into small, partially isolated populations.

Some species have experienced population size reductions (**bottlenecks**), but have since recovered. The Mauritius kestrel was reduced to a single pair but has now recovered to 400–500 birds (Box 8.1). Northern elephant seals dropped from many thousands to 20–30 but now number over 100 000 (Box 8.2), while the Lord Howe Island woodhen declined to 20–30 individuals but has since built up to about 200 birds. These populations pay a genetic cost for their bottlenecks; they have reduced genetic diversity, higher levels of inbreeding, lower reproductive fitness and compromised ability to evolve (Box 8.1).

Box 8.1	A population size bottleneck in the Mauritius kestrel and its genetic consequences (after Groombridge et al. 2000)

The decline of the Mauritius kestrel began with the destruction of native forest and the plunge towards extinction resulted from thinning of eggshells and greatly reduced hatchability following use of DDT insecticide beginning in the 1940s. In 1974, its population numbered only four individuals, with the subsequent population descending from only a single breeding pair. Under intensive management the population grew to 400–500 birds by 1997, but it experienced six generations at numbers of less than 50.

While this is a success story, the Mauritius kestrel carries genetic scars from its near extinction. It now has a very low level of genetic diversity for 12 microsatellite loci, compared to six other kestrel populations (see below). The Mauritius kestrel has 72% lower allelic diversity and 85% lower heterozygosity than the mean of the non-endangered kestrels. Prior to its decline, the Mauritius kestrel had substantial genetic diversity, based on ancestral museum skins from 1829–94, but even then its genetic diversity was lower than the non-endangered species. The Seychelles kestrel went through a parallel decline and recovery and also has low genetic diversity. It was rare during the 1960s and had become extinct on many outlying islands. However, it has now recovered to a population size of over 400 pairs.

Species	A	H_e	Sample size
Endangered			
Mauritius kestrel			
Restored	1.41	0.10	350
Ancestral	3.10	0.23	26
Seychelles kestrel	1.25	0.12	8
Non-endangered			
European kestrel	5.50	0.68	10
Canary Island kestrel	4.41	0.64	8
South African rock kestrel	5.00	0.63	10
Greater kestrel	4.50	0.59	10
Lesser kestrel	5.41	0.70	8

The reproductive fitness of the Mauritius kestrel has been adversely affected by inbreeding in the early post-bottleneck population; it has lowered fertility and productivity than comparable falcons and higher adult mortality in captivity.

Small population size is a pervasive concern in conservation biology. Not only do such populations suffer the genetic constraints described above and have an increased probability of extinction, but also the evolutionary process in small populations is fundamentally different from that in large populations. Consequently, it is critical that we consider the special evolutionary problems confronted by small populations.

Mutation, selection and migration have essentially deterministic effects in large populations. Replicate populations and replicate loci subject to them behave in the same way. The effects of chance are generally minimal, except for neutral alleles. Conversely, in small populations, the role of chance predominates and the effects of selection are typically reduced or even eliminated. Chance introduces a random, or **stochastic**, element into the evolution of populations, i.e. replicate loci and populations exhibit a diversity of outcomes. Small populations also become inbred at a faster rate than do large populations, as inbreeding is unavoidable.

Mutation, migration, selection and chance are responsible for evolution in both small and large populations. However, the role of chance is much greater and the impact of selection less, in small than large populations

We begin by considering the effects of chance alone. Following that we will, in turn, consider inbreeding, selection, mutation and mutation–selection equilibrium in small populations. The role of migration in small populations is deferred to Chapter 13 where we consider population fragmentation.

Impact of small population size: chance effects

Chance effects arise from random sampling of gametes in small populations

When a small population reproduces, the subsequent generation is derived from a sample of parental gametes. Each offspring receives one allele, selected at random, from each parent. Just by chance, some alleles, especially rare ones, may not be passed on to the offspring and may be lost. The frequencies of alleles that are transmitted to the following generation are likely to differ from those in the parents (Fig. 8.1). Over multiple generations allele frequencies change, or drift, from one generation to the next, a process termed random **genetic drift**.

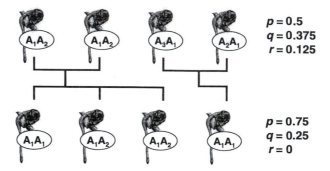

Fig. 8.1 Genetic drift in allele frequencies in a small population of golden lion tamarins. *Allele A_3 is lost by chance. Further, the frequencies of A_1 and A_2 change from one generation to the next, with A_1 rising and A_2 falling.*

$p = 0.5$
$q = 0.375$
$r = 0.125$

$p = 0.75$
$q = 0.25$
$r = 0$

Genetic drift

Genetic drift has major impacts on the evolution of small populations

It may seem that chance effects would have minor impacts on the genetic composition of populations. However, random sampling of gametes within small populations has three consequences of major importance in evolution and conservation:
- Random changes in allele frequencies from one generation to the next
- Loss of genetic diversity and fixation of alleles within populations
- Diversification among replicate populations from the same original source (e.g. fragmented populations).

The effects of chance are greater in small than in larger populations

The above three features are illustrated in the flour beetle populations (Fig. 8.2). First, individual populations show random fluctuations in allele frequencies from generation to generation. For example, in the $N = 10$ population marked with an asterisk in the upper panel the wild-type allele begins at a frequency of 0.5, drops in frequency for three generations, and goes through regular rises and falls until generation 20 when its frequency is approximately 0.65. Note that the fluctuations in frequencies for populations of size 10 are much greater than for

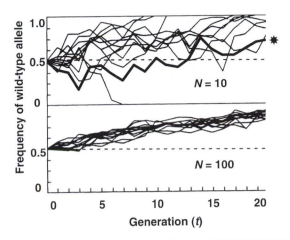

Fig. 8.2 Random genetic drift of the wild-type and black alleles at a body colour locus in the red flour beetle. Two population sizes $N = 10$ and $N = 100$ were used, with 12 replicates of each. All populations began with frequencies of 0.5 for the two alleles and were maintained by random sampling of either 10 or 100 individuals to be parents of each succeeding generation (after Falconer & Mackay 1996). *Large variation in allele frequencies occurred in the small ($N = 10$) populations due to random genetic drift both among replicates and from generation to generation in individual replicates. Conversely, allele frequencies in the large populations showed greater consistency. Selection favoured the wild-type allele over the black mutation.*

populations with $N = 100$, clearly illustrating that genetic drift is greater in smaller populations.

Second, there is random diversification among replicate populations, particularly in the $N = 10$ populations. These populations all began with allele frequencies of 0.5, yet end up with frequencies ranging from 0 to 1. Again, the diversification among replicate populations is much less for the $N = 100$ populations.

Third, some populations lose genetic diversity and become fixed. Seven of the 12 $N = 10$ populations became fixed over 20 generations. Six of the seven populations became fixed for the wild-type allele (all $+/+$) and one for the black allele (all b/b). On average, we expect equal numbers of each type to be fixed if the alleles are not subject to selection, given that the two alleles were equally frequent initially. None of the large populations became fixed over the 20 generations.

Modelling drift in allele frequencies

The characteristics of chance effects can be understood by modelling the sampling process in the absence of selection, mutation and migration (Fig. 8.3). Let us first consider sampling alleles for an offspring from a selfing individual with genotype A_1A_2. This is akin to tossing two coins. The possible outcomes are two heads, two tails, a head and a tail, or a tail and a head, all with probabilities of ¼. The chance that only heads (or only tails) are obtained as $(½)^2 = ¼$. Thus, if only one offspring is produced,

Genetic drift can be predicted using binomial sampling theory

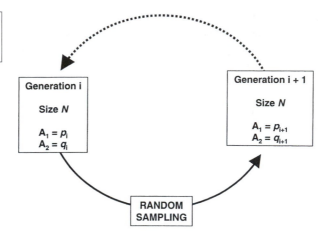

Fig. 8.3 Simple model of a small population with no mutation, migration or selection.

there is a 50% chance that one or the other allele will not be passed on. With N offspring, there are $2N$ coins tossed and the chance that all are heads (or tails) is now $(\frac{1}{2})^{2N}$. Consequently, it is much less likely that A_1 or A_2 will be lost if N is large. Further, the allele frequencies in the offspring will be more similar to that of the parent in larger populations. Just as in statistical theory, a larger (genetic) sample size always provides a better estimate (of parental allele frequencies) than a smaller one.

This simple case shows that basic probability theory can be used to calculate changes in allele frequency from one generation to the next due to random sampling of alleles. In the following discussion, we assume that populations breed randomly, which is equivalent to stating that the alleles in the offspring are a random sample of the parental gene pool.

When a population of size N reproduces, $2N$ gametes are sampled to produce subsequent generations (Fig. 8.3). We can predict the outcome of sampling of gametes using **binomial sampling** theory with replicate populations. Replicate populations are needed because the sampling process is stochastic and we cannot predict the outcome of any one sample. Hence, by considering what would happen if we applied the same sampling process to replicate populations, we can evaluate the full range of possible outcomes. The concept of using replicate populations and loci to estimate the range of possible outcomes from stochastic factors in experimental and theoretical situations is frequently used in conservation genetics.

> The extent of variation in allele frequencies among replicate populations or loci depends on the allele frequencies and on the population size.

If the population being sampled has two alleles A_1 and A_2 at initial frequencies of p_0 and q_0, respectively (and there are no other forces), the mean frequency of the A_1 allele in the next generation (p_1) over a large number of replicate populations is unchanged

$$p_1 = p_0$$

However, there will be random variation among replicate populations in their allele frequencies. In the simple case where $N = 2$ (Example 8.1), the expected distribution of allele frequencies in replicate populations are given by terms of the binomial expansion of $(p+q)^4$. There are five possible outcomes, the first and the last outcomes are homozygous (fixed). Consequently, the average heterozygosity across all replicate populations is reduced (see below). However, the mean allele frequency is unchanged from that in the source population.

Example 8.1 | Expected distribution of allele frequencies in populations of size $N = 2$

If we take many samples of 2 individuals ($= 4$ gametes) from the same population where alleles A_1 and A_2 have frequencies of p and q, respectively, the expected distribution of allele frequencies is given by the terms of the binomial expansion $(p+q)^4$. The power of 4 is the number of gametes sampled, twice the number of individuals sampled. The terms of this expansion are given below, along with the frequencies for the case where $p = 0.6$ and $q = 0.4$.

Outcome	p	frequency (f)	Example $(p = 0.6, q = 0.4)$	
$4\,A_1, 0\,A_2$	1.00	p^4	0.6^4	$= 0.1296$
$3\,A_1, 1\,A_2$	0.75	$4p^3q$	$4 \times 0.6^3 \times 0.4$	$= 0.3456$
$2\,A_1, 2\,A_2$	0.50	$6p^2q^2$	$6 \times 0.6^2 \times 0.4^2$	$= 0.3456$
$1\,A_1, 3\,A_2$	0.25	$4pq^3$	$4 \times 0.6 \times 0.4^3$	$= 0.1536$
$0\,A_1, 4\,A_2$	0.00	q^4	0.4^4	$= 0.0256$
Totals		1		1.0000

Thus, we expect five outcomes with frequencies of A_1 of 1, 0.75, 0.5, 0.25 and 0. For the example with initial base population frequencies of $p = 0.6$ and $q = 0.4$, the proportions of each outcome are expected to be 12.96%, 34.56%, 34.56%, 15.36% and 2.56%, respectively.

The mean frequency is

$$\text{Mean } p = \Sigma p_i f_i$$
$$= (1 \times 0.1296) + (0.75 \times 0.3456) + (0.5 \times 0.3456) + (0.25 \times 0.1536) + 0$$
$$= 0.6$$

Thus, the mean frequency is unchanged.

For a population with size N, the expected distribution of outcomes for a locus with two alleles is given by the terms of the binomial expansion $(p+q)^{2N}$ (akin to the tossing of a biased coin). The probability that a population has all A_1 alleles is p^{2N}, while the probability that it has all A_2 alleles is q^{2N}. These two situations correspond to populations that have lost all their genetic diversity. The probability that a population has $r\,A_1$ alleles and $2N - r\,A_2$ alleles is

$$\binom{2N}{r} p^r q^{2N-r}$$

where $\binom{2N}{r}$ is the binomial function $2N! / [r!\,(2N-r)!]$.

The expected distributions of allele frequencies over many replicate

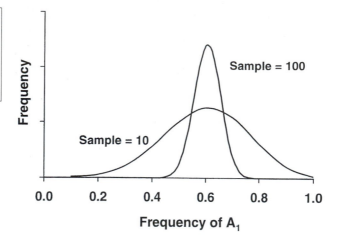

Fig. 8.4 Expected distribution of allele frequencies when many replicate samples of sizes 10 and 100 are taken from a population with an allele frequency for A_1 of 0.6.

populations of sizes 10 and 100 are shown in Fig. 8.4. Among replicate populations (or loci), the variance around the mean allele frequency is given by the binomial sampling variation:

$$\sigma_p^2 = \frac{p_0 q_0}{2N} \qquad (8.1)$$

Consequently, the variance in allele frequency depends on the allele frequencies and the population size. Variance is higher in small than large populations. Further, the variance is greatest when the two alleles have frequencies of 0.5, and less when allele frequencies are unequal. When there are two alleles, $\sigma_p^2 = \sigma_q^2$.

Sampling occurs in every generation in small populations, and the effects are cumulative. This can be seen in Fig. 8.2, where the replicate populations of size 10 diverge more with passing generations. The cumulative effects of genetic drift with time are extremely important in conservation genetics. However, the theory is more complex, and is deferred until Chapters 10, 11 and 13.

Fixation

The probability of losing an allele in a single generation is higher in a small than in a large population and greater for rare than for common alleles

Genetic drift will ultimately cause all except one allele to be lost. The surviving allele is fixed. In each generation there is a probability that each allele will become fixed, or lost. The probability of losing an allele is dependent on its frequency and on the population size. In the two allele case, the probability of losing one allele is the probability of fixing the other allele.

The probability that a gamete does not contain allele A_1 is $(1-p)$. Consequently, the probability that a random mating population loses allele A_1 (all individuals in the population become $A_2 A_2$) in a single generation is the probability that a gamete does not contain allele A_1 raised to the power of the number of gametes sampled, namely

$$\Pr(\text{losing } A_1) = (1 - p)^{2N}$$

Similarly, the chance of losing allele A_2 (all individuals becoming A_1A_1), is $(1 - q)^{2N}$. For example, for a population of size 4, with alleles A_1 and A_2 at initial frequencies of 0.25 and 0.75, respectively, the chance of losing A_1 in one generation of sampling is $(1 - 0.25)^8 = 0.100$. The probability of losing A_2 is $(1 - 0.75)^8 = 1.53 \times 10^{-5}$. Note that the rarer allele has a far greater probability of being lost. For a population of size 100, the chance of losing alleles with these frequencies in one generation is essentially zero. Thus, the probability of losing an allele is dependent on the population size.

Effects of population bottlenecks

Genetic diversity is typically lost as a consequence of short periods at small sizes (bottlenecks), or continued small population sizes. The northern elephant seal suffered a bottleneck due to over-hunting and has no allozyme genetic diversity (Box 8.2) and many endangered species have been bottlenecked (Table 8.1). Bottlenecks often occur during the founding of island populations. Founders may be as few as a single pair (inseminated female) of animals, or a single plant propagule capable of self-fertilizing or asexual reproduction. For example, the Isle Royale gray wolves were founded in about 1950 by a single pair that reached the island in Lake Superior, during an extremely cold winter, by crossing an ice bridge from the mainland (Wayne *et al.* 1991).

Genetic diversity is reduced by population size reductions

Box 8.2	Population bottleneck in the northern elephant seal

Northern elephant seals were hunted for their fur and oil, and suffered such a severe decline that they were thought to be extinct. Fortunately, a small population of about 20–30 survived on Isla Guadalupe in the Pacific. This species has large harems, so it may have been reduced to only a single harem. (Illustration from Austin & Short 1984.)

In their classic study, Bonnell & Selander (1974) showed that this bottlenecked population had no genetic diversity at 20 allozyme loci, while the related southern elephant seal had normal levels of genetic diversity. Subsequently, Hoelzel *et al.* (1993) found that the northern elephant seal had only two mtDNA variants compared to 23 in southern elephant seals.

Following protection from hunting, the northern elephant seal has recovered to numbers of over 100 000 and it has been removed from the endangered species list. This demonstrates that a population size bottleneck does not necessarily doom a species to immediate extinction. However, the loss of genetic diversity is likely to make it more prone to extinction from new diseases or other environmental changes. Further, the population will be partially inbred (Chapter 11), and is likely to have reduced reproductive fitness as a consequence (Chapter 12). An important feature of such bottleneck events is the large chance element in the outcome. Some situations will be relatively harmless if few deleterious mutations are, by chance, present in the remaining population. In other cases, populations are not so lucky; deleterious mutations are fixed and they decline to extinction.

Table 8.1 | Bottlenecks in endangered species (numbers of founders breeding in captivity)

Species	Bottleneck size	Reference
Mammals		
Arabian oryx	10	1
Black-footed ferret	10	2
European bison	13	3
Indian rhinoceros	17	3
Père David's deer	~5	4
Przewalski's horse	12 (+ 1 domestic mare)	5
Red-ruffed lemur	7	5
Siberian tiger	25	3
Birds		
California condor	14 (3 clans)	6
Chatham Island black robin	5	7
Guam rail	12	8
Mauritius kestrel	2	9
Mauritius pink pigeon	6	10
Nene (Hawaiian goose)	17	11
Puerto Rican parrot	13	12
Whooping crane	14	13

References: 1, Marshall *et al.* (1999); 2, Russell *et al.* (1994); 3, Hedrick (1992); 4, Ballou (1989); 5, Hedrick & Miller (1992); 6, Geyer *et al.* (1993); 7, Ardern & Lambert (1997); 8, Haig *et al.* (1994); 9, Groombridge *et al.* (2000); 10, Wayne *et al.* (1994); 11, Rave *et al.* (1994); 12, Brock & White (1992); 13, Glenn *et al.* (1999).

The impact of single pair bottlenecks on allele frequencies in experimental populations of fruit flies is shown in Fig. 8.5. Note the loss of alleles, particularly of rare alleles. Allele frequencies have changed from those in the parent population. Replicate bottlenecked populations varied in the allele they lost and in the frequencies of the alleles that remained. On average, heterozygosity dropped from 0.61 in the base population to 0.44 in the bottlenecked populations, and the number of alleles from 6.7 to 2.4. Note that the cumulative effects of $N_e = 100$ over 57 generations has resulted in a similar loss of genetic diversity. In what follows we present the theory relating to the effects of single generation population bottlenecks, while the effects of sustained small population size are deferred until Chapter 10.

> Population bottlenecks result in loss of alleles (especially rare ones), reduced genetic diversity and random changes in allele frequencies

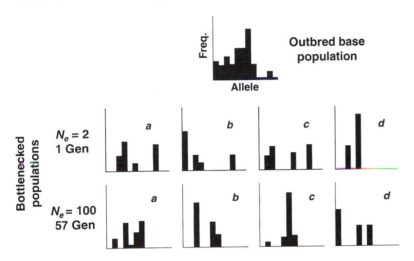

Fig. 8.5 Effect of single pair population bottlenecks on experimental populations of fruit flies (England 1997). The distribution of allele frequencies at a microsatellite locus is shown in the large outbred base population, in four replicate populations subjected to a bottleneck of one pair of flies, and in four populations maintained at $N_e = 100$ for 57 generations. *Alleles are lost, especially rare ones, and allele frequencies distorted in the bottlenecked populations.*

The impact of a bottleneck on heterozygosity is simplest to derive for a single pair bottleneck (Table 8.2). From that we can generalize to larger sized bottlenecks. Following a single pair bottleneck heterozygosity is reduced from $2pq$ to $1.5pq$, a decline of 25%. In general, the proportion of initial heterozygosity retained after a single generation bottleneck is

$$H_1 / H_0 = 1 - (1/2N) \tag{8.2}$$

where H_1 is the heterozygosity immediately after the bottleneck, and H_0 that before. Upon rearrangement we obtain an expression for the change in heterozygosity between the two generations (ΔH):

$$\Delta H = H_1 - H_0 = -(1/2N) H_0 \tag{8.3}$$

A proportion $1/(2N)$ of the original heterozygosity is lost. Thus, single generation bottlenecks have to be severe before they have a substantial impact on heterozygosity. A bottleneck of $N = 25$ only reduces heterozygosity by 2%, while a bottleneck of 100 reduces it by only 0.5%. Loss of genetic diversity arises predominantly from sustained reductions in population size, rather than single generation bottlenecks (Chapter 10).

The impact of a bottleneck on allelic diversity is often greater, although correlated. Overall, the number of alleles (A) retained following a single generation bottleneck is

Table 8.2 Effect on heterozygosity of a single pair, single generation bottleneck. The heterozygosities given are the Hardy–Weinberg equilibrium H_e following the single pair bottleneck. The base population has two alleles A_1 and A_2 at frequencies p and q, respectively (and a heterozygosity of $2pq$)

Possible alleles in samples of two individuals	Frequency (f)	Heterozygosity (H_e)	$f \times H_e$
$4\,A_1$	p^4	0	0
$3\,A_1 : 1\,A_2$	$4p^3q$	0.375	$1.5\,p^3q$
$2\,A_1 : 2\,A_2$	$6p^2q^2$	0.5	$3\,p^2q^2$
$1\,A_1 : 3\,A_2$	$4pq^3$	0.375	$1.5\,pq^3$
$4\,A_2$	q^4	0	0
Total	1		$1.5\,pq\,(p^2 + 2pq + q^2)$ $= 1.5\,pq$

Mean heterozygosity in bottlenecked populations $H_1 = 1.5\,pq$
Consequently, $H_1 / H_0 = 1.5pq\,/\,2pq = 0.75 = [1 - (1\,/\,2N)]$.

Thus, a single pair bottleneck, on average, reduces heterozygosity by 25% of the initial value.

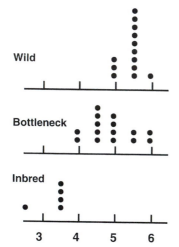

Wild

Bottleneck

Inbred

3   4   5   6

NaCl %

Fig. 8.6 Effects of population bottlenecks on evolutionary potential in fruit flies (Frankham et al. 1999). Populations were subjected to a single pair bottleneck for one generation. These populations, their base population and highly inbred (homozygous) populations from the same stock were all increased to the same population size, placed in cages and subjected to a regime of increasing concentrations of NaCl until extinction. Extinction concentrations for the three treatments are plotted. *Evolutionary potential was significantly reduced in the bottlenecked populations and they were more variable than the base population.*

$$A = n - \sum_{i=1}^{\substack{\text{No. of} \\ \text{alleles}}} (1 - p_i)^{2N} \qquad (8.4)$$

where n is the number of alleles before the bottleneck and p_i is the frequency of the ith allele. The sigma term is the number of alleles lost.

Loss of heterozygosity and allelic diversity in the bottlenecked fruit fly populations (Fig. 8.5) are close to those expected from the theory above. For example, the heterozygosity was predicted to fall from 0.61 to $0.61 \times (1 - \frac{1}{4}) = 0.45$ in the bottlenecked populations. The observed change was to 0.44. In the Mauritius kestrel, heterozygosity declined 57% from 0.23 to 0.10 as a result of single pair bottleneck (Box 8.1). This was greater than expected from a single pair bottleneck. However, the population suffered several generations of bottlenecks. Additional genetic diversity would have been lost during the six generations it spent at sizes of less than 50.

Many threatened wildlife populations show evidence of loss of genetic diversity due to population size bottlenecks (Chapter 3). For example, polymorphism is significantly reduced in artiodactyls (swine, hippopotamus, ruminants, deer and bison) that have suffered known bottlenecks (Hartl & Pucek 1994). In contrast, the Indian rhinoceros in Chitwan, Nepal has gone through a recent bottleneck of 60–80 individuals but retains a high level of genetic diversity (9.9% heterozygosity for allozymes; Dinerstein & McCracken 1990). Such a bottleneck is too large to generate any detectable reduction in heterozygosity within a few generations (see Problem 8.5).

Effect of population bottlenecks on quantitative genetic diversity

For quantitative characters showing only additive genetic variation, the expected loss of quantitative genetic variation due to a bottleneck is also a $1/(2N)$ proportional reduction in variation. This expectation has been verified in several selection experiments in fruit flies (Frankham 1980). The situation is more complex for characters exhibiting non-additive genetic variation, as bottlenecks can actually increase additive genetic variation due to increased homozygosity for rare recessive alleles (Robertson 1952). Increases in additive genetic variation in bottle-necked population for characters exhibiting non-additive variation have been reported by Bryant *et al.* (1986) and by Lopez-Fanjul & Villaverde (1989), but their relevance to evolutionary potential is questionable as the mean values for the characters dropped due to the inbreeding involved. A direct test of the impact of population bottle-necks on evolutionary potential in fruit flies found clear reductions due to the bottleneck (Fig. 8.6). The bottlenecked populations also showed a greater variance in evolutionary potential among populations than did the outbred controls (see also Whitlock & Fowler 1999).

> Population size bottlenecks reduce evolutionary potential

Inbreeding

In small populations, matings among relatives (inbreeding) is inevitable. With time, every individual becomes related so that no matings between unrelated individuals are possible. This is illustrated in the Mexican wolf pedigree (Fig. 8.7). Every individual beyond the third generation has parents that are related, i.e. they are all inbred. This is not a result of deliberate mating of relatives, it is simply a consequence of the small number of founders and the small population size. Inbreeding also becomes inevitable in larger populations, but it takes longer. For example, a population of size 100 over 57 generations becomes, on average, as inbred as the progeny of a brother–sister mating (Chapter 10).

> Inbreeding is unavoidable in small populations and leads to reductions in reproduction and survival

Inbreeding is of profound importance in conservation biology as it leads to reductions in heterozygosity, to reduced reproduction and survival (inbreeding depression) and to increased risk of extinction (Chapter 2, 11 and 12).

Measuring population size

Natural populations have many different structures and breeding systems that have different genetic consequences. For example, some populations of small mammals fluctuate wildly in size. Further, species vary in mating system (e.g. monogamy, harems), and from approximately random mating to selfing and asexual reproduction. The same

3 Founders

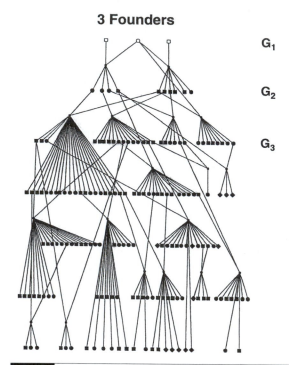

Fig. 8.7 Inbreeding is unavoidable in small populations. Pedigree for the Certified population of Mexican wolves (from Hedrick, Miller, Giffen & Wayne, © 1997 *Zoo Biology*, vol. 16, 47–69, reprinted by permission of Wiley–Liss, Inc., a subsidiary of John Wiley and Sons, Inc.). Square – males, circles – females, diamonds – unknown sex. *Within a few generations parents of all individuals share common ancestors, i.e. progeny are inbred.*

number of individuals may result in very different genetically effective population sizes, depending on population structure and breeding system. Consequently, we must define what we mean by population size in conservation genetics. We do this by comparing real populations to an idealized population we define below.

The idealized population

The idealized population, to which all other populations are compared, is a closed random mating population with discrete generations, constant population size, equal sex-ratio and Poisson variation in family sizes

We define population size in terms of the equivalent size of a standardized population, the **idealized population** (Fig. 8.8). We begin by assuming a large (essentially infinite) random mating base population, from which we take a sample of size N adults to form the ideal population. The idealized population is maintained as a random mating, closed population in succeeding generations. Alleles may be lost by chance, and allele frequencies may vary due to sampling variation. The simplifying conditions applying to the idealized population are:

• There is no migration
• Generations are distinct and do not overlap

Generation

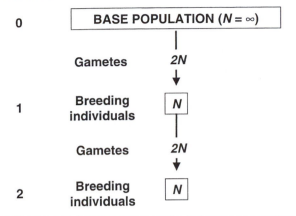

0   BASE POPULATION ($N = \infty$)

Gametes   2N

1   Breeding individuals   N

Gametes   2N

2   Breeding individuals   N

Fig. 8.8 Idealized population. From the very large base population a sample of N adults is taken and this population is maintained as a random mating, closed population with constant number of parents in each generation.

- The number of breeding individuals is the same in all generations
- All individuals are potential breeders
- All individuals are hermaphrodites (both sexes in each individual)
- Union of gametes is random, including the possibility of selfing
- There is no selection at any life cycle stage
- Mutation is ignored
- Number of offspring per adult averages 1, and has a variance of 1.

Within the population, breeding individuals contribute gametes equally to a pool from which zygotes are formed. Survival of zygotes is random, so that the contributions of families to the next generation are not equal. The mean number of offspring per adult is 1. These conditions result in a variance in family size of 1, so that family sizes may be 0, 1, 2, 3, 4, etc. This distribution of family sizes is described by the terms of the **Poisson distribution**.

The theoretical characteristics of the idealized population are well defined because of these assumptions, and a large body of theory has been derived for idealized populations. Consequently, by equating real populations to the idealized population, this theory can be utilized to make practical predictions.

Effective population size (N_e)

We can standardize the definition of population size by describing a population in terms of its **effective population size** (N_e). The effective size of a population is the size of an idealized population that would lose genetic diversity (or become inbred) at the same rate as the actual population. For example, if a real population loses genetic diversity at

> The effective population size is the number of individuals that would give rise to the calculated inbreeding coefficient, loss of heterozygosity or variance in allele frequency if they behaved in the manner of an idealized population

the same rate as an ideal population of 100, then we say the real population has an effective size of 100, even if it contains 1000 individuals. Thus, the N_e of a population is a measure of its genetic behaviour, relative to that of an ideal population.

It follows that the genetic consequences of small population size depend on the effective population size, rather than on the absolute number of individuals. In practice, the effective size of a population is usually less than the number of breeding adults. Real populations deviate in structure from the assumptions of the idealized population by having unequal sex-ratios, high variation in family sizes, variable numbers in successive generations, and in having overlapping generations. Details of how to calculate N_e are given in Chapter 10. For the time being, we shall simply recognize that it is the effective size, and not the actual number of individuals (N), that should be used in most equations (e.g. 8.2–8.4).

> The genetic consequences in small populations depend on the effective population size rather than on the number of individuals in the population

Selection in small populations

> Selection is less effective in small than large populations

Large populations show greater adaptive evolutionary capabilities than small, endangered populations. Pest insect species numbering in the millions have successfully evolved to combat a wide range of assaults (e.g. insecticides) that humans use to combat them. Conversely, many small island populations have been driven to extinction by the impacts of introduced predators, competitors and diseases.

Selection operating on body colour in the red flour beetle was more effective in large than in small populations (Fig. 8.2). There was a consistent increase in frequency of the wild-type allele in all the large ($N = 100$) populations. However, the effect of selection in the small populations ($N = 10$) was much more variable in outcome. Despite selection against the black allele, one population even became homozygous for this deleterious allele. This provides a critical insight for conservation genetics; selection is less effective in small than in large populations.

> Small populations show less response to directional selection for quantitative characters than larger populations

Small populations lose genetic diversity each generation so selection response should reduce compared to large populations. From a model of this process, Robertson (1960) predicted that the total amount of selection response (the limit) to directional selection would depend on the product of effective population size and the selection differential.

These predictions have been verified for several different quantitative characters in a range of species including fruit flies, mice, chickens and maize (Frankham & Weber 2000). Response to selection for bristle number in fruit flies, over 50 generations, was greatest in populations with 40 pairs of parents per generation, intermediate in those with 20 pairs of parents, and least in those with 10 pairs of parents (Fig. 8.9).

The evolutionary potential of endangered species is seriously compromised, compared to non-endangered species, as they have less initial

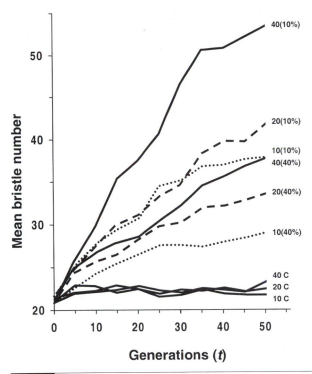

Fig. 8.9 Response to directional selection for increased abdominal bristle number (a quantitative character) over 50 generations in populations of fruit flies maintained at different sizes (10, 20 and 40 pairs of parents) and selected at different intensities (10%, 40% and unselected controls) (after Jones *et al.* 1968). Lines marked C are unselected controls of different sizes. All populations were derived from the same outbred base population. Treatment means are plotted. *Selection response was greater in larger than in smaller populations and in the more intensely selected treatment within each population size.*

genetic diversity (Chapter 3) and they lose genetic diversity at a greater rate in each generation. We elaborate on this issue in Chapter 14.

An important implication of the lower efficiency of selection in small than in large populations is that deleterious alleles are less likely to be removed by natural selection and may even become fixed. This can lead directly to reduction in reproductive fitness and increased extinction risk (Chapters 12 and 14).

Deleterious alleles are more likely to be fixed in small than large populations

Mutation in small populations

The occurrence of a particular new mutation at a locus in a finite population will be a rare event, unlikely to be repeated in a long time. In a population of size N, a new mutation will have a frequency of $1/(2N)$, and will be rare unless the population is very small. If the mutation is neutral (i.e. functions as well as, but no better than, the pre-existing allele) then its ultimate probability of fixation due to genetic drift will

Most new mutations in small populations are lost by chance

be its initial frequency $1/(2N)$. Its ultimate probability of loss will be $1 - 1/(2N)$. Consequently, the most likely fate of a new mutation in a finite population will be loss of the allele, unless the population is very small.

For a neutral mutation to reach fixation it must rise in frequency from $1/(2N)$ to 1 purely by chance events. The average time for this to occur is approximately $4N$ generations.

Mutation–selection equilibrium in small populations

Equilibrium frequencies for deleterious alleles are, on average, lower in small populations than in large populations

Mutation–selection balance maintains deleterious mutations in populations at low frequencies at many loci (Chapter 7). However, the equilibrium frequencies for deleterious alleles are, on average, lower in small populations than in large populations (Fig. 8.10). In smaller populations, the frequency of homozygotes is higher, leading selection against recessives to be more efficient than in larger populations. The expected equilibrium frequencies for a recessive lethal allele with a mutation rate of 10^{-5} is 3×10^{-3} in a very large population (Table 7.4), but less than 10^{-4} in populations of size 10. The relationship with population size is weaker for partially recessive lethals. For example, a partially recessive lethal, with a 2.5% decrement in heterozygote fitness, has an equilibrium frequency of 4×10^{-4} in a very large population, and about 10^{-4} in a population with an effective size of 10.

While the average frequency of deleterious alleles is reduced in small populations, the variance in frequencies will be high. Many loci will have no deleterious alleles, but some will have relatively high frequencies by chance. We saw this in the case of chondrodystrophy in California condors, where the lethal allele has a frequency of about 17% (Chapter 4). Such a deleterious allele is expected to have a mutation–selection equilibrium frequency of about 0.3% (Chapter 7). Other endangered species have been found to have elevated frequencies of alleles causing genetic diseases (Ryder 1988). Founding events have led to elevated frequencies of alleles causing a range of genetic diseases in various human populations (Diamond & Rotter 1987).

Fig. 8.10 Equilibrium frequencies for recessive lethal alleles in populations of different sizes. A mutation rate of 10^{-5} is assumed. The solid line is for a completely recessive lethal, and the dashed line for a partially recessive lethal allele that reduces reproductive fitness by 2.5% in heterozygotes (after Crow & Kimura 1970).

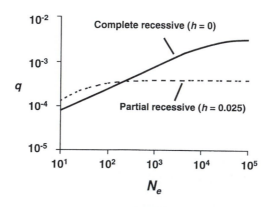

Computer simulation

Due to the stochastic nature of genetic drift, the impacts of selection on allele frequencies in small populations are difficult to model algebraically. Consequently, computer simulations are often used to study the impacts of chance and selection (Box 8.3). For example, the flour beetle experiment described in Fig. 8.2 has been simulated (Fig. 8.11). Selection on allele frequencies were simulated for replicate populations with two different population sizes ($N = 10$ and 100) for an additive locus with a selection coefficient of 0.1. Note the similarity of the results with the experimental result. Replicates diverged in frequencies more in smaller than larger populations, variation in frequencies from generation to generation were greater in smaller than in larger populations, and selection has a more predictable effect in larger than in smaller populations.

Computer simulation is used to investigate problems that are difficult to solve mathematically, such as the impact of selection or mutation in small populations

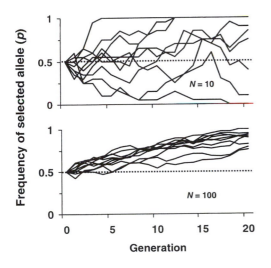

Fig. 8.11 Computer simulation illustrating the operation of selection in replicate populations with sizes of $N = 10$ and $N = 100$. Selection is for an additive model with $s = 0.1$. These simulations were conducted using a random number generator in spreadsheet software.

Box 8.3 | Complex models and computer simulation

The joint impacts of chance with selection, migration, or mutation rapidly become complicated to investigate using algebraic models. These are investigated either by using relatively complex mathematics, such as diffusion equations, or by building stochastic computer models. Computer models that include chance are called Monte Carlo simulations, after the famous casinos in that principality. Monte Carlo simulations yield a distribution of outcomes, rather than a single outcome, as shown in Fig. 8.11.

Computer simulations are used in several different ways in conservation genetics. They may be used to:
- verify the results of mathematical models
- provide numerical solutions for expressions produced by stochastic mathematical models
- check the validity of approximate mathematical solutions to problems

- suggest a solution to a problem that may subsequently be solved mathematically
- investigate problems that are too complex to solve with mathematical models.

In the latter context, computer simulation provides links between simple tractable mathematical models (with many simplifying assumptions) and experiments with real living organisms in all their complexity. Computer simulations can include a reasonable level of reality and complexity. For example Lacy (1987) used computer simulations to evaluate the likely effects of drift, selection, migration and population subdivision on small populations of endangered species. For complex pedigrees, the probabilities that alleles are lost, or retained, over time are typically determined using 'gene drop' computer simulations (MacCluer et al. 1986). Further, Ballou & Lacy (1995) used computer simulation to evaluate the effects on retention of genetic diversity and inbreeding of alternative genetic management schemes proposed for endangered species. Their simulations followed many replicates over several generations for a single locus, based on starting populations with different pedigrees. There were still simplifying assumptions as they used only one locus, and thus ignored linkage, linkage disequilibrium, mutation and selection. Their work led to a new procedure (minimizing kinship) being instituted for genetic management of captive population (Chapter 17). Their computer results were subsequently verified in experiments with fruit flies.

More complex computer models are used to assess extinction risk due to all important threatening processes – a procedure called population viability analysis (Chapter 20). The results in Fig. 2.2 were based on such analyses.

Summary

1. Populations of conservation concern are small or declining.

2. Mutation, migration, selection and chance determine the evolution of both small and large populations.

3. Evolution in small populations involves a greater impact of chance, and more inbreeding, than in large populations

4. Chance effects (genetic drift) arise from random sampling of gametes.

5. Genetic drift results in random fluctuations in allele frequencies, diversification among replicate populations, fixation and loss of genetic diversity.

6. The genetic consequences of small populations depend upon the effective population size, rather than on the actual number of individuals .

7. Selection is less effective in small than in large populations.

8. The equilibrium frequencies for deleterious alleles due to mutation–selection balance are generally lower in small than in large populations.

FURTHER READING

Crow & Kimura (1970) *Introduction to Population Genetics Theory*. Relatively advanced treatment of the theory relating to evolution in small populations.

Falconer & Mackay (1996) *Introduction to Quantitative Genetics*. Chapter 3 provides a very clear introduction to the topics in this chapter.

Frankel & Soulé (1981) *Conservation and Evolution*. Classic book covering much of the material on the evolution in small populations in a conservation context.

Hartl & Clark (1997) *Principles of Population Genetics*. Topics in this chapter are covered in this widely used textbook.

Lacy (1987) An evaluation of the likely impacts of drift, selection, migration and population subdivision on small populations of endangered species, done using computer simulation.

PROBLEMS

8.1 Probability of chance loss of an allele: If a heterozygous Brown's banksia plant with genotype A_1A_2 has three offspring by selfing, what is the probability that allele A_1 is absent in the offspring?

8.2 Probability of chance loss of an allele: If two Siberian tiger parents with genotypes A_1A_2 and A_1A_3 have four offspring, what is the probability that allele A_1 is absent in the offspring? That A_2 is absent in the offspring? That A_3 is absent in the offspring?

8.3 Probability of chance loss of an allele: If a Guam rail population has two alleles A_1 and A_2 at frequencies of 0.9 : 0.1, respectively, (a) what is the probability that A_2 is lost in the subsequent generation if 12 offspring are produced? (b) What is the probability that A_2 is lost in the subsequent generation if 100 offspring are produced? Compare (a) and (b).

8.4 Probability of retaining alleles under random sampling: How many offspring would be needed to be 95% certain that both alleles were sampled from the first individual in the top line of the golden lion tamarin pedigree in Fig. 8.1?

8.5 Loss of genetic diversity: What proportion of the initial heterozygosity is lost due to a single generation bottleneck in (a) a single plant of *Pritchardia munroi*, an endemic Hawaiian palm? (b) The Chatham Island black robin reduced to five individuals? (c) Whooping crane reduced to 14 individuals? (d) Indian rhinoceros population in Chitwan, Nepal reduced to about 70 individuals? (e) Southern bluefin tuna reduced to 300 000 individuals?

8.6 Loss of allelic diversity: What is the probability that an allele with an initial frequency of q is lost following a single-generation bottleneck when (a) $q = 0.1$ in one plant of *Castalleja ulinogosa*? (b) $q = 0.1$ in two Mauritius kestrel? (c) $q = 0.1$ in 50 northern hairy-nosed wombats? (d) $q = 0.05$ in 25 Siberian tigers?

PRACTICAL EXERCISE: COMPUTER SIMULATIONS

The following computer simulation exercises are designed to assist readers to understand aspects of the evolution in small populations. They can be completed using a package such as POPGEN.

1. Genetic drift and diversification: Compare the proportion of populations (a) still polymorphic, (b) going to fixation ($q = 1$) and (c) losing the A_2 allele ($q = 0$) in populations of different sizes (10 vs. 50) over 100 generations, beginning at frequencies of $q = 0.5$ and $q = 0.1$.

These require 50–100 replicates and can be done individually, or compiled as the sum of replicates from all the students in a class.

Simulation	Fixed $q = 1$	Polymorphic	Lost $q = 0$
$q_0 = 0.5\ N = 50$			
$q_0 = 0.5\ N = 10$			
$q_0 = 0.1\ N = 50$			
$q_0 = 0.1\ N = 10$			

How do the results differ with different starting frequencies?

2. Adaptive evolution with strong selection: Industrial melanism in peppered moths (favoured dominant allele). Industrial melanism increased in frequency from an allele frequency $q = 0.005$ (allele 2 of POPGEN) in 1848 to about 0.90 in 1900 (52 generations). The relative fitnesses are approximately as follows:

	Typical tt	Melanic Mt	Melanic MM
Relative fitnesses	0.7	1	1

Simulate this case for 100 generations with $N = 50$ and record the results in the table below.

Simulation	Fixed $q = 1$	Polymorphic	Lost $q = 0$
$q_0 = 0.005\ N = 50$			

In what proportion of cases was the deleterious allele fixed? Compare these results with the deterministic case from Chapter 6.

3. Adaptive evolution with weak selection: For a partially dominant locus with following fitnesses (akin to an allozyme locus or a MHC allele), simulate changes in allele frequencies over 2000 generations with $N = 50$ and $N = 10$, beginning with $q = 0.1$.

A_1A_1	A_1A_2	A_2A_2
0.99	0.992	1.0

Record your results in the table below

Simulation	Fixed $q = 1$	Polymorphic	Lost $q = 0$
$q_0 = 0.1\ N = 50$			
$q_0 = 0.1\ N = 10$			

In what proportion of cases was the deleterious allele fixed? Compare these results with the deterministic case by running the same fitnesses and starting frequencies.

Chapter 9

Maintenance of genetic diversity

Levels of genetic diversity result from the joint impacts of mutation and migration adding variation, chance and directional selection removing it, and balancing selection impeding its loss. The balance between these factors depends strongly on population size and differs across characters

Terms:
Associative overdominance,
balancing selection,
effectively neutral,
frequency-dependent selection,
heterozygote advantage,
inversions,
intron,
neutral mutation,
non-synonymous substitutions,
overdominance,
pseudogene,
synonymous substitutions,
transient polymorphisms,
trans-species polymorphism

Malaria and genetic diversity in humans. (a) Distribution of falciparum malaria and the frequencies of alleles that confer resistance to the disease, (b) sickle cell anaemia, (c) thalassaemia and (d) G6pd deficiency (after Allison 1961 and Strickberger 1985).

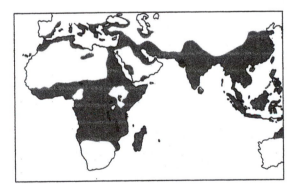

(a) Falciparum malaria

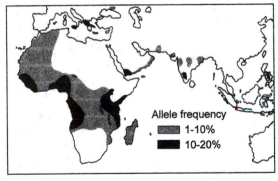

Allele frequency
1-10%
10-20%

(b) Sickle cell anaemia

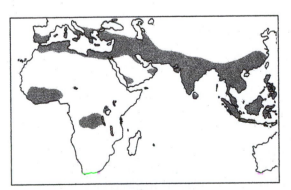

(c) Thalassaemia

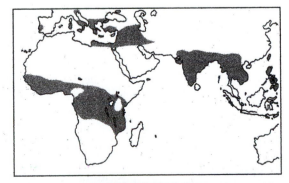

(d) G6pd deficiency

Conservation of genetic diversity

Maintenance of genetic diversity is a major objective in conservation programs, as genetic diversity represents evolutionary potential

Conservation biologists need to understand how genetic diversity is maintained through natural processes if conservation programs are to be designed for its maintenance in managed populations of endangered species. So far, we have considered the impacts of mutation, migration, selection and chance on genetic diversity, and have largely treated them as independent factors. Here we consider in detail how these factors interact to produce the different levels of genetic diversity observed in diverse species. If selection removes deleterious alleles and fixes favourable alleles, while genetic drift removes alleles, why do we observe so much genetic diversity? Why do small populations, including endangered species, generally have lower genetic diversity than large non-endangered species? Maintenance of extensive genetic diversity in natural populations is one of the most important, largely unresolved, questions of evolutionary genetics (Prout 2000).

These questions lead us to consider the nature, extent and relevance of balancing selection, which actively maintains variation within populations, and to contrast this with random processes.

Genetic diversity arises from mutation, or is introduced by migration, and is lost by genetic drift in small populations and by directional selection. Balancing selection generally impedes the loss of genetic diversity

Populations vary in their levels of genetic diversity (Chapter 3). Most large, widespread species have high levels of genetic diversity. Conversely, smaller populations, island populations and endangered species often display much lower levels. These differences are a direct result of the interacting processes of selection, genetic drift, mutation and migration operating within particular breeding systems. The level of diversity therefore depends on which process predominates and this varies for different characters.

We now consider the mechanisms that can maintain genetic diversity, and consider their likely roles for different characters, namely untranslated DNA, translated DNA, protein polymorphism, quantitative characters, chromosomal inversions and visual polymorphisms.

There are two main explanations for maintenance of genetic diversity, neutral mutations undergoing random genetic drift, and balancing selection

Before considering the contributions of balancing selection and neutral mutation/random genetic drift to maintenance of genetic diversity, we need to consider the selective values associated with different classes of mutations.

Fate of different classes of mutations

Most of the genetic diversity observed in populations is likely to represent neutral alleles and alleles subject to balancing selection

The major classes of mutations are:
- deleterious mutations,
- beneficial mutations,
- neutral mutations, and
- mutations whose effects are favoured in some circumstances, but not in others (Chapter 7).

The fate of each of these is considered below.

The majority of newly arisen mutations are deleterious. Deleterious mutations are removed by selection but continue to be added by mutation

While we do not know the precise proportions of the four types of mutations, there is no doubt that those with effects on the phenotype are overwhelmingly deleterious. Deleterious mutations are continually removed by selection. The balance between mutation and selection generally keeps deleterious alleles at very low frequencies (Chapter 7).

A (very) small proportion of mutations is beneficial. These increase in frequency until they reach fixation, provided they are not lost by chance when rare in the early generations. Loci with such alleles will be observed as polymorphic during the phase when the alleles are rising in frequency prior to reaching fixation. During this phase they are referred to as **transient polymorphisms**. Loci with such mutations will rarely be observed as polymorphic as they represent a rare class of mutations and the alleles are fixed relatively rapidly.

Beneficial mutations are fixed by natural selection

A proportion of mutations is **neutral**, i.e. they have the same impact on reproductive fitness as pre-existing alleles. Many mutations in untranslated DNA (regions between loci, and introns) and DNA base substitutions that do not result in amino acid changes (synonymous substitutions) are expected to fall into this category. These drifting alleles also create transient polymorphisms. The fate of neutral mutations is determined by genetic drift alone so they do not enter into our discussion of the maintenance of genetic diversity for reproductive fitness. Their fate depends entirely on population size.

Many mutations outside functional regions and some within them are neutral

The fourth class of mutations is favoured by selection in some circumstances, and selected against in others. This is termed **balancing selection**. These alleles are maintained in the population at relatively intermediate frequencies, resulting in polymorphisms.

Mutations subject to any form of balancing selection are actively retained in large populations

There are different forms of balancing selection. Some alleles are advantageous in heterozygotes and disadvantageous in homozygotes (**heterozygote advantage** or **overdominance**), while others are advantageous when rare, and disadvantageous when common (subject to **frequency-dependent selection**). Finally, some of these mutations have selective values that are advantageous in some environments and disadvantageous in others conditions, e.g. one season versus another, one environmental niche versus another, or in captive versus native habitats. Such alleles display genotype × environment interactions (Chapter 5).

Since both deleterious and favourable mutations are lost or rapidly go to fixation, the polymorphisms observed in natural populations are primarily a result of alleles that are neutral plus those subject to balancing selection.

Maintenance of genetic diversity in large populations

The balance of forces maintaining genetic diversity differs between large and small populations. Selection has major impacts in large populations. However, its impacts are reduced in small populations, where genetic drift has an increasingly important role.

We begin discussion of the maintenance of genetic diversity in large populations by considering the fate of neutral mutations under genetic drift, then consider the extent of selection on different loci and characters, discuss balancing selection and conclude with maintenance of

The relative importance in maintenance of genetic diversity of balancing selection versus neutral alleles undergoing random genetic drift depends on the relationship between selection and population size. Selection is more effective in larger populations, while drift is most important in small populations

genetic diversity for fitness characters. Maintenance of genetic diversity in small populations (i.e. those of conservation concern) is treated in the latter part of the chapter so that we can compare and contrast it with the situation for large populations.

Neutral mutations under random genetic drift

The fate of neutral mutations is determined by random sampling in finite populations (genetic drift). Most neutral mutations are lost within a few generations of origin (because they start at such low frequencies). However, new mutations continue to be produced. A small proportion rise in frequency just by chance, and some (a proportion $1/2N$) go to fixation (Fig. 9.1). The flux of these alleles is such that, at any one time, some loci are likely to be polymorphic. The late Motoo Kimura from Japan was a major proponent of the view that DNA and protein polymorphisms were predominantly neutral and that levels of genetic diversity for such loci were primarily due to neutral alleles undergoing genetic drift (Kimura 1983). This is referred to as the **neutral theory** of molecular evolution.

Fig. 9.1 Neutral mutation/random genetic drift (after Crow & Kimura 1970). The figure illustrates the flux of neutral mutations over a very large number of generations in a very large population. Most mutants are lost within a few generations (thin lines). Occasional mutants increase in frequency. Some of these increase to eventual fixation (heavy lines), while others are lost (dotted lines). *At any point in time there are polymorphic loci (transient polymorphisms).*

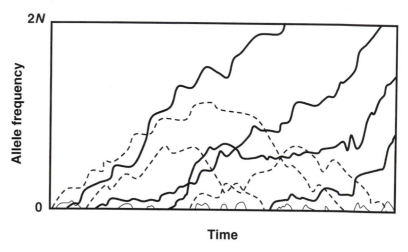

Kimura and his co-workers marshalled several lines of evidence in support of the neutral theory (Kimura 1983). We shall consider some of these below.

The neutral theory predicts that the rate of amino acid substitution in proteins, and of base substitutions in DNA, will occur at constant rates for particular proteins or sequences of DNA. The derivation of this relationship is as follows. The number of neutral mutations per generation in a population of size N_e is $2N_e u$, where u is the neutral mutation rate. However, the probability of fixing a neutral mutation is its initial frequency, $1/2N_e$ (Chapter 8). Consequently, the rate of substitution at a steady state is the product of these two values $2N_e u \times 1/2N_e = u$. Thus, the rate of substitution of amino acids, or of DNA bases, is expected to be

constant in different sized populations and to equal the neutral mutation rate. This derivation leads to constancy per generation. However,
Kimura has argued that the rate should be constant per year, as the
number of germ line generations is approximately constant per year,
regardless of generation length. Whether the rate of molecular evolution should be constant per year or per generation remains a matter of
controversy.

The evidence favours an approximate constancy in rates of amino
acid substitution in proteins (Fig. 9.2; Kimura 1983, but see Gillespie
1991).

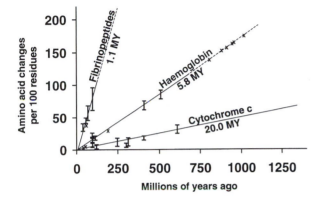

Fig. 9.2 Rate of nucleotide substitutions versus palaeontological time (after Hartl & Clark 1997). The rate is approximately constant as predicted by the neutral theory, but differs among proteins. Different rates are expected for proteins with different degrees of functional constraint, as they have different neutral mutation rates.

Regions of the genome that have little function are expected to have
higher neutral mutation rates than regions coding for essential functions, such as the active site of enzymes, or folding sites in proteins.
Consequently, the neutral theory predicts higher polymorphism for
non-translated sections of the genome such as introns or regions
between loci (excluding regulatory sequences) than for coding
sequences that are transcribed and translated. Evidence supports this
prediction (Hartl & Clark 1997). Polymorphism in non-translated DNA
(synonymous mutations at the third position of codons, introns and
pseudogenes – non-functional loci) is higher than in regions of DNA with
obvious function, as predicted by the neutral theory. Further, levels of
protein polymorphism are related to the size of proteins, as predicted by
the neutral theory (Ward *et al.* 1992). Larger proteins would be expected
to have higher average neutral mutation rates than smaller ones.

The neutral theory predicts higher levels of polymorphism for regions of the genome subject to fewer functional constraints

Under the neutral theory, drift, rather than selection, determines
the number of alleles and the heterozygosity. The balance between
mutation adding alleles and drift removing them determines levels of
genetic diversity. Since alleles drift to fixation more rapidly in small
than in large populations, neutral theory predicts that the expected
heterozygosity (H_e), and effective number of alleles (n_e) will be higher in
larger than in smaller populations:

The neutral theory predicts that there will be a positive relationship between genetic diversity and population size

$$H_e = 4N_e u / (4N_e u + 1) \tag{9.1}$$

$$n_e = 4N_e u + 1 \tag{9.2}$$

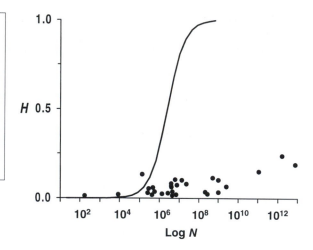

Fig. 9.3 Predicted relationship between heterozygosity and population size according to the neutral theory, and experimentally determined relationship (after Nei 1987). The curve is the predicted relationships with a mutation rate of 10^{-7}, and dots are observed data points. *Observed heterozygosities are much lower than those predicted by the neutral theory.*

where N_e is the effective population size (defined in Chapter 8), and u the neutral mutation rate. Thus, genetic diversity is expected to be related to effective population size (Fig. 9.3).

The neutral mutation rate is lower than the overall mutation rate as it excludes deleterious and favourable mutations. A typical rate for protein loci is 10^{-9} per amino acid position per year, but it varies widely for different proteins according to the functional constraints on the molecule (Kimura 1983). For a protein composed of 100 amino acids this translates into a mutation rate of 10^{-7} per year for the whole locus, compared to typical single locus total mutation rates of 10^{-5} per generation. Example 9.1 illustrates the use of equation 9.1 to predict heterozygosities and effective numbers of alleles for different sized populations. The equilibrium heterozygosity is 0.8 for a population of 10 million, but only 4×10^{-5} for a population with an effective size of 100.

While there is strong evidence for a relationship between genetic diversity and population size both across species and within species (Frankham 1996), the shape of the relationship is not of the form predicted by the neutral theory (Fig. 9.3). Equally, the observed relationship does not conform to that predicted by balancing selection, but a model of near neutral mutations, as described below, can account it for.

Example 9.1	Predicted heterozygosities and effective number of alleles in different sized populations according to the neutral theory

Let us consider two populations, one with an effective size of 100 and the other of 10 million, and a neutral mutation rate of 10^{-7} for a locus. Heterozygosity for the smaller population is predicted to be

$$H_{small} = 4N_e u / (4N_e u + 1)$$
$$= (4 \times 100 \times 10^{-7}) / (4 \times 100 \times 10^{-7} + 1) = 4 \times 10^{-5}$$

while that for the larger populations is

$$H_{\text{large}} = (4 \times 10^7 \times 10^{-7}) / (4 \times 10^7 \times 10^{-7} + 1) = 0.8$$

The effective number of alleles in the smaller population will be

$$n_{e\,\text{small}} = 4N_e u + 1 = 4 \times 100 \times 10^{-7} + 1 = 1.00004$$

while that in the larger population is expected to be

$$n_{e\,\text{large}} = 4 \times 10^7 \times 10^{-7} + 1 = 5$$

Consequently, a stable population of 10 million is expected to have much greater heterozygosity and allelic diversity than a population of 100.

There are good reasons to reject a purely neutral theory of molecular evolution (see Kreitman & Akashi 1995; Hey 1999). For example, the relationship between genetic diversity and population size is not as predicted (Fig. 9.3). The near neutral theory, where both strictly neutral and mildly deleterious alleles are included, is more plausible (Ohta 1992, 1996). The near neutral theory considers that most new mutations are deleterious, and most mutations with very small effects are likely to be very slightly deleterious. Such mutations are selected against in large populations, but behave as if neutral in small populations. Thus there is a flux of mutations entering populations and being lost, or fixed, as for the neutral theory. However, only a small proportion is neutral and most are very mildly deleterious mutants. Most mildly deleterious alleles are removed from large population by selection, but they are effectively neutral in small populations.

> A purely neutral theory does not adequately explain molecular evolution, or genetic diversity, and it does not apply to fitness characters

However, neither neutral or near neutral theories apply to all loci. There is clear evidence for balancing selection on some protein polymorphisms (Powers *et al.* 1991), on the MHC, on self-incompatibility loci, and on essentially all inversion and visual polymorphisms. The neutral theory clearly does not apply to genetic diversity for reproductive fitness, a major conservation focus. The magnitude of selection varies widely with the character being observed.

Selection intensities vary among characters

The range of selective values for different characters is illustrated in Fig. 9.4. The great majority of mutations in untranslated DNA are believed to be neutral, or nearly so. Most mutations resulting in amino acid substitutions are deleterious and removed by natural selection. For those changes in amino acid sequence that persist as protein polymorphisms, some may be neutral, and some subject to balancing selection (Brookfield & Sharp 1994; Kreitman & Akashi 1995). A very small

> The selective force on different characters varies, being very weak or absent for untranslated DNA, weak for most translated DNA and protein polymorphisms, modest for gene clusters, and strong for visual polymorphisms and reproductive fitness

Fig. 9.4 Intensities of selection on different characters.

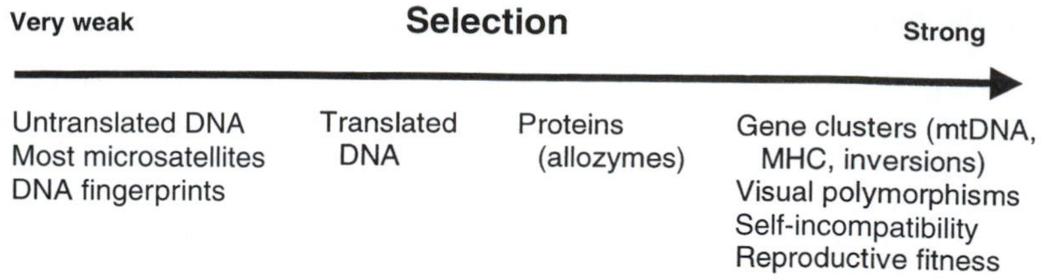

Very weak   **Selection**   Strong

→

Untranslated DNA	Translated	Proteins	Gene clusters (mtDNA,
Most microsatellites	DNA	(allozymes)	MHC, inversions)
DNA fingerprints			Visual polymorphisms
			Self-incompatibility
			Reproductive fitness

proportion of amino acid substitutions is advantageous. Even where there is evidence for selection on protein polymorphisms, the selective forces are usually weak (see Kimura 1983; Gillespie 1991; Hey 1999).

For some loci, or clusters of loci, there is clear evidence of selection. This is particularly true for groups of loci found in single selective units (mtDNA, inversions, and clusters of loci in linkage disequilibrium such as the MHC). Alleles involved in determining self-incompatibility in plants are clearly subject to frequency-dependent selection (rare advantage). There is clear evidence for natural selection operating on visual polymorphisms (e.g. for banded vs. non-banded, and yellow vs. brown snail shells, polymorphic mimics and speckled vs. melanic colouration in moths), and often the forces of selection are strong. Reproductive fitness is the focus of selective forces acting on individuals, so it too is subject to relatively strong selection.

Balancing selection

Balancing selection generally impedes the loss of genetic diversity

The three main forms of balancing natural selection, i.e. heterozygote advantage, frequency-dependent selection, and selection of varying direction in time and space, are considered below. Each of these actively maintains genetic diversity through natural selection.

Heterozygote advantage (overdominance)

Heterozygote advantage results in an equilibrium that actively retains polymorphism

Heterozygote advantage or overdominance arises where heterozygotes have higher fitness than either homozygote (see Fig. 6.5). A classic example is sickle cell anaemia in humans living in areas where malaria is endemic (Box 9.1). Heterozygotes show increased resistance to malaria, while homozygous normal individuals suffer elevated mortality from malaria, and those homozygous for the sickle allele suffer very high mortality from anaemia.

Box 9.1 | Overdominant selection and balanced polymorphism for sickle cell anaemia in humans

Sickle cell anaemia is due to an abnormal allele of haemoglobin (S) that results in low survival of SS homozygotes due to severe anaemia. However, the S allele provides protection against malarial infection in heterozygotes. Balancing selection was first inferred from correlations between the distribution of the sickle cell allele and malaria across Africa, the Mediterranean and Asia (see chapter frontispiece).

AA　　　　　　　　**AS**　　　　　　　　**SS**

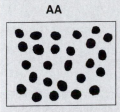 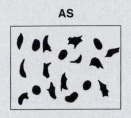 

Blood cells of the AA, AS and SS genotypes under oxygen starvation.

Allison (1956) verified that selection was favouring heterozygotes in malarial areas of Africa. He determined the frequencies of the three genotypes among infants and adults, and estimated the relative fitnesses of the three genotypes as shown below (after Falconer & Mackay 1996). The population is in Hardy–Weinberg equilibrium at birth, but selection leads to an excess of heterozygotes in adults (Problem 9.1).

	Genotype			
	AA	AS	SS	Frequency (S)
Number of infants	189	89	9	
Number of adults	400	249	5	
Frequency in infants	0.659	0.310	0.031	0.186
Frequency in adults	0.612	0.381	0.008	0.198
Relative survival (adult frequency/ infant frequency)	0.929	1.228	0.242	
Fitness relative to AS	0.929/1.228	1.228/1.228	0.242/1.228	
	0.757	1	0.197	
Selection coefficient	$s_1 = 1 - 0.76$		$s_2 = 1 - 0.20$	
	$= 0.24$		$= 0.80$	

Thus, there is strong selection favouring heterozygotes. The frequency of the S allele is similar in infants and adults, as expected for a population in equilibrium.

For a locus subject to overdominant selection, a stable equilibrium is reached. This depends only on the selection coefficients against the two homozygotes. For a locus with two alleles, the equilibrium is obtained by equating the expression for Δq from Table 6.2 to zero, as follows:

The equilibrium frequency with heterozygote advantage depends only on the relative values of the selection coefficients against the two homozygous genotypes

$$\Delta q = \frac{pq\,(s_1 p - s_2 q)}{(1 - s_1 p^2 - s_2 q^2)} = 0$$

this occurs when the bracketed portion of the numerator is zero, so

$$s_1 p = s_2 q$$

and after rearrangement and substitution of $p = 1 - q$, the expression for the equilibrium frequency of the S allele is:

$$\hat{q} = \frac{s_1}{(s_1 + s_2)} \tag{9.3}$$

Thus, the equilibrium frequency depends only on the relative values of the selection coefficients. For example, when $s_1 = s_2$, the equilibrium frequency is 0.5. In Example 9.2, this equation is used to predict the equilibrium frequency for sickle cell anaemia, based on mortality data. The predicted equilibrium of 0.23 for the S allele is close to that observed in malarial areas of Africa.

This is a stable equilibrium. Populations begun at the equilibrium frequency remain at that frequency, while those with frequencies above or below the equilibrium move towards it (Example 9.3).

Example 9.2 | Predicted equilibrium frequency for sickle cell anaemia, a case of heterozygote advantage

The selection coefficients against the normal and sickle cell homozygotes are approximately 0.24 and 0.80, as shown in Box 9.1. The predicted equilibrium is obtained as follows:

$$\hat{q} = \frac{s_1}{(s_1 + s_2)} = 0.24 / (0.24 + 0.80) = 0.23$$

Consequently, the predicted equilibrium frequencies are 0.23 for the sickle cell allele and $1 - 0.23 = 0.77$ for the normal haemoglobin allele. These are close to observed frequencies.

Example 9.3 | Stable equilibrium with heterozygote advantage

We can test whether the equilibrium for sickle cell anaemia in malarial areas is stable by determining what happens to Δq when the frequency is perturbed to values above and below the equilibrium. If the equilibrium is stable, then selection moves frequencies back towards the equilibrium. For example, if we perturb the frequency for S from 0.23 (equilibrium), to values of 0.5 and 0.1, Δq will be $-$ for $q = 0.5$, and $+$ for $q = 0.1$. (If Δq was $+$ for $q = 0.5$ and $-$ for $q = 0.1$, the equilibrium would be unstable.)

The values of Δq when the frequency of the S allele is 0.5, 0.23 and 0.1 are determined below ($s_1 = 0.24$ and $s_2 = 0.80$; Box 9.1).
For $q = 0.5$, $p = 0.5$

$$\Delta q = \frac{pq\,(s_1 p - s_2 q)}{(1 - s_1 p^2 - s_2 q^2)} = \frac{0.5 \times 0.5\,(0.24 \times 0.5 - 0.8 \times 0.5)}{(1 - 0.24 \times 0.5^2 - 0.8 \times 0.5^2)} = -0.095$$

For $q = 0.23$, $p = 0.77$

$$\Delta q = \frac{pq\,(s_1 p - s_2 q)}{(1 - s_1 p^2 - s_2 q^2)} = \frac{0.77 \times 0.23\,(0.24 \times 0.77 - 0.8 \times 0.23)}{(1 - 0.24 \times 0.77^2 - 0.8 \times 0.23^2)} = 0$$

For $q = 0.1, p = 0.9$

$$\Delta q = \frac{pq\,(s_1 p - s_2 q)}{(1 - s_1 p^2 - s_2 q^2)} = \frac{0.9 \times 0.1\,(0.24 \times 0.9 - 0.8 \times 0.1)}{(1 - 0.24 \times 0.9^2 - 0.8 \times 0.1^2)} = 0.015$$

The perturbed frequencies move towards the equilibrium, while a population at the equilibrium frequency remains there. Thus, the equilibrium is stable.

Other polymorphisms that are probably associated with heterozygote advantage for resistance to malaria include thalassaemia, and the sex-linked glucose–6-phosphate dehydrogenase deficiency (Ruwende *et al.* 1995) (see chapter frontispiece).

Tests based on DNA sequence data indicate that some protein polymorphisms are influenced by balancing selection (perhaps overdominance), including the alcohol dehydrogenase locus in fruit flies (Fig. 3.2; Kreitman 1983). In addition, the warfarin resistance polymorphism in rats shows overdominance, as do most visual polymorphisms. However, several lines of evidence indicate that only a small proportion of loci exhibit overdominance (Kimura 1983; Falconer & Mackay 1996). Convincing evidence for it has been found for few loci. Further, haploid organisms have similar (or higher) levels of allozyme diversity to diploids, but do not have heterozygotes.

Frequency-dependent selection

Frequency-dependent selection occurs when an allele or genotype is favoured when at one frequency, but disadvantaged when at another frequency. When alleles are favoured when rare, but selected against when common, a balanced polymorphism results (Hedrick 2000).

> A balanced polymorphism results if an allele is favoured when rare, but disadvantaged when common

Frequency-dependent selection may arise under a range of realistic circumstances. For example, if genotypes have slightly different resource use, one genotype may be favoured when rare, as its resource is abundant, but disadvantaged when common as its resource is over-exploited. Genotypes that differ in disease resistance may be subject to frequency-dependent selection, as pathogens adapt to infect the most common genotype, leaving rare genotypes least affected (Lively & Dybdahl 2000).

The MHC has a major role in fighting disease in vertebrates. There is strong evidence that balancing selection is retaining the high levels of genetic diversity at the MHC in humans and other vertebrates (Box 9.2). However it is not clear whether this selection is through heterozygote advantage, or frequency dependence, although the latter is likely to be partly involved. Clearly, maintenance of genetic diversity at the MHC is important to species' survival and of concern in conservation biology.

Predation will often yield frequency-dependent selection on prey species displaying visual polymorphism. Birds form searching images based on common prey phenotypes, such that rarer phenotypes have greater survival. However, when the previously rare types become most plentiful, they become the basis for searching images (Clarke 1969). In spite of these examples, frequency-dependent selection seems to be maintaining genetic diversity at only a small proportion of loci (Falconer & Mackay 1996).

Box 9.2	Balancing selection on the major histocompatibility complex (MHC) (after Hedrick & Kim 2000)

The human MHC (called the HLA) contains over 100 loci covering a region of nearly 4 million bases of DNA. Loci fall into three main groups termed class I, II and III. Within each there are closely related loci that have arisen by gene duplication.

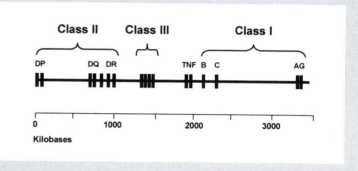

These are the major loci involved in fighting disease, combating cancer and controlling transplant acceptance/rejection (see Hughes & Yeager 1998; Hedrick & Kim 2000).

MHC loci exhibit the highest polymorphism of all known functional loci in vertebrates. For example, humans have 67, 149 and 35 alleles at the class I HLA-A, HLA-B and HLA-C loci, and 69, 29 and 179 at the class II DPB, DQB and DRB loci, respectively (Hedrick & Kim 2000).

There are several lines of evidence that variation at MHC loci is maintained by balancing selection:

1. There are excesses of non-synonymous substitutions (causing amino acid changes) over synonymous substitutions in the functionally important peptide binding regions (PBR) of six human HLA loci, as illustrated for HLA-A, HLA-B and HLA-C below (after Hughes & Yeager 1998). This contrasts with other loci (and the non-PBR regions of these loci) where there is a strong excess of synonymous over non-synonymous substitutions.

2. Allele frequencies at MHC loci are more even than expected for neutral alleles.

3. Polymorphisms are very ancient and extend beyond species boundaries (**trans-species polymorphism**). For example, at both the HLA-A and HLA-B

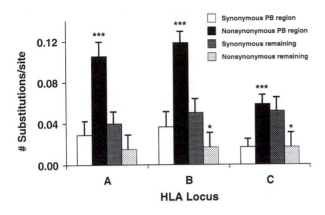

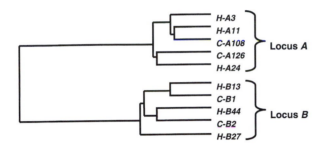

loci, each chimpanzee (C) allele is more closely related to a human (H) allele than to other chimpanzee alleles, as illustrated by the gene tree below (after Nei & Hughes 1991).

4. Excesses of heterozygotes at MHC loci have been reported in South American Indian populations, mice and pheasants, but not in bighorn sheep (Black & Hedrick 1997; Hedrick & Kim 2000).

5. There is linkage disequilibrium among loci in MHC (see Box 4.2) that may be due to selection.

6. Several examples of direct associations between MHC genotypes and resistance to pathogens have been reported. For example, heterozygosity at HLA-A, HLA-B and HLA-C is associated with longer survival in humans infected with HIV. Further, particular MHC alleles are associated with resistance/susceptibility to HIV, malaria, hepatitis B and C, tuberculosis, leprosy and venereal diseases in humans, to gut worms in sheep, to *Theileria parva* and mastitis in cattle and to Marek's disease (tumor caused by a virus) in chickens (Chan *et al.* 1979; Nicholas 1987; Mejdell *et al.* 1994; Taracha *et al.* 1995; Singh *et al.* 1997; Stear *et al.* 1997; Carrington *et al.* 1999). Heterozygote advantage for particular MHC loci has been demonstrated in humans for responses to hepatitis B and HIV infections (Thurz *et al.* 1997; Carrington *et al.* 1999).

Other selective forces may also operate on the MHC. Spontaneous abortion rates are higher for couples who share MHC alleles than for those who do not (Hedrick & Kim 2000). Further, mice, and probably humans, avoid mating with individuals sharing their MHC alleles, so it may have a role in inbreeding avoidance (Potts et al. 1994).

In spite of the strong evidence for balancing selection on the MHC, the selection coefficients are often small, being 4.2%, 1.9%, 1.5%, 0.85%, 0.28%, 0.26% and 0.07% for different loci (Satta et al. 1994). Conversely, in some cases, very strong selection has been reported (Black & Hedrick 1997). These differences may relate to how recently and frequently populations were subject to serious disease epidemics. The relative importance of the various forms of balancing selection operating on the MHC remains unclear.

The clearest case of frequency-dependent selection occurs at self-incompatibility (SI) loci in plants (Box 9.3). These along with MHC loci are among the most highly polymorphic loci known (Charlesworth & Awadalla 1998). Self-incompatibility systems have important implications in conservation biology as loss of S alleles in small populations leads to reduced reproductive fitness (Chapter 10).

| **Box 9.3** | Maintenance of self-incompatibility alleles in plants by frequency-dependent selection (after Wright 1969; Richman & Kohn 1996; Richards 1997; Charlesworth & Awadalla 1998) |

Self-incompatibility (Chapter 2) has evolved independently several times as it is based on different functional loci in different plant groups. We will describe multi-allelic gametophytic self-incompatibility due to a single locus. This is found in Scrophulariaceae, Onagraceae, Papaveraceae, Solanaceae, Rosaceae and several other flowering plant families.

Gametophytic self-incompatibility has the following characteristics:
- The compatibility of matings is controlled by S alleles at a single locus
- Populations contain many S alleles (about 66 in poppies and 400 in evening primroses and clovers)
- Matings between plants carrying the same SI genotypes are incompatible ($S_1S_2 \times S_1S_2$)
- Matings between plants sharing one SI allele are 50% compatible ($S_1S_2 \times S_1S_3$)
- Matings between plants with different SI genotypes are compatible ($S_1S_2 \times S_3S_4$)
- Self-incompatibility polymorphisms are very ancient; sequence variants have been maintained since before related species speciated (see Klein et al. 1998)
- Frequency-dependent selection maintains the polymorphism for self-incompatibility alleles.

An example of the operation of this system is given below for a three allele system (after Hedrick 2000). If an allele is rare, it will have a great advantage in pollination success as pollen containing the rare allele will seldom encounter maternal genotypes with the same allele. Conversely, if an allele is common it will frequently encounter maternal genotypes with the same allele and make reduced contributions to the next generation. The table below gives the relationships between genotype frequencies in succeeding generations. Since only heterozygotes can form, $P_{12} + P_{13} + P_{23} = 1$.

Female parent	Pollen	Frequency	Offspring S_1S_2	S_1S_3	S_2S_3
S_1S_2	S_3	P_{12}	—	$\frac{1}{2}P_{12}$	$\frac{1}{2}P_{12}$
S_1S_3	S_2	P_{13}	$\frac{1}{2}P_{13}$	—	$\frac{1}{2}P_{13}$
S_2S_3	S_1	P_{23}	$\frac{1}{2}P_{23}$	$\frac{1}{2}P_{23}$	—
			$\frac{1}{2}(1-P_{12})$	$\frac{1}{2}(1-P_{13})$	$\frac{1}{2}(1-P_{23})$

The frequencies of the three genotypes in the next generation are

$$P'_{12} = \frac{1}{2}P_{13} + \frac{1}{2}P_{23} = \frac{1}{2}(1-P_{12})$$

$$P'_{13} = \frac{1}{2}P_{12} + \frac{1}{2}P_{23} = \frac{1}{2}(1-P_{13})$$

$$P'_{23} = \frac{1}{2}P_{12} + \frac{1}{2}P_{13} = \frac{1}{2}(1-P_{23})$$

The change in genotypic frequency for S_1S_2 is

$$\Delta P_{12} = P'_{12} - P_{12} = \frac{1}{2}(1-P_{12}) - P_{12}$$
$$= \frac{1}{2}(1-3P_{12})$$

The equilibrium genotype frequency is obtained by setting $\Delta P_{12} = 0$, yielding

$$\hat{P}_{12} = 1/3$$

The equilibrium frequencies for P_{13} and P_{23} are also 1/3, so the equilibrium frequencies for the S_1, S_2 and S_3 alleles are all 1/3. This equilibrium is reached rapidly as the selection is strong. When there are n alleles, the equilibrium frequency of each allele is $1/n$.

The frequency dependence of the fitness of pollen genotypes can be illustrated using an example. If the three female parents have equal frequencies, but S_1, S_2 and S_3 pollen have unequal frequencies of 1/2, 1/3 and 1/6 (above, at, and below equilibrium, respectively), then all alleles will have a frequency of 1/3 in the next generation. Consequently, pollen alleles with frequencies above the equilibrium have relative fitnesses of less than 1, alleles with frequencies less than the equilibrium have relative fitnesses of greater than 1 and alleles at the equilibrium frequency have fitnesses of 1, i.e. the fitnesses are dependent on allele frequencies.

Selection in different directions in heterogeneous environments

Selection may change over seasons. For example, selection that varied with seasons was described for an inversion polymorphism in fruit flies in California (Fig. 9.5). The CH inversion is favoured in June and the ST in March and October. Such selection may lead to a stable polymorphism (Haldane & Jayakar 1963).

Selection may differ among habitats within the range of a species, such that one allele is favoured in one environment and selected against in another. If there is migration between habitats, then polymorphism may result. Gene flow will usually be related to the distance among the populations, resulting in a cline (Chapter 7). Box 9.4 details a cline in

Selection that differs across seasons may lead to retention of genetic diversity

When there is differential selection in different habitats and migration among them, a polymorphism may result

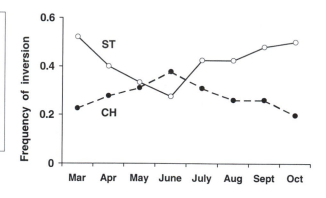

Fig. 9.5 Changes with season in the frequency of chromosomal inversions (ST and CH) segregating in fruit flies at Pĩnon Flats, California (Dobzhansky *et al.* 1977). *This polymorphism showed a similar pattern in different years, confirming that it is a stable polymorphism.*

glaucousness (leaf waxiness) with elevation in several species of eucalypt tress in Tasmania, Australia. A balance between migration and selection maintains this polymorphism. Selection for frost tolerance favours glaucous individuals at higher elevation, but selection due to insect defoliation acts against them at lower elevation. Pollen flow across sites reintroduces alleles that are selected against. Clines due to migration–selection balance have been found for heavy metal tolerance in colonial bent grass plants between old heavy metal mine waste sites and nearby pastures in Wales (Chapter 7), for industrial melanism in peppered moths across gradients from polluted to unpolluted areas (Bishop & Cook 1975) and for alleles at several allozyme loci (Powers *et al.* 1991). Clines in morphological characters are relatively common, some being so pervasive that they are referred to as ecogeographic rules (Chapter 7).

Conditions for maintenance of genetic diversity by mechanisms involving spatial or temporal variation in selection are considered to be rather restricted (Prout 2000).

| **Box 9.4** | Clines in leaf glaucousness in several species of eucalypt trees in Tasmania, Australia due to differential selection at high and low altitudes and pollen flow (Barber 1955; Barber & Jackson 1957; Thomas & Barber 1974) |

Some eucalypt trees have leaves with a distinct waxy (glaucous) layer on them. At least eight species of eucalypts (gum trees) in Tasmania have parallel clines of glaucousness with higher frequencies of waxy leaves at higher, frosty, altitudes. Further, some species show similar clines in different locations. Glaucous leaves have greater survival in heavy frosts. At lower elevations, glaucous plants suffer greater defoliation through insect attacks. Selective differences have been demonstrated by showing that frequencies differ between seeds and adult plants (see lower figure). Pollen flow between populations results in mixing of alleles from different elevations, while selection operating between seed and adult stages of the life cycle re-establishes differences among elevations.

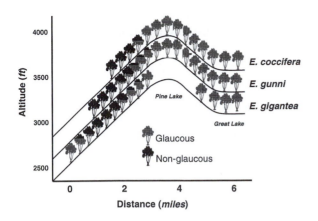

Parallel clines in glaucousness up mountains in Tasmania, Australia in different species of eucalypt trees (after Barber & Jackson 1957).

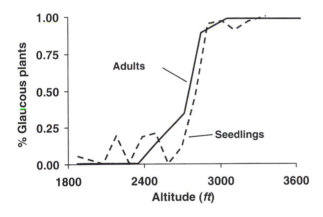

Changes in frequencies of glaucous plants and seedlings with altitude in the urn gum. Difference in glaucous frequencies between seeds and adult plants demonstrate the operation of selection (after Barber 1955).

Reproductive fitness

Genetic diversity for loci affecting reproductive fitness can be maintained by
- mutation-selection equilibrium,
- balancing selection, or
- either of the above interacting with genetic drift.

Neutral mutations do not, by definition, contribute to genetic variation for fitness.

Half, or more, of the genetic diversity for fitness characters is due to mutation–selection balance (Falconer & Mackay 1996; Charlesworth & Hughes 2000). The remainder is maintained by balancing selection, with selection in heterogeneous environments the most probable mechanism (Charlesworth 1998). Neither overdominance nor frequency-dependent selection are considered to be important means for maintaining quantitative genetic diversity for fitness (Falconer & Mackay 1996; Charlesworth & Hughes 2000).

Mutation–selection balance is widely acknowledged as an important factor maintaining genetic diversity for reproductive fitness, accounting for one half, or more, of the genetic diversity

Maintenance of genetic diversity in small populations

Genetic drift has a larger impact, and balancing selection is less effective, in smaller populations, so genetic diversity will generally be lower in small than in large populations

Genetic diversity is often lower in small populations than in large populations (Chapter 3). In large populations genetic diversity is maintained through slow drift of neutral alleles, by mutation–selection balance and by balancing selection. The situation differs in small populations. Five crucial points emerge:

- Drift fixes alleles more rapidly in smaller populations
- Loci subject to weak selection in large populations approach effective neutrality in small populations
- Mutation–selection equilibria are lower in small than in large populations
- The effect of finite population size on balanced polymorphisms depends on the equilibrium frequency; the fixation of intermediate frequency alleles is retarded, but balancing selection accelerates fixation of low frequency alleles
- Balancing selection can retard loss of genetic diversity, but it does not prevent it in small populations.

The consequence of these effects is that genetic diversity in small populations is lower for both neutral alleles and those subject to balancing selection.

Selection and drift in small populations

Genetic drift has a major impact in small populations even for loci that are subject to balancing selection

The balance between selection and drift depends on the population size and the intensity of the selection. When both factors are operating, selection predominates in very large populations, while drift predominates in small populations. For example, in Fig. 8.2 the small populations ($N = 10$) showed a wide variation in behaviour, with one population going to fixation for the deleterious allele, and six for the favoured allele, with five remaining polymorphic. Conversely in the large populations ($N = 100$), all replicates showed similar increases in the frequency of the wild-type allele, with no populations reaching fixation after 20 generations.

Drift may negate the influence of selection

An allele is considered to be effectively neutral if its selection coefficient is less than about $1/(2N_e)$

In small populations, alleles which have effects on fitness may behave as if they are not subject to selection, and drift randomly in frequency from one generation to the next (Wright 1931). Thus, weakly selected alleles in small populations, plus strictly neutral alleles, are referred to as **effectively neutral** (or selectively neutral).

The conditions for effective neutrality depend on the relationship between the selection coefficient and the effective population size (Fig.

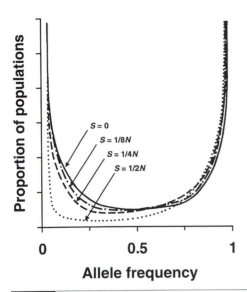

Proportion of populations (y-axis)

S = 0
S = 1/8N
S = 1/4N
S = 1/2N

Allele frequency (x-axis: 0, 0.5, 1)

Fig. 9.6 Distributions of allele frequencies in different sized populations subject to different strengths of directional selection (after Dobzhansky *et al.* 1977, based on Wright). The proportions of populations with different allele frequencies are shown for populations that have reached a steady state. *The distributions with weak selection are similar to those for no selection (s = 0), until the selection coefficient equals or exceeds approximately* $1/(2N_e)$.

9.6). The distributions of allele frequencies for weakly selected loci are very similar to those for neutrality ($s = 0$) until $s > 1/2N$. Consequently, Kimura (1983) defined an effectively neutral allele as one where

$$s < \frac{1}{2N_e} \tag{9.4}$$

For example, a selection coefficient of 5%, which would be considered a very strong deterministic force in a large population, becomes effectively zero in a population of effective size < 10. Further examples of population sizes required for alleles to be effectively neutral are given in Example 9.4. These indicate that most allozyme loci will be effectively neutral in populations with effective sizes of less than 300. MHC alleles may often behave as if neutral in populations with effective sizes of 50 of less. These effective population sizes may correspond to actual sizes of perhaps 10 times larger (Chapter 10). Thus, for most populations of conservation concern, allozyme and DNA polymorphisms will behave as if they are neutral, or very nearly so.

Example 9.4 | In what sized populations are alleles effectively neutral?

Selection coefficients are often on the order of 0.15% or less on allozymes (Kreitman 1996), and often less than 1% on MHC variants. At what population sizes are these effectively neutral? Allozymes will be effectively neutral when $s < 1/(2N_e)$, thus

$$0.0015 < \frac{1}{2N_e}$$

i.e. when

$$N_e < \frac{1}{2 \times 0.0015} < 333$$

Thus, allozyme alleles will be effectively neutral in populations with effective sizes of about 300 or less. This typically corresponds to an actual population size of up to 3000 adults (Chapter 10). Consequently, allozymes will be effectively neutral in most threatened species.

A MHC allele with a 1% selection coefficient will be effectively neutral when

$$0.01 < \frac{1}{2N_e}$$

i.e. when

$$N_e < \frac{1}{2 \times 0.01} < 50$$

Thus, an allele with a selection coefficient of 1% will be effectively neutral in a population with an N_e of less than 50. This typically corresponds to an actual population size of up to 500 adults, so such alleles will be effectively neutral in many endangered species.

While Equation 9.4 suggests that there is a threshold population size below which effective neutrality occurs, the effectiveness of selection declines in a more-or-less continuous fashion as effective population size is reduced (Fig. 9.7). The effectiveness of selection is less sensitive to reductions in population size for alleles with large, as opposed to those with small, selection coefficients. An allele with a selection coefficient

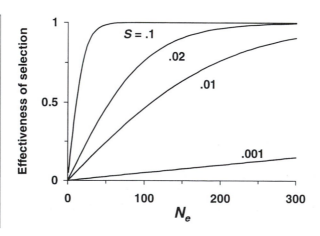

Fig. 9.7 Selection is less effective in small than in large populations. Plot of the effectiveness of selection against N_e for alleles with different selection coefficients (s). An allele with an effectiveness of 1 has the same probability of fixation as that in an infinite population. Effectiveness is defined as ($P_{fixation}$ − p) / ($1 - p$), where p is the initial frequency of the allele and $P_{fixation}$ is the probability of fixation for the allele in populations of particular sizes.

of 10% is selected as effectively as in an infinite population size until N_e drops below 50. Below this the effectiveness of selection drops rapidly as N_e reduces and the allele becomes effectively neutral. An allele with a selection coefficient of 1% is not selected with complete efficiency even at a population size of 300, and its selective effectiveness drops incrementally as the population size declines.

Balancing selection and drift in small populations

Balancing selection may slow the loss of genetic diversity in small populations, but it cannot normally prevent it, i.e. even strongly selected balanced polymorphisms for the MHC, inversions, self-incompatibility alleles and visual polymorphisms are not immune from the effects of genetic drift. For example, MHC diversity is subject to genetic drift, as it is correlated with allozyme diversity across species, and with DNA fingerprint diversity across different sized populations of pocket gophers (Fig. 9.8). Related evidence has been reported for the Australian bush rat (Seddon & Baverstock 1999). Inversions are subject to genetic drift (Montgomery *et al.* 2000). Further, there is evidence that visual polymorphisms in snail shells are affected by genetic drift in small populations (Lamotte 1959).

> Even strongly selected balanced polymorphisms for the MHC, inversions, self-incompatibility alleles and visual polymorphisms lose genetic diversity due to genetic drift in small populations

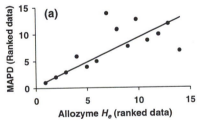 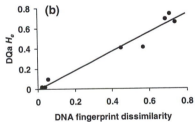 

Fig. 9.8 Loss of genetic diversity due to drift at MHC loci. Correlation of MHC diversity and allozyme or DNA fingerprint diversity across species and populations, indicating that the MHC loses diversity due to genetic drift (Zegers 2000). (a) Plot of MHC diversity (MAPD) against allozyme diversity for a range of different species. (b) Plot of MHC diversity (DQa locus) against DNA fingerprint diversity for different populations of pocket gophers. *These correlations are expected with genetic drift, but not with selection. Genetic drift affects all neutral (and effectively neutral) loci in the same way. Conversely, selection affects different loci in different ways.*

Loss of alleles at self-incompatibility loci has also been documented in several small plant populations (Les *et al.* 1991; Demauro 1993; Young *et al.* 2000). Theoretical models predict that there will be a close relationship between number of SI alleles and effective population size (Fig. 9.9).

To understand the loss of genetic diversity for loci under balancing selection, we now consider the impacts of heterozygote advantage selection in small populations.

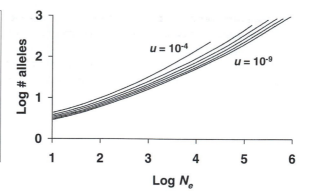

Fig. 9.9 Smaller plant populations are expected to have fewer self-incompatibility alleles than larger populations. Predicted number of S alleles in populations with different effective sizes (N_e) for various mutation rates (u) (after Richman & Kohn 1996). The model involves drift, mutation and self-incompatibility selection.

Heterozygote advantage impedes fixation for alleles with equilibrium frequencies in the range 0.2–0.8, but accelerates fixation for alleles outside this range when compared to neutral alleles

A critical point about balanced polymorphisms in small populations is that maintenance of genetic diversity by overdominant selection depends on the equilibrium frequency (Fig. 9.10). Robertson (1962) demonstrated that heterozygote advantage impedes fixation for alleles with equilibrium frequencies in the 0.2–0.8 range. Conversely, for alleles with equilibrium frequencies outside this range, overdominance actually *increases* the rate of fixation, compared to neutral alleles. This counter-intuitive result occurs because alleles that drift to more intermediate frequencies are moved back towards their more extreme equilibrium frequencies by selection, thus making them more prone to loss by drift. In other words, selection 'discourages' these rarer alleles from drifting to higher frequencies. Many alleles at polymorphic DNA and allozyme loci fall into this frequency range. This equilibrium frequency effect probably applies to all forms of balancing selection.

Even for alleles with equilibria of 0.2–0.8, there are effects of genetic drift unless selection coefficients are large and population sizes very large. For example, there is a relationship between genetic diversity and population size up to an effective population size of 1000 (perhaps $N = 10\,000$) for alleles with selection coefficients $s_1 + s_2 = 0.04$ (Robertson 1962). DNA sequence polymorphisms, allozymes and even MHC diversity are likely to fall within this range of selective values in threatened populations.

The conservation implications of the above are clear and extremely important.

Weakly selected loci in small populations become effectively neutral, so that drift is a major concern in maintaining genetic diversity in species of conservation concern

Evolutionary processes are changed when a species declines from a large size to become small and endangered. For example, the impact of natural selection on both American and European bison has been substantially reduced since their numbers have been depleted by overexploitation. Similar processes are occurring in African elephants and rhinoceroses as their population sizes are reduced, and they exist in small, isolated fragments. The impact of natural selection is reduced for any population that has decreased in size. We see the worrying implication that small populations are less able to evolve to cope with environmental changes, such as new diseases, even if they have the same amounts of genetic diversity initially.

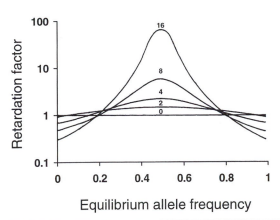

Fig. 9.10 Reduction (retardation) in fixation probability in finite populations, compared to that for a neutral locus, for loci exhibiting overdominant selection with different equilibrium frequencies (after Robertson 1962). When the retardation factor exceeds 1.0, selected loci show greater retention of genetic diversity than neutral loci, but when it is less than 1.0 they show accelerated fixation compared to neutral loci. The numbers on the curves represent different values of the product of selection coefficients and effective population size [$N_e(s_1 + s_2)$]. *Overdominant selection retards fixation in the range 0.2–0.8, but accelerates it outside this range of equilibrium frequencies.*

Associative overdominance

In small populations, a further interaction between balancing selection and drift arises. Linkage disequilibrium develops over generations in small populations, as chromosomal types are lost by chance (Fig. 9.11). As essentially all chromosomes contain at least one deleterious allele, chromosomal homozygotes are homozygous for one or more deleterious alleles. However, different chromosomes contain deleterious recessive alleles at different loci, so chromosomal heterozygotes are heterozygous for deleterious alleles. Consequently, chromosomal homozygotes are deleterious, while heterozygotes have higher reproductive fitness (Fig. 9.11). When this occurs, the fate of an allele is determined by the loci around it. The neutral locus (A) in the figure is apparently exhibiting overdominance, as it is non-randomly associated with the deleterious alleles m_2 and m_6. This apparent overdominance due to linkage disequilibrium is termed **associative overdominance**.

Linkage disequilibrium only develops gradually over several generations after population size has been reduced. It does not impede the initial loss of genetic diversity (e.g. there has been fixation at loci m_1, m_3, m_4, and m_5 in Fig. 9.11).

The selective forces involved here are likely to be much stronger than those experienced by most single loci, i.e. the major selective force in small populations will usually be associative overdominance.

Associative overdominance slows loss of genetic diversity in small populations. Allozyme diversity was lost at only about 80% of the rate

In small populations, linkage disequilibrium develops over generations. This results in blocks of loci containing different deleterious alleles, showing heterozygous advantage (associative overdominance)

Associative overdominance slows the subsequent loss of genetic diversity, but does not prevent it

Fig. 9.11 Development of associative overdominance in small populations. The gene pool for a large population is shown with an array of chromosomes that exhibit linkage equilibrium between deleterious alleles (m) and a neutral marker locus (A). In a small population, genetic drift over generations leads to the loss of all except two chromosomal haplotypes, leading to linkage disequilibrium (recombination is insufficient to prevent this in small populations). The resulting genotypes exhibit overdominance, as each chromosomal homozygote is homozygous for a different recessive deleterious allele (m_2 or m_6), while the chromosomal heterozygotes are heterozygous for both deleterious alleles. Consequently, neutral alleles (A_1 vs. A_2) on the chromosomes behave as if they have heterozygote advantage (associative overdominance).

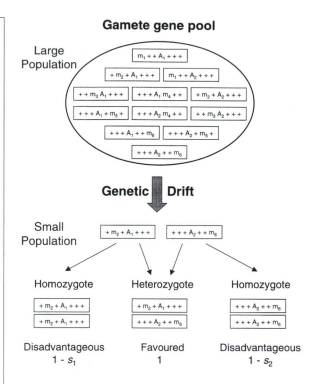

expected for neutral loci in fruit fly populations of size $N = 2$ (Rumball *et al.* 1994). Similarly, linkage disequilibrium eventually developed and slowed fixation, even in fruit fly populations with effective sizes of about 50 (Latter *et al.* 1995). Computer simulations with many loci indicate that linkage disequilibrium, coupled with either deleterious alleles, or loci showing overdominance, slows fixation at linked neutral loci, but does not prevent eventual fixation (Latter 1998).

Genetic diversity for reproductive fitness in small populations

Genetic diversity for reproductive fitness will be lost through genetic drift in small populations, but rates of loss may be less than for neutral loci

The magnitudes of selective forces acting on individual polymorphic loci affecting fitness are unknown, as the number of polymorphic loci contributing to the observed variation in fitness is unknown. However, selective forces on most loci are presumed to be small, as many loci are involved. If selection is weak, then genetic drift in small populations will reduce genetic diversity at these loci.

Loci contributing to genetic variation for fitness traits through mutation–selection balance will carry deleterious alleles at very low frequencies. Rare alleles are very sensitive to genetic drift, and variation will be readily lost in small populations. Even lethal alleles are not immune to the effects of genetic drift, as we saw in the previous chapter. Since lethals represent the most strongly selected alleles, most alleles affecting fitness will be even more affected by genetic drift.

Components of genetic variation for fitness, maintained by balancing selection, will be less sensitive to population size reduction than neutral variation. However, they too will not be immune to the effects of genetic drift.

There can be no doubt that genetic variation for reproductive fitness is lower in small than in large populations. Evolutionary potential has been shown to be reduced in bottlenecked laboratory populations and to be related to size in populations maintained for 50 generations at different sizes (Chapter 10, Frankham *et al.* 1999).

Summary

1. Genetic diversity is of major concern in conservation biology as populations require the capacity to evolve with environmental changes.

2. Genetic diversity arises by mutation and is lost through directional selection and genetic drift.

3. Balancing selection impedes loss of genetic diversity. This may take the form of heterozygote advantage, frequency-dependent selection, or selection of varying direction over space or time.

4. The relative contributions of selection versus drift in determining levels of genetic diversity depend on the population size and the character being considered.

5. Drift effects predominate in small populations, while selection is most effective in large populations.

6. Selection is more important for visual polymorphisms and reproductive fitness than for untranslated DNA, with protein polymorphisms intermediate. Drift has the opposite pattern of importance.

7. Genetic variation for reproductive fitness seems to be maintained by mutation–selection balance for half, or more, of its variation, and by some form of balancing selection for the remainder.

8. Population size is a major determinant of genetic diversity for all loci and characters in small populations and species of conservation concern.

FURTHER READING

Gillespie, J. (1991) *The Causes of Molecular Evolution*. An exposition on the topic that takes a very strong selectionist view.

Hughes & Yeager (1998) A review of mechanisms maintaining genetic diversity at MHC loci in vertebrates.

Kimura (1983) *The Neutral Theory of Molecular Evolution*. A fine exposition of the neutral theory for maintenance of genetic diversity.

Kreitman & Akashi (1995) A review of the evidence for selection on molecular variation.

Richman & Kohn (1996) An excellent review of the evolutionary biology of self-incompatibility.

Singh & Krimbas (2000) *Evolutionary Genetics*. A recent collection of excellent advanced reviews, several relating to topics in this chapter. See especially chapters by Schaeffer & Aguade, Hedrick & Kim, Prout, and Charlesworth & Hughes.

PROBLEMS

9.1. Genetic diversity under neutrality: What are the predicted equilibrium heterozygosities and effective number of alleles under neutrality for a locus with a neutral mutation rate of 10^{-7} in a population with an effective size of 20?

9.2 Excess heterozygosity due to selection: Do the genotype frequencies at the haemoglobin locus for adults differ from Hardy–Weinberg equilibrium expectations for the data in Box 9.1? Do the infant genotype frequencies differ from Hardy–Weinberg equilibrium expectations?

9.3 Heterozygote advantage: If relative fitnesses are 0.99, 1 and 0.97 for genotypes A_1A_1, A_1A_2 and A_2A_2, respectively, what are equilibrium frequencies for the two alleles?

9.4 Heterozygote advantage: The locus that confers resistance to the anti-coagulant poison warfarin in wild rats shows heterozygote advantage; resistant homozygotes survive the poison, but many die from vitamin K deficiency, heterozygotes are resistant to poison and do not suffer from vitamin K deficiency, while susceptible homozygotes have higher mortality due to the poison. What is the equilibrium frequency for the warfarin resistant R allele in rats, given the following survival rates of the three genotypes (modified from Greaves *et al.* 1977)? (Assume that the only selection is for survival.)

RR	RS	SS
0.3	0.8	0.56

9.5 Heterozygote advantage: If the relative fitnesses of the three genotypes A_1A_1, A_1A_2 and A_2A_2 at a locus are 0.7, 1 and 0.9, what will be the final state of populations beginning with a frequency of A_1 of (a) 0.1? (b) 0.3? (c) 0.9?

9.6 Equilibrium frequency with heterozygote advantage: Derive the expression for the equilibrium frequency due to selection favouring heterozygotes at a locus. Assume that the starting frequencies for alleles A_1 and A_2 are p and q.

	Genotypes			
	A_1A_1	A_1A_2	A_2A_2	Total
Frequencies at fertilization				
Relative fitnesses	$1-s_1$	1	$1-s_2$	
After selection				
Adjust so total is 1				
New frequency of $A_1 = p_1 =$				
$\Delta p =$				
At equilibrium $\Delta p =$				

9.7 Self-incompatibility: For the system described in Box 9.3, determine the relative fitness of each S allele in pollen in a population with equal frequencies of three genotypes in females, but frequencies of S_1, S_2 and S_3 alleles of 1/6, 1/3 and 1/2 in pollen.

9.8 Self-incompatibility: What will the relative fitness of a new S_4 allele be in pollen in the case described in Box 9.3, if the three female genotypes have equal frequencies and alleles S_1, S_2, S_3 and S_4 have frequencies of 0.33, 0.33, 0.33 and 0.01, respectively, in pollen?

9.9 Selective neutrality: At what population size is an allele with a selection coefficient of 2% effectively neutral?

PRACTICAL EXERCISES: COMPUTER SIMULATIONS

Maintenance of genetic diversity due to heterozygote advantage Use POPGEN or a similar software package to simulate aspects of the maintenance of genetic diversity in large vs. small populations.

1. Strong selection Simulate the allele frequency trajectories for sickle cell anaemia, beginning at different allele frequencies, using the following relative fitnesses observed by Allison in 1956:

AA	AS	SS
0.76	1	0.20

Commence runs with S allele frequency 0.1 and run for 100 generations with (a) an infinite population (deterministic option in POPGEN) (b) $N = 100$ and (c) $N = 10$, doing 20 replicates of each of the latter. Compare the outcomes at the three population sizes.

2. Weak selection: equilibrium $q = 0.5$ Simulate the allele frequency changes for the following model of heterozygote advantage with weak selection:

A_1A_1	A_1A_2	A_2A_2
0.99	1	0.99

Commence runs with $q = 0.5$ and run for 100 generations (a) an infinite population (deterministic option in POPGEN) (b) $N = 100$ and (c) $N = 10$. Run 50 replicates of the latter two cases. Repeat the runs for same population sizes with neutrality (relative fitnesses of all genotypes of 1). Compare the proportion of populations polymorphic at generation 100 for the neutral cases with those for balancing selection and across population sizes. Does balancing selection slow fixation, or speed it up?

3. Weak selection: equilibrium $q = 0.1$ Simulate the allele frequency changes for the following model of heterozygote advantage with weak selection:

A_1A_1	A_1A_2	A_2A_2
0.99	1	0.999

Commence runs with $q = 0.1$ and run for 100 generations with (a) an infinite population (deterministic option in POPGEN) (b) $N = 100$ and (c)

$N = 10$. Run 50 replicates. Repeat the runs for the same population sizes with neutrality. Compare the proportion of populations polymorphic at generation 100 for the neutral cases with those for balancing selection, and across population sizes. Does balancing selection slow fixation, or speed it up?

Section II

Effects of population size reduction

Threatened species have small, or declining populations. Once small, they suffer loss of genetic diversity, inbreeding (with consequent reduction in reproductive fitness) and accumulation of deleterious mutations. All these factors increase the risk of extinction. Consequently, Section II considers these factors in detail, as they represent the major genetic issues in conservation biology, and provide the essential background material for the genetic management of threatened species in Section III.

Factors reducing population size

Humans are reducing the size and distribution of wild populations through clearing and fragmentation of habitat, over-exploitation, pollution and the impact of introduced species. Of these, habitat loss is having the greatest impact. Species are becoming extinct before they are described, and unknown numbers of invertebrate and plant species will be exterminated.

Loss of genetic diversity

Loss of genetic diversity in small populations reduces the ability to evolve in response to ever-present environmental change. There are four threats to genetic diversity:
- Extinction of populations or species
- Extinction of alleles due to sampling in small populations
- Inbreeding reducing heterozygosity (redistributing genetic diversity among homozygous individuals and populations)

• Selection reducing genetic diversity by favouring one allele at the expense of others, leading to fixation.

Overwhelmingly the major threat to genetic diversity is extinction of alleles in finite populations by genetic drift. The adverse genetic effects of population size reduction, loss of genetic diversity, inbreeding, and accumulation of deleterious mutations all depend on the effective population size, rather than the census size. The effective population size is reduced by unequal sex-ratios, high variation in family sizes, and by fluctuations in population sizes. **Chapter 10** deals with the effects of small population size on genetic diversity and the factors that influence effective population size.

Inbreeding

Inbreeding is an inevitable consequence of small population size. Eventually all individuals become related, so that matings amongst relatives cannot be avoided. **Chapter 11** describes how inbreeding is measured, and its rate of increases in finite populations. Inbreeding exposes deleterious mutations and reduces reproductive fitness and so increases extinction risk. **Chapter 12** documents the extent of inbreeding depression and discusses its genetic basis.

Population fragmentation

Habitat fragmentation reduces population sizes and increases isolation of population fragments. Completely isolated population fragments suffer elevated rates of inbreeding and loss of genetic diversity, and consequently have elevated extinction risks, compared to single populations of the same total size. The impacts of population fragmentation depend critically on population structure and gene flow. **Chapter 13** deals with the genetic consequences of population fragmentation and with the means for measuring population differentiation and inferring gene flow.

Genetically viable populations

The section concludes with **Chapter 14**, 'Genetically viable populations'. This is concerned with the questions: How large do populations need to be to avoid inbreeding depression? To avoid loss of evolutionary potential? To avoid accumulation of deleterious mutations? These sizes are compared with actual population sizes for endangered species and size targets for de-listing species. Current goals for genetic management of captive populations represent a compromise that recognizes that there will be modest genetic deterioration over time.

Chapter 10

Loss of genetic diversity in small populations

Sustained restrictions in population size are the main reason for loss of genetic diversity. Losses in closed populations depend on the effective population size (N_e) and on the number of generations. N_e is usually much less than the number of adults in a population

Terms:

Effective population size (N_e),
harmonic mean,
idealized population

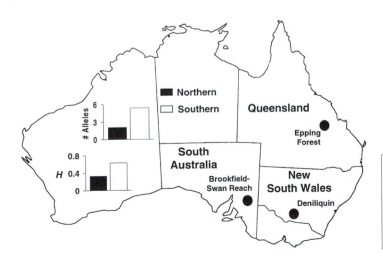

Low genetic diversity in the critically endangered northern hairy-nosed wombat, compared to its nearest relative, the southern hairy-nosed wombat (after Smith & Wayne 1996).

Changes in genetic diversity over time

The current genetic status of a population derives from cumulative effects over many previous generations. Predictions of future changes must also encompass many generations

In Section I, we examined the origin, extent and fate of genetic variation for both single locus and quantitative traits. In particular, we explored the evolutionary forces which influence genetic diversity and contrasted their importance in small versus large populations. Our major conclusions are:

- Genetic diversity provides the raw material for evolutionary adaptive change
- Mutation is the ultimate source of all genetic variation
- Mutation, and migration from conspecific populations or closely related species, are the only mechanisms for restoring lost diversity. As mutation rates are always very low, this factor is inconsequential for genetically depauperate endangered species
- Genetic diversity can be estimated by a variety of laboratory techniques and expressed by the related parameters of percentage of loci exhibiting polymorphism, allelic diversity or average heterozygosity. Heterozgosity is the most useful parameter as it can be compared across species for single locus variation and is directly correlated with additive genetic variance for quantitative traits
- Some adaptive genetic variation is maintained within populations by balancing selection
- The influence of the deterministic forces of natural selection is directly related to population size. The fate of alleles in most small populations of endangered species is predominated by random factors
- Inbreeding, with consequent loss of fitness, becomes inevitable in small populations
- Effective population size (N_e), as opposed to the observed census size, determines loss of genetic diversity and inbreeding.

For simplicity, we have primarily considered single generation changes due to deterministic and random factors. However, the current genetic status of a population is a consequence of cumulative effects over many previous generations. Equally, our predictions of future changes, in both managed and un-managed populations, must extend over many generations.

At first it may seem that loss of genetic diversity is only of concern in long-term evolutionary adaptation. However, there are immediate short-term implications of loss of genetic diversity as well. In self-incompatible plants there is a direct relationship between loss of genetic diversity at self-incompatibility loci and reduction in reproductive fitness that we explore below. Further, loss of genetic diversity is intimately related to the average increase in inbreeding in outbreeding populations. Increased inbreeding will lead to reductions in average reproductive fitness for populations, i.e. concerns about loss of genetic diversity in conservation biology are actually concerns about both loss of evolutionary potential and short-term loss of fitness due to inbreeding depression.

Relationship between loss of genetic diversity and reduced fitness

The self-incompatibility in many plant species is genetically controlled by one or more multi-allelic self-incompatibility (SI) loci (Box 9.3). Computer simulations show that these S alleles are lost in small populations and that this can lead to extinctions (Byers & Meagher 1999). This arises because the proportion of the pollen that can successfully fertilize increases with the number of S alleles (Fig. 10.1). If there is a shortage of pollen, or pollen of all types is not dispersed to all plants, this leads to reduced fitness in populations with reduced numbers of S alleles. In very small populations, all reproduction may cease, leading to effective extinction even when a handful of plants remains.

Losses of S alleles in small self-incompatible plant populations and consequent reductions in population fitness have been documented in three species (Les *et al.* 1991; Demauro 1993; Young *et al.* 2000); the case of the endangered grassland daisy is described in Box 10.1. All threatened self-incompatible plant species are susceptible to similar problems.

> Loss of alleles at self-incompatibility loci in small plant populations reduces population reproductive fitness

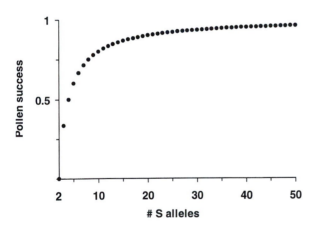

Fig. 10.1 Predicted relationship between maximum proportion of pollen that can succeed in fertilizing and number of S alleles in plants with gametophytic self-incompatibility.

Box 10.1	Relationship between loss of S allele diversity and reproductive fitness in the endangered self-incompatible grassland daisy (Young *et al.* 2000; Young personal communication)

Direct evidence of loss of S alleles and reduced reproductive fitness has been found in small populations of the endangered grassland daisy in eastern Australia. S allelic diversity (and allozyme diversity) declined with population size in five population fragments of the daisy with sizes from 5 to 70 000 plants. Number of seeds per plant was related to log N. This relationship between seeds/plant and population size was not due to a shortage of pollinators in small populations as there were about 50 pollen per stigma and only a single ovule to fertilize. Use of pollen from other populations increased seed set in small populations, confirming that the small number of S alleles in small populations caused the reduced seed set.

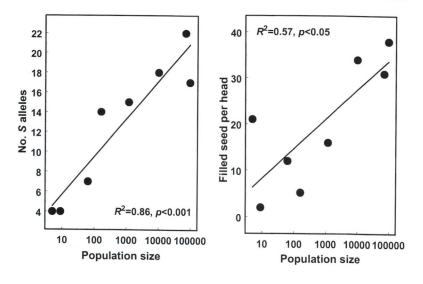

Loss of genetic diversity in small populations is related to inbreeding, so it is often related to reduced reproductive fitness

Within most large random mating populations there is little relationship between heterozygosity of individuals and their reproductive fitness, as such relationships depend upon occurrence of heterozygote advantage or frequency-dependent selection. These are rare, except for MHC and for SI loci (Carrington *et al.* 1999). When relationships are observed between individual heterozygosity and fitness they generally seem to be due to inbreeding (see Hedrick & Savolainen 1996; David 1998).

However, small populations of naturally outbreeding species suffer both losses of genetic diversity and inbreeding over time. Since inbreeding reduces reproductive fitness (Chapters 2, 11 and 12), loss of genetic diversity from small populations is expected to be associated with reductions in reproductive fitness. A recent meta-analysis of 33 data sets has confirmed that such a relationship exists; the average correlation between population fitness and heterozygosity was 0.40 (Reed & Frankham, 2001). Disease resistance/tolerance has also been shown to be related to genetic diversity in a range of animal and plant species (see Chapter 2).

Below, we first consider the impact on genetic diversity of small population size, sustained over many generations. Second, we consider means for measuring effective population size, especially by evaluating the impacts of unequal sex-ratio, variable family sizes and fluctuations in population size over generations on N_e. Details of the impacts of population size restriction on inbreeding are deferred until Chapters 11 and 12.

Effects of sustained population size restrictions on genetic diversity

There are five mechanisms by which genetic diversity is lost:
- Extinction of species and populations
- Fixation of favourable alleles by selection
- Selective removal of deleterious alleles
- Random loss of alleles by inter-generational sampling in small populations
- Inbreeding (such as selfing) within populations reducing heterozygosity.

The first two are relatively infrequent events, while the drift and inbreeding are common events related to population size.

In Chapter 8 we saw that loss of genetic diversity resulted from drastic reductions in population size (bottlenecks) over one or a few generations. However, equally serious loss of variation can accumulate with modest population restriction. A population of effective size 100 (a size typical for vulnerable species – see below) loses 25% of its heterozygosity over 57 generations, the same loss as a single generation bottleneck of one pair (Fig. 8.6). Since severe bottlenecks are relatively uncommon, while more modest population size restrictions are a regular feature of threatened species, the major significance of small population size to genetic diversity is not usually single generation bottlenecks, but the insidious loss of genetic diversity over many generations. For example, the Illinois population of the greater prairie chicken dwindled from several million to fewer than 50 individuals over a 130-year period. This led to reduced genetic diversity (Box 10.2).

Below we develop the theory to predict the sustained impacts of many generations of small population size.

> Genetic diversity is lost primarily due to sustained restrictions in effective population size

---

| **Box 10.2** | **Loss of genetic diversity due to population size reduction in the greater prairie chicken** (Bouzat et al. 1998) |

The greater prairie chicken is a North American grassland/prairie species with limited dispersal. During the last century many populations have become increasingly affected by loss of natural habitats through human activities. Populations in Illinois were estimated to be in the millions in the 1860s, but subsequently declined to 25 000 birds in 1933, 2000 in 1972, 76 in 1990 and to fewer than 50 in 1993. In contrast, extant populations in Kansas, Minnesota and Nebraska remained comparatively large (4000 to more than 100 000 birds).

Data were obtained for six microsatellite loci, with pre–1960 Illinois samples being obtained from museum specimens. The current Illinois population has fewer alleles per locus than that in the current populations from Kansas, Minnesota and Nebraska.

Further, it has lost alleles since 1960; all the alleles shown in bold below for the pre-1960 samples are now absent from the Illinois population.

Population	Locus 1	2	3	4	5	6	Allelic diversity
Illinois							
now	ABC-	ABCD-	A--D-F-H	ABC---	-B--E--	--C-EFGHI---	3.67
pre-1960	AB---	-BCD**E**	A--D-F---	ABC-**E**-	-**BCDEFG**	-**BCDEFG**-I--**L**	5.12
Kansas	ABCD	-BCDEF	A-CDEFGH	ABCDE-	ABCDE--	ABCDEFGHI---	5.83
Minnesota	ABCD	ABCD--	ABCDEFGH	ABC-E-	-BCDE--	-BCDEFGHI---	5.33
Nebraska	ABCD	ABCDE-	ABCDEFGH	-BC-EF	-BCDE--	-BCDEFGHIJK-	5.83

Loss of heterozygosity is a process of continuous decay that is more rapid in smaller than larger populations

In each generation, a proportion $1/(2N_e)$ of neutral genetic diversity is lost, as we saw in Chapter 8. Such effects occur in every generation and losses accumulate with time. We dealt with loss of genetic diversity due to the impact of a single reduction in population size in Chapter 8.

If population size is constant in each generation, we can extend Equation 8.2 to obtain an expression for the effects of sustained population size restriction in heterozygosity, as follows:

$$H_1 = [1 - 1/(2N_e)] H_0$$

and

$$H_2 = [1 - 1/(2N_e)] H_1$$

so by substituting the initial expression for H_1 in the second equation

$$H_2 = [1 - 1/(2N_e)]^2 H_0$$

By extension, the predicted heterozygosity at generation t becomes

$$H_t = [1 - 1/(2N_e)]^t H_0$$

This is usually expressed as the predicted heterozygosity as a proportion of the initial heterozygosity:

$$H_t / H_0 = [1 - 1/(2N_e)]^t \sim e^{-t/2N_e} \tag{10.1}$$

Predicted declines in heterozygosity with time in different sized populations are shown in Fig. 10.2. The important points of this relationship are:

• Loss of genetic diversity depends on the effective population size, rather than the census size
• Heterozygosity is lost at a greater rate in small than large populations
• Loss depends on generations, not years
• Loss of heterozygosity continues with generations, in an exponential decay process

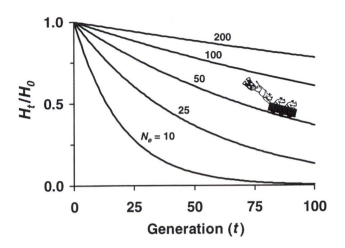

Fig. 10.2 Predicted decline in heterozygosity over time in different sized populations (after Foose 1986).

• Half of the initial heterozygosity is lost in 1.4 N_e generations.

We elaborate on some of these points below.

Example 10.1 demonstrates that populations with effective size 500 will lose only about 5% of their initial heterozygosity over 50 generations, while populations with $N_e = 25$ loses 64% of their initial heterozygosity.

The shorter the generation length, the more rapid in absolute time will be the loss. Consequently, similar sized populations of black-footed ferrets with generation lengths of two years will lose genetic diversity more rapidly than elephants with generation lengths of 26 years.

This theory leads us to expect lowered genetic diversity in endangered species, and in small populations generally. This is the case (Chapter 3).

| **Example 10.1** | Expected loss of heterozygosity due to sustained population size reduction |

The expected proportion of heterozygosity retained over 50 generations in a population of effective size 500 from Equation 10.1 is

$$H_t / H_0 = [1 - 1 / (2N_e)]^t = [1 - 1 / (2 \times 500)]^{50} = (999/1000)^{50} = 0.951$$

i.e. this large population will lose only about 5% of its initial heterozygosity in 50 generations.

For a population with $N_e = 25$, the proportion of initial heterozygosity retained at generation 50 is expected to be

$$H_t / H_0 = [1 - 1 / (2N_e)]^t = [1 - 1 / (2 \times 25)]^{50} = (49/50)^{50} = 0.364$$

Consequently, this small population will lose 64% of its initial heterozygosity in 50 generations.

In small populations
heterozygosity for allozyme loci is
lost approximately as predicted by
simple neutral theory

Does this theory agree with loss of genetic diversity in real populations? We have assumed that alleles are neutral and that they are unlinked – assumptions that may not apply in practice. Allozyme variation is indeed lost approximately as described by Equation 10.1 (Fig. 10.3).

Equation 10.1 predicts the expected (i.e. average) fate of heterozygosity, but the behaviour of individual loci will be highly variable because of the stochastic properties involved, especially in small populations. Note that the variation among replicate populations is greater for smaller populations than for larger populations (Fig. 10.3). Heterozygosity estimates derived from the average of several loci will yield results closer to predictions than those based on a single locus. The extent of the variation among replicate populations is addressed in Chapter 13.

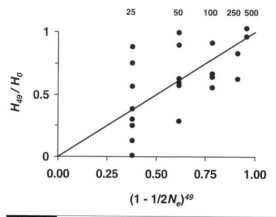

Fig. 10.3 Comparisons of observed and predicted heterozygosities after 49 generations in populations of different size. Heterozygosity for allozyme loci at generation 49, as a proportion of initial heterozygosity (H_{49}/H_0), in populations of fruit flies with different sizes (N_e) plotted against $(1 - 1/2N_e)^{49}$ (after Montgomery et al. 2000). Numbers at the top are effective population sizes. The line on the figure indicates the neutral prediction. *The observed relationship does not differ significantly from expectations.*

Small populations lose genetic
variation for reproductive fitness

As genetic variation for reproductive fitness is subject to strong natural selection, the equations for neutral loci do not apply to it. Is this component of genetic diversity also lost in small populations? As there are many loci involved, and many deleterious alleles are very rare, it is most probable that the alleles involved are affected by genetic drift, and that evolutionary potential is compromised in small populations (Chapter 9). An experimental test with fruit flies showed that the ability of populations to evolve in the face of a changing environment (evolutionary potential) is related to population size (Fig. 10.4).

When populations fluctuate in size
over generations, loss of genetic
diversity is most strongly
influenced by the minimum size

So far in our development of the theory, we have only considered populations with constant sizes. However, most real populations fluctuate in size from generation to generation. Familiar examples are 'plague species', such as locusts and domestic mice. Such fluctuations have profound influences on heterozygosity (equation below), on effective population size (see below) and on inbreeding (Chapter 11).

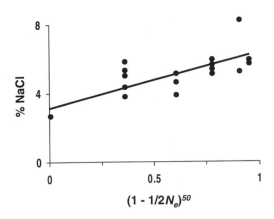

$$H_t / H_0 = \prod_{i=1}^{t} [1 - 1/(2N_{e_i})] \tag{10.2}$$

Fig. 10.4 Relationship between population size and evolutionary potential in fruit flies (Frankham, Lowe, Woodworth, Montgomery & Briscoe, unpublished data). Populations founded from the same source population were maintained at different effective sizes for 50 generations. Equal numbers were used to establish large cage populations that were forced to evolve in response to increasing concentrations of NaCl. The concentrations of NaCl at extinction are plotted against $[1 - 1/(2N_e)]^{50}$. *Extinction concentrations, on average, increase with population size.*

Reductions in heterozygosity are most strongly dependent on the generation with the smallest effective population size. For example, a population with effective sizes of 10, 100, 1000 and 10 000 over four generations loses 5.5% of its heterozygosity (Example 10.2). Almost all of the loss (5%) is due to the generation with $N_e = 10$.

Example 10.2 | Loss of heterozygosity with fluctuating population sizes

The expected proportion of heterozygosity retained in a population with effective sizes of 10, 100, 1000 and 10 000 over four generations is determined using Equation 10.2, as follows:

$$H_t / H_0 = \prod^{t} [1 - 1/(2N_{e_i})]$$

$$= [1 - (1/20)][1 - (1/200)][1 - (1/2000)][1 - (1/20\,000)]$$

$$= 0.95 \times 0.995 \times 0.9995 \times 0.99995 = 0.945$$

Consequently, the population loses 5.5% of its heterozygosity over the four generations, the great majority (5%) being due to the population size of 10.

Relationship between population size and genetic diversity in wild populations

Based on Equations 10.1 and 10.2, correlations between population size and genetic diversity in wild populations are expected. This depends upon two assumptions. First, that most genetic diversity is neutral in small populations, or at most weakly selected and subject to genetic

There is overwhelming evidence that levels of genetic diversity are related to population size, both across species and among populations within species

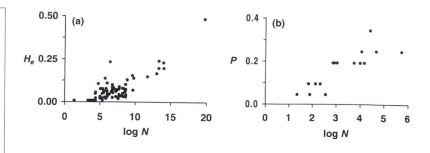

Fig. 10.5 Relationship between genetic diversity and population size among and within species. (a) H_e and logarithm of population size across species (after Frankham 1996), and (b) percent polymorphism and population size among populations within the New Zealand conifer *Halocharpus bidwilli* (after Billington 1991).

drift (Chapter 9). Second, that current population sizes reflect historic effective population sizes.

A strong relationship has been found between genetic diversity and population size across a wide array of species (Fig. 10.5a), with population size explaining around one-half of the variation in heterozygosity among species.

Correlations of genetic diversity with population size were positive in 22 of 23 studies within species of plants and animals (Frankham 1996). An example of one large study is given in Fig. 10.5b. Further, geographic range, a factor likely to reflect population size, is the major factor explaining levels of genetic diversity within plant species (Hamrick & Godt 1989). While the data above relate mainly to allozyme diversity, mtDNA also shows a significant relationship with population size across species.

Not all studies show significant relationships between population size and genetic diversity. This is due to three causes. First, many studies are so small that they lack the statistical power required to detect significant relationships. For example, one study with a correlation of 0.75 was not significant as it was based on only four populations! Meta-analyses, which overcome lack of statistical power, reveal clear associations (Frankham 1996). Second, current population size does not always reflect historic effective population size. Third, the relationship is 'noisy' (Fig. 10.3). Many loci need to be evaluated to obtain a representative picture for the whole genome. Alternatively, many replicate populations are required to obtain an adequate representative average. In spite of these complications, there is overwhelming evidence for associations between population size and genetic diversity, both within and across species (Frankham 1996).

Endangered species typically have lower genetic diversity than related non-endangered species

Endangered species, by definition, have small or declining population sizes, and are therefore expected to have lower genetic diversity than non-endangered species (with larger population sizes). This has been found (Chapter 3). For example, the critically endangered northern hairy-nosed wombat from Australia, with a population size of only 75, has less genetic diversity than its non-endangered relative, the southern hairy-nosed wombat (Box 10.3). The magnitude of the difference in genetic diversity between endangered and non-endangered species is substantial. On average, endangered species have only about 60% the microsatellite heterozygosity of related non-endangered species and around half the number of alleles (see Table 3.5).

Box 10.3	Low genetic diversity in the critically endangered northern hairy-nosed wombat (Taylor *et al.* 1994; Beheregaray *et al.* 2000)

The northern hairy-nosed wombat exists as a single population of approximately 75 individuals in Epping Forest, central Queensland, Australia (see chapter frontispiece for locations). This population has had a low population size for a considerable period of time. Based on 28 microsatellite loci, the population had lower levels of genetic diversity than its nearest relative, the southern hairy-nosed wombat, that exists in larger numbers further south in the continent.

Species	A	H_e
Northern	2.1	0.32
Southern	5.9	0.71

Loss of genetic diversity for haploid, sex-linked and polyploid loci

Species differ in the number of chromosomal sets they contain, from haploid (n), through diploid ($2n$), to polyploid (triploid – $3n$, tetraploid – $4n$, etc.). Many plant and a few animal species are polyploid, while bacteria are usually haploid. Since loss of genetic diversity is a sampling process, the rate of loss depends on the number of gene copies per individual (Bever & Felber 1994). While this is two in the diploids considered above, it is one in haploids, one in males and two in females for sex-linked loci (and haplo-diploid species) and four in tetraploids, etc. Further, chloroplast and mitochondrial genomes are typically maternally transmitted. Equations for loss of genetic diversity for a range of non-diploid loci are compared with that for diploids in Table 10.1.

Loss of genetic diversity due to genetic drift in populations of the same size is fastest for mtDNA and chloroplast DNA loci, followed in order by haploids, sex-linked loci, diploids and tetraploids

Table 10.1	Rates of loss of expected heterozygosity (H_e) per generation in populations of the same size for neutral loci that are haploid, sex-linked, diploid, or tetraploid, or in mtDNA or chloroplast DNA. N_e is effective population size and N_{ef} is the effective number of females. It is assumed that only one mtDNA or chloroplast genome per gamete contributes to the next generation.

Mode of inheritance	Rate of loss of genetic diversity (H_e)
Haploid	$1 / N_e$
Sex-linked (or haplo-diploid)	$1 / 1.5 N_e$
Diploid	$1 / 2 N_e$
Autotetraploid	$1 / 4 N_e$
Allotetraploid	$1 / 4 N_e$
Chloroplast DNA	$1 / N_{ef}$
mtDNA	$1 / N_{ef}$

Source: Wright (1969).

There is an inverse relationship between loss of genetic diversity and ploidy. Loss is greatest per generation for haploids and least for tetraploids. The most rapid rate of loss is for mtDNA and chloroplast DNA loci as only females transmit them. Example 10.3 illustrates rates of loss in a single generation in a population with five males and five females.

Example 10.3 | Loss of genetic diversity for haploid, sex-linked, diploid, tetraploid and mtDNA loci in a small population

We consider rates of loss of genetic diversity in a population composed of only five males and five females. For comparative purposes, genetic diversity is measured as the Hardy–Weinberg heterozygosity expected for a random mating diploid (H_e). The losses of genetic diversity are:

Haploid loss $= 1/N_e = 1/10 = 10\%$

Sex-linked loss $= 1/(1.5N_e) = 1/15 = 0.067 = 6.7\%$

Diploid loss $= 1/(2N_e) = 1/20 = 0.05 = 5\%$

Tetraploid loss $= 1/(4N_e) = 1/40 = 0.025 = 2.5\%$

mtDNA loss $= 1/N_{ef} = 1/5 = 20\%$

Thus, the rates of losses of genetic diversity compared to the diploid case are four times for mtDNA and cpDNA genomes, double for haploids, 33% greater for sex-linked, and half for tetraploids.

Loss of genetic diversity in small populations is slower in polyploids than for equivalent sized diploids

There is less concern about reductions in evolutionary potential for polyploid species than for diploid ones as:
- Polyploids tend to have higher polymorphism and allelic diversity than diploids
- Polyploids have higher heterozygosity for the same allele frequencies than equivalent diploids (Chapter 4)
- Polyploids lose genetic diversity at slower rates than diploids (Table 10.1)
- Allopolyploids at complete homozygosity may have fixed heterozygosity (see below).

Autotetraploid populations of the endangered grassland daisy have greater polymorphism and allelic diversity than related diploid populations (Brown & Young 2000). This seems to apply to a variety of tetraploids. However, some recently formed polyploids may have gone through bottlenecks at foundation that reduced their genetic diversity.

As predicted from Table 10.1, the relationship between population size and genetic diversity appears to be weaker in tetraploids than diploids in a range of threatened plant species (Maki *et al.* 1996; Prober *et al.* 1998; Brown & Young 2000; Buza *et al.* 2000).

Allopolyploids may have duplicate loci fixed for different alleles even when completely inbred, such that they display fixed heterozygosity. Allotetraploids at complete fixation have the same expected heterozygosity as a random mating diploid (Example 10.4).

Example 10.4 | Comparing loss of heterozygosity in allotetraploids and diploids

If we consider two loci each with two alleles A_1 and A_2 at initial frequencies of p and q, then the heterozygosity is $2pq$ for a diploid and $2pq(2-pq)$ for a tetraploid with duplicated loci (Chapter 4). At complete fixation, due to inbreeding ($F=1$) or long-term finite population size, all loci will be homozygous. In the diploid species, genotype frequencies across many replicate populations will be:

	A_1A_1	A_1A_2	A_2A_2	Heterozygosity
At fixation	p	0	q	0

In an allotetraploid, the situation is the same at each of the duplicated loci, but the two duplicated loci may be fixed for the same or for different alleles, as follows:

		Locus 1		
		A_1A_1	A_1A_2	A_2A_2
Locus 2	A_1A_1	p^2	0	pq
	A_1A_2	0	0	0
	A_2A_2	pq	0	q^2

Resulting in genotypes with frequencies	$A_1A_1A_1A_1$ p^2	$A_1A_1A_2A_2$ $2pq$	$A_2A_2A_2A_2$ q^2

Thus, the allotetraploid will have a heterozygosity of $2pq$ at complete fixation, (the same as the diploid prior to inbreeding), while the diploid will have no heterozygosity. If the two contributing genomes in an allotetraploid have different allele frequencies, then the increased heterozygosity of allotetraploids over diploids will be even higher than in this example.

Effective population size

In this chapter we express population size as the genetically effective population size (N_e), rather than the actual numbers of individuals in the population (N, the census size) (Wright 1931). All of the adverse genetic consequences of small populations depend on the effective population size. Further, most of the theoretical predictions in conservation genetics are couched in terms of effective population size. Thus, it is fundamentally important to have a clear understanding of the concept of effective population size and how it differs from census size.

The effective size of a population is usually less than the number of breeding adults as real populations deviate in structure from the assumptions of the idealized population in sex-ratio, distribution of family sizes, constancy of numbers in successive generations, and in having overlapping, rather than discrete generations

We defined effective population size in Chapter 8 as *the number of individuals that would give rise to the calculated loss of heterozygosity, inbreeding or variance in allele frequencies if they behaved in the manner of an idealized population.* What factors cause the effective size to differ from the number of adults in the population? Fundamentally any characteristic of a real population that deviates from the characteristics of an ideal population (Chapter 8) will cause the census size to be different from N_e. The primary factors are unequal sex-ratio, high variance in family sizes and fluctuating population sizes over generations. In general, these factors deviate such that $N_e < N$.

By how much do effective population sizes differ from census sizes? Are the differences large enough to be important? What factor(s) have most impact? Below we review evidence on N_e/N ratios and conclude that they are usually much less than 1. Later we consider in turn the factors influencing N_e and examine their impacts. This leads us to the means for measuring N_e in real populations.

N_e/N ratios

Estimates of effective population size that encompass all relevant factors average only 11% of census sizes

The census population size (N) is usually the only information available for most threatened species. However, it is the effective population size that determines loss of genetic diversity and inbreeding. Consequently, it is critical to know the ratio of effective to census population size (N_e/N), so that effective size can be inferred.

Values of N_e/N that include all relevant factors (comprehensive estimates) average only 11%, based on a meta-analysis (Fig. 10.6). Thus, long-term effective population sizes are substantially lower than census sizes. For example, the threatened winter run of chinook salmon in the Sacramento River of California has about 2000 adults, but its effective size was estimated to be only 85 ($N_e/N = 0.04$), much lower than previously recognized (Bartley *et al.* 1992). Genetic concerns are much more immediate with an effective size of 85 than with 2000.

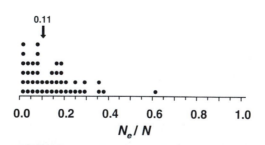

Fig. 10.6 Distribution of effective/actual population size (N_e/N) ratios. The estimates include the effects of fluctuations in population size, variance in family sizes, and unequal sex-ratios, and thus reflect long-term effective population sizes (after Frankham 1995c). *The mean of estimates (arrow) is only 11%.*

The sobering implication is that long-term effective population sizes are, on average, about 1/10 of actual sizes. Endangered species with 250 adults have effective sizes of about 25, and will lose half of their current heterozygosity for neutral loci in 34 generations. By this time, the population will become inbred to the point where inbreeding will increase their extinction risks (Chapter 11 and 12). Threatened populations with $N = 1000$ will have N_e of about 100 and lose half of their heterozygosity in 138 generations.

The most important factor reducing the N_e/N ratio is fluctuation in population size, followed by variation in family size, with variation in sex-ratio having a smaller effect (Frankham 1995c). Overlapping versus non-overlapping generations has no significant effect, nor do life history attributes. There were no clear or consistent differences in the ratio between major taxonomic groups, but such differences may well emerge with more data.

> Fluctuations in population size have greatest impact on reducing N_e, followed by variation in family sizes

Measuring effective population size

Since $N_e \ll N$ we need to measure the impacts on the effective population size of unequal sex-ratio, variation in family size, fluctuations in population size over generations, and overlapping generations. These impacts are described below, with derivations and further details given in Crow & Kimura (1970).

> Effective population size can be estimated from demographic data on sex-ratio, variance in family sizes and fluctuations in population size over generations

Unequal sex-ratio

In many wild populations the numbers of breeding females and males are not equal. Many mammals have harems (polygamy) where one male mates with many females, while many other males make no genetic contribution to the next generation. This occurs in an extreme form in elephant seals where a single male may have a hundred or more females in his harem. In a few species, the situation is reversed (polyandry). The equation accounting for the effects of unequal sex-ratio is

> Unequal sex-ratios reduce the effective size of the population towards the number of the sex with fewer breeding individuals

$$N_e = 4 N_{ef} N_{em} / (N_{ef} + N_{em}) \text{ (approx.)} \tag{10.3}$$

where N_{ef} is the effective number of breeding females and N_{em} the effective number of breeding male parents. This is the single generation effective population size due to this factor alone; all other characteristics are assumed to be as in an idealized population.

As the sex-ratio deviates from 1:1 in either direction, the N_e/N ratio declines (Fig. 10.7). For example, an elephant seal harem with one male and 100 females has an effective size of only 4 (Example 10.5). However, it is the lifetime sex-ratio over a generation that matters. In practice, harem masters often have limited tenure so that the average sex-ratio over a complete generation is usually much less skewed than that occurring during a single breeding season. While harems average about 40

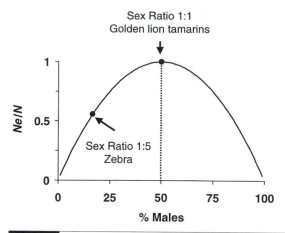

Sex Ratio 1:1
Golden lion tamarins

Sex Ratio 1:5
Zebra

Fig. 10.7 Effects of unequal sex-ratios on the N_e/N ratio. As the sex-ratio deviates from 1:1 in either direction the N_e/N ratio declines.

females in any one breeding season in elephant seals (Jewell 1976), genetic data indicate that the sex-ratio over a generation is only about 5 females:1 male in southern elephant seals (Slade *et al.* 1998). The predicted effects of unequal sex-ratio on loss of genetic diversity and inbreeding have been verified in experiments using fruit flies (Briton *et al.* 1994).

| **Example 10.5** | Reduction in effective size due to unequal sex-ratio in elephant seals (illustration from Austin & Short 1984) |

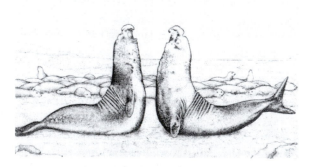

If a harem has one male and 100 females, the effective size is

$$N_e = 4 N_{ef} N_{em} / (N_{ef} + N_{em}) = 4 \times 100 \times 1 / (100 + 1) = 3.96$$

Thus the effective size of the harem is 3.96, approximately 4% of the actual size of 101.

Sex-ratios may be distorted by the mating system (as above), by sex deter-mining mechanisms that result in more of one sex than the other, by small population size (stochastic variation), or even by human actions. For example, poaching of Asian elephants had a large impact on sex-ratio in a southern Indian population. The sex-ratio in adults was 605 females : 6 males (Sukumar *et al.* 1998). This resulted in an effective size of only 24 (Problem 10.5), yielding a N_e/N ratio of 0.04. Global warming may be distorting sex-ratios in turtles, crocodilians and other reptiles where sex is determined by incubation temperature.

Overall, unequal sex-ratios have modest effects in reducing effective population sizes below actual sizes, resulting in an average reduction of 36% (Frankham 1995c).

Variation in family size

Family sizes (lifetime production of offspring per individual) in wild populations typically show greater variation than the expected (Poisson) for the idealized population. In a stable population of a ran-domly breeding monogamous species, the mean family size (k) is 2 (an average of one male and one female to replace each parent) and the variance (V_k) is 2. Note that the variance equals the mean for a Poisson distribution, so $V_k/k = 1$ for a population with an idealized structure. With this distribution the proportions of families with 0, 1, 2, 3, 4 and 5 offspring are 0.135, 0.271, 0.271, 0.180, 0.090 and 0.036, respectively. In non-monogamous species, we treat the two sexes separately (see below).

Table 10.2 illustrates variances in family sizes for a range of threat-ened species. All have V_k/k ratios in excess of the value of 1 assumed for the idealized population, with most values being much greater than 1. High variation in family sizes in wildlife is partly due to individuals that contribute no offspring to the next generation. Similar but less extreme effects arise from very large and very small families.

The effect of variation in family sizes in a population otherwise having the structure of an idealized population is

$$N_e = (4N - 2) / (V_k + 2) \tag{10.4}$$

This is the single generation effective population size due to family size alone. In the idealized population, $V_k = 2$, so that $N_e \sim N$.

This equation indicates that the higher the variance in family size, the lower the effective population size. For example, in Darwin's cactus finch high variance in family size (6.74), compared to the Poisson expec-tation (2) reduces the effective population size to 46% of the number of breeding pairs (Example 10.6). Over a range of species, variation in family sizes reduced effective population sizes to an average of 54% of census sizes (Frankham 1995c).

> When variation in family size exceeds that of the Poisson distribution, effective population size is less than the number of adults

Table 10.2 | Variance in lifetime reproductive success (V_k) and mean family size (k) for a range of species, many threatened. When the ratio V_k/k is greater than 1, variance is greater than for the Poisson distribution and effective size will be less than census size.

Species	Captive(c) or wild (w)	Sex	V_k	k	V_k/k	Reference
Mammals						
Asiatic lion	c	m	31.10	1.64	19.0	1
	c	f	34.00	1.67	20.4	
Eastern barred bandicoot	w	f+m	11.6	1.0	11.6	2
Golden lion tamarin	c	m	12.10	1.7	7.1	3
	c	f	13.5	1.6	8.4	
Golden-headed lion tamarin	c	m	7.27	1.07	6.8	1
	c	f	5.74	1.05	5.5	
Grevy's zebra	c	m	34.00	1.90	17.9	1
	c	f	1.20	1.14	1.1	
Przewalski's horse	c	m	23.44	1.18	19.9	1
	c	f	9.92	1.27	7.8	
Scimitar-horned oryx	c	m	127.90	1.48	86.4	1
	c	f	10.44	1.24	8.4	
Sumatran tiger	c	m	22.50	2.46	9.1	4
		f	16.61	2.09	7.9	
Birds						
Darwin's cactus finch	w	f+m	6.74	1.8	3.7	5
Darwin's large cactus finch	w	f+m	0.53	0.3	1.8	6
Darwin's medium ground finch	w	f+m	7.12	1.6	4.5	5
Pink pigeon	c	m	31.24	1.54	20.3	1
	c	f	5.74	1.05	5.5	1
Red-crowned crane	c	m	9.10	1.76	5.2	1
	c	f	4.80	1.64	2.9	1

References: 1, Dobson *et al.* (1992); 2, Sherwin & Brown (1990); 3, Ballou & Foose (1996); 4, Ballou & Seidensticker (1987); 5, Grant & Grant (1992); 6, Grant & Grant (1989).

Example 10.6 | Reduction in effective population size through high variance in family size in Darwin's cactus finch

The variance in family sizes for Darwin's cactus finch is 6.74, compared to the value of 2 assumed for an idealized population (Table 10.2). Equation 10.4 can be rearranged to give

$$N_e/N \sim 4/(V_k+2)$$

If we insert the observed value into this equation, we obtain

$$N_e/N \sim 4/(6.74+2) = 0.46$$

Thus, high variation in family size in Darwin's cactus finch reduces effective population size to only 46% that of the observed number of potential breeders.

If populations vary in size, the equation describing the influence of variation in family size on effective size becomes:

$$N_e = (Nk - 1) / [k - 1 + (V_k / k)] \qquad (10.5)$$

where N is the number of adults in the previous generations and k is the mean family size (this is again a single generation N_e). All other factors are assumed to conform with those of an idealized population. Note that when $k = 2$, this equation reduces to Equation 10.4.

This effect is illustrated for a captive Asiatic lion population (Example 10.7). Variation in family sizes results in a 92% reduction in effective size compared to the actual size.

Example 10.7 | Reduction in effective population size in Asiatic lions due to high variation in family sizes

Asiatic lions in captivity have an average family size of 1.65 and a variance in family size of 32.65 (Table 10.2). We rearrange Equation 10.3 to give an expression for N_e/N, by dividing both sides of the equation by N:

$$N_e/N = (Nk - 1) / N [k - 1 + (V_k / k)] \sim k / [k - 1 + (V_k / k)]$$

Substituting the observed values into this equation gives

$$N_e/N \sim k / [k - 1 + (V_k / k)] = 1.65 / [1.65 - 1 + (32.65 / 1.65)] = 0.081$$

Thus, variation in family size reduces the effective size of the Asiatic lion population to 8% of the number of adults.

If family sizes are equalized, $V_k = 0$. By substitution of this into Equation 10.4 we obtain $N_e \sim 2N$. In other words, the effective size of a population can be approximately twice as high as the number of parents if all individuals contribute equally to the next generation. It can be understood by recalling that the idealized population assumes that there is variance in family size ($V_k = 1$ for each sex), i.e. by chance some individuals do not reproduce and do not pass alleles they possess to the next generation. Further, other families vary in size at random, and make unequal contributions to the next generation. When all families contribute alleles equally to the next generation, there is minimal distortion in allele frequencies and the proportion of the genetic diversity passed on is maximized. Equalization of family sizes (EFS) also allows inbreeding to be minimized (Chapter 11).

This observation is of critical importance to captive breeding management. Equalization of family sizes potentially allows limited captive breeding spaces for endangered species to be effectively doubled. The benefits of equalizing family sizes in minimizing loss of genetic diversity and inbreeding have been verified in experiments with fruit flies (Box 10.4). EFS forms part of the recommended management regime for captive populations of endangered species (Chapter 17).

Equalization of family sizes (EFS) leads to an approximate doubling of the effective population size, compared to the actual size of the population

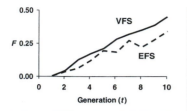

Levels of inbreeding in the EFS and VFS treatments.

Box 10.4 | An experimental evaluation of the effects of variable versus equal family sizes on loss of genetic diversity, inbreeding, and reproductive fitness, using fruit flies (Borlase et al. 1993)

From a large population of fruit flies, 20 replicate populations were founded, 10 being managed with equal family sizes (EFS), and 10 with variable family sizes (VFS). The experiment was run for 10 generations. Four female and four male parents were used in each generation ($N = 8$). Variances in family sizes were manipulated to be 0 for EFS, while normal variances were allowed for VFS (expected to be 2). Thus, the effective population sizes for the two treatments were expected to be 16 for EFS and 8 for VFS, based on Equation 10.4. Consequently, the EFS treatment was expected to lose less genetic diversity, have lower inbreeding and experience less reduction in reproductive fitness than the VFS treatment.

Each of these predictions was verified, as shown for allozyme heterozygosity (below left), inbreeding levels (in margin), and reproductive fitness (below right). Quantitative genetic variation was also higher in EFS than in VFS treatments (Frankham 2000a).

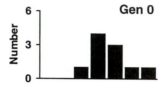

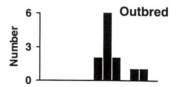

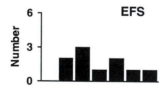

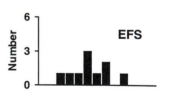

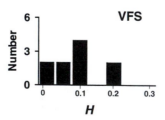

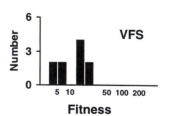

Distribution of average allozyme heterozygosities for the founding lines at generation 0, and for the EFS and VFS lines at generation 10.

Distribution of reproductive fitnesses at generation 11 in the EFS and VFS populations, and in the outbred base population.

Fluctuations in population size

Wild populations vary in numbers as a consequence of variation in food availability, climatic conditions, disease epidemics, catastrophes, predation, etc. For example, lynx and snowshoe hare populations fluctuate in size, the hare showing about a 30-fold difference between high and low years and the lynx about an 80-fold difference (Fig. 10.8). Small mammals often show severe fluctuations in population size, and large mammals exhibit similar variation to small mammals when both are measured on a per-generation basis (Sinclair 1996). Young (1994) has shown that declines of size of 70%–90% are not uncommon for large mammals in Africa.

Fluctuations in population size, over generations, reduce N_e below the average number of adults

The effective size in a fluctuating population is not the average, but the **harmonic mean** of the effective population sizes over t generations:

$$N_e = t / \Sigma(1/N_{e_i}) \quad \text{(approx.)} \tag{10.6}$$

where N_{e_i} is the effective size in the ith generation. This is the long-term, overall effective population size.

The long-term effective size is closest to the size of the generation with the smallest single generation N_e. For example, the northern elephant seal was reduced to 20–30 individuals, but has since recovered to over 100 000. Its effective population size over this time is about 60 (Example 10.8). This is far closer to the minimum population size than to the mean or the maximum. This relationship can best be explained by noting that an allele lost in a generation of low population size is not regained when the population size rises. Similarly, the inbreeding effects of small population size are not reduced when the population increases in size.

The order of the population sizes is irrelevant to the final outcome. It does not matter whether the order of population size is 10 000, 1000, 100, 10, or 1000, 10, 10 000, 100, etc. – all suffer the same loss of heterozygosity and inbreeding. N_e computed using Equation 10.6 can be used in Equation 10.1, to obtain the equivalent answer to use of Equation 10.2.

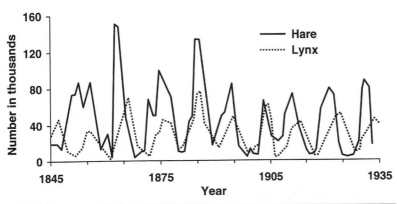

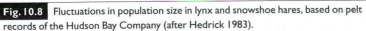

Fig. 10.8 Fluctuations in population size in lynx and snowshoe hares, based on pelt records of the Hudson Bay Company (after Hedrick 1983).

The predicted effects of fluctuations in population size on loss of genetic diversity, inbreeding and reproductive fitness have been verified in experiments with fruit flies (Woodworth *et al.* 1994). As indicated above, fluctuations in population size are the most important factor reducing N_e, on average reducing it by 65% (Frankham 1995c).

Example 10.8 | Reduction in N_e due to fluctuations in popular size

The northern elephant seal was reduced to 20–30 individuals by hunting. It has since recovered to over 100 000. For simplicity we assume that the population declined from 100 000 to 20 and recovered to 100 000 over three generations and that these were the effective sizes for each of the generations. The effective size of the population is

$$N_e = t/[(1/N_{e_1}) + (1/N_{e_2}) + (1/N_{e_3})]$$
$$= 3/[(1/100\,000) + (1/20) + (1/100\,000)]$$
$$= 60$$

The effective size of 60 is much closer to the minimum size than the mean size (66 673), being only 0.09% of the mean size over the three generations.

Exclusion of matings between close relatives

Self-fertilization is not possible in dioecious species, and many species avoid incestuous matings between close relatives. However, these deviations from the assumptions of the idealized population do not have major impacts on loss of genetic diversity, or on the overall rate of inbreeding, as the probability of selfing or sib-mating is very low in random mating populations unless they are very small. The effects of these exclusions on the single generation effective size (for populations otherwise behaving as idealized populations) are given below:

Self-fertilization excluded:

$$N_e = N + \tfrac{1}{2} \quad \text{(approx.)} \tag{10.7}$$

Sib-mating also excluded:

$$N_e = N + 2 \quad \text{(approx.)} \tag{10.8}$$

Exclusion of matings between close relatives cannot prevent loss of genetic diversity and inbreeding (Chapter 11). In a small population, every individual soon becomes related to every potential mate.

Inbred populations

Inbreeding reduces effective population size (Li 1976):

$$N_e = N / (1 + F) \tag{10.9}$$

In the special case of a completely inbred population ($F = 1$), the effective population size is half the actual size and the population consists of a number of different homozygous genotypes. The rare North American Pacific yew tree illustrates the use of Equation 10.9. The yew has an inbreeding coefficient of 0.47 (El-Kassaby & Yanchuk 1994). Thus, $N_e/N = 1/(1+0.47) = 0.68$, i.e. inbreeding reduces its effective size by 32%.

Overlapping generations

Most natural populations have overlapping, rather than the discrete generations assumed for idealized populations. The effects on N_e of overlapping generations are not clearly in one direction. However, overlapping generations are more likely to reduce N_e. Equations exist to evaluate its effects (Lande & Barrowclough 1987), but they are rarely used in practical situations. Relatively complex computer models are more frequently used (Allendorf *et al.* 1991).

Overlapping generations do not have a consistent directional effect on N_e

Combinations of factors

Ultimately we wish to determine the effective population size resulting from the combined impact of all factors. Example 10.9 illustrates the determination of the combined impacts of variance in family sizes plus unequal sex-ratios for golden lion tamarins. When more factors are taken into account, the net impact of all factors on loss of genetic diversity or inbreeding can be determined (sometimes using computer models) and the overall effective population size estimated as described below.

| Example 10.9 | Computing N_e in captive golden lion tamarins due to the combined impacts of variance in family sizes and unequal sex-ratios (after Ballou & Foose 1996) |

The numbers of female and male golden lion tamarins and the mean (k) and variance (V_k) of the numbers of offspring they contributed to the next generation are:

	Females	Males
Adult numbers	275	269
k	1.6	1.7
V_k	13.5	12.1

The effective size in females (N_{ef}) due to variation in family sizes, using Equation 10.5, is

$$N_{ef} = (N_f k - 1)/[k - 1 + (V_k/k)]$$
$$= (275 \times 1.6 - 1)/[1.6 - 1 + (13.5/1.6)] = 48.6$$

The effective size in males (N_{em}) due to variation in family sizes is

$$N_{em} = (N_m k - 1) / [k - 1 + (V_k / k)]$$
$$= (269 \times 1.7 - 1) / [1.7 - 1 + (12.1 / 1.7)] = 58.4$$

The overall N_e is obtained by taking into account the unequal sex-ratio, as follows:

$$N_e = 4N_{ef}N_{em} / (N_{ef} + N_{em}) = (4 \times 48.6 \times 58.4) / (48.6 + 58.4)$$
$$= 106.1$$

Thus, the effective size of the golden lion tamarin population is 106, while its actual size is 544, giving a N_e/N ratio of 0.2.

Inbreeding and variance effective sizes

Different effective population sizes are required to predict inbreeding and loss of genetic diversity. Often these are very similar, but may differ, when there are large changes in population size over time

So far we have discussed effective population size as though it was a single parameter. However, there are three, the inbreeding, eigenvalue and variance effective sizes (Templeton & Read 1994). Strictly, the effective size determining loss of genetic diversity is the eigenvalue effective size. The inbreeding effective size determines the rate of inbreeding, and the variance effective size, as the name implies, determines diversification among replicate populations. Often the three effective sizes have very similar values, but, in some circumstances, they can be quite different, especially when there are major changes in population size over time. Readers are referred to Crow & Kimura (1970) and Templeton & Read (1994) for details of this somewhat complex issue.

Estimating N_e

A variety of methods are used in practical situations to estimate N_e, including:

Demographic methods
These are based on Equations 10.3–10.9 above. They require extensive demographic data that often are not available.

Genetic methods
A variety of genetic methods have been devised that are often more practical. These methods are based on equations relating N_e and:
• loss of heterozygosity over generations (Equation 10.1)
• changes in allele frequencies over time due to genetic drift (Chapter 13)
• rate of decay in linkage disequilibrium among loci (Hill 1981). This has been used in chinook salmon and other fish (Bartley *et al.* 1992)
• rate of increase in pedigree inbreeding coefficient (Equation 11.3)
• loss of allelic diversity (Saccheri *et al.* 1999).

Example 10.10 illustrates the estimation of N_e from loss of genetic diversity over time in the endangered northern hairy-nosed wombat. The effective size was approximately 7, compared to the actual size of about 75.

For more detail, readers are referred to Caballero (1994) for a review of demographic estimation procedures and to Neigel (1996) and Schwartz *et al.* (1998) for reviews of genetic methods of estimating N_e.

Example 10.10	Estimation of N_e from loss of genetic diversity over time in the critically endangered northern hairy-nosed wombat (Taylor *et al.* 1994)

The northern hairy-nosed wombat declined over the last 120 years from more than 1000 individuals to 25 in 1981 and had recovered to about 70 individuals by the early 1990s. It has retained about 41% of its heterozygosity over this period. The generation length is approximately 10 years. The loss of genetic diversity has therefore occurred over about 120/10 = 12 generations.

We can estimate the long-term effective population size for this species using Equation 10.1, as follows:

$$H_t / H_0 = 0.41 \sim e^{-t/2N_e} = e^{-12/2N_e}$$

Taking $\log_e$, we obtain

$$\ln(0.41) = -12/2\,N_e$$

and by rearranging

$$N_e = -12/[2\ln(0.41)] = 6.7$$

Thus, the effective population size of the endangered northern hairy-nosed wombat over the last 120 years has been about 7.

Summary

1. Reductions in population size result in loss of genetic diversity, inbreeding and consequently increased extinction risk.

2. Genetic diversity decays over generations in small closed populations at a rate dependent on the effective population size.

3. The effective population size (N_e) is the number of individuals that would give rise to the observed loss of heterozygosity, or to the calculated inbreeding coefficient, if they behaved in the manner of the idealized population.

4. N_e is typically much less than adult population sizes; long-term N_e values average about 10% of the census sizes.

5. The effective population size is reduced by unequal sex-ratios, high variance in family size and especially by fluctuations in population size across generations.

6. Effective population sizes are measured either using a series of demographic equations that account for the variables in 5, or from equations for rates of loss of genetic diversity over time, etc.

FURTHER READING

Crow & Kimura (1970) *Introduction to Population Genetics Theory*. An advanced treatment of the theory of effective population size, and the prediction of the effects of small size on genetic diversity.

Falconer & Mackay (1996) *Introduction to Quantitative Genetics*. Provides a clear treatment of effective population size and the expected loss in genetic diversity in small populations.

Frankham (1995c) A review and meta-analysis of N_e/N ratios and factors that affect the ratio.

Frankham (1996) Review and meta-analysis of evidence on the relationship between population size and genetic diversity.

Hedrick (1992) Conservation orientated review of the issues in this chapter.

Lande & Barrowclough (1987) Conservation orientated review of the issues in this chapter.

Wright (1969) *Evolution and the Genetics of Populations*, vol. 2. A scholarly review of effective population size from the person who defined the concept.

PROBLEMS

10.1 Loss of heterozygosity in small populations: (a) What proportion of its initial genetic diversity will be retained after 100 years in the Javan rhinoceros that has a population size of 60 and a generation length of about 20 years? (b) What proportion of the initial heterozygosity will be retained if the effective population size is only 10?

10.2 Loss of heterozygosity: Use Equation 10.1 to determine the time taken for a population of size N_e to lose (a) 50% of its initial heterozygosity (set $H_t/H_0 = 0.5 = e^{-t/2N_e}$, then take ln of both sides of the equation and rearrange), and (b) 95% of its initial heterozygosity.

10.3 Loss of heterozygosity with a fluctuating population size: Compare the loss of heterozygosity in a population that fluctuates 100, 10, 100, 200 with one that fluctuates 200, 100, 100, 10.

10.4 Heterozygosity in tetraploids and diploids: What will be the heterozygosities in an allotetraploid and its diploid ancestors at complete fixation for a locus with two alleles at initial frequencies of 0.1 and 0.9?

10.5 Effective population size: What is the effective size of the Asian elephant population in Periyar, southern India where poaching has resulted in an adult sex-ratio of 6 males to 605 females? What would the effective size be with a 'normal' adult elephant sex-ratio of 1:3 (202 males:605 females)?

10.6 Effective population size: What is the effective population size in a population of red-crowned cranes with four families that contribute 0, 1, 2 and 5 offspring to the next generation?

10.7 Effective population size: What is the effective population size in a population of British field crickets if its size fluctuates as follows: 10, 100, 1000, 250?

10.8 Effective population size: What is the ratio of effective to census size in the endangered Brown's banksia from Western Australia due to inbreeding? It has an inbreeding coefficient of about 18% (Sampson *et al.* 1994).

10.9 Effective population size: If the adult population of Sumatran tigers consists of 60 males and 80 females, use the data in Table 10.2 to determine its N_e due to the combined effects of variance in family sizes and unequal sex-ratio.

10.10 Estimating N_e from loss of genetic diversity: Rearrange equation 10.1 and use it to estimate the effective population size for the Mauritius kestrel, given that it has lost 57% of its heterozygosity in about 17 generations (Groombridge *et al.* 2000).

PRACTICAL EXERCISES: COMPUTER SIMULATIONS

Use POPGEN or an equivalent computer simulation package to complete the following:

1. Using initial frequencies of $p = q = 0.5$, run 50 replicate simulations with population sizes of 10, 50 and 100 each for 50 generations. Compare them for proportion of the populations fixed at generation 50 ($p = 0$, or $p = 1$) and average heterozygosities at generation 50.

2. Using initial frequencies of $p = q = 0.9$, run 50 replicate simulations with population sizes of 10, 50 and 100 each for 50 generations. Compare these results with those for practical exercise 10.1 for proportion of the populations fixed ($p = 0$, or $p = 1$) at generation 50 and average heterozygosities at generation 50.

Inbreeding

Inbreeding is the mating of individuals related by ancestry. It is measured as the probability that two alleles at a locus are identical by descent (F). Inbreeding increases homozygosity and exposes rare deleterious alleles

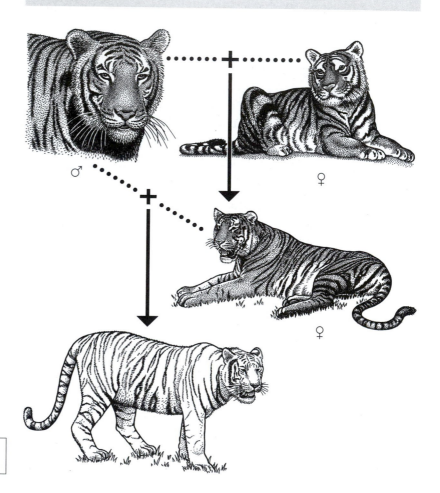

Father–daughter mating resulting in a white tiger (India).

What is inbreeding?

When the parents of an individual share one or more common ancestors (i.e. are related), the individual is inbred. A case of inbreeding, a father–daughter mating in tigers, is illustrated on the chapter frontispiece. Inbred matings include self-fertilization, mating of brother with sister, father with daughter, mother with son, cousins, etc.

> Inbreeding is the mating of individuals related by ancestry

Inbreeding is unavoidable in small populations as all individuals become related by descent over time. For example, Box 11.1 shows the early generations of the pedigree for the endangered Przewalski's horse population. As this population is presumed to derive from only 12 remaining individuals plus one domestic mare (a closely related species), complete avoidance of inbreeding is impossible.

Box 11.1 | Inbreeding in the endangered Przewalski's horse

The Przewalski's horse (Mongolian wild horse) became extinct in the wild, primarily through hunting and competition from domestic animals (Ehrlich & Ehrlich 1981). It existed only in captivity for many years, but it is being reintroduced into its natural range in Mongolia. The population is presumed to derive from only 12 individuals plus one domestic mare. The early pedigree is shown below with their studbook numbers (after Thomas 1995). Circles represent females, squares males and diamonds individuals who have not yet reproduced. Diamonds may represent several sibs. The 13 founders (individuals without connections to ancestors) are labelled; most are near the top of the figure, except for 231, in the middle. DOM is the domestic mare.

There are many inbred individuals in this pedigree. For example, in the top left-hand side, male 11 produced a daughter with female 12 and a son with DOM; these

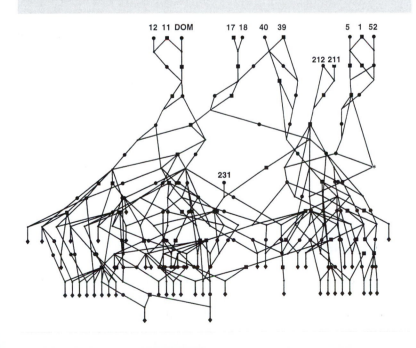

half-siblings mated to produce an inbred son and an inbred daughter. Analyses indicated that inbreeding was associated with deleterious changes in number of offspring per mare and longevity (Frankel & Soulé 1981). Genetic management initially minimized the genetic contribution of the domestic mare, and since 1970 has also tried to minimize inbreeding.

The increase in numbers and in average inbreeding in the captive Przewalski's horse population is shown below (after Volf 1999).

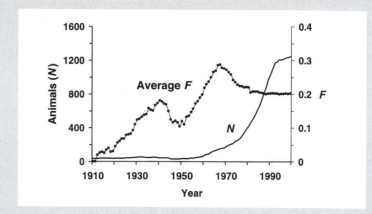

Recent molecular genetic analyses indicate that there are errors in this pedigree and that more than one domestic horse has contributed (Chapter 19).

Conservation concerns with inbreeding

Inbreeding results in a decline in reproductive fitness (inbreeding depression)

Inbreeding reduces reproductive fitness in essentially all well-studied populations of outbreeding animals and plants. For example, Ralls & Ballou (1983) found higher mortality in inbred progeny than in outbred progeny in 41 of 44 mammal populations (Fig. 11.1). In the pygmy hippopotamus, inbred offspring had 55% juvenile mortality, while outbred offspring had 25% mortality. On average, progeny of brother–sister (full-sib) matings resulted in a 33% reduction in juvenile survival. Full details of inbreeding depression and its causes are deferred until the next chapter. In this chapter we define methods for measuring inbreeding and describe the genetic impacts of inbreeding on genotype frequencies.

Why is inbreeding so detrimental in small and endangered populations? To understand this, we must first consider the measurement of inbreeding, and then determine the genetic impacts of inbreeding on genotype frequencies.

Inbreeding coefficient (*F*)

The inbreeding coefficient of an individual (*F*) is the probability that it carries alleles at a locus that are identical by descent

The consequence of matings between relatives is that offspring have an increased probability of inheriting alleles that are recent copies of the same DNA sequence. These recent copies of the same allele are

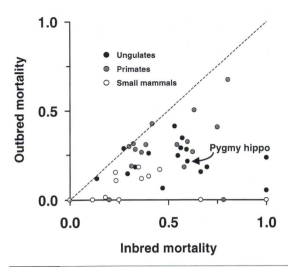

Fig. 11.1 Inbreeding depression for juvenile survival in 44 captive mammal populations (Ralls & Ballou 1983). Juvenile mortality in outbred individuals is plotted against that in inbred individuals from the same populations. The line represents equal survival of inbred and outbred individuals. *Most populations fall below the line, indicating that inbreeding is deleterious (inbreeding depression).*

referred to as **identical by descent**, or **autozygous**. For example, in Fig. 11.2 A_1A_1 or A_2A_2 offspring resulting from self-fertilization have inherited two alleles which are identical by descent. The two identical copies of an allele do not need to come from an individual in the previous generation, but may come from a common ancestor in a more remote generation. For example, in Fig. 11.2 an offspring resulting from a brother–sister mating may inherit two copies of allele A_1 from its grandparent. The grandparents are said to be **common ancestors**, meaning that they are ancestors of both the mother and the father of the individual.

The **inbreeding coefficient** (*F*) is used to measure inbreeding. The inbreeding coefficient of an individual is the probability that both alleles at a locus are identical by descent. As *F* is a probability, it ranges from 0 to 1, the former being outbreds and the latter completely inbred.

Identity by descent is related to, but distinct from homozygosity. Individuals carrying two alleles identical by descent are, of course, homozygous. However, not all homozygotes carry alleles that are identical by descent, i.e. homozygotes include both autozygous and **allozygous** types (where the two alleles do not originate from a recent common ancestor). For example, referring back to Fig. 3.3, an individual carrying Adh copies 7 and 8 would be homozygous for Adh-F. However, these alleles differ in DNA sequence at nine bases, and are not recent copies of the same allele, i.e. they are allozygous. Conversely, an individual carrying two copies of Adh 7 that were inherited from a recent common ancestor of both its parents would be autozygous, i.e. the two alleles would be identical by descent.

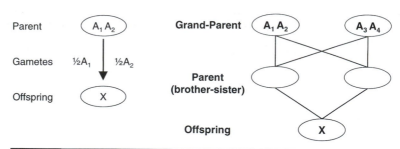

Fig. 11.2 Inbreeding coefficients for individuals resulting from self-fertilization and full-sib mating.

The inbreeding coefficient of an individual resulting from self-fertilization (selfing) is ½ and that for an individual resulting from brother–sister (full-sib) mating is ¼ (Fig. 11.2). To calculate inbreeding coefficients from first principles, each non-inbred ancestor is labelled as having unique alleles (A_1A_2, A_3A_4, etc.) (Fig. 11.2). The probability that an individual inherits two alleles identical by descent (A_1A_1, or A_2A_2, etc.) is computed from the paths of inheritance, assuming normal Mendelian segregation. For example, with selfing the inbreeding coefficient is the probability that offspring X inherits either two A_1 alleles by descent, or two A_2 alleles. Individual X has ½ chance of inheriting A_1 in the ovule and ½ chance of inheriting it through the pollen. Consequently, the probability that X inherits two identical A_1 alleles is ½ × ½ = ¼. Similarly the chance that X inherits two A_2 alleles is also ½ × ½ = ¼. The inbreeding coefficient is then the probability of inheriting either A_1A_1 or A_2A_2 = ¼ + ¼ = ½.

The inbreeding coefficient, as described above, measures the probability of alleles at a locus being identical by descent within an individual. Inbreeding coefficients can also refer to the level of inbreeding averaged across all individuals within a population (Box 2.1).

What are the genetic consequences of inbreeding? We next establish that inbreeding increases the frequency of homozygotes, and so exposes deleterious recessives. We then consider levels of inbreeding in small populations, for individuals with different pedigrees, and for regular systems of inbreeding (selfing, full-sib mating, etc.).

Genetic consequences of inbreeding

Inbreeding increases levels of homozygosity and exposes deleterious recessive alleles

Inbreeding increases the probability that an individual is homozygous at a locus. Since naturally outbreeding populations contain deleterious alleles (mostly partially recessive) at low frequencies in mutation–selection balance (Chapter 7), inbreeding increases the risks of exposing them as homozygotes. We saw in Fig. 4.2 that selfing increases the level of homozygosity. Other forms of inbreeding also increase homozygosity, but more slowly. Quantitative expressions for the magnitude of these effects are given below.

Table 11.1 | Genotype frequencies under random mating compared to those in populations with inbreeding coefficients (F) of 1 and F.

Population	F	+/+	+/m	m/m
			Genotypes	
(a) Random mating (N = ∞)	0	p^2	$2pq$	q^2
(b) Fully inbred	1	p	0	q
(c) Partially inbred	F	$p^2(1-F)+Fp$ p^2+Fpq	$2pq(1-F)+F\times0$ $2pq(1-F)$	$q^2(1-F)+Fq$ q^2+Fpq

To determine the genetic consequences of inbreeding, we begin with a random mating population with two alleles $+$ and m at a locus with frequencies of p and q. Table 11.1 shows the derivation of the effects of inbreeding on genotype frequencies. Table 11.1a gives the Hardy–Weinberg equilibrium genotype frequencies expected under random mating, and Table 11.1b shows a fully inbred population ($F=1$), where all uniting gametes are identical by descent, so only homozygotes are produced. These occur in proportion to the allele frequencies, namely p of $+/+$ and q of m/m.

A partially inbred population (inbreeding coefficient $=F$) consists of genotypes generated in two ways:

(a) those due to random union of gametes: proportion $1-F$

(b) those due to union of gametes identical by descent: proportion F. The overall genotype frequencies are the sum of these two components. Thus, the frequency of heterozygotes is $2pq(1-F)$ from (a) and $0\times F$ from (b), totalling $2pq(1-F)$. The frequency of m/m homozygotes is $q^2(1-F)+Fq=q^2+Fpq$ upon rearrangement. Similarly, the frequency of $+/+$ homozygotes is p^2+Fpq.

Inbreeding decreases heterozygosity and increases homozygosity (Table 11.1). The ratio of heterozygosity in an inbred population ($H_I=2pq(1-F)$) relative to that in a random breeding population ($H_o=2pq$) is:

> Inbreeding reduces the frequency of heterozygotes in proportion to the inbreeding coefficient

$$H_I/H_o = 2pq(1-F)/2pq = 1-F$$

Thus, reduction in heterozygosity due to inbreeding is directly related to the inbreeding coefficient F. We can estimate the level of inbreeding by comparing observed heterozygosity with that expected under random mating.

$$F = 1 - (H_I/H_o) \tag{11.1}$$

There is a deficiency of heterozygotes at the lemma colour locus in wild oats, a species that is largely self-pollinating (Table 11.2). We can estimate from Equation 11.1 that the population has an inbreeding coefficient of $1-(0.071/0.486)=0.85$. We will see later that measuring

Table 11.2 Deficiency of heterozygotes at the locus controlling black versus grey lemma colour in wild oats, a species that often self-fertilizes (Hedrick 2000 after Jain & Marshall). Observed genotype frequencies and those expected with random mating (Hardy–Weinberg equilibrium) are shown

	Genotype		
	BB	Bb	bb
Observed	0.548	0.071	0.381
Hardy–Weinberg expectation	0.340	0.486	0.173

changes in heterozygosity over time can also be used to estimate the level of inbreeding in a population.

While inbreeding changes genotype frequencies, it does not change allele frequencies. We can illustrate this by calculating allele frequencies from the genotype frequencies in Table 11.1 (Example 11.1). The frequencies of the $+$ and m alleles remain at p and q, respectively. When inbreeding is due to small population size, allele frequencies in individual populations will change due to genetic drift, but the average frequency over a large number of replicate populations will be unchanged.

Inbreeding does not change allele frequencies

Example 11.1 | Allele frequencies under inbreeding

The frequency of the $+$ allele in the inbred population, p_1, is obtained by allele counting, as follows:

$$p_1 = [2 \times \text{freq}(+/+) + \text{freq}(+/m)] / 2$$
$$= [2 \times (p^2 + Fpq) + 2pq(1 - F)] / 2 = p^2 + Fpq + pq - Fpq$$
$$= p^2 + pq = p(q + p) = p$$

$$\therefore p_1 = p$$

Thus, there is no change in the frequency of the $+$ allele. The frequency of the m allele is also unchanged at q.

Inbreeding exposes rare deleterious alleles

A major practical consequence of inbreeding is that homozygotes for deleterious recessives are more frequent than in a random mating population. This is illustrated for chondrodystrophy in California condors in Table 11.3. Note that the frequency of homozygous dw/dw is more than doubled in a population with an inbreeding coefficient of 25% and almost six times as common in a completely inbred population. In general, the ratio of frequencies of rare recessive homozygotes under inbreeding versus random mating is

$$\text{Ratio} = [q^2 + Fpq]/q^2$$
$$= 1 + (Fp/q)$$

where q is the frequency of the rare allele.

Table 11.3 | Expected genotype frequencies under inbreeding at the chondrodystrophy locus in California condors. The deleterious recessive allele has a frequency of about 17%, and the normal allele a frequency of 83% (Example 4.5). Genotype frequencies are shown for random mating, complete inbreeding and full-sib mating ($F = 0.25$) determined using the formulae in Table 11.1. The ratios of frequencies of dw/dw in inbred to outbred populations are also given

| | Genotypes | | | |
	+/+	+/dw	dw/dw	Ratio
Random mating	0.6889	0.2822	0.0289	
Inbred $F = 1$	0.83	0	0.17	5.9
Partially inbred $F = 0.25$	0.7242	0.2116	0.0642	2.2

Thus, the ratio increases with the amount of inbreeding and is greater for rare than for common alleles.

Lethal allele frequencies are rarely as high as 17%. A more typical frequency for a lethal allele that is partially recessive and in mutation–selection balance would be $\sim 5 \times 10^{-4}$ (Chapter 7). In a population with an inbreeding coefficient of 25% due to full-sib mating, the ratio of the lethal homozygote frequency to that with no inbreeding would be

$$\text{Ratio} = 1 + (Fp/q) = 1 + [0.25 \times (1 - 5 \times 10^{-4}) / 5 \times 10^{-4}] = 501$$

Thus, the frequency of lethal homozygotes after one generation of full-sib mating would be about 500 times higher than with random mating.

The frequency of lethal homozygotes under random mating with the above equilibrium frequency (q^2) is 25×10^{-8}, while that following full-sib mating ($q^2 + Fpq$) is $25 \times 10^{-8} + 1.25 \times 10^{-4}$. In the inbred population, most of the lethal homozygotes are due to the inbreeding. The additional frequency of lethal homozygotes at a locus due to inbreeding is Fpq which is approximately Fq when we are dealing with very rare alleles (i.e. $p \sim 1$). Consequently, there will be only $0.25 \times 5 \times 10^{-4} = 1.25 \times 10^{-4}$ extra homozygotes in the example above. Such effects are very small at any single locus. However, they occur across all loci in the genome that are segregating for lethal alleles.

There are about 35 000 functional loci in the mammalian genome and 5000–26 000 can produce lethal mutations in mice (Miklos & Rubin 1996). Consequently, we need to consider the cumulative impacts of at least 5000 loci. Example 11.2 suggests that about 47% of all zygotes from full-sib matings will be homozygous for at least one such lethal allele.

The value of 47% is greater than the 33% reduction in juvenile survival found for full-sib mating in mammals (Ralls & Ballou 1983). However, many lethals will cause mortality prior to birth and not be recorded as juvenile mortality. Consequently, a sizeable proportion of zygotes must be homozygous for lethal alleles when the population is inbred.

In addition to the increase in lethal homozygotes, there will be many other less deleterious alleles, whose homozygosity will reduce the reproductive fitness of inbred populations. Consequently, increased homozygosity of deleterious partially recessive alleles provides an obvious mechanism by which inbreeding reduces reproductive fitness in naturally outbreeding species (see Chapter 12).

Example 11.2 | Overall frequency of individuals homozygous for lethal alleles in inbred populations

To obtain the frequency of individuals homozygous for one or more lethal alleles in an inbred population, we need to know the number of loci, the mutation–selection equilibrium frequency for lethal alleles, and the average inbreeding coefficient (F). There are around 35 000 loci in mammals, and at least 5000 of them can mutate to produce lethal alleles in mice. The typical mutation–selection equilibrium frequency for a partially recessive lethal is 5×10^{-4} (Chapter 7).

To do the computation we need to consider the probability that a zygote is *not* homozygous for a lethal at a single locus under random mating. This is $1 - q^2$. We then raise this to the power of the number of loci likely to be segregating for lethal alleles (5000 in this example). Thus:

$$P(\text{not a lethal homozygote}) = (1 - q^2)^{5000}$$

and after substituting for q, we have

$$P(\text{not a lethal homozygote}) = [1 - (5 \times 10^{-4})^2]^{5000} = 0.99875$$

Thus, only about 0.125% of zygotes will be homozygous for a lethal in a random mating population.

The situation for zygotes resulting from full-sib mating is determined in a similar manner. The probability that an individual is not homozygous for a lethal is $1 - q^2 - Fpq$ at each locus. The probability that an individual is not homozygous for any lethal due to inbreeding is:

$$P(\text{not lethal homozygote}) = (1 - q^2 - Fpq)^{5000}$$

For progeny of full-sib matings ($F = 0.25$), this probability is:

$$P(\text{not lethal homozygote}) = [1 - (5 \times 10^{-4})^2 - (0.25 \times 5 \times 10^{-4})]^{5000}$$
$$= 0.53$$

Consequently, the probability that an individual is homozygous for lethal alleles at one or more loci is $1 - 0.53 = 0.47$. We expect 47% of zygotes from full-sib mating to be homozygous for a lethal allele for a least one locus in mammals.

Inbreeding in small populations

While a minority of plants routinely self-fertilize (Richards 1997), animals normally do not self. In spite of many opportunities for relatives to mate due to the proximity of siblings, offspring or parents, inbred matings are generally less than expected from proximity of potential mates, as many species have evolved inbreeding-avoidance mechanisms (see later). In species that do not deliberately inbreed, the majority of inbreeding arises as an inevitable consequence of small population sizes.

In small closed populations all individuals eventually become related by descent, so inbreeding is unavoidable. This is evident in the pedigree for Przewalski's horse (Box 11.1). This can be understood by considering numbers of ancestors. We each have two parents, four grandparents, eight great-grandparents and 2^t ancestors t generations in the past. The number of ancestors rapidly exceeds the historical population size, so individuals must have common ancestors and be related. For example, 10 generations back we each have 1024 ancestors. Our parents each have 512 ancestors, so the minimum population size for them to have no common ancestors 10 generations ago would be 1024. If the population size was less than this, then our parents must share common ancestors, and we must be inbred to some degree. Many threatened species have population sizes less than this (a size below 1000 adults is sufficient for a population to be included in the IUCN vulnerable category), or have had generations where the size was less than this.

Consequently, individuals are more likely to be inbred in small than in large populations. In a very large random mating population, inbreeding is close to zero as there is very little chance of mating with a relative.

In naturally outbreeding species, inbreeding arises predominantly from small population size

Inbreeding is unavoidable in small closed populations

Theory of inbreeding in small populations

The effects of population size on the level of inbreeding can be determined by considering the probability of identity by descent in the idealized random mating population (Chapter 10). We begin by assuming that all founding individuals (generation 0) are non-inbred, unrelated, and carry unique alleles, with their progeny constituting generation 1. Consider a hermaphroditic marine species that sheds gametes into the sea; there are N individuals producing equal numbers of gametes that unite at random, and there are $2N$ ancestral alleles $A_1, A_2, A_3, ... A_{2N}$ in the gene pool. Each individual in the next generation is formed by sampling with replacement two alleles at random from this pool. If the first allele sampled is A_6, the probability that the second is also A_6 (identical by descent) is $1/2N$. For any individual, the probability that they have two alleles identical by descent is $1/2N$. Consequently, the inbreeding coefficient in the first generation is $1/2N$.

Inbreeding in a random mating population of size N_e increases at a rate of $1/(2N_e)$ per generation

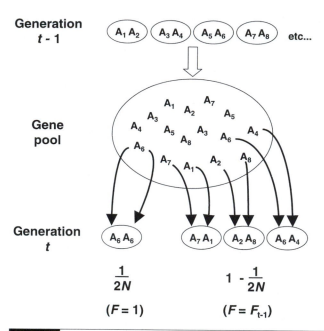

Generation
t - 1

$A_1 A_2$ $A_3 A_4$ $A_5 A_6$ $A_7 A_8$ etc...

Gene
pool

A_1 A_7
A_3 A_2 A_5
A_4
A_5 A_3 A_6 A_4
A_6
A_7 A_1 A_2 A_8

Generation
t

$A_6 A_6$ $A_7 A_1$ $A_2 A_8$ $A_6 A_4$

$\dfrac{1}{2N}$ $1 - \dfrac{1}{2N}$

$(F = 1)$ $(F = F_{t-1})$

Fig. 11.3 Inbreeding due to small population size. The ellipses above and below represent different genotypes in generations $t-1$ and t, respectively. Taking a random sample of $2N$ gametes from the generation $t-1$ gene pool involves a probability of $1/2N$ that two identical alleles are sampled and a probability of $1-1/2N$ that two distinct alleles are sampled.

In following generations, there are two ways that identical alleles can be sampled to create a zygote (Fig. 11.3):
• From the sampling of two copies of the same allele (as above) with probability $1/2N$
• from sampling two alleles that are identical from previous inbreeding. The probability of sampling two different alleles is the remaining proportion, $1 - 1/2N$. However, a proportion F of these alleles is identical by descent due to the previous inbreeding. Therefore the inbreeding due to previous inbreeding is $F_{t-1} \times [1 - 1/(2N)]$

Taken together the probability of creating a zygote in generation t with both alleles identical by descent (F_t) is the sum of these:

$$F_t = 1/(2N) + [1 - 1/(2N)] F_{t-1} \qquad (11.2)$$

where F_{t-1} is the inbreeding coefficient in generation $t-1$. Thus inbreeding is made up of two parts, an increment $1/(2N)$ due to new inbreeding, plus that attributable to previous inbreeding. Even if there is no new inbreeding, as may occur if population size increases, the population does not lose its previous inbreeding.

The increment in inbreeding per generation (the rate of inbreeding) is:

The increment in inbreeding per generation is equal to the loss of heterozygosity

$$\Delta F = 1/(2N) \qquad (11.3)$$

Recall from Equation 8.2 that loss of heterozygosity in one generation is also $1/(2N)$. Thus, the increment in inbreeding equals the loss of heterozygosity per generation, illustrating the close relationship between inbreeding and loss of genetic diversity in random mating species.

So far, we have expressed the inbreeding coefficient as a function of that in the previous generation. However, we often wish to predict the accumulated inbreeding over several generations. If the population size is constant over generations, we can obtain the required expression for F_t by rearranging Equation 11.2:

$$1 - F_t = 1 - \{1/(2N) + [1 - 1/(2N)]F_{t-1}\} = [1 - 1/(2N)](1 - F_{t-1})$$

and

$$1 - F_t = [1 - 1/(2N)]^t (1 - F_0)$$

When the initial population is not inbred ($F_0 = 0$), the inbreeding coefficient in any subsequent generation t is:

$$F_t = 1 - [1 - 1/(2N)]^t \tag{11.4}$$

Thus, inbreeding accumulates with time in all closed finite populations, at a rate dependent on their population sizes. Inbreeding increases more rapidly in small than in large populations (Fig. 11.4).

Example 11.3 illustrates the rapid accumulation of inbreeding in a small closed population with only four individuals per generation. The population reaches an average inbreeding coefficient of 74% by generation 10. This is approximately equivalent to the level of inbreeding due to two generations of selfing or six generations of full-sib mating – but it was achieved in a random mating population. Since captive populations of endangered species within individual zoos are often of this size, individuals have to be moved between institutions if rapid inbreeding is to be minimized (Chapter 17).

> Inbreeding accumulates over time and does so more rapidly in smaller than in larger populations

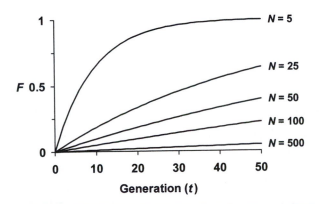

Fig. 11.4 Increase in inbreeding coefficient F with time in finite populations of different sizes (N). *Inbreeding increases more rapidly in smaller than in larger populations.*

Example 11.3 | Accumulation of inbreeding in a small closed captive population

Many captive populations of threatened species in individual zoos are small, and would accumulate inbreeding rapidly if they were kept closed, i.e. no individuals exchanged between zoos. If a zoo started a breeding program with four unrelated individuals, and kept the breeding population at four parents per generation over many generations, the inbreeding coefficient would increase as follows:

Generation 0 $F = 0$

Generation 1 $F = 1 - (1 - 1/2N)^1 = 1 - (1 - 1/8) = 0.125$

Generation 2 $F = 1 - (1 - 1/2N)^2 = 1 - (1 - 1/8)^2 = 0.234$

Generation 3 $F = 1 - (1 - 1/2N)^3 = 1 - (1 - 1/8)^3 = 0.33$

Generation 4 $F = 1 - (1 - 1/2N)^4 = 1 - (1 - 1/8)^4 = 0.41$

Generation 10 $F = 1 - (1 - 1/2N)^{10} = 1 - (1 - 1/8)^{10} = 0.74$

Thus, the inbreeding coefficient increases rapidly and reaches 74% by generation 10.

For populations that do not have idealized structures, N_e is used in place of N in prediction equations

Inbreeding will usually increase at a more rapid rate than indicated above, as populations generally have smaller genetically effective sizes than census sizes (Chapter 10). If the population does not have the structure of an idealized population (and few, if any, will) the increase in F in any population of constant size can be obtained by substituting N_e for N in the earlier equations.

If population sizes fluctuate among generations, as occurs in real populations, the expression for the inbreeding coefficient at generation t is:

$$F_t = 1 - \prod_{i=1}^{t} [1 - 1/(2N_{e_i})]$$

(11.5)

where N_{e_i} is the effective size in the ith generation. Example 11.4 illustrates the use of this equation to estimate the minimum inbreeding level in the northern elephant seal following a bottleneck of 20–30 individuals. Alternatively, the harmonic mean N_e could be used in Equation 11.4 to give the same result.

Example 11.4 | Inbreeding in a fluctuating population

The northern elephant seal population declined to 20–30 individuals and has since recovered to over 100 000. If we consider, for simplicity, that its effective numbers in three successive generations were 100 000, 20 and 100 000 then its inbreeding coefficient from Equation 11.5 would be

$$F_t = 1 - \prod_{i=1}^{t} [1 - 1 / (2N_{e_i})]$$

$$= 1 - [1 - 1 / (2 \times 100\,000)] \times [1 - 1 / (2 \times 20)]$$
$$\times (1 - 1 / (2 \times 100\,000)]$$

$$= 1 - 0.975 = 0.025$$

Thus, the northern elephant seal has an inbreeding coefficient of at least 2.5% as a result of its previous bottleneck, even though its current population size is over 100 000 individuals. Its actual inbreeding level will be much greater than this as it has a polygamous mating system and it existed at small population sizes for much more than a single generation.

An alternative approach is to compute the harmonic mean population size (Chapter 10), and use it in Equation 11.4. The harmonic mean population size is 60, so the inbreeding coefficient after three generations at this size is

$$F_t = 1 - [1 - 1 / (2N_e)]^t = 1 - [1 - 1 / (2 \times 60)]^3 = 0.025$$

This yields the same inbreeding coefficient as above.

Indirect estimates of population inbreeding coefficients

In most populations, levels of inbreeding are unknown. However, the relationship between genotype frequencies and inbreeding coefficients (Table 11.1) can be used to estimate levels of inbreeding. A deficiency of heterozygotes provides an indication that a population is inbreeding, rather than mating randomly. The deficiency of heterozygotes, compared to Hardy–Weinberg equilibrium expectations, provides an estimate of F.

A second estimate of the average inbreeding coefficient for a population can be obtained from the loss of genetic diversity over time. From Equations 10.1 and 11.4,

$$H_t / H_0 = (1 - 1/2N_e)^t = 1 - F \qquad (11.6)$$

The effective inbreeding coefficient F_e can be estimated as

$$F_e = 1 - (H_t / H_0) \qquad (11.7)$$

Levels of inbreeding in island populations were inferred using this approach by comparing allozyme heterozygosities in island and mainland populations (Fig. 2.6; Frankham 1998). Box 11.2 illustrates the estimation of the effective inbreeding coefficient for the endangered Isle Royale population of gray wolves in North America. The estimate of 55% indicates that this endangered island population is highly inbred, as its history would lead us to suspect.

An indirect estimate of inbreeding coefficients can be obtained from the ratio of observed to expected heterozygosity

Box 11.2	Inbreeding due to low founder numbers and small population sizes in the endangered population of Isle Royale gray wolves (after Wayne *et al.* 1991)

Gray wolves became established on Isle Royale in Lake Superior in about 1949, during an extreme winter when the lake froze. Moose, their main prey, had previously become established on the island. The moose and wolf populations and their interactions have been studied extensively. The wolf population is presumed to have been established by a single pair. The wolf population rose to 50 in 1980, but subsequently declined to 14 in 1990. This decline could have been due to reduced availability of prey, to disease, or to deleterious effects of inbreeding, or a combination of these factors.

The island population must be inbred due to low founder numbers and subsequent small population sizes (2–3 breeding pairs). All individuals have the same rare mtDNA genotype, consistent with foundation of the population from the progeny of a single female. DNA fingerprint data indicate that the island wolves are as similar as sibs in a captive population of wolves. Allozyme heterozygosity, based on 25 loci, was 3.9% for Isle Royale, compared to 8.7% in wolves from nearby mainland populations. Using Equation 11.7, the effective inbreeding coefficient is

$$F_e = 1 - (H_{island}/H_{mainland}) = 1 - (0.039/0.087) = 0.55.$$

Consequently, this endangered island population is highly inbred. Gray wolves suffer reductions in reproductive fitness due to inbreeding (Laikre & Ryman 1991). The Isle Royale population has small litters and poor juvenile survival.

Many polymorphic loci should be used to estimate effective inbreeding coefficients. This is particularly important if the inbreeding coefficient of an individual is being estimated, as there is wide variation in homozygosity among loci due to the chance effects involved in Mendelian segregation. For example, a locus in the progeny of a full-sib mating (Fig. 11.1) has a 0.25 probability of being identical by descent. As a corollary, 0.75 of loci in such individuals are not identical by descent. Thus, the measurement of identity by descent has a mean of 0.25 and a standard error of $\sqrt{(0.75 \times 0.25 / n)} = 0.43 / \sqrt{n}$, where n is the number of loci sampled. Consequently, many loci are required to obtain a reliable estimate of the effective inbreeding coefficient for an individual.

Deviations of genotype frequencies from Hardy–Weinberg equilibrium for allozyme or DNA markers are widely used to determine selfing rates in plants (Richards 1997). If a proportion S of the population selfs, the frequency of heterozygotes is $2pq (1 - \frac{1}{2}S)$ following similar logic to that used in Table 11.1. Consequently, the selfing rate will be twice the deviation of heterozygote frequencies from Hardy–Weinberg equilibrium (Chapter 19).

Pedigrees

Pedigrees can be used to determine the inbreeding coefficient of an individual, as we saw above. In this way we can evaluate the effects of inbreeding on survival or reproduction rates, etc. at the level of individuals. Computation of F from first principles becomes impractical when dealing with complex pedigrees such as that for Przewalski's horse (Box 11.1). Consequently, simpler alternative methods have been devised for complex pedigrees.

Simple methods exist for determining inbreeding from pedigrees

We begin by considering an example where we can determine the inbreeding coefficient from first principles, and then illustrate how the method can be simplified for more complex pedigrees. Figure 11.5 illustrates a pedigree where there is mating between half-sibs. The parents of individual X are related through their common parent A. They are not related in any other way, so we only have to consider the transmission of alleles from A through D and E to X. The inbreeding coefficient of individual X is determined by labelling the alleles in individual A as A_1 and A_2, and computing the probability that individual X is either A_1A_1 or A_2A_2, i.e. that it has two alleles identical by descent. The probability that A_1 is transmitted from grandparent A to parent D is ½ based on normal Mendelian segregation, and that it is then transmitted from D to X is a further ½. Similarly, the probability that A_1 is passed from A to parent E is ½, and from E to X another ½. Thus, the probability that X is A_1A_1 is the product of the probabilities for four paths:

$$P(X \text{ is } A_1A_1) = (\tfrac{1}{2})^4 = 1/16$$

Similarly, the probability that X is A_2A_2 is $(\tfrac{1}{2})^4 = 1/16$. Thus, the probability that X is either A_1A_1 or A_2A_2 is the sum of the above two probabilities:

$$P(X \text{ is } A_1A_1 \text{ or } A_2A_2) = (\tfrac{1}{2})^4 + (\tfrac{1}{2})^4 = 1/8$$

The probability of X being homozygous represents the new inbreeding arising from A as a common ancestor of D and E.

However, if A is already inbred (i.e. A_1 and A_2 have a probability F of being identical by descent), an additional amount of homozygosity occurs. Individuals inheriting A_1 from their mother and A_2 from their father may be inheriting identical alleles, as are individuals inheriting A_2 from mother and A_1 from father, i.e. they are autozygous. The probability of the former is:

$$P(X \text{ inherits } A_1 \text{ from father and } A_2 \text{ from mother}) = (\tfrac{1}{2})^4$$

for the same reason as above. Thus, the probability of either one or the other of these situations is $(\tfrac{1}{2})^4 + (\tfrac{1}{2})^4 = (\tfrac{1}{2})^3$. The probability that A_1 is identical by descent with A_2 is A's inbreeding coefficient F_A. Thus, the probability that X is identically homozygous through previous inbreeding is:

$$P(X \text{ is identically homozygous through past inbreeding}) = (\tfrac{1}{2})^3 F_A$$

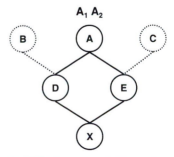

Fig. 11.5 Pedigree with mating between half-sibs.
$P(A_1A_1) = 1/16$
$P(A_2A_2) = 1/16$
$P(A_1A_2) = 1/8$

The overall inbreeding coefficient of X due to both new and previous inbreeding is:

$$F_X = (\tfrac{1}{2})^3 + (\tfrac{1}{2})^3 \, F_A = (\tfrac{1}{2})^3 \, (1 + F_A).$$

Thus, if a common ancestor is already inbred, inbreeding is increased further down the pedigree.

> The inbreeding coefficient for an individual can be calculated from the number of individuals in each path connecting one parent to the other through each common ancestor, and the inbreeding coefficient of each common ancestor

The inbreeding coefficient can be obtained by counting the individuals in the path from mother to father through the common ancestor (including both parents), and raising $\tfrac{1}{2}$ to this power. For example, there are three individuals connecting parents of individual X through their common ancestor A in Fig. 11.5, i.e. through D, A and E. The inbreeding coefficient of X is $(\tfrac{1}{2})^3$, if A is not inbred.

In more complex pedigrees, the parents may be related through more than one common ancestor, or from the same ancestor through different paths. Each common ancestor, and each path, contributes an additional probability of the progeny having identity by descent. The inbreeding coefficient is the sum of the probabilities contributed by each different path to each common ancestor, as follows:

$$F = \Sigma \, (\tfrac{1}{2})^n \, (1 + F_{ca}) \tag{11.8}$$

where n is the number of individuals in the path from one parent to a common ancestor and back to the other parent, and F_{ca} is the inbreeding coefficient of the particular common ancestor. These contributions to inbreeding are summed for each different path linking both parents to each common ancestor.

We apply this method to the simple pedigree in Fig. 11.6 and then to a more complex case in Fig. 11.7. In Fig. 11.6, the individuals to count from one parent to the other through the common ancestor (A) are F, D, B, A, C, E and G, making $n = 7$ steps. Thus F_X in Fig. 11.6 is $(\tfrac{1}{2})^7 (1 + F_A)$, being 1/128 if individual A is not inbred.

Calculation of the inbreeding coefficient for the Dorcas gazelle shown in Fig. 11.7 is more complex as it involves summing six different paths, two of them involving inbred common ancestors (Example 11.5). The inbreeding coefficient is 0.266. The paths through E, the most recent common ancestor, contribute most of this. Distant ancestors contribute little to the inbreeding coefficient.

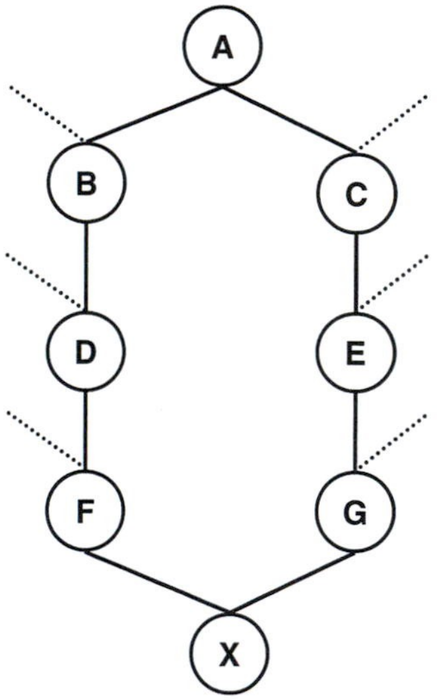

Fig. 11.6 Pedigree with a more remote common ancestor. The dotted lines represent paths to other ancestors that are not on the path to the common ancestor A.

Example 11.5	Determining the inbreeding coefficient for Dorcas gazelle X in the pedigree shown in Fig. 11.7

To calculate the inbreeding coefficient of individual X, we must identify all the common ancestors of the parents H and I, and all the paths to them. Individuals A, B and E are common ancestors causing relationships between H and I. The paths of relationship, the number of individuals in paths joining parents through common ancestors (n), the inbreeding coefficients of common ancestors, and the contribution of each of the paths to the inbreeding coefficient F_X (rounded to four decimal places) are shown below. A, B and F are all assumed to be unrelated and non-inbred. Individual E is the results of a parent (B) – offspring (C) mating and has an inbreeding coefficient of $(\frac{1}{2})^2 = 0.25$. The overall inbreeding coefficient of X is 0.2656.

Paths of relationship (common ancestors are in bold)	n	F of common ancestor	Contribution to F_X	
HE**CA**DGI	7	0	$(\frac{1}{2})^7$	$= 0.0078$
HE**CB**DGI	7	0	$(\frac{1}{2})^7$	$= 0.0078$
HE**B**DGI	6	0	$(\frac{1}{2})^6$	$= 0.0156$
HE**G**I	4	$\frac{1}{4}$	$(\frac{1}{2})^4 \times 5/4$	$= 0.0781$
HE**I**	3	$\frac{1}{4}$	$(\frac{1}{2})^3 \times 5/4$	$= 0.1563$
			F_X	$= 0.2656$

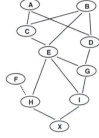

Fig. 11.7 Complex pedigree for male Dorcas gazelle 102796 (X) at the Smithsonian National Zoological Park, Washington, DC.

Other procedures and computer programs are available to calculate inbreeding coefficients for more complex situations on pedigrees stretching over many generations (Ballou 1983; Lacy *et al.* 2000)

Breeding systems in nature

There are many circumstances where it would be easier for an individual to mate with relatives. They are nearby and mating with them would avoid the risks associated with dispersal to find unrelated mates (e.g. predation, competition and starvation). In plants, there is a cost involved in long-distance pollen dispersal, as more pollen will be wasted. However, only a small proportion of species practise regular inbreeding. These usually have life histories that involve large benefits from mating with relatives, such as in colonizing species.

Most species of animals are thought to avoid inbreeding (Ralls *et al.* 1986). Many species of birds and mammals have dispersal patterns that reduce inbreeding. Often only one sex disperses, as in the yellow-bellied marmot (Koenig *et al.* 1996). In at least some mammals, individuals avoid mating with other individuals carrying the same MHC alleles, promoting outbreeding (Penn & Potts 1999).

Plants have more diverse breeding systems, but perhaps 50% have self-incompatibility systems that result in avoidance of selfing (Chapters 9 and 10). Further, selfing appears to be an unstable evolutionary strategy; it has evolved many times, but its taxonomic distribution in plants, terrestrial slugs and marine invertebrates suggests that it is an evolutionary dead end (Frankham 1995a).

Many species have evolved mechanisms that result in avoidance of inbreeding

Regular systems of inbreeding

About 40% of flowering plant species can and do self-fertilize (self) and 20% may do so routinely (Richards 1997). For example, endangered

Some species routinely reproduce by selfing

Brown's banksia from Western Australia exhibits about 30% self-fertilization, a high rate for this genus (Sampson *et al.* 1994).

Consequently, we need to consider the outcomes of repeated deliberate inbreeding over generations. We consider selfing, full-sib mating, and repeated backcrossing. The first two are the most extreme forms of inbreeding possible in self-fertile and naturally non-selfing species, respectively. Repeated backcrossing can be used to recover a sub-species that has declined to a single individual by crossing to a related sub-species, followed by repeated backcrossing to the remaining individual.

Fig. 11.8 Increase in inbreeding coefficients arising from repeated generations of selfing, full-sib mating and backcrossing to a single individual.

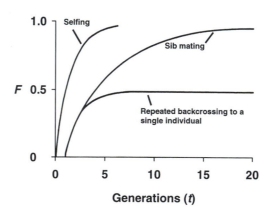

Figure 11.8 illustrates the increase in inbreeding over generations due to selfing, full-sib mating and backcrossing to a parent. The recurrence relations for these cases are given in Table 11.4 (derivations are given in Falconer & Mackay 1996). The use of the recurrence relationship for a selfing plant is shown in Example 11.6 and that for full-sib mating is given in Example 11.7 using the naked mole rat as an example. Backcrossing is of practical conservation interest as it can be used to recover sub-species that have been reduced to a single individual (Fig. 11.9). The survivor A is mated to B (from a different sub-species), and their offspring C is backcrossed to A, then D is backcrossed to A, etc. Backcrossing to the original parent increases the genetic representation of the threatened sub-species in the offspring. However, this is done at the expense of increased inbreeding. For example, the one remaining

Table 11.4 Recurrence relations for regular systems of inbreeding. F is the inbreeding coefficient and t is the generation

Form of inbreeding	Recurrence relationship
Self-fertilization	$F_t = \frac{1}{2}(1 + F_{t-1})$
Full-sib mating	$F_t = \frac{1}{4}(1 + 2F_{t-1} + F_{t-2})$
Repeated backcrossing to a single individual, A	$F_t = \frac{1}{4}(1 + F_A + 2F_{t-1})$

Example 11.6 | Accumulation of inbreeding over generations in a selfing plant species

The rise in inbreeding coefficient for a species with continual selfing can be computed using the recurrence relationship from Table 11.4:

$$F_t = \tfrac{1}{2}(1 + F_{t-1})$$

If the initial population is non inbred, $F_{t\,1} = 0$, then

$$F_1 = \tfrac{1}{2}(1 + 0) = 0.5$$

$$F_2 = \tfrac{1}{2}(1 + 0.5) = 0.75$$

$$F_3 = \tfrac{1}{2}(1 + 0.75) = 0.875$$

and the population rapidly becomes highly inbred approaching $F \sim 1$ (complete inbreeding).

Example 11.7 | Accumulation of inbreeding with repeated full-sib mating

In a few species, such as the colonial naked mole rat, full-sib inbreeding appears to be a regular part of the mating system (Reeve *et al.* 1990). Repeated full-sib mating is also used to generate inbred populations of animals for experimental purposes. The rise in F can be calculated using the recurrence relationship in Table 11.4, as follows:

$$F_t = \tfrac{1}{4}(1 + 2F_{t-1} + F_{t-2})$$

If we assume no prior inbreeding (F_{t-1} and $F_{t-2} = 0$), then

$$F_1 = \tfrac{1}{4}(1 + 0 + 0) = 0.25$$

$$F_2 = \tfrac{1}{4}(1 + 2 \times 0.25 + 0) = 0.375$$

$$F_3 = \tfrac{1}{4}(1 + 2 \times 0.375 + 0.25) = 0.5$$

Consequently, the inbreeding coefficient with full-sib mating reaches a value of 0.5 after three generations, the same value achieved after one generation of selfing. The inbreeding coefficient continues to rise with continued sib mating until $F \sim 1$.

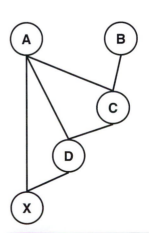

Fig. 11.9 Pedigree for repeated backcrossing to the same individual.

female Norfolk Island boobook owl has been crossed to its nearest related sub-species from New Zealand. If she lives long enough to be used for four generations of backcrossing to be completed (unlikely, but useful as an example), her progeny in successive generations will have the inbreeding coefficients given in Example 11.8. Such a backcrossed population has an inbreeding coefficient approaching 50% after four generations of backcrossing.

Example 11.8 | Inbreeding with repeated backcrossing to one individual

The one remaining female Norfolk Island boobook owl has been crossed to males from the related New Zealand sub-species. By backcrossing to the female, wildlife managers could generate a population with a gene pool consisting mostly of Norfolk Island boobook alleles. What effect will this have on the inbreeding coefficients of the progeny?

Let us first assume that the one remaining female owl is not inbred. The hybrid offspring will have an inbreeding coefficient of 0. The progeny of the first generation backcross of the hybrids to the Norfolk Island female will have an inbreeding coefficient:

$$F_1 = 0.25$$

since $F_{t-1} = 0$

$$\text{and } F_2 = ¼\,(1 + 2F_1) = ¼\,(1 + ½) = 0.375$$

$$F_3 = ¼\,(1 + 2F_2) = ¼\,(1 + ¾) = 0.4375$$

$$F_4 = ¼\,(1 + 2F_3) = ¼\,(1 + 7/8) = 0.46875$$

Thus, the regenerated boobook owl population would have an inbreeding coefficient of almost 47% after four generations of backcrossing.

The proportion of the genotype deriving from the Norfolk Island boobook owl is 50% in the first cross and 75%, 87.5%, 93.75% and 96.9% after 1, 2, 3 and 4 generations of backcrossing, respectively.

If the one remaining female owl was, herself, the offspring of a full-sib mating ($F_A = ¼$), the first generation hybrid offspring would still have an $F = 0$, but the following generations have higher inbreeding coefficients than above.

$$F_1 = ¼\,(1 + ¼) = 0.3125$$

$$F_2 = ¼\,(1 + ¼ + 2F_1) = ¼\,(1 + ¼ + 0.625) = 0.4688$$

$$F_3 = ¼\,(1 + ¼ + 2F_2) = ¼\,(1 + ¼ + 0.9375) = 0.5469$$

$$F_4 = ¼\,(1 + ¼ + 2F_3) = ¼\,(1 + ¼ + 1.09375) = 0.5859$$

In this case, the inbreeding coefficient in the final generation would be almost 59%, compared to about 47% if she was non-inbred. In reality, the one remaining owl is likely to be partially inbred.

Mutation–selection balance with inbreeding

Selfing species are expected to have lower equilibrium frequencies for deleterious alleles

Since some species routinely self-fertilize and others do so sometimes, we need to determine the mutation–selection equilibria for inbreeding species. Inbreeding increases the frequency of homozygotes and increases the opportunity for deleterious alleles to be removed by

Table 11.5 Mutation–selection equilibria for deleterious alleles, comparing selfing with random mating. u is the mutation rate, s the selection coefficient against homozygotes for deleterious alleles, hs the selection coefficient against heterozygotes and F the inbreeding coefficient

	Inbreeding	Random mating
Complete recessive	$\sim [\sqrt{(F^2 + 4u/s)} - F]/2$	$\sqrt{(u/s)}$
Partial recessive	$\sim u/[s(h + F)]$	u/hs
Highly inbred (irrespective of dominance)	$\sim u/s$	

Source: Li (1955); Crow & Kimura (1970).

selection. This is referred to as **purging**. Table 11.5 presents equilibrium frequencies due to mutation–selection balance under inbreeding.

Equilibrium frequencies for inbreeding species are lower than those for outbreeding species (Example 11.9). The reduction in frequency of a lethal allele is most pronounced for a complete recessive and somewhat less for a partial recessive. With very high levels of inbreeding (such as continual selfing), the equilibrium frequency for all cases (irrespective of the level of dominance) is approximately u/s. For a lethal allele, this results in equilibrium frequencies that are only 1/50 that for a partially recessive lethal, and 1/300 that for a fully recessive lethal, under random mating. These examples indicate that purging of lethal alleles greatly reduces their frequencies under inbreeding. However, the situation is rather different for mildly deleterious alleles in small populations. Purging has very little impact on removal of mildly deleterious alleles under full-sib inbreeding (Hedrick 1994).

Purging occurs in threatened species that suffer inbreeding as a result of small population sizes, but its impacts appear to be relatively small (see Chapter 12).

Example 11.9 Comparison of mutation–selection equilibria for a lethal allele under inbreeding versus random mating

Inbreeding exposes deleterious recessives as homozygotes and increases the opportunity for selection to remove them. In assessing the impact of inbreeding on mutation–selection equilibria, we first consider a completely recessive lethal with a mutation rate of 10^{-5}. In a random mating population its equilibrium frequency will be

$$q = \sqrt{(u/s)} = \sqrt{(10^{-5}/1)} = 3 \times 10^{-3}$$

By contrast, in a population with an equilibrium F of 0.33 (50% selfing), a recessive lethal will have an equilibrium frequency of

$$q \sim [\sqrt{(F^2 + 4u/s)} - F]/2 = [\sqrt{(0.33^2 + 4 \times 10^{-5}/1)} - 0.33]/2$$
$$= 3 \times 10^{-5}$$

Thus, the equilibrium frequencies for recessive lethal alleles in a population with an equilibrium inbreeding coefficient of 33% is 1/100 that in a random mating population.

For a partially recessive lethal allele with $hs = 0.02$ ($s = 1$, $h = 0.02$), the equilibrium in a random mating population is

$$q = u/hs = 10^{-5}/0.02 = 5 \times 10^{-4}$$

while for a population with an inbreeding coefficient of $F = 0.33$, the equilibrium frequency is

$$q = u/[s(h + F)] = 10^{-5}/[1(0.02 + 0.33)] = 2.86 \times 10^{-5}$$

Thus, the frequency of a partially recessive lethal in a population at equilibrium with $F = 0.33$ is only about 1/17 that in a random mating population.

For a highly inbred population, for example, one with continual selfing where F approaches 1, the equilibrium frequency is approximately

$$q \sim u/s \sim 10^{-5}$$

Consequently, inbreeding reduces the equilibrium frequencies to 1/50 that for a partial recessive and to 1/300 that for a complete recessive in random mating populations.

Inbreeding in polyploids

Inbreeding reduces heterozygosity more slowly in polyploids than in diploids

Since many plants and some animals are polyploid, we must consider the impact of inbreeding in them. We restrict consideration to autotetraploids, as this is sufficient to illustrate the principles involved. Since each locus has four copies in tetraploids, all four must be identically homozygous for a complete recessive to be exposed. Consequently, we might expect that inbreeding would have a lesser impact in polyploids than in diploids.

The details of segregation in autotetraploids are more complex than in diploids, as it depends upon the position of a locus relative to the centromere. Gametic output for two situations is given in Table 11.6. Crossing-over between the centromere and the locus makes it possible to produce AA gametes from Aaaa parents and aa gametes from AAAa parents, while these gametes are not possible with random chromosome assortment.

The impact of selfing in an autotetraploid is shown in Table 11.7. In contrast to a diploid, where selfing of an Aa heterozygote produces 25% aa recessive homozygotes, selfing of an AAaa autotetraploid produces only 2.8% aaaa recessive homozygotes with chromosome segregation and 4.6% aaaa recessive homozygotes with random chromatid segregation. With continual selfing of an AAaa individual, heterozygosity (AAAa + AAaa + Aaaa) drops from 100% initially to 94.4%, 80.6%, 67.4% and 56.3% over four generations with random chromosomal segrega-

Table 11.6 Gametic output for different genotypes in an autotetraploid for loci close to, and distant from, the centromere (referred to as random chromosome and random chromatid assortment, respectively)

| | Gametic output | |
| | Distance from centromere | |
Parent genotype	Close	Distant
AAAa	1AA: 1Aa	15AA: 12Aa: 1aa
AAaa	1AA: 4Aa: 1aa	3AA: 8Aa: 3aa
Aaaa	1Aa: 1aa	1AA: 12Aa: 15aa

Source: After Bever & Felber (1994).

Table 11.7 Phenotypic ratios produced by selfing for different genotypes in an autotetraploid, for loci close to and distant from the centromere. One A allele is assumed to produce the dominant A phenotype

| | Phenotype ratios | |
| | Distance from centromere | |
Parent genotype	Close	Distant
AAA	All A	All A
AAAa	All A	783A: 1a
AAaa	35A: 1a	20.8A: 1a
Aaaa	3A: 1a	2.5A: 1a
aaaa	All a	All a

Source: After Allard (1960).

tion (Li 1976). This is a much slower decline in heterozygosity than that produced by selfing in a diploid, where heterozygosity drops from 100% initially to 50%, 25%, 12.5% and 6.25% over four generations. Heterozygosity halves each generation with selfing in a diploid, but for an autotetraploid locus close to the centromere it eventually settles down to a reduction of 1/6 of the current value per generation, and slightly more than 1/5 for a distant locus (Bever & Felber 1994). Consequently, inbreeding in tetraploids is anticipated to have a lesser impact on reproductive fitness than in diploids (Chapter 12).

Relationships between inbreeding, heterozygosity, genetic diversity and population size

It is important to recognize that the connections between inbreeding, small population size and expected heterozygosity are a feature of

The close relationship between inbreeding and loss of heterozygosity found in small random mating populations is often not found in habitually inbreeding species

random mating populations, but not of populations that naturally inbreed. In a random mating population of stable size, loss of genetic diversity equals the inbreeding coefficient. Further, loss of heterozygosity is closely related to loss of allelic diversity and loss of polymorphism.

Conversely, a large plant population that reproduces by selfing may have a high inbreeding coefficient in each individual, a very low heterozygosity, but high overall genetic diversity as alleles are distributed among, rather than within individuals. Loss of genetic diversity as measured by polymorphism and allelic diversity is due to sampling effects, rather than to inbreeding. Thus, inbreeding and loss of genetic diversity are connected through the effects of finite population size in small random mating populations, but their relationship is more complex in habitually inbreeding species.

Summary

1. Inbreeding is the mating of individuals that are related by descent.

2. Inbreeding is of conservation concern as it reduces reproductive fitness in inbred populations and increases the risk of extinction.

3. Inbreeding is measured using the inbreeding coefficient (F), the probability that an individual has two alleles at a locus that are identical by descent.

4. Inbreeding reduces heterozygosity and exposes deleterious recessive alleles.

5. Inbreeding is an inevitable consequence of small population size.

6. Mutation–selection equilibria under inbreeding for partially recessive alleles of large effect are lower than under random mating, but may show little difference for alleles of small effect.

7. Inbreeding increases homozygosity more slowly in polyploids than in diploids and so is expected to have less impact in them.

FURTHER READING

Charlesworth & Charlesworth (1987) An excellent scholarly review of both the theory and empirical issues relating to the impact of inbreeding.

Crow & Kimura (1970) *Introduction to Population Genetics Theory*. Fairly advanced treatment of inbreeding theory.

Falconer & Mackay (1996) *Introduction to Quantitative Genetics*. Provides a clear treatment of inbreeding.

Malecot (1969) *The Mathematics of Heredity*. The classic work that defined inbreeding in probability terms.

Ralls & Ballou (1983) Highly influential study describing deleterious effects of inbreeding on captive wildlife.

Richards (1997) *Plant Breeding Systems*. Provides a comprehensive overview of plant breeding systems and their consequences.

Wright (1969) *Evolution and the Genetics of Populations*, vol. 2. A scholarly review of inbreeding theory by the person who developed much of it.

PROBLEMS

11.1 Inbreeding coefficients: What is the inbreeding coefficient for the white tiger on the front of this chapter that resulted from a father–daughter mating?

11.2 Inbreeding in small populations: What is the average inbreeding coefficient for the Isle Royale gray wolf with an effective population size of 5 for 10 generations?

11.3 Inbreeding in fluctuating populations: Compute the inbreeding coefficient for a population of Mauritius kestrels that fluctuates in size as follows: 2, 100, 2, 100.

11.4 Genotype frequencies with inbreeding: Determine the genotype frequencies for the chondrodystrophy locus in California condors for progeny that would result if they could self (see Table 11.3).

11.5 Inbreeding and homozygosity: By what factor is the frequency of deleterious recessive homozygotes increased in children of (a) full-sib mating and (b) first-cousin mating, compared to random mating when the allele has a frequency of 1%?

11.6 Recurrent inbreeding: What is the inbreeding coefficient for the first five generations using repeated full-sib mating in the naked mole rat?

11.7 Inbreeding and heterozygosity: What will be the frequency of heterozygotes at the Mdh–2 locus with alleles F and S at frequencies of 0.4 and 0.6 in a population of Pacific yew with an inbreeding coefficient of 0.47 (El-Kassaby & Yanchuk 1994)?

11.8 Effective inbreeding coefficient: The microsatellite heterozygosity in the black bears on the Island of Newfoundland is 36%, while that in the population on the Canadian mainland is 79.2% (Paetkau & Strobeck 1994). What is the effective inbreeding coefficient for the Newfoundland population, relative to the mainland population?

11.9 Pedigree inbreeding: Determine the inbreeding coefficient of individual X in the pedigree in the margin above (the results of a double first-cousin mating).

11.10 Pedigree inbreeding: What is the inbreeding coefficient for individual X in the pedigree shown (after Hedrick 1983)?

11.11 Pedigree inbreeding: What is the inbreeding coefficient for the Nigerian giraffe (individual X) in Paris Zoo (Box 2.1)?

11.12 Deleterious effects of inbreeding: What is the probability that individuals resulting from selfing are homozygous for at least one lethal allele in an outbreeding plant species with 20000 loci, 10% of which can mutate to produce lethals? Assume that deleterious alleles at each of 2000 loci have equilibrium frequencies of 5×10^{-4}. Compare this with the probability for a random mating population.

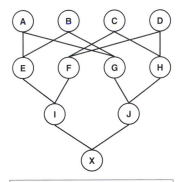

Problem 11.9

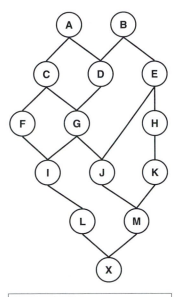

Problem 11.10

Chapter 12

Inbreeding depression

Terms:

Dominance,
epistasis,
heterosis,
inbreeding depression,
lethal equivalents,
overdominance,
purging

Inbreeding reduces reproduction and survival in essentially all well-studied naturally outbreeding species and to a lesser extent in selfing species. Outcrossing reverses its deleterious effects

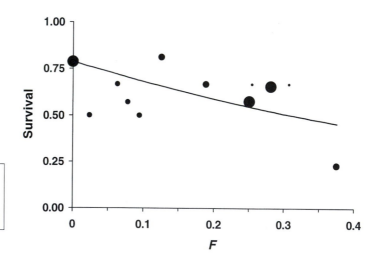

Inbreeding depression: survival of juvenile pygmy hippopotamus from Africa declines with increasing inbreeding (*F*).

Inbreeding depression in naturally outbreeding species

Reductions in population size increase the rate of inbreeding in closed populations. In normally outbreeding species, inbreeding results in a decline in the mean for reproductive fitness characters, termed **inbreeding depression**. The deleterious effects of inbreeding were recognized before the Mendelian basis of inheritance was established. Darwin (1876) clearly documented inbreeding depression, in studies of 57 species of plants from 52 genera and 30 families. Inbred plants were on average shorter, weighed less, flowered later and produced fewer seeds (Table 12.1). The effects of inbreeding were substantial. On average, selfed plants showed a 41% reduction in seed production and a 13% decline in height. Not all species showed inbreeding depression for all characters studied, but virtually all cases showed inbreeding depression for most characters.

Inbreeding in naturally outbreeding populations of animals and plants results in a decline in reproductive fitness, termed inbreeding depression

Table 12.1 Effects of inbreeding by self-fertilization (I) versus outcrossing (O) on several characters in 57 species of plants

Characters	Number of species	Number of experiments	O > I	O < I	Similar[a]	Difference (O − I)
Height	54	83	57	8	18	13%
Weight	8	11	8	1	2	
Flowering time	32	58	44[b]	9	5	
Seed production	23	33	26	2	5	41%

Notes:
[a]Darwin considered comparisons to be similar if they lay within 5% of each other.
[b]Outbreds flowered earlier than inbreds.
Source: Darwin (1876).

Subsequently, inbreeding depression has been documented in laboratory animals, domestic animals, outbred plants and humans (Table 12.2; Wright 1977; Charlesworth & Charlesworth 1987; Thornhill 1993; Falconer & Mackay 1996; Roff 1997; Lynch & Walsh 1998). Despite the overwhelming evidence from laboratory and domestic species, there has been considerable scepticism that inbreeding depression occurs in wildlife. However, Ralls & Ballou (1983) found higher mortality in inbred versus outbred progeny in 41 of 44 mammals (Fig. 11.1). On average, progeny of full-sib matings displayed a 33% reduction in juvenile survival (Ralls *et al.* 1988). This was the first convincing evidence that inbreeding does have deleterious effects across a variety of wildlife species of conservation interest. Since then, inbreeding depression has been found in essentially all well-studied naturally outbreeding species (Lacy 1997; Roff 1997; Lynch & Walsh 1998).

Table 12.2 | Inbreeding depression for different components of fitness in animals and plants due to a 25% increase in the inbreeding coefficient. Inbreeding depression is expressed as % reduction in mean of inbreds compared to outbreds

Species	Character	Inbreeding depression (%)	Species	Character	Inbreeding depression (%)
Humans			*Non-domesticated species*		
	Height at age 10	4			
	IQ score	11	Deer mice		
				Litter size	15
Domesticated species				Age at 1st reproduction	−17
				Survival to weaning	8
Cattle			House mice (wild)		
	Milk yield	8		Litter size	10
Sheep				Body weight at 53 days	−10
	Fleece weight	14		Nesting behaviour	10
	Body weight at 1 year	9	Japanese quail		
Pigs				Reproduction and survival	64
	Litter size	8		Fertility	21
	Body weight at 154 days	11		Survival 0–5 wks	10
Mice				Body weight	4
	Litter size	18	Chukar partridges		
	Body weight at 6 wks	2		Reproduction and survival	58
Chickens				Egg production	16
	Reproduction and survival	26		Body weight	1
	Egg production	10	Rainbow trout		
	Body weight	5		Hatchability	−10, 9, 14
Turkeys				Fry survival	8, 11
	Reproduction and survival	38		Weight at 150 days	12
	Egg production	10	Zebra fish		
	Body weight	10		Hatchability	89
Maize				Survival to 30 days	43
	Yield of seed (full-sib)	14		Length at 30 days	11
	(selfing)	17	Channel catfish		
	Plant height (full-sib)	5		Hatchability	−11
	(selfing)	6		Body weight at 4 wks	43
				Body weight at 12 wks	7

Source: After Abplanalp (1990); Falconer & Mackay (1996); Rolf (1997).

Inbreeding depression in the wild

There is clear and compelling evidence for inbreeding depression in the majority of wild populations investigated, including vertebrates, invertebrates and plants

There is now clear and irrefutable evidence for inbreeding depression in wild populations, despite earlier scepticism. Crnokrak & Roff (1999) reviewed 35 papers investigating inbreeding depression in nature for 34 taxa that included 157 valid data sets. In 141 cases (90%) inbred individuals had poorer attributes than comparable outbreds (inbreeding depression), two were equal and only 14 were in the opposite direction. Inbreeding depression was significant for 88 data sets. Significant inbreeding depression has also been reported in at least another 15 other taxa, including five species of fish, great reed warblers, blue tits, harbour seals, greater prairie chickens, Soay sheep, rock wallabies, red-cockaded woodpeckers, Arabian oryx, mice, and red deer (Frankham 2000b). For example, in endangered golden lion tamarins in the wild in Brazil, survival of inbred individuals is lower than that for outbred individuals (Fig. 12.1). Overall, the evidence is compelling, especially considering the inevitable small sample sizes and lack of verified paternities in many of these studies. The desert topminnow fish (Box 12.1) provides an excellent case study of inbreeding depression in the wild.

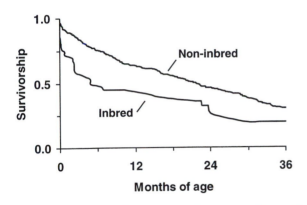

Fig. 12.1 Inbreeding depression for survival of endangered golden lion tamarins in natural habitats in Brazil (after Dietz *et al.* 2000).

Some studies have failed to detect inbreeding depression, but these are usually very small studies, or cases where paternity has not been verified. For example, Rowley *et al.* (1993) found no inbreeding depression in splendid fairy wrens from Western Australia, but later paternity studies revealed that at least 64% of progeny were not fathered by the group male(s), to whom paternity had previously been attributed. Komdeur *et al.* (1998) detected no inbreeding depression in Seychelles warblers, but the study involved only 12 outbred and 17 inbred matings.

The deleterious impacts of inbreeding depression are substantially greater, on average, in more stressful wild habitats than in captivity. Inbreeding depression for mammals is 6.9 times higher in the wild than in captivity (Crnokrak & Roff 1999). The impacts of inbreeding depression in the wild are usually very large when the entire life cycle is considered. For example, Meagher *et al.* (2000) found a 57% reduction in total offspring production by inbred (from full-sib matings), compared to outbred, wild house mice.

Box 12.1 | Inbreeding depression in desert topminnow fish in the wild (after Vrijenhoek *et al.* 1992; Vrijenhoek 1994)

Robert Vrijenhoek and his students have studied populations of desert topminnow fish in Sonora, Mexico. The upper pools in the Plátanos were completely desiccated during a severe drought in 1975. By 1978, these pools had been recolonized, but their populations became quite inbred as they were founded by a single gravid female. Prior to the drought, the topminnows co-existed with a clonal, parthenogenetic fish of the same genus, with the forms representing 76% and 24% of the fish density, respectively. After the populations were re-founded and the sexual form inbred, the frequency of sexual topminnows was only 5% to the clone's 95%, indicating 93% inbreeding depression. No corresponding changes in relative abundance occurred in downstream populations where topminnows did not become inbred. The inbred population of topminnows showed spinal curvature and other deformities, and poorer resistance to low oxygen (manifestations of inbreeding depression).

In 1983, 30 genetically variable female topminnows from the downstream mainstream pool were exchanged with 30 inbred topminnow females from the upstream Heart Pool. By 1985, the topminnow had re-established its numerical dominance

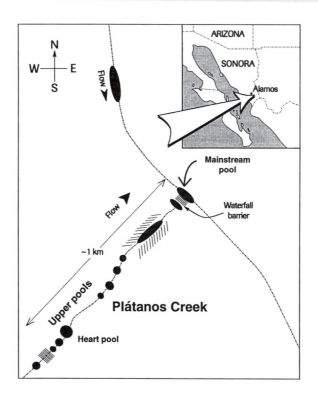

over the clonal genotype and represented about 80% of the fish. Adding outbred fish to the population had reversed inbreeding depression.

Another manifestation of inbreeding depression in these fish is their susceptibility to a monogean trematode parasite (the black spots on the fish illustrated above). The parasite load is least in outbred fish and highest in inbred and clonal fish (Lively *et al.* 1990).

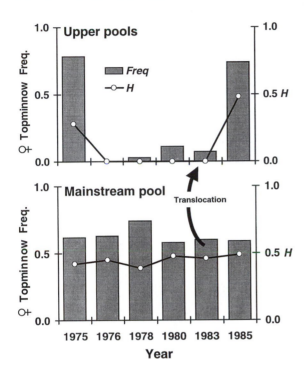

Inbreeding depression due to small population size

Inbreeding becomes inevitable in small populations (Chapter 11). Consequently, small isolated populations are expected to accumulate inbreeding depression. Small random mating populations of plants (three species), fruit flies, house flies, black-footed rock wallabies, euros (a kangaroo), greater prairie chickens, and a snake species have all exhibited reduced population fitness due to inbreeding (Polans & Allard 1989; Frankham 1995a; Heschel & Paige 1995; Madsen *et al.* 1996; Fischer & Matthies 1998; Eldridge *et al.* 1999, personal communication;

Inbreeding due to small population size results in inbreeding depression

Westemeier *et al.* 1998; Bryant *et al.* 1999). For example, Box 12.2 details inbreeding depression for litter size and abnormal offspring in a small Swedish population of adders.

Box 12.2 | **Inbreeding depression in a small isolated population of adders in Sweden** (Madsen *et al.* 1996)

A small isolated population of fewer than 40 individuals and fewer than 15 adult adders in Sweden has been separated from the main distribution of the snake for at least a century. Allozyme variability and DNA fingerprints confirmed that it had low levels of genetic diversity, and so was inbred compared to other large populations of the species.

The small population showed evidence of inbreeding depression. It displayed lower litter size and more abnormal offspring than the large snake population. While these differences could have been due to different environmental conditions, this explanation was ruled out for frequency of abnormal offspring; the progeny of an introduced male from the large population, when mated to females from the small population, exhibited reduced frequency of abnormalities. Further, analyses of soil samples ruled out heavy metal contamination as a reason for the difference, and food supply was similar in the two localities.

Inbreeding and extinction

Inbreeding will increase the risk of extinction for most species under a wide range of circumstances

Since inbreeding reduces reproductive fitness, it is expected to increase the risk of extinction. Inbreeding clearly increases extinction risks in captive populations (Frankham 1995b, 2001). For example, the incremental proportion of populations surviving declines with inbreeding coefficient in populations of mice and fruit flies (Fig. 12.2). There is a threshold; extinctions do not begin until intermediate levels of inbreeding. Population growth rates must become negative for extinctions to occur in captive populations and inbreeding must accumulate to a critical level before that occurs.

Since there has been scepticism about the effects of inbreeding, it is no surprise that there is also scepticism about the relative importance of genetic factors as a cause of extinction in wild populations. Much of this doubt is due to lack of direct evidence identifying genetic factors as common causes of extinction. In Chapter 2 we discussed the relationship between inbreeding and extinction. We showed that inbreeding is likely to increase extinction risk for a range of life histories under circumstances that are realistic for threatened species. This is especially true when genetic effects interact with other threatening factors. These findings (see Chapter 2; Frankham & Ralls 1998) are based upon:

• Direct evidence of inbreeding increasing extinction risk of butterfly and plant populations

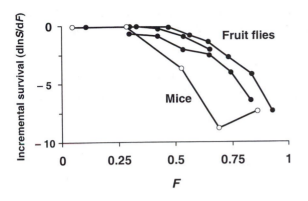

Fig. 12.2 Relationship between inbreeding and extinction in captive populations of mice and fruit flies (Frankham 1995b). Incremental survival (dlnS/dF) is plotted against the inbreeding coefficient (F). *Inbreeding increases extinction rates, but not until intermediate levels of inbreeding are reached, i.e. there is a threshold.*

- Circumstantial evidence that inbreeding may contribute to the extinction proneness of island populations
- Computer projections using real life histories with all threatening processes included, which indicate that inbreeding increases extinction risks under a wide range of realistic circumstances.

Characteristics of inbreeding depression

Inbreeding has been shown to adversely affect all aspects of reproductive fitness. This includes offspring numbers, juvenile survival, longevity, interbirth interval, mating ability, sperm quantity and quality, maternal ability, competitive ability and developmental time in animals. In plants, pollen quantity, number of ovules, amount of seed, germination rate, growth rates and competitive abilities all exhibit inbreeding depression (see Tables 12.1 and 12.2). This applies not only to domesticated species, but also to wild species, including those of conservation interest. For example, sperm abnormalities were higher, and sperm motility lower, in small inbred populations of lions and Florida panthers than in related large populations (Wildt 1996). Sperm numbers and quality were negatively related to inbreeding within the endangered Cuvier's gazelle population in Spain (Roldan *et al.* 1997). In old-field mice, inbred dams were less likely to breed and, of those that did, less likely to have a second litter. Their litters were smaller, survival of inbred offspring from birth to weaning was lower (69% vs. 93%), mass of inbred pups at weaning was lower and overall mass of progeny produced was reduced when compared to outbred dams (Lacy *et al.* 1996).

Inbreeding depression is most prominent for characters associated with reproductive fitness and least for characters peripherally associated with reproductive fitness (Mousseau & Roff 1987; Roff & Mousseau 1987: Falconer & Mackay 1996; Lynch & Walsh 1998). For example, seed production/grain yield show greater inbreeding depression than height in plants (Tables 12.1 and 12.2). Similarly, reproduction, survival and litter size typically show more inbreeding depression than body size in animals (Table 12.2).

All components of reproductive fitness are subject to inbreeding depression

Characters most closely related to reproductive fitness show greater inbreeding depression than those that are peripherally related to fitness

Unfortunately, relatively few studies have documented the extent of inbreeding depression on total reproductive fitness. Most studies typically assess only a few components of fitness, while all aspects of reproductive fitness, including survival, fecundity, mating ability, behaviour and maternal ability are subject to inbreeding effects. Frankel & Soulé (1981) noted that over a wide range of species each 10% increase in inbreeding coefficient caused approximately a 5%–10% decline in the mean of components of reproductive fitness, and a 25% decline in total fitness. For example, greater inbreeding depression for overall fitness than for its components has been found for old-field mice, house mice, chickens, turkeys, Japanese quail and chukar partridges (Table 12.2; Beilharz 1982; Abplanalp 1990; Lacy *et al.* 1996; Meagher *et al.* 2000). Impacts of inbreeding on total fitness are often very large. For example, Meagher *et al.* (2000) found a 57% reduction in total fitness in mice due to full-sib inbreeding vs. outbreeding in semi-wild conditions.

As might be expected, the impact of inbreeding depression is usually greater in harsher environments (Hoffmann & Parsons 1991; Roff 1997; Lynch & Walsh 1998). In plants, inbreeding depression is typically greater in the field than in greenhouses. For example Dudash (1990) found that selfed progeny of the rose pink plant exhibited 75% inbreeding depression in the field, but only 55% in the greenhouse (Fig. 12.3). Inbreeding depression in the scarlet gilia plant was greater when populations were stressed by transplanting and clipping, than when they were 'unstressed' (Heschel & Paige 1995). Inbreeding reduced survival in Soay sheep under conditions of high population densities, due to gastro-intestinal nematodes, but the effect was not found at low densities, or in sheep cleared of nematodes (Coltman *et al.* 1999). Further, experiments with fruit flies have shown that inbreeding depression is greater under stressful than benign conditions, leading to elevated extinction rates of inbred populations in stressful environments (Bijlsma *et al.* 2000).

Inbreeding depression is also generally greater in wild than in captive populations, presumably because captive environments are optimized (see Frankham 1995a). Based upon a meta-analysis, Crnokrak & Roff (1999) calculated that the impact of inbreeding was 6.9 times greater in the wild than in captivity. Meagher *et al.* (2000) found it to be 4.5 times greater in mice. Consequently, inbreeding depression is likely to be substantially greater in nature than estimates from captive populations of animals and plants would lead us to believe.

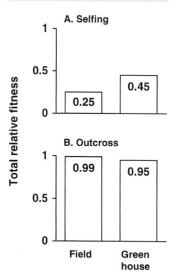

Fig. 12.3 Inbreeding depression in the rose pink plant is greater in more stressful conditions (after Dudash 1990). Relative fitnesses in propagules resulting from self-pollination, and cross-pollination between populations when grown in the greenhouse, and field conditions.

Variability in inbreeding depression

Since inbreeding depression depends on the frequency of deleterious alleles, it is expected to have a large stochastic element. As small inbreeding populations are subject to genetic drift, the same deleterious allele may be absent in one population and present at high frequency in another. Furthermore, individuals with the same expected F will have a range of actual levels of heterozygosity due to the sampling involved in Mendelian inheritance. Different loci will become homozygous in different individuals, just by chance. Consequently, different species, populations within a species, families within populations, and individuals within families will differ by chance in their complement of deleterious alleles, and show differences in their susceptibility to inbreeding depression. Since many loci affect reproductive fitness, it is highly improbable that fixation of deleterious alleles will be avoided at all loci. This accounts for the ubiquitous but highly variable nature of inbreeding depression.

The study by Ralls & Ballou (1983), across 44 different mammal species, found substantial variation in inbreeding effects (Fig. 11.1). Variation in inbreeding depression among lineages within species has been reported in old-field mice, dairy cattle, fruit flies and flour beetles (see Hohenboken *et al.* 1991; Montgomery *et al.* 1997), and is expected to be found in all outbreeding species. For example, Fig. 12.4 illustrates variation in inbreeding depression among three sub-species of old-field mice, and among three samples within each sub-species. Such effects appear to be common, although there have been few systematic comparisons. For example, Kärkkäinen *et al.* (1996) reported geographic variation in inbreeding depression in the Scots pine.

> Species, populations and families differ in inbreeding depression

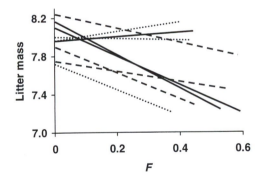

Fig. 12.4 Differences in inbreeding depression among three sub-species of old-field mice and of three samples within each sub-species for total mass of progeny weaned per pair (after Lacy *et al.* 1996). Regression lines relating fitness and inbreeding coefficient for each replicate of each sub-species are plotted. The three sub-species are designated by solid, dashed and dotted lines.

The stochastic nature of inbreeding depression also suggests that different species and populations will vary in the components of fitness that are affected by inbreeding. Captive populations of Mexican and red wolf do not exhibit inbreeding depression for juvenile survival (Kalinowski *et al.* 1999), but do show inbreeding depression in adult survival (Wilcken 2001). Similarly, replicates differed in the fitness components affected by inbreeding in the study of old-field mice (Lacy *et al.* 1996).

In contrast to the differences within species, little variation among major taxonomic groups has been found in susceptibility to inbreeding. No differences were found among mammalian orders in inbreeding

> Major taxa show similar inbreeding depression for natural outbreeders

depression for juvenile survival (Ralls *et al.* 1988). Inbreeding depression was very similar across birds, mammals, poikilotherms and plants (Crnokrak & Roff 1999). Further, no differences were found among mammals, birds, invertebrates and plants in susceptibility to extinction due to inbreeding (Frankham unpublished meta-analysis).

The one systematic difference found so far is between gymnosperms and angiosperms (64% vs. 39% reduction in fitness traits due to selfing) (Husband & Schemske 1996). While the reason for this is not clear, Lynch & Walsh (1998) suggested that mutation rates are higher in long-lived conifers than in short-lived angiosperms, due to differences in number of cell divisions per sexual generation. Alternatively, it could be related to the very different rates of polyploidy in gymnosperms and angiosperms (see below).

Inbreeding depression in species that regularly inbreed

Species that naturally inbreed show inbreeding depression, but the magnitude is generally less than that found in naturally outbreeding species

Since the opportunity for selection against deleterious recessives is greater in populations that regularly inbreed (Chapter 11), naturally inbreeding species are expected to suffer less from inbreeding depression. Species of plants that self usually show inbreeding depression, but of a lesser magnitude than for outbreeding plants. In a meta-analysis, the reductions in fitness due to self-fertilization were 0.23 for selfers and 0.53 for outbreeders (Husband & Schemske 1996). Further, there was a negative correlation between inbreeding depression and selfing rate.

Lower inbreeding depression in species that self could be due either to prior inbreeding, or to natural selection having previously removed deleterious alleles. The evidence above does not differentiate these effects. The extent of inbreeding depression due to one generation of inbreeding depends on the increase in inbreeding coefficient (ΔF) from one generation to the next. For selfing from an outbred population, ΔF is ½, while it is only ¼ for selfing from a plant that is itself the product of self-fertilization in the previous generation. If the selfing species analysed by Husband & Schemske (1996) had been subjected to only one generation of prior selfing, this could explain most of the difference in inbreeding depression between them and the outbreeding species.

Genetic basis of inbreeding depression

The magnitude of inbreeding depression depends upon heterozygosity for deleterious alleles ($2pq$), the dominance deviations for alleles (d) and the amount of inbreeding (F)

An understanding of the genetic basis of inbreeding depression is essential if we are to devise means for minimizing and reversing it. The fundamental cause of inbreeding depression is that inbreeding increases the frequency of homozygotes and decreases that of heterozygotes (see Chapter 11).

Table 12.3 | Impact of inbreeding on the mean of a population: single locus model

Genotype	Value	Genotype frequencies		Genotype frequency $\times$ value	
		Random mating	Inbred	Random mating	Inbred
A_1A_1	a	p^2	$p^2 + Fpq$	p^2a	$p^2a + Fpqa$
A_1A_2	d	$2pq$	$2pq(1-F)$	$2pqd$	$2pqd(1-F)$
A_2A_2	$-a$	q^2	$q^2 + Fpq$	$-q^2a$	$-q^2a - Fpqa$
			Means	$a(p-q) + 2pqd$	$a(p-q) + 2pqd - 2dpqF$
				M_0	$M_F = M_0 - 2dpqF$

The effects of inbreeding on the mean of a character can be illustrated using a simple model with no selection. Let us consider a population with an inbreeding coefficient of F and two alleles A_1 and A_2, with frequencies of p and q. The genotype frequencies are shown in Table 12.3. If the genotypes A_1A_1, A_1A_2 and A_2A_2 have genotypic values of a, d, and $-a$ (Fig. 5.4), then the mean of the inbred population is obtained by multiplying the frequencies of the genotypes by their values, and summing them. Consequently, the inbred population has a mean M_F of:

$$M_F = a(p-q) + 2dpq(1-F)$$

Since a random mating outbred population has a mean $M_0 = a(p-q) + 2pqd$, then:

$$M_F = M_0 - 2pqdF$$

Consequently, the inbreeding depression (ID) is:

$$ID = 2pqdF \qquad (12.1)$$

Inbreeding depression depends upon heterozygosity (for deleterious alleles), dominance deviation (d) (for deleterious alleles) and the inbreeding coefficient. As inbreeding depression is directly proportional to the amount of inbreeding, this leads us to expect a linear relationship between inbreeding depression and F, an issue we address below.

Deleterious alleles must be partially or completely recessive (and favourable alleles dominant, or partially so), or show overdominance to contribute to inbreeding depression (Example 12.1), i.e. a locus will only contribute to inbreeding depression if $d > 0$. Whether inbreeding depression results from dominance or overdominance is an important issue. While both mechanisms cause inbreeding depression, they respond differently to natural selection. With dominance, selection can reduce the frequency of deleterious alleles, but it cannot do this with overdominance (see 'Purging', below). Dominance of favourable alleles, rather than overdominance, is considered to make the major contribution to inbreeding depression (Falconer & Mackay 1996; Lynch & Walsh 1998; Charlesworth & Charlesworth 1999).

> Inbreeding depression only occurs when there is dominance, or overdominance

---

Example 12.1 | Effect of different levels of dominance on inbreeding depression

The values of d (dominance deviations for the heterozygotes) for additive, dominant and overdominant loci are 0, a and $2a$, respectively (Fig. 5.4). If we consider a locus with two alleles at frequencies of 0.99 for A_1 and 0.01 for deleterious A_2, with an effect of 10% on survival ($a = 0.05$), then the inbreeding depression for a full-sib mating ($F = 0.25$) will be:

For a locus with additive effects ($d = 0$), inbreeding depression (ID)

$$ID = 2pqdF = 2 \times 0.01 \times 0.99 \times 0 \times 0.25 = 0$$

For a locus showing complete dominance ($d = a = 0.05$), inbreeding depression

$$ID = 2 \times 0.01 \times 0.99 \times 0.05 \times 0.25 = 2.47 \times 10^{-4}$$

An equivalent, partially dominant, locus would cause inbreeding depression in an amount proportional to the dominance. If it showed intermediate dominance ($d = 0.05/2 = 0.025$), the inbreeding depression would be half that for a fully dominant locus. The inbreeding depression for a locus showing overdominance is expected to be higher as the allele frequencies will probably be more intermediate, yielding a higher value for $2pq$. Further, the value of d for the overdominant case is greater than that for the dominant cases, being $2a$.

Thus, dominance is required for inbreeding depression, there being none for an additive locus. The magnitude of inbreeding depression may seem very low for a single locus, but it must be remembered that the effects accumulate over all loci.

Effects of inbreeding depression accumulate over all polymorphic loci affecting a trait

Numerous loci will generally be involved in causing inbreeding depression for fitness, and its components. While the number of loci involved is unknown, it may well be thousands. An equation equivalent to 12.1 can be derived for the sum of many loci. If the combined genotypic values are given by the sum of the effects of the individual loci, the population mean is:

$$M_F = \sum_{i=1}^{\substack{\text{no. of} \\ \text{loci}}} [a_i(p_i - q_i) + 2d_i p_i q_i(1 - F)]$$

$$= M_0 - 2F \sum_{i=1}^{\substack{\text{no. of} \\ \text{loci}}} d_i p_i q_i$$

and inbreeding depression will be

$$ID = 2F \sum_{i=1}^{\substack{\text{no. of} \\ \text{loci}}} d_i p_i q_i \tag{12.2}$$

Thus, inbreeding depression depends on F, the number of loci polymorphic for deleterious alleles, the dominance of the alleles, and on their frequencies. For inbreeding to change the mean, dominance (d) must be directional, i.e. deleterious alleles must be partially to completely reces- sive, rather than an equal mixture of dominants and recessives. This will almost certainly be the case as natural selection reduces the frequency of dominant deleterious alleles relative to recessives (Table 7.4). Inbreeding depression is closely related to the dominance variance (V_D) (Chapter 5). Both depend upon $2pqd$. Dominance variance is greater for fitness char- acters than for peripheral ones and so is inbreeding depression.

The cumulative effects of multiple loci are illustrated for loci with lethal alleles in Example 12.2. Lethals alone can account for high levels of inbreeding depression with realistic numbers and effects of loci. In practice, inbreeding depression is due to a combination of alleles with effects ranging from lethal to mildly deleterious. In fruit flies, the only genus for which we have reasonable data, inbreeding depression is about equally due to lethals and deleterious alleles of small effect (Simmons & Crow 1977; Lynch & Walsh 1998).

| **Example 12.2** | Inbreeding depression due to multiple loci with lethal alleles |

Following Example 11.2, we will consider 5000 loci, each with lethals in mutation–selection equilibrium frequencies of 5×10^{-4}. Lethal alleles (l) typically reduce the fitness of heterozygotes by about 2%, giving the following genotypic values:

	$+/+$	$+/l$	l/l
Genotypic values	1	0.98	0

Yielding

$$a = (1 - 0)/2 = 0.5$$

and

$$d = 0.98 - 0.5 = 0.48$$

If we consider a population with an inbreeding coefficient of 0.25 as a result of full-sib mating, then the inbreeding depression due to one locus is

$$ID = 2pqdF = 2 \times (1 - 5 \times 10^{-4}) \times (5 \times 10^{-4}) \times 0.48 \times 0.25$$
$$= 1.2 \times 10^{-4}$$

To accumulate these effects over 5000 loci, we take the fitness effects of each locus and multiply them together, as follows:

$$\text{Fitness due to inbreeding at 1 locus} = 1 - ID = 1 - 1.2 \times 10^{-4}$$
$$= 0.99988$$

And the cumulative effects over 5000 loci are

$$\text{Overall fitness} = (0.99988)^{5000} = 0.55$$

so

$$\text{Total } ID = 1 - 0.55 = 0.45$$

Thus, lethal alleles alone could result in inbreeding depression of 45% in survival from fertilization to adult in a vertebrate species with an inbreeding coefficient of 25%. This is similar to the answer we found in Example 11.2, using a related approach. At an inbreeding coefficient of 0.5, the inbreeding depression for survival would be 70%. In both cases there will be an additional contribution to inbreeding depression due to deleterious alleles of smaller effects. These are likely to be substantial. Further, there will be effects on fecundity as well as survival.

Linearity of inbreeding depression with *F*

Simple theory predicts that there will be a linear relationship between the mean value of a character and the inbreeding coefficient

If effects of different loci combine additively, then inbreeding depression is expected to be linearly related to the inbreeding coefficient F (Equation 12.2). For survival, where we expect to multiply the fitness effects of different loci, the logarithm of survival should show a linear relationship with inbreeding, as discussed below. More complex models of inbreeding depression involving interactions among loci (epistasis) suggest that there may be an additional, quadratic effect, depending on F^2.

Available data generally indicate an approximately linear relationship between the mean and the inbreeding coefficient (Lynch & Walsh 1998). For example, grain yield and height in maize show essentially linear declines with inbreeding (Fig. 12.5). However, a few cases do show a quadratic relationship with the mean dropping proportionately less at a low and more at higher levels of inbreeding. Even fewer cases show the reverse trend – a decrease of inbreeding depression per unit F at high F values.

There are methodological problems in distinguishing between

Fig. 12.5 Inbreeding depression in maize. Change in mean height and mean grain yield with inbreeding, expressed as a percentage of the non-inbred mean (after Falconer & Mackay 1996, based on data from Hallauer & Sears [dotted lines] and Cornelius & Dudley [continuous and dashed lines]). The dotted and dashed lines refer to consecutive selfing and the solid line to full-sib mating. *The declines are approximately linearly related to F, and more severe for yield than height.*

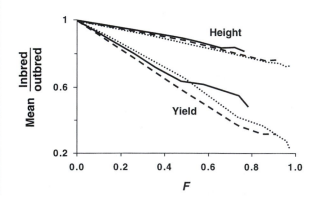

linear and curvilinear relationships, as extinctions occur at higher levels of inbreeding (Fig. 12.2), such that the samples of populations are not equivalent at low and high inbreeding.

Effects of ploidy

Since inbreeding depression is directly related to the expression of deleterious alleles and to the frequency of heterozygotes, it is no surprise that inbreeding depression is different for haploids, diploids and tetraploids. It is absent in haploids as there are no hidden deleterious alleles. The relative impact of inbreeding in diploids and tetraploids depends on the relative rates of fixation, on the genetic loads and on whether overdominance or dominance is causing inbreeding depression.

> Ploidy has a major effect on inbreeding depression; haploids lack inbreeding depression, while polyploids may exhibit less than diploids

The most plausible models lead us to expect less inbreeding depression in tetraploids than in diploids for similar degrees of inbreeding. First, the rate of fixation is slower in tetraploids than diploids (Chapter 11). Second, genetic loads for partially recessive alleles are expected to be similar in diploids and tetraploids (Chapter 11). Thus, there should be fewer deleterious alleles fixed and less inbreeding depression in the genome of a tetraploid than in a diploid for the same amount of inbreeding. If overdominance was a major cause of inbreeding depression (unlikely), then inbreeding depression is predicted to be greater for tetraploids than for diploids (Husband & Schemske 1997).

The most carefully performed experimental study of this issue revealed that inbreeding depression due to selfing was greater in diploid than in tetraploid forms of the plant *Epilobium angustifolium*. For cumulative fitness, inbreeding depression due to selfing was 0.95 in diploids and 0.68 in tetraploids (Husband & Schemske 1997). Overall, there is a paucity of data to evaluate the issue.

Purging

Rare deleterious recessive alleles are exposed by inbreeding and can therefore be more effectively removed by natural selection (Chapter 11). However, purging does not operate on the component of genetic load due to overdominant loci, as selection continually favours heterozygotes, maintaining deleterious alleles in the population. Further, the operation of purging depends on the magnitude of allele effects, being highly effective for alleles of large effect (e.g. lethals), but much less so for alleles of small effect, as they approach selective neutrality. In fact, deleterious alleles of small effect are likely to be fixed due to genetic drift in small populations (Chapter 8), so purging regimes (i.e. intentional inbreeding to remove deleterious alleles) can actually reduce reproductive fitness, rather than increasing it (Hedrick 1994).

> Inbreeding depression may be reduced, or purged, by selection against deleterious alleles. Purging may ameliorate inbreeding depression, but it is unlikely to eliminate it

The relative levels of inbreeding depression expected for different

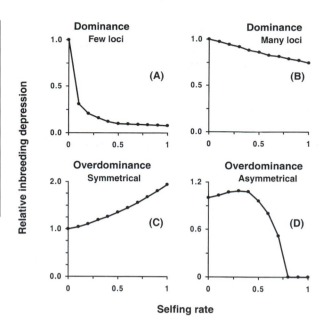

Fig. 12.6 Relationship between inbreeding depression and selfing rate under models assuming different genetic bases for inbreeding depression (from Barrett & Kohn 1991). The assumed bases of inbreeding depression are: (A) lethal or highly deleterious recessive alleles; (B) many loci, each with small deleterious effects; (C) symmetrical overdominance; (D) asymmetrical overdominance.

genetic models in populations with different selfing levels are shown in Fig. 12.6. Purging is highly effective with recessive lethals or detrimentals with large effects (A), but much less so for the many loci with alleles having small detrimental effects yield much smaller purging effects (B). Conversely, with symmetrical overdominance (C) inbreeding depression actually increases with selfing level (the opposite of purging). Associative overdominance is also likely to result in this pattern. The asymmetrical overdominance model (D) exhibits modest enhancement of inbreeding depression up to intermediate frequencies, and strong purging effects at higher F values. The proportion of alleles falling into categories A–D is not known precisely, but A and B will form the majority and be about equally important. In small populations, associative overdominance develops over time, so C is likely to rise in importance. Further details are given by Charlesworth & Charlesworth (1987).

Purging has been documented in selfing plants, mice, birds, and fruit flies, and in the many experimental populations of species where highly inbred lines have been developed (Frankham 1995b; Husband & Schemske 1996; Ballou 1997).

Four factors contribute to purging:
• Genetic basis of inbreeding depression (discussed above)
• Natural selection reducing the frequency of deleterious alleles
• Effects of prior inbreeding in reducing the amount of new inbreeding
• Impact of new mutations.

These issues are now discussed and their impacts evaluated.

We would expect to detect the effects of purging by comparing inbreeding depression in populations with different levels of selfing, and in studies of the effect of inbreeding depression with different rates of inbreeding. We use these cases to illustrate the extent of purging, and the contribution of the processes described above.

Inbreeding and selection

For large populations, the impact of selection under inbreeding can be determined by modelling selection against a deleterious partially recessive allele (frequency q) with genotypic fitnesses $A_1A_1 = 1$, $A_1A_2 = 1 - hs$ and $A_2A_2 = 1 - s$. The decrease in the frequency of the deleterious A_2 allele is then:

$$\Delta q = \Delta q_{outbred} + spqF(1 - 2h) \tag{12.3}$$

Selection against deleterious recessives is more effective under inbreeding, but its impact depends upon the size of effect of the alleles and on the population size

where $\Delta q_{outbred}$ is the change in allele frequency expected due to selection in an outbred population and the term on the right is the additional change due to inbreeding. Thus, selection against a deleterious partial recessive is more effective in a large inbred population than in a large outbred population, by an amount that depends on the inbreeding level (F), the selection coefficient (s), the allele frequencies and the dominance of the allele (h). Note that there is no difference for an additive allele ($h = 0.5$).

In small populations subject to inbreeding, selection is less effective, and only deleterious alleles of large effect will be effectively purged (Hedrick 1994). Deleterious alleles of small effect will be effectively neutral and their fate will be dominated by genetic drift. They will approach mutation–drift equilibrium. If we compare the overall levels of genetic diversity for rare deleterious alleles in small and large populations we expect that small population will have:

- Lower frequencies of deleterious alleles of large effect due to purging (fate determined by selection)
- Slightly lower frequencies of partially recessive deleterious alleles of moderate effect due to mutation–selection–drift balance
- A higher frequency of mildly deleterious alleles as they are effectively neutral in small populations and are therefore in mutation–drift equilibrium, rather than mutation–selection–drift equilibrium
- A lower frequency of very mildly deleterious alleles that are effectively neutral in both small and large populations.

Consequently, the net effect depends on the proportion of alleles falling into the four classes of effects. In fruit flies, deleterious alleles of large effect cause about half of the inbreeding and alleles of smaller effect the remaining half (Simmons & Crow 1977). However, the proportions falling into the remaining categories are unclear and are dependent upon the population size. Overall, genetic diversity for deleterious alleles is likely to be less in smaller than in larger populations, but the differences may be modest, rather than very large.

Relationship of inbreeding depression to rate of inbreeding

Slower inbreeding generally causes less inbreeding depression than an equivalent amount of rapid inbreeding, but the difference is often small

We have dealt mainly with the impacts of rapid inbreeding due to selfing, or full-sib mating. However, much of the inbreeding in endangered species in nature results from the cumulative impacts of small population size, i.e. slow inbreeding. The time, in generations, taken to reach similar levels of inbreeding is longer for small populations than for self-fertilization or brother–sister mating. For example, the time taken to reach an inbreeding coefficient of 0.5 is one generation with selfing, three generations with continued brother–sister mating and 34, 69 and 138 generations with random mating populations of size 25, 50 and 100, respectively.

Since the opportunities for natural selection to act are greater with slower inbreeding, the effects of a similar amount of inbreeding are predicted to be less with slower inbreeding. This prediction has proved to be generally correct (see Frankham 1998), although the effects are usually small (as illustrated for the comparison of selfing and full-sib mating in Fig. 12.5).

Inbreeding depression in species/populations with historically small populations

A prior history of small population size is likely to reduce subsequent inbreeding depression, but it is most unlikely to remove it completely

Even in normally outbreeding species, the theory of purging predicts that inbreeding depression can be purged if the population has been small and has become inbred over a long period of time. This expectation has led some authors to predict that populations that have been small for many generations are not expected to demonstrate further inbreeding depression, or that populations or species with low levels of heterozygosity should not show inbreeding depression if inbred further. However, experimental evidence indicates that purging effects are modest and that small partially inbred populations usually continue to exhibit inbreeding depression when inbred further, even when they have low genetic diversity. Brewer et al. (1990) found no correlations between either historical population size or amount of heterozygosity with the severity of inbreeding depression in populations of deer mice. Ballou (1997) detected only slight reductions in inbreeding depression in progeny from parents that were related and subject to prior inbreeding, versus progeny of related parents with no prior history of inbreeding. In populations of fruit flies that had been inbred slowly ($N_e \sim 50$) over a period of about 150 generations ($F = 0.5$–0.6), further inbreeding to near homozygosity still caused substantial inbreeding depression (Latter et al. 1995). The effects of prior inbreeding are not always consistent; in three populations of deer mice effects ranged from reduced inbreeding depression (purging), through no effect to enhanced inbreeding depression (Lacy & Ballou 1998).

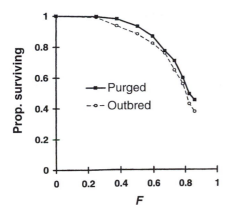

Fig. 12.7 Effect of purging on extinctions due to inbreeding. The proportion of populations remaining at different inbreeding coefficients in outbred and purged populations subject to continuous full-sib mating are given. The purged populations were formed from four-way crosses among highly inbred populations (20 generations of full-sib mating prior to crossing) from the outbred population (after Frankham et al. in press). *The difference in extinction rates with inbreeding between purged and non-purged populations was small and non-significant.*

An extreme case illustrates the small impact that natural selection may have on inbreeding depression, through purging. The impact of purging can be determined by comparing inbreeding depression in populations derived from an outbred base, with that in populations from crosses between highly inbred populations. In the latter case, the highly inbred populations should be purged, and this treatment should lead to less inbreeding depression. The results of such an experiment yielded a small and non-significant difference between the two treatments (Fig. 12.7).

One reason for the persistence of inbreeding depression in small populations and those which habitually inbreed is the steady recurrence of deleterious mutations. While selection may remove deleterious alleles, they are continually replenished by mutation. The effect of persistent small population size (or recurrent inbreeding) on inbreeding depression depends on its effect on mutation–selection equilibrium. As we saw in Chapter 8 (Fig. 8.13), the effect of population size on mutation–selection equilibrium for partial recessives (probably the predominant mutations contributing to inbreeding depression) is relatively small. Thus, a prior history of small size (or recurrent inbreeding) may reduce subsequent inbreeding depression, but is unlikely to eliminate it.

New deleterious mutations are being added to populations each generations

Detecting and measuring inbreeding depression

Survival and reproduction are strongly influenced by environmental conditions (Chapter 5). Consequently, we cannot compare the fitness of inbred and non-inbred individuals except under the same environmental conditions at the same time. For example, the deleterious effects of inbreeding on captive mammals were studied by comparing the juvenile survival of inbred and outbred offspring matched for zoo, enclosure in zoo, year of birth and density of population (Ballou & Ralls 1982). Another excellent example of a well-designed comparison involved deer

Contemporary comparisons of inbred and outbred individuals (or populations) maintained under the same environmental conditions are required to detect inbreeding depression

Fig. 12.8 Effect of inbreeding depression on reintroduction success increases with age in deer mice. Inbred and outbred individuals were released into the wild and their survival followed over time (after Jimenez *et al.* 1994). Survival of inbreds ($F = 0.25$) relative to the survival of non-inbreds is plotted against time since release.

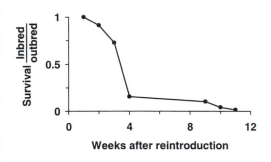

mice. Jimenez *et al.* (1994) captured animals, and bred them in captivity to produce inbred and outbred offspring. They released both types of offspring of the same age into the wild at the same time and followed their subsequent survival and weights. Inbreds exhibited substantially poorer survival than outbreds (Fig. 12.8). Chen (1993) used a similar experimental design with snails.

An alternative approach for detecting inbreeding depression is to outcross populations suspected of suffering inbreeding depression. If the outcrossed progeny display increased fitness (**heterosis**), then the original population is suffering inbreeding depression. This method has been used for topminnow fish by Vrijenhoek (Box 12.1), by Westemeier *et al.* (1998) on greater prairie chickens, and by Madsen *et al.* (1999) on adders (see Fig. 12.10 below).

An approach that does not require capture, and/or arranged breeding, is to use genetic markers such as multiple microsatellite loci to infer the degree of inbreeding of individuals, and to compare inbreds and outbreds in the same environment. This has recently been used to detect inbreeding depression in harbour seals, Soay sheep and red deer (Coltman *et al.* 1998, 1999; Slate *et al.* 2000)

Cheetahs illustrate problems that can arise in testing for inbreeding depression. The cheetah has a low level of genetic diversity, and it is presumed to be inbred. There is, however, controversy as to whether the cheetah, as a species, is suffering from inbreeding depression (see May 1995). The issue cannot be resolved, as there are no genetically variable, outbred, control cheetahs to compare with. However, it is possible to ask if the current cheetah population suffers from inbreeding depression by comparing individuals resulting from recent inbreeding with those that have no recent inbreeding in their ancestry. The captive cheetah population does exhibit inbreeding depression based upon such a comparison (Hedrick 1987).

Fluctuating asymmetry (FA) measures differences within individuals between bilateral features. It has been suggested that FA provides a simple indication of the presence of inbreeding depression, as more fit individuals may have greater developmental stability (see Clarke 1995). Unfortunately, FA has proven to be too inconsistent to be a reliable indicator (Vollestad *et al.* 1999; Gilligan *et al.* 2000).

Measuring inbreeding depression

A general measure of inbreeding depression (δ) is the proportionate decline in mean due to a given amount of inbreeding, as follows:

$$\delta = 1 - \frac{\text{fitness of inbred offspring}}{\text{fitness of outbred offspring}} \qquad (12.4)$$

Inbreeding depression is usually measured as the proportionate decline in mean per unit increase in inbreeding coefficient

This is simply the *ID* measure defined previously (Equation 12.1), divided by the mean of the outbred population, i.e. ID/M_0. This formula does not specify the level of inbreeding, and this must be defined. Example 12.3 illustrates the use of Equation 12.4 to estimate inbreeding depression in Dorcas gazelle. A compilation of estimates of inbreeding depression due to sib-mating ($F = 0.25$) is presented in Table 12.2.

δ is most often used in plants. Since many plants can be selfed, the usual estimate of inbreeding depression is obtained by comparing selfed and outcrossed progeny; this encompasses the impact of inbreeding due to an inbreeding coefficient of 50%.

Example 12.3 | Inbreeding depression in Dorcas gazelle (Ralls & Ballou 1983)

Juvenile survival rates of 50 outbred and 42 inbred Dorcas gazelle were 72.0% and 40.5%. The inbreeding depression (δ) for juvenile survival in this species is:

$$\delta = 1 - \frac{\text{fitness of inbred offspring}}{\text{fitness of outbred offspring}} = 1 - \frac{0.405}{0.720} = 0.44$$

Lethal equivalents

The usual means for expressing and comparing the extent of inbreeding depression for survival in animals is **lethal equivalents**. This is obtained from the regression of survival on level of inbreeding, as detailed below. This measures the impact of complete inbreeding ($F = 1$). A lethal equivalent is defined as a group of detrimental alleles that would cause on average one death if homozygous, e.g. one lethal allele, or two alleles each with 50% probability of causing death, etc. The probability of surviving, S, can be expressed as a function of inbreeding F (Morton *et al.* 1956):

$$S = e^{-(A+BF)} \qquad (12.5)$$

If we take natural logarithms (ln) this becomes

$$\ln S = -A - BF \qquad (12.6)$$

where e^{-A} is fitness in an outbred population, F is the inbreeding coefficient, and B is the rate at which fitness declines with a change in

Table 12.4 Data on survival levels for offspring with different levels of inbreeding (F) in the okapi

F	Lived	Died
0	86 (61%)	55 (39%)
0.125	5 (71%)	2 (29%)
0.25	12 (40%)	18 (60%)
0.375	1 (17%)	5 (83%)

Source: de Bois *et al.* (1990).

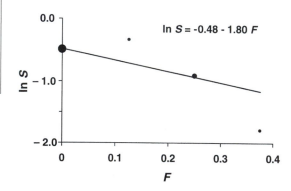

$$\ln S = -0.48 - 1.80\ F$$

inbreeding (Hedrick 1992). B measures the additional genetic damage that would be expressed in a complete homozygote ($F = 1$). Thus, B is the number of lethal equivalents per gamete, and $2B$ the number per individual. This model assumes a linear relationship between logarithm of survival and the inbreeding coefficient F.

To estimate lethal equivalents, data are collected on survival rates of individuals with different levels of F and weighted linear regression (or maximum likelihood methods) used to estimate A and B. Table 12.4 illustrates such data for the okapi. Figure 12.9 shows the relationship between ln S and inbreeding coefficient for the okapi, with the regression line inserted. The slope of the line (B) is -1.80, indicating that the population contains 1.8 haploid and 3.6 diploid lethal equivalents. Ralls *et al.* (1988) found that the median number of lethal equivalents for 40 captive mammal populations was 1.57 (B) per haploid and 3.14 ($2B$) per diploid, although species varied widely. These values indicate that each gamete contains deleterious mutations equivalent to between one and two lethals when homozygous. Similar values have been calculated for other animal populations, including humans.

The effects of inbreeding on population viability are complex and will interact with other factors affecting population growth, or population fluctuations, but they will be deleterious in the long term

Inbreeding and population viability

Scepticism has been expressed about the significance of inbreeding to population viability (Caro & Laurenson 1994; Caughley & Gunn 1996).

Reference is often made to highly inbred populations with no apparent inbreeding depression. For example, a number of small, presumably inbred, island populations persist. This is particularly evident in bird species, such as Chatham Island black robin, Hawaiian crow, Mauritius kestrel, Mauritius pink pigeon, red-tailed hawk and Seychelles robin (Box 8.1; Dhondt & Mattysen 1993; Craig 1994). Further, several bottle-necked populations, including the northern elephant seal, have recovered without apparent ill effects (Box 8.2). Since there are often no controls with which to compare these populations, it is difficult to evaluate the effects of inbreeding in these populations. Nevertheless, it is important to consider the probable impacts of inbreeding on population viability.

Inbreeding interacts with basic parameters of population viability, population growth rate and variation in population size. While these interactions may be complex, inbreeding in naturally outbreeding species will always be deleterious to closed populations in the long term, even if the impacts on population size are not evident initially. For example, a healthy outbred population (with a positive r) beginning at a small size and having a potential size of K due to limited carrying capacity, will rapidly grow to its carrying capacity (Box 12.3). A mildly inbred population will also grow to size K, but more slowly. A moderately inbred population will grow to the same carrying capacity even more slowly. However, a highly inbred population with a negative growth rate will decline to extinction. Whilst the first three populations reach a similar K, they have quite different capacities to recover from population catastrophes (droughts, floods, fires, etc.). They also have different capacities to absorb new impacts from introduced pests, parasites, diseases or predators. In all cases, the inbred populations will be inferior to the outbred population.

> Inbreeding depression does not necessarily cause declines in population size

Adverse effects of inbreeding on population growth rates have been described in eastern mosquito fish and in red flour beetles, and probably occur in all naturally outbreeding species. Populations of mosquito fish founded from brother–sister pairs exhibited 56% lower growth in numbers than populations founded from unrelated pairs (Leberg 1990a). McCauley & Wade (1981) found strong reductions in population growth in flour beetle populations inbred due to small numbers; they detected adverse effects at an F of only 0.1.

An example of a population that grew in size despite inbreeding is provided by the northern elephant seal (see Box 8.2). Despite the bottleneck of 20–30 individuals, it has recovered to over 100 000. The reasons for this are two-fold. First, the decline in numbers was due to over-hunting, which has been stopped by legislative protection (i.e. the environment has improved). Second, the inbreeding did not result in a negative population growth rate.

The susceptibility to extinction of populations with different growth rates (r), through inbreeding, will depend on the way in which inbreeding affects them. Populations with lower growth rates will be more susceptible to inbreeding depression than those with more rapid growth, as relatively small reductions in r may produce negative growth rates (Mills & Smouse 1994). Populations with major fluctuations in size (which will themselves increase levels of inbreeding) will also generally be more susceptible to the effects of inbreeding.

Box 12.3 | Impact of inbreeding on population viability

To illustrate the probable effects of inbreeding on population viability, we compare growth over time in small populations – outbred, mildly inbred, moderately inbred and highly inbred.

The effects of inbreeding on population growth can be illustrated using equations of population growth from ecology (see Wilson & Bossert 1971 or any modern ecology textbook). A small population of size N in a constant environment with a large amount of available habitat is expected to show exponential growth. The rate of growth in terms of increments of population size (dN) per increment of time (dt) depends on the difference between the birth (b) and death rates (d), r, and the population size N, as follows:

$$dN/dt = (b-d)N = rN$$

and the population size at time t, N_t, is

$$N_t = N_0 e^{rt}$$

We can consider the effects of inbreeding on population growth by considering a non-inbred population with a growth rate r of 0.04. Inbreeding will reduce r. Using the value of 25% decrease in total fitness per 10% increase in F from Frankel & Soulé (1981), the r for a mildly inbred population with an inbreeding coefficient of 20% would be 0.04 (1 − 2.5 × 0.2) = 0.02 (i.e. a 50% decrease), while r for a moderately inbred population ($F = 0.3$) would be 0.01. Finally a highly inbred population with an F of 0.5 would have a negative growth rate of −0.01.

Populations usually exist in a habitat with a limited carrying capacity. Such populations show logistic population growth (see below). The outbred and the mildly and moderately inbred populations grow to the same carrying capacity K, i.e. they will eventually have the same population sizes. Conversely the highly inbred population declines towards extinction. An important implication is that populations exhibiting inbreeding depression may have the same sizes (K) as related non-inbred populations. However, inbred populations take different times to reach the carrying capacity.

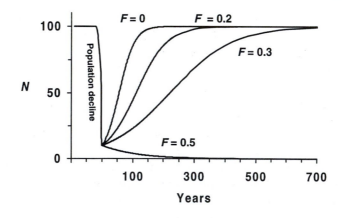

An important aspect of the different growth rates of outbred and mildly and moderately inbred populations is that they will take different times to recover from catastrophes. For example, consider populations with an initial size of $\frac{1}{2}K$ that are subjected to a catastrophe resulting in a 90% reduction in population size. Such impacts have been observed for many species in nature (Young 1994). The approximate times for the populations to recover to their original sizes ($N_t = 10 N_0$) can be determined by rearranging the second equation, as follows:

$$N_t / N_0 = 10 = e^{rt}$$

Taking natural logarithms and rearranging this yields:

$$t = \ln(10) / r$$

By substituting for r, we obtain 57.6 years for the outbred population to recover its original size, 115 years for mildly inbred population, and 230 years for the moderately inbred population. The highly inbred population ($F = 0.5$) that is declining in population size ($r = -0.01$) will decline and eventually become extinct. While the mildly and moderately inbred populations will eventually recover to their original size, another catastrophe may strike them before they have done so.

Recovering from inbreeding depression

The remedy for inbreeding depression is to outcross the inbred population to another unrelated population (Falconer & Mackay 1996). Such crosses can be made with an outbred population. In many cases of conservation concern no other outbred populations exists. If other, independent, inbred populations exist they will usually allow recovery of fitness. For example, if one population is inbred and fixed for deleterious allele a and another inbred population is fixed for deleterious allele b, crosses between the two will result in multiple heterozygotes (AaBb), and fitness will be restored, or even enhanced above the original non-inbred levels of fitness. This is termed heterosis, and applies to all loci fixed for different alleles in the two inbred populations. Fitness will be reduced in subsequent generations, as segregation of alleles produces homozygotes.

Inbreeding depression is reversed by outcrossing

Outcrossing has frequently been used to help populations recover from inbreeding depression, especially in laboratory and agricultural species, and more recently in small, inbred populations of several species of plants and animals. For example, Heschel & Paige (1995) found that small, presumably inbred, plant populations increased in fitness when outcrossed (while large populations that were presumably not inbred showed no change in fitness with outcrossing). Similarly, Madsen *et al.* (1999) found reductions in the proportion of abnormal offspring in adders when they outcrossed, and a subsequent increase in the recruitment rate and the population size (Fig. 12.10a). A similar increase in fitness and numbers following introductions of immigrants from larger populations was shown in the Illinois population of greater prairie chickens (Fig. 12.10b) and in small inbred populations of topminnow fish (Box 12.1). Partial recovery can be obtained

(a) Adders

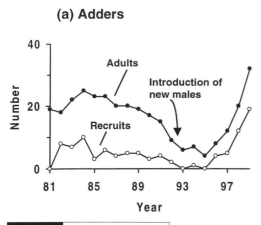

(b) Prairie chickens

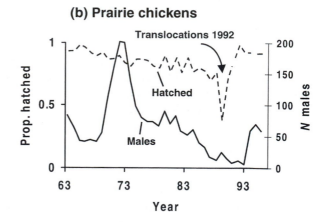

Fig. 12.10 Recovery of reproductive fitness due to introduction of immigrants into small partially inbred populations of (a) adders in Sweden (after Madsen et al. 1999), and (b) greater prairie chicken in Illinois – translocations began in 1992 (after Westemeier et al. 1998).

by introducing unrelated inbred immigrants into populations. Introduction of a single immigrant into partially inbred populations ($F = 0.5$) of fruit flies resulted in about a 50% recovery of reproductive fitness towards that in the outbred base population (Spielman & Frankham 1992).

Fitness rebounds following bottlenecks

Reproductive fitness usually declines following severe population bottlenecks, but may recover (partially) due to natural selection removing deleterious alleles

When populations suffer severe bottlenecks they become inbred and usually suffer inbreeding depression. If the population size recovers rapidly, reproductive fitness may recover partially through natural selection. As a result of the bottleneck, some deleterious alleles are fixed, some are lost and most change in frequency. Those that are fixed cause a reduction in the mean fitness of the population and this contribution remains relatively constant subsequently. Those that became lost increase fitness by a minuscule amount (as they were mostly heterozygous). Deleterious alleles that are increased in frequency due to the bottleneck event will subsequently decrease in frequency due to natural selection, especially if they have large effects. Thus fitness may rebound over time following a bottleneck.

Partial recovery of fitness following severe bottlenecks has been reported in house flies, butterflies and fruit flies (Bryant et al. 1990; Saccheri et al. 1996; Fowler & Whitlock 1999). Typically it involves only partial, rather than complete, recovery of fitness. In fruit flies, there was 28% reduction at generation 3 in the mean fitness of populations due to a single pair bottlenecks, and the depression was still 21% at generation 20. Further, the recovery may only occur in one environment; inbred fruit fly populations that had been artificially purged showed depressed fitness in a different stressful environment (Bijlsma et al. 1999).

Summary

1. Inbreeding results in a decline in reproductive fitness (inbreeding depression), in essentially all well-studied naturally outbreeding populations of animals and plants.

2. All components of reproductive fitness are subject to inbreeding depression.

3. Inbreeding depression is much greater for total fitness than for its components.

4. The expression of inbreeding depression is typically greater in harsher environments than benign ones.

5. Inbreeding depression has a large stochastic element due to different contents of deleterious alleles in different species, families and populations and to the chance element of Mendelian inheritance in their probabilities of fixation versus loss.

6. Inbreeding depression is due to the fixation of partially recessive deleterious or overdominant alleles.

7. The extent of inbreeding depression is $\Sigma 2pqdF$. Thus, it depends on the number of loci heterozygous for deleterious alleles and the directional dominance for them, and is proportional to the amount of inbreeding.

8. Inbreeding depression is measured by lethal equivalents, or as the proportionate change in mean (δ) for a given level of inbreeding.

9. Deleterious alleles of large effect may be purged (reduced in frequency) from inbred populations, but mildly deleterious alleles are likely to remain.

10. Inbreeding depression occurs in selfing species, but is generally of a lesser magnitude than that found in naturally outbreeding species.

11. Outcrossing reverses the effects of inbreeding.

FURTHER READING

Charlesworth & Charlesworth (1987, 1999) Excellent scholarly reviews of both the theory and empirical issues relating to the impact of inbreeding and the causes of inbreeding depression.

Crnokrak & Roff (1999) A review and meta-analysis of inbreeding depression in populations in wild habitats.

Falconer & Mackay (1996) *Introduction to Quantitative Genetics*. Provides a clear treatment of the theory of inbreeding, as well as experimental evidence from domestic plants and animals.

Hedrick & Kalinowski (2000) A review on inbreeding depression and its importance in conservation biology.

Lacy (1997) Fine review on the importance and impacts of inbreeding in mammals.

Lynch & Walsh (1998) *Genetics and Analysis of Quantitative Traits*. Chapter 10 has a wide-ranging review of both theory and experimental evidence on inbreeding depression.

Ralls *et al.* (1988) Highly influential study on the effects of inbreeding depression for captive wildlife.

Roff (1997) *Evolutionary Quantitative Genetics.* Considers both the theory of inbreeding and its impacts.

Thornhill (1993) *The Natural History of Inbreeding and Outbreeding: Theoretical and Empirical Perspectives.* A collection of reviews on both the theoretical and experimental issues relating to inbreeding; especially see Chapter 15 by Lacy *et al.* Has a range of controversial chapters, so requires critical reading.

Wright (1977) *Evolution and the Genetics of Populations*, vol. 3. A scholarly review of evidence on the impacts of inbreeding by one of the pioneers of the field.

PROBLEMS

12.1 Inbreeding depression: What determines the level of inbreeding depression experienced by a population?

12.2 Inbreeding depression: What effect does inbreeding have on a haploid organism?

12.3 Inbreeding depression: How much inbreeding depression in survival is expected due to selfing for the following three loci, each with allele frequencies of $0.9 + : 0.1\ m$?

	$+/+$	$+/m$	m/m
(a) Survival % (partial dominant)	90	89	70
(b) Survival % (overdominant)	80	90	70
(c) Survival % (additive)	90	80	70

12.4 Inbreeding depression δ: The juvenile survival rates of inbred and outbred offspring in the pygmy hippopotamus were 45% and 75%, respectively (see Fig. 11.1). What is the inbreeding depression as measured by δ?

12.5 Lethal equivalents: How many lethal equivalents are found in Parma wallabies, given survival of individuals with inbreeding coefficients F of 0, 0.625, 0.125, 0.25 and 0.375 are 80%, 68%, 59%, 43% and 31%; the regression equation relating juvenile survival (S) and inbreeding coefficient (F) is

$$\ln S = -0.221 - 2.52\ F$$

(a) Lethal equivalents per haploid genome =
(b) Lethal equivalents per diploid genome =

12.6 Lethal equivalents, survival and inbreeding depression: For a mammal with a typical number of lethal equivalents (3.14 per diploid genome), what is the ratio of survival of inbred young to non-inbred young for the progeny of brother–sister matings? What is the inbreeding depression?

12.7 Lethal equivalents, survival and inbreeding depression: For the case in Example 12.2, determine the impact of selfing on inbreeding depression for survival with 5000 loci segregating for partially recessive lethal alleles.

Chapter 13

Population fragmentation

The genetic impacts of population fragmentation depend critically upon gene flow among fragments. With restricted gene flow, fragmentation typically leads to greater inbreeding and loss of genetic diversity within fragments. There is genetic differentiation among fragments, and greater risks of extinction, in the long term, than for a single population of the same total size

Terms:
F_{ST},
F statistics,
metapopulation,
single large or several small (SLOSS),
source–sink,
Wahlund effect

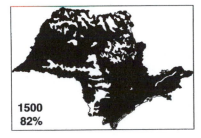

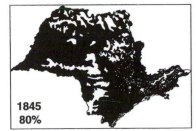

1500
82%

1845
80%

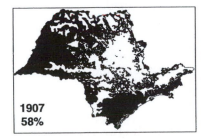

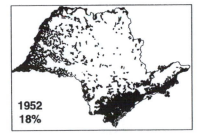

1907
58%

1952
18%

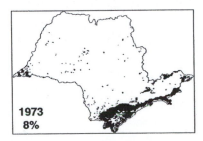

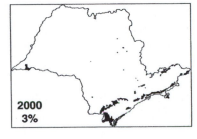

1973
8%

2000
3%

Fragmentation of Atlantic forest in São Paulo State, Brazil, from 82% forest cover in 1500, to 3% in the year 2000 (from Oedekoven 1980).

Habitat fragmentation

Habitat fragmentation is the conversion of once-continuous habitat into a patchwork with reduction of total habitat area, and isolation of different patches in a landscape of now-inhospitable terrain

Habitat fragmentation includes two processes, a reduction in total habitat area and creation of separate isolated patches from a larger continuous distribution. These are evident for the Atlantic forest in São Paulo State, Brazil (see chapter frontispiece), and similar examples abound throughout the world. Human-induced habitat loss and fragmentation, through land clearing, forestry and damming of rivers, are recognized as the primary causes of biodiversity loss (WCMC 1992).

Habitat fragmentation leads to overall reductions in population size for most species, and to reduced migration (gene flow) among patches. Deleterious consequences of reduced population size on genetic diversity, inbreeding and extinction risk have been addressed in Chapters 2 and 10–12.

This chapter focuses on the genetic effects of **population fragmentation**, the separation of a population into partially or completely isolated fragments. We address the genetic impacts of individuals being distributed in several fragments in comparison with a single population of the same total size. This is known as '**Single Large or Several Small**' (SLOSS).

Population fragmentation

The genetic consequences of population fragmentation depend critically upon gene flow. With restricted gene flow, fragmentation is usually highly deleterious in the long term

The impacts of population fragmentation on genetic diversity, inbreeding, differentiation and extinction risk depend on the level of gene flow among fragments. These in turn depend on:
- Number of population fragments
- Distribution of population sizes in the fragments
- Geographic distribution or spatial pattern of populations
- Distance between fragments
- Dispersal ability of the species
- Migration rates between fragments
- Environment of the matrix among the fragments and its impact on dispersal
- Time since fragmentation.

All of the issues we have previously discussed in this book, with respect to reduced population size, come into play when populations are fragmented. In fragmented populations with reduced gene flow, these adverse effects are usually more severe than in a non-fragmented population of the same total size. Fragmentation often results in elevated extinction risks.

The endangered red-cockaded woodpecker in the eastern USA illustrates many of the features and genetic problems associated with fragmentation of the habitat for a species with a once continuous distribution (Box 13.1). Isolated and small woodpecker populations show loss of genetic diversity compared to large populations.

Differentiation among populations in different patches is evident, with nearby populations generally being more similar than more distant ones. The small populations are expected to suffer from inbreeding depression.

Box 13.1	Impact of habitat fragmentation on the endangered red-cockaded woodpecker metapopulation in southeastern USA (Stangel et al. 1992; Kulhavy et al. 1995; Daniels et al. 2000)

The red-cockaded woodpecker was once common in the mature pine forests of the southeast United States. It declined in numbers, primarily due to habitat loss, and was placed on the US endangered species list in 1970. It now survives in scattered and isolated sites within the US southeast (see map from James 1995). A species recovery plan is being implemented to manage the species.

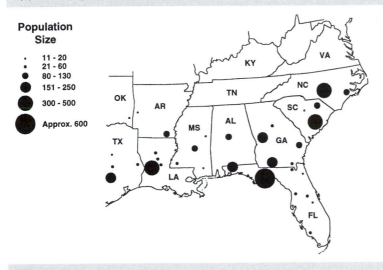

There is little migration among isolated sites. Populations would therefore be expected to diverge genetically from each other, and lose genetic diversity, with smaller populations showing the greatest loss of genetic diversity and the most divergence, as observed below (after Meffe & Carroll 1997).

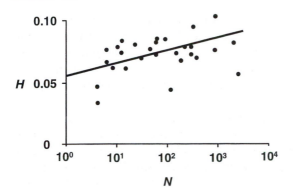

State

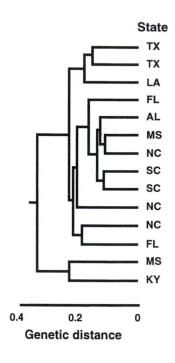

TX
TX
LA
FL
AL
MS
NC
SC
SC
NC
NC
FL
MS
KY

```
0.4        0.2         0
```
Genetic distance

Moderate divergences in allele frequencies exist among woodpecker populations. Differentiation, measured as F_{ST} (a value of zero indicates no differentiation, and 1.0 indicates complete isolation; described later in this chapter), is 0.14 based on allozyme data, and 0.19 based on RAPD data. Both data sets show a general tendency for closer genetic similarity among geographically proximate populations – shown in the cluster analysis of genetic distances among 14 populations in the margin (after Haig & Avise 1996).

Computer simulations indicate that the smallest woodpecker populations are likely to suffer from inbreeding depression in the near future (Daniels et al. 2000).

The distribution and density of the woodpeckers are restricted by their requirement for old-growth forest providing nest holes. Steps have been taken to preserve old-growth forest for the woodpeckers. However, hurricanes damage old-growth forest and kill birds. In 1989 Hurricane Hugo destroyed 87% of the active woodpecker nesting trees in the Francis Marion National Forest in South Carolina, previously the second largest population, and killed 63% of the birds. This population has recovered by 33% by 1992, due mainly to the installation of artificial cavities for nesting.

In response to the threats posed by fragmentation, management of the woodpeckers involves habitat protection, improvement of habitat suitability by constructing artificial nest holes, reintroductions into suitable habitat where populations become extinct, and augmentation of small populations to minimize inbreeding and loss of genetic diversity. Recovery guidelines specify an effective size of 500 for population viability for each major fragment. This is one of the most extensive management programs for a fragmented population anywhere in the world.

This chapter begins by examining alternative population structures, followed by considering the genetic impacts of completely isolated fragments (the most extreme case). We then consider the impact of migration and gene flow, means for measuring genetic divergence and inferring rates of gene flow (F statistics) and finally the genetic impacts of different population structures.

Population structure

The impact of population fragmentation depends on the details of the resulting population structure

The genetic impacts of population fragmentation may range from insignificant to severe, depending upon the details of the resulting population structures and migration patterns among fragments. Several potential fragmented population structures can be distinguished:
- Totally isolated population fragments with no gene flow ('islands')
- Effectively single large – fragments where gene flow is sufficient to result effectively in a single large population
- Island models where migration is equal among equally sized islands
- Linear stepping-stone models where only neighbouring populations exchange migrants (as in riparian habitat along rivers)

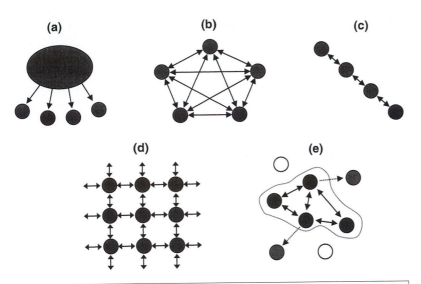

Fig. 13.1 Five different fragmented population structures: (a) a mainland–island (or source–sink) situation where the 'mainland' (source) provides all the input to the island (sink) populations, (b) an island model where migration is equal among equal sized islands, (c) a linear stepping-stone model where only neighbouring populations exchange migrants, (d) a two-dimensional stepping-stone model where neighbouring populations exchange migrants (all after Hedrick 1983), and (e) a metapopulation (after Hanski & Gilpin 1997).

- Two-dimensional stepping-stone models where only surrounding populations exchange migrants
- Mainland–island or source–sink models, and
- Metapopulations.

The last five cases are illustrated in Fig. 13.1.

Metapopulations differ from the other structures in that there are regular extinction and recolonization events, while no extinction is assumed in the simpler forms of the other structures. The endangered Glanville fritillary butterfly population in Finland (Box 2.2) provides a good example. There are about 1600 suitable meadows for the butterfly, 320–524 being occupied in 1993–96. The population turnover rate is high, with an average of 200 extinctions and 114 colonizations per year. There has been a recent shift towards considering fragmented populations as metapopulations, as extinctions of fragments are an ever-present risk (Hanski & Gilpin 1997). In general, the genetic consequences of a metapopulation structure are more deleterious than for other population structures (apart from completely isolated fragments), as described below.

Extensive population genetic theory has been developed to model genetic processes within different kinds of structures. We use this theory to describe how fragmentation impacts on issues of conservation concern.

Completely isolated population fragments

Fragments that are completely isolated suffer increased inbreeding, loss of genetic diversity and extinction risk, compared to a single large population of the same total size

Completely isolated population fragments, lacking gene flow, are the most severe form of fragmentation, and the easiest to understand. There is no gene flow among such population fragments. As each population fragment has a smaller population size than a single, large, unfragmented population, this isolation has significant deleterious effects on inbreeding, loss of genetic diversity and extinction risk. This form of fragmentation has many parallels with oceanic island populations.

In Fig. 13.2 four single small isolated fragments (SS) are compared to a single large population (SL) of the same initial total size. The large population (1) possesses four alleles, A_1-A_4. In the short term the four SS populations (2) rapidly become homozygous and lose fitness through inbreeding depression. Loss of genetic diversity is slower in the single large population (3) – it only loses allele A_4. However, fixation in the SS populations is at random, so that overall all four alleles are retained, while the SL population has lost the A_4 allele. Thus, as long as there are

Fig. 13.2 The genetic consequences of a single large population (SL) versus several small (SS) completely isolated population fragments of initially the same total size (SLOSS) over different time frames. (1) A_1–A_4 represent four alleles initially present in the population. In the short term, without extinctions, the several small populations (2) are expected to go to fixation more rapidly, but to retain greater overall genetic diversity than the single large population (3). The chances are greater that an allele will be totally lost from the large population, than from all small populations combined. However, the SS populations will each be more inbred than the SL population.

In the longer term, when extinctions of small, but not large populations occur, the sum of the small surviving populations (4) will retain less genetic diversity than the single large population (5). A metapopulation with extinctions and recolonizations is similar to (4).

Initial populations

(1)

Short-term, no extinctions

Several small

(2)

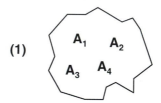

Single large

(3)

Long-term, extinction of some small populations

(4)

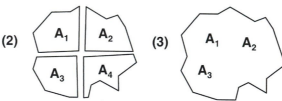

(5)

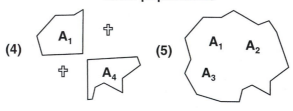

no extinctions of SS populations, they retain greater overall allelic diversity than the SL population (Varvio *et al.* 1986; Lande 1995b). This expectation has been verified in experiments with fruit flies (Margan *et al.* 1998).

However, in the long term, extinction rates will be greater in smaller than in larger population fragments due to environmental and demographic stochasticity, catastrophes (Chapter 20) and genetic factors. With extinction of some SS populations (4), the SL population retains more genetic diversity and has higher reproductive fitness than all the SS populations combined (now only two populations). We later derive many of these predictions algebraically.

Isolated population fragments as 'islands'

Since fragmentation creates 'islands' from once-continuous habitat, its effects parallel those in oceanic island populations. As we have described earlier, island populations are often inbred, have lower genetic diversity and elevated extinction risks compared to mainland populations (Chapter 2).

Isolated population fragments share many of the features found in island populations

For example, island populations of black-footed rock wallabies in Western Australia possess fewer microsatellite alleles per locus than mainland populations – most island populations are fixed at each locus (Table 13.1). Further, the island populations differ in the alleles they contain, in a more or less random manner. The one population whose fitness has been examined (Barrow Island – BI), exhibits inbreeding depression, when compared with mainland populations (Box 2.3). While these island populations have been isolated for thousands of years, loss of genetic diversity can occur on a much shorter time-scale. Loss of genetic diversity is already evident in three species of mammals on islands created, in 1987, by damming a river in Thailand (Srikwan & Woodruff 2000).

Consequences of fragmentation in an idealized population

We begin by considering an idealized fragmented population (Fig. 13.3) and evaluating the impacts of totally isolated populations (all of equal sizes) on (a) diversity in allele and genotype frequencies among fragmented populations and (b) divergence of these frequencies over time. Later the assumption of equal size and no migration will be relaxed. In dealing with an idealized population, we are assuming that allelic variation is selectively neutral.

Deleterious genetic impacts within isolated fragments accumulate with time and become increasingly deleterious with smaller fragments

When a population is subdivided, individual alleles and genotypes are distributed among fragments. Population fragments will be genetically differentiated from the very beginning. It is useful to consider fragmentation as occurring in two steps:

Table 13.1 | Loss of genetic diversity in populations fragmented on islands by post-glacial sea level rises 8000–15 000 years ago. Alleles present (+) and absent (−) at four microsatellite loci in populations of black-footed rock wallabies on the mainland of Australia and on six offshore islands.

Island populations contain many fewer alleles than mainland populations, but they are usually a sub-set of alleles found on the mainland. Different island populations often contain different alleles, as expected due to genetic drift

			Islands					
Locus	Allele	Mainland	BI	SI	PI	MI	Wil	Wel
Pa297	102	+	−	−	−	−	−	−
	106	+	−	−	−	−	−	−
	118	+	−	−	−	−	−	−
	120	−	−	−	+	−	−	−
	124	+	−	−	−	+	−	−
	128	+	−	+	−	−	+	+
	130	+	−	−	−	−	−	−
	136	+	+	−	−	−	−	−
Pa385	157	+	−	−	−	−	−	−
	159	+	−	−	+	−	+	+
	161	+	−	+	−	−	−	−
	163	+	−	−	−	+	−	−
	165	+	−	−	−	−	−	−
	173	−	+	−	−	−	−	−
Pa593	105	+	−	−	−	−	+	+
	113	−	+	−	−	−	−	−
	123	+	−	−	−	−	−	−
	125	+	−	−	+	−	−	−
	127	+	−	−	−	−	−	−
	129	+	−	−	−	−	−	−
	131	+	−	+	−	−	−	−
	133	+	−	−	−	−	−	−
	135	+	−	−	−	−	−	−
	137	−	−	−	−	+	−	−
Me2	216	+	−	−	−	−	−	−
	218	+	−	−	−	+	+	−
	220	+	+	−	−	−	−	+
	222	+	−	+	−	−	−	−
	224	+	−	−	−	−	−	−
	230	−	−	−	+	−	−	−

Source: Eldridge *et al.* (1999).

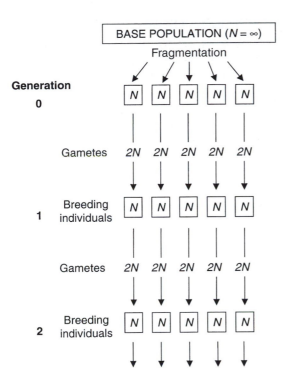

BASE POPULATION ($N = \infty$)

Fragmentation

Generation
0

N N N N N

Gametes $2N$ $2N$ $2N$ $2N$ $2N$

1   Breeding
    individuals N N N N N

Gametes $2N$ $2N$ $2N$ $2N$ $2N$

2   Breeding
    individuals N N N N N

Fig. 13.3 Model of fragmentation in an idealized population. The base population is infinite, the populations founded from it are of equal size, and there is no migration among populations. Each of the individual fragmented populations is itself an idealized population (after Falconer & Mackay 1996).

1. Fragmentation resulting in an initial genetic sub-division of a population, and

2. Cumulative diversification, through genetic drift and inbreeding over time in each of the population fragments.

Distribution of alleles among fragments

When a population is fragmented, different fragments will have different initial allele frequencies just by chance. The extent of diversification in allele frequencies can be measured as variances in allele frequencies (Box 5.2). The variance due to the initial fragmentation can be predicted for neutral alleles from the binomial sampling variance. Consider a single locus with two alleles, A_1 and A_2, at frequencies of p and q in the base population. For each fragment, we sample N individuals ($2N$ gene copies) from the base population. If a large number of samples of size $2N$ are taken, the resulting allele frequencies across all fragments will be unchanged. The variance in the frequencies of A_1 among the fragments, σ_p^2, is

> Differentiation in allele frequencies among fragmented populations is greater for small than for large fragments

$$\sigma_p^2 = pq/2N \qquad (13.1)$$

Thus there will be greater variance, and larger differentiation of allele frequencies, among small fragments than among large fragments (Example 13.1). Further, variance is greatest when initial allele frequencies are equal (0.5), as pq is at a maximum with these frequencies.

As we shall see below, the degree of dispersion is also related to loss of heterozygosity and to the level of inbreeding.

Example 13.1 | Variance in allele frequencies in different sized population fragments

Consider a locus with initial allele frequencies of 0.6 and 0.4. In fragments with sizes of 100, the variance in allele frequencies among fragments is (Equation 13.1):

$$\sigma_p^2 = pq/2N = 0.6 \times 0.4/(2 \times 100) = 0.0012$$

Fragments of size 10 have a variance in allele frequency of:

$$\sigma_p^2 = pq/2N = 0.6 \times 0.4/(2 \times 10) = 0.012$$

Thus, variance in allele frequencies after sampling to form fragments is directly proportional to sample size.

Distribution of heterozygosities among fragments

Heterozygosity in a fragmented population will be lower than in the original continuous population and will vary among fragments

Fragmented populations have, on average, reduced heterozygosity and increased variance in heterozygosity across loci within populations. The average reduction in heterozygosity due to sampling from the base population is $1/(2N)$ (Equation 8.3). This initial reduction is minor unless the population fragments are very small (e.g. less than 10). This effect was illustrated in Table 8.2 for population fragments each founded with a single pair of parents.

Degree of fragmentation

The larger the number of population fragments for the same total size, the greater becomes the rate of inbreeding and loss of genetic diversity over time within fragments

With increasing fragmentation, population size within each population fragment becomes smaller and differentiation among isolated populations will be greater. Inbreeding and inbreeding depression will be more rapid within smaller fragments, as will genetic drift and loss of genetic diversity. As predicted, reproductive fitness was lower in smaller populations than in larger ones (Woodworth 1996; Bryant et al. 1999).

For a population of total size N, separated into f totally isolated, equal sized fragments, the size of each fragment is N/f. Each of the fragments will become inbred and lose genetic diversity at a rate dependent upon N/f. A single population of the same total size will become inbred and lose genetic diversity at a slower rate dependent upon its size, N. For example, the proportion of initial heterozygosity retained after t generations in each of the small SS fragments is

$$H_t/H_{0\,SS} = [1 - 1/(2N/f)]^t \sim e^{-tf/2N}$$

While for the single large (SL) population of the same total size N, the proportion of initial genetic diversity retained is

$$H_t/H_{0\,SL} = [1 - 1/(2N)]^t \sim e^{-t/2N}$$

The ratio of these proportions for SS and SL ($H_t/H_{0\,SS/SL}$) is

$$H_t/H_{0\,SS/SL} \sim (e^{t/2N})^{1-f} \qquad (13.2)$$

If we take natural logarithms

$$\ln[H_t/H_{0\,SS/SL}] = (1-f)\,t/2N \qquad (13.3)$$

Thus, the proportional retention of heterozygosity in several small population fragments, compared to a single large population, declines with the number of fragments and increases with generations. The rate of decline is greater with smaller than larger total population size.

For a given aggregate population size, inbreeding and the loss of genetic diversity within population fragments increase with the number of (equally sized) fragments. Consider, for example, a single population with a constant size of size 500 individuals per generation. Over 50 generations, a single population of size 500 loses 5% of its initial heterozygosity, while two populations of size 250 each lose 10%, five populations of size 100 each lose 22%, ten populations of size 50 each lose 39% and twenty populations of size 25 each lose 64% of their initial genetic diversity.

Such loss of genetic diversity has been documented in many small isolated population fragments, including black-footed rock wallabies (Table 13.1), greater prairie chickens (Box 10.1), adders (Box 12.2), Glanville fritillary butterflies (Box 2.2) and grassland daisies (Box 10.2). Inbreeding depression has also been documented in these cases and in isolated populations of royal catchfly and scarlet gilia plants (Menges 1991; Heschel & Paige 1995).

Divergence in allele frequencies over time

Loci in small isolated population fragments will differentiate at random due to genetic drift, even if they began with identical genetic compositions. This has two important conservation consequences. First, it indicates that fragmentation causes genetic differences among otherwise similar populations. Second, the degree of differentiation provides a means for inferring levels of gene flow.

> Allele frequencies within fragments drift randomly, resulting in further diversification in frequencies among fragments over time

In an idealized fragmented population we are considering multiple populations of the same size, each undergoing genetic drift independently. A particular allele may increase in frequency in some fragments and decrease in others. Even fragments that are initially identical will differentiate genetically over time.

Dispersion in allele frequencies among small isolated fruit fly populations over generations is illustrated in Fig. 13.4. All populations began

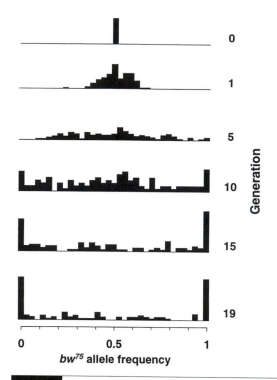

Fig. 13.4 Divergence in allele frequencies over time due to population fragmentation in fruit flies. The frequency distribution for the bw^{75} allele is shown over 19 generations in 105 replicate populations maintained with 16 parents per generation. All populations began with initial frequencies of 0.5 (after Buri 1956).

with frequencies of 0.5 for each allele. Eventually many populations reached fixation. Dispersion in allele frequencies among populations is also evident in red-cockaded woodpeckers (Box 13.1) and black-footed rock wallabies (Table 13.1).

Diversification in allelic frequencies continues, generation by generation, until eventually, all populations are fixed ($p = 1$, or 0). The effects of continual isolation can be predicted using binomial sampling theory, by extending Equation 13.1 over multiple generations. The expected variance in allele frequencies among fragments after t generations is:

$$\sigma_p^2 = p_0 q_0 \{1 - [1 - 1/(2N)]^t\} \tag{13.4}$$

where p_0 and q_0 are the initial allele frequencies and the fragment size (N) is constant over time.

From this equation, we predict that the variance in allele frequencies will

• increase with generations, and
• increase faster in small than in large populations.

These predictions are illustrated numerically in Example 13.2. The theoretical distributions of p expected after different numbers of generations are shown for two different initial values of p in Fig. 13.5. With time, the distributions become flattened as allele frequencies disperse, resulting in an essentially uniform distribution after $2N$ generations (excluding the fixed populations). The observed distribution for fruit fly populations (Fig. 13.4) is similar to that expected. When the number of generations is very large and all populations have become fixed, the variance is $p_0 q_0$.

Example 13.2 | Increase in variance of allele frequencies with time

Buri's classic fruit fly experiment (Fig. 13.4) began with $p = q = 0.5$ and each of the populations had 16 parents per generation. The expected variances in allele frequencies can be computed using Equation 13.4. After the first generation

$$\sigma_p^2 = pq \{1 - [1 - 1/(2N)]^t\} = 0.5 \times 0.5 \{1 - [1 - 1/(2 \times 16)]^1\}$$
$$= 0.0078$$

After two generations

$$\sigma_p^2 = pq \{1 - [1 - 1/(2N)]^t\} = 0.5 \times 0.5 [1 - (31/32)^2] = 0.015$$

and after 19 generations

$$\sigma_p^2 = pq \{1 - [1 - 1/(2N)]^t\} = 0.5 \times 0.5 [1 - (31/32)^{19}] = 0.113$$

The variance in allele frequencies increases progressively and reaches its maximum value of $pq = 0.25$ when all populations have become fixed.

   The observed variance in this fruit fly experiment increased more rapidly than predicted, as the effective population size was less than the 16 parents used.

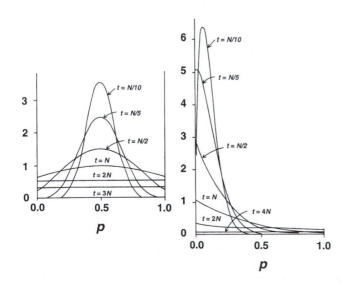

Fig. 13.5 Predicted changes in allele frequency distributions with generations among fragmented populations, after different numbers of generations (t), expressed in terms of the population size of the fragments (N). In the left-hand figure $p_0 = 0.5$, and in the right $p_0 = 0.1$. Populations are excluded from the figure after they have become fixed. The horizontal axis is the allele frequency (p) in any line. The vertical axis is the probability, scaled to make the area under each curve equal to the proportion of unfixed lines (after Falconer & Mackay 1996).

Divergence and loss of heterozygosity

As heterozygosity is lost within fragments and allele frequencies drift among fragments, there is a deficiency of heterozygotes when compared to Hardy–Weinberg expectations for the entire population. Loss of heterozygosity in fragmented populations can be treated as either a drift, or an inbreeding process (Table 13.2).

Under drift, the reduction in heterozygosity is equal to twice the variance in allele frequency (Falconer & Mackay 1996). When fragmentation is treated in terms of inbreeding, heterozygosity is reduced in proportion to the inbreeding level (Equation 11.1). Example 13.3 illustrates the equivalence of the inbreeding and drift approaches.

Table 13.2 Genotype frequencies in the total population (combination of all population fragments) treated as genetic drift, or inbreeding processes (p_0 and q_0 are allele frequencies before fragmentation). Note that $\sigma_p^2 = Fp_0q_0$.

Genotype	Frequency before fragmentation	Frequencies in the total population after fragmentation	
		Genetic drift	Inbreeding
A_1A_1	p_0^2	$p_0^2 + \sigma_p^2$	$p_0^2 + Fp_0q_0$
A_1A_2	$2p_0q_0$	$2p_0q_0 - 2\sigma_p^2$	$2p_0q_0(1-F)$
A_2A_2	q_0^2	$q_0^2 + \sigma_p^2$	$q_0^2 + Fp_0q_0$

Reduction in heterozygosity, averaged over all population fragments, can be illustrated using a simple numerical example. Imagine a number of fragments, each founded with initial frequencies $p = q = 0.5$. Heterozygosity is maximal ($2pq = 0.5$) at the outset. However, as drift occurs in each fragment, away from $p = q = 0.5$, then $2pq$ is inevitably reduced (e.g. if $p = 0.3$, $q = 0.7$ in a fragment, then $2pq = 0.42$). If there are large numbers of fragments, then p and q will still remain close to 0.5 in the total population of fragments, but average heterozygosity will be reduced. This is referred to as the **Wahlund effect** after its discoverer.

Lower than expected heterozygosity can be used to diagnose populations that are genetically fragmented. For example, the endangered spreading avens plant has a heterozygosity of 0.052, averaged across five populations in the eastern USA, but an expected heterozygosity of 0.098 (Hamrick & Godt 1996). Analyses using F statistics (see later) indicate that the deficiency of heterozygotes is due to a combination of population fragmentation and inbreeding within populations.

So far, we have only considered the effect of fragmentation on single loci. However, quantitative characters also exhibit diversification due to random genetic drift (Fig. 13.6). Diversification among fragments in

---

Example 13.3 | Reduced heterozygosity in fragmented populations

For a locus with two alleles at frequencies of 0.7 and 0.3, the expected Hardy–Weinberg heterozygosity under random mating H_e is $2 \times 0.7 \times 0.3 = 0.42$. However for a population with an inbreeding coefficient F of 0.64, this is reduced to

$$H_F = 2 \times 0.7 \times 0.3 \times (1 - 0.64) = 0.15$$

The reduction in heterozygosity of $(0.42 - 0.15)/0.42 = 64\%$ is directly proportional to the inbreeding coefficient.

If a group of fragmented populations, all with effective sizes 10 per generation, were isolated from each other for 20 generations ($F = 0.64$), the expected variance in allele frequency would be

$$\sigma_p^2 = 0.7 \times 0.3 \,\{1 - [1 - 1/(2 \times 10)]^{20}\} = 0.135$$

These populations would be expected to have an overall heterozygosity of

$$H_{\text{frag}} = 2p_0 q_0 - 2\sigma_p^2 = 0.42 - 2 \times 0.135 = 0.15$$

Again the heterozygosity is reduced below Hardy–Weinberg random mating expectations. Consideration of fragmentation as either an inbreeding or a drift process yields identical answers.

---

phenotype mean increases with generations just like allele frequencies. Since we cannot distinguish the individual loci and follow the frequencies of their alleles, changes in additive genetic variances are measured. Additive genetic variation (V_A) among fragments increases and that within populations decreases. For additive loci (no dominance) the genetic variance among populations increases to $2FV_A$, whilst the genetic variance within populations decreases to $V_A(1 - F)$ (Falconer & Mackay 1996). With dominance the situation is more complex. However, the genetic variation among populations increases with F,

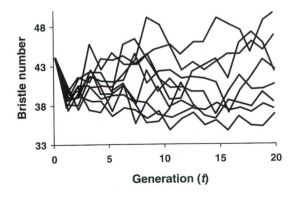

Fig. 13.6 Random genetic drift for abdominal bristle number in fruit flies (after Falconer & Mackay 1996, based on Rasmuson). The figure shows the mean bristle number in 10 populations, all founded from the same base population, and reproduced from a single pair of parents in each generation. *Means drift over time for individual populations and divergence among population means generally increases with time.*

while the variation within populations may increase initially with F before declining to zero at high values of F.

Since quantitative characters reflect the effects of many loci, it is important to consider the effects of fragmentation across loci. Each individual locus undergoes drift independently. Some attain fixation, while others remain polymorphic. The combined effect across all loci in the genome will closely reflect the average effects we defined above (Tables 13.2 and 13.3), i.e. an overall reduction in heterozygosity. However, replicate fragments from the same initial population will have diverse genetic constitutions as they will have different alleles fixed at loci, and different loci still polymorphic.

Measuring population fragmentation: F statistics

The degree of differentiation among fragments can be described by partitioning the overall inbreeding into components within and among populations (F statistics)

Inbreeding resulting from population fragmentation can be used to measure the degree of differentiation that has occurred among population fragments. Differentiation among fragments or sub-populations is directly related to the inbreeding coefficients within and among populations (Table 13.2). Sewall Wright used inbreeding coefficients to describe the distribution of genetic diversity within and among population fragments. He partitioned inbreeding of individuals (I) in the total (T) population (F_{IT}) into that due to (Wright 1969):

- Inbreeding of individuals relative to their sub-population (S) or fragment, F_{IS}, and
- Inbreeding due to differentiation among sub-populations, relative to the total population, F_{ST}.

F_{IS} is the probability that two alleles in an individual are identical by descent. It is inbreeding coefficient, F (Chapter 11), averaged across all individuals from all population fragments.

F_{ST}, the **fixation index** (sometimes referred to as G_{ST}), is the effect of the population sub-division on inbreeding. It is the probability that two alleles drawn randomly from a population fragment (either from different individuals, or from the same individual) are identical by descent. With high rates of gene flow among fragments, this probability is low. With low rates of gene flow among fragments, populations diverge and become inbred, and F_{ST} increases.

F_{IT}, F_{IS} and F_{ST} are referred to as F statistics (Wright 1969). The relationship between these quantities is given below:

$$F_{IT} = F_{IS} + F_{ST} - (F_{IS})(F_{ST}) \qquad (13.5)$$

Since we wish to use F_{ST} to measure population differentiation, we rearrange Equation 13.5 to obtain

$$F_{ST} = (F_{IT} - F_{IS}) / (1 - F_{IS}) \qquad (13.6)$$

The F statistics can be calculated using the relationship between heterozygosity and inbreeding: $F = 1 - (H_t/H_0)$ (Equation 11.7). This allows F statistics to be determined from genetic markers using the following equations (Nei 1987):

$$F_{IS} = 1 - (H_I / H_S) \qquad (13.7)$$

$$F_{ST} = 1 - (H_S / H_T) \qquad (13.8)$$

$$F_{IT} = 1 - (H_I / H_T) \qquad (13.9)$$

where H_I is the observed heterozygosity averaged across all population fragments, H_S is the expected heterozygosity averaged across all population fragments, and H_T is the expected heterozygosity for the total population (equivalent to H_e). F_{ST} ranges from 0 (no differentiation between fragments) to 1 (fixation of different alleles in fragments).

The application of F statistics is illustrated using a hypothetical example in Table 13.3. Case (a) shows two population fragments with identical allele frequencies, but with inbreeding in fragment 2. F_{IS} is therefore greater than zero. When allelic frequencies are very similar in different fragments, as would be the case when migration is high, or

Table 13.3 A hypothetical example demonstrating calculation of F statistics from genotype data

Fragment	Genotypes A_1A_1	A_1A_2	A_2A_2	Allele frequency	F	H_e $(=2pq)$
(a) $F_{IS} = 0.3; F_{ST} = 0; F_{IT} = 0.3$						
1	0.25	0.5	0.25	$p = 0.5$ $q = 0.5$	0	0.5
2	0.4	0.2	0.4	$p = 0.5$ $q = 0.5$	0.6	0.5
Combined		$H_I = 0.35$		$p = 0.5$ $q = 0.5$		$H_S = 0.5$ $H_T = 0.5$
(b) $F_{IS} = 0; F_{ST} = 0.099; F_{IT} = 0.099$						
1	0.25	0.5	0.25	$p = 0.5$ $q = 0.5$	0	0.5
2	0.04	0.32	0.64	$p = 0.2$ $q = 0.8$	0	0.32
Combined		$H_I = 0.41$		$p = 0.35$ $q = 0.65$		$H_S = 0.41$ $H_T = 0.455$
(c) $F_{IS} = 0.244; F_{ST} = 0.099; F_{IT} = 0.319$						
1	0.25	0.5	0.25	$p = 0.5$ $q = 0.5$	0	0.5
2	0.14	0.12	0.74	$p = 0.2$ $q = 0.8$	0.625	0.32
Combined		$H_I = 0.31$		$p = 0.35$ $q = 0.65$		$H_S = 0.41$ $H_T = 0.455$

the populations have only recently fragmented, then divergence is low and $H_S \sim H_T$, and $F_{ST} \sim 0$. In (b) there is no inbreeding within either population fragment. The observed heterozygosity is equal to the expected heterozygosity ($H_I = H_S$), and $F_{IS} = 0$. However, the population fragments have different allele frequencies, as will occur with severely restricted gene flow. H_T exceeds H_S, and $F_{ST} > 0$. In (c) there is both divergence in allele frequencies and inbreeding, F_{IS} and F_{ST} are greater than zero and the total inbreeding, F_{IT}, reflects the effect of both (Equation 13.5).

F_{ST} can be estimated using allozyme heterozygosity data, but is less suitable for use with microsatellite data with many alleles, where the related measure R_{ST} is often considered more suitable (Slatkin 1995).

Example 13.4 illustrates the calculation of the F statistics based on heterozygosities for the endangered Pacific yew in western North America. This species exhibits inbreeding within populations ($F_{IS} > 0$) and differentiation among populations ($F_{ST} > 0$).

Example 13.4 | Computation of F statistics for the rare Pacific yew

This example is based on genotype frequencies and heterozygosities for 21 allozyme loci in nine Canadian populations (El-Kassaby & Yanchuk 1994). Average observed heterozygosity (H_I) across the nine populations was 0.085, while the average expected heterozygosity for these populations (H_S) was 0.166. Consequently, inbreeding within populations F_{IS} is

$$F_{IS} = 1 - (H_I / H_S) = 1 - (0.085/0.166) = 0.49$$

This is a high level of inbreeding, but it is not due to selfing as the species is dioecious. It is probably due to clustering of relatives (offspring establishing close to parents) and clumping of individuals from bird and rodent seed caches. The expected heterozygosity for the total nine populations (H_T) was 0.18, so inbreeding due to population differentiation (F_{ST}) is

$$F_{ST} = 1 - (H_S / H_T) = 1 - (0.166/0.180) = 0.078$$

This indicates only a modest degree of population differentiation. The total inbreeding due to both inbreeding within populations and differentiation among them (F_{IT}) is

$$F_{IT} = 1 - (H_I / H_T) = 1 - (0.085/0.18) = 0.53$$

F_{ST} increases with time in fragmented population at a rate dependent on population size

Since F_{ST} values measure population divergence, they are expected to increase over time in the absence of migration. Smaller populations should diverge more rapidly than larger populations (Fig. 13.7). Typically, an F_{ST} above about 0.15 is considered to be an indication of significant differentiation among fragments.

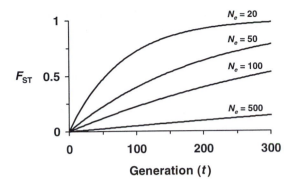

Fig. 13.7 Increase in F_{ST} with generations in isolated fragments with different population sizes.

Fragmentation in non-idealized populations

In real populations, the size of the population fragments may differ, there may be different rates of migration among fragments, fragments may have been separated at different times, the individual populations may not have idealized structures, and there may be impacts of natural selection. For example, the Indian rhinoceros population is fragmented into eight groups in widely separated geographic locations with population sizes ranging from 1300 down to 5 (Box 14.1).

Most populations have $N_e < N$, often by substantial proportions (Chapter 10). The impacts of fragmentation on genetic divergence, inbreeding and loss of genetic diversity will therefore usually be greater than expected from the census population size. If effective population sizes in different fragments vary, then the fragments will become inbred and lose genetic variation at different rates, with the smallest populations being most affected. The interactions between these factors can be complex and their effects difficult to predict using theory alone. Computer simulations are often used to explore the genetic implications of fragmentation in real populations.

The theory we have just explored is based on selective neutrality of alleles. If alleles are subject to balancing selection, then the rate of diversification will be lower than predicted. If selection differs among patches, such that one allele is favoured in some patches and detrimental in others, then the rate of diversification may be greater than predicted. However, if populations are small and selection is weak, then alleles will be effectively neutral (Chapters 8 and 9).

For non-idealized populations, the effective population size N_e is substituted for N in the appropriate equations

Gene flow among population fragments

So far we have ignored migration in dealing with fragmented populations. Many populations have some migration among fragments, but less than in the previous continuous population. Migration reduces the

Gene flow reduces the genetic effects of population fragmentation

impact of fragmentation by an extent dependent on the rate of gene flow. With sufficient migration a fragmented population will behave just like a single large population of the same total size.

Sewall Wright obtained the surprising result that a single migrant per generation among idealized populations was sufficient to prevent complete differentiation (and fixation) (Wright 1969). Initially we consider an 'island model' where migration rates are equal among identically sized population fragments (other, more realistic, situations are examined later). Figure 13.8 illustrates the theoretical equilibrium distributions of allele frequencies across population fragments for different migration rates. The migration rate m is the proportion of a population derived from migrants per generation (Chapter 7). Thus Nm is the number of migrants per generation. Populations with migration rates of more than one migrant per generation ($Nm = 2$ and 4) exhibit no fixations, while those with less than one migrant per generation ($Nm = 1/2$ and $1/4$) differentiate to the extent that some populations are fixed for alternative alleles.

> A single migrant per generation is considered sufficient to prevent the complete differentiation of idealized populations, irrespective of their size

These results are independent of population size. One migrant has as much impact on the equilibrium in a large population as in a small population. This appears paradoxical until it is recognized that although only one migrant is involved, the migration rate (m) is proportionally much higher in smaller than in larger populations. The higher migration rates in smaller populations counteract their greater loss of variation due to drift.

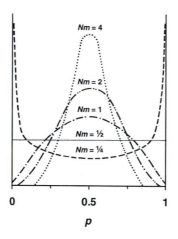

Fig. 13.8 illustration, with curves labelled $Nm = 4$, $Nm = 2$, $Nm = 1$, $Nm = 1/2$, $Nm = 1/4$; x-axis from 0 to 1 labelled p with 0.5 at centre.

Fig. 13.8 Distribution of allele frequencies in finite populations of size N with different levels of migration (m) among them (after Wright 1940). *Populations with one or more migrants per generation do not differentiate completely (no populations become fixed), while populations with lower migration rates differentiate with a proportion of populations reaching temporary fixation.*

> In real (non-ideal) populations, more than one migrant per generation is required to prevent fixation in population fragments

The conclusions above assume that migrants and residents are equally likely to successfully produce offspring, and that all population fragments have idealized structures, apart from the occurrence of migration. These assumptions are unlikely to be realistic. More than one migrant per generation may therefore be required. Lacy (1987) suggested around 5 migrants per generation to prevent differentiation, while Mills & Allendorf (1996) suggested 1–10 migrants per generation was more realistic in practice. Vucetich & Waite (2000) concluded that more than 10 immigrants were required to compensate for increased diversification due to typical fluctuations in population size.

Migration and inbreeding

Inbreeding accumulates over generations in completely isolated population fragments. This can be substantially reduced by introduction of individuals from other fragments (Chapter 12). This occurs even when the immigrants are themselves inbred, as long as they come from genetically distinct populations.

> Inbreeding is reduced by migration among population fragments

Equilibrium between migration and inbreeding

We have previously established that small population size increases divergence, while migration reduces divergence among populations. With constant population sizes and migration rates, these forces reach an equilibrium where the reduction in divergence due to migration balances the increase due to drift. This equilibrium can be measured using F_{ST}. Equilibrium inbreeding is related to the effective population size and the migration rate (m) in such a population (Wright 1969) as:

> Inbreeding in population fragments depends on the effective population size and the migration rate

$$F_{ST} = 1/(4 N_e m + 1) \qquad (13.10)$$

This equation applies when m is small. Figure 13.9 illustrates the relationship between the number of migrants per generation ($N_e m$) and the inbreeding coefficient. With one migrant per generation, $F_{ST} = 1/(4 + 1) = 0.2$. Conversely, the inbreeding coefficient rises rapidly with less than one migrant per generation, and reaches 1.0 (complete divergence – fixation of populations) when there is no migration.

The deleterious effects of inbreeding on reproductive fitness and extinction risk are expected to be largely alleviated in populations with one or more migrants per generation (Fig. 13.8). Experimental studies support this prediction. Populations of the annual canola plant maintained at sizes of five individuals per generation for five generations, with 0, 1 and 2.5 migrants per generation had inbreeding coefficients of

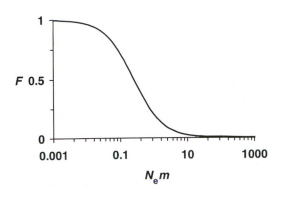

Fig. 13.9 Relationship between inbreeding coefficient and the number of migrants per generation ($N_e m$) for an island model at equilibrium between drift and migration.

0.33, 0.08 and 0, respectively, and average seed numbers per plant of 35, 75 and 79 (Newman 1995). Related results were obtained by Bryant *et al.* (1999) in house flies. A single migrant per generation reduced extinction rates and fitness declines.

Measuring gene flow

Gene flow can be estimated from the degree of genetic differentiation among populations

Migration rates are notoriously difficult to measure by direct tracking of individuals, pollen, etc. Further, immigrants may not breed in their new habitat. Consequently gene flow, rather than migration rate, needs to be estimated.

Gene flow can be inferred from patterns of differentiation among populations by calculating F statistics. F_{ST} is related to population size and migration rate by Equation 13.10. This is an approximation based on the island model (Fig. 13.1). Related expressions have been derived for other models of migration (see Neigel 1996).

Equation 13.10 can be rearranged and used to estimate the migration rate. For example, for the Pacific yew

$$Nm = [1 / F_{ST} - 1] / 4 = [1 / 0.078 - 1] / 4 = 2.96$$

On average about 3 migrants per generation are entering Pacific yew populations. This value reflects historical evolutionary rates of gene flow in equilibrium circumstances, so it may not reflect current gene flow (Steinberg & Jordan 1998).

While populations often do not strictly adhere to the details of the island model, F_{ST} is widely used to measure restrictions in gene flow. The exact estimates of migration rates obtained from this equation are not necessarily reliable, but they do indicate the relative rates of gene flow that populations would have if they adhered to the island population structure. Other means for inferring rates of migration and gene flow are discussed in Chapter 19.

Dispersal and gene flow

Gene flow among fragmented populations is related to dispersal ability

Since differentiation among populations is dependent on levels of gene flow, we would expect this to be related to the dispersal abilities of species and the degree of isolation among populations. Thus, the degree of genetic differentiation among populations (F_{ST}) is expected to be greater for populations:

• In species with lower vs. higher dispersal rates
• In sub-divided vs. continuous habitat
• In distant vs. closer fragments
• In smaller vs. larger population fragments
• In species with longer vs. shorter divergence times (in generations)
• With adaptive differences vs. those without.

Observations generally confirm these predictions (Hastings & Harrison 1994; Hamrick & Godt 1996).

Table 13.4	Fixation index (F_{ST}) in a range of taxa	
Species	F_{ST}	Reference
Mammals (57 species)	0.24	1
Birds (23 species)	0.05	2
Reptiles (22 species)	0.26	1
Amphibians (33 species)	0.32	1
Fish (79 species)	0.14	1
Insects (46 species)	0.10	1
Plants		
Selfing	0.51	3
Mixed selfing and outcrossing – animal pollination	0.22	3
– wind pollination	0.10	3
Outbreeding – animal pollination	0.20	3
– wind pollination	0.10	3

References: 1, Ward *et al.* (1992); 2, Evans (1987); 3, Hamrick & Godt (1989).

There is a strong negative correlation between F_{ST} and the dispersal ability of species, as predicted; the average rank correlation was −0.73 in a meta-analysis involving 333 species across 20 animal groups (Bohonak 1999). Examples of mean F_{ST} values for major groups of organisms are given in Table 13.4. Taxa that can fly, such as birds and insects, have lower F_{ST} values than those that do not. Further, F_{ST} is higher in plants that self (low pollen dispersal) than in outcrossing plants (Table 13.4).

Gene flow and distance between fragments

Dispersal rates typically reduce with distance, as illustrated in acorn woodpeckers (Fig. 13.10). Consequently, distant islands are expected to receive fewer migrants than near islands (Wright 1969; Jaenike 1973). Allozyme variability for island populations generally declines with distance from the mainland in lizards and several species of mammals (Frankham 1997). For mainland population fragments, distant habitat patches are expected to receive fewer migrants than nearby habitat

Distant population fragments show reduced gene flow and greater extinction risk than closer population fragments, for the same sized fragments

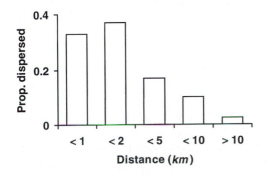

Fig. 13.10 Dispersal distances in acorn woodpecker males in North America (after Koenig *et al.* 1996). *Dispersal rates decline rapidly with distance.*

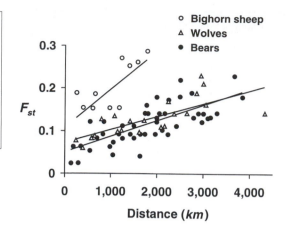

Fig. 13.11 Isolation with distance. Relationship between degree of genetic differentiation (F_{ST}) at microsatellite loci and geographic distance among bighorn sheep, brown bear and gray wolf populations in North America (after Forbes & Hogg 1999). F_{ST} *increases with distance in all three species.*

patches, but this effect depends upon the nature of the surrounding matrix and its influence on dispersal rates. Genetic differentiation and gene flow are associated with geographic distance in bighorn sheep, gray wolves and bears in North America (Fig. 13.11). Similarly, the red-cockaded woodpecker and the northern spotted owl show relationships between distance and genetic differentiation (Box 13.1; Haig *et al.* 2001), as do many other species.

Impacts of different population structures on reproductive fitness

The overall consequences of different population structures on reproductive fitness will depend primarily on the inbreeding coefficient in each fragment. The single large unfragmented population (SL) becomes the standard for comparison. Consequences of different population structures are:

- In the island and stepping-stone models, inbreeding and fitness will depend critically upon the migration rates and upon the variation in population sizes on different islands (Nunney 1999). When there is no gene flow, inbreeding will depend upon the effective population sizes of the individual populations, and will be greater than for SL. Conversely, when there is ample migration among populations, inbreeding will depend upon the effective size of the total population, and be similar to SL.
- In source–sink (or mainland–island) structures, the effective population size will depend on N_e in the mainland (source) populations, rather than that for the total populations. Thus, inbreeding and loss of fitness are likely to be much higher with this structure than for SL.
- Metapopulations typically have effective sizes that are markedly less than the number of breeding adults, due to cycles of extinction and recolonization (Hanski & Gilpin 1997; Pannell & Charlesworth 1999; Wang & Caballero 1999). Their inbreeding will typically be greater

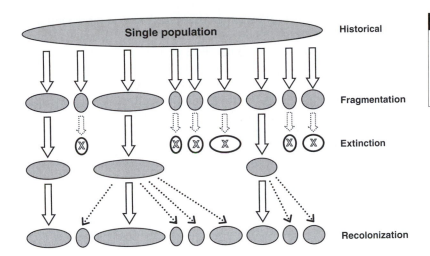

than in other fragmented and non-fragmented structures and the fitness in fragments the lowest.

Since metapopulations have features not already considered, further consideration of them follows.

Metapopulations

Effects on inbreeding and genetic diversity in metapopulations differ from previous examples because of extinctions and recolonizations, and depend on details of the population structures. Figure 13.12 illustrates extinctions of fragments and bottlenecks during recolonization in a metapopulation. The effective size will approximate the sum of the effective sizes of fragments following extinctions, rather than the sum of all effective sizes. Bottlenecks during recolonization will subsequently reduce N_e still further.

If there are frequent extinctions and recolonizations mainly from a few large fragments, the structure approaches that of a source–sink, and less genetic diversity is retained than in a single large population of the same total size (Gilpin 1991). Conversely, a metapopulation with sufficient migration and low rates of local extinctions approaches the characteristics of a single large population. In general, the higher the rates of extinction and recolonization, the more deleterious is the metapopulation.

> Metapopulations typically have effective sizes that are much less than the sum of their parts, due to extinctions and bottlenecks during recolonizations. They are likely to suffer much more rapid inbreeding and fitness reduction than single large populations, and the effects are likely to be worse with higher rates of extinction and recolonization

Summary

1. Population fragmentation usually has deleterious genetic consequences in the long term, compared to a similar sized unfragmented population.

2. The genetic effects of fragmentation for the same total population size depend critically upon gene flow. This in turn depends on the number of fragments, details of population structure, distance among fragments and the dispersal characteristics for the species.

3. Inbreeding and reduced fitness in population fragments are more severe with increased fragmentation, with lower gene flow, and these effects increase with time.

4. Fragmented populations diverge in allele frequencies and heterozygosities.

5. Fragmented populations with restricted gene flow share many of the features of island populations, including elevated extinction risk.

6. Metapopulation structures, with extinctions and recolonizations of population fragments, are likely to be particularly deleterious.

7. F statistics are frequently used to measure differentiation among populations and to infer historic levels of gene flow.

FURTHER READING

Hanski & Gilpin (1997) *Metapopulation Biology*. A fine collection of relevant papers on metapopulations. See especially the chapters by Hedrick & Gilpin, Barton & Whitlock and Giles & Goudet.

Hedrick (2000) *Genetics of Populations*. Chapter 7 provides a clear treatment of many of the genetic issues relating to population fragmentation.

McCullough (1996) *Metapopulations and Wildlife Conservation*. A fine collection of papers on metapopulations with many case studies, some including genetic issues. See especially the chapters by Hedrick, Gutiérrez & Harrison, Stith *et al.* and McCullough *et al.*

Quammen (1996) *The Song of the Dodo*. An interesting and stimulating book written for a popular audience; it has a fine coverage of island biogeography and its relevance to extinctions.

Saccheri *et al.* (1998) This outstanding study evaluated the effects of inbreeding on extinction rates in a butterfly metapopulation.

Wright (1969) *Evolution and the Genetics of Populations*, vol. 2. A scholarly treatment of the genetics of population fragmentation, including F statistics, which the author devised. Relatively advanced.

Young & Clarke (2000) *Genetics, Demography and the Viability of Fragmented Populations*. An excellent collection of studies on fragmented populations of animals and plants.

PROBLEMS

13.1 Fragmentation: What are the genetic impacts of population fragmentation?

13.2 Variance in allele frequencies: Calculate the variance in allele frequencies for populations with allele frequencies 0.1, 0.2, 0.2, 0.3, 0.3, 0.3, 0.4, 0.4, 0.5 (see Box 5.2 for variances).

13.3 Variance in allele frequencies: For population fragments all derived from an initial population with two alleles at frequencies of 0.3 and 0.7, and maintained as isolated populations with effective sizes of 50, what is the expected variance in allele frequencies (a) after 20 generations? (b) after 100 generations?

13.4 Determining migration rates: Calculate Nm among spotted owl sub-species, given that F_{ST} is 0.2.

13.5 Population structure: Calculate H_I, H_S and H_T for each of the three situations in Table 13.3.

13.6 Population differentiation and F statistics: Five populations of the spreading avens, an endangered plant endemic to mountaintops in the eastern USA, were typed for 25 allozyme loci. Observed and expected heterozygosities for each population and for the total of the five populations are given below (Hamrick & Godt 1996). Calculate F_{ST}, F_{IS} and F_{IT} for this data set and explain what each F statistic means. Interpret the population structure.

Population	Observed heterozygosity	Expected heterozygosity
PMT	0.056	0.091
RMT	0.050	0.086
GMT	0.049	0.066
CTP	0.054	0.064
CGG	0.050	0.061
Population means	0.052 (H_I)	0.074 (H_S)
Species		0.098 (H_T)

13.7 Population differentiation and F statistics: Three populations of the threatened swamp pink plant in the eastern USA showed the following allozyme heterozygosities (Hamrick & Godt 1996). Calculate F_{ST}.

Population	Observed heterozygosity	Expected heterozygosity
Appalachian region	0.038	0.061
Virginia region	0.028	0.045
New Jersey region	0.021	0.033
Species		0.053

13.8 Inbreeding and population differentiation: If populations are maintained either as a single population of effective size 50, or two isolated populations of effective size 25 for 30 generations, what are their inbreeding coefficients? What is the inbreeding coefficient in the population created by pooling the two populations of size 25?

Chapter 14

Genetically viable populations

As resources for threatened species are limited, it is important to define the minimum size needed to retain genetic 'health.' To avoid inbreeding depression and retain fitness in the short-term $N_e \gg 50$ is required. For threatened species to permanently retain their evolutionary potential N_e of 500–5,000 is required. Current sizes of threatened species are typically too small to avoid genetic deterioration

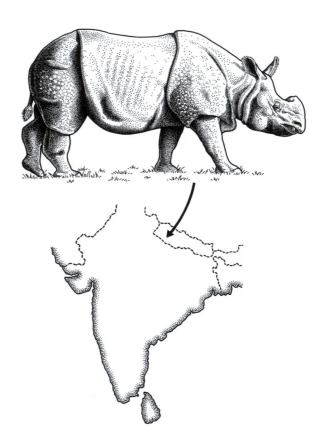

Endangered Indian one-horned
rhinoceros.

Shortage of space for threatened species

Habitat loss is equivalent to loss of living space for threatened species. Substantial proportions of mammals (56%), birds (53%), reptiles (62%), amphibians (64%), fish (56%), gymnosperms (32%) and angiosperms (9%) are threatened, largely through this reduction (Chapter 1). The financial and physical resources required to conserve them are enormous. Providing reserves, such as national parks, is costly, and often conflicts with human demands for increased land use. Captive breeding programs have been suggested as a partial solution. However, there is also a shortage of resources for this strategy. About 2000 endangered vertebrate species require captive breeding, but space exists for only about 800 species (Tudge 1995). Pragmatic decisions must be made in allocating scarce breeding spaces. Retention of too few individuals will lead to the deleterious genetic effects we have discussed, and ultimately jeopardize the outcome of programs. Conversely, allocating too many resources to one species will be at the expense of others, for which no space will be available.

> There is a severe shortage of space for threatened species, both in wild reserves and in captivity

Consequently, there is an urgent need to define the minimum population size required for species to be viable in the long term. This chapter addresses the question: 'How large must populations be, to be genetically viable?' This issue has been discussed under the title of **minimum viable population size** (MVP), yet the population sizes are not necessarily minimum, nor viable. Rather, we are considering the minimum size required to maintain a population that suffers no reduction in reproductive fitness or evolutionary potential over thousands of years. This does not signify that populations of lesser size have no future, only that their reproductive fitness and evolutionary potential are likely to be compromised, and they have an increased risk of extinction. As Soulé (1987) noted 'there are no hopeless cases, only people without hope and expensive cases.'

For a particular population or species, the question above reduces to:

- Is the population size large enough to avoid loss of reproductive fitness?
- Does the species have enough genetic diversity to evolve in response to environmental change?

These questions are illustrated for the endangered Indian rhinoceros and the northern elephant seal in Box 14.1.

Box 14.1	Is the species genetically viable in the medium to long term?

IS THE RHINOCEROS POPULATION SIZE LARGE ENOUGH?
The Indian one-horned rhinoceros, like many wildlife populations, numbered many hundreds of thousands. With habitat reduction and fragmentation and poaching for

horns, the numbers have been reduced to about 2200 individuals in eight geo-graphically separated areas, shown in the figure and table below (International Rhino Fund personal communication). This species has normal levels of allozyme genetic diversity (Dinerstein & McCracken 1990). The largest population is 1300 and the smallest 5. For the entire species, are there sufficient individuals to avoid extinction due to inbreeding and compromised ability to undergo adaptive evolu-tionary change? Regrettably, the arguments presented in this chapter lead us to anticipate that the one-horned rhinoceros will undergo slow genetic deterioration in the long term.

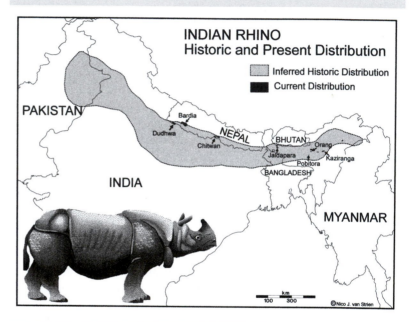

Area	Population size (1999)
Areas with large populations	
Kaziranga (India, Assam)	~ 1300
Chitwan (Nepal)	~ 600
Areas with smaller populations	
Pobitora (India, Assam)	76
Dudhwa/Bardia (Nepal/India)	72
Jaldapara (India, W. Bengal)	53
Orang (India, Assam)	46
Goruma (India, W. Bengal)	19
Mamas (India, Assam)	~ 5
Total	*2175–2225*

DOES THE NORTHERN ELEPHANT SEAL HAVE ENOUGH GENETIC DIVERSITY?
The northern elephant seal underwent a population size bottleneck of about 20–30 individuals, but has since recovered to well over 100000 individuals and is no longer

listed as endangered. However, it displays no allozyme genetic diversity (Bonnell & Selander 1974; Hoelzel et al. 1993) and only two mtDNA haplotypes (compared to 23 in related southern elephant seals). Many other threatened species lack genetic diversity (Chapter 3). Are these species doomed to extinction? Below we will see that such species are likely to have compromised ability to evolve in response to environmental change and thus increased extinction risk. However, they are not predicted to become extinct in the near future, unless they experience an unexpected catastrophe (e.g. a new disease).

How large?

How large do populations need to be to ensure their genetic 'health'? This involves three critical genetic goals:
- Retaining reproductive fitness by avoiding inbreeding depression
- Retaining the ability to evolve in response to changes in the environment (evolutionary potential)
- Avoiding the accumulation of new deleterious mutations.

Various predictions of population sizes required to achieve these goals are given in Table 14.1. We consider each of these issues below.

Table 14.1 How large must populations be to retain genetic 'health'? Various estimates of the required effective population size (N_e) are given. The times to recover normal levels of genetic diversity following complete loss of diversity are also given in generations

Goal	N_e	Recovery time (generations)	Reference
Retain reproductive fitness	50		1, 2
Retain evolutionary potential	500	$10^2 - 10^3$	1, 3
	5000		4
	570–1250		5
Retain single locus genetic diversity	$10^5 - 10^6$	$10^5 - 10^7$	3
Avoid accumulating deleterious mutations	1000		4
	100		6
	12		7

References: 1, Franklin (1980); 2, Soulé (1980); 3, Lande & Barrowclough (1987); 4, Lande (1995a); 5, Franklin & Frankham (1998); 6, Lynch et al. (1995); 7, Charlesworth et al. (1993).

Retaining reproductive fitness

Small populations of naturally outbreeding species become inbred and suffer reductions in reproductive fitness (Chapter 12). What amount of inbreeding can be tolerated without significant inbreeding depression?

No finite population is immune from eventual inbreeding depression

Franklin (1980) and Soulé (1980) both suggested that an effective population size of 50 was sufficient to avoid inbreeding depression, in the short term, based on the experience of animal breeders.

Is there a population size that is immune from inbreeding depression? Since inbreeding increases at a rate of $1/2N_e$ per generation, all finite closed populations eventually become inbred. Further, as inbreeding depression is linearly related to the inbreeding coefficient (Chapter 12), there is no threshold below which inbreeding is not deleterious. Even low levels of inbreeding are expected to result in some low level of inbreeding depression. Based upon the median number of lethal equivalents of 3.14, as found in captive mammals (Ralls *et al.* 1988), we would expect about 2% inbreeding depression when $F = 0.005$, 4% when $F = 0.01$, and 15% when $F = 0.05$ for juvenile survival alone.

An effective size of 50, suggested by Franklin and Soulé, corresponds to an increase in inbreeding coefficient of 1% per generation. The context of their predictions was that over a period of perhaps 5–10 generations, there would be little detectable inbreeding depression when the N_e was 50. However, little relevant data were available at the time of their predictions.

Subsequently, inbreeding depression was described in fruit fly populations maintained at effective sizes of about 50 for 210 generations. One-quarter of the populations became extinct (Latter *et al.* 1995). Inbreeding depression was also evident in fruit fly populations maintained with effective sizes of 50, or less, for 50 generations (Fig. 14.1). In housefly populations inbreeding depression was evident in populations with $N_e = 50$ after 12 generations, and even in those of $N_e \sim 90$ after only five generations (Bryant *et al.* 1999; Reed & Bryant 2000).

We do not know precisely how large populations must be to avoid meaningful inbreeding depression in the long term, but the required size is clearly much greater than an effective size of 50. Disturbingly, about one-half of all captive populations of threatened mammals have N of less than 50 (Magin *et al.* 1994), and are likely to suffer inbreeding depression relatively soon.

At what point will inbreeding become sufficient to cause extinctions? Estimated times to extinction for different sized housefly populations approximated the effective size in generations, i.e. 480 generations for $N_e = 500$, 80 for $N_e = 87$, 54 for $N_e = 50$ and 32 for $N_e = 15$ (Reed & Bryant 2000). Extinction risks in rapidly inbred populations of mice and fruit flies increase markedly at $F = 0.5$ and beyond (Fig. 12.2). F values for the housefly populations at extinction were 0.38 to 0.66, consistent with the fruit fly data.

In practice, wild populations that were listed as endangered in 1985–91 numbered 100–1000 individuals (Wilcove *et al.* 1993). Similarly, the IUCN scheme for categorization of extinction risk lists 50, 250 and 1000 adults as cut-offs for the critically endangered, endangered and vulnerable categories (IUCN 1996). Since N_e/N ratios are about 0.1, many of these populations will have effective sizes of 50 or less and are at risk

Populations with effective sizes of 50 in fruit flies and 90 in houseflies show inbreeding depression

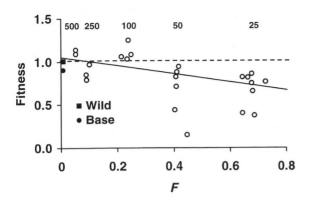

Fig. 14.1 How large must populations be to avoid inbreeding depression? Reproductive fitness of populations of fruit flies maintained for 50 generations with different effective sizes (numbers at the top of the figure), compared to the wild population from which they were founded (after Woodworth 1996). There is a significant regression of fitness on inbreeding coefficient, F, as indicated by the fitted line. *All populations with sizes of 50 or less had lower fitness than the wild population (dotted line).*

of extinction from inbreeding depression (without considering other factors) unless their sizes are substantially increased.

Retaining evolutionary potential

Since our objective is conservation of species as dynamic entities capable of evolving to cope with environmental change, evolutionary potential must be retained. While there is a range of estimates of the size of populations required, there is general agreement that it is an N_e of at least 500 (Table 14.1). Since the debate about this issue has major implications for the genetic management of wild and captive populations, we consider the estimations in some detail.

Effective population sizes of 500–5000 have been suggested as necessary to maintain evolutionary potential

In his classic paper, Franklin (1980) predicted that an effective size of 500 was required. He argued that additive genetic variation, rather than allelic diversity, determined evolutionary potential, and this is directly related to heterozygosity (Equation 5.3). Finally Franklin assumed that the level of additive genetic variation for peripheral characters at equilibrium was dependent on the balance between loss of quantitative genetic variation and its replenishment by mutation.

The N_e required to balance additive genetic variation lost by drift and with that gained by mutation (under a neutral model), is obtained as follows:

$$\Delta V_A = V_m - V_A / 2N_e \tag{14.1}$$

where ΔV_A is the change in additive genetic variation in one generation, V_m the gain in genetic variation per generation due to mutation, and V_A the additive genetic variation. The $V_A/2N_e$ term is the loss of additive genetic variation per generation due to drift. At equilibrium, $\Delta V_A = 0$, so

$$N_e = V_A / 2V_m \tag{14.2}$$

Thus, the required population size depends upon the initial additive genetic variation and the rate at which it is regenerated by mutation.

Franklin (1980) noted that $V_m \sim 10^{-3} V_E$ for bristle characters in fruit flies (one of the few estimates of V_m then available), where V_E is the environmental variation for the quantitative character. Upon substituting this value into Equation 14.2, he estimated the required N_e as

$$N_e = V_A / [2 \times 10^{-3} \times V_e] = 500 \, V_A / V_E \qquad (14.3)$$

and since the heritability $h^2 = V_A / V_P \sim V_A / (V_A + V_E)$

$$N_e = 500 \, h^2 / (1 - h^2) \qquad (14.4)$$

To obtain his estimate of N_e, Franklin (1980) assumed a heritability of 50%. This is a reasonable estimate of the heritability for peripheral characters (Table 5.3). Consequently, Franklin predicted that an effective size of 500 was required to retain additive genetic variation and long-term evolutionary potential.

Lande and Barrowclough (1987) reached a similar conclusion, based on a model involving an equilibrium between stabilizing selection, drift and mutation. However, Lande (1995a) later revised his estimate and suggested that a value of 5000 was required. He argued that only about 10% of newly generated mutations are useful for future genetic change because most newly arisen mutations are deleterious (based on data from Lopez & Lopez-Fanjul 1993). Since V_m has been found to be approximately $10^{-3} V_E$ for a wide range of quantitative characters (Table 7.1), Lande adjusted for the deleterious mutations by using $V_m = 10^{-4} V_E$. Upon substituting this value into equation 14.2, he estimated N_e as:

$$N_e = V_A / [2 \times 10^{-4} \times V_E] = 5000 \, h^2 / (1 - h^2) \qquad (14.5)$$

Like Franklin (1980), Lande (1995a) also assumed a heritability of 50%. This yielded an estimate of 5000 to retain evolutionary potential.

Reservations have been expressed about this estimate (Frankham & Franklin 1998). First, estimates of $V_m = 10^{-3} V_E$ already include, in part, a correction for deleterious alleles. Some estimates are derived from long-term experiments, which provide the opportunity for unconditionally deleterious mutations to be eliminated, i.e. many of the 90% of deleterious mutations have already been excluded in obtaining the estimate.

Second, by introducing the issue of deleterious mutations, Lande was beginning to consider fitness, rather than peripheral characters. For these, heritabilities are often much less than 0.5 (see Tables 5.2 and 5.3). Heritabilities for fitness characters are typically 10%–20%, or less. If we use a heritability of 10%, and $V_m = 10^{-4} V_E$, then $N_e \sim 560$, and for a heritability of 20% is $N_e = 1250$ (Franklin & Frankham 1998).

Third, the effects of mutations depend on environmental conditions. Mutations that are deleterious in the current environment may be favourable under altered conditions in the future. For example, genetic adaptation to captivity in fruit flies seems to be due to rare alleles that are deleterious in the wild (Woodworth 1996). Since evolutionary potential is concerned with the capacity to adapt to environmental change, the genetic diversity that must be preserved may be deleterious, or neutral, in the current environment. We do not know what proportion of mutations are unconditionally deleterious versus those that are deleterious in some conditions and beneficial in others.

The calculations above are based on models that ignore natural selection, or do not consider it adequately. Reproductive fitness is the central character for evolutionary potential, as it is fitness that is involved in evolutionary change. The above expressions are of dubious validity when applied to reproductive fitness subject to directional natural selection. There is currently no theory allowing us to predict the equilibrium additive genetic variation under a model of mutation, drift and natural selection operating on reproductive fitness. The issue must be resolved empirically. Preliminary experimental estimates from fruit flies indicate that the effective population sizes required to retain evolutionary potential are from several hundred to several thousand (Gilligan 2001).

We should emphasise that estimates of the required N_e are very approximate. There are uncertainties about mutational variances for reproductive fitness, and especially about the proportion of mutations that are deleterious (Keightley 1996). Further, the above estimates assume that heterozygosity determines evolutionary potential. Some authors argue that allelic diversity may be critical (Allendorf 1986; Fuerst & Maruyama 1986). For example, particular alleles may confer disease, pest or parasite resistance. If allelic diversity is important in determining evolutionary potential, the sizes required to preserve it (particularly for rare alleles) are much larger than those required to preserve heterozygosity (see below).

What population size is required to maintain evolutionary potential for wild populations in nature? Only very rarely is N_e known for wild populations. Since comprehensive estimates of N_e/N are about 0.1 (Chapter 10), census sizes in wild populations must be about one order of magnitude higher than the N_e values we have calculated, i.e. 5000–50000. This sets a lower limit for the minimum size to maintain long-term viability (Soulé 1987), and is within the range of values reached from consideration of other threats (Chapter 20).

> Wild populations in nature require adult census sizes about 10 times larger than the N_e values estimated above, i.e. several thousand to tens of thousands

How large are threatened populations?

We have concluded that effective sizes of at least 500 and actual numbers of adult census sizes of at least 5000 are required to retain genetic diversity and to minimize inbreeding depression in perpetuity. However, we operate in a climate of severely restricted resources. The following section examines the population sizes being recommended in practical endangered species programs.

The population size criteria used in the IUCN (1996) system for categorizing endangerment of species reflect the current scientific consensus on the relationship between population size and degree of endangerment (Chapter 1). Under this system, populations (species) are considered critically endangered, endangered, or vulnerable if populations sizes are less than 50, 250 or 1000 mature individuals, respectively. These

> The population size criteria used by IUCN to define endangerment are well below the 5000 minimum required to retain long-term genetic health

correspond to N_e of about 5, 25 and 100, respectively, all within the range where inbreeding and loss of genetic diversity will undoubtedly occur over a relatively short period of time. These will certainly impact on the viability of populations within the time frames specified for the endangered IUCN categories (Table 1.3). For example, the critically endangered category refers to three generations. A critically endangered species with $N_e = 5$ would have an inbreeding coefficient in excess of that for full-sib mating after three generations and would suffer substantial inbreeding depression. An endangered species with $N_e = 25$ would have $F = 0.18$ after the 10-generation time frame specified by the IUCN.

> Population sizes of endangered species are usually smaller than those required to meet genetic objectives

Actual census population sizes for a variety of endangered species are given in Table 14.2. Most of these have population sizes of less than 500 and, presumably, effective population sizes much less than this.

What happens to species with $N_e < 500$?

> Species with effective sizes of less than 500 are not doomed to extinction, but will become increasingly vulnerable with time, and have increased extinction risk

Species with effective sizes insufficient for long-term maintenance of genetic diversity are not doomed to immediate extinction. On average they will suffer depletion of genetic diversity and suffer reduced ability to evolve in response to novel environmental threats. They will slowly become inbred, with consequent reduction in reproduction and survival rates, and require increasing human intervention to ensure their survival. This may take the form of providing them with more benign environments (isolating them from competitors, avoiding introduction of diseases and improving their environment), or managing them to increase reproduction and survival.

Reduced long-term evolutionary potential in endangered species

> Endangered species have substantially compromised ability to evolve in response to environmental change, as long-term evolutionary potential depends on N_e and reproduction rates, in addition to initial additive genetic variation

The long-term ability of populations to evolve is proportional to the effective population size, both for evolutionary change due to current genetic variation in the population and for changes due to new mutations. This dependence arises through the impact of drift on current genetic diversity and because more new mutations occur in larger populations. The combination of these effects puts a limit on the extent of adaptation to novel environmental conditions that can be wrought by natural selection. We now extend several of the concepts relating to quantitative genetic variation and selection response in small populations, first presented in Chapter 5 and 8.

For genetic variation from the initial population, the total response to selection in the long term (R_{Limit}, the limit to selection) is predicted to be approximately (Robertson 1960)

$$R_{Limit} = 2N_e S h^2 \tag{14.6}$$

where S = selection differential and h^2 = heritability (Chapter 5).

Table 14.2 | Population sizes in the wild (N) and category of endangerment for a variety of threatened taxa. The categories are based primarily on the IUCN system and account for more than population sizes (Chapter 1)

Species	Location	Category[a]	N[b]	Reference
Mammals				
Asiatic lion	India	E	284	1
Baiji dolphin	China	Cr. E	150	2
Eastern barred bandicoot	Australia (mainland)	Cr. E	200[c]	3
Ethiopian wolf	Ethiopia	Cr. E	<500	4
Darwin's fox	Chile	E	<500	4
Florida panther	USA	Cr. E	30–50	5
Giant panda	China	E	1,000	6
Golden lion tamarin	Brazil	Cr. E	600 (+ 200[d])	7
Humpback whale	Oceans	V	6000	8
Javan rhinoceros	Indonesia	Cr. E	60	9
Javan rhinoceros (different sub-species)	Vietnam	Cr. E	5	9
Northern hairy-nosed wombat	Australia	Cr. E	70	10
Northern right whale	N. Oceans	E	350	6
Tana River crested mangabey	Kenya	E	12000–15000	11
Birds				
Attwater's prairie chicken	USA	E (USA)	42	12
Bali starling	Indonesia	Cr. E	25	5
Black stilt	New Zealand	Cr. E	70	13
Kirtland's warbler	USA	V	1530	14
Lord Howe Island woodhen	Australia	E	20–30[c]	15
		E (NSW V)	211	15
Mauritius pink pigeon	Mauritius	Cr. E	<20	16
Puerto Rican parrot	Puerto Rico	Cr. E	~ 40	5
Seychelles magpie robin	Seychelles	Cr. E	22	17
Seychelles warbler	Seychelles	Cr. E	26	18
		V	~1500	18
Red-cockaded woodpecker	USA	V (USA E)	9270	19
Whooping crane	N. America	E	160 (+73[d])	20
Reptiles				
Aruba Island rattlesnake	Caribbean	Cr. E	350	21
Komodo dragon	Indonesia	V	<3000	22
Invertebrates				
Palo Verdes blue butterfly	California	E (USA)	200	23
Plants				
Apalachicola rosemary	Florida	E	555[c]	24
Bidens micrantha kalealaha	Hawaii	E	2000	25
Catalina mahogany	California	E	6[c]	27
Corrigan grevillea	Australia	E	27	28
Mauna Kea silversword	Hawaii	E	~ 24[c]	24
Schiedea haleakalensis	Hawaii	E	100–200	25
Small whorled pogonia	N. America	V	2600	24

Table 14.2 (cont.)				
Species	Location	Category[a]	N[b]	Reference
Texas snowbell	Texas	E	39[c]	24
Wollemi pine	Australia	E (NSW)	~ 40 adults	28

Notes:

[a]Cr. E = critically endangered, E = endangered, and V = vulnerable.

[b]Numbers reflect those at the time of the study, and are not necessarily current.

[c]Prior to captive breeding and reintroduction program.

[d]From reintroduction.

References: 1, O'Brien *et al.* (1996); 2, Zhou *et al.* (1994); 3, Clark *et al.* (1994); 4, Wayne (1996); 5, Seal (1991); 6, Primack (1998); 7, Ballou *et al.* (1998); 8, McIntosh (1999); 9, Pain (1998); 10, Taylor *et al.* (1994); 11, Kinnaird & O'Brien (1991); 12, Anonymous (1996); 13, Millar *et al.* (1997); 14, Richter (1996); 15, Brook *et al.* (1997a); 16, Craig (1994); 17, Komdeur (1996); 18, Komdeur *et al.* (1998); 19, Kulhavy *et al.* (1995); 20, Glenn *et al.* (1999); 21, Seal (1992); 22, Ciofi & Bruford (1998); 23, Nelson (1995); 24, Falk *et al.* (1996); 25, Loope & Medeiros (1994); 26, Rieseberg & Swenson (1996); 27, Rossetto *et al.* (1995); 28, NPWS (1998).

In practice, this overestimates the total response to selection, but experiments in a range of species have demonstrated greater selection response in larger, compared to smaller, populations (Chapter 8).

For evolutionary change due to new mutations, the asymptotic rate of response per generation after mutation and drift reach equilibrium is predicted to be (Hill 1982)

$$R_{\mathrm{mutation}} = 2N_{\mathrm{e}} S V_{\mathrm{m}} / V_{\mathrm{P}} \qquad (14.7)$$

where V_{P} is the phenotypic variance. This provides a reasonable prediction of response, although not a precise one (Frankham 1983; Mackay *et al.* 1994).

Importantly, both prediction equations show that evolutionary potential is proportional to N_{e}. In practice, it is proportional to log N_{e} (Fig. 14.2). There is a clear increase in selection response until at least $N_{\mathrm{e}} = 300$, after which response may be asymptoting.

The ability of large populations to adapt genetically is amply illustrated by pest insects that have evolved resistance to a wide range of

Fig. 14.2 Observed relationship between long-term response to directional selection and effective population size (Weber & Diggins 1990). The *y* axis is the cumulative response at generation 50, divided by the response in the first generation (R_{50}/R_1) for selection on a diversity of characters in mice, fruit flies, red flour beetles and maize. This is plotted against log N_{e} for the populations. The dotted exponential curve is the predicted limit to selection based on Equation 14.6, while the two asymptotic curves represent 50-generation predictions based on Equation 14.8 with mutation added using Equation 14.7 (higher curve) and without it (lower curve). *Selection response is proportional to log N_{e}.*

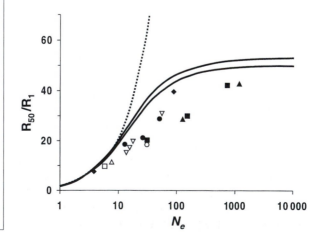

insecticides (McKenzie & Batterham 1994). Conversely, an endangered species such as black rhinoceros, which now has an effective size of perhaps 100, may have only one-third the ability for long-term evolution that it had previously. Example 14.1 illustrates the potential impacts of population size on evolutionary potential in small populations of gray wolves.

Example 14.1 | Impact of population size on evolutionary potential

We can illustrate the impact of many of the variables affecting evolutionary potential, using the Isle Royale gray wolf as an example (Wayne *et al.* 1991). A single pair is believed to have founded the gray wolf population on Isle Royale in Lake Superior. Consequently, heterozygosity of the island population will be $(1 - 1/2N) = (1 - \frac{1}{4}) = \frac{3}{4}$ of that on the mainland. Since heritability is proportional to heterozygosity, this bottleneck at foundation reduces the evolutionary potential by about one-quarter through its impact on h^2.

Differences in reproductive rate impact on evolutionary potential through effects on the selection differential (S). These effects are more difficult to quantify. The Isle Royale population is expected to suffer reduced reproduction and survival rates due to inbreeding depression. With an initial inbreeding coefficient of 25%, the reduction in lifetime production of offspring reaching sexual maturity is likely to be about 50% (Frankel & Soulé 1981). Assuming that the mainland population has 30 pups per pair over five years, the island population will have only 15. If the population is stable in size, then one pair of pups from each pair contributes to the next generation. This represents 6.7% of the mainland population breeding and 13.3% of the island population, giving selection differentials (S) of 1.9 and 1.6 (using tables in Becker 1984), respectively. The island population would have a 16% lower selection differential and thus a 16% reduced selection response (due to S alone).

Response (R) to several generations (t) of selection is predicted as:

$$R = Sh^2 \sum [1 - (1/2N_e)]^{t-1} \tag{14.8}$$

where h^2 is the heritability. The sigma term on the right-hand side reflects erosion of genetic diversity each generation due to genetic drift.

The impact of population size on evolutionary potential over five generations depends on the $(1 - 1/2N_e)^{t-1}$ term. If the mainland population of wolves is 5000 breeding individuals and the Isle Royale population 25 potentially breeding individuals per generation, then, with a conservative N_e/N ratio of 0.2, the effective sizes are 1000 and 5. Consequently, the loss of genetic diversity for the mainland population will be very small [$(1 - 1/2000)$ per generation], and, after 20 generations, only 1% of the initial heterozygosity will be lost. However, with only five effective individuals breeding on the island

10% of the existing genetic variation will be lost each generation. Thus, the response to selection R in the Isle Royale population over the first five generations will be

$$R_1 = \tfrac{3}{4}\,h^2 \times 1.6 = 1.2\,h^2$$

$$+R_2 = \tfrac{3}{4}\,h^2 \times 1.6 \times [1-(1/10)] = 1.08\,h^2$$

$$+R_3 = \tfrac{3}{4}\,h^2 \times 1.6 \times 0.9^2 = 0.97\,h^2$$

$$+R_4 = \tfrac{3}{4}\,h^2 \times 1.6 \times 0.9^3 = 0.87\,h^2$$

$$+R_5 = \tfrac{3}{4}\,h^2 \times 1.6 \times 0.9^3 = 0.79\,h^2$$

The cumulative response over the five generations will be 4.91 h^2 in the Isle Royale gray wolf.

In contrast, response to selection in the large mainland population in the first and subsequent generations will be

$$R_1 = h^2 \times 1.9 = 1.9\,h^2$$

The cumulative response to selection in the mainland population over five generations will be 9.5 h^2.

Thus, response in the Isle Royale population will be only 4.91/9.5 = 52% that of the mainland population. The proportionate response in the island population continues to decline with time compared to that in the mainland population.

N_e is the major factor causing differences in medium to long-term evolutionary potential when comparing closely related endangered and non-endangered species with similar life histories, or endangered and non-endangered populations within species. Differences in genetic diversity may often make a contribution, but its effects are likely to be much smaller. There may be an even smaller contribution from differences in selection differentials as endangered species may have lower reproductive rates than related non-endangered species due to inbreeding depression. The overall loss of evolutionary potential in very small populations is likely to be substantial, and much worse than that due to low initial genetic diversity.

The arguments in Example 14.1 emphasize the importance of expanding the population sizes of endangered species to minimize inbreeding and loss of genetic variation and to improve their ability to evolve in response to environmental changes.

Retaining single locus genetic diversity in the long term

Effective population sizes of 10^5–10^6 are required to retain single locus diversity due to the balance between mutation and drift

We now move to considering what population size is required to maintain genetic diversity at a single locus. Some loci, such as self-incompatibility loci in plants and MHC loci in vertebrates, are of such importance to survival that we must retain their genetic diversity. Population sizes required to retain single locus diversity are much larger than those for quantitative characters. Mutation rates are lower for individual loci (10^{-5}–10^{-6}) than for quantitative characters ($10^{-3} \times V_E$), but both types of variation lose similar proportions of genetic diversity due to drift each generation. Consequently, the equilibria between drift and mutation will result in lower genetic diversity for single loci than for quantitative characters for the same effective population sizes.

Based on mutation–drift equilibrium, Lande & Barrowclough (1987) suggested that effective population sizes of 10^5–10^6 were required to retain single locus diversity. These sizes are unattainable goals for most species (especially vertebrates) of conservation concern, given current habitat availability and conservation resources. Population sizes required to maintain diversity at loci subject to balancing selection (e.g. SI and MHC loci) will be less than this, but may also be unattainable goals.

Time to regenerate genetic diversity

Loss of genetic diversity would not be of great concern if it were regenerated rapidly. The regeneration times for different forms of genetic diversity depend on their mutation rates (Chapter 7). Since mutation rates are very low, times to regenerate genetic diversity are very long (Table 14.1). Single locus diversity with a mutation rate of 10^{-5}–10^{-6} per generation takes 100 000 to 10 million generations to regenerate. Quantitative genetic variation has a mutation rate of $10^{-3} V_E$ per generation, and requires only 100–1000 generations to regenerate – still about 2600–26 000 years for elephants! Clearly, we cannot rely on mutation to regenerate genetic diversity in time spans of conservation concern. The implication is that every effort must be made to prevent loss of current genetic diversity.

> If genetic diversity is lost, it is only regenerated very slowly by mutation, with recovery of original levels taking hundreds to thousands of generations

Avoiding accumulation of new deleterious mutations

Recall that alleles of small effect become effectively neutral in small populations (Chapter 9). Thus, a proportion of mildly deleterious mutations will be fixed by chance in small populations, resulting in reduced reproductive fitness that may result in a decline to extinction (**mutational meltdown**). The deleterious alleles that are fixed may have been in the population for some period of time, or may be recent mutations. Both forms of mutation are fixed through inbreeding, or drift, so this topic is closely related to inbreeding depression. Here we consider the impact of newly arisen mutations.

> Some mildly deleterious mutations are fixed by chance in small populations, and result in reduced reproductive fitness. The size of populations required to avoid such effects is unclear

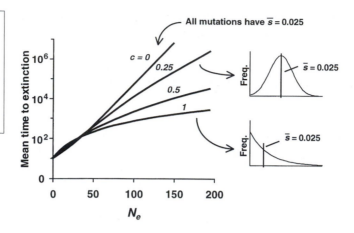

Fig. 14.3 Mean times to extinction (in generations) as a function of effective population size due to fixation of new mutations (after Lande 1995a). The values of c reflect different assumptions about the variation in the effects of new mutations, as illustrated.

Since mutation rates are low, they accumulate slowly. Thus, the threat due to accumulation of newly arisen mutation is only evident in the long term. Nevertheless, there is considerable evidence that mutational accumulation causes declines in asexual populations (de la Peña *et al.* 2000). In contrast, in sexual populations, recombination allows natural selection to more effectively oppose fixation of deleterious alleles, as progeny can be produced that have higher reproductive fitness than that of their parents.

The significance of mutational accumulation in sexually reproducing populations is controversial. Lande (1995a) suggested that effective population sizes below 1000 will suffer serious declines from the chance fixation of new, mildly deleterious mutations (Fig. 14.3), while Lynch *et al.* (1995) argued that it would cause problems in populations with sizes up to $N_e = 100$. In contrast, Charlesworth *et al.* (1993) did not consider this factor to be a serious threat to sexual populations unless population sizes were less than $N_e = 12$.

Direct tests for mutational accumulation in fruit fly populations maintained for 45–50 generations at effective sizes of 25, 50, 100, 250 and 500 found no evidence of mutational accumulation (Gilligan *et al.* 1997). It is unclear whether this was due to the long times that may be required to observe the effects of mutational accumulation, or to uncertainties about the rates and effects of new mutations affecting reproductive fitness. Nevertheless, mutational accumulation does not appear to be of major importance in the time frame of most conservation concern in naturally outbreeding species (100–200 years). In practice inbreeding depression is likely to cause extinction before mutational accumulation is a serious issue. For example, while effects of mutational accumulation were not detected, inbreeding depression was evident in the populations of $N_e = 25$ and 50 studied by Gilligan *et al.* (1997) (Fig. 14.1).

Mutational accumulation cannot be discounted as a factor in the long term, or in asexually reproducing species. Naturally inbreeding species are likely to be more sensitive to declines in fitness due to mutational accumulation than outbreeders. Their known susceptibility to inbreeding depression is probably primarily due to relatively recent mutations.

Genetic goals in the management of wild populations

We are only aware of a few management plans for endangered species in the wild where genetic objectives are defined. In the golden lion tamarin, the objective is to retain 98% of genetic diversity for 100 years, corresponding to an effective population size of about 400 (Example 14.2). Currently there are about 630 wild individuals, plus 360 animals resulting from reintroductions, in the wild. Five hundred individuals are maintained in captivity. The N_e/N ratio must exceed 0.31 to attain this goal based on all animals, or 0.5 for wild animals. Since this is unlikely, the genetic goal is not being achieved. Lack of available habitat to allow expansion of the population is the primary obstacle to reaching these goals.

Few management programs for endangered species in the wild include genetic objectives

---

Example 14.2 | Effective population size required to retain 98% of genetic diversity for 100 years in the golden lion tamarin

To obtain the required population size we use Equation 10.1:

$$H_t/H_0 = (1 - 1/2N_e)^t \sim e^{-t/2N_e}$$

Substituting $H_t/H_0 = 0.98$ and $t = 100/6 = 16.7$ (tamarins have a generation length of 6 years), we obtain

$$0.98 = e^{-16.7/2N_e} = e^{-8.333/N_e}$$

After taking natural logarithms (ln) of both sides, we obtain

$$\ln 0.98 = -8.33/N_e$$

and

$$N_e = -8.33/\ln 0.98 = 412$$

Thus, the effective size required to meet the goal of retaining 98% of genetic diversity for 100 years in wild golden lion tamarins is over 400.

In practice, the N_e needed to reach this goal is estimated using computer simulations, taking into consideration all the relevant life and population structure details (Ballou *et al.* 1998).

Recovery targets for population sizes used to de-list species

Populations size targets for de-listing endangered species vary, but are generally smaller than the above genetic considerations would suggest

Recovery programs for endangered species often identify a target population size, the size at which the species would be removed from the

Table 14.3 | Population size targets specified for de-listing a range of endangered species

Species	Target population size for de-listing	Reference
Mammals		
Asian rhinoceros	2500 ($N_e > 500$) in 10+ populations	1
Black-footed ferret	1500 adults in 10+ populations	2
Sea otter	2650	3
Birds		
Attwater's prairie chicken	5000 in 3 different areas	4
Bald eagle	3900 pairs	5
California condor	2 × 150 wild + 150 captive	6
Lord Howe Island woodhen	200 (endangered to threatened)	7
Peregrine falcon	456 breeding pairs	8
Red-cockaded woodpecker	5 populations of 500 = 2500	9
Plants		
Lakeside daisy	1000 plants	10

References: 1, Foose *et al.* (1995); 2, Clark (1994); 3, Ralls *et al.* (1996); 4, Bowdoin & Williams (1996); 5, Millar (1999); 6, Ralls *et al.* (2000); 7, Brook *et al.* (1997a); 8, Mesta (1999); 9, Kulhavy *et al.* (1995); 10, Demauro (1994).

endangered list (Table 14.3). Target sizes are based on many considerations, but frequently ignore genetic concerns. While most target sizes are in the thousands, they are generally less than genetic arguments require, based on a N_e/N ratio of about 0.1. The numbers for peregrine falcons and California condors are particularly alarming at about 900 and 450. The peregrine falcon has now been de-listed as it exceeded its target population size.

Genetic goals in management of captive populations – a compromise

Captive populations of endangered species are usually managed to retain 90% of their genetic diversity for 100 years

There are many fewer captive breeding resources available than would be required to maintain all the species deserving captive breeding, especially if the numbers recommended above are used (e.g. $N_e = 500$ per species). Zoos house about 540 000 mammals, birds, reptiles and amphibians. At most, only half of the spaces are suitable for propagating endangered animals (Conway 1986). It is estimated that about 2000 vertebrate species require captive breeding to save them from extinction (Tudge 1995). To maintain each of these species at an effective size of 500 (assuming $N_e/N = 0.3$ in captivity) would require 3.3 million animal spaces, about 12 times the space available for captive breeding. At an average population census size of 500, only 540 species can be accommodated. Currently only 15% of mammal spaces in zoos house threatened species (Magin et al. 1994), and the situation is even worse than indicated above. There is a trade-off. If some loss of genetic diversity is accepted, smaller populations of more species can be accommodated.

The current compromise is to manage endangered species in captivity to conserve 90% of the wild population's genetic diversity for 100 years. The background to the 100 years time frame is that wild habitat may become available following the predicted human population decline in 100–200 years (Soulé et al. 1986). This requires different sized populations for species with different generation lengths. An approximate expression for the required size can be obtained using Equation 10.1, as follows:

$$H_t/H_0 = (1 - 1/2N_e)^t \sim e^{-t/2N_e}$$

Upon taking natural logarithms, substituting 0.9 for H_t/H_0, $100/L$ for t (where L is generation length in years), and rearranging, we obtain

$$N_e = 475/L \qquad (14.9)$$

Consequently, the required size is inversely proportional to the generation length for the species in question. A range of examples is given in Table 14.4. For example, the effective size required to maintain 90% of the original heterozygosity is 475 for a species with one generation per year, 18 for Caribbean flamingos with a generation time of 26 years and 1759 for the white-footed mouse with a generation length of 14 weeks. This is one of the few circumstances where long-lived species are at an advantage.

Maintaining 90% of genetic diversity for 100 years is a reasonable practical compromise. However, even with this compromised goal, it is unlikely that all the species requiring captive breeding can be accommodated. Species are being maintained with lesser goals (and smaller sizes) due to shortage of resources.

The cost of this compromise is increased inbreeding and reduced reproductive fitness. From Chapter 11:

$$F = 1 - (H_t/H_0)$$

The accepted 10% loss of heterozygosity corresponds to an increase of F of 10%, with consequent inbreeding depression. After 100 years, individuals will be related to each other to a degree somewhere between that of first cousins ($F = 0.0625$) and half-siblings ($F = 0.125$). This will reduce juvenile survival on average by about 15% and total fitness by about 25%, in captivity (Chapter 12). The fitness costs are likely to be much greater if species are subsequently reintroduced into harsher wild environments (Crnokrak & Roff 1999). Thus, captive breeding programs are balancing the cost of permitting a moderate degree of inbreeding over 100 years against the benefits of maintaining additional endangered species within the limited resources available.

Table 14.4 | Effective population sizes required to retain 90% of original heterozygosity for 100 years in 11 different species with different generation times

Species	Generation time (years)	N_e
White-footed mouse	0.27[a]	1759
Striped grass mouse	0.75	633
Partula snail	5[b]	95
Brush-tailed bettong	6	79
Bullfrog	7	68
Siberian tiger	7	68
Nyala	8	58
Arabian oryx	10	48
African black-necked cobra	10	48
Mauritius pink pigeon	10	48
Indian rhinoceros	18	26
Caribbean flamingo	26	18
White-naped crane	26	18

Notes:
[a]Millar & Zammuto (1983).
[b] P. Pearce-Kelly (personal communication).
Source: Modified from Conway (1986).

Population sizes required to retain 90% of genetic diversity for 100 years are affected by small founder numbers, by rates of population growth and by N_e/N ratios less than unity

The discussion above ignores the bottleneck associated with founding populations and assumes that population numbers can immediately be raised to the desired size. Captive populations typically have few founders and grow slowly to their final sizes. Together these factors lead to greater losses of genetic diversity early in the captive breeding program than predicted above. Consequently, effective population sizes required to retain 90% of genetic diversity for 100 years are typically greater than given above. Box 14.2 illustrates the required size for the captive population of golden lion tamarins.

Box 14.2 | **Determining the effective population size required to maintain 90% of genetic diversity for 100 years in golden lion tamarins**

Calculating the N_e required to maintain 90% heterozygosity for 100 years (the target effective population size) requires knowledge of generation length, number of founders and potential population growth rate (to model the growth of the population from the founders to the required N_e).

Golden lion tamarins have a generation length (average age of reproduction) of about 6 years, started with about 15 effective founders and the population can grow as rapidly as 20% per year, although a more realistic value might be 10% per year. How does population growth rate affect the N_e required to meet these objectives?

Figure A, left panel, shows population (N_e) increase over time for the two different growth rates. Number of founders is set at 15. The right panel shows the loss of heterozygosity over time. The slower-growing population needs more time to reach a larger final size ($N_e = 312$) than the faster-growing population ($N_e = 155$). This is because the slower-growing population loses more heterozygosity early in its history than does the more rapidly growing population, and needs to grow to a larger final size to compensate for the early loss of heterozygosity.

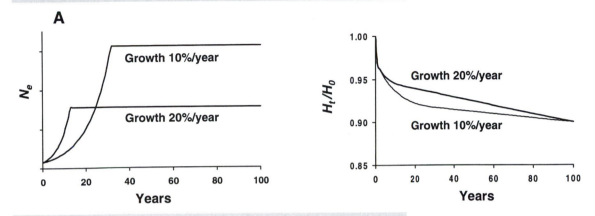

The number of founders also affects the required N_e. Figure B illustrates this bottle-neck effect on the target population size for two populations with the same growth rate (20% per year) but with different numbers of founders (15 and 30). The population with the fewer founders must reach a larger size ($N_e = 155$) than the population founded with 30 individuals ($N_e = 98$) due to loss of heterozygosity during its more severe founding bottleneck.

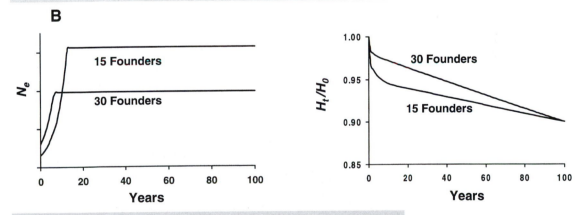

Genetic management of captive populations, by planned matings, allows N_e/N ratios to be higher than those in the wild. Typical N_e/N for captive populations is about 0.3. Thus, from the example above, the population size required to maintain 90% hetero-zygosity for 100 years in golden lion tamarins might range from 326 for a well-founded and rapidly growing population, to 1040 for a slow-growing population started with a small number of founders. The current population is being managed at about 500 individuals (Box 18.1).

Frequently, the desired population size is larger than the number of spaces available. This is often the case for small mammals with short generation lengths. Black-footed ferrets require over 19 000 individuals to maintain 90% of their heterozygosity for 100 years. Their generation length is about 2.5 years and they started with only eight effective founders.

When requirements exceed the available resources, the program must accept either that the population will become more inbred than 10%, or that the time frame for management is shorter than 100 years. For example, with black-footed ferrets, the captive management objectives were adjusted to 90% retention of heterozygosity for 50 years. The shorter time frame was justified because a reintroduction program was implemented within the first three generations of founding the captive population (Ballou & Oakleaf 1989). Detailed treatment of genetic issues concerned with captive breeding and reintroduction is given in Chapters 17 and 18.

The fallacy of small surviving populations

The persistence of a few small populations following severe bottlenecks does not contradict the conclusions that inbreeding and loss of genetic diversity are normally deleterious and that population sizes in the thousands are usually required for long-term viability

Several species have survived bottlenecks of a few individuals, while others have survived at small sizes for considerable periods of time (Craig 1994) (although many more have gone extinct). For example, the golden hamster and Mauritius kestrel went through a bottleneck of a single pair (Groombridge *et al.* 2000). The northern elephant seal was reduced to 20–30 individuals. Several island birds, including the Chatham Island black robin and Seychelles warbler, have gone through serious bottlenecks and recovered (Dhondt & Mattysen 1993; Komdeur *et al.* 1998). The Mauritius pink pigeon has persisted at a population size of less than 20 for over 150 years, while the Socorro Island red-tailed hawk survived with 20 pairs of adults for over 120 years (Walter 1990). These and similar cases have led some authors to question the importance of inbreeding and loss of genetic diversity in population viability (see Craig 1994; Elgar & Clode 2001).

Do these cases refute the requirement for population sizes in the thousands for long-term viability? It is fallacious to argue from a few surviving bottlenecked populations, that bottlenecks do not lead to extinctions (Soulé 1987). This is akin to arguing that 'Granddad smoked 30 a day and lived to 80, so smoking doesn't contribute to cancer' (Sunnucks 2000a). While some bottlenecked populations have survived, we must not ignore those (the majority?) that have failed to do so (Laikre *et al.* 1997), or those that are trapped in the vortex leading to extinction (Fig. 2.3). An unbiased quantitative assessment of the relationship between population size and extinction rate in bighorn sheep found that small populations were more extinction prone than larger ones (Fig. 2.4).

The effects of inbreeding have a large stochastic element as they depend on the chance fixation of deleterious alleles. A modest proportion of populations deliberately inbred to essentially complete homozygosity survive in benign laboratory conditions (Frankham 1998). The small surviving populations of wildlife are not a random sample. They are likely to be the few exceptional survivors, i.e. they are analogous to the few highly inbred lines that survive, or the few heavy smokers who live long lives. Most of these small inbred wild populations will be highly vulnerable, as the extinction proneness of island populations attests (Frankham 1998).

Further, many remnant populations have benefited from intensive management. For example, northern elephant seals recovered following protection from hunting, Mauritius kestrels following banning of DDT use, European bison herds following protection from hunting and provision of supplementary feeding during winter and Seychelles warblers following translocation to nearby islands with greater food supplies.

Some island populations of threatened species survive as they lack the predators or diseases that drive mainland populations to extinction. For example, black-footed rock wallabies are being decimated on mainland Australia by introduced red foxes, but foxes are absent from the islands where the wallabies are found. Several island populations survive and some are numerically larger, but they show evidence of severe genetic problems (loss of genetic diversity and inbreeding depression; Eldridge *et al.* 1999; Groombridge *et al.* 2000).

We should not let the occasional persistence of genetically impoverished populations mislead us. We wish to conserve the majority of threatened species, rather than permitting extinction of many species and conserving only a few exceptional cases.

The conclusions in this chapter set minimum population sizes only for genetic viability. They do not ensure sizes that are sufficient to minimize extinction risk in natural settings. In natural populations, demographic and environmental stochasticity and catastrophes, as well as genetic factors, combine to cause extinctions. The relative roles of these factors and their interactions will be considered in Chapter 20.

Summary

1. Since resources for maintaining threatened species in the wild and in captivity are limited, attempts have been made to define minimum sizes for genetically viable populations.

2. The size of populations required to avoid inbreeding depression is much greater than $N_e = 50$. All small populations of outbreeding species are likely to eventually suffer inbreeding depression. Times to extinction (in generations) due to inbreeding depression (in captivity) approximate the effective size of populations.

3. To retain evolutionary potential, effective population sizes of 500–5000 have been recommended, corresponding to actual population sizes of 5000–50000 in the wild.

4. Essentially all threatened species have reduced long-term evolutionary potential, as this is related to the logarithm of N_e, as well as to genetic diversity and reproductive rate.

5. The size of population required to avoid accumulation of new deleterious mutations is unclear and is a matter of controversy.

6. Current population sizes for most threatened species in the wild and in captivity are typically too small to avoid genetic deterioration within time frames of conservation concern.

7. Due to space and resource constraints, captive populations of endangered species are typically managed to retain 90% of the genetic diversity for 100 years.

8. The existence of a few cases where small populations have survived does not contradict the general rule that small populations are at a high risk of extinction.

FURTHER READING

Franklin (1980) The classic paper that provided the foundation for considering the genetic issues involved in defining viable populations for conservation.

Franklin & Frankham (1998) A response to Lande's (1995a) estimate that $N_e = 5000$ is required to retain evolutionary potential.

Lande (1995a) Revised the N_e required to maintain evolutionary potential from 500 to 5000. Also considers the likely impact of mutational accumulation.

Soulé (1987) *Viable Populations for Conservation*. A series of chapters considering different aspects of 'How large', both genetic and ecological. See especially Lande & Barrowclough's chapter and Soulé's Introduction and concluding remarks.

Soulé *et al.* (1986) Seminal paper on the issues described in this chapter. Proposed the captive breeding goal of retaining 90% of genetic diversity for 200 years (later modified to 100 years).

PROBLEMS

14.1 Evolutionary potential: If V_m is $3 \times 10^{-3} V_E$ and the heritability is 15%, what N_e is required to preserve short-term evolutionary potential?

14.2 Evolutionary potential: If 90% of mutations are deleterious, what N_e is required under the conditions in Problem 14.1?

14.3 Maintenance of genetic diversity: Derive the expression for the effective size required to maintain 95% of genetic diversity for 100 years.

14.4 Maintenance of genetic diversity: How large does a bank vole population, with three generations per year, need to be to retain 90% of its genetic diversity for 100 years?

14.5 Maintenance of genetic diversity: How large a population is required for the endangered palm cockatoo (generation length of 20 years) to retain 90% of its genetic diversity for 100 years?

14.6 Maintenance of genetic diversity: How many elephants (26 years per generation) and deer mice (three generations per year) are needed to maintain (a) 95% of the diversity for 100 years (b) 90% of original diversity for 50 years?

14.7 Evolutionary potential: The population size goal for the California condor recovery program is 150 birds in each of three populations (two wild and one captive). This is substantially less than the N_e needed to maintain evolutionary potential. Will the California condor go extinct because of this?

Section III

From theory to practice

In Sections I and II we covered the evolutionary genetics of populations and the deleterious genetic consequences of population size reduction. In Section III we apply this information to the genetic management of threatened populations and species.

Taxonomic uncertainties and management units

A critical first step in conserving a species is to gain a clear understanding of its taxonomy. Is the population of interest a unique species? Does it actually consist of multiple cryptic species? Or is it simply another population of a common species? Without this knowledge endangered species may be denied protection, or resources wasted on populations of common species. The use of genetic techniques to assist in resolving taxonomic uncertainties is described in **Chapter 15**. To do this we must first define what is meant by a species and consider briefly how speciation occurs. Populations within species may be so distinct that crosses suffer reduced reproductive fitness (outbreeding depression). Consequently, they may require management as separate entities. The chapter concludes by considering means for defining management units within species.

Management of wild populations

The genetic management of wild populations is considered in **Chapter 16**. Typically wild population management is concerned with increasing population sizes and alleviating the effects of population fragmentation. Species with inadequate gene flow among population fragments will suffer an insidious process of inbreeding depression, loss of genetic diversity and eventually population extinctions, unless gene flow is re-established. Sadly, there is limited activity in this area. Genetic management of fragmented populations represents the greatest unmet genetic challenge in conservation biology. The chapter also addresses the different management regimes required for species varying in breeding systems.

Captive management and reintroduction

A large and increasing number of species have had their numbers reduced to the point where they are at risk of extinction unless there is benign human intervention. In many cases the only way to save species from extinction is by *ex situ* **conservation**, i.e. to preserve species away from their natural habitats. About 2000 species of terrestrial vertebrates alone require captive breeding to save them from extinction. *Ex-situ* conservation takes many forms; it includes captive breeding in zoos, wildlife parks and aquaria, conservation of plants in botanical gardens and arboreta, seed storage, cryopreservation of animals, plants, cell cultures and gametes. However, space, numbers, costs, continuity and adaptation to captivity limit *ex-situ* conservation. It is most appropriate for large vertebrates and for plants. **Chapter 17** covers the genetic management of captive populations. Captive breeding of animals has been highly successful, with hundreds of captive breeding programs underway for threatened species. Maintaining viable populations with the potential for reintroduction to the wild is an objective of many of the programs. **Chapter 18** considers the genetic management of captive populations to minimize genetic changes that adversely affect reintroduction success, as well as the genetic issues involved in the reintroduction process itself. Reintroduction is a difficult and expensive process and, so far, has a relatively low success rate.

Use of molecular genetics in forensics and to understand species biology

Molecular genetic methods are being used in forensics to detect illegal hunting and trade in endangered species. These methods are also helping us understand the basic biology of species, knowledge necessary for their conservation (**Chapter 19**). Genotyping endangered species can be done following non-destructive sampling of hair, skin, egg shells, faeces, etc., and PCR amplification of DNA. Genetic markers can be used for resolving paternity, sexing birds and marine mammals, determining mating systems, population structure, dispersal rates, population size and diet, and detecting disease and hybridization with other species. Gene trees and coalescence provide powerful techniques for understanding many aspects of species biology.

The broader context

Wild populations in natural habitats suffer human impacts (habitat loss and degradation, over-exploitation, pollution and introduced species) and stochastic threats (demographic, environmental and genetic stochasticity, and catastrophes) that contribute to extinctions. **Chapter 20** discusses the combined impacts of all threatening processes, and so provides a connection between conservation genetics and broader issues in conservation biology. This chapter provides an introduction to the use of population viability analysis (PVA) for predicting the risk of extinction due to the combination of human impacts and stochastic factors, and as a tool to compare management options for species recovery.

Chapter 15

Resolving taxonomic uncertainties and defining management units

Taxonomic status must be accurately established so that endangered species are not denied protection, nor effort wasted on abundant species. Genetic information assists in resolving taxonomic uncertainties and is used to define management units within species

Terms:
Allopatric,
allopolyploidy,
autopolyploidy,
biological species concept,
coadapted gene complex,
conspecific,
evolutionarily significant units (ESU),
genetic distance,
lineage sorting,
management unit,
monophyletic,
outbreeding depression,
polyphyletic,
sibling species,
speciation,
sympatric,
taxa

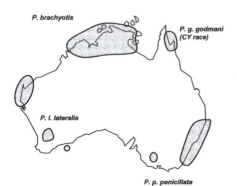

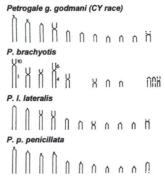

Rock wallabies in Australia, along with the chromosomes from a sample of species (after Eldridge 1991). Many are endangered.

Importance of accurate taxonomy in conservation biology

Many inappropriate conservation decisions can be made if the status of taxa is incorrect

The taxonomic status of, and relationships among, many taxa are unresolved. This is particularly true for lower plants and invertebrate animals, but also applies to large and obvious animals including deer, wallabies and wolves.

In conservation, many erroneous decisions may result if the taxonomic status of populations is not correctly assigned. These include:
- Unrecognized endangered species may be allowed to become extinct
- Incorrectly diagnosed species may be hybridized with other species, resulting in reduced reproductive fitness
- Resources may be wasted on abundant species, or hybrid populations
- Populations that could be used to improve the fitness of inbred populations may be overlooked
- Endangered species may be denied legal protection while populations of common species, or hybrids between species, may be granted protection.

This chapter explores the rationale and methodologies for defining taxonomic status. A similar approach can be used for practical definition of management units within species – genetically differentiated populations whose crossing can result in reduced population fitness (outbreeding depression). Further, taxonomic and phylogenetic distinctiveness may provide means for setting conservation priorities. For example, the unique tuataras are considered to have greater conservation value than an endangered species within a speciose genus (Crozier 1997).

Taxonomic uncertainties result from inadequate data. It is somewhat disconcerting that many species and sub-species descriptions trace to limited information on the geographic distribution of a small number of (usually morphological) traits of unknown genetic basis (Avise 1996). Velvet worms (Phylum Onychophora) in Australia provide an extreme example. Only seven named species were recognized in a 1985 review, based on morphology. However, over 100 clearly diverged species were identified using allozymes (Briscoe & Tait 1995).

Incorrect 'lumping' of several distinct species into one recognised species has denied protection to endangered species. The threatened tuataras in New Zealand, the only surviving members of an ancient reptilian order, are now known to include two species; one of which was at serious risk of extinction (Box 15.1). Likewise, the endangered Kemp's Ridley sea turtle is a genetically distinct species, rather than a form of a related non-endangered species, as was previously thought. It is now being afforded protection (Bowen & Avise 1996). The Office of Endangered Species in the USA ignored *Helianthus exilis,* a sunflower from California, as it was considered to be closely related to a sympatric sunflower with which it hybridized. However, allozymes, cpDNA and rDNA identified *H. exilis* as a distinct endangered species deserving conservation (Rieseberg 1991).

Conversely, 'splitting' of one species into two or more recognized taxa may lead to erroneous conservation decisions. Two rare flightless chafer beetles in New Zealand, previously considered to be different species, have been shown to belong to a single species, based on allozyme data (Emerson & Wallis 1994). Similarly, there is no genetic differentiation among the eight recognized morphological sub-species of North American pumas, including the critically endangered Florida panther (Box 15.1). The controversial northern spotted owl also involves questionable splitting (Box 1.1; Haig *et al.* 2001).

Probably the greatest confusion, and often acrimony, has arisen when hybrids among common species have been mis-identified as rare species deserving conservation. Examples include the Texan sunflower *Helianthus paradoxus* (Rieseberg 1991) and, more controversially, the red wolf (Fig. 15.1). Hybridization between populations whose taxonomy is incorrect has created problems in some conservation efforts. For example, while the last Norfolk Island boobook owl was successfully hybridized with its closest relative from New Zealand (Norman *et al.* 1998), the sole remaining dusky seaside sparrow was unsuccessfully hybridized with an inappropriate seaside sparrow sub-species and became extinct (Avise 2000). Ryder *et al.* (1989) found that infertility in a captive population of dik-dik was due to mixing of different chromosome races (probably undescribed species). A similar problem has been found in owl monkeys (Templeton 1986). Lack of recognition of the degree of genetic differentiation between the Bornean and Sumatran sub-species (possibly separate species) of orangutans previously led to their hybridization in many zoos (Box 15.2). Concerns about potential hybridization have influenced management decisions in the opposite direction. For example, two populations of Mexican wolf were kept separate from the one known small and inbred 'pure' population as it was suspected that they had hybridized with dogs, coyotes or gray wolves (Hedrick *et al.* 1997) (see Chapter 19).

Box 15.1	Taxonomic uncertainty in tuataras and North American pumas and their conservation implications (Daugherty *et al.* 1990; Culver *et al.* 2000)

TUATARA

The threatened tuataras in New Zealand are the only survivors of the ancient reptilian Order Rhynchocephalia, and were thought to be a single species. Studies of different island populations, using both 25 allozyme loci and morphology, revealed that the 'species' consists of three distinct groups, *Sphenodon punctatus punctatus* in the north, a western Cook Straits sub-species (*S. p. western*), and *S. guntheri*. The latter was being neglected and at serious risk of extinction without active conservation management.

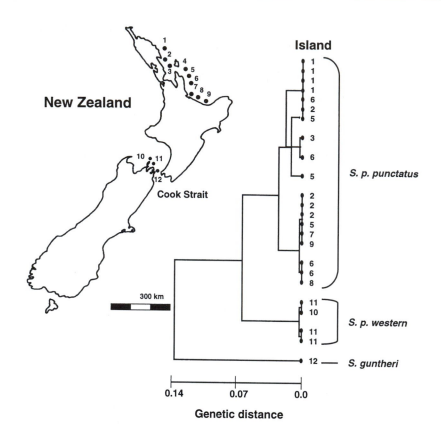

NORTH AMERICAN PUMAS

Mammalogists have recognized approximately eight morphological sub-species of North American pumas (also referred to as cougars, panthers and mountain lions), including the critically endangered Florida panther. However, microsatellite and mtDNA analyses found no significant differentiation among the populations, but did separate these from a number of South American sub-species.

An important conservation implication is that the number of separate sub-species requiring conservation is reduced. Further, the recent controversial decision to augment Florida panthers with individuals from the Texas sub-species, to remove inbreeding depression, can now be recognized as a logical management action involving only simple translocation of animals.

In practice, the taxonomy of particular groups of populations can usually be resolved with sufficient morphological, reproductive and genetic data. Genetic markers including chromosomes, microsatellites, allozymes, mtDNA and DNA fingerprints can frequently help. However, to appreciate this use of genetic markers, we must first review what is meant by a biological species, what we seek to conserve and how populations differentiate and speciate.

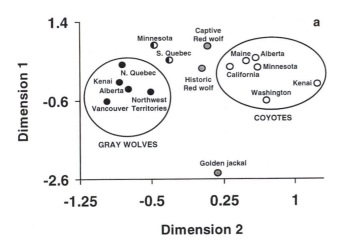

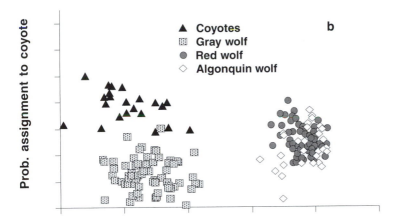

Fig. 15.1 Is the red wolf a distinct species, or a hybrid between wolves and coyotes? (Wayne 1996; Wilson *et al.* 2000).

The endangered red wolf in the southern USA has variously been considered to be either a separate species, or a hybrid population between gray wolves and coyotes. It is subject to a captive breeding and reintroduction program requiring substantial financial resources. Using 10 microsatellites and mtDNA, Wayne and colleagues concluded that the red wolf was a hybrid population, derived from gray wolves and coyotes. The red wolf contained no alleles that were not also present in gray wolves or coyotes. The microsatellite data revealed that red wolves were intermediate between gray wolves and coyotes, consistent with it being a hybrid.

(a) Two-dimensional scaling of microsatellite data for red wolves, gray wolves and coyotes. The gray wolf circle encompasses non-hybridizing populations, while the Minnesota and southern Quebec populations have introgression from coyotes. The red wolves are intermediate between 'pure' gray wolves and coyotes, as expected if they are a hybrid population (from Wayne 1996).

(b) Recent work has reopened this controversial case. Wilson *et al.* (2000) have suggested that a small-bodied (Algonquin) wolf in eastern Canada is distinct from the gray wolf but very similar to the red wolf. Microsatellite data and mtDNA sequence data both indicated clustering of Algonquin and red wolves as a distinct group from coyotes and gray wolves.

What is a species?

Most named species have been delineated, on the basis of morphological characteristics, as groups of individuals that are distinct from all other groups. However, morphological definitions of species may have limited connection to genetics or evolution. Some groups of individuals, for example the Australian velvet worms, initially appear morphologically indistinguishable, but are composed of two or more distinct species (cryptic or **sibling species**). Chinese and Indian muntjac deer are morphologically similar, yet the former has 46 chromosomes, while the latter has 6 in males and 7 in females, and they are clearly distinct species (Ryder & Fleischer 1996).

Confusingly, there is no universally accepted definition to answer the question 'What is a species?' At least 22 definitions exist (Claridge *et al.* 1997). These include morphological species, through ecological and genetic species to biological, evolutionary and phylogenetic species. Some definitions can, and have, classified the sexes of one species as separate species. Other definitions are based on evolutionary units and gene flow.

The **biological species concept** has been the most influential definition of species in population and evolutionary genetics and in conservation biology. This defines a species as a group of actually, or potentially, interbreeding individuals and natural populations that cannot interbreed with individuals from all other such groups (Simpson 1961; Mayr 1963). Dobzhansky *et al.* (1977) defined species in similar terms: 'In sexually reproducing organisms species can be defined as Mendelian populations, or arrays of Mendelian populations, between which the gene exchange is limited or prevented by reproductive isolating mechanisms. An isolating mechanism is any genetically conditioned impediment to gene exchange between populations.' Both of these definitions recognize that individuals within a species can exchange genes, while those from different species normally do not.

These definitions provide practical means for delineating species genetically. Groups of individuals sharing the same area will be exchanging genes if they are **conspecifics**, but not if they belong to separate species. Geographically separated populations of the same species will be capable of crossing and producing fertile offspring in the first and subsequent generations. Conversely, populations of different species will either fail to mate, or produce offspring with reduced survival or fertility. For example, lions and tigers can be hybridized, but their progeny are sterile.

The biological species concept does not deal adequately with asexual, parthenogenetic and habitually inbreeding forms, becomes blurred for species that hybridize and has little relevance to classification of fossil specimens. Given these limitations, it is not surprising that the biological species concept is less accepted by botanists than zoologists (Briggs & Walters 1997). The evolutionary species concept also encapsulates much of what we wish to define. Here a species is 'an entity composed of organisms which maintains its identity from other such entities through time and over space, and which has its own independent evolutionary fate and historical tendencies' (Mayden 1997). While this concept has much to recommend it, it is not as widely applied as it deserves. The evolutionary species concept perhaps accords best with the entities we seek to conserve, followed closely by the biological species concept. The US Endangered Species Act is based on the biological species concept, but it has encountered difficulties by excluding hybrids from conservation and by not dealing adequately with asexual forms. Lack of a universally recognized definition of species creates enormous difficulties in conservation biology. The World Conservation Union has devised objective criteria for defining endangerment (Chapter 1). It is to be hoped that the Union, or an equivalent body, will now address the issue and formulate an internationally acceptable definition of species for conservation usage.

Sub-species

Threatened **sub-species** are frequently accorded legislative protection, and are the focus of substantial conservation effort. Sub-species are groupings of populations, within a species, that share a unique geographic range or habitat and are distinguishable from other subdivisions of the species by multiple, independent, genetically based traits (Avise & Ball 1990; O'Brien & Mayr 1991). Members of different sub-species do not normally exhibit marked reproductive isolation. They can usually produce fertile offspring, although there may be some reduction in fertility or survival of crossed offspring. Crosses between the Bornean and Sumatran sub-species of orangutans produce fertile offspring with no apparent reduction in survival rates.

> Sub-species are partially differentiated populations within a species

The concept of sub-species is more subjective than that of species. They may best be considered as populations partway through the evolutionary process of divergence towards full speciation. By some definitions, such as the phylogenetic species concept (Claridge *et al.* 1997), sub-species would be raised to the status of species.

Higher taxonomic categories

Higher taxonomic categories (genus, family, order, class, phylum, superphylum and kingdom) are used to organize organisms into hierarchical groups that (preferably) reflect their evolutionary origins. They have been based previously upon a largely unspecified mix of similarity by resemblance and similarity by descent (Avise & Johns 1999). However, there has been considerable movement, over the last few decades, towards **monophyletic** classifications. In these, all members of a particular taxon are descended from a single common ancestor. Taxa containing members from diverse ancestral lineages are termed **polyphyletic**.

> There are no objective criteria to define higher taxonomic categories of genus, family, order, class, phylum and kingdom

The inclusiveness of higher taxonomic categories is very arbitrary. For example, some species of fruit flies within the genus *Drosophila* last shared a common ancestor over 40 million years ago, whereas some primates, currently placed in different families, only separated within the last few million years. Some cichlid fish placed in different genera diverged within the last few thousand years. Recently, Avise & Johns (1999) proposed that taxonomic categories, above the species level, be defined by times since isolation from a common ancestor, and that times be determined using a molecular clock based on multilocus DNA sequence data complemented by fossil evidence. This proposal has much to recommend it, but there is no current agreement to implement it. Such an approach would facilitate proposals to use diversity in DNA information content in setting conservation priorities (Crozier 1997). Phylogenetic and taxonomic distinctiveness would correspond and provide the basis for comparing the conservation value of different species.

How do species arise?

Speciation involves the genetic divergence of populations until they are reproductively isolated

Species arise in two ways. The first is gradual change within a lineage, i.e. a species changes so much over time that it is considered to be a different species at a later time. The second is diversification, when a prior species gives rise to two or more descendant species. This occurs when populations genetically differentiate, become reproductively isolated and are said to have speciated. Speciation frequently involves, at least partial, physical isolation. We are concerned with the diversification of species in this chapter.

Isolating factors

Populations may become isolated by geographic features (allopatry), or a change (e.g. host shifts) within the same environment (sympatry)

Physical isolating factors often result from geographic phenomena (mountain uprises, desertification, river changes, sea-level rises and continental drift) or from spread of organisms to novel territories. In this case speciation is termed **allopatric**. This is a very common form of speciation (Mayr 1963). Mayr suggested that all speciation was allopatric, based largely on his studies of speciation in birds, but this is no longer widely accepted (Howard & Berlocher 1998).

Speciation may also occur within the range of the ancestral species, **sympatric** speciation, such as host shifts. For example, hawthorn flies court and mate on the developing fruits of their host plants. They began to utilize apples in 1864 and cherries in 1960 (Howard & Berlocher 1998). As these trees have somewhat different fruiting times, this provided an isolating mechanism and selective forces driving differentiation among populations on the different hosts. Bush (1975) suggested that this is a common form of speciation in parasites. Evidence for the importance of sympatric speciation is accumulating (Howard & Berlocher 1998). While both forms of speciation occur, definitive evidence on their relative importance is not yet available.

Other mechanisms for speciation have been suggested. White (1978)

considered that chromosomal change was fundamental to speciation, and was attracted to the idea that reduced fitness in hybrids produced at the overlap of chromosomal races provided a driving force for evolution of reproductive isolation. However, as most species lack chromosomal races, and some related species have identical chromosome configurations, this is unlikely to be a universal speciation mechanism.

Recent evidence indicates that adaptation to distinct environments has an important, or even predominant, role in leading to reproductive isolation (Schemske 2000). For example, three-spine stickleback fish in three isolated lake populations in western Canada independently evolved benthic (bottom dwelling) and limnetic (open water) forms with different sizes and diets, following glacial retreat 10 000 years ago (Rundle *et al.* 2000). Tests of mating preference revealed that benthics from different lakes were not reproductively isolated, nor were limnetics from different lakes. However, benthics and limnetics from the same or different lakes showed reproductive isolation.

> Reproductive isolation arises from adaptation to different environments

'Instant' speciation

Many plant species have arisen 'instantly' via **polyploidy** (Ramsey & Schemske 1998) when the chromosome number increases by a multiple greater than 2 of the basic haploid number (n) to $3n$ (triploid), $4n$ (tetraploid), $6n$ (hexaploid), $8n$ (octoploid), etc. These forms are, to a large degree, isolated from their diploid (or other) progenitors. For example, the giant California redwood tree is a hexaploid with 66 chromosomes while its closest related living relative has $2n = 22$ (Lewis 1980).

> Many plant species have been formed due to polyploidy

Two forms of polyploidy occur, **autopolyploidy** and **allopolyploidy**, the latter being much more important in nature (Futuyma 1998). Autopolyploids form by increasing the number of sets of chromosomes from within a species, presumably by production of diploid gametes. For example, there are both diploid ($2n = 22$) and autotetraploid ($4n = 44$) forms of the endangered grassland daisy in eastern Australia (Young & Murray 2000).

Allopolyploid species form by combining the complete chromosomal constitutions from two pre-existing species, as described for the rare allotetraploid Hong Kong lady's tresses orchid in Fig. 15.2.

The frequency of polyploidy varies among plants, being 47%–70% in angiosperms, 95% in pteridophytes (ferns), but only 5% in gymnosperms overall and 1.5% in conifers (Lewis 1980; Grant 1981). Polyploidy is much rarer in animals (especially mammals and birds) than in plants. Sexually reproducing polyploids are known in a few groups of fish and frogs, but polyploid animals are more frequently parthenogenetic (asexual), for example some amphibians, reptiles and insects (Lewis 1980). Polyploid animals of conservation concern include many tetraploid salmonid fish (Allendorf & Waples 1996). In this family 22 species, including Apache trout, cutthroat trout, Gila trout, sockeye salmon and chinook salmon are listed as threatened.

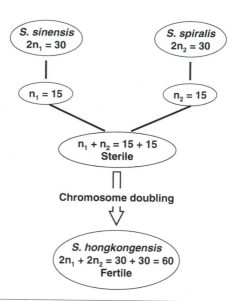

Fig. 15.2 'Instant' speciation in the rare Hong Kong lady's tresses orchid through allopolyploidy (after Sun 1996). The rare orchid *Spiranthes hongkongensis* is an allotetraploid with 60 chromosomes. It arose from the hybridization of two diploid ancestors each with 30 chromosomes (*S. sinensis* and *S. spiralis*) which have distributions that overlap in the Himalayas.

The probable mode of formation for *S. hongkongensis* is indicated above. The initial cross between the diploid progenitor species yielded a sterile hybrid. A spontaneous doubling of chromosome numbers, presumably in a flower meristem (or production of rare diploid gametes), generated gametes that yielded a fertile allopolyploid. Evidence from allozymes indicates that allotetraploid *S. hongkongensis* formed only once as almost all individuals have the same multilocus genotype. This orchid can cross with its diploid progenitor *S. sinensis*, but the progeny are infertile triploids.

Speciation is generally slow

Speciation takes at least thousands of years and generally millions of years, apart from that due to polyploidy

Most speciation occurs gradually over long periods of time, presumed to be thousands to millions of years (Futuyma 1998). For example, some plant populations that have been geographically isolated for at least 20 million years, such as American and Asian sycamores and plantains, form fertile hybrids. Similarly, European and American forms of birds, such as tits, creepers and ravens are so similar that they are classified as the same species. Some cases of speciation have been more rapid, but still involve many thousands of years. For example, some populations, including polar bears and voles, separated by Pleistocene glaciation 1.8 million years ago have developed at least partial reproductive isolation. On average, fruit flies (the best-studied group) take 1.5–3.5 million years of separation to speciate (Coyne & Orr 1989). However, Hawaiian fruit flies have speciated in as little as 500 000 years. Hawaiian honeycreepers

(Chapter 3 frontispiece) diverged and speciated from a finch-like ancestor in 3–5 million years. One of the most rapid cases of speciation is the development of endemic species of cichlid fish in Lake Nabugabo, Africa that has only been isolated from Lake Victoria for 4000 years. About 170 species of cichlids evolved in Lake Victoria itself, even though it is only 500 000 to 750 000 old. They are now being exterminated by an introduced carnivorous fish.

As evolution is an ongoing process, some populations will be observed partway through the speciation process. They are partially differentiated, show some reproductive isolation and are very difficult to classify. Sub-species may typically represent populations progressing towards full species status. Rock wallabies in Australia, many of which are endangered, are examples of populations 'caught in the act' of speciating (Eldridge & Close 1992, 1993). Populations and species across Australia show varying degrees of differentiation in chromosomes, allozymes and mtDNA and often have only partial reproductive isolation. Several hybrid zones have been discovered.

Use of genetic markers in delineation of sympatric species

Sympatric populations share the same, or overlapping, geographic distributions. According to the biological species concept, sympatric populations of the same species should exchange alleles, while distinct species sharing the same geographic region should not. Consequently, if any genetic marker shows lack of gene exchange, two sympatric populations belonging to different species have been identified. In practice, several loci are required for such diagnoses. For example, two sympatric forms of potoroos (small marsupials) in southeastern Australia were shown to be different species based on their different chromosome numbers and the lack of shared alleles at five allozyme loci (Fig. 15.3). Clearly, the two forms are reproductively isolated. The long-footed potoroo exists in very low numbers and is an endangered species. Morphologically similar velvet worms from the same log in the Blue Mountains inland from Sydney, Australia had fixed differences at 86% of 21 allozyme loci. Consequently, they were clearly different species that had diverged millions of years ago. Subsequently, many cryptic sympatric species of velvet worm have been revealed using electrophoresis (Briscoe & Tait 1995). Many of these are likely to be threatened species.

If two sympatric populations share alleles at all loci, then the hypothesis that they are the same species cannot be rejected. If sufficient loci are studied, then conspecificity is confirmed. For example, two rare, different-coloured sympatric chafer beetles from New Zealand were found to belong to the same species based on allozymes and morphology (Emerson & Wallis 1994).

> Genetic markers can be used to provide a definitive diagnosis of the taxonomic status of sympatric populations

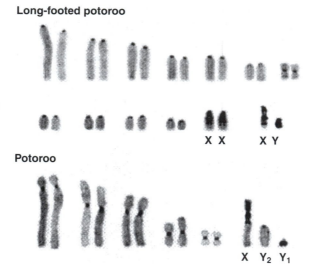

Long-footed potoroo

Potoroo

X Y₂ Y₁

Fig. 15.3 Two sympatric potoroos (macropods) in southeastern Australia belong to separate species, as indicated by lack of gene exchange (Seebeck & Johnson 1980). Potoroos are small nocturnal marsupials, akin to pint-sized kangaroos. Between 1967 and 1978, four potoroos were collected in southeastern Australia that appeared to differ from the potoroo species known to occur in that area. These specimens had longer hind feet and were about twice the size of the other sympatric potoroos. The presence of two species was confirmed by chromosome analyses showing that the long-footed potoroo had 24 chromosomes, while the previously described potoroo had 12 in females and 13 in males (chromosomes from Johnston et al. 1984). Further five of 22 allozyme loci show no electrophoretic alleles in common.

Allopatric populations that differ chromosomally are normally distinctive species. However, the use of other genetic markers is less definitive, and requires calibration against genetic differentiation of other recognized species

Use of genetic markers in delineation of allopatric species

Physical isolation of allopatric populations may deny opportunity for exchange of genetic material. In this case, the biological species concept would require evidence from crosses between the populations. Hybrid sterility, or markedly reduced survival, would indicate separate species. Conversely, if the hybrids were fully viable and fertile through several generations, then the populations belong to the same species. Such crosses are often impractical, especially in threatened species.

Consequently, genetic markers are often used to delineate allopatric species. Fixed chromosomal differences normally provide definitive evidence for distinct species status, as many chromosomal differences result in partial sterility in heterozygous individuals. Chinese and Indian muntjac deer are morphologically similar, but are clearly distinct species as the former has 46 chromosomes, while the latter has 6/7 (Ryder & Fleischer 1996). Similarity of chromosomes in allopatric populations is not definitive evidence that they belong to the same species.

Classification based on molecular markers is more arbitrary than for sympatric species, as it is based on inferred reproductive isolation. In practice, two populations are considered to be different species if they are as genetically differentiated as are two well-recognized species in a related group. For example, Bornean and Sumatran orangutans differ in mtDNA, proteins and DNA fingerprints, and by a pericentric chromosomal inversion, and are as different as other well-known primate species. Consequently, it has been suggested that they be classified as different species, as opposed to two sub-species (Box 15.2). However, crosses between the two forms are viable and fertile in the F_1 and F_2. Genetic markers have been used to establish that newly discovered forms of mammals in Vietnam and Laos are distinct from known species. For example, the saola or Vu Quang bovid has been identified as a distinct species based on morphology and DNA analyses (Whitfield 1998). Only a few hundred individuals of this species seem to exist, so it is probably endangered.

| Box 15.2 | Genetic differentiation between Bornean and Sumatran orangutans. Are they separate species? (Xu & Arnason 1996; Zhi et al. 1996) |

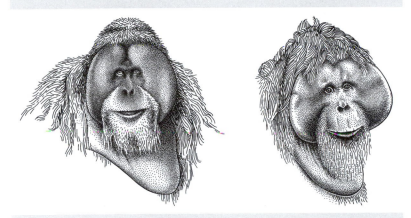

Bornean and Sumatran orangutans are restricted to their respective islands in Southeast Asia. They differ in morphology and behaviour, and have been designated as sub-species. Bornean and Sumatran orangutans differ by a pericentric chromosomal inversion (a reversed chromosomal segment), and in protein coding nuclear loci, DNA fingerprints and mtDNA sequences. Estimates of time since divergence from a common ancestor average 1.7 million years, far more ancient than the separation of Borneo and Sumatra by rising sea levels 10 000–20 000 years ago. As they differ genetically by at least as much as do the clearly recognized chimpanzees and bonobos, full species status for the two forms has been suggested. However, recent

Sumatran

```
  1 TTCTTTCATGGGGGACCAGATTTGGGTGCCACCCCAGTACTGACCCATTTCTAACGGCCTATGTATTTCGTACATTCCTGCTAGCCAACATGAATATCAC
  1 .............T..........A...........C..........C.G........................C...............
  1 .............T..........A...........C..........C.G........................C...............
  1 .............T..........A...........C..........C.G........................C...............
```

Bornean

```
101 CCAACACAACAATCGCTTAACCAACTATAATGCATACAAAACTCCAACCACACTCGACCTCCACACCCCGCTTACAAGCAAGTACCCCCCCATGCCCCCC
101 ......................C.....CA........G.C.A.T.....C.A....T..C.......................
101 ......................C.....CA........G.C.A.T.....C.A....T..C.......................
101 .............A........C.....CA........G.C.A.T.....C.A.....A.........................
```

morphological studies reveal an even more complex story. Skulls of individuals from southwestern Borneo were as distinct from skulls from the remainder of Borneo as those were from Sumatra (Groves *et al.* 1992).

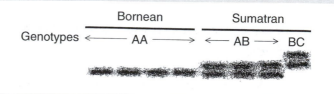

Hybrids are found in many zoos and are viable and fertile in the F_1 and F_2 generations (Muir *et al.* 1998). Consequently, they cannot be recognized as distinct species according to the biological species concept, but they can be so recognized under other definitions of species. This illustrates the confusion created by different species definitions, and the proposal to classify them as separate species has been challenged (Muir *et al.* 1998). Regardless of their formal taxonomic status, they represent different evolutionary units and should be managed as separate entities.

If differentiation between allopatric populations is much less than that between two well-recognized species in the same or related genera, then the populations are considered to be conspecific. For example, the colonial pocket gopher population from Georgia, USA consisted of fewer than 100 individuals in the 1960s and was listed and managed as an endangered species. Subsequent analyses based on morphology, allozymes, chromosomes and mtDNA revealed no consistent differences between this population and nearby populations of the common southeastern pocket gopher. On this basis, the colonial pocket gopher does not warrant recognition as a separate species (Laerm *et al.* 1982).

There is only limited evidence on the ability of morphology, chromosomes, allozymes, nuclear DNA markers and mtDNA to correctly predict taxonomic status as determined by breeding experiments. Data on rock wallabies in Australia suggest that chromosomes provide better predictions of hybridization results than allozymes (Eldridge & Close 1992), as do data on Australian rodents (P. Baverstock *et al.* personal communication). Unfortunately, chromosomal analysis is currently out of favour for delineating taxonomic status.

Mitochondrial DNA is one of the most commonly used genetic markers to delineate taxa. However, it has a number of limitations. First, mtDNA differentiation can be produced by lack of female dispersal, while male dispersal may be keeping populations genetically undifferentiated. Second, mtDNA patterns in different populations can also be misleading as a result of selection (Box 15.3). Third, mtDNA behaves as only a single inherited unit. If the foundation population, before divergence, is polymorphic, then drift can lead to incorrect phylogenies (Box 15.3; Nei 1996). Consequently, it is unwise to use mtDNA as the sole basis for delineating taxonomic status.

In the absence of crossing data, the most convincing delineations of species are based on chromosomes, or the concordance of a wide array of information including morphology, breeding behaviour, nuclear markers (allozymes, DNA markers) and mtDNA.

Measuring differences between populations: genetic distance

The extent of reproductive isolation among populations is correlated with their genetic differentiation (Table 15.1; Coyne & Orr 1989). To delineate allopatric populations as separate species on the basis of similar genetic differentiation to that among 'good' species in related groups, we require a measure of genetic differentiation, or **genetic distance**. The most commonly used measure is Nei's genetic distance D_N (Nei 1987). First we define Nei's index of genetic similarity I_N

> Nei's genetic distance is the most commonly used measure of genetic differentiation among populations and species

$$I_N = \sum_{i=1}^{m} (p_{ix} p_{iy}) \Big/ \left[\left(\sum_{i=1}^{m} p_{ix}^2 \right) \left(\sum_{i=1}^{m} p_{iy}^2 \right) \right]^{1/2} \quad (15.1)$$

and then transform this to obtain Nei's genetic distance

$$D_N = -\ln (I_N) \quad (15.2)$$

where p_{ix} is the frequency of allele i in population (or species) x, p_{iy} is the frequency of allele i in population (or species) y, and m is the number of alleles at the locus. I_N is related to the correlation in allele frequencies between populations.

When allele frequencies are similar in two populations ($p_{ix} = p_{iy}$), the genetic similarity approaches 1, and the genetic distance approaches zero. Conversely, when the two populations share no alleles, the index of genetic similarity is zero and the genetic distance is infinity.

Example 15.1 illustrates calculation of genetic distance from an allozyme locus in endangered red-cockaded woodpeckers. Estimates should be based on numerous polymorphic loci to provide reliable estimates of genetic distances (Nei & Takezaki 1994). The method for combining information for different loci is given by Nei (1987).

Example 15.1 | Calculation of Nei's genetic distance

Three populations of endangered red-cockaded woodpeckers have the following frequencies at the lactate dehydrogenase (Ldh) locus (from Stangel *et al.* 1992).

	Frequencies		
Ldh allele	Vernon	Apalachicola	Gameland
B	0.023	0.019	0.981
C	0.977	0.885	0.019
D	0.000	0.096	0.000

To calculate the genetic distance we need to compute the squares of the allele frequencies and the products of their frequencies between populations.

For the Vernon population the sum of the squared frequencies is

$$\Sigma\, p_{ix}^2 = 0.023^2 + 0.977^2 + 0.000^2 = 0.955$$

and for Apalachicola

$$\Sigma\, p_{iy}^2 = 0.019^2 + 0.885^2 + 0.096^2 = 0.793$$

The numerator is the sum of the cross products, as follows:

$$\Sigma\, (p_{ix}\, p_{iy}) = 0.023 \times 0.019 + 0.977 \times 0.885 + 0 \times 0.096 = 0.865$$

Consequently, Nei's genetic similarity for the Vernon and Apalachicola comparison is

$$I_N = \Sigma\, (p_{ix}\, p_{iy}) / [(\Sigma\, p_{ix}^2)\,(\Sigma\, p_{iy}^2)\,]^{1/2} = 0.865 / \sqrt{[0.955 \times 0.793]}$$

$$= 0.865/0.870 = 0.994$$

and the genetic distance is

$$D_N = -\ln (I_N) = -\ln (0.994) = 0.006$$

Consequently, the genetic distance between the Vernon and Apalachicola populations of the woodpeckers is 0.006, a very small genetic distance. Calculations of the genetic distances for Vernon–Gameland and Apalachicola–Gameland are given as Problems.

How large are genetic distances for 'good' species?

Genetic distances generally increase with level of reproductive isolation, but the relationship is very 'noisy'

Genetic distances generally increase as we progress up the taxonomic hierarchy from populations within species, to species, to genera, to families, etc. For example, average allozyme genetic distances increase with the level of reproductive isolation among forms of fruit flies (Coyne & Orr 1989). Genetic distances in the *Drosophila willistoni* species complex increases on average from geographically isolated populations (mean $D = 0.03$), to sub-species ($D = 0.23$), to sibling species ($D = 0.66$) and are highest for non-sibling species ($D = 1.04$).

Genetic distances for a range of species in different taxa are given in Table 15.1. Average genetic distances, for the same taxonomic hierarchy, differ markedly among groups (Table 15.1; Fig. 3.3). For example, differentiation among sub-species of peppers largely overlaps that among species of macaques, and genera of Galapagos finches. This emphasizes the arbitrary nature of taxonomic rankings. Designations of the status of taxa on the basis of genetic distance for allozyme loci are imprecise. A similar conclusion applies to mtDNA genetic distances in vertebrates (Johns & Avise 1998).

Table 15.1 Genetic differences (for allozyme loci) between local races, sub-species, species, genera and families, using Nei's genetic distance, D_N

Comparison	D_N
Local races	
Humans	0.011 − 0.029
Mice	0.010 − 0.024
Lizards	0.001 − 0.017
Fish	0.000 − 0.003
Horseshoe crabs	0.001 − 0.013
Drosophila willistoni group	0.008 − 0.049
Sub-species	
Red deer	0.016
Mice	0.194
Pocket gophers	0.004 − 0.262
Ground squirrels	0.103
Lizards	0.335 − 0.351
Drosophila willistoni group	0.228 ± 0.026
Plants (peppers)	0.02 − 0.07
Species	
Macaques	0.02 − 0.10
Ground squirrels	0.56
Gophers	0.12
Birds (*Catharus*)	0.01 − 0.028
Galapagos finches	0.004 − 0.065
Lizards (*Anolis*)	1.32 − 1.75
Lizards (*Crotaphytus*)	0.12 − 0.27
Amphisbaenian	0.61 − 1.01
Salamanders	0.18 − 3.00
Teleosts (*Xiphophorus*)	0.36 − 0.52
Teleosts (*Hypentelium*)	0.09 − 0.33
Fruit flies	
Sibling species	
Drosophila willistoni group	0.54 ± 0.05
pseudoobscura vs. *persimilis*	0.05
Non-sibling species	
obscura group	0.29 − 0.99
willistoni group	1.21 ± 0.06
Hawaiian species	0.33 − 2.82
Plants (peppers)	0.05 − 0.79
Genera	
Insectivora	0.42 − 1.10
Birds (Parulidae)	0.05 − 0.69
Galapagos finches	0.04 − 0.14
Fish (Scaenidae)	1.1 − 2.8
Fish (Plectonectidae)	0.47 − 1.3
Families	
Human–chimpanzee	0.62

Source: After Nei (1987).

Constructing phylogenetic trees

Information from genetic or morphological markers can be used to construct phylogenetic trees

We often wish to identify the most closely related population or sub-species to use in crossing programs to recover threatened species. Phylogenetic trees reflecting evolutionary relationships among species (or populations) can be constructed using genetic data (Hillis *et al.* 1996; Avise 2000; Nei & Kumar 2000). Example 15.2 provides a simple illustration of tree-building based on mtDNA sequence data for the Norfolk Island boobook owl and its nearest presumed relatives.

A large number of statistical methods are now available for deriving trees from molecular markers or from morphology, including distance matrix methods (UPGMA), maximum parsimony and maximum likelihood methods (Nei 1987; Hillis *et al.* 1996). Software packages are available for computation (e.g. PAUP, PHYLIP, HENNIG86, MacClade; Futuyma 1998). These methods have limited statistical foundation, but generally yield reliable trees if there is sufficient information, i.e. number of loci, number of nucleotides or amino acids or number of morphological characters, or preferably a combination of these (Nei 1996).

Example 15.2 | Building a phylogenetic tree from DNA sequence data

mtDNA sequence differences in the Norfolk Island (NI) boobook owl and its nearest presumed relatives are given below. The NI boobook owl declined to a single individual, and the best recovery option was to cross it to its most closely related sub-species. Crosses of the remaining female to a male from a related New Zealand (NZ) sub-species has yielded 16 F_1 offspring. Subsequent analyses of mtDNA sequences (298 bases of the cytochrome *b* locus) confirmed that the sub-species chosen for crossing was the most closely related and conformed with morphological data (Norman *et al.* 1998).

Comparison	mtDNA base pair differences
NI boobook – NZ boobook	2
NI boobook – Tas boobook	8
NZ boobook – Tas boobook	8
Powerful owl – rufous owl	13
NI boobook – powerful owl	21
NI boobook – rufous owl	23

By placing the nearest relatives closest together, we obtain the following tree. The lengths of the segments are proportional to the number of base differences between taxa, and therefore should approximate the evolutionary time since divergence. Thus, the branch lengths to the node below NI boobook and NZ boobook are 1 each (total of 2 differences between them). These differ from Tas boobook by 8 bases, so we attribute 4 to the segment from Tas boobook to the node below it, and 4 from the node to NI boobook and NZ boobook; 1 has already been attributed to the distance to the node to NI boobook and NZ boobook, so 3 is attributed to the section from their node to the joint node with Tas boobook. Half of the difference of 13 between powerful owl and rufous owl (6.5) is attributed to each path to their node. Finally the NI boobook–powerful owl and NI boobook–rufous owl average 22 bases different, so we attribute half of this (11) to each path to the lowest node. On the left-hand side we have already attributed 4, leaving 7 for the section to the lowest node. On the right-hand side, 6.5 has been allocated to the path to the first node, leaving 4.5 to allocated to the path from this node to the lowest node.

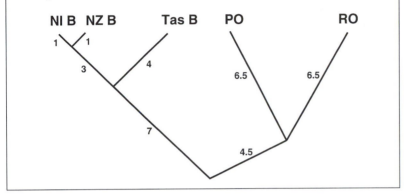

Box 15.3 illustrates hypothetical cases of sequence evolution and the phylogenetic trees that are inferred from their DNA sequences. Trees will accurately reflect evolutionary relationships only if the foundation population is monomorphic, rates of evolution in different lineages are constant (A) and selection does not operate on the markers. When rates of evolution are not equal in different lineages (B), the inferred tree does not agree with the real tree. Unequal rates of evolution could occur as a result of unequal rates of neutral mutations, or different rates of selective substitutions in different lineages, for example, if one lineage changed its habitat such that amino acid substitutions at a locus are favoured and driven to fixation by natural selection. For example, in predatory snails, neurotoxin genes show high rates of evolution, presumably as a result of natural selection (Duda & Palumbi 1999), and would be likely to yield incorrect phylogenies.

When the starting population is polymorphic (C), as will frequently be the case, fixation of different initial sequences in different lineages (termed **lineage sorting**) may lead to incorrect inferred phylogenies. This situation can be resolved if data are available from many independent loci; Nei & Takezaki (1994) recommended about 30 polymorphic allozyme loci or 20 microsatellite loci. For example, problems have been encountered in inferring primate phylogenies. mtDNA data yielded phylogenies that are inconsistent with a wide array of morphological, behavioural and chromosomal evidence. The consensus phylogeny based on several nuclear loci is concordant with the other evidence (Herbert *et al.* 1999).

Trees based on genetic markers will only accurately reflect evolutionary relationships if rates of evolution are constant in different lineages, markers are neutral and the foundation population is monomorphic (or there are many independently inherited markers)

Box 15.3 | Use of DNA sequence data to build phylogenetic trees

The following hypothetical examples indicate the conditions where DNA sequence data are likely to result in reliable phylogenetic trees, and those where they are not. In each example, an initial sequence evolves as we move down the page, so that mutations (Δ, ∇) accumulate over time.

The correct phylogeny is only inferred in A with a monomorphic initial population and a constant rate of evolution in each lineage (branch). Conversely, incorrect phylogenies are likely when there is either unequal rates of evolution (B), or a polymorphic initial population (C). The latter problem can be overcome by using sufficient independently segregating loci (Nei & Takezaki 1994).

A. Monomorphic founding population.
   Constant rate of evolution

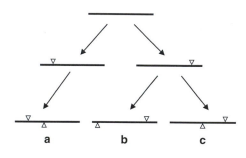
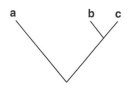

B. Monomorphic founding population.
   Unequal rate of evolution (higher in lineage c)

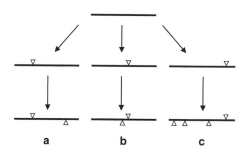
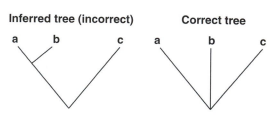

C. Polymorphic founding population.
   Constant rate of evolution

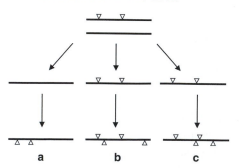
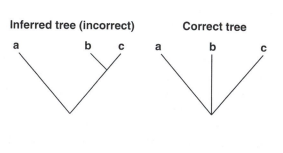

Phylogenetic trees, or 'gene trees', are used for many other purposes in conservation biology (Chapter 19).

Outbreeding depression

A perceived concern with crossing of genetically differentiated populations is the risk that hybrid offspring in the F_1 and subsequent generations will suffer deleterious consequences termed **outbreeding depression**. A major reason for resolving taxonomic uncertainties is to avoid unwitting production of such crosses.

For example, there is reduced reproductive fitness and production of developmentally abnormal offspring in a zone of hybridization between two populations of velvet worms in eastern Australia (Sunnucks & Tait 2001). A less severe case of outbreeding depression is found in corroboree frogs in the mountains of southeastern Australia (Osborne & Norman 1991). Allopatric populations in the north and south of the range have subtle differences in colour pattern and skin alkaloids and exhibit a genetic distance of 0.17–0.49. Hybrids between the populations are fertile and viable, but display 17% larval abnormality, compared to < 4% in crosses within regions.

Currently, great caution is expressed about mixing populations. For example, Shields (1983) doubted the wisdom of crossing different populations of gray wolves, even though they clearly belong to the same species. Many population geneticists consider that concerns over outbreeding depression, for species whose taxonomy is clearly understood, are being taken unnecessarily far. Outbreeding depression is frequently mentioned, but the benefits of crossing are understated.

> Outbreeding depression describes the situation when crossing of populations results in reduced reproductive fitness

Extent of outbreeding depression in animals and plants

The extent and significance of outbreeding depression is a matter of controversy. Evidence for outbreeding depression in mammals and birds is scarce, apart from cases where the taxonomy has not been adequately resolved (Frankham 1995a). The most widely quoted, but anecdotal, example is ibex in the Tatra Mountains of Czechoslovakia (Turcek 1951). Following extinction of the previous population, animals were successfully re-established by translocating Austrian animals of the same sub-species. However the population was eliminated by subsequent introduction of desert-adapted animals of different sub-species from Turkey and from Sinai. The cause of extinction was disruption of the breeding cycle, with maladapted hybrids rutting in early autumn and, fatally, giving birth in February, the coldest month.

Lacy (1998) detected outbreeding depression for some traits in experimental crosses between different sub-species of mice, but this was small in comparison to the beneficial effects of crossing (heterosis).

> Outbreeding depression in crosses between populations within species has been documented in few cases in animals, but may be more common in plants

The endangered Arabian oryx is suffering simultaneously from both inbreeding depression and outbreeding depression, but there are chromosomal differences segregating in this population (Benirschke & Kumamoto 1991; Marshall & Spalton 2000). Outbreeding depression has been clearly documented in an intertidal copepod that shows marked genetic differentiation, and limited dispersal, over relatively short geographic distances (Burton *et al.* 1999). F_2 populations showed reduced fitness (i.e. hybrid breakdown) in developmental time and response to osmotic stress.

In several cases where outbreeding depression has been detected in animals, the presumed taxonomy proved to be erroneous. For example, crosses between different populations of owl monkeys and dik-diks resulted in sterile offspring (Templeton 1986). In both cases the two contributing forms came from different localities, had different chromosome numbers, and were most probably undescribed species or sub-species.

Outbreeding depression is more frequent when crosses occur between populations that have undergone significant adaptation to local conditions and when dispersal is limited. Not surprisingly, most evidence for outbreeding depression comes from plants with these characteristics (ecotypes) (Waser 1993; Dudash & Fenster 2000).

Dispersal rates are often lower in plants than in animals, especially for inbreeding species of plants. Dudash & Fenster (2000) found simultaneous inbreeding and outbreeding depression in an outbreeding legume in the USA, but outbreeding depression was only notable in crosses between populations from locations 2000 km apart. Badly needed, quantitative, estimates of the frequency, magnitude and distribution of outbreeding depression are not available.

Species and many well-defined sub-species have diverged to the point where crosses among them result in reduced fitness. Outbreeding depression in crosses between sub-species from widely different environments, such as those between ibex adapted to the environments of Austria or Sinai, is hardly surprising. As an extreme example, crosses between Bengal and Siberian tigers would not be expected to produce offspring fit for either environment.

> Outbreeding depression may be expected in crosses between different sub-species or species

Genetic basis of outbreeding depression

> Outbreeding depression may arises from combining alleles from populations adapted to different environments, so that the hybrid population is not well adapted to either environment

Outbreeding depression may arise due to two different mechanisms. First, outbreeding depression is usually attributed to genotype × environment interactions when populations are adapted to different environmental conditions (Fig. 15.4). The hybrid population will then contain genotypic combinations of alleles that may be less suited to either environment. Reduced fitness can be due to additive, dominant or more complex effects arising from the interactions among alleles from the different source populations. This may explain the case of the ibex. The F_1 hybrids between the European and Middle Eastern ibex calved at a time intermediate between those of the two parent populations (i.e. the

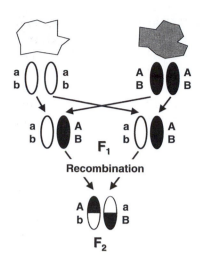

Fig. 15.4 Genetic mechanisms of outbreeding depression. The pedigree shows how genotypes and sets of loci (coadapted gene complexes) adapted to different local environments (shaded vs. unshaded) could reduce fitness of F_1 and F_2 hybrids (after Templeton & Read 1984). Here genotypes aabb and AABB are adapted to two different environments. Furthermore, the two loci a/b and A/B form a coadapted gene complex that has high fitness only when containing alleles from the same source population.

Fitness reductions in the F_1 can results when alleles from different populations form genotypes maladapted to the environment in which the F_1 reside. For example, aa and AA are adapted to their original environments, while the F_1 genotype Aa is adapted to neither. Fitness can be further reduced in the F_2 when recombination might break up the coadapted gene complex. After recombination, a is with B, and A is with b, the loci are no longer paired with alleles from the same source population.

alleles from the different source populations had an additive interaction). However, this was in mid-winter and all offspring died. In a similar manner, hybrids between two populations can be deleterious if the F_1 manifests the dominant phenotype of one parent, but this is deleterious in the environment of the population to which it has been introduced.

A more complex type of outbreeding depression occurs when different populations have evolved different **coadapted gene complexes**. Coadapted gene complexes are groups of loci whose fitness depends on interactions between loci (epistatic interactions). Particular combinations of alleles at different loci are needed to produce favourable effects. Recombination in hybrid populations produces new combinations of alleles that are deleterious. Outbreeding depression resulting from disruption of coadapted gene complexes has been shown in a copepod, mice and in the highly outcrossing legume *Chamaecrista fasciculata* (Lacy 1998; Burton *et al.* 1999; Dudash & Fenster 2000).

This form of outbreeding depression can also occur in crosses between different populations adapted to the **same** environmental conditions. For example, one population may have evolved genotype aabb and the other AABB (Fig. 15.4) because alleles a and b are beneficial together, as are A and B. When they are crossed, recombination among

Populations that have adapted utilizing different sets of interacting alleles (coadapted gene complexes) may show outbreeding depression as alleles are deleterious when recombined. This may occur for populations adapted to the same, or different environments

the genomes in hybrid populations produces new allelic combinations (e.g. AAbb and aaBB genotypes), that are deleterious.

Inbreeding depression and outbreeding depression due to disruption of coadapted gene complexes may be confused, as both are first manifested in the F_2 generation. However, techniques are available to distinguish and separate the two phenomena, whether the data being analysed are from population crosses (Lynch 1991) or from molecular markers (Coulson *et al.* 1998).

Even where outbreeding depression does occur when two partially inbred and differentiated populations are crossed, it will not be a long-term phenomenon. Unless the F_1 hybrid individuals are sterile, or of very low fitness, natural selection will act upon the extensive genetic variation in the hybrid population adapting it to its environment (Lewontin & Birch 1966). The hybrid population will usually, at worst, go through a temporary decline in fitness, and then increase.

> Even if crosses of populations result in outbreeding depression, natural selection will usually lead to rapid recovery and often higher eventual fitness

Defining management units within species

Species clearly require management as separate units. However, populations within species may be on the path to speciation. If they show significant adaptive differentiation to different habitats (ecological niches), or significant genetic differentiation, then they may justify management as separate evolutionary lineages for conservation purposes. The desirability of separate management depends on the balance between the cost of keeping two (or more) populations versus one, and risks of outbreeding depression, or benefits accruing from hybridizing the populations.

> Populations within species may be sufficiently differentiated in adaptive characteristics or genetic composition to require separate management

Defining **management units** within species is more difficult and controversial than defining species. Below we outline the concept of evolutionarily significant units, together with a more recent proposal to define such units.

Evolutionarily significant units (ESU)

Many authors believe that genetically differentiated populations within species should not be merged and require separate genetic management (see Moritz 1995). These populations are referred to as evolutionarily significant units. Initially the concept was applied to populations with reproductive and historical isolation and adaptive distinctiveness from other populations within the species (Crandall *et al.* 2000). Moritz (1995) suggested that genetic markers be used to define management units within species. If mtDNA shows significant divergence between populations, and monophyly within them, and nuclear loci show significant divergence of allele frequencies, then they should be defined as separate ESUs and managed separately. In broad terms this often means that well-defined sub-species are the unit of management, but such may not be the case in little-studied groups.

> An evolutionarily significant unit (ESU) is a population that has a high priority for separate conservation

While many ESUs have been defined in threatened species, the concept has been criticized on semantic and practical grounds. First, Cracraft (1997) has argued that evolutionarily significant units are essentially equivalent to, and should be abandoned in favour of, phylogenetic species. The second, and more serious criticism, is that genetically defined ESUs ignore adaptive differences (Crandall *et al.* 2000). ESUs are unlikely to be detected within species with high gene flow, even though populations may have adaptive differences and warrant separate management. Conversely, in taxa with low gene flow, populations that have differentiated by genetic drift may be designated as separate ESUs, even though they may not be adaptively distinct – in this case they may benefit from gene flow.

Defining management units on the basis of exchangeability

Crandall *et al.* (2000) proposed that populations be classified according to whether they show recent or historical ecological or genetic exchangeability. This proposal attempts to delineate whether there is adaptive differentiation, whether there is gene flow, and whether the gene flow is historical, or due to recent admixture. It then leads to management recommendations based upon the assessment. The authors claim that this system deals more adequately with many cases where the ESU process yielded outcomes of doubtful justification.

> Management units can be defined using ecological and genetic exchangeability

In practice, the populations are given + or − classifications in each of four cells, representing recent and historical genetic and ecological exchangeability (Fig. 15.5). This results in 16 categories of divergence between two populations (Fig. 15.5). In general, the more + scores the greater the differentiation. Genetic exchangeability is concerned with the limits of spread of new genetic variation through gene flow. Exchangeability is rejected (+) when there is evidence of restricted gene flow between populations ($Nm < 1$), while it is accepted (−) when there is evidence of ample gene flow. Evidence for gene flow is ideally based on multiple nuclear loci (allozymes, microsatellites, etc.), but could also be based on mtDNA or cpDNA.

Ecological exchangeability is based on the factors that define the fundamental niche and the spread of new genetic variants through genetic drift and natural selection. Ecological exchangeability is rejected (+) where there is evidence for population differentiation due to genetic drift or natural selection. Evidence can be based on difference in life history traits, morphology, habitat, QTL and loci under selection, and such differences should, ideally, be demonstrably heritable. We interpret this as primarily reflecting adaptive differentiation.

The recent and historical time frames are designed to distinguish natural evolutionary processes of limited gene flow (+ in the historical–genetic category) from recent population isolation (+ in recent–genetic). Further, they distinguish secondary contact (− in recent–genetic) from long-term gene flow (− in historical–genetic).

Recommended management actions are given for each of the eight categories in Fig. 15.5. Example 15.3 illustrates the application of the

Fig. 15.5 Defining management units within species on the basis of genetic and ecological exchangeability (Crandall et al. 2000). This method has been proposed for measuring categories of population distinctiveness, and consequent management actions recommended for each of the categories. Categories of population distinctiveness are based on rejection (+) or failure to reject (−) the null hypothesis of genetic and ecological exchangeability for both recent and historical time frames. As the number on the left-hand side of the table increases there is decreasing evidence for significant population differentiation.

H_o Exchangeability

	Genetic	Ecological
Time frame		
Recent		
Historical		

Relative strength of evidence (indicated by number)	Evidence of adaptive distinctiveness	Recommended management action
1	$\begin{array}{c c} + & + \\ + & + \end{array}$	Are separate species
2	$\begin{array}{c c c} + & + & + & + \\ - & + & + & - \end{array}$	Treat as separate species
3	$\begin{array}{c c} - & + \\ + & + \end{array}$	Treat as distinct populations (recent admixture, loss of genetic distinctiveness)
4	$\begin{array}{c c} + & - \\ + & + \end{array}$	Natural convergence on ecological exchangeability − treat as single population; or anthropogenic convergence − treat as distinct population
5	(a) (b) (c) $\begin{array}{c c c} + & + & - & + & - & - \\ - & - & - & + & + & + \end{array}$	(a) and (b) Recent ecological distinction, so treat as distinct populations; (c) Allow gene flow consistent with current population structure
6	$\begin{array}{c c} - & + \\ - & - \end{array}$	Allow gene flow consistent with current population structure; treat as distinct populations
7	$\begin{array}{c c} + & - \\ + & - \end{array}$	Allow gene flow consistent with current population structure; treat as a single population
8	$\begin{array}{c c c} + & - & - & - & - & - \\ - & - & - & + & + & - \end{array}$ $\begin{array}{c c c} + & - & - & + & - & - \\ - & + & + & - & - & - \end{array}$	Treat as single populations; if exchangeability is due to anthropogenic effects, restore to historical condition; if natural, allow gene flow

methodology to black rhinoceros, African elephants, Cryan's buck-moth and puritan tiger beetles. This methodology seems to provide a logical means for delineating populations that justify separate management, without having an excessive number of management units that do not show adaptive differentiation. By contrasts, the term ESU has been applied to every category in Fig. 15.5, leading to a very large number of management units, some with doubtful justification. For example, mtDNA analyses resulted in separate ESUs within African elephants, while the criteria of Crandall *et al.* (2000) treated this as due to genetic drift and so did not recommend separate management units. In a survey of 98 published studies, Crandall *et al.* (2000) found that over half fell into category 8 and so did not justify separate management units, while separate ESUs had been recommended for some of these.

Example 15.3	Assignment of black rhinoceros, African elephants, Cryan's buckmoth and puritan tiger beetles to the categories defined by Crandall *et al.* (2000)

BLACK RHINOCEROS

For the black rhinoceros in Africa, there are insufficient grounds to reject either genetic exchangeability or ecological exchangeability. Populations show gene flow and their habitats are similar. Consequently, it is classified as category 8 ($\frac{-}{-}\frac{+}{-}$), leading to the recommendation that the species be managed as a single population. Conversely, O'Ryan *et al.* (1994) used mtDNA data to argue for two sub-species with separate management.

AFRICAN ELEPHANT

Georgiadis *et al.* (1994) found a reciprocal monophyletic relationship among mtDNA of African elephants. These populations would be distinct ESUs according to the definition of Moritz (1995). However, Georgiadis *et al.* (1994) argued that the genetic divergence was simply isolation by distance due to drift across their geographic range. The habitat of different populations is sufficiently similar to accept ecological exchangeability. According to the categorization scheme of Crandall *et al.* (2000), the elephants would fall into category 8 ($\frac{+}{-}\frac{-}{-}$) and be managed as a single population, as recommended by Georgiadis *et al.* (1994).

CRYAN'S BUCKMOTH

For Cryan's buckmoth, Legge *et al.* (1996) found no evidence to reject genetic exchangeability based on either mtDNA or allozymes (there was adequate gene flow), yet there was evidence to reject recent, but not historical ecological exchangeability among populations ($\frac{-}{-}\frac{+}{-}$; category 6). Both the authors and Crandall *et al.* (2000) argued for the adaptive significance of the ecological differentiation and thus for the recognition of separate management units, although gene flow consistent with current population structure is allowable.

PURITAN TIGER BEETLE

Puritan tiger beetles from Connecticut River and Chesapeake Bay, USA are not genetically exchangeable, based on mtDNA (low gene flow and significant differentiation). Further they are not ecologically exchangeable based on habitat parameters. Thus they were classified as category 2 ($\frac{+}{+}|\frac{+}{-}$), indicating strong adaptive differentiation and the recommendation to manage the two populations as separate units for conservation purposes.

Summary

1. Correct diagnosis of taxonomic status of populations is critical for conservation purposes so that undiagnosed species are not left to become extinct, undiagnosed species are not hybridized with deleterious consequences, and resources are not wasted on populations belonging to common species, or hybrid populations that are not distinct species.

2. There is no universally accepted definition of species.

3. The biological species concept has been highly influential in population and conservation biology. It defines species as groups of actually, or potentially, interbreeding individuals that are isolated from other such groups.

4. According to this concept, genetic markers can be used to definitively diagnose species within sympatric populations as different species will not be exchanging genes.

5. For allopatric populations, definitive diagnosis of species requires information on the fertility and viability of crosses between populations. Chromosomal differences usually also lead to definitive classification. Molecular markers can also be used to assist in diagnosing taxonomic status, but this is more subjective and must be calibrated against genetic differentiation of known species in related groups of organisms.

6. Outbreeding depression is the reduction in fitness that can occur when some populations are crossed. It is more likely when there is local adaptation to different environments and restricted gene flow.

7. Populations within a species may justify management as separate units if they show adaptive genetic differentiation. Delineation of such populations requires information on their genetic and ecological exchangeability – if they show significant differentiation in both, they should be managed separately.

FURTHER READING

Avise (2000) *Phylogeography*. Recent textbook covering molecular methods in taxonomy.

Avise & Hamrick (1996) *Conservation Genetics*. Advanced scientific reviews that describe many cases of resolving taxonomic uncertainties with the aid of molecular genetic techniques.

Crandall *et al.* (2000) Newly proposed method for using genetic and ecological differences between populations within species as a basis for deciding on whether they deserve separate management.

Dudash & Fenster (2000) Excellent review paper on impacts of inbreeding and outbreeding in fragmented populations, with a plant emphasis.

Futuyma (1998) *Evolutionary Biology*. A textbook with an excellent readable coverage of speciation and the genetic processes underlying it.

Hillis *et al.* (1996) *Molecular Systematics*. A major book on inferring phylogenies using genetic markers.

Howard & Berlocher (1998) *Endless Forms*. Recent volume containing reviews on many aspects of speciation, with a heavy emphasis on sympatric speciation. Schemske (2000) provides an outstanding perspective on speciation in his review of this book.

Nei & Kumar (2000) *Molecular Evolution and Phylogenetics*. Textbook on genetic distances and building phylogenies.

Smith & Wayne (1996) *Molecular Genetic Approaches in Conservation*. A book containing scientific review chapters, many with cases where taxonomic uncertainties have been resolved with the aid of molecular genetic techniques.

PROBLEMS

15.1 Taxonomic uncertainties: Why are taxonomic uncertainties of conservation concern?

15.2 Taxonomy: What is meant by sympatric?

15.3 Taxonomic uncertainties: Sympatric populations show the following characteristics. Are they the same or different species? Why?

(a) Diploid chromosome number 20 in population A and 22 in population B.

(b) Allozyme frequencies at the Adh locus of SS in one population, and FF in the other (S and F represent slow and fast electrophoretic mobility).

(c) Microsatellite genotypes 11, 12 and 22 in one population and 33, 34 and 44 in another (1, 2, 3 and 4 are microsatellite alleles with different sizes).

(d) Microsatellite genotypes 11, 12 and 22 in one, and 11 in the other.

15.4 Taxonomy: What is meant by allopatric?

15.5 Taxonomic uncertainties: Allopatric populations show the following characteristics. Are they the same or different species? Why?

(a) Giant redwood trees in California have 66 chromosomes in all individuals, while a morphologically related plant population in China has 22 chromosomes in every individual (Lewis 1980).

(b) Tigers have an extensive distribution on the Asian mainland, while the Sumatran population is on an island isolated by rising water levels 6000–10000 years ago. Separation based on morphology is minimal, at best. Crosses between tiger sub-species are fertile. For mtDNA sequences in the cytochrome *b* locus, three bases out of 1140 show distinct differences between mainland and Sumatran tigers (Cracraft *et al.* 1998).

(c) Two populations of velvet worm (an invertebrate with limited dispersal), one from the Blue Mountains and the other from the

Border Range about 600 km away, show fixed differences at 70% of 20 loci surveyed (D. A. Briscoe & N. N. Tait personal communication).

15.6 Genetic distance: Calculate Nei's genetic distance for two populations x and y with the following frequencies for alleles at a single locus:

	Allele		
	1	2	3
(a) Population x	0.1	0.2	0.7
Population y	0.1	0.2	0.7
(b) Population x	0.5	0.5	0.0
Population y	0.0	0.0	1.0
(c) Population x	0.5	0.5	0.0
Population y	0	0.7	0.3

15.7 Genetic distance: Calculate Nei's genetic distances (a) between the Vernon and Gameland populations using the data in Example 15.1, (b) between the Apalachicola and Gameland populations.

15.8 Management units: Use the exchangeability method of Crandall *et al.* (2000) to categorize three coho salmon populations. Two populations differ significantly from a third in microsatellite frequencies and in heritable characters likely to be of ecological significance (morphology, swimming ability and age at maturation). How would you recommend the three populations be managed?

15.9 Management units: Use the method of Crandall *et al.* (2000) to categorize northern and California spotted owl populations using data from Box 1.1.

PRACTICAL EXERCISE: BUILDING A PHYLOGENETIC TREE
Use DNA sequence data to build a phylogenetic tree using a computer software package, such as PAUP or PHYLIP. Suitable DNA sequence data on primates can be found in Hayasaka *et al.* (1988), while sequences for other species can be found in GENBANK.

Chapter 16

Genetics and the management of wild populations

Genetic management in wild populations involves increasing population size, the recovery of small inbred populations, management of fragmented populations, alleviating genetic 'swamping' due to hybridization with related species, and minimizing the deleterious impacts of harvesting

Terms:
Clones, corridor, introgression, translocation

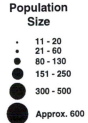

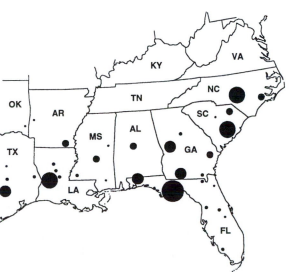

Population Size

·   11 - 20
·   21 - 60
●   80 - 130
●   151 - 250
●   300 - 500
●   Approx. 600

The endangered red-cockaded woodpecker and its current fragmented distribution in southeastern USA (from James 1995).

Genetic issues in wild populations

Genetic management of
threatened populations in nature
is in its infancy

There has been limited application of genetics in the practical management of threatened taxa in natural habitats. Genetic issues are not unimportant in wild population, but are rarely considered. We have already referred to most examples of genetic management of wild populations. Some are presented in more detail here.

As we continue to draw together observations and theoretical genetic predictions with the practicalities of management strategies, it is instructive to summarize the current situation. On the one hand, we may have comprehensive knowledge of the natural history, distributions, behaviour and ecology of many species, particularly for 'charismatic' species – the flowering plants, mammals, birds and butterflies that so attract human attention. This is underpinned by ecological, demographic and wildlife-management theory and the invaluable insights of the practitioners who maintain our natural reserves and manage endangered species in the wild.

On the other hand, genetic research is providing increasingly powerful molecular techniques for estimating genetic diversity, and a growing database for many endangered and non-endangered species. These complement an extensive theoretical base that has not been fully utilized for wild populations. This chapter endeavours to integrate these knowledge bases. Failure to achieve this integration into comprehensive management strategies will doom small and fragmented populations to the 'extinction vortex', increasing genetic impoverishment and greatly elevated extinction risks.

As we have discussed previously, the key genetic contributions to conservation biology are:

- Resolution of taxonomic uncertainties such that managers are confident of the status of, and relationships among, the populations they strive to maintain (Chapter 15)
- Delineation of any distinct management units within species, as biologically meaningful entities for conservation (Chapter 15)
- Recognition that the effective sizes of populations, that determine the genetic future of populations, are frequently about an order of magnitude lower than census sizes
- Detection of declines in genetic diversity. Sensitive genetic markers, particularly microsatellites, have the power to detect reductions in heterozygosity and allelic diversity in small and fragmented populations
- Development of theory to describe past, and predict future, changes in genetic variation. All such theories have a common, central, element – genetic diversity is dependent on N_e
- Recognition that the genetic diversity underlying the quantitative variation in reproductive fitness is the raw material for adaptive evolution through natural selection. Loss of this class of genetic variation reduces the capacity of populations to evolve in response to environmental change

- Direct evidence for inbreeding depression in endangered species in natural habitats
- At a practical level, potential inbreeding depression may be inferred from its correlation with reduction in genetic variation, assessed by markers
- Degree of fragmentation and rates of gene flow can be inferred from the distribution of genetic markers within and among populations and calculation of F statistics.

Many of these issues are illustrated by the example of the Florida panther (Box 16.1).

This chapter follows approximately the order of genetic management actions for wild populations:

- resolve any taxonomic uncertainties and delineate management units
- increase population size
- diagnose genetic problems
- recover small inbred populations with low genetic diversity in naturally outbreeding species
- genetically manage fragmented populations.

These are followed by genetic issues in the design of reserves, introgression and hybridization, and the impact of harvesting in wild populations. The chapter concludes by examining management of species that are not naturally outbreeding diploids.

| Box 16.1 | Identification of genetic problems in the Florida panther and genetic management to alleviate them (Roelke *et al.* 1993; Barone *et al.* 1994; Land & Lacy 2000) |

The endangered Florida panther is restricted to a small relict population of approximately 60–70 individuals in southern Florida, primarily in the Big Cypress and adjoining Everglades National Park ecosystems. Prior to European settlement, they ranged across the entire southeast of the United States, and other sub-species (called panthers, pumas, cougars, catamounts, or mountain lions) were spread throughout North and South America. Since 1973, the main causes of deaths have been road kills, illegal hunting or injuries. A population viability analysis in 1989 (see Chapter 20) predicted that this population had a high probability of extinction within a short time, unless remedial actions were taken (Seal & Lacy 1989). A more recent assessment is more optimistic (Maehr *et al.* 2001).

Analyses using mtDNA, allozymes and morphology revealed that a portion of the population had received genetic input (introgression) from a South American puma sub-species, at some time in the past. Subsequently, records revealed that South American animals had been released into the population by a private breeder between 1956 and 1966. Hybrid animals are located in areas away from most 'authentic' animals.

The authentic Florida panther population has very low levels of allozyme, DNA fingerprint and mtDNA genetic diversity compared to the hybrids, other puma populations and felids generally.

Sub-species	Allozymes		DNA fingerprint heterozygosity %
	P % (range)	H_e % (range)	
Florida (authentic)	4.9	1.8	10.4
Florida (introgressed)	7.3	1.8	29.7
Western US	9.85 (4.9–17.1)	4.3 (2.0–6.7)	46.9
Other felids	8–21	3–8	
Domestic cat			45.9

Authentic Florida panthers also display evidence of inbreeding depression. They exhibit morphological abnormalities ('cow lick' patterns in their fur and kinked tails), cardiac defects, the poorest semen quality of any felid (see figure below; J. Howard & B. Pukazhenthi) and a high level of cryptorchidism. All 'pure' males have at least one undescended testis. This problem has become progressively worse since 1975. Florida panthers also suffer a high prevalence of infectious disease.

How can the authentic Florida panther be recovered? Since it displays both the genetic and physical hallmarks of inbreeding depression, its fitness should be

Normal

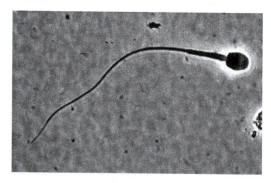

Coiled tail, bent acrosome

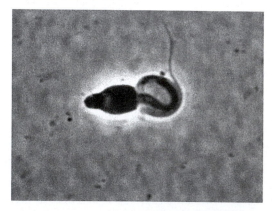

increased by introduction of immigrants from another population. As no other population of Florida panthers exists, the only source of individuals was from another sub-species of puma. The nearest sub-species is from Texas, a population that was contiguous with the Florida population, before its decline. The Florida and Texas populations probably had historical gene exchange.

Following extensive consultations, the decision was made to introduce 6–8 females of the Texas sub-species into the Florida panther population. Outbreeding depression is unlikely as there is no evidence for it either in the hybrid Florida population or in mixed populations of captive pumas. Further, Culver *et al.* (2000) have subsequently shown that all North American panthers/cougars are genetically very similar for molecular markers and suggested that they be reclassified as a single sub-species.

The first eight individuals from Texas have now been introduced. Three of the imports died, but 25 surviving outcrossed progeny are known, including some second generation offspring from hybrids. The F_1 hybrid kittens lack cowlicks and kinked tails and appear to be more robust than authentic Florida panthers.

Resolving taxonomy and management units

As we have seen in Chapter 15, it is not possible to properly manage wild populations (genetically, or otherwise) if the taxonomy is not correct. The first step in the genetic management of wild populations of threatened species is to ensure that the species' taxonomy is correctly assigned and that any distinct management units are defined. For the rest of this chapter, we will assume that taxonomic uncertainties and management have been resolved, and address genetic management within management units.

> The first step in the management of any wild population is to ensure that any questions about the taxonomy and management units within species are resolved

Increasing population size

The first objective of threatened species management is to halt decline and increase the size of populations. This alleviates all of the stochastic threats to species (demographic, environmental, catastrophic and genetic). If populations have only recently declined from far larger sizes, and are now rapidly expanded from short-term effective population sizes of, say fifty to several hundred, then the genetic impacts are minimal. Despite the bottleneck, short-term reductions of this magnitude allow little opportunity for variation to be lost through genetic drift.

The first step in this process is in the domain of wildlife biologists and ecologists – identification of the causes of the decline. Actions taken to arrest population declines and recover species include legislative controls on hunting and harvesting, designation of reserves, reduction of pollutants, improvement of habitat quality and eradication of

> A primary objective in managing wild populations is to increase the sizes of small populations

predators and competitors. Such actions benefit all of the biodiversity in the managed region. In this respect, the endangered species acts as a 'flagship' for an entire community.

A number of success stories illustrate the benefits arising from these forms of management. Indian rhinoceroses have increased from 27 to about 600 in Chitwan National Park, Nepal following bans on hunting and designation of the royal hunting reserve as a national park. Similarly, the northern elephant seal has increased from 20–30 to over 100 000 following cessation of hunting and United States legislation protecting of all marine mammals (Halley & Hoelzel 1996). The northern hairy-nosed wombat has increased slowly in population size following designation of its only remaining habitat at Clermont in Queensland, Australia as a national park and improvement of food resources by exclusion of cattle (Taylor *et al.* 1994). As insecticides accumulate to the highest concentrations at the top of the food-chain, birds of prey frequently suffer most from their effects. Mauritius kestrel, bald eagle and peregrine falcon populations have all increased following control of DDT usage (Groombridge *et al.* 2000). Peregrine falcons have been removed from the endangered species list, following DDT control and a reintroduction program.

The Chatham Island black robin has increased from five to over 140 following protection, cross-fostering and translocations (Butler & Merton 1992). The Lord Howe Island woodhen has recovered from a size of 20–30 following eradication of their primary threat, pigs, and a short-term captive breeding and release program (Brook *et al.* 1997a). The recovery program for Seychelles warblers has been especially well-considered and successful (Komdeur *et al.* 1998). From a low of 26–29 birds on Cousin Island between 1959 and 1968, it reached a carrying capacity of about 320 birds in 1982 and has maintained this level. In 1988 and 1990, 29 birds were translocated to each of the nearby Aride and Cousine Islands. By 1996, these had grown into populations of 1000 and 186, respectively. In plants, recovery has followed legislative protection to minimize harvest, creation of reserves and removal of herbivores (Bowles & Whelan 1994; Primack 1998). Where numbers are extremely small, forms of *ex-situ* conservation have been used, followed by reintroductions (Chapters 17 and 18).

While genetic information may help to alert conservation biologists to the extent of endangerment, the management actions above involve little, or no, genetics. However, recovery in numbers of highly inbred populations can be substantially enhanced following introduction of additional genetic variation (Fig. 12.11).

Insecure wild populations can be augmented using captive bred individuals. The nene (Hawaiian goose) has been subject to a long program of augmentation from captivity, as its wild population does not appear to be self-sustaining (Black 1995). Such programs may be counterproductive in the long run if the captive population adapts to reproduction in captivity, and its reproductive ability in the wild is reduced. This is clearly a problem in fish where long-term captive popu-

Some wild populations are regularly augmented from captive populations, but this is likely to be genetically deleterious in the long term

lations, used to stock wild habitats, have lower reproductive fitness in the wild than residents (Hindar *et al.* 1991). Genetic adaptation to captivity is considered in Chapter 18.

Diagnosing genetic problems

A necessary precursor to genetic management of wild populations of threatened species is to diagnose their status. We need to answer three questions:

- Has a threatened species/population lost genetic diversity?
- Is it suffering from inbreeding depression?
- Is it genetically fragmented?

The means for carrying out these diagnoses have been discussed in Chapters 3, 12 and 13. Many threatened species have been examined to evaluate their status. In fact, such diagnoses have been the main genetic contributions to the conservation of wild populations, so far. However, using this information to plan conservation management is still in its infancy. Below, we consider the genetic management actions that should be taken to alleviate genetic problems.

> Most of the genetic contribution to management of wild populations has been to diagnose the genetic status of threatened species and populations

Recovering small inbred populations with low genetic diversity

An effective management strategy in the recovery of small inbred populations with low genetic diversity is to introduce individuals from other populations to improve their reproductive fitness and restore genetic diversity. There is extensive experimental evidence that this approach can be successful. For example, it improved fitness in natural populations of greater prairie chickens, Swedish adders and a desert topminnow fish (Chapter 12). In the scarlet gilia plant, outcrossing improved seed mass for small inbred populations, but not for large non-inbred populations (Fig. 16.1). Similar benefits have been demonstrated in experimental populations of fruit flies, rye grass and *Silene alba* and numerous domestic animals and plants (Polans & Allard 1989; Spielman & Frankham 1992; Richards 2000).

> Small, inbred populations can be recovered by introducing unrelated individuals

In spite of the clear benefits of outcrossing to recover small inbred populations, there are very few cases where it is being done (see below).

Source of unrelated individuals for genetic augmentation

The individuals chosen for introduction to inbred populations, for recovery of fitness and genetic diversity, may be either outbred (if available), or inbred but genetically differentiated from the population to

> Individuals to augment small inbred populations with low genetic diversity can come from outbred populations, from inbred but genetically unrelated populations, or from related inter-fertile taxa

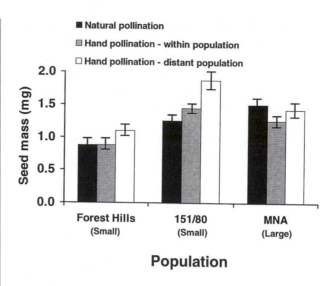

Fig. 16.1 Alleviating inbreeding depression in the scarlet gilia plant by outcrossing (after Heschel & Paige 1995). Seed mass per plant (±SE) is shown for natural pollination, hand pollination within populations, and hand pollinations using pollen from distant populations, for populations at three localities. Small populations (Forest Hills and 151/80) exhibit inbreeding depression for seed mass. The different mean seed masses in the different locations are due to different environmental conditions. *Outcrossing improved the seed mass in the small inbred populations, while the large MNA population did not change with outcrossing.*

which they are being introduced. An example of the latter situation is provided by Australian wallabies (Table 13.1). The black-footed rock wallaby has several inbred island populations that could be combined to increase genetic diversity and improve reproductive fitness. The combined genetic material from all the island populations contains most of the microsatellite alleles found within the mainland populations. There are 66 alleles at 10 microsatellite loci in mainland populations and 47 in the pool of six island populations (Eldridge *et al.* 1999). Mainland populations are threatened by fox predation. In the future, it may be necessary to use crosses among island populations to reconstitute a new population for reintroduction to mainland localities once foxes are eliminated. This approach is not yet being used in practice.

Where no unrelated individuals of the same taxon are available, individuals from another sub-species can be used to alleviate inbreeding depression. This has been done for the Florida panther (Box 16.1) and the Norfolk Island boobook owl (Example 10.4).

If an endangered species exists as only a single population, then the only possible source of additional genetic material is from a related, interfertile species. American chestnuts have been crossed to the Chinese chestnut to introduce genetic variation for resistance to blight that severely depleted the American species. China is the source of the blight disease and the Chinese chestnut possesses resistance (Hebard 1994).

The option of crossing a threatened species to a related species requires very careful consideration. The potential benefits need to be very large, as there may be a serious risk of outbreeding depression. However, inter-species crosses have been found to have equal probabilities of having beneficial or deleterious effects on reproductive fitness (Arnold & Hodges 1995). Such crosses must be evaluated on an experimental basis, to ensure that hybrids are fertile in F_1 and subsequent generations, prior to full implementation. Even where some outbreeding depression occurs, inbreeding depression will be greatly reduced. Further, natural selection will eventually remove most or all of the outbreeding depression, particularly if the hybrid population has a large reproductive excess. Given that the extent of genetic differentiation among species varies considerably across higher taxa, inter-species crosses in some taxa will only be equivalent to crosses between subspecies in other taxa (Table 15.1).

Management of species with a single population lacking genetic diversity

From a genetic perspective, the worst situation is where an endangered species exists as a single, inbred population, with no sub-species or related species with which to hybridize. Information on the level to which genetic diversity has been reduced is useful only as an indication of the fragility of the species. The lower the genetic diversity, the lower becomes evolutionary potential, and the higher becomes the probability that the species has compromised ability to cope with changes in its physical or biotic environment. For fragile species, management regimes should be instituted to

- increase their population size (see above)
- establish populations in several location (to minimize the risk of catastrophes)
- maximize their reproductive rate by improving their environment (e.g. removing predators and competitors)
- insulate them from environmental change.

The latter regime should include quarantining from introduced diseases, pests, predators and competitors, and monitoring, so that remedial action can be initiated as soon as new environmental threats arise. For example, the recently discovered and endangered Wollemi pine in Australia entirely lacks genetic diversity at several hundred loci within and among populations (Chapter 3). The recovery plan (NPWS 1998) calls for (a) restricting access to the populations by keeping their location secret, (b) restricting access to the site to approved people, (c) instituting strict hygiene protocols to avoid introducing disease, (d) fire management and (e) maintaining *ex-situ* samples of each plant in botanic gardens. Further, commercial propagation of the species is increasing population size and reducing stochastic risks. Ironically, in such a case, retention of just one individual retains the entire gene pool of the species, although this would clearly be foolhardy in terms of increased extinction risk from non-genetic causes. Plant species in this situation have an advantage over animals, in that many can be propagated by cuttings.

In the less extreme case of the black-footed ferret, where there is low genetic diversity, the recovery plan calls for the re-establishment of 10 wild populations, in different locations, to minimize the risks of disease and other environmental catastrophes.

For species consisting of a single population with reduced genetic diversity, the only options are to improve their environment and minimize risks associated with changed environments (especially disease) and small population size

Restoration of genetic diversity in species with a single population with low fitness and limited quantitative genetic variation can only be through mutation, or introgression from another species.

Genetic management of fragmented populations

The adverse genetic consequences of population fragmentation can be alleviated by increasing gene flow among population fragments, by improving habitat quality and by re-establishing populations in areas where they have become extinct

Many threatened species have fragmented habitats, of the type illustrated for the giant panda (Fig. 16.2). The management options for fragmented populations to maximize genetic diversity and minimize inbreeding and extinction risk are to
* increase the habitat area
* increase the suitability of available habitat (increase density)
* artificially increase the migration rate by translocation
* re-establish populations in suitable habitat where they have gone extinct
* create habitat corridors.

Gene flow must be re-established to reduce the risk of extinction in genetically isolated fragments

To alleviate or prevent deleterious genetic consequences in isolated fragments, gene flow needs to be re-established by moving individuals (**translocation**) or gametes (usually sperm or pollen), or by establishing migration **corridors**. The benefits of immigration have been established in many cases (Chapters 12 and 13). In the small scabious plant, between-population crosses had fitnesses 2.5 times that of the within-

Fig. 16.2 Habitat fragmentation for the giant panda in China. Both its current and previous distributions are shown.

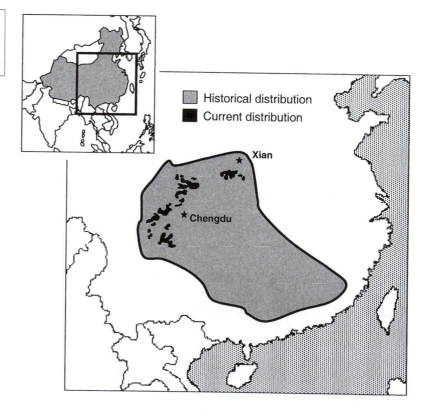

Historical distribution
Current distribution

Xian

Chengdu

population crosses (van Treuren *et al.* 1993). Computer projections indicate that immigration will reduce the extinction risks for two small black rhinoceros populations in East Africa (Box 16.2). Similarly, computer projections demonstrated migration among population fragments to be beneficial in the management of fragmented tule elk populations in California (McCullough *et al.* 1996).

Translocation of individuals among populations may be costly, especially for large animals, and carries the risks of injury, disease transmission and behavioural disruption when individuals are released. For example, introduced male lions regularly kill cubs. Further, sexually mature males of many species may kill intruders. The cost of translocations can be reduced by artificial insemination for species where this technique has been perfected. The same care to avoid outbreeding depression, discussed previously, must be exercised in planning translocations.

Corridors among habitat fragments (frequently recommended for non-genetic reasons) can re-establish gene flow among isolated populations. Species vary in their requirements for a corridor to be an effective migration path (Lindenmayer & Nix 1993). The most ambitious proposal of this kind is 'The Wildlands Project' – to provide corridors from north to south in North America (Davis 1992). The corridors will link existing reserves and surround both reserves and corridors with buffer zones that are hospitable to wild animals and plants. The time frame for achieving this vision is hundreds of years, given the political, social and financial challenges. None the less, such systems are essential if we are to conserve biodiversity in the long term. With global climate change, plants and animals need to alter their distributions to cope with moving climatic zones. At present, such movement is largely prevented by inhospitable habitat between reserves and protected areas.

Box 16.2	Modelling the effects of inbreeding depression and immigration on the survival of black rhinoceros populations in Kenya (after Dobson *et al.* 1992)

Black rhinoceros populations are threatened across their entire range due, predominantly, to poaching. In East Africa, no single population numbered more than 60 animals when this work was done (the situation is probably worse now). The population is fragmented and there is no migration among most, or all, of the fragments. Several of the populations are in protected sanctuaries or reserves.

Dobson and co-workers investigated the demographic and genetic factors likely to contribute to extinction risk, and the factors that must be taken into consideration in managing the populations. The study involved stochastic computer projections that followed the history of each individual from birth to death, as well as their reproductive output (Chapter 20). Input files contained the identity and parentage of each individual, age and sex-specific rates of survival and reproduction as well as

rates of immigration of different age and sex classes. Data from rhinoceros populations in sanctuaries were used as input.

Populations at Lewa Downs and Nakuru National Park, Kenya were modelled for 200 years with (a) no immigration and no inbreeding depression (only demographic and environmental stochasticity), (b) inbreeding depression with no immigration and (c) with inbreeding depression and immigration of one immigrant every 10 years for the next 50 years. Inbreeding depression was applied to survival at a level of 2.0 lethal equivalents per haploid genome (4.0 per diploid), approximating the average value observed for captive mammals by Ralls et al. (1988). The initial population sizes of the two populations were set at their actual sizes, 10 females and 3 males (5 and 1 being adults) at Lewa Downs and 7 females and 11 males (5 and 8 being adults) at Nakuru National Park. Carrying capacities were estimated at 20 for Lewa Downs and 71 for Nakuru. Rates of breeding were adjusted by a function incorporating density dependence.

The results, based on 200 simulations of the three situations are given below. Scenario (a) yielded an extinction risk of over 50% after 200 years in the smaller Lewa Downs population, but less than 10% in the larger Nakuru population, both due to stochastic factors. Scenario (b) yielded increased extinction risk over those in (a) in both populations, the extinction probabilities rising to 76% and 22%, respectively. Thus, both of these isolated population fragments are susceptible to extinction from inbreeding depression, as well as to demographic and environmental stochasticity. Extinction risks were lowest with scenario (c) being about 40% and 5%, respectively. Consequently, immigration is predicted to reduce extinction risk in these fragmented rhinoceros populations. Additional migration after year 50 would result in further reductions in extinction risks. Consequently, clear benefits of immigration on population persistence were predicted.

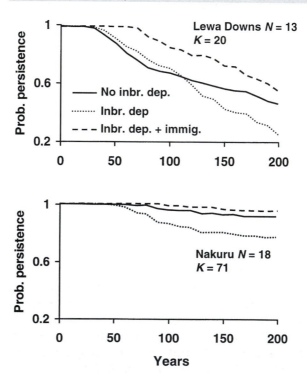

Despite the widespread fragmentation of populations of threatened species, we are only aware of three cases in animals and two cases in plants, where immigration is being used as a practical measure to alleviate inbreeding and loss of genetic diversity in the wild. Individuals from other populations are being introduced to small populations of endangered red-cockaded woodpeckers, as computer simulations have predicted their likely extinction without augmentation (Haig *et al.* 1993). The other animal cases are the endangered and inbred Florida panther (Box 16.1) and the golden lion tamarin (Box 20.1).

> Genetic management of fragmented populations is the greatest unmet challenge in conservation genetics

The two botanical examples involve self-incompatible plants where loss of alleles at self-incompatibility loci results in reduced fitness due to shortage of compatible pollen (Chapter 10). The threatened lakeside daisy population in Illinois was incapable of reproducing as all individuals contained the same S allele. It has now been outcrossed to Ohio plants, and seeds from Ohio and Ontario populations have been introduced, to increase diversity of S alleles and recover reproductive fitness (Demauro 1994). The endangered Mauna Kea silversword was reduced to 50 adult plants through overgrazing by sheep (Rieseberg & Swensen 1996). Subsequently, 450 plants were raised and outplanted to augment the populations. However, genetic analyses revealed that all the outplanted individuals were the progeny of two female plants and had lower genetic diversity than the original wild population (Robichaux *et al.* 1997). As this is a self-incompatible plant, the outplanted individuals produced only a 20% seed set. This rose to 60% when they were pollinated by unrelated individuals from the natural population, which presumably carried different S alleles. To alleviate these problems, outplanted individuals have been cross-pollinated using pollen from unrelated individuals from the natural population.

We now consider two practical decisions that must be made when genetic augmentation of small, inbred populations is contemplated – the source of the immigrants and the rate of input.

Managing gene flow

Managing gene flow involves considerable complexity as many issues must be addressed, including:
- Which individuals to translocate?
- How many?
- How often?
- From where to where?
- When should translocations begin?
- When should they be stopped?

> In managing translocations, many variables must to optimized. This requires continuous genetic monitoring, computer projections to optimize management options, and adaptive management

Answering these questions requires that the population be genetically monitored. Since there are so many variables to optimize, computer projections of the type given in Box 16.2 will often be required to define (and refine) the required management. The objective is to identify a regime that maintains genetically viable populations with acceptable costs and that fits within other management constraints.

Re-establishing extinct populations

To maximize population sizes and minimize extinction risks, populations that have become extinct should be re-established from extant populations, if the habitat can still support the species.

Which populations should be used to re-establish extinct populations? To minimize inbreeding and maximize genetic diversity, the re-founding population should be sampled from most, or all, extant populations. A case of poor choice of populations is provided by the koala in southeastern Australia (Box 16.3). Island populations with low genetic diversity were used for reintroduction, as ample individuals were available from those sources. Genetic issues were ignored and deleterious genetic consequences have resulted.

Where there is evidence of adaptive genetic differentiation among extant populations (e.g. many plants), the translocated individuals should normally come from populations most likely to be the best adapted to the reintroduction habitat. This is frequently the geographically closest extant population.

Care should taken when island populations are being considered as source populations for translocation as they typically have low genetic variation and are inbred (Frankham 1997, 1998). For example, Eldridge et al. (1999) demonstrated that small isolated mainland populations of black-striped rock wallabies in Western Australia had much higher levels of microsatellite diversity than the numerically larger population on Barrow Island. Further, there was evidence that the reproductive rate was lower in the island population. This population would be an unwise choice as a source for translocation.

Genetic diversity in populations available for restocking should be compared and the most diverse population with the highest reproductive fitness, or a cross among populations, chosen.

| **Box 16.3** | Reintroduction of koalas in southeastern Australia: a poorly designed program with adverse genetic impacts (Houlden et al. 1996; Sherwin et al. 2000) |

The koala is a unique marsupial endemic to Eastern Australia. It is both a cultural icon and an important contributor to tourist income. It once ranged down the East Coast from Queensland to Victoria and South Australia (see map), but its numbers have been reduced by hunting, habitat loss and disease. At the peak of hunting in 1924, 2 million animals were shot. By the 1930s, koalas inhabited less than 50% of their former range. They had disappeared in South Australia, and were nearly extinct in Victoria. However, they were still considered common in Queensland where they subsequently recovered without large-scale assistance. The fur trade ceased by the 1930s when koalas were given legal protection in all states. Subsequently, much effort has gone into koala conservation.

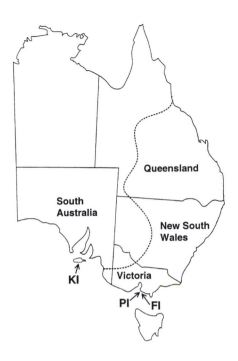

Extensive translocations of animals occurred in the southeast. A population was founded from as few as 2–3 individuals on French Island (FI) in Victoria late in the 19th century. This population grew rapidly in the absence of predators and rapidly reached carrying capacity. Surplus animals from this population were used to found an additional population on Kangaroo Island (KI) (18 adult founders plus young) in 1923–25, and to supplement a population founded on Phillip Island (PI) in the 1870s. The French and Phillip Island populations were used widely to supplement mainland Victorian populations and the Kangaroo Island population to restock mainland South Australia. The restocked South Australia mainland population has gone through three bottlenecks, mainland Victoria→French Island→Kangaroo Island→mainland South Australia. Since 1923, 10000 animals have been translocated to 70 locations.

Stocking of populations using individuals from bottlenecked populations is expected to result in loss of genetic diversity and inbreeding. As predicted, the southeastern populations in Victoria and South Australia have about half the genetic diversity found in the less-perturbed populations further north; 5.3 versus 11.5 microsatellite alleles per locus and heterozygosities (H_e) of 0.44 versus 0.85. DNA fingerprints and RAPD analyses provide similar conclusions. As expected, the Kangaroo Island populations had the lowest genetic diversity of all surveyed populations. All southeast populations showed similar microsatellite allele frequencies, and similar mtDNA haplotypes, while the more northerly populations exhibited considerable genetic differentiation among populations.

Translocations using animals with low genetic diversity have reduced genetic diversity and distorted natural allele frequencies. The translocations may have contributed to reductions in reproductive fitness, including lowered resistance to

Chlamydia infection, to a lowering of sperm concentrations and motility, and to an increased frequency of a testicular abnormality (aplasia) (Seymour *et al.* in press).

What might have been done to avoid such problems? Loss of genetic diversity and inbreeding depression would have been averted if the French Island population had been founded with more individuals, or if its genetic diversity had been augmented to give it a greater base. The situation would have been much better if the more diverse Phillip Island population had not been 'swamped' with French Island individuals.

What can be done to reverse the current problems? The most efficient strategy would be to introduce more genetic diversity into the southeastern populations (both island and mainland). Since the koala population is somewhat differentiated, this would best be done from nearby populations. The ideal solution would be discovery of a remnant population in Victoria with high genetic diversity. If none exists, then the best source of genetic diversity is from New South Wales. Genetic diversity should be checked in source populations before they are used for translocation.

Genetic issues in reserve design

Reserves need to be sufficiently large to support the target species, and contain habitat to which the species is adapted. Natural or artificial gene flow must occur between reserves

There are many biological, ecological, political and genetic considerations to balance when considering the design of nature reserves. Soulé & Simberloff (1986) are among the few authors to consider the genetic issues. They suggested that three steps are involved in the ecology and genetics of reserve design: (a) identify target, or keystone species, whose loss would significantly decrease the value of biodiversity in the reserve, (b) determine the minimum population size needed to guarantee a high probability of long-term survival for these species, and (c) using known population densities for these species, estimate the area required to sustain minimum numbers. The genetic issues in reserve design are:
- Is the reserve large enough to support a genetically viable population?
- Is the species adapted to the habitat in the reserve?
- Should there be one large reserve, or several smaller reserves?

From the arguments given in Chapter 14, a reserve of sufficient size to maintain an effective population size of at least several hundred and an actual size of several thousand is required. Detailed computer projections support this contention (Chapter 20).

Should a threatened species be maintained in a single large reserve, or in several smaller reserves? The issue of single large versus several small (SLOSS) reserves was addressed in Chapter 13. In general, a single large reserve is more desirable from the genetic point of view, if there is a risk that populations in small reserves will become extinct (a likely scenario for many species). However, protection against catastrophes dictates that more than one reserve is preferable, or even obligatory. The best compromise is to have more than one sizeable reserve, but to ensure that there is natural or artificial gene flow among them. In practice, the choice of reserves has often been a haphazard process, determined more by local politics, alternative land uses and the need for reserves to serve multiple purposes (e.g. recreation), than by biological principles.

Introgression and hybridization

Introgression is the flow of alleles from one species, or sub-species, to another. Typically, hybridizations occur when humans introduce exotic species into the range of rare species (Ellstrand *et al.* 1999), or alter habitat so that previously isolated species are now in secondary contact. Introgression is a threat to the genetic integrity of a range of canid, duck, fish, plant, and other species (Rhymer & Simberloff 1996).

Introgression can be detected using a wide range of genetic markers, including allozymes, microsatellites, DNA fingerprints, RAPDs and, where appropriate, chromosomal studies. Allozyme analyses of captive Asiatic lions indicated that they contained alleles from African lions (O'Brien 1994). Endangered Florida panthers consist of two populations, one of which resulted from introgression from a South American sub-species of panthers (Box 16.1). Females of the highly endangered Ethiopian wolf have been shown to hybridize with male domestic dogs, with the levels varying in different populations (Gottelli *et al.* 1994). This finding was based on microsatellite and mtDNA analyses. Conversely, microsatellite data on Mexican wolf populations showed no evidence of introgression from dogs or coyotes (Hedrick *et al.* 1997). Widespread evidence of introgression has been detected in salmonid fish based on studies with genetic markers (Ryman *et al.* 1995; Allendorf & Waples 1996). Allozyme studies indicate that there has been extensive hybridization between the endangered Hawaiian duck and introduced mallard ducks on the island of Oahu (Haig & Avise 1996).

Introgression has also been detected in plants. Extensive introgression into the Galapagos Islands endemic tetraploid cotton from introduced cultivated cottons has been detected using data from 59 allozyme loci (Wendel & Percy 1990). Further, hybridization of the Catalina mahogany, California's rarest tree, with two related species has been documented (Rieseberg 1991).

A particularly deleterious form of hybridization is that between related diploid and tetraploid populations, resulting in sterile triploids. This has been reported in the endangered grassland daisy in Australia (Young & Murray 2000).

Some species are endangered due to genetic 'swamping' by interbreeding with common related species. Genetic markers can be used to detect introgression and hybrid individuals

Alleviating introgression

The Catalina mahogany (Box 16.4) provides an example of management of a species subject to hybridization. The major part of this management program involves protection of the remaining plants and increasing their numbers. In this case, genetic information was critical in defining

Introgression can be alleviated by removing the hybridizing species, by eliminating hybrid individuals, or by expanding the number of 'pure' individuals

the hybridization problem, and in identifying hybrid individuals, but had a limited role in the recovery process.

Options for addressing this problem include eliminating the introduced species, or translocating 'pure' individuals into isolated regions or into captivity. Success for these options is hard to achieve. It will not be practical to remove all dogs from the habitat of the Ethiopian wolf. In the case of native salmon in the Pacific Northwest, other salmonids have already been introduced. In theory, fish could be exterminated in closed lakes and re-stocking carried out with 'pure' native fish. However, control of fish dispersal is notoriously difficult, as fishermen often undertake illegal stocking.

| Box 16.4 | Catalina mahogany: identification of hybridization with a related species and institution of a recovery plan (Rieseberg & Swensen 1996) |

The Catalina mahogany is a small endangered tree restricted almost entirely to a single gully on Santa Catalina Island in the Channel Islands off California. The species is extremely rare, having declined from 40 to 11 plants by 1996. Its decline was largely a consequence of introduction of goats. The grazing and rooting by goats, pigs and recently introduced bison and mule deer remain a serious threat, despite efforts to control introduced species. Active management began in the late 1970s. A botanical inventory of the island identified several individuals that resembled mountain mahogany (a separate species), or were intermediate. Genetic studies using allozymes and RAPDs identified six of 11 adult trees as 'true' Catalina mahogany, and the other five as hybrids with mountain mahogany. In addition, one mainland plant was identified as either a relict, or a relict that had hybridized with mainland mountain mahogany.

The management of the Catalina mahogany began with the fencing of two trees, following by fencing an area of 0.4 hectares (1 acre) around these trees. This resulted in the production of about 70 seedlings that were mostly 'pure', based on allozyme analyses. Several cuttings from the 'pure' trees have been propagated at the Rancho Santa Anna Botanic Gardens and 16 of these have been planted on the island. Survival of outplanted trees has been high (about 90%). A major remaining problem is the lack of protection against introduced pests at most localities. Genetics has been critical in identifying the hybridization problem and in providing a method for detecting hybrids during the recovery process.

Impacts of harvesting

Harvesting may alter sex-ratio, N_e, breeding system, generation length, or gene flow, and result in inbreeding and loss of genetic diversity

Many species of wild animals and plants are harvested. This may alter effective population size, genetic diversity and generation length. Usually the effects are deleterious genetically. For example, Ryman *et al.* (1981) showed that hunting of moose and white-tailed deer would severely reduce genetic diversity even within short periods. Hunting regimes reduced the effective population size by 64%–79% in moose and by 58%–65% in the deer, depending on the regime and assumptions made. Poaching has had a devastating impact on sex-ratio and reproductive rate in Asian elephants (Box 16.5). Hunting for bighorn sheep primarily targets large-horned rams. Since rams with larger horns have higher heterozygosity, hunting may reduce genetic diversity (Fitzsimmons *et al.* 1995). Hunting the greywing francolin in South Africa had a limited genetic impact; the reduction in local population size in hunted populations was balanced by increased immigration following hunting (Little *et al.* 1993).

Logging of forest trees may alter the breeding system. In a comparison of logged and nearby unlogged forest, Murawski *et al.* (1994) showed that logging increased the level of inbreeding in a rare tree in Sri Lanka from 15% selfing in primary forest to 35% in logged forest. Gene flow has been reduced by fragmentation in the royal mahogany tree from Central and South America (Dayanandan *et al.* 1999).

Box 16.5	Impact of poaching on sex-ratio, effective population size, reproductive fitness and population viability in Asian elephants (Sukumar *et al.* 1998)

Poaching for ivory has had a devastating impact on sex-ratios, as only male Asian elephants have tusks. Poaching over the last 20 years in Southern India has so decimated the male population that in Periyar Reserve there are only six adult males to 605 adult females. The effective size of this population is only 24. Further, with such a small number of males, female reproduction rates have declined. Females that do not breed early remain reproductively barren throughout the rest of their life. Thus, harvesting not only affects the sex-ratio and effective population size, but it also reduces reproductive fitness. Modelling suggests that the impact of this poaching over the next 20 years will cause a population decline of between 0.6% and 1.5% per year. This further reduction in population size will only exacerbate the genetic problems, driving the population into an extinction vortex.

Many wild species are selectively harvested by humans who favour particular phenotypes within the population. These include elephants, rhinoceroses, deer, moose, fish, whales, crustaceans, forest trees and many other plants. This may result in selection pressures that change the phenotype of the species, conflicting with forces of natural selection and reducing the overall fitness of the population. For example, males with large antlers are the favoured prey of hunters. This is expected to select for smaller antlers, conflicting with natural selection favouring large antlers in males. Similarly, the frequency of tuskless male elephants is rising in several populations in Africa and Asia, because of ivory poaching (Dobson *et al.* 1992; Sukumar *et al.* 1998). Tuskless elephant males may be less successful than tusked males in finding mates and less able to ward off lions and other predators.

Selective harvesting by humans may change the genetic composition and phenotypes of populations

The obvious solution to the impacts of selective harvesting is to change regulations to make it more random, but this may be very difficult to achieve in practice. Harvest of elephant ivory is itself already an illegal activity that is not controllable. Despite many international

Impacts of selective harvest may be alleviated by changing harvest regimes, or by preserving a portion of the species without harvest

agreements, total fish catches are difficult to regulate, as the collapse of so many fisheries attests. As harvested species often occur in large, though frequently declining numbers, an option is to preserve a proportion of the population from harvest. In this way, fully wild stock is maintained to introduce into harvested areas so that the genetic impacts of harvest are reduced.

The genetic and evolutionary impacts of selective harvesting deserve more attention.

Genetic management of species that are not outbreeding diploids

Species that are not diploid outbreeders require modified genetic management as they differ in distributions of genetic diversity, in rates of loss of genetic diversity and in responses to inbreeding

In the material above, we have concentrated on diploid outbreeding species. However, many species of plants, and some animals, have diverse breeding systems that require modified management regimes. These include:
- asexual reproduction
- self-fertilization
- haplo-diploidy (in Hymenoptera)
- polyploidy (as found in many plants and a few animals).
The remainder of this chapter is concerned with their characteristics and the modifications to genetic management that this entails.

Asexual species

In asexual species, many individuals may have identical genotypes, so that great care is required to sample the diversity of clones within the species

Many species of plants are capable of vegetative reproduction, via runners, bulbs, corms, etc. Species with exclusively asexual reproduction typically exist as one or a few **clones**. Several endangered Australian species exist as single clones, including the triploid shrub King's lomatia, the Meelup mallee tree, and the Wollemi pine (Lynch *et al.* 1998; Rossetto *et al.* 1999; Hogbin *et al.* 2000). The endangered *Limonium dufourii* plant from Spain consists of several triploid clones (Palacios & González-Candelas 1997).

In a fully clonal species, there is no concern with inbreeding. However, species that only exist as a single clone will have severely compromised ability to adapt in response to environmental changes, in a similar manner to highly inbred populations of outbreeding species. This fragility requires management of the type used for the Wollemi pine (see above).

In species that show a mixture of sexual and asexual reproduction, the number of genetically distinct individuals may be far less than the number of individuals. For example, 53 individuals of endangered Australian shrub *Haloragodendron lucasii* consisted of only seven clones (Hogbin *et al.* 2000). Consequently, genetic diversity was much more restricted than in an equivalent sexually reproducing species. Partially clonal reproduction is also found in several other threatened plants, including lakeside daisy, false poison sumac, and Santa Cruz Island bush mallow in North America (Demauro 1994; Hamrick & Godt 1996; Rieseberg & Swensen 1996).

Maintenance of genetic diversity in asexually reproducing species requires that the structure of such populations be recognized for *in-situ* conservation, in re-establishing extinct populations, and in sampling for *ex-situ* conservation. Genetic diversity may occur among clones, but individuals within clones are very similar, or identical. The major conservation need is to identify and maintain as many distinct clones as possible. In theory, one individual is sufficient to capture the genetic diversity of the entire clone. However, mutation generates low levels of genetic diversity within clones. Thus, several members of each clone should be preserved.

Self-fertilizing species

About 20% of plant species habitually self-fertilize and another 40% do so occasionally. Further, some invertebrates (e.g. some slugs and snails) also self (Chapter 11). The endangered Malheur wirelettuce is an obligate inbreeder (Falk *et al.* 1996), while Brown's banksia is partially self-fertilizing (Sampson *et al.* 1994).

Predominantly self-fertilizing species are typically less heterozygous than outbreeding species, with a higher proportion of their genetic diversity being distributed among populations compared to within populations (Chapter 3; Liu *et al.* 1998). Consequently, wide sampling of selfing species is required to encompass their total genetic diversity (Falk & Holsinger 1991). The loss of individual populations is likely to have more serious consequences than the loss of individual populations of outbreeding species.

Inbreeding is less of an issue in selfing species, as they typically suffer less inbreeding depression than outbreeding species (Chapter 12). However, selfing populations often outcross at intervals, so the opportunity to do so in threatened species should be maintained.

Habitat loss and fragmentation may have greater impacts on selfing species than on outcrossing species since more of their genetic diversity is distributed among populations and less within. Reduced gene flow as a result of population fragmentation is less important in naturally inbreeding species, as they are already highly fragmented due to restricted gene flow. To retain genetic diversity within populations, and heterozygosity within individuals, small fragmented populations need to be augmented with individuals from other fragments.

> Selfing species have less heterozygosity within populations and more differentiation among populations than outbreeders. Consequently, much greater effort is required to preserve diverse populations than for outbreeders

Haplo-diploids

More than 15% of animal species, primarily Hymenoptera (ants, bees and wasps), have a haplo-diploid method of reproduction (Hedrick & Parker 1997). In Hymenoptera, females are diploid and males haploid, and all loci behave as if they are sex-linked. The effective size for a

> Haplo-diploid species have lower effective population sizes and less genetic diversity than diploid outbreeders. They require larger population sizes to retain genetic diversity than outbreeders

haplo-diploid is only three-quarters that of a diploid of the same population size, when there is an equal sex-ratio (Table 10.1). Consequently, they have lower genetic diversity than a diploid species (Hedrick & Parker 1997).

In haplo-diploid species, equilibrium frequencies of deleterious mutations in mutation–selection equilibrium are expected to be lower than in diploid species, so they are expected to show less inbreeding depression than diploids (Hedrick & Parker 1997).

Management of haplo-diploid species requires larger population sizes to maintain equivalent proportions of genetic diversity than for a diploid species. However, there is less concern about inbreeding depression.

Polyploids

Genetic management issues for polyploid species are similar to those for diploid species, but concerns about small population size and inbreeding are less

Genetic management of polyploids (the majority of plants) follows the same principles as for diploids with similar breeding systems. However, there is generally less genetic concern than for equivalent diploids (Brown & Young 2000; Buza *et al.* 2000). Polyploids probably suffer less inbreeding depression than diploids (Chapter 12). Further, loss of genetic diversity in small populations is less in polyploids than in similar sized diploid populations (Chapter 10). Consequently, polyploids should tolerate lower population sizes than diploids. However, the sizes required to avoid demographic and environmental stochasticity and catastrophes will be similar to those for diploids (see Chapter 20).

Hybridization of polyploids with related diploids (where they occur) is likely to reduce population viability. Crosses of tetraploids to diploids yield sterile triploids, and reduce overall reproductive output, as has been documented in the endangered grassland daisy (Young & Murray 2000). Triploid individuals were found in a re-established tetraploid population because of hybridization with a nearby diploid population. Genetic management should aim to minimize hybridization of polyploids and diploids.

Summary

1. Genetic management of wild populations involves increasing population sizes, recovery of small inbred populations, management of fragmented populations, alleviating genetic 'swamping' due to hybridization with related species and minimizing the genetic impacts of harvesting.

2. Small inbred populations with low genetic diversity can be recovered by adding immigrants from other populations (where they exist), and by increasing their sizes to minimize further genetic deterioration.

3. Fragmented populations with inadequate gene flow require translocations, or creation of corridors, to avoid genetic deterioration. Further, extinct populations should be re-established to maximize population size.

4. Hybridization with common related species is a threat to some mammals, birds and plants, and numerous fish species. Management is required to minimize hybridization by reducing the common species or by protecting 'pure' populations.

5. Selective harvesting genetically alters species. Harvest regimes should be designed so that they are as non-selective as possible, or segments of the population should be maintained without harvest.

6. Species that are not outbreeding diploids have altered susceptibility to loss of genetic diversity and inbreeding depression and require modified genetic management regimes.

FURTHER READING

Avise & Hamrick (1996) *Conservation Genetics*. Contains case histories on wild management of threatened species.

Bowles & Whelan (1994) *Restoration of Endangered Species*. Covers both the conceptual issues in restoration and case studies for animals and plants.

Clark *et al.* (1994) *Endangered Species Recovery*. Describes case histories on endangered species recovery, but contains little genetics.

Falk & Holsinger (1991) *Genetics and Conservation of Rare Plants*. Contains a number of chapters on management of wild threatened plant species.

Woodford (2000) *The Wollemi Pine*. An interesting, well-written popular book on the discovery, conservation and genetics of the Wollemi pine.

PROBLEMS

16.1 Recovering inbred populations: How would you alleviate the genetic problems of a moderate sized, but inbred population of euros on Barrow Island? Other non-inbred populations exist on the mainland.

16.2 Recovering inbred populations: Which population would you choose to recover a small inbred population with a heterozygosity of zero, and a genotype of $A_1A_1B_1B_1C_1C_1$? (a) A large population with genotype $A_1A_1B_1B_1C_1C_1$, or (b) a small one with $A_2A_2B_1B_1C_2C_2$?

16.3 Recovering inbred populations: Which population would you choose to recover a small inbred population with zero heterozygosity, and a genotype of $A_1A_1B_1B_1C_1C_1$? (a) A large population with zero heterozygosity, or (b) a small one with 2.5% heterozygosity?

16.4 Genetic management: How would you address the problem of loss of alleles at the self-incompatibility locus and consequent sterility in small populations of the endangered grassland daisy (Young *et al.* 2000)? Other populations of this plant exist.

16.5 Genetic management: How would you address the problem of fragmentation among isolated island populations of the endangered black-footed rock wallaby?

16.6 Managing fragmented populations: Which species in a fragmented habitat is expected to require most translocations to maintain reproductive fitness and genetic diversity in local populations? A bird, a snail, or a rodent (assume that all have the same effective sizes in each patch)?

16.7 Selective harvesting: What effect would you expect from the selective harvesting of the largest trees in a forest tree species over a long period?

16.8 Genetic management: How would you address the genetic management of the asexual plant King's lomatia in Tasmania, Australia? All individuals belong to a single clone (Lynch *et al.* 1998).

Chapter 17

Genetic management of captive populations

Captive breeding provides a means for conserving species that are incapable of surviving in their natural habitats. Captive populations of endangered species are managed to retain high levels of genetic diversity over long periods. Minimization of kinship is the current recommended genetic management strategy

A selection of endangered species that have been saved from extinction by captive breeding: Guam rail, Franklin tree (North America), *Partula* snail (Tahiti), Potosi pupfish (Mexico), Socorro dove (Mexico), Père David's deer (China) and European bison.

Why captive breed?

For terrestrial vertebrates alone, it is estimated that 2000–3000 species will require captive breeding over the next 200 years to save them from extinction (Soulé *et al.* 1986; Seal 1991; Tudge 1995). Already, 25 animal species, including addax, Arabian oryx, black-footed ferret, California condor, Père David's deer, Przewalski's horse, scimitar-horned oryx, and 11 species of *Partula* snail and several plants, including the Franklin tree and Cooke's kok'io, have been preserved in captivity following extinction in the wild. Further, many threatened species have captive populations that act as insurance against extinction in the wild. Traditionally, the objective of captive breeding programs was simply preservation of species, sometimes ironically called 'living museums', and increase of numbers. Now managers of zoos, botanic gardens and wildlife parks almost universally accept the necessity to retain species as dynamic evolutionary entities and to maintain their genetic 'health' both for long-term viability and, hopefully, for subsequent release back to their natural habitats.

The World Conservation Union (IUCN 1987) has recognized the critical value of captive breeding programs. They assist conservation by:
• Establishing populations in secure *ex-situ* locations
• Educating and engaging the public on conservation issues
• Providing a focus for funding-raising efforts for conservation
• Providing animals for research on the basic biology of species, knowledge that can then be applied to conservation of species in the wild
• Providing animals for reintroduction programs, where applicable.
Techniques and management strategies in *ex-situ* conservation range from relatively simple cultivation of plants and husbandry of animals to high-technology procedures such as artificial insemination and cryopreservation of organisms, cells and gametes. These are being applied to a wide variety of animals and plants. Most emphasis is placed on the more charismatic species, flowering plants, mammals and birds, with lower plants and invertebrates only rarely receiving attention.

Extent of captive breeding and propagation activity

Approximately 1150 zoos and aquaria worldwide currently house about 1232000 individual animals, including 584000 individual fish, 202000 mammals, 351000 birds, 74000 reptiles and 21000 amphibians (Magin *et al.* 1994). Perhaps 5%–10% of the available spaces are used for endangered species (Seal 1991). With changes in priority, there could be breeding space for about 800 endangered species in zoos and wildlife parks. In contrast, an estimated 2000–3000 species of terrestrial vertebrates alone will require captive breeding within the foreseeable future. As of 1989/90 245 threatened vertebrate species were being bred in captivity,

174 mammals (34% of threatened species), 32 birds (3%), 34 reptiles (20%) and 5 amphibians (9%) (Magin *et al.* 1994).

Perhaps 30% of all vascular plants are represented in the collections of approximately 1500 botanic gardens worldwide (Briggs & Walters 1997). The Royal Botanic Gardens at Kew, UK alone houses about 10% of all vascular plants; and 2700 out of about 25 000 threatened species (Primack 1998). The Center for Plant Conservation in the USA now maintains 480 endangered US plants in protective cultivation or seed storage (Falk *et al.* 1996).

Zoos in the 21st century

The menageries of the late 1800s and early 1900s were consumers of wildlife. They exhibited small collections of exotic species, primarily as single individuals or single pairs. Zoo collections changed dramatically in the 1970s (Ginsberg 1993). Wildlife populations were declining, legislation was being adopted to limit the trade in endangered species (e.g. US Endangered Species Act in 1972; CITES in 1973), and a conservation ethic was growing, partly as a result of public exposure to wildlife through television. The late Gerald Durrell, charming author, broadcaster and founder of the Jersey Wildlife Preservation Trust and Jersey Zoo, was a leading figure in recognizing and promoting the role of zoos and captive breeding in conservation. Consequently, zoos began to maintain larger collections and to devote more effort to breeding endangered species in captivity. However, each zoo can only maintain a certain number of individuals and these small breeding groups can rapidly become inbred and potentially non-viable. By the early 1980s, zoo managers recognized that their contribution to conservation could best be made through regional and international cooperative breeding programs and through collaborations with *in-situ* conservation programs.

> The menageries of the 19th century are now zoological parks and the best are major animal conservation centers

During the last 20 years, the role of zoos has expanded substantially, with active participation in a wide range of collaborative captive breeding and conservation activities. In North America, Species Survival Plans (SSP), co-ordinated by the American Zoo and Aquarium Association, were first developed in 1981. SSPs involve co-ordinated management of all captive individuals held by co-operating institutions, and are now in place for many endangered species. Regional and international studbooks (computer databases containing the pedigree and life history of all individuals in the population) are used to make recommendations on which animals should breed, with whom, how often and where. Individual institutions permit their animals to be managed under one genetic and demographic objective, determined by the co-ordinator, and animals are frequently moved among participating institutions for breeding to optimize genetic management. Similar programs have also been developed in Australia, Europe, Japan, New Zealand, South Africa and Central America.

> Zoos are now involved in a wide range of collaborative captive breeding programs and in general conservation activities

Information on pedigrees, individual histories, breeding experiences and health records are collected at each zoo and maintained by the International Species Information System (ISIS) in Minnesota. ISIS provides a central repository, with 1.4 million records on 7600 species from 554 zoos and wildlife parks in 56 countries (as of early 2000). To better collect and manage the information, ISIS has developed record keeping software such as the Animal Record Keeping System (ARKS), Single Population Analysis and Record Keeping System (SPARKS) and Medical Animal Record Keeping System (MEDARKS).

Zoos also contribute to both *ex-situ* and *in-situ* conservation through involvement with the Conservation Breeding Specialist Group (CBSG) of the Species Survival Commission of IUCN, led by Ulysses Seal. Their programs include (a) Conservation Assessment and Management Plans (CAMPs) that provide initial assessments of the global status of species and initial research and management recommendations, (b) population and habitat viability assessments (Chapter 20) that provide detailed quantitative assessment, evaluation of management options, and recommendations for conservation action, (c) zoo conservation planning, (d) providing expertise relating to captive breeding, and (e) co-ordinating meetings and workshops on topics required to advance conservation, etc. Their CAMPs provided much of the recent information for the *Red List of Threatened Animals* (IUCN 1996). In many very difficult cases, CBSG has facilitated resolution of disputes among agencies and groups involved in high profile conservation programs (e.g. the cases of Florida panthers, black-footed ferrets and giant pandas).

A long-term goal for many captive breeding programs is to eventually reintroduce species back into the wild

Captive populations can provide animals for reintroduction programs. While reintroduction programs exist for many species, habitats are not available, and threatening processes continue for the majority (Primack 1998). The next chapter details the genetic issues involved in reintroducing species to the wild.

Stages in captive breeding and reintroduction

Captive breeding and reintroduction may be viewed as a process involving six stages (Fig. 17.1):
• Decline of the wild population and its genetic consequences
• Founding a captive population
• Growing the captive populations to a secure size
• Managing the captive population over generations
• Selecting individuals for reintroduction
• Managing the reintroduced population (probably fragmented) in the wild.

Genetic issues of importance in the first stage are the rate of decline of the wild population, the size to which it declines, and the resulting loss of genetic diversity and inbreeding that it has suffered prior to captive breeding. The first four issues were introduced in Chapters 10–14 and their management implications are discussed here. Additional aspects

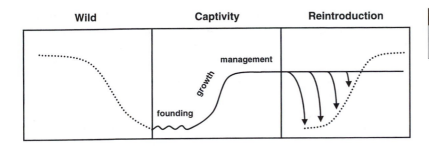

Fig. 17.1 Captive breeding and reintroduction as components of a six-stage process.

of the fourth issue, and genetic management of reintroductions, are deferred until the next chapter.

Captive populations must be managed through three phases, foundation, growth and maintenance. Management during each of these phases focuses on different priorities. During foundation, population size is usually small, and knowledge of the husbandry of the species lacking. Management focuses on basic research to develop husbandry techniques and efforts to ensure reproduction of the founders.

During the growth phase, the focus is on rapid reproduction and expansion of the population to multiple facilities. During the maintenance phase, the population is managed at zero population growth, at a size determined by the genetic goals of the program. Typically, animals are not removed from the captive population (e.g. for reintroduction) until the population size approaches this target size. The growth of the captive population of golden lion tamarins over these three phases is illustrated in Fig. 17.2.

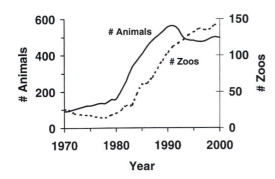

Fig. 17.2 Growth of the golden lion tamarin captive population (Ballou & Mickelberg, unpublished data). Foundation was from 1970 to 1980, growth from 1980 to 1990 and the population has been stably maintained with intense genetic management from 1990 to 2000.

The following sections discuss the genetics of captive breeding in more detail.

Founding captive populations

Potential founders may come from different sources or be of unknown origin. It is therefore essential to resolve any taxonomic uncertainties, or the need for separate management units prior to foundation (Chapter 15). This avoids outbreeding depression or a population of

Many captive populations of endangered species have been founded with few individuals, such that considerable genetic diversity has been lost and rapid inbreeding cannot be avoided

undesirable hybrids. It was not until late in the program that it was discovered that several of the founders of the Asiatic lion captive breeding program were identified as actually African lions, resulting in termination of the program, but only after substantial resources had been expended in its development and support.

The founding process sets the genetic characteristics for, and ultimately affects the conservation value of, the captive population. If the population is to encompass the genetic diversity in the wild and minimize subsequent inbreeding, then a fully representative sample of founders is required. Some selection is also inevitable during foundation as typically only a moderate proportion of wild-caught individuals successfully breed in captivity. For example, 242 wild-caught animals entered the golden lion tamarin captive population (mostly before it was being managed), but only 48 individuals contributed to the current living gene pool. Furthermore, two-thirds of the gene pool prior to management was derived from just one prolific breeding pair (Box 18.1).

There are economic trade-offs among the number of founders, the cost of starting captive populations and the subsequent size required to maintain 90% of genetic diversity for 100 years (the current objective of captive management). With few founders, the initial cost of obtaining individuals is minimized, but large populations are required to maintain genetic variation and avoid inbreeding. Subsequent costs will be much greater. With large founder numbers, the initial costs are higher, but subsequent costs are reduced, yielding substantial savings in the long term.

The need to acquire a solid genetic base, the effects of selection in reducing the number of contributing founders, and economics all argue for establishing populations with a large number of founders.

Unfortunately, most captive populations have been established using an inadequate number of founders. Some captive populations were only founded when the endangered species was 'at the last gasp', when few founders were available. Founders for most other captive breeding programs were the few animals (or ancestors of animals) that were already in captivity at the time the program was formalized (Table 17.1).

Captive populations should be established before the wild population approaches extinction, if we are to avoid serious genetic impacts. Consequently, IUCN (1987) recommended that captive populations be founded before wild populations drop below 1000 individuals. Benefits of this include (a) the ability to obtain wild founders with low inbreeding levels, (b) removal of animals will be less detrimental to wild populations than when they are smaller, and (c) it provides time to develop suitable husbandry techniques.

> IUCN recommends that captive populations be established when wild populations drop below 1000

Genetic consequences of small founder numbers

> Small founder numbers lead to loss of genetic diversity and to rapid rates of inbreeding and inevitable inbreeding depression

Population size bottlenecks at foundation lead to loss of genetic diversity, result in inbreeding, and reduced reproductive fitness (Chapters 8

Table 17.1	Founder numbers in captive populations of endangered species. *Many species have fewer than the recommended minimum of 20–30 founders*

Species	Number of founders
Mammals	
Arabian oryx	9
Black-footed ferret	18
European bison	13
Golden lion tamarin	242 (current population descended from only 48)
Indian rhinoceros	17
Przewalski's horse	12 (+ 1 domestic mare)
Red-ruffed lemur	7
Siberian tiger	25
Snow leopard	7
Speke's gazelle	4 (1♂,3♀)
Birds	
California condor	14 (3 clans)
Guam rail	21 (only 9 bred)
Lord Howe Island woodhen	6 (3 pairs)
Mauritius pink pigeon	6
Plain pigeon	21
Puerto Rican parrot	13
Invertebrates	
British field cricket	12 (6 pairs)

Source: Ryder (1988); Brock & White (1992);; Hedrick & Miller (1992); Haig *et al.* (1994); Olney *et al.* (1994); Tongue (1999).

and 10–12). To avoid bottlenecks, it is recommended that a minimum of 20–30 contributing (i.e. genetically effective) founders be used. Most of the captive populations of endangered species referred to in Table 17.1 had fewer founders than recommended and so will have lost genetic diversity and become inbred more rapidly than desirable.

The relationship between number of founders and the proportion of the heterozygosity that they capture is shown in Fig. 17.3. The proportion of heterozygosity retained is $[1 - (1 / 2N_e)]$ (Equation 8.2). Thus, even 10 contributing founders capture 95% of the heterozygosity in an outbreeding species, while 30 founders capture over 98%.

The number of founders required to capture allelic diversity depends on the number and frequencies of alleles, but typically requires more individuals than needed to capture heterozygosity. More founders are needed if rare alleles are to be sampled. Marshall & Brown (1975) recommended that the number of founders be sufficient to obtain, with a 95% certainty, all the alleles at a random locus occurring in the target population with a frequency greater than 0.05.

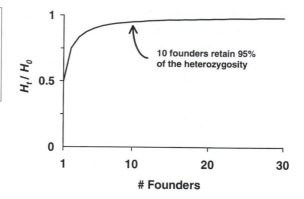

Fig. 17.3 Relationship between the number of founders and the proportion of the heterozygosity that they capture. *20–30 founders will capture most of the heterozygosity in the source population.*

For a locus with two alleles, the probability that a random sample of n founders contains at least one copy of each allele $P(A_1, A_2)$ is given by:

$$P(A_1, A_2) = 1 - (1 - p)^{2n} - (1 - q)^{2n} \tag{17.1}$$

where p is the frequency of allele A_1 and q is the frequency of A_2. $P(A_1, A_2)$ is plotted against founder number in Fig. 17.4 for a locus with allele frequencies at (0.05, 0.95) and (0.01, 0.99). At least 30 founders are needed to meet Marshall & Brown's recommendations (95% certainty of capturing an allele with frequency of 0.05). For the rarer allele, at a frequency of 1%, even 50 founders only have about a 60% chance of capturing the allele. Rare alleles are unlikely to be sampled unless founder numbers are very high.

Fig. 17.4 Probability of sampling at least one copy of each allele against number of founders for loci with alleles at frequencies of $p = 0.05$ and $p = 0.01$.

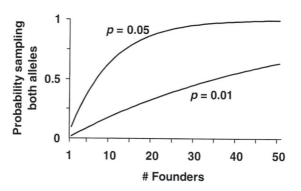

Growth of captive populations

The second phase of captive breeding programs is to multiply the population size as rapidly as possible up to the desired size set by the genetic and demographic objectives of the program. This also meets the need to create a demographically secure population. The primary objective is to grow the population as fast as possible. Genetic management is de-emphasized during this phase as it may conflict with the goal of rapid population

During the growth phase for captive populations, priority is on rapid population growth as opposed to intense with minimal genetic management growth. Offspring must be produced from all adults, not just the genetically most valuable. Some animals display strong mating preferences and may refuse to mate in genetically ideal crosses. If a genetically undesirable pairing is broken up in a monogamous species, new pairings may not mate for several years, slowing population growth. Genetic management during this phase is usually limited to avoid pairing between close relatives. This will also be desirable for demographic reasons, as inbreeding will reduce reproductive and survival rates.

During the growth phase in golden lion tamarins, black-footed ferrets and California condors (still growing), limited genetic management was applied, but subsequently these programs have been subjected to intensive genetic management (as detailed below).

How is the target population size set?

The current goal of most captive breeding programs for endangered species is to retain 90% of genetic diversity for 100 years (Chapter 14). For a population with a stable size, the effective size required to meet this goal is inversely proportional to the generation length, $N_e = 475/L$ where L is the generation length in years (Box 14.2). For example, it takes an effective population size of 475 for a species with a generation a year, but only 21 to retain 90% of the genetic variation in a species, such as mountain gorillas, with a generation length of 23 years. Conversely, an insect with 10 generations per year requires a population of 4750. In practice, demographic security would dictate a size larger than 21 for gorillas.

> The target size is the population size required to retain 90% of genetic diversity for 100 years

The founding phase has a significant impact on the required N_e, and it is likely to be greater than the value above (Chapter 14). The required number of animals depends critically on the founder effects, N_e/N ratio, the generation length, and on how quickly the population increases after the bottleneck. The N_e/N ratio depends on variance in family size, sex-ratio, mating system and fluctuations in N (Chapter 10). Computer programs are available to estimate the required N_e for these cases (Lacy *et al.* 2000).

Genetic management of captive populations

Genetic deterioration in captivity

As the population approaches its target size, the focus increasingly shifts to more intense genetic management. The objective becomes maintaining demographic stability and counteracting deleterious genetic changes including:

- inbreeding depression
- loss of genetic variation
- accumulation of new deleterious mutations

> Captive populations deteriorate genetically through inbreeding depression, loss of genetic diversity, accumulation of new deleterious mutations and through genetic adaptations to captivity that are deleterious in the wild

- genetic adaptations to captivity that are deleterious in the wild
- outbreeding depression.

These factors have different impacts, operate over different time scales, and have different relationships with population size. Inbreeding depression, loss of genetic diversity and genetic adaptation to captivity are expected in all closed captive populations. The accumulation of new deleterious mutations is only a long term concern and is of unknown importance. The most immediate threat during foundation is inbreeding depression.

The effects of inbreeding depression, loss of genetic diversity and mutational accumulation are all more severe in smaller than in larger populations. Conversely, genetic adaptation to captivity is more extensive in larger than smaller populations. While this is beneficial in captivity, its deleterious effects are only felt when the population is returned to the wild. All deleterious changes in captivity are likely to be more deleterious when populations are reintroduced into harsher wild environmental conditions (Chapter 18).

Inbreeding and inbreeding depression

Many captive populations of threatened species are too small to avoid inbreeding depression even within relatively few generations

Inbreeding and inbreeding depression are unavoidable in small closed captive populations of endangered species (Chapter 8, 11 and 12). For example, the endangered Przewalski's horse has an inbreeding coefficient of about 20% (Box 11.1), despite intensive genetic management.

For many endangered species, the effective sizes of captive populations (Fig 17.5) are so low that they will suffer inbreeding depression and significant loss of genetic diversity over relatively short time spans. Individual zoos frequently have populations of only a few individuals. For example if just two pairs were maintained as a closed population, then inbreeding would accumulate rapidly and the population would be at serious risk of extinction within about five generations. To minimize such problems, the total captive population of an endangered species is often managed as a single unit under regional (e.g. SSPs) or global management plans (e.g. golden lion tamarin). These involve interchange of animals among zoos to minimize inbreeding.

Despite interchange, these pooled populations are still not large. The SSP programs have a mean effective population size of only 41,

Fig. 17.5 Distribution of effective population sizes in SSP programs for endangered species (from Hodskins 1997). This assumes an N_e/N ratio of 0.3.

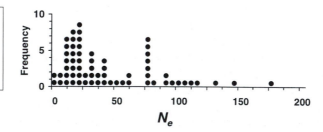

smaller than sizes where inbreeding depression due to finite size has been observed (Chapter 12). A population with $N_e = 41$ will have an inbreeding coefficient of 12% after 10 generations, and one of 26% after 25 generations, i.e. after 25 generations the population average F is greater than that arising from one generation of full-sib mating. It is not surprising that Ralls *et al.* (1988) and many others have found substantial evidence of inbreeding depression in zoo populations.

Loss of genetic diversity

Captive populations of threatened species lose genetic diversity at foundation, and because of small subsequent population size. Equation 10.1 can be recast to illustrate both the effect of N_e/N ratio and the effect of founder, versus subsequent population, numbers, as follows:

$$H_t / H_0 = \{1 - 1 / [2N (N_e/N)]\}^t \tag{17.2}$$

This can be partitioned in terms of the founder effect, and the subsequent size effects, as:

$$H_t / H_0 = [1 - (1 / 2N_{fo})] \{1 - 1/[2N (N_e / N)]\}^{t-1} \tag{17.3}$$

where N_{fo} = number of effective founders. The first term reflects the founder effect and the second term is the effect of subsequent population size restrictions. From Equation 17.3 genetic variation in captive breeding programs can be retained by:
- Maximizing the initial genetic variation by using adequate numbers of founders
- Minimizing the number of generations by breeding from older animals, or using cryopreservation
- maximizing population size
- maximizing N_e/N.

Captive populations lose genetic diversity at foundation, and due to subsequent small population sizes

Current genetic management of captive populations

The goal of genetic management is to preserve to the greatest extent possible the genetic diversity of the wild source population. Since the founders are presumed to be a representative sample of the wild population (frequently not the case), this goal translates into minimizing any changes to the founder gene pool from one generation to the next, in other words 'freezing' evolution in the captive population.

The current target of genetic management is a loss of genetic diversity, and a concomitant increase in inbreeding coefficient, of no more than 10% over 100 years (see Chapter 14). Unfortunately, such goals are unattainable in many populations (due to small founder numbers, and/or limitations in space), and the genetic objective is often relaxed. Targets may be lowered to 80% for 100 years, or 90% for 50 years. If

Captive populations are managed to minimize genetic changes that might occur in captivity

reintroduction appears feasible, the length of a program may be shortened. It is disturbing that there has been a continuing relaxation of goals since they were first defined. The original proposal was to retain 90% of genetic diversity for 200 years (Soulé *et al.* 1986), but goals as low as 80% for 50 years are now appearing. Conversely, some programs have made genetic goals stricter. For the black lion tamarin, the goal is to maintain 95% of genetic diversity in perpetuity. This is being achieved by periodic infusion of new founders from the wild. This goal was selected as the captive population is seen as one population contributing to the wild metapopulation in this species.

The remainder of this chapter addresses genetic management strategies that maximize retention of genetic diversity and avoidance of inbreeding such that genetic diversity can be kept as high as possible.

Maximizing N_e/N

As captive breeding resources are clearly limited, and the number of species requiring captive breeding to save them from extinction is increasing, it is important to maximize the N_e for each species using the minimum number of individuals. The following procedures can be used to maximize N_e/N ratios:

- Equalizing family sizes so that $N_e \sim 2N$ (Chapter 10). This recommendation can double the effective captive breeding resource and it is being applied in practice.
- Equalizing the sex-ratio of breeders, i.e. avoiding harems if possible. This is difficult to achieve in mammals as most are polygamous and many breed best with harem structures. Many mammals are maintained in harems to avoid injury and deaths from male–male aggression, and this is sometimes practiced for species that do not naturally have harems. Maintaining an equal sex-ratio is generally a lesser problem in birds, as many adapt well to being maintained as pairs.
- Equalizing population sizes across generations. Following the foundation and growth phases, captive populations are typically maintained at relatively stable sizes (Fig. 17.2).
- Maximizing generation length. This may be done by (a) allowing parents to reproduce from sexual maturity, with successive euthanasia of offspring as new siblings are produced (not ethically acceptable to many), (b) retaining all offspring, but only using later-born siblings to be parents of subsequent generations (wasteful in terms of resources), (c) delaying reproduction until they are older; this risks death, or sterility before breeding, (d) breeding parents when young, and then avoiding reproduction (often contracepting) until older, and breeding them again, or (e) cryopreservation of embryos, or gametes; often the technology to do this is not available for the species (see later). These procedures, while theoretically sound, are not widely practiced, although there is some use of (d).

Table 17.2 Effective population size to census size (N_e/N) ratios in captive populations of endangered species

Endangered species	N_e/N	Reference
Mammals		
Arabian oryx	0.14	1
Black-footed ferret	0.35	2
Cheetah	0.21	3
Golden lion tamarin	0.22	2
Grevy's zebra	0.28	1
Okapi	0.38	2
Red panda	0.42	2
Rodriguez fruit bat	0.18–0.43	1
Scimitar-horned oryx	0.20	1
Tiger	0.05–0.08	4
Birds		
California condor	0.21	2
Cinereous vulture	0.37	5
Hooded crane	0.24	5
King penguin	0.36	5
Red-crowned crane	0.45	1
Spix macaw	0.14	5
White-winged wood duck	0.05–0.09	1

References: 1, Frankham (1995c); 2, values computed from studbooks by J. D. Ballou; 3, Marker & O'Brien (1989); 4, Ballou & Seidensticker (1987); 5, L. Bingaman Lackey personal communication

The benefits of genetic management of captive populations in terms of increasing the N_e/N ratio can be very large. The N_e/N ratio is approximately 0.11 in unmanaged populations (Frankham 1995c). Ratios of close to 2 can be achieved in experimental populations by equalizing family sizes, sex-ratios and numbers in different generations (Borlase *et al.* 1993). Thus, an 18-fold improvement is possible.

In captive populations of endangered species, N_e/N ratios of 0.2–0.4 appear common (Mace 1986). Ratios for a range of endangered species are given in Table 17.2. These range from 0.065 in the tiger to 0.45 in the red-crowned crane and average 0.26. These figures are in part low as total population size is often used as N and about 1/3 of populations are juveniles. To adjust for this, we multiply by a factor of 4/3, yielding an average of 0.35. These values are about three times higher than for wild populations because of stricter control over breeding, but there is still considerable room for improvement. Practical considerations (mate incompatibility, compliance with recommendations and stochastic factors) will probably always limit N_e/N to some extent.

Maximum avoidance of inbreeding

Probably the greatest contribution of genetics to captive population management is the design of mating schedules that minimize inbreeding and loss of genetic diversity. A maximum avoidance of inbreeding scheme is shown in Fig. 17.6. This scheme involves equalization of family sizes, which doubles the effective population size (Chapter 10). It also delays inbreeding for as long as possible using a circular mating system.

The example has eight unrelated founders, and female 1 mates with male 2, female 3 with male 4, etc. Each of the four matings produces one female and one male. In the next generation, the female from 1×2 mates to the male from 3×4, the female from 5×6 mates with the male from 7×8, etc. In the succeeding generation, the female from $(1 \times 2) \times (3 \times 4)$ mates with the male from $(5 \times 6) \times (7 \times 8)$. After this point, inbreeding cannot be avoided. To be fully effective, however, the scheme only works when applied from the first (founder) generation and it requires that equal numbers of breeding females and males are produced to become parents of the next generation.

Unfortunately, this scheme is very difficult to apply to captive populations of threatened species. First, genetic management in the vast majority of cases begins with individuals several generations removed from the founders. Second, the scheme must be followed precisely to be effective, with no practical allowance for problems such as mortality of offspring and parents, incompatibility of breeders, reduced fertility, etc. Captive breeding programs are confronted with complex pedigrees

Fig. 17.6 Maximum avoidance of inbreeding.

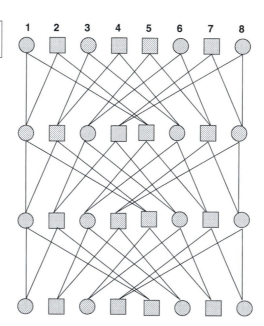

with unequal founder representation, possibly already high levels of inbreeding, and loss of genetic diversity. Managing populations by minimizing mean kinship is the most effective way to deal with these problems.

Minimizing kinship

The individuals used to found captive populations typically make very unequal contributions to subsequent generations. As we have already noted, two-thirds of the pre-genetic-management gene pool of the golden lion tamarin was derived from just one breeding pair. A range of procedures, including maximum avoidance of inbreeding, genome uniqueness, founder importance and minimizing kinship have been recommended and used in captive management of threatened species. What is the optimum way to manage pedigreed captive populations of threatened species?

> The recommended genetic management regime is to choose parents to minimize kinship

Ballou & Lacy (1995) compared the above procedures using both theoretical predictions and computer simulation and found that minimizing kinship was best for retaining genetic variation. In brief, minimization of kinship involves choosing individuals with the lowest relationship in the population to be parents of the subsequent generation. It reduces inequalities in founder contributions. When it is applied, beginning with unrelated founders, it involves equalization of family sizes and is very similar to maximum avoidance of inbreeding. We formally define kinship and show how it is calculated in the next section. In the subsequent section, mean kinship is defined together with an example of its use.

The **kinship** (or **coancestry**) of two individuals is directly related to inbreeding, and, in fact, is the inbreeding coefficient of their offspring (if they had them). Example 17.1 illustrates the computation of kinship coefficients.

> The kinship of two individuals is the probability that two alleles taken at random, one from each, will be identical by descent

---

| Example 17.1 | Pedigree for a small golden lion tamarin population and the computation of kinships |

The kinship of Robert (next page) to the other named individuals is zero; he shares no common ancestors with them.

$$k_{\text{Ro-Ri}} = k_{\text{Ro-Th}} = k_{\text{Ro-L}} = 0$$

The kinship of Rita with Robert and Robert with Rita are the same.

The kinship of Louise and Rita is most easily obtained by computing the inbreeding coefficient of hypothetical offspring X from a mating between them (hypothetical as they are both female). Using the pedigree method (Chapter 11), we have the following paths through their common ancestors, A and B:

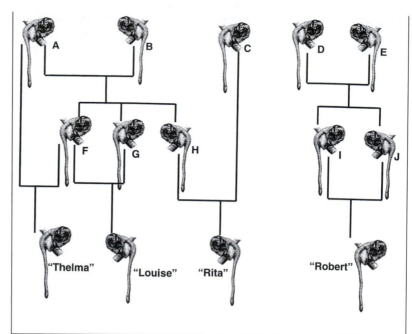

Paths	n	$F_{\text{common ancestor}}$	Contribution to F_X
LF**A**HR	5	0	$(\frac{1}{2})^5$
LG**A**HR	5	0	$(\frac{1}{2})^5$
LF**B**HR	5	0	$(\frac{1}{2})^5$
LG**B**HR	5	0	$(\frac{1}{2})^5$
			$F_X = 4/32 = 1/8$

Thus,

$$k_{\text{L-Ri}} = k_{\text{Ri-L}} = F_X = 1/8$$

The kinship of Rita with herself is the probability that two random gametes from her contain alleles that are identical by descent. As Rita is not inbred, she does not herself contain alleles that are identical by descent. If she is labelled with a genotype of A_5A_6, then Rita's kinship with herself is

$$k_{\text{Ri-Ri}} = P(\text{both } A_5) + P(\text{both } A_6) = \frac{1}{4} + \frac{1}{4} = \frac{1}{2}$$

This is the same value as the F for the progeny of selfing, as we expect.

Robert is inbred, so his kinship with himself is increased, as follows:

$$k_{\text{Ro-Ro}} = \frac{1}{2}(1 + F_{\text{Ro}})$$

and since Robert results from a full-sib mating, his inbreeding coefficient $F_{\text{Ro}} = \frac{1}{4}$, and

$$k_{\text{Ro-Ro}} = \frac{1}{2}[1 + \frac{1}{4}] = 5/8$$

Computation of other kinship values are given as Problems at the end of the chapter.

The **mean kinship** is:

$$mk_i = \sum_{j=1}^{N} k_{ij} / N \qquad (17.4)$$

where k_{ij} = kinship between i and j, and N is the number of individuals in the population. Example 17.2 illustrates the computation of mean kinship for the named individuals in Example 17.1.

> The mean kinship for individual i (mk_i) is the average of kinship values for that individual with every individual in the population, including itself

---

Example 17.2 | Computation of mean kinships

The kinship and mean kinship for the named individuals in the pedigree from Example 17.1 are:

	Thelma	Louise	Rita	Robert	Mean kinship
Thelma	5/8	9/32	1/8	0	0.258
Louise	9/32	5/8	1/8	0	0.258
Rita	1/8	1/8	½	0	0.187
Robert	0	0	0	5/8	0.156

For example, the mean kinship for Thelma is $(5/8 + 9/32 + 1/8 + 0)/4 = 0.258$.

The distribution of mean kinship in the entire population of 480 golden lion tamarins is given in Fig. 17.7 below.

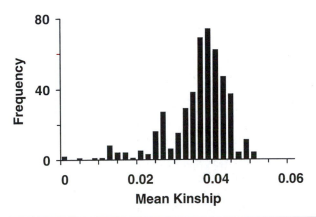

Fig. 17.7 Distribution of kinship values of 480 golden lion tamarins. The individuals with the lowest mean kinships are recently acquired founders ($mk = 0$) and F_1 descendents of founders in Brazilian zoos that have yet to reproduce.

The rationale behind the use of mean kinship in genetic management is illuminated by noting the relationship of average mean kinship to genetic diversity (H_t/H_0):

> Mean kinship for a population is inversely related to genetic diversity

$$1 - \overline{mk} = H_t/H_0 \tag{17.5}$$

where $\overline{mk}$ is the average mean kinship in the population (Ballou & Lacy 1995). Consequently, *if kinship is minimized, heterozygosity is maximized*.

Individuals with low mean kinship are the most valuable. They have fewer relatives in the population than individuals with high mean kinship and therefore carry fewer common alleles. For the pedigree in Example 17.1, Robert has the lowest mean kinship and he is the most valuable animal in his generation as he is unrelated to Rita, Louise and Thelma. In numerical terms, he has a mean kinship of 0.156, while the other named individuals have values that are greater than this. Conversely, Thelma and Louise share most genes with the rest of the population, and are least valuable genetically. Their mean kinship is 0.258, the highest value amongst the named individuals. Under a mean kinship breeding program, animals with lower mean kinship are given breeding priority. Managing by mean kinships would then increase the contribution of genes from Robert and decrease those of Thelma and Louise.

An extreme case may help to illustrate management by mean kinship (i.e. management that minimizes mean kinship). A pedigree involving 10 founders with maximum distortion of founder representation is shown in Fig. 17.8a. One individual in generation 3 is unrelated to the remaining individuals, and represents eight founders that are otherwise unrepresented. The other seven individuals in that current generation trace to only two founders. Consequently, management by mean kinship involves mating the single unrelated male with the four females on the left, as shown in Fig. 17.8b. In this way his genetic contribution and that of his eight ancestors is increased, while the contribution of the two over-represented founders is decreased.

When all animals are unrelated, or related with the same kinship, all individuals have the same mean kinship and managing by mean kinship becomes equalization of family sizes, which approximately doubles the effective population size (Chapter 10).

Populations of fruit flies, with the initial pedigree illustrated in Fig. 17.8, and subsequently managed by minimizing kinship retained more genetic diversity than those managed with maximum avoidance of inbreeding, or unmanaged populations (Montgomery *et al.* 1997). However, there were no significant differences among treatments in reproductive fitness, although the kinship treatment was best or equal best in fitness.

Applying mean kinship breeding strategies

When applying minimizing kinship to a threatened population, the mean kinship for each individual is calculated from pedigrees. Parents to be used for breeding are chosen as those with the lowest mean kinships. Two additional considerations are required to determine specific matings. First, mates are chosen such that matings between individuals

(a)

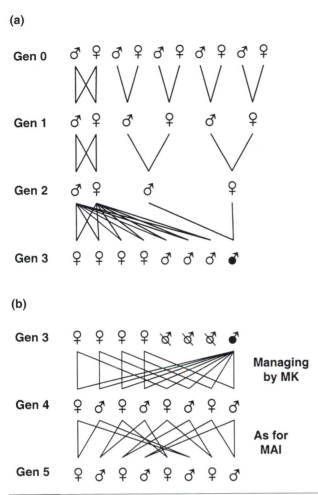

(b)

Fig. 17.8 Management by minimizing kinship. (a) A pedigree with 10 founders and maximum distortion of founder representation, and (b) the matings that would be set up using mean kinship management. At generation 3, seven progeny come from only two founders following two generations of full-sib mating, while the remaining individual (filled male symbol) is outbred and represents the contributions of the other eight founders. To minimize kinship, the single outbred male is mated to the four inbred females, and the three inbred males are not used for breeding.

with quite different mean kinships are avoided as they limit management options in the future. If a valuable individual is mated to one of low value, increasing the contribution of the under-represented individual also increases the contribution of its over-represented mate (unless the valuable individual is subsequently remated to another individual). Second, mating of close relatives is avoided to minimize inbreeding. For example, two sibs with low mean kinships should not be mated to each other. In complex pedigrees mean kinship, inbreeding, and genome uniqueness (see below) are computed using software, such as SPARKS (Scobie 1997) in combination with PM2000 (Lacy et al. 2000).

Genome uniqueness

Genome uniqueness is used to identify individuals carrying unique founder alleles

A second procedure is often used in addition to minimizing kinship to identify individuals who are the sole carriers of founder alleles. For example, an offspring with one parent carrying very common alleles and the other parent carrying rare alleles might not have a low enough mean kinship to readily identify the offspring as carrying some rare alleles. Such offspring can often be identified using **genome uniqueness**. Genome uniqueness (gu) is the probability that an allele chosen at random from that individual is unique in the population (i.e. no other copies of the alleles exist). Further details of gu are given by Ballou & Lacy (1995).

Incomplete pedigree information

Both the minimizing mean kinship and genome uniqueness protocols require that the pedigree of the population is completely known. However, in many captive populations, ancestry is not known with complete certainty. Records on parentage may not have been kept during the early years of the pedigree, while some species may require multiple breeders in an enclosure at the same time. Molecular genetic techniques can be used to determine parentage when putative mates and offspring are available for sampling (Chapter 19), but unknown ancestry in many generations past can be difficult to rectify. Methods have been developed to estimate mean kinship when part of the parentage is unknown, but this does not provide optimal management of genetic diversity (Ballou & Lacy 1995).

Limitations of management by minimizing kinship

Minimizing kinship in a single large population does not address all the genetic concerns in captive breeding. However, its use in partially fragmented populations is likely to be optimal

While minimizing kinship maximizes retention of genetic diversity in a single population, it is not the only defensible means for managing captive populations. Management of the entire captive population as a single large unit involves frequent movement of animals among institutions. Such translocations entail high costs and risks of disease spread. Further, a single population is not the optimal way to maximize retention of genetic variation (Chapter 13). Loss of genetic variation is least in populations split into sub-populations, provided none of the sub-populations suffers extinction. As endangered species already exist in fragmented populations spread over many zoos, alternative management involving partially fragmented populations (each managed using minimizing kinship) is considered in the next chapter.

Minimizing kinship does not directly address probable changes in reproductive fitness. It does not necessarily minimize inbreeding, but it is very close to a minimization of inbreeding strategy.

Genetic adaptation to captivity is a concern for populations destined for reintroduction to the wild (Chapter 18). Equalization of family sizes (a component of minimizing kinship) minimizes genetic adaptation to captivity for a given sized population (Frankham *et al.* 2000). However, maximization of N_e in a single large population promotes genetic adaptation to captivity. A partially fragmented population structure (with each fragment managed using minimizing kinship) will reduce genetic adaptation to captivity, as we describe in Chapter 18.

Captive management of groups

Pedigrees are usually not available for populations that are maintained in groups. Some species breed best in multi-female, multi-male groups, where paternities are unknown. For example, chimpanzees and many ungulates breed best in groups, while other species live in colonies (social birds and mammals, many fish and corals). Consequently, effective populations sizes, inbreeding and loss of genetic diversity cannot be accurately predicted and minimizing kinship cannot be used.

For group breeders, strategies have been devised to minimize inbreeding by exchanging individuals among groups on a regular basis (Box 17.1). These procedures utilize the maximum avoidance of inbreeding (MAI) scheme described above (Fig. 17.6), but applied to groups rather than to individuals. They are similar to the equalization of family sizes that is used when founder representation is not distorted. Contributions of groups to be parents of the following generation are equalized and individuals are regularly exchanged among groups. In Box 17.1 eight groups are shown. In the first generation, males are moved one group in a clockwise direction. In the second generation, males are moved two groups in a clockwise direction. In this example, inbreeding cannot be avoided after the third generation

Group genetic management is also an option that can be used for non-threatened species, as a less intensive procedure when resources are insufficient for full-scale genetic management using minimizing kinship. It is also suitable for management of small wild populations, but the form shown in Box 17.1 with the movement of all males would be expensive.

Genetic management of groups is one of the poorest-understood areas in captive population management. This and the problem of genetic adaptation to captivity are badly in need of further consideration.

> Where pedigrees are unavailable, management of groups by maximum avoidance of group inbreeding is recommended

Box 17.1	Low intensity genetic management for groups using maximum avoidance of inbreeding (Princée 1995)

This procedure involves applying maximum avoidance of inbreeding to groups, rather than to individuals. Maximum avoidance of inbreeding (MAI) in pedigreed populations involves equalization of family sizes and a mating system that avoids mating between relatives for as long as possible (Wright 1969; Crow & Kimura

1970). Application of MAI to groups is illustrated with eight groups in the two figures below.

Maximum avoidance of inbreeding for eight breeding groups in the first generation is shown in the figure. Maternal and paternal lineages are indicated with letters AB, CD, ..., OP. Boxes represent breeding groups. Arrows indicate transfer of males from natal groups to host groups. Bloodlines of males are shown near the arrows. The operation of the MAI system can be illustrated by following group 1. In generation one, males are moved to the next group in a clockwise direction. Group 1 starts with lines A and B. Males of group 1 (bloodlines AB) are moved to group 2. Male offspring of group 8 (bloodlines OP) are moved into group 1.

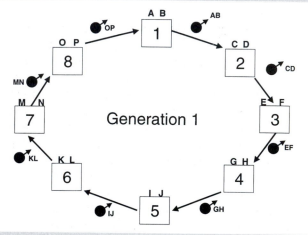

In the second generation, male offspring are moved two groups in a clockwise direction. This is necessary, as moving males by one group would result in inbreeding. For example, moving males of group 1 (bloodline ABOP) to group 2 (ABCD) is akin to cousin mating. Moving males by two groups results in group 1 males (ABOP) being mated to group 3 females (CDEF), thus avoiding inbreeding, i.e. no original breeding group is genetically represented in both males and females.

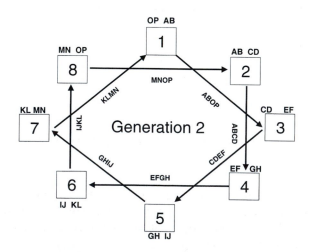

In the third generation, males are moved four groups in a clockwise direction, 1 to 5, 2 to 6, 3 to 7 and 4 to 8. This avoids inbreeding. Inbreeding can no longer be avoided after the third generation as all groups have bloodlines ABCDEFGHIJKLMNOP. Exchange of individuals in generation 4 reverts to that in generation 1 and the cycle is repeated.

Detailed guidelines for applying this system to different numbers of groups are provided by Princée (1995).

Ex-situ conservation of plants

Genetic management of captive plant populations is not nearly as complex an issue as it is in animals. Many plants can be stored as seeds, and some can be cryopreserved. Consequently, they progress through fewer generations in captivity and suffer little inbreeding, loss of genetic diversity, mutational accumulation or genetic adaptation due to captive propagation. However, preservation of seeds is not successful for about 15% of species, mainly tropical species that lack seed dormancy (Briggs & Walters 1997).

Most *ex situ* conservation of plants is done by seed storage with occasional captive propagation to regenerate seed. Thus, the emphasis is on collecting germplasm to maximize genetic diversity

The major issues for most plants are the sampling regime involved in collecting specimens for captive propagation or storage (Frankel *et al.* 1995). Two features of sampling are the size of samples and ensuring that collected material is representative and encompasses the full genetic diversity of the species. Concern about representation is greater for plants than for animals, and if the species is selfing, as a higher proportion of genetic diversity is often distributed among populations, particularly for adaptive genetic variation (Chapters 3 and 16).

In brief, recommended sampling regimes involve collecting 10–50 individuals from each of five separate threatened plant populations, with 1–20 seeds per individual (Falk & Holsinger 1991). Such sampling would also be desirable in founding captive populations of animals, but in practice, the luxury of time or resources is not available.

The emphasis in plants has been on conservation of species of known or potential commercial value, especially domesticated plants and their wild relatives. Recently, endangered plants have received increasing conservation effort (Falk & Holsinger 1991; Bowles & Whelan 1994; Falk *et al.* 1996).

Reproductive technology and genome resource banks

Reproductive technologies, developed for use in domestic animals, promise to have significant input to conservation of threatened species. These techniques include artificial insemination, cryopreservation and various cloning techniques.

Reproductive technology and genome resource banking can contribute significantly to genetic management, but have only limited current use

Artificial insemination (AI)

AI can be used to capture the genetic contribution of individuals that are unable to breed naturally, and this technique is being applied to black-footed ferrets, giant pandas and whooping cranes.

Artificial insemination with frozen semen can be used in transportation of genetic material, rather than animals, with great reductions in cost. It can also be used to equalize sex-ratios of breeders by inseminating females with semen from males other than the local dominant, or sole, male.

To our knowledge, artificial insemination is only being used routinely in the management of four threatened species, the black-footed ferret, cheetah, giant panda and whooping crane, and its use is just beginning in elephants. It is proving valuable in these species.

Cryopreservation

Cryopreservation of gametes, embryos, seeds or tissues has many potential benefits for conservation, as it literally deep-freezes tissue, and the genes they contain, away from deleterious environmental and genetic influences.

In threatened species, cryopreservation of sperm or embryos in genome resource banks provides a valuable means for extending the generation interval, and slowing inbreeding and loss of genetic diversity (Johnston & Lacy 1995). This is similar to the use of seed banks in plants. In animals, a live animal population must still be maintained, so that females are available to be inseminated, or to raise embryos. In a few cases, related domestic species can act as surrogate mothers. This has been carried out with an African wildcat and Indian desert cat (into domestic cats), gaur (into cattle), and mouflon sheep (into domestic sheep) (Lanza *et al.* 2000). However, most species are unlikely to be able to be raised in abundant domestic surrogates.

Cryopreservation of germ cells and embryos is currently only applicable to a small proportion of animals, as the technology needs to be customized for each species, and is available mainly for domestic mammals and their close relatives. Cryopreservation of seeds and of cultured cells seems to be more generally applicable for plants, and so has more immediate value to a wide range of species. For example, seed from 68 of 90 native Western Australian plant taxa germinated after storage in liquid nitrogen (Touchell & Dixon 1993). The authors suggested that at least 40% of threatened Western Australian plant taxa could be maintained in this way.

Cloning

Cloning has the potential to aid in conservation of threatened species. This is easily achieved via cuttings or tissue culture in plants, where many copies of each individual can be made. This has been carried out for Wollemi pine in Australia to preserve the genetic material of the last 40 individuals (Woodford 2000).

In animals, nuclear transplanting has been used to clone a variety of domestic animals, and the endangered gaur (Lanza *et al.* 2000). Cloning may contribute to the conservation of endangered animals in the future. For example, biopsies can be collected from endangered animals and used to expand numbers rapidly in captivity, whilst retaining the wild population. The founders could be used to generate the target population size with essentially no loss of genetic diversity.

However, at this stage, cloning of animals is not possible for any but a few species that are closely related to domestic animals (as with the gaur), and it is very expensive. Further, the technology requires surrogate mothers and an ample supply of these is unlikely to be available for threatened species.

Genome resource banks

Cryopreserved animal cells, embryos and gametes stored in genome resource banks can provide genetic material for future use, as indicated above. Animal cells provide the potential for regenerating individuals in the future via cloning, in a similar manner to tissue culture of plant cells. Gene banking of purified DNA serves as an invaluable source of material for research, but is most unlikely to contribute to living populations (Ryder *et al.* 2000). A number of such DNA banks are already in existence. They will in the future allow tests to determine whether genetic diversity has been lost, in a similar manner to studies using museum specimens.

Managing inherited diseases in endangered species

Populations derived from small number of founders have a high probability of carrying some genetic disorders at much increased frequencies. This is found in human isolates such as the Amish, Afrikaners and Finns. Several endangered populations that have originated from few founders exhibit conditions presumed to be inherited diseases (Ryder 1988; Roelke *et al.* 1993; Seymour *et al.* in press). Examples include undescended testes in Florida panthers, dwarfism in California condors, hernias in golden lion tamarins, hairless offspring in red-ruffed lemurs, malabsorption of vitamin E in Przewalski's horse and missing testicles (aplasia) in koalas.

It may appear initially that inherited defects should be eliminated from populations of threatened species. However, this comes at the cost of individuals being eliminated from the breeding population, leading to loss of genetic diversity and increased rates of inbreeding. Consequently, detailed cost–benefit analyses must be undertaken. The

> Populations of endangered species, initiated with few founders, are likely to exhibit genetic disorders at relatively high frequencies

management options are to (a) eliminate the deleterious condition, (b) minimize its phenotypic frequency, or (c) ignore it.

The impact of a program to remove a deleterious allele depends on the mode of inheritance of the defect. If it is dominant, then it will be possible to eliminate the defect by simply removing affected individuals with it. However, most inherited defects are recessive, and most individuals carrying the allele are heterozygotes. Consequently, elimination of a recessive defect is very difficult as carriers are not phenotypically detectable and removal of suspected carriers, based on pedigrees, is likely to eliminate an unacceptably large proportion of the endangered population, along with their genetic diversity. Management of a recessive genetic disorder is exemplified by chondrodystrophy in California condors (Box 17.2).

The California condor has had several hatchlings with chondrodystrophy, an autosomal recessive condition with skeletal dwarfing defects (Example 4.5). A detailed comparison of the management options (a)–(c) above for this lethal allele revealed that there would be an unacceptably large genetic and demographic cost to eliminating the condition at this stage. The proportion of the population that will be homozygous for this recessive defect is low (about 3%) and natural selection will reduce its frequency. Consequently, there is little cost in ignoring the condition and maintaining all founders in the population. The recommendation in this case was to reduce the frequency of affected individuals by avoiding matings between potential carriers, and by re-pairing individuals that have an affected offspring.

| **Box 17.2** | Managing a genetic disease in the California condor (modified after Ralls *et al.* 2000) |

We have used the autosomal recessive genetic disorder chondrodystrophy several times previously. Here we discuss practical genetic management of the condition.

Recall that we estimated the condition had a frequency of 0.17 by assuming Hardy–Weinberg equilibrium (Example 4.5). Ralls *et al.* (2000) computed the allele frequency using a gene drop analysis by an alternative method (that only accounted for alleles in known carriers and their relatives) and obtained an estimate of 0.09. The true estimate will lie between 0.09 and 0.17, but the difference does not affect the management conclusions reached. For simplicity, we use the former estimate in frequency computations below.

All affected individuals die, so natural selection is expected to reduce the gene frequency from 17.2% at hatching to 14.7% after selection (Example 6.1). With random mating, the expected frequency of affected individuals in the next generation is $q_1^2 = 0.147^2 = 2.2\%$. If there were 100 hatchings in the next generation, about 2 would be affected.

However, by avoiding matings between known and suspected carriers, it should be possible to further reduce the phenotypic frequency. In subsequent generations, it will eventually be impossible to avoid matings between all individuals that may be carriers. However, the frequency of affected hatchlings can still be kept low by splitting up pairs that have an affected offspring, and pairing them with another individual with a low risk of being a carrier.

A detailed examination of the pedigree indicated that it would be possible to reduce the frequency of the gene to zero in the next generation if that was desirable. However, to exclude all potential carriers would involve removing 77 of 146 condors from the current reproductive pool, far too high a cost for an endangered species. The low frequency of affected individuals and the cost of trying to remove the gene in terms of demography, loss of genetic diversity and increased future inbreeding meant that it was not considered wise to eliminate the chondrodystrophy allele. The figure below shows the impacts of removing suspected carriers on allele frequency and genetic diversity (after Ralls *et al.* 2000).

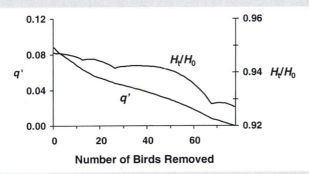

Consequently, the recommendation in this case was to separate the pair that produced the four affected individuals, and to pair them with other individuals presumed to be totally free of the *dw* allele (this has been done). In future, pairings should be made to minimize the risk of producing affected individuals, while at the same time maximizing retention of genetic diversity by managing by mean kinship.

Summary

1. Many species have to be captive bred to save them from extinction.

2. The genetic goal of such programs is to minimize deleterious genetic changes that might occur in captivity.

3. Captive populations deteriorate genetically due to inbreeding depression, loss of genetic diversity, accumulation of deleterious mutations and genetic adaptation to captivity (leading to reduced adaptation to the wild environment).

4. Captive populations should be initiated with a minimum of 20 contributing founders to establish an adequate genetic base for the population. This should be done before the wild population drops below 1000 individuals.

5. Minimizing kinship is recommended to maximize retention of genetic variation for endangered species in captivity.

6. Group breeding schemes, based upon maximum avoidance of group inbreeding, are recommended for group breeding species where pedigrees are unknown.

7. Technologies such as artificial insemination, cryopreservation and cloning have the potential to enhance genetic management of captive populations in the future, but they have limited current use.

8. By chance, rare deleterious alleles can reach relatively high frequencies in populations derived from few founders. Detailed cost–benefit analyses are required to determine appropriate management for such conditions.

FURTHER READING

Ballou *et al.* (1995) *Population Management for Survival and Recovery*. Advanced treatment of topics relating to captive breeding and reintroduction; see especially the chapters by Ballou & Lacy on use of recommendation to minimize kinship in the captive management, and by Princée on genetic management of groups of endangered species.

Botting (1999) *Gerald Durrell: The Authorised Biography*. An entertaining and informative biography of a highly influential figure in leading zoos to be involved in conservation via captive breeding of endangered species.

Falk & Holsinger (1991) *Genetics and Conservation of Rare Plants*. Considers issues relevant to *ex-situ* conservation of threatened plants.

Kleiman *et al.* (1996) *Wild Mammals in Captivity*. Detailed treatment of most aspects of managing captive populations of mammals in zoos.

Olney *et al.* (1994) *Creative Conservation*. Considers many of the issues dealt with in this chapter and has several case studies.

Tudge (1991) *Last Animals at the Zoo*. An enjoyable book written for a popular audience on the role of captive breeding in conservation.

PROBLEMS

17.1 Captive breeding: By what means do captive populations deteriorate genetically?

17.2 Kinship: What is the kinship coefficient between individuals G and H in the following pedigree?

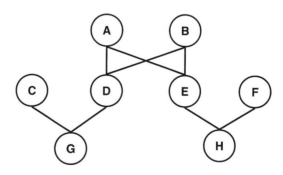

17.3 Kinship: Compute the kinship between Thelma and Rita in Example 17.1.

17.4 Kinship: Compute the kinship between Thelma and herself in Example 17.1.

17.5 Kinship: Compute the mean kinship for Rita in Example 17.2.

17.6 Group breeding schemes: In a group breeding scheme with four populations, show the recommended mating in the first two generations and the genetic composition of the resulting populations.

17.7 Cloning: What is the role of cloning in plant conservation? What is the role of cloning in animal conservation now? What role might cloning assume in animal conservation 20 years hence?

17.8 Management of genetic diseases: All 125 red-ruffed lemurs in captivity trace their ancestry to seven individuals, three of whom contribute more than 70% of the genes in the current population. Some inbred families segregate for a hairless condition due to an autosomal recessive (Ryder 1988). How would you genetically manage this condition? Assume that the recessive allele occurs at a frequency of about 10% in the captive population.

Chapter 18

Genetic management for reintroduction

Terms:
Reintroduction, supportive breeding, translocation

Captive populations provide a source of individuals for reintroductions. Reintroductions should establish self-sustaining populations with high reproductive fitness in the wild environment and ample genetic diversity

A selection of endangered species that have been captive bred or propagated and reintroduced into the wild: Mauna Kea silversword (Hawaii), California condor, black-footed ferret (North America), Arabian oryx and Przewalski's horse (Mongolia).

Reintroductions

An important role of the captive population for some conservation programs is to supply animals for reintroduction. Reintroduction is the process of releasing captive-born animals back into the wild to re-establish or supplement existing wild populations. While reintroduction programs currently exist for many species, conditions are not suitable for reintroduction for the majority as wild habitat is not available or threats to wild populations still exist (Kleiman *et al.* 1996). Nevertheless, many captive breeding programs aim to retain sufficient levels of genetic diversity and demographic viability over the long term to eventually reintroduce animals back into the wild – if and when the situation presents itself (Soulé *et al.* 1986).

While some reintroductions are carried out after brief periods in captivity (e.g. black-footed ferrets, Lord Howe Island woodhen), many may occur after long periods in captivity. The scenario envisaged with captive breeding and reintroduction is that humans will go through a demographic transition within 100–200 years, resulting in population decline that releases wild habitat for the reintroduction of endangered species. The success of reintroductions is jeopardized by genetic deterioration in captivity.

In the previous chapter, we viewed species-rescue programs as a six-stage process, commencing with recognition of demographic and genetic deterioration in the wild populations, through foundation, expansion and maintenance of captive populations, and concluding with release and management of the species in its natural environment. In that chapter, we discussed issues in the genetic management of captive species from foundation to maintenance. Here we focus on ways to limit genetic change during captivity in populations destined for reintroduction to maximize their long-term viability in the wild. Further, we consider practical questions in reintroduction; which and how many individuals should be released, where and how many wild populations should be re-established, and what management should be applied to the new populations.

At the outset, we note that the option of release is, regrettably, being de-emphasized in some programs. This may be considered a 'policy of despair'. None the less, we argue that reintroduction must remain the ultimate goal for the vast majority of captive-bred species. The success of reintroductions is jeopardized by genetic deterioration in captivity. We have discussed many of the issues in previous chapters. Here we particularly concentrate on the, often-overlooked, effects of genetic adaptation to captive environments.

There are three genetic scenarios for captive populations (Frankham *et al.* 1986). First, the threatening process in the wild may be controlled with relative ease, for example by the extermination or exclusion of introduced predators or competitors on an island. In this case, the endangered species may be reintroduced after only a few generations of population expansion in captivity (e.g. black-footed ferrets, Lord Howe

Many captive populations of threatened species are managed to preserve the option of eventual reintroduction to the wild

Island woodhen). The only genetic issues are representative sampling during foundation and avoidance of inbreeding. Any genetic deterioration has already occurred as the wild population declined. A second scenario represents the other extreme. Loss or degradation of habitat may be so severe that reintroduction is not a realistic proposition. This may be the case for some species of large, naturally wide-ranging mammals. Here genetic management may, sadly, be 'domestication', deliberate selection of passive animals, capable of tolerating close proximity to humans and other animals, and easily maintained on cheap, non-specialist diets. Non-threatened species kept in zoos for display may also be managed in this way. The majority of captive endangered species lie between these extremes and constitute the third scenario. They require many generations of captive breeding, but release remains a viable option. The third scenario is the focus of this chapter.

The case of the golden lion tamarin represents, arguably, the most extensively managed captive breeding and reintroduction program and illustrates many of the features above (Box 18.1).

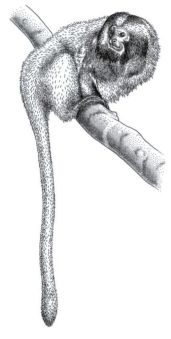

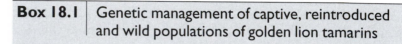

Box 18.1 | Genetic management of captive, reintroduced and wild populations of golden lion tamarins

Golden lion tamarins are small, arboreal, monogamous primates from Brazil. Their habitat in the Atlantic rainforest has been fragmented and reduced to less than 2% of the original area. Consequently, tamarin numbers have declined to endangerment. The Golden Lion Tamarin Conservation Program is a collaborative program involving the Smithsonian National Zoological Park, the Golden Lion Tamarin Conservation Association and the Brazilian Government. It involves the largest global captive breeding and reintroduction program. The program has developed a multi-disciplinary approach to preserving the species and its habitat, by integrating captive breeding, reintroduction, translocation, studies on the ecology of wild tamarins, habitat restoration and community conservation education (Kleiman et al. 1991).

The captive population consists of about 500 individuals located in 140 zoos worldwide. The concept of managing by mean kinship to maximize retention of genetic diversity was originally developed for genetic management of this complex population. Although descended from 48 founders, about two-thirds of the genes in the population had derived from just one prolific breeding pair, prior to genetic management (see pedigree below; after Ballou & Lacy 1995). However, due to subsequent careful genetic management, the level of inbreeding in the population is now only 1.9%.

The wild population consists of about 600 individuals dispersed among 11 isolated populations (see map), the largest being Poço das Antas Biological Reserve containing about 350 tamarins. Translocation of animals from the most severely threatened populations to a newly established reserve is underway. Molecular genetic analyses are also being used to determine the genetic uniqueness of the isolated populations and the degree of genetic differentiation among wild and captive populations (Grativol et al. 2001). This information will be used to define a program of regular translocations of animals among fragments to keep inbreeding to a minimum and to maximize the effective size of the entire population. This is impor-

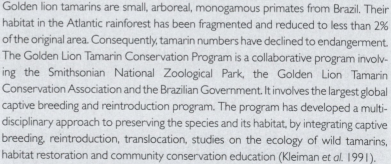

tant, as ecological and behavioural studies of wild groups in the Poço das Antas Reserve have shown that inbreeding significantly reduces juvenile survival in this species (Fig. 12.1).

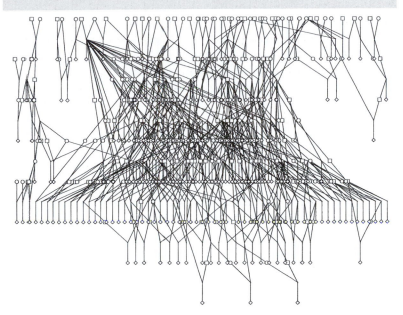

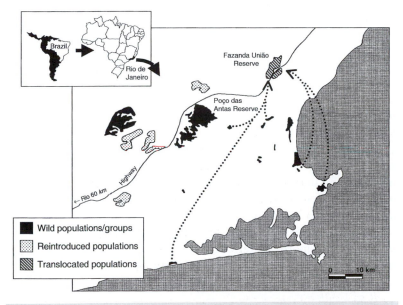

A reintroduction program, initiated in 1983, is also being used to re-establish populations in areas of their former range. Since 1984, over 145 tamarins have been released, and the reintroduced population has flourished, growing at a rate of 25% per year in recent years. Initially there was high mortality in released animals, associated with lack of foraging ability and orientation. Modified protocols have solved many of these early problems and offspring born to reintroduced tamarins have survival comparable to wild tamarins.

The reintroduced population is genetically managed in much the same way as a zoo population. Weekly monitoring permits tracking of parentage, birth and death dates, as well as migration events among groups. These are recorded in a studbook database and used to identify genetic relationships in the population. These data are also used to select individuals for reintroduction. From pedigrees of both the reintroduced and captive populations, it is possible to avoid reintroducing animals that are (a) genetically valuable to the captive population, or (b) closely related to the reintroduced animals. Similar approaches are used to select reintroduction candidates for the black-footed ferret and California condor reintroduction programs.

Genetic changes in captivity that affect reintroduction success

Inbreeding depression, loss of genetic diversity, genetic adaptation to captivity, relaxation of natural selection and perhaps accumulation of new deleterious mutations reduce reintroduction success

Captive populations typically deteriorate in ways that reduce reintroduction success. The means by which captive populations deteriorate are:

- Loss of genetic diversity
- Inbreeding depression
- Accumulation of new deleterious mutations
- Genetic adaptation to captivity.

In the previous chapter, we discussed genetic deterioration in captivity due to the first three factors. In this chapter, we will consider the impact of genetic adaptation to captivity and means for minimizing it.

These factors have different impacts, operate over different time-scales, and have different relationships with population size (Fig. 18.1). Inbreeding depression, loss of genetic diversity and genetic adaptation to captivity are expected in all closed captive populations. The accumulation of new deleterious mutations is a much longer-term concern and is of unknown importance.

The effects of inbreeding depression, loss of genetic diversity and mutational accumulation are all more severe in smaller than in larger populations. Conversely, genetic adaptation to captivity is more extensive in larger than in smaller populations (Chapter 6). While this is beneficial in captivity, its deleterious effects are only felt when the population is returned to the wild. All deleterious changes in captivity are likely to be more deleterious when populations are reintroduced into harsher wild environmental conditions (Fig. 18.1).

Genetic adaptation to captivity

Genetic adaptations to captivity typically reduce reproductive fitness when populations are returned to the wild

While genetic adaptation to captivity has been recognized since the time of Darwin (domestication), it has, until recently, been considered only a minor problem in captive breeding. However, there is now compelling evidence that it can be a major threat to the success of reintroductions. All populations adapt to their local environmental conditions (Chapter 6). When we compare populations across a range of environ-

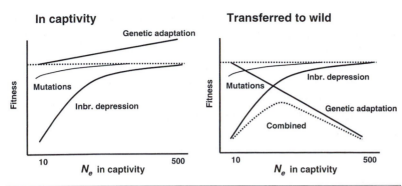

In captivity

Transferred to wild

Fig. 18.1 Genetic deterioration in captivity and its impact on reintroduction success. Predicted relationships of reproductive fitness with effective population size (N_e) due to impacts of inbreeding depression, accumulation of deleterious mutations and genetic adaptation to captivity. Reproductive fitness under captive conditions is shown on the left, and for captive populations transferred to the wild on the right. The dotted line is the fitness of a large wild population. The curve labelled 'Combined' is the cumulative impact of inbreeding depression and genetic adaptation to captivity. A long-term time frame is being considered (~ 50 generations). The magnitudes of effects will vary among species and environments, but the directions of change will be consistent.

ments, we usually observe that they have highest fitness in their own environment and perform least well in other environments (genotype × environment interactions) (Chapters 5 and 6). Thus, for populations maintained in captivity for many generations, adaptation to this novel environment may severely reduce their performance upon return to natural environments. This is evident in introduced pest species, such as rabbits and European starlings, where release of captive stock has often failed, while introductions with wild stock have been more 'successful' (Fenner & Ratcliffe 1965; Fyfe 1978). Less anecdotal evidence comes from reintroductions of captive populations of turkeys, biocontrol insects and, especially, fish (Hindar *et al.* 1991; Frankham 1995d). Genetic adaptation is expected to occur in all species in captivity.

When wild populations are brought into captivity, the forces of natural selection change. Populations are naturally or inadvertently selected for their ability to reproduce in the captive environment. Selection for tameness is favoured by keepers and flighty animals such as antelope, gazelle, wallabies and kangaroos may kill themselves by running into fences. Predators are controlled, as are most diseases and pests. Carnivores are no longer selected for their ability to capture prey. Further, there is usually no competition with other species in captivity, and limited competition for mates within species. Natural selection on all of these characters will be relaxed, or, if there are trade-offs with other aspects of reproductive fitness, they may actually be selected against (Bryant & Reed 1999).

Genetic adaptation to captivity has been described in mammals, fish, several species of fruit flies, plants and bacteria (see Chapter 6; King 1939; Frankham & Loebel 1992; Arnold 1995; Woodworth 1996; Behr *et*

Captive populations of threatened species adapt to reproduce in their captive environment. This adaptation is deleterious when they are returned to the wild

al. 1999) and it is likely to occur in all species. The extent of change may be very large. Wild rats showed about a three-fold increase in reproductive output over 25 generations in captivity (King 1939). Similarly, wild fruit fly populations kept in large populations under regular laboratory conditions increased in fitness by over three-fold over 84 generations (Gilligan 2001).

Response to selection and hence genetic adaptation to captivity is greater in larger than smaller populations (Fig. 18.1). If genetic adaptation to captivity causes major reductions in fitness when captive populations are reintroduced, then large captive populations will actually have lower fitness in the wild than smaller ones. When both inbreeding depression and genetic adaptation to captivity are occurring, we expect a curvilinear relationship between population size and fitness when returned to the wild (Fig. 18.1).

> Genetic adaptation to captivity is more extensive in large than in small populations

It is therefore critical that we experimentally evaluate the combined impacts of inbreeding depression, genetic adaptation to captivity and accumulation of deleterious mutation on fitness, both in captivity and when following reintroduction. At what rate do captive populations deteriorate genetically? How large an impact does each of the factors have? To evaluate these issues, Woodworth (1996) maintained captive populations of fruit flies at effective sizes of 25, 50, 100, 250 and 500 for 50 generations under benign uncrowded conditions designed to minimize genetic adaptation to captivity. After 50 generations, the patterns of reproductive fitness in the different populations under captive and 'wild' conditions (Fig. 18.2) reflected those predicted in Fig. 18.1. Under benign captive conditions, reproductive fitness was related to population size. Smaller populations generally displayed lower fitness and the large populations had higher fitness. Some larger populations had evolved greater fitness, under these conditions, than the wild population from which all populations had been founded, i.e. they had adapted to the captive environment.

> Genetic adaptation to captivity may be an important determinant of reintroduction success

However, when the same populations were evaluated under crowded, competitive conditions, designed to mimic conditions in the wild, major genetic deterioration in reproductive fitness was observed. All populations had declined in fitness, under these conditions, by at least 67%. There was a curvilinear relationship between 'wild' fitness and population size; populations with intermediate size ($N_e = 100$) had highest fitness in the 'wild'. This is only expected when genetic adaptation to captivity is causing genetic deterioration at greater rates in larger populations, and inbreeding depression is causing most deterioration in small populations. The largest populations ($N_e = 500$) had lost 86% of their reproductive fitness over 50 generations, i.e. a decline of approximately 1.7% per generation. Similar genetic changes in captivity have been reported in other large fruit fly populations (Shabalina *et al.* 1997), in fish and in insect biological control programs. This issue is emerging as a major concern in captive breeding programs where the option of reintroduction to the wild is envisaged.

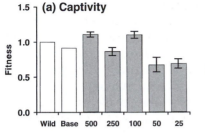 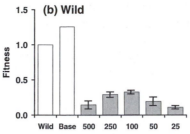

Fig. 18.2 Genetic deterioration in captivity (Woodworth 1996). Reproductive fitness (±SE) of fruit fly populations maintained in benign captive conditions for 50 generations with effective population sizes of 25, 50, 100, 250 and 500. Fitness was measured at generation 50 under benign captive conditions (captivity), and when the populations were raised under crowded, competitive 'wild' conditions. Genetic deterioration under captive conditions was due to inbreeding depression, but was lessened by genetic adaptations to the captive conditions. Genetic deterioration under 'wild' conditions was due to inbreeding depression and to genetic adaptations that had evolved over the 50 generations of benign captive environmental conditions. Genetic adaptation was greatest in larger populations, while inbreeding depression was most severe in the smaller populations, yielding a curvilinear relationship between fitness and population size in the 'wild'. No contribution from accumulation of new deleterious mutations was found in these populations (Gilligan et al. 1997).

What determines the rate of genetic adaptation to captivity?

To minimize the deleterious impacts of adaptation to captivity on reintroduction success, we need to consider what factors determine the annual rate. These include:

- Number of generations in captivity (years / generation length: y / L)
- Selection differential in captivity (S)
- Additive genetic variation for reproductive fitness (as heritability: h^2)
- Effective population size of the captive population (N_e)
- Proportion of the population derived from migrants (m)
- Generation length in years (L).

Rates of genetic adaptation (GA) can be predicted from:

> Genetic adaptation to captivity depends upon genetic diversity, selection in captivity, the effective population size, the number of generations in captivity, and the difference between the captive and wild environments

$$GA \sim \frac{Sh^2}{L} \sum_{i=1}^{y/L} [1 - 1/(2N_e)]^{y/L} (1 - m_i) \qquad (18.1)$$

where m_i is the proportion of the genetic material from immigrants in the *ith* generation.

Selection in captivity is dependent upon the mortality rate and upon the variance in family sizes. Under conditions of extremely high density and mortality, captive fitness doubled over eight generations in a fruit fly population (Frankham & Loebel 1992), while changes were much less over 50 generations under the benign captive conditions described above (Fig. 18.2). The extent of the difference between captive and wild environments drives the adaptive differentiation in captivity. If the captive environment is very different from the wild, selection in captivity will be strong and the population will evolve rapidly to adapt.

As selection is more effective in large than in small populations (Chapters 8 and 14), genetic adaptation to captivity is greater in large than in small populations. If genetic adaptation causes major genetic deterioration for released captive populations, then large captive populations will actually display lower fitness in the wild than smaller ones. This suggests a management strategy to minimize it (see later).

Immigrants, introduced from the wild, will slow the rate of genetic adaptation. However, for many endangered species wild individuals are either not available at all (extinct in the wild), or too valuable to use in augmenting a captive population.

Species with shorter generation lengths show faster genetic adaptation per year than ones with longer generations, e.g. elephants will adapt more slowly to captivity (per year) than native mice, if all other factors are the same.

Minimizing genetic adaptation to captivity

Genetic adaptation to captivity can be minimized by reducing the number of generations in captivity, selection and size of captive populations

We have just discussed the factors that promote adaptation to captivity. Consequently, adaptation can be reduced by:
- Minimizing number of generations in captivity
- Minimizing selection in captivity
- Minimizing the heritability of reproductive fitness in captivity
- Minimizing the size of captive populations
- Maximizing the proportion of wild immigrants and the recency of introducing immigrants
- Maximizing generation length.

Minimizing time in captivity has both genetic and non-genetic benefits. Low numbers of generations in captivity have been utilized for Lord Howe Island woodhens (about four years in total), black-footed ferrets and California condors, although, in the latter cases, the wild populations are not yet self-sustaining. Conversely, Père David's deer has been in captivity for hundreds of years and Przewalski's horse for most of the 20th century.

Cryopreservation has the potential to be highly effective in minimizing generations in captivity. However, it is currently only available for a small number of animal species, mostly those closely related to domestic animals (Chapter 17). Breeding from older animals can also extend the generation interval, but is not easy to achieve in practice (Chapter 17).

Selection can be minimized by making the captive environment as similar to the natural habitat as possible. The heritability of fitness is likely to increase with the difference between the natural and captive environments (Sgrò & Hoffmann 1998). However, duplicating a natural environment (habitat, diet, endemic diseases, predators, competitors, etc.) is extremely difficult. It is also difficult to justify in captive breeding of a threatened species as the first priority is to establish a secure, viable population, i.e. to reduce the threatening processes.

Genetic adaptation can also be reduced by managing the population to ensure equal representation of founder alleles and avoiding preferential breeding of individuals. Managing for equal representation of founder alleles ensures that some lineages or alleles are not selected in favour of others. The strategy of breeding to minimize mean kinship is designed to accomplish this objective as decisions on who should breed and how many offspring should be produced is based on pedigree information as opposed to reproductive performance or phenotype. However, selection within families is unavoidable and cannot be compensated for by management using mean kinship. For example, all siblings in a family initially have the same mean kinship, yet they differ in the alleles they receive from their parents. If sibs carrying a particular allele show higher survival, selection will not be prevented by mean kinship. Nevertheless, genetic management using mean kinship can halve the intensity of selection. This has been verified in fruit flies under breeding programs that equalized family sizes (the equilibrium state of a mean kinship breeding program; Frankham *et al.* 2000). However, this type of breeding program is insufficient to prevent substantial genetic deterioration in captivity, as it was used in the experiment described in Fig. 18.2.

> Minimizing kinship can halve genetic adaptation to captivity

Population fragmentation as a means for minimizing genetic adaptation to captivity

The competing requirements to maintain genetic diversity and avoid severe inbreeding depression, but also to avoid genetic adaptation to captivity, indicate that neither large nor small populations are ideal for breeding in captivity, when reintroduction to the wild is envisaged. Small populations suffer loss of genetic variation and inbreeding depression, but minimize genetic adaptation to captivity. Large populations retain genetic variation and have only slow inbreeding, but suffer most from genetic adaptation to captivity.

> Fragmented populations with occasional exchanges of individuals show reduced genetic adaptation to captivity and retain more overall genetic diversity than in a single population of the same total size

A compromise could be achieved by maintaining a large overall population, but fragmenting it into partially isolated sub-populations, as shown in Fig. 18.3. The sub-populations are maintained as separate populations until inbreeding builds to a level where it is of concern. This will most probably be at an F of 0.1–0.2, although populations should be monitored for signs of fitness decline. Immigrants are exchanged among sub-populations at this point. The sub-populations are then maintained as isolated populations until inbreeding again builds up. This structure is expected to maintain more genetic diversity than a single population of the same total size and to exhibit less deleterious changes due to genetic adaptation to captivity. There might be low levels of inbreeding depression, but these should be tolerable.

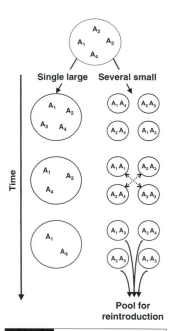

Time

Single large   Several small

Pool for
reintroduction

Fig. 18.3 Single large or several small: alternative genetic management options for captive populations. *Several partially isolated fragmented sub-populations, when pooled, should maintain more genetic variation, show less genetic adaptation to captivity and have a lower inbreeding coefficient than a single large population with the same total size.*

If all sub-populations are combined (e.g. to produce animals for reintroduction) the pooled population has a lower level of inbreeding and more genetic diversity than a single large population of the same total size (Margan *et al.* 1998). A critical requirement in the use of fragmentation is that none of the sub-populations becomes extinct due to inbreeding depression or other reasons. For this reason, this strategy is not recommended for wild populations in nature, as it is very difficult to avoid extinctions of sub-populations. Further, we wish to maximize adaptation to wild environments.

This structure satisfies other requirements in captive breeding. Captive populations are already fragmented. Individual zoos and wildlife parks have limited capacity and endangered species are dispersed over several institutions to minimize risk from catastrophes (fires, tornadoes, disease, etc.). Currently, individuals are moved among institutions to create, effectively, a single large population. The fragmented structure will reduce costs and the risk of injury, and reduce disease transmission.

How would the fragmented structure be implemented? Initially it is envisaged that movement of animals among institutions for genetic management will cease, but that populations within institutions will be managed by mean kinship. When inbreeding levels reach 0.1–0.2, nearby zoos will exchange animals. This may happen in two generations for zoos with only one pair. For example, they might exchange all breeding males. The new outbred populations will again be maintained in isolation until inbreeding rises to 0.1–0.2. At this point exchange of animals will be with zoos that are more distant. This process will be continued in a manner similar to the maximum avoidance of inbreeding with groups (Box 17.1).

When inbreeding has accumulated and there are no additional 'unrelated' populations within regions, transfer of individuals among captive breeding programs in different regions or countries may be envisaged. The number of generations between animal transfers will depend on the N_e of different populations, and will be more frequent for smaller populations than larger ones.

Does population fragmentation work as a genetic management strategy? The predicted benefits of fragmentation on 'wild' fitness have been demonstrated in fruit flies, using the populations described in Fig. 18.2. Populations were maintained under benign captive conditions as either fragmented populations (and pooled after 50 generations), or as single large populations e.g. four populations of size 25 versus two of 50 versus one of 100. These populations were 'reintroduced' by placing them in more stressful, crowded, competitive conditions. The fragmented/pooled populations exhibited superior fitness in the stressful 'wild' environment, indicating that the smaller population fragments had adapted to the captive environment to a lesser extent than the single large populations (Fig. 18.4). The fragmented populations also had more overall genetic diversity than the single large populations.

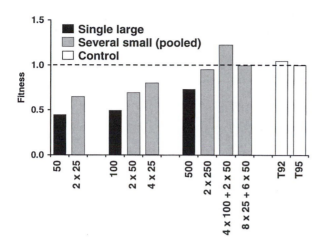

Fig. 18.4 Experimental evaluation of population fragmentation for the captive management of populations destined for reintroduction. Reproductive fitness under crowded, competitive 'wild' conditions for fruit fly populations previously maintained for 50 generations under benign captive conditions is shown for single large populations, compared to several small pooled populations of equivalent total size. The several small populations were pooled after generation 50 (Margan et al. 1998). *In all cases the fitness under 'wild' conditions was greater in the pool formed from the several small populations, than in the single large populations.*

This strategy has only recently been advocated and experimentally validated, and it is not yet the recommended genetic management for captive populations of endangered species. However, it has much to commend it.

Genetic management of reintroductions

Reintroductions and introductions are designed to re-establish self-sustaining wild populations. There are many practical considerations when a reintroduction is contemplated. Genetics may play a relatively minor role in some decisions (Kleiman *et al.* 1994). However, genetic considerations should not be ignored, as often occurs, as reintroductions have a higher probability of success if all issues are considered (see below). Genetics can contribute to:
- choice of sites for reintroduction
- choice of individuals, and numbers to release
- deciding upon the number of release sites
- genetic management of released populations.

These issues are considered in turn below.

> The genetic objective of reintroduction programs is to re-establish wild populations with maximum genetic diversity using individuals predicted to have maximal reproduction fitness in the wild habitat

Choosing sites for reintroduction

Sites for reintroduction should maximize the chances of successful re-establishment in the wild. The environment should match, as closely as possible, the environment to which the population was adapted, prior to captive breeding. Reintroductions should therefore be carried out within the previous range of the species and ideally into prime, rather than marginal, habitat. This minimizes the adaptive evolution required in the reintroduction site.

For example, in butterfly reintroductions it is important that the site

> Reintroductions and introductions should be carried out in sites where the species has the best chance of surviving in the wild

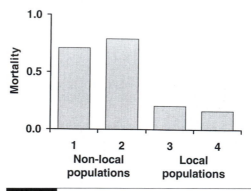

Fig. 18.5 Populations adapted to local conditions have higher fitness than those from distant sites. Mortality in four *Nasella pulchra* plant populations planted at Winters, California (Knapp & Dyer 1998).

contains the food-plants to which the species is best adapted. It is important that reintroduced plants be genetically adapted to the soil, day length and climatic conditions. For example, mortality in the plant *Nasella pulchra* was greater in non-local than local populations planted at Winters, California (Fig. 18.5). Similar results have been found in several other plant studies (Guerrant 1996; Montalvo & Ellstrand 2000). Similar principles apply to vertebrates. However, the extent of local adaptation in vertebrates is generally less than in invertebrates and plants, and a wider variety of sites may be acceptable.

Reintroduction from populations maintained in captivity for long periods may face challenges due to changes in the wild habitat. This also suggests that time in captivity be minimized.

Choosing individuals to reintroduce

> Reintroduction programs should use healthy individuals with as much reproductive ability and genetic variation as possible

Individuals used for reintroductions should maximize the chances of re-establishing a self-sustaining wild population. Thus, healthy individuals with high reproductive potential, low inbreeding coefficients and high genetic diversity are ideal. Inbred deer mice, snails and American kestrels were found to have lower survival than their outbred counterparts when released into the wild (Chen 1993; Jiménez *et al.* 1994; Frankham 1995a). Populations of rose clover with higher genetic variation had greater success in colonizing new environments than populations with less genetic variation (Martins & Jain 1979). Similarly, fish populations with more genetic diversity had higher population growth rates than those with lower genetic diversity (Leberg 1990a). The plant *Lysimachia minoricensis* lacks genetic diversity for RAPD and allozymes. Efforts to reintroduce it back into the Balearic Islands (Minorca) have failed (Calero *et al.* 1998).

> When choosing animals for reintroduction, the genetic impacts of adding them to the reintroduced population, and of removing them from the captive population, must both be evaluated

When an individual is transferred to the wild, its genetic diversity is added to the reintroduced population, but removed from the captive population. Both these effects must be assessed when evaluating indi-

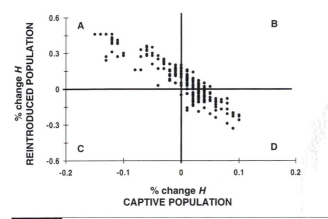

Fig. 18.6 Changes in genetic diversity in the captive and reintroduced populations resulting from reintroducing individual golden lion tamarins. Each point shows how reintroducing that individual will affect the heterozygosity of the reintroduced population and how its removal will affect the heterozygosity of the captive population.

viduals for reintroduction. Since survival in the natural habitat is expected to be much lower than in captivity, it is undesirable to deplete the captive population of genetically valuable animals to benefit the wild population. This is particularly important at the beginning of a reintroduction program as mortality is frequently high. Conversely, the reintroduced population is highly related to its source captive population and an otherwise ideal reintroduction candidate may be closely related to animals previously released. Its reintroduction may actually reduce the genetic diversity of the reintroduced population.

Often the interests of the two populations conflict, as illustrated for golden lion tamarins in Fig. 18.6. Individuals (points) in segment A are those reintroductions that would benefit the reintroduced population, but be harmful to the captive population. These are genetically valuable captive animals with few relatives in the reintroduced population. Reintroduction of individuals in segment B will benefit both the reintroduced and the captive population. These are genetically over-represented captive animals with few reintroduced relatives. Reintroduction of individuals in quadrant C would be detrimental to both captive and reintroduced populations (valuable in the captive population but with lots of reintroduced relatives). Reintroducing individuals from sector D is beneficial to the captive population, but detrimental to the reintroduced population (over-represented in both populations).

Because of the high risks of mortality commonly associated with reintroduction programs, individuals of type D should be used initially. This has been practiced in reintroduction programs for golden lion tamarins, California condors, black-footed ferrets and Przewalski's horses. When survival and reproduction in the reintroduced population has improved, more valuable animals may be added until the full range of genetic diversity in the captive population is represented in the wild.

This can only be done if survival and reproduction of individuals in the reintroduced population are carefully monitored. All phases of this process have now occurred for the golden lion tamarin reintroduction program.

Choice of individuals to reintroduce when several populations exist

When several captive populations exist, individuals for reintroduction may come from a single population, a pool of populations, or from crosses among individuals from different populations

Several captive populations may be able to supply individuals for reintroductions, especially in plants. From which population(s) should individuals for reintroduction be taken? The options are for individuals to be taken from:
• a single population
• a combination of populations
• crosses between populations.
The decision rests on evaluating which of these options maximizes the probability of reintroduction success (Guerrant 1996).

A single population may be selected if the species shows strong local adaptation and one captive population was derived from the environment where the reintroduction is planned. This presumes that there are accurate records of the sources of populations, and that the environment has not changed. The latter presumption is often untrue, as the initial endangerment of the species frequently arises from environmental deterioration. If the environment has changed, reintroduction success is improved by using individuals that represent a combination of populations, or ideally, crosses among populations.

If the species is a natural outbreeder and the captive populations are inbred, then crosses between populations should improve reproductive fitness and genetic variation and thus improve reintroduction success. There are suggestions that wild turkeys resulting from crosses among populations had higher reproductive fitness in the wild than those from single populations (Leberg 1990b). Reintroduction of individuals from several small differentiated populations, each with low genetic diversity, has been used in reintroduction for collared lizards in Missouri, USA (Templeton 1986). However, care must be taken to avoid outbreeding depression in such cases. The most prudent approach is to proceed with reintroductions on an experimental basis, monitoring survival and reproductive success of pure and hybrid individuals. This is being undertaken for the Florida panther, following the introduction of individuals from the Texas sub-species. These data can then be used to decide upon the best approach for further reintroductions.

How many reintroduced populations should be established?

There are genetic and non-genetic advantages in establishing several reintroduced populations

Where several suitable reintroduction sites and ample excess captive-bred individuals are available, a number of reintroduced populations should be established to maximize the numbers of reintroduced individuals (Leberg 1990b). This minimizes loss of genetic diversity and will minimize inbreeding if individuals are translocated among the different sites. Having several populations reduces the risk of extinction due to natural hazards and disease and may reduce the risks from environmental stochasticity. For example, at least 10 reintroduced populations of the black-footed ferret are recommended to minimize extinction risk (Chapter 16).

Genetic management of reintroduced populations

As the probability of success of the reintroduced population increases, animals of type B, and then of type A should be added to the wild population (Fig. 18.6), to provide the wild population with all the genetic diversity available from the captive population. Further, this will serve to minimize the inbreeding in the population and so should increase its reproductive fitness. Subsequent genetic management follows that for wild populations, discussed in Chapter 16.

Once populations are reintroduced and self-sustaining, the full range of genetic diversity should be added to them

How successful are reintroductions?

Reintroduction of threatened species is a relatively recent activity. It is a complex process that involves considerable understanding of species' biology and ecology. Even introductions of widespread and successful pest species, such as rabbits and European starlings, have failed (Fenner & Ratcliffe 1965; Fyfe 1978). For example, several introductions of domesticated rabbits into Australia failed before the 'successful' introduction of wild rabbits resulted in a serious pest problem.

Reintroduction is a complex process that, so far, has a relatively low success rate

Surveys of success rates for translocations or reintroductions indicate that they have a relatively low success rate. Wolf *et al.* (1996) reported an overall success rate of 67%, but 53% for translocations of threatened mammal and birds (Table 18.1). Success was defined as producing a self-sustaining wild population. Translocations of native game species were more successful than those for threatened species. Success rates increased with the quality of the release habitat and were higher for releases in the core of the historical habitat than in the periphery or outside. There was a trend for translocation of wild-caught animals to be more successful than reintroduction of captive-reared individuals. Translocations of omnivores were more successful than those of carnivores or herbivores. Successful translocations released more animals than unsuccessful translocations. Genetic factors were not evaluated in the survey, as they have rarely been considered in decisions involving reintroduction.

A second, more restricted, survey was carried out by Beck *et al.* (1994) based purely upon reintroductions of captive-born animals into or near the species' historical range to establish or augment wild populations. This survey covered 145 projects involving reintroduction of over 13

Table 18.1 | Success rates of intentional translocations and reintroductions of native birds and mammals to the wild in Australia, Canada, New Zealand and the USA as of 1993. Data came from 77 translocations of mammals and 105 translocations of birds; factors associated with success of translocations are indicated

Variable	Success (%)
Threatened, endangered or sensitive species	53
Native game	81
Release area habitat	
Excellent	79
Good	69
Fair or poor	45
Location of release	
Core of historic range	75
Periphery or outside	46
Wild-caught	71
Captive-reared	50
Adult food habit	
Carnivore	65
Herbivore	61
Omnivore	80
Early breeder, large clutch	67
Late breeder, small clutch	71
Potential competitors	
Congeneric	71
Similar	60
Neither	72

Source: After Wolf *et al.* (1996).

million animals of 126 species; 44% of projects involved threatened species. Programs were defined as successful if reintroduced populations reached at least 500 individuals, free of human support. Only 11% of projects were considered successful to that date. The 16 successful cases were wood bison, plains bison (two projects), Arabian oryx, Alpine ibex, bald eagle, Harris' hawk, peregrine falcon, Aleutian goose, bean goose, lesser white-fronted goose, wood duck, gharial, Galapagos iguana, pine snake and Galapagos tortoise. Success rates were 11% for mammals and birds, 17% for reptiles and amphibians and zero for fish and invertebrates. Successful projects released animals for longer (11.8 years) than other projects (4.7 years) and released more animals (average of 726 versus 336). Successful projects more frequently provided local employment and community education programs than other projects. Rather surprisingly, successful projects used veterinary screening and pre-release provisioning less often than other projects.

The relatively low success rates for reintroductions are not surprising since programs may have had insufficient time to succeed. Further, some programs have been rather cursory – animals have been reintroduced and left to fend for themselves without training for coping with the wild. Reintroduction success should improve substantially as the science behind it advances.

We are not aware of any surveys of reintroduction success in plants. However, plant data provide more insights into the probable role of genetic factors in reintroduction success. The desirability of high genetic variation in reintroduced populations is widely accepted (Huenneke 1991). Experiments with sweet vernal grass demonstrated an advantage of genetically variable (sexual) progeny in survivorship, fecundity and growth over genetically uniform (asexual) progeny, under natural field conditions (Ellstrand & Antonovics 1985). Further, genetic uniformity increases the susceptibility of populations to pathogens (Fiedler & Karieva 1998). In a reciprocal transplant experiment with Guadalupe Island lupine, differences in fitness were found among three source populations (Helenurm 1998). The poorest success was with seed from the smallest of three natural populations, a result that could reflect inbreeding depression.

Supportive breeding

Some wild populations that are not self-sustaining are maintained by regular augmentation from captive populations (supportive breeding). For example, the wild population of the nene (Hawaiian goose) is not self-sustaining and is continuously augmented using captive-bred animals (Black 1995). Restocking began in 1960 and by 1990 2100 individuals had been released. Hatchery fish stocks are widely used to augment a large number of wild fish species, especially those favoured by anglers.

Such supportive breeding typically has deleterious impacts in the long term on the genetic composition and reproductive fitness of the wild stock. It is likely to lead to (a) reduced effective population sizes, (b) reduced reproductive fitness resulting from genetic adaptations to captivity that are deleterious in the wild, and perhaps to (c) inbreeding depression. For example, Hindar et al. (1991) concluded that the fitness of captive stock was inferior to wild stock, when compared in the wild, in all nine cases they examined.

A reintroduction was proposed in Amur leopards to reinforce a small remnant population of only about 30 animals. However, the captive animals to be used descended mostly from two founders and one of these may have come from a different sub-species (Foose 1991). Consequently, the reintroduction program could have added animals that could have actually reduced the genetic diversity of the wild population. The solution proposed was to augment the captive population with individuals from the wild, to conserve genetic diversity in the more secure captive environment. Subsequently, this captive population could be used to provide substantial numbers of animals for reintroduction to the wild. Ryman et al. (1995) urged caution in allowing continuous gene flow from captive to wild populations, where a wild

Some wild populations are augmented regularly using captive-bred animals

population still exists, due to concerns about genetic adaptation to captivity, and greater inbreeding and loss of genetic diversity.

Case studies in captive breeding and reintroduction

Arabian oryx

The Arabian oryx was driven to near extinction in the wild because of hunting with increasingly sophisticated weapons. The species was saved by capture of the last few wild oryx in 1962, followed by a captive breeding program. The captive population originated from nine founders. These were bred predominantly at the Phoenix Zoo in Arizona where there was a steady increase in numbers and implementation of a genetic management program. With funding and co-operation from the Sultan of Oman, a successful reintroduction program has been carried out (Stanley Price 1989). Ten animals were initially introduced into pens in the oryx's native range, followed by gradual release. Local tribesmen were employed to assist in management and tracking of the oryx. Released animals showed good survival and reproduction, and relatively normal behaviour. They increased substantially in numbers and by 1995, there were approximately 280 animals in the wild, ranging over 16 000 km² of desert.

Unfortunately, poaching returned and the wild population was depleted to 138 individuals in 1998 (Gorman 1999). At that point, 40 individuals were taken back into captivity. After further poaching, just 11 wild females and 85 males remained in Oman. Another reintroduction program is in Saudi Arabia, where poaching is currently less of a threat.

Genetic analyses of the Arabian oryx using microsatellites have revealed loss of alleles due to the bottleneck, errors in the pedigrees and the occurrence of simultaneous inbreeding and outbreeding depression in the species (Marshall *et al.* 1999; Marshall & Spalton 2000). The population is polymorphic for a chromosomal translocation that probably explains the outbreeding depression (Benirschke & Kumamoto 1991).

Black-footed ferret

The black-footed ferret was reduced in numbers through habitat loss and especially from vigorous efforts by cattle ranchers to exterminate their prairie dog prey (Clark 1994). The last wild population was found in Wyoming in 1981 and a captive breeding program begun in 1985. Distemper was then found to be killing individuals and the last wild individuals were captured. The captive breeding program was founded from 18 individuals. These contributed unequally so that by 1993 there were effectively only 4.1 founders (Russell *et al.* 1994). The captive population has increased to about 250 adults, and has been subject to genetic management based on minimizing kinship.

A reintroduction program commenced in 1991 with surplus animals from the captive population. Since then, all females in the captive population are routinely bred to produce animals for reintroductions. Currently reintroduction has established six populations, Wyoming, Montana (two separate sites), South Dakota, Arizona, and the Utah/Colorado border, with another planned for South Dakota. Between 1991 and 1999, about 1185 ferrets have been introduced into the wild. In 2000, over 85 litters were born in the wild, but only two of the reintroduced populations have been particularly successful so far. The objective is to eventually establish 10 populations with a total of at least 1500 animals.

Przewalski's horse

Przewalski's horses have been restricted to captivity for much of the 20th century (Boyd & Houpt 1994). A captive population was founded from 12 individuals, plus one domestic mare (a different species with a different chromosome number). Numbers in captivity are now approximately 1500. The captive population has an average inbreeding coefficient of $F = 0.20$ (Box 11.1). It has been managed to minimize inbreeding, equalize founder representation, and to reduce the genetic inputs from the domestic mare. Horses have been reintroduced into Mongolia at the site where the species was last seen in the wild (Van Dierendonck et al. 1996). As of mid-2000, 47 individuals existed in the wild. A recent genetic marker analysis has cast serious doubts on the accuracy of the pedigree, suggesting that more than one domestic mare contributed (see Chapter 19).

California condor

The California condor was reduced in population size due to habitat loss, DDT pollution and lead poisoning from eating shot wildlife carcasses (see Ralls et al. 2000). After much controversy, the last birds in the wild were captured and a captive breeding and reintroduction program instituted at the San Diego Wild Animal Park and Los Angeles Zoo. Fourteen founders from three related clans were available for the program. Captive numbers have steadily increased and a limited number of releases have occurred. The major initial concern has been to increase the size of the population as rapidly as possible. Reintroduction to the wild initially met with limited success. Deaths occurred from lead poisoning, hitting electricity powerlines and poisoning due to ingestion of antifreeze from vehicle radiators. Recently, reintroduction to the Grand Canyon has been undertaken to avoid problems associated with proximity to humans. These birds are provided with supplementary feeding. At the end of 1998, the population consisted of 146 individuals, 98 captive birds, 26 wild birds in California and 22 in Arizona (Ralls *et al.* 2000).

Guam rail

The Guam rail is a flightless omnivorous bird restricted to the island of Guam in the Pacific. It numbered about 80 000 in the 1960s. However, it was extinct in the wild by 1986, due to predation from introduced brown tree snakes. The brown tree snake was introduced inadvertently during World War II, and drove seven of 11 native forest species to extinction and depleted other species. The Guam rail was saved from extinction by a captive breeding program that was based upon 21 founders rescued from the wild just prior to extinction. Nine of these did not breed. Five strategies for selecting breeders to produce young rails for reintroduction were compared by Haig *et al.* (1990): random choice, selecting for fitness, maximizing allozyme diversity by equalizing allele frequencies, equalization of family sizes and minimizing mean kinship. They concluded that the last approach was best and this was implemented. Founder relationships were evaluated using DNA fingerprints and resulted in six individuals being placed in two different sib groups (Haig *et al.* 1994). The captive breeding program has been highly successful. Further, reintroductions have been made onto nearby Rota Island where the brown tree snake is absent. After initial difficulties, reintroduced birds are now surviving and breeding. From 1989 to the end of 2000, 384 rails have been released on Rota (S. Medina, personal communication). Second generation birds have not been observed and detailed censuses are underway. In 1998, a reintroduction program was commenced in Guam, where birds were put into an enclosure designed to exclude the brown tree snake.

Lord Howe Island woodhen

The Lord Howe Island woodhen has been described as a classic case of captive breeding and reintroduction (Caughley & Gunn 1996). The endangered population on Lord Howe Island, off the East Coast of Australia, fell to 20–30 individuals mainly because of predation by introduced pigs (Brook *et al.* 1997a). The only three known breeding pairs were captured and bred in enclosures on the island and feral pigs were exterminated. Following reintroduction of 86 birds over four years, the population increased to about 200 and stabilized, so that a downgrading of its status has been recommended.

Whilst the ecological side of this program is regarded as a model, the genetic management was far from optimal. As only three pairs contributed to the captive breeding program, the total population will be much more inbred than prior to the program, and genetic variation is likely to be lost due to the distorted contributions of the available individuals. In hindsight, it would have been desirable to enhance the genetic base of the captive breeding program once it was known to be successful, i.e. by adding further fertile individuals to the captive breeding program. Unfortunately, no genetic data on the population have been reported, no remedial action is planned, and routine monitoring has ceased.

Mauna Kea silversword

A situation similar to that of the Lord Howe Island woodhen occurred with the reintroduction of the Mauna Kea silversword plant. By the late 1970s, only a small remnant natural population remained, following grazing pressure by introduced ungulates. Since 1973, 450 plants have been outplanted to promote recovery of this population. However, genetic analysis using RAPDs indicates that all outplanted individuals are derived from only two maternal founder plants, resulting in a major reduction in genetic variation in the total population (Robichaux *et al.* 1997). Since this species is self-incompatible, the restricted genetic base was affecting mating success for reintroduced individuals. Natural pollination of these only results in a 20% seed set, while deliberate outcrosses to the remaining wild individuals increases it to 60%. A remedial program to outcross the outplanted individuals to the remaining wild individuals is underway to broaden the genetic base of the population.

Summary

1. Captive populations provide a source of individuals to reintroduce and supplement wild populations of threatened species.

2. The success of reintroduction is jeopardized by genetic deterioration in captivity due primarily to inbreeding depression, loss of genetic variation, and genetic adaptation to captivity (leading to reduced adaptation to the wild environment).

3. Genetic adaptation may pose a serious threat to reintroduction success.

4. The optimum means for managing captive populations for reintroduction is to maintain them as small partially isolated subpopulations, with occasional migration. This is also the optimum means for retaining genetic diversity (but is not currently used). In addition, this management reduces costs and risk of disease transfer.

5. Individuals for reintroduction should have maximum genetic diversity and maximum reproduction fitness in the wild environment. However, the risks involved dictate that reintroduction programs should begin with genetically surplus individuals with many relatives in the captive population, so that the captive population is not compromised.

6. The initial priority with reintroduced populations is to increase numbers.

7. Once successful, the wild population should be augmented until the full complement of genetic diversity is represented in the wild.

8. Reintroductions have a relatively low success rate, to date.

FURTHER READING

Ballou *et al.* (1995) *Population Management for Survival and Recovery*. Advanced treatment of topics relating to captive breeding and reintroduction.

Bowles & Whelan (1994) *Restoration of Endangered Species*. A fine collection of papers on animal and plant restorations, including discussions of genetic issues and case studies.

Falk *et al.* (1996) *Restoring Diversity*. Wide-ranging coverage of plant reintroductions with several case studies.

Gipps (1991) *Beyond Captive Breeding*. Proceedings of a conference on reintroductions that encompasses a broad range of issues, and includes case studies.

Leberg (1990b) Discusses genetic considerations in the design of animal introduction and reintroduction programs.

Margan *et al.* (1998) Model experiment in fruit flies that demonstrates genetic advantages for a fragmented population strategy for genetic management of captive populations for reintroductions.

Olney *et al.* (1994) *Creative Conservation*. Considers many of the issues dealt with in this chapter and has case studies for animals.

Serena (1995) *Reintroduction Biology of Australian and New Zealand Fauna*. A collection of papers on animal reintroductions that covers theoretical concepts, practical considerations and many case studies.

Stanley Price (1989) *Animal Re-Introductions*. Provides detail of the classic reintroduction of the Arabian oryx into Oman and a perspective on reintroductions generally.

PROBLEMS

18.1. Genetic adaptation: What are the reasons for concerns about genetic adaptation to captivity in captive breeding and reintroduction programs?

18.2. Genetic adaptation: What determines the rate of genetic adaptation to captivity?

18.3. Reintroductions: What are the genetic issues in reintroduction programs?

18.4. Reintroductions: Why would release of a genetically over-represented captive animal (one with a high mean kinship) actually benefit genetic diversity in the captive population? Describe the effect of the release on mean kinship and heterozygosity in the captive population.

Chapter 19

Use of molecular genetics in forensics and to understand species biology

Genetic markers contribute to the conservation of species by aiding in detection of illegal hunting and by resolving important aspects of species biology; they have been used to detect bottlenecks and other demographic events in a population's history, estimate effective size, detect selection, determine parentage, sex, mating systems, population structures, dispersal rates, population sizes, diet, disease status and to detect introgression. Coalescence and gene tree analyses provide useful tools for understanding many of these factors

Terms:
Biparental inbreeding,
clade,
coalescence,
forensics,
gene trees,
haplotype network,
introgression,
selective sweep

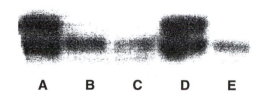

Eggs from same clutch

Multiple paternity in loggerhead turtles (tropical and temperate oceans) revealed using allozyme electrophoresis (gel from Harry & Briscoe 1988).

Forensics: detecting illegal hunting and collecting

PCR-based genetic markers can be used to detect illegal hunting or collecting

Poaching and illegal harvest are threats to a wide variety of endangered species, especially large cats, elephants, bears, rhinoceroses, parrots, whales and some plants. Most countries have laws to protect threatened plants and animals. However, it is often difficult to obtain evidence to convict individuals suspected of illegally taking or trading in threatened species. For example, a person wearing a vest containing eggs suspected of belonging to threatened bird species was apprehended at an Australian airport. The person simply squashed the eggs so that they could not be identified and thus avoided prosecution. Molecular genetic methods can be used in such cases to identify the origin of the biological material, including ivory, horns, eggs, turtle shells, meat, organs, feathers, hair and plant materials.

Molecular genetic techniques have assumed an important and growing role in the detection of illegal hunting of wildlife. For example, the US Fish and Wildlife Service has established the Clark Bevin Forensics Laboratory in Oregon specifically for the purposes of providing evidence in cases involving illegal imports, exports and hunting of endangered species. One of the more fascinating cases of molecular forensics involved the detection of meat from protected species of whales on sale in Japan and Korea (Box 19.1). Analyses of mtDNA established that some of the whale meat was not from minke whales, for which Japan engages in 'scientific' whaling, but from protected blue, humpback, fin, and Bryde's whales. In addition, some 'whale' meat was from dolphin, porpoise, sheep and horse. Not only was illegal whaling suspected, but consumers were being misled. In a related context, PCR-based mtDNA analyses have revealed that 23% of caviar samples in New York was mislabelled (Birstein *et al.* 1998). The sources have conservation implications, as most of the 27 members of the sturgeon group are endangered due to overfishing and habitat degradation. The identity of a poached endangered Arabian oryx was confirmed by microsatellite analyses (Marshall *et al.* 1999) and mtDNA-based methods are being developed to detect tiger products in Asian medicines (Holden 2000).

Forensic DNA methods have been used to determine the source of poached chimpanzees. Sequencing of mtDNA established that 26 confiscated chimpanzees in Uganda belonged to the eastern sub-species (Goldberg 1997). This identified the region where poaching was taking place, and where these animals could be reinstated into the wild.

Box 19.1	Detecting sale of meat from protected whales (after Baker & Palumbi 1996; Dizon *et al.* 2000)

Following many years of commercial exploitation, the numbers of most whale species collapsed. This led the International Whaling Commission (IWC) to institute

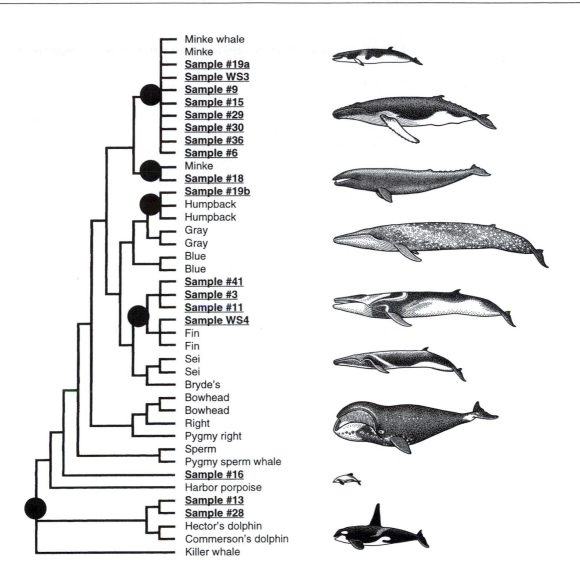

Minke whale
Minke
Sample #19a
Sample WS3
Sample #9
Sample #15
Sample #29
Sample #30
Sample #36
Sample #6
Minke
Sample #18
Sample #19b
Humpback
Humpback
Gray
Gray
Blue
Blue
Sample #41
Sample #3
Sample #11
Sample WS4
Fin
Fin
Sei
Sei
Bryde's
Bowhead
Bowhead
Right
Pygmy right
Sperm
Pygmy sperm whale
Sample #16
Harbor porpoise
Sample #13
Sample #28
Hector's dolphin
Commerson's dolphin
Killer whale

a global moratorium on commercial whaling that took effect in 1985/86. Some IWC members have continued to hunt a few whale species (primarily minke whales) for 'scientific' purposes and the whale meat can be sold for human consumption. There were suspicions that protected whale species were being marketed as species that could be taken legally. At the request of Earthtrust, Baker & Palumbi developed a system for monitoring trade in whale and dolphin products using mtDNA sequencing following PCR. They reliably distinguished a variety of whale species from each other and from dolphins using mtDNA control region sequences (see figure above).

Samples of whale products were subsequently purchased in retail markets in Japan and Korea. To avoid the possibility of violating laws governing transport of endangered species, Baker & Palumbi set up a portable PCR laboratory in their hotel room and amplified the mtDNA control region from the samples. The amplified

DNA was taken back to their laboratories in New Zealand and the USA and sequenced.

Results from the initial 16 purchases are shown in the figure. They are fitted into a mtDNA phylogenetic tree along with known whale and dolphin samples. Nine samples near the top of the tree were indistinguishable from minke whale and could be attributed to legal 'scientific' whaling. However, samples #19b, 41, 3, 11, and WS4 were from protected species. Sample #19b was from a humpback whale, while samples #41, 3, 11 and WS4 were from fin whales. Further, samples #16, 13 and 28 were from porpoise and dolphins, so consumers were being misled.

By 1999, 954 samples of 'whale meat' had been purchased in Japan and Korea and analysed by scientific groups (Dizon *et al.* 2000); 773 were from whales, approximately 9% coming from protected species whales (including blue, humpback, fin and Bryde's whales). The samples that were not from whales included dolphins, porpoises, sheep and horses. Not only were consumers being misled, but there were questions about the origin of the meat. The possibility that meat from protected species had been sourced from frozen stores collected prior to bans on whaling cannot be excluded, but this explanation does not apply to fresh meat. This has led to stricter controls over the distribution of 'scientifically harvested' whale meat and demands that legally harvested whales and meat stockpiled prior to whaling bans be genetically typed to monitor distribution.

An understanding of species biology is critical to its conservation

Molecular genetic markers and analyses help resolve many aspects of species biology that are important in conservation

An understanding of species biology is critical to effective conservation. Critical aspects of species biology are often unknown, as details of life histories are often difficult and time-consuming to determine directly. For example, paternities are notoriously difficult to assign without genetic data and genetic population structures cannot be determined without use of genetic markers. Introgression can only be suspected, but never verified from morphology. Dispersal and migration rates are hard to determine by direct observation and are often unreliable, as migrants do not necessarily breed.

Analyses of sequence differences among populations and individuals can resolve paternity, define population structure, detect introgression from another species, evaluate sources of new founders for small endangered populations, and indicate sites for reintroductions. Comparisons of DNA sequences may also be used to detect bottlenecks, migration patterns and the demographic histories of populations. For example, life history characteristics have been determined and a potential reintroduction site identified using microsatellites in northern hairy-nosed wombats (Box 19.2).

The remainder of this chapter examines the methods used, and presents examples of practical issues that have been resolved. More advanced technical treatments can be found in Smith & Wayne (1996), Hoelzel (1998) and Avise (2000).

Box 19.2	Censusing the critically endangered northern hairy-nosed wombat and inferring aspects of its biology following non-intrusive sampling of hair (Taylor et al. 1994, 1997; Beheregaray et al. 2000; Sloane et al. 2000)

Northern hairy-nosed wombats from Australia are nocturnal, fossorial, and difficult to study directly. Trapping has been used to estimate population size and sex-ratio, but is traumatic to the animals, risks possible injury or death, necessitates construction around burrows and is time-consuming and unreliable.

Twenty-eight microsatellite loci have been identified in the northern hairy-nosed wombat. Using DNA from hair collected using adhesive tape on frames at the entrance to wombat burrows, Sloane et al. (2000) were able to genetically characterize the population for up to 20 microsatellite loci. This allowed each individual in the population to be identified. Individuals have also been sexed following amplification of X and Y chromosome loci. Thus, the population can be routinely censused without trapping.

Tissue from museum skins was used to characterize an extinct population from Deniliquin (see Chapter 10 frontispiece for locations). This established that the Deniliquin population was of the northern species, rather than the southern species that is currently found nearer to this location. Consequently, Deniliquin should be suitable for establishing a reintroduced population as a hedge against catastrophes in the Queensland population.

Microsatellites have been used to infer aspects of the biology of the northern hairy-nosed wombats. Individuals of the same sex sharing burrows are often relatives, but males and females sharing burrows are not closely related. Dispersal patterns have also been inferred. The N_e/N ratio was estimated to be 0.1, based on loss of genetic diversity compared to the southern species. Parentage analyses based on 8–9 microsatellite loci were not particularly successful due to low genetic variation, but this will be improved with use of additional loci that have subsequently been developed.

Table 19.1 lists available methodologies and their applicability to the issues considered here (Chapter 3; Sunnucks 2000b). In general, DNA-based methods such as mtDNA sequence analysis, RAPDs, DNA fingerprints and, especially microsatellites are suitable for most of the purposes listed in Table 19.1. Further, RAPDs, mtDNA and microsatellites can be analysed using specimens from non-intrusive sampling and PCR (Chapter 3).

Gene trees and coalescence

Coalescence and gene trees derived from data on sequence differences among individuals and populations are important tools for exploring evolutionary processes and demographic events in a species' past.

Gene trees and coalescence analyses provide information on many aspects of species biology necessary for effective conservation

Table 19.1 Methods available for genetically characterizing individuals and populations and their applicability to each issue. Techniques with + can be used for the purpose specified, with several + indicating that the technique has higher utility, ? are cases where the technique is useful in only some cases, while − indicates that the technique is not useful in this context

Issue	Morphology	Chromosomes	Allozymes	mtDNA	RAPD	Microsatellites	DNA fingerprint
Non-intrusive sampling	−	−	−	+++	++	+++	−
Forensics	−	−	+	+++	++	++	++
Population size	+	−	−	+++	+	+	?
Estimating N_e	−	−	++	++[a]	−	+++	?
Demographic history	−	−	−	++	−	+	?
Detecting and dating bottlenecks	−	−	++	++[a]	++	+++	?
Detecting selection	+	+	+	+++	+	+++	++
Migration and gene flow	?	−	++	+[a]	++	+++	++
Individual identification and tracking	+	−	−	++	+	+++	−
Population structure	?	−	++	+?	++	+++	++
Phylogeography	−	−	−	+++	−	+++	−
Source populations to recover endangered species	+?	−	++	+	++	+++	+++
Introgression	+	+	++	+[a]	++	+++	++
Secondary contact	−	−	−	+++	−	+++	+
Taxonomic status	+	+++	++	++	+++	+++	+++
Sites for reintroduction	−	−	−	+	+	+++	−
Populations for reintroduction	+?	−	++	+	++	+++	+++
Reproductive systems	−	−	++	−	+	+++	?
Paternity	−	−	+	−	+	+++	+++
Founder relationships	−	−	?	−	+++	++	+++
Sources of new founders for endangered populations	+?	−	++	+	++	+++	++
Sexing birds	?	+++	−	−	−	?	?
Detecting disease	−	−	−	++?	++	+	++
Diet	−	−	−	+++	++	++	++

Note:

[a] Can detect only female contributions.

Based on the neutral theory, they provide a null hypothesis against which to test data and to discriminate possible reasons for deviations (Chapter 9). Moreover, coalescent methods work backwards in time and allow time dimensions (generations) to be added to the analyses. Consequently, they are more powerful than conventional analyses that use only current distributions and patterns of DNA sequence differences.

Coalescence is based on the concept that current allelic sequences in a population can be traced back through time to a point at which they **coalesce** to a single individual sequence (Fig. 19.1). Other alleles, once

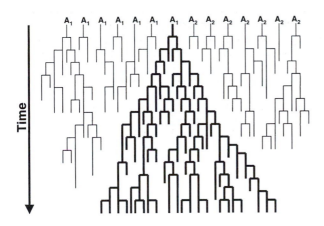

A_1 A_1 A_1 A_1 A_1 A_1 A_1 A_2 A_2 A_2 A_2 A_2 A_2 A_2

Time

Fig. 19.1 Gene trees and coalescence. A possible history of descent of DNA sequences in a population that began at time 0 (top of figure) with 14 copies, representing two alleles. Some sequences leave one or more copies in the subsequent generation while others become extinct. Sequences present at the bottom are all descended from (coalesce to) a single ancestral copy of the A_1 allele (this lineage is shown in the heavier black lines in the figure). If the failure of the ancestral sequences to leave descendants was random, the final sequences could equally well have come from any other ancestral copy at generation 0 (after Futuyma 1998).

present in the past, have been lost by genetic drift or selection, and new alleles have been generated through mutation. The evolutionary pattern of the extant distribution of alleles at a locus can be represented as the branches of a tree coalescing back to a single ancestral allelic sequence.

Coalescent patterns are usually depicted using **gene trees**, which show the genealogy of the alleles in the current population. The nodes (coalescence events) and branch lengths in the tree reflect the origins and time frames involved in deriving the observed patterns. Gene trees trace the evolutionary history of the alleles (e.g., mtDNA haplotypes) in the same manner as tracing the origin, or loss, of alleles through pedigrees. For example, the sex-linked haemophilia allele in the royal families of Europe can be traced back to Queen Victoria of the United Kingdom.

The basis of the coalescence method is that DNA sequence differences among alleles at a locus retain information about the evolutionary history of those sequences (Futuyma 1998). For example, two alleles that differ by two bases are more closely related and diverged more recently than two alleles that differ by 11 base pairs. In Fig. 3.3, alcohol dehydrogenase alleles 1-S and 2-S differ by two bases, while 1-S differs from 7-F by 11 bases. Clearly, we infer that 1-S and 2-S diverged recently and 1-S and 7-F diverged in the more distant past. An example of building a gene tree from DNA sequence information was given in Example 15.2.

Neutral theory allows us to predict the time in generations back to coalescence, thus adding a time dimension to analyses. Under neutral theory, two alleles may descend from the same ancestral allele in the previous generation with a probability $1/N_{ef}$ for mtDNA, or $1/2N_e$ for a nuclear diploid locus. Alternatively, two alleles may derive from two different alleles in the previous generation (or derive from the same allele many generations ago) with probabilities $1 - 1/N_{ef}$, or $1 - 1/2N_e$. This is the same reasoning used to determine loss of genetic diversity (Table 10.1). Under this neutral model of genetic drift, the coalescence process takes a characteristic time. In a diploid population with k alleles at a

Coalescence is the analysis of the distribution and differences among DNA sequences for alleles and the events and time frames involved in developing these sequences

Coalescence provides theory to model the survival and spread of alleles over time in the lineages of a population

Fig. 19.2 Gene trees and coalescence times. An example of a gene tree for 5 sample alleles. The large circles indicate coalescent events (after Hedrick 2000). T_i is the length of time it takes for the i alleles present to coalesce into $i -$ 1 alleles, and intervals are shown proportional to their expected times.

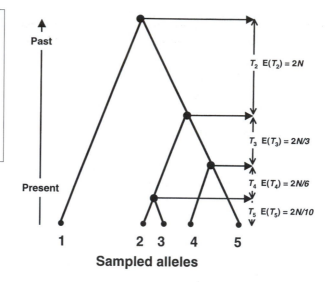

neutral locus, the average time T_k back to the previous coalescent event (i.e. where there were $k - 1$ alleles) is (Hedrick 2000):

$$T_k = 4N_e / [k(k-1)] \text{ generations} \tag{19.1}$$

Thus, the times during which there are 5, 4, 3 and 2 lineages are $2N_e/10$, $2N_e/6$, $2N_e/3$ and $2N_e$ generations, respectively. The time for all alleles in the population to coalesce is $4N_e[1 - (1/k)]$ generations (Fig. 19.2). Thus, the coalescence is quicker, and gene trees shorter, in smaller than larger populations.

We can immediately see an application of gene tree analysis. It can provide details about differences in historical population size for different populations, or species. Example 19.1 illustrates the calculation of coalescence times in diploid populations with effective size 50 and 100. Note that the coalescence times increase in direct proportion to population size.

Example 19.1 | Estimating coalescence times

In a population of $N_e = 50$ with 3 alleles, the expected time to its previous coalescence (when the population only had 2 alleles) is:

$$T_3 = 4N_e/[k(k-1)] = (4 \times 50)/(3 \times 2) = 33 \text{ generations.}$$

Thus, 3 alleles coalesce to 2 alleles on average in 33 generations in a population of size $N_e = 50$.

For $N_e = 100$ coalescence takes:

$$T_3 = 4N_e/[k(k-1)] = (4 \times 100)/(3 \times 2) = 67 \text{ generations.}$$

Thus, the coalescence takes twice a long in a population with twice the size.

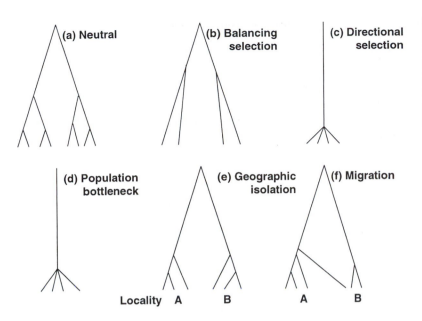

Fig. 19.3 Gene trees showing coalescence patterns for (a) neutrality, (b) balancing selection, (c) directional selection (selective sweep), (d) population bottlenecks, (e) geographic isolation and (f) migration.

The structure of gene trees and patterns of coalescence are strongly influenced by deviations from neutrality and random mating (Fig. 19.3). For example, different forms of selection affect the coalescence time in characteristic ways; directional selection reduces the coalescence time, while balancing selection increases it, compared to the expectation with genetic drift. Coalescence of alleles in the MHC or SI loci (that are subject to balancing selection) often extend back prior to speciation events (trans-species polymorphism) (Chapter 9).

After long periods of isolation and lack of gene flow, populations show deep divisions among them (Fig. 19.3e). Migration yields characteristic signatures when gene trees are mapped onto geographic location (Fig. 19.3f); alleles characteristic of one geographic region are found in another, partially isolated, region (Slatkin & Maddison 1989) Fluctuations in population size or population bottlenecks foreshorten coalescence time (Fig. 19.3d). Mutations generate sequence differences, slowing coalescence times.

When patterns are similar, such as those for directional selection to fixation (**selective sweeps**) and population bottlenecks, additional information is required to resolve the cause. For example, information on multiple unlinked loci allows discrimination of selective sweeps and bottlenecks (Fig. 19.3c and d); population bottlenecks affect all loci in a similar manner, while a selective sweep will affect a locus in a different manner to the behaviour of other loci.

Differences in DNA sequences, gene tree structure and coalescence rates allow us to infer details about population structure and evolution that are not easily, or less accurately, found using other techniques. Analysis of gene trees, using coalescence analysis, have been used to:

• Estimate effective population sizes (using selectively neutral sequences)

> Alterations in coalescence patterns allow detection of selection, isolation among populations, migration, and changes in population size

- Measure neutral mutation rates
- Infer selection and determine its form
- Determine migration events and measure migration rates
- Determine phylogenetic relationships among geographically separated populations (and make comparisons among species to determine whether patterns are similar)
- Detect secondary contact of diverged populations
- Estimate divergence times among populations
- Infer changes in population size (bottlenecks, exponential growth versus constant size)
- Detect recombination in disease organisms
- Reconstruct the origins and history of disease epidemics.

To this point, most coalescent analyses have used mtDNA data, as recombination is essentially absent, inheritance is maternal (in most species) and mtDNA has a higher mutation rate than nuclear loci. Nuclear DNA sequences have just begun to be used. Analyses of gene trees, coalescence and phylogeographic patterns have become a discipline in their own right. Readers are referred to Harvey *et al.* (1996) and Avise (2000) for further details.

The following sections provide examples illustrating the diverse uses of molecular genetic methods to determine aspects of species biology that are critical in conservation biology. These include applications involving gene trees and coalescence analyses, as well as other molecular approaches. These are rapidly developing fields where new methods are appearing regularly (Luikart & England 1999; Sunnucks 2000b). Consequently, we are only able to describe a sample of the methods and applications.

Population size and demographic history

Population size

Minimum estimates of population size can be obtained from the number of unique genotypes

It is difficult to directly estimate population sizes in nocturnal, fossorial, rare and shy animal species. Minimum estimates of their population size can be made by identifying individuals using multilocus DNA fingerprints or microsatellites. DNA can be 'remotely' sampled by collecting hair, skin or faeces, and microsatellites typed following PCR amplification. For example, a minimum population size of one female and four males was estimated for endangered Pyrenean brown bears using sex-specific markers and microsatellites to distinguish unique genotypes (Taberlet *et al.* 1997).

PCR-based genetic markers can be used to identify species when using faeces to estimate population size

Scat (faeces) counts have been used to estimate population sizes for many species, e.g. bears and coyotes. However, this cannot be applied where more than one species with similar scats exists in an area. To estimate population sizes for endangered San Joaquin kit foxes in California, their scats must be distinguished from those of red foxes,

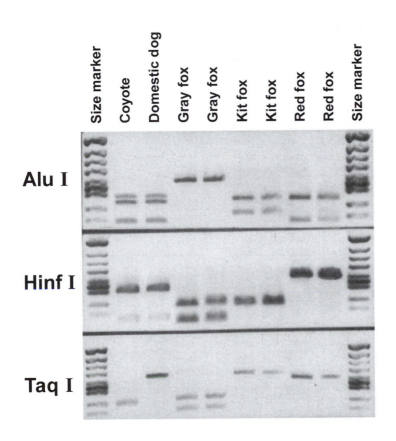

Fig. 19.4 Distinguishing scats of endangered San Joaquin kit foxes from those of other canids using mtDNA analyses (from Paxinos *et al.* 1997). PCR was used to amplify mtDNA from scats by using canid-specific primers for the cytochrome *b* gene. DNA, cut with three restriction enzymes (Alu I, Hinf I and Taq I), revealed patterns that distinguishes kit foxes from other canid species, as shown below. The second lane for each fox species utilized DNA from a scat.

gray foxes, coyotes and dogs. This can be achieved using mtDNA analyses (Fig. 19.4). DNA analyses have also been used to authenticate bear scats in Europe (Höss *et al.* 1992). Similarly, five microsatellite markers and one sex-specific marker were used on seal faecal samples to identify species, individuals and sex-ratios at a mixed-species 'haul-out' (Reed *et al.* 1997).

Demographic history

The distribution of the number of sequence differences between pairs of alleles (a 'mismatch' analysis) has characteristic shapes for populations with different demographic histories. Populations with historically stable population size, exponentially growing populations, population bottlenecks or populations experiencing secondary contact leave different signals (Fig. 19.5). Exponential growth is expected to generate a smooth unimodal distribution, while stable populations yield geometric distributions. Bottlenecks yield either a bimodal distribution, or a distribution close to zero, depending on whether the bottleneck reduced genetic diversity, or completely removed it (so that the

> The distribution of sequence differences between pairs of alleles can be used to distinguish between stable, growing and bottlenecked populations

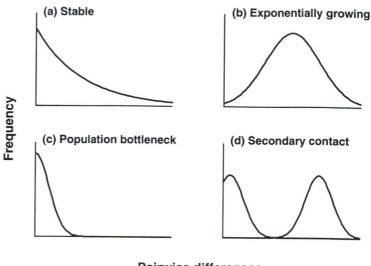

Fig. 19.5 Distributions of pairwise sequence differences between alleles in populations with different histories (after Avise 2000). (a) Population with stable size, (c) population showing exponential growth, (b) population subject to a recent bottleneck and (d) secondary contact and fusion.

diversity represents mutations since that point). Humans exhibit a unimodal distribution characteristic of exponential growth, which accords with known human history.

Characterizing and dating bottlenecks

Signals of past population bottlenecks can be detected using molecular genetic analyses

Undocumented past bottlenecks can be detected and their severity inferred from the loss of genetic diversity. Even when there are no samples of the pre-bottleneck population, they can often be identified using information from multiple microsatellite loci (Luikart & Cornuet 1998).

Koalas exhibit signals of a population bottleneck, together with isolation-by-distance, in their mtDNA sequences (Fig. 19.6). Most populations from Victoria and South Australia are indistinguishable. These were established by individuals translocated from island populations that had experienced bottlenecks (Box 16.3). The patterns of similarities among other mainland populations suggest isolation-by-distance, with populations from nearby localities generally being more similar than those from distant localities.

Bottleneck effects have been measured by comparing microsatellite genetic diversity from the current populations with that from museum specimens for Mauritius kestrels and the Illinois population of greater prairie chickens (Boxes 8.1 and 10.1).

The size and duration of bottlenecks can be inferred from loss of genetic diversity

Not only can bottlenecks in population size be detected, but also the size of the bottleneck can often be inferred from loss of genetic diversity. For example, the size of the population bottleneck experienced by the northern elephant seal has been inferred from the loss of mtDNA

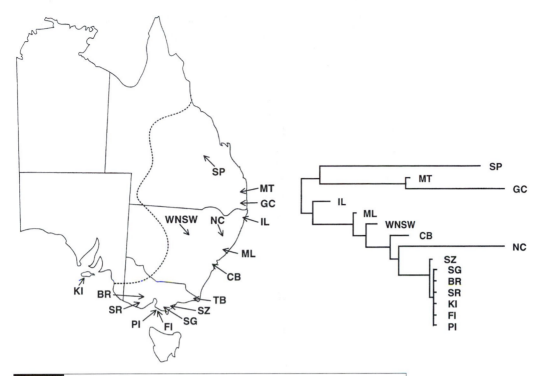

Fig. 19.6 Gene tree for koala populations, based on mtDNA sequence divergence (after Houlden *et al.* 1998). *Populations from Victoria and South Australia (bottom), derived mainly from bottlenecked island populations, are essentially indistinguishable. The remaining populations generally show their closest affinities with geographically adjacent populations, as expected with isolation-by-distance.*

genetic diversity (Box 19.3). It can be accounted for by a single generation bottleneck of 10–20 effective females. However, a bottleneck of this size is not severe enough to account for the complete absence of allozyme variation.

A particularly elegant example of the use of ancient DNA is provided by a study of the nene in Hawaii (Paxinos *et al.* in press). There is only a single mtDNA haplotype present in extant birds, largely the same haplotype in museum specimens and subfossil bones aged 100–500 years, but seven haplotypes occur in subfossil bones aged 850–2540 years. Thus, the major decline in genetic diversity did not result from Western colonization but from earlier Polynesian settlement. Modelling of the type illustrated in Box 19.3 indicates that the population probably declined to fewer than 10 females over 50–100 generations.

The 13 species of Darwin's finches on the Galapagos Islands were thought to have diverged from the progeny of a single pair. However, MHC sequence diversity indicated that they probably diverged from a founding group of at least 30 individuals (Vincek *et al.* 1997).

Box 19.3 | Estimating bottleneck size in northern elephant seals (after Hedrick 1995a)

Northern elephant seals underwent a bottleneck due to hunting. The last major hunt occurred in 1884. Subsequently, the population expanded to 350 in 1922, to 15 000 in 1960 and to well over 100 000 by the year 2000. During this bottleneck, the seals lost both nuclear and mtDNA genetic diversity. Only two mtDNA haplotypes occur in post-bottleneck northern elephant seals, while 23 haplotypes are found in related southern elephant seals. No allozyme variation was found in the northern elephant seal, while the average heterozygosity is 0.03 in southern elephant seals. The actual size and duration of the bottleneck is unknown. Since loss of genetic diversity is related to population size (Chapter 10), we can estimate the bottleneck size and duration. The expected loss of mtDNA diversity is:

$$H_t = H_0 \prod_{i=1}^{t} (1 - 1/N_{ef_i})$$

where N_{ef_i} is the effective number of females in generation i and t is the number of generations from the beginning of the bottleneck until the population is censused. This is similar to Equation 10.2, but $2N_e$ is replaced with N_{ef} as mtDNA is maternally inherited and genetic diversity is lost at a rate of $1/N_{ef}$ (Table 10.1). The mtDNA diversity in southern elephant seals is 0.980 (assumed to represent H_0), while that in northern elephants seals is 0.409 (H_t).

Many combinations of bottleneck sizes and durations can fit these data, but only a limited range will allow realistic growth in population numbers. A single generation bottleneck would require the effective number of females to be

$$H_1/H_0 = (1 - 1/N_{ef}) = 0.409/0.980 = 0.417$$

yielding

$$N_{ef} = 1.7$$

Thus, the effective number of females would be less than 2. This is not compatible with the observed population growth, which requires a minimum of about 12 females, unless the ratio of effective number of females to actual number is 0.14. Further, additional genetic diversity is lost during approximately 14 generations between the bottleneck and 1960. Hedrick assumed that N_{ef}/N_f ratios lay between 0.25 and 0.125.

The combinations of parameters that best fit both the loss of mtDNA diversity and the changes in population size were (a) a single generation female bottleneck of 12.4 with $N_{ef}/N_f = 0.25$ ($N_{ef} = 3.1$), or (b) a bottleneck of three generations with 44 females and $N_{ef}/N_f = 0.125$ ($N_{ef} = 5.5$). In both cases population numbers were projected to be close to those observed in 1922 and 1960. Halley & Hoelzel (1996) reached similar conclusions, based on detailed computer simulations. This bottleneck is not sufficient to account for complete absence of allozyme variation. Other factors must have come into play to explain this.

It has been hypothesized that the cheetah lost substantial genetic diversity due to a population size bottleneck. The presumed bottleneck was estimated to have occurred about 10 000 years ago, by comparing levels of genetic variation for allozymes (low mutation rate), with mtDNA, DNA fingerprints and microsatellites (higher mutation rates) (O'Brien 1994). However, there are alternative interpretations for low allozyme genetic diversity in this case (Hedrick 1996).

> The timing of bottlenecks can be inferred from genetic data

Estimating evolutionary effective population size

The use of genetic markers to estimate effective population size from changes in heterozygosity was considered in Chapter 10. Coalescence theory allows effective size for females to be estimated from mtDNA as (Futuyma 1998):

> Long-term effective population size can be determined using coalescence theory if mutation rates are known

$$N_{ef} = PS/2u \qquad (19.2)$$

where PS is the average proportion of nucleotide sites that differ between random pairs of haplotypes and u is the mutation rate. The effective population size for female red-winged blackbirds in the USA was estimated by utilizing similar methods (Avise 2000). RFLP analyses of mtDNA from 127 birds identified 34 haplotypes. The mutation rate per base is 10^{-8} per generation. From these, an estimate of 36 700 females was derived, much less than the current number of 20 million breeding females. The most probable explanation is that numbers were much lower during Pleistocene glaciation (as recently as 10 000 years ago) and that numbers have increased markedly since then from a refuge population. Effective sizes in females are typically much less than the current number of adult females in a wide range of species (Avise 2000).

Gene flow and population structure

Population structure

Genetic management recommendations vary significantly depending on population structure. Populations in different habitat fragments may be totally isolated, partially isolated, effectively a single population, or a metapopulation, depending on the extent of gene flow and population extinction rates (Chapters 13 and 16). Small and totally isolated populations may experience severe inbreeding. The delineation of population structure is usually only possible using genetic data.

> Genetic markers can be used to determine population structure

The degree of population differentiation can be determined using F_{ST} and related measures for any type of polymorphic genetic marker (Chapter 13). More powerful and informative analyses are possible using gene trees. Population structure can be identified by mapping the sequences of different alleles onto geographic locations (Templeton

1998). The cause of genetic differentiation, restricted gene flow, past fragmentation or range expansion can then be determined. East African populations of buffalo and impala show similar F_{ST} values of 0.08 and 0.10. However, the distribution of mtDNA haplotypes over geographic locations is entirely different in the two species, as shown in the **haplotype networks** in Fig. 19.7. The distribution of Chobe haplotypes (Chobe is the most isolated location) is random in buffalo, but tightly clustered in impala. Consequently, buffalo exhibit recurrent genetic maternal interchange between Chobe and more northerly populations. Conversely, impala have restricted female gene flow that either reflects isolation-by-distance or isolation of the Chobe population from the northern populations.

Differentiated maternally inherited components of the genome can be revealed with mtDNA or cpDNA (plants). The vulnerable ghost bat populations in Australia (Fig. 19.8) illustrate marked differentiation among colonies, and no haplotypes are shared between colonies. This is

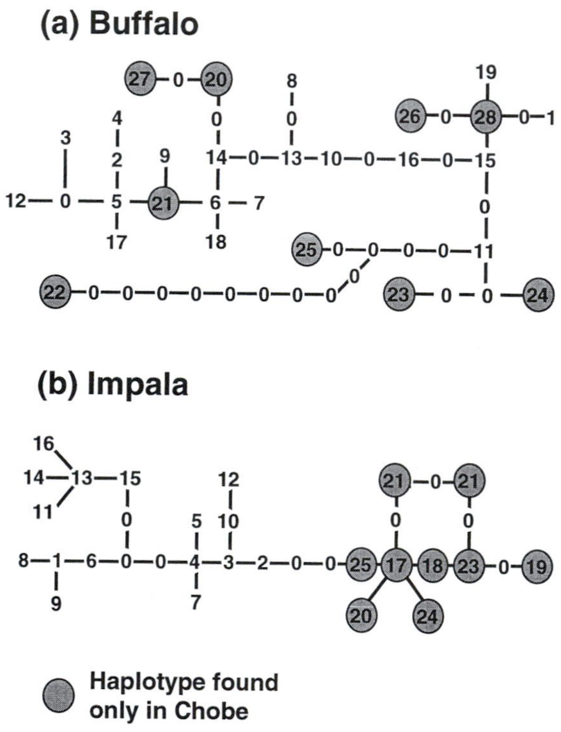

(a) Buffalo

(b) Impala

Haplotype found only in Chobe

Fig. 19.7 Haplotype networks for mtDNA for buffalo and impala (after Templeton 1998). Each line in the network represents a single mutational change. '0' indicates a node in the network that was absent in the sample. These nodes are inferred intermediates between the two nearest neighbour haplotypes in the network that differed by two or more mutations. Haplotype numbers are those given in the original reference. *Chobe haplotypes, from the most isolated and southerly location, are tightly clustered for impala but interspersed throughout the buffalo network.*

consistent with mark–release–recapture studies in the field. The extent of sequence differences among colonies suggests that isolation is not recent (or that effective population sizes are very small). Further, microsatellite analyses also revealed substantial differentiation between populations. Despite the bat's flying ability, each population now represents a closed population, at least for females. Consequently, extinct colonies are unlikely to be recolonized by natural migration. Moritz *et al.* (1996) recommended that each colony be managed as a separate management unit for conservation purposes.

In another application, studies in the long-finned pilot whale revealed a pod structure consisting of single extended matrilineal

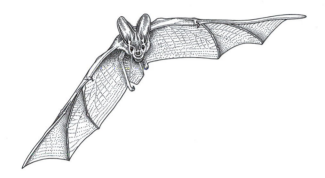

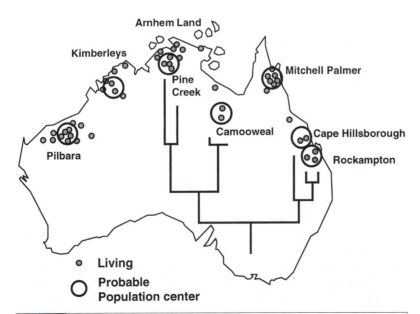

Fig. 19.8 Population structure of ghost bat populations revealed by mtDNA (after Worthington-Wilmer *et al.* 1994, Moritz *et al.* 1996). This species lives in caves and abandoned mines and was once widespread, but has contracted northward. *There is clear differentiation among populations. No haplotypes were shared between populations.*

families, often containing more than 100 individuals (Amos *et al.* 1993). Neither sex of offspring disperses. However, there was not significant inbreeding, as determined using nuclear genetic markers. This apparent contradiction was resolved when members of different pods were observed to mate when they encountered each other.

Dispersal and gene flow

Dispersal rates can be inferred from genetic differentiation among populations

Dispersal rates are difficult to study by direct observation, as rates may be low and long-distance dispersal too rare to measure with precision. An increasing number of studies use genetic markers to infer dispersal patterns. With no dispersal, mating will not be at random, and there will be an overall deficiency of heterozygotes (Table 8.2). For example, mice maintain territories within barns and so do not mate at random, resulting in overall deficiencies of heterozygotes compared to Hardy–Weinberg expectations (Selander 1970).

Genetic studies often reveal a picture of dispersal differing from that suggested by direct observations. For example, observations of territorial North American pikas indicated that they rarely dispersed, and long-distance dispersal was not observed at all. Consequently, they were thought to regularly mate with close relatives. However, DNA fingerprinting studies revealed that close inbreeding was not common and that dispersal occurred over short, medium and long distances (Peacock 1997). Mark–release–recapture methods are often inadequate to characterize long-term dispersal.

Dispersal patterns of turtles have been followed using mtDNA markers. Females frequently return to lay their eggs in the beach where they hatched. Haplotypes in loggerhead turtles are distinct in populations on nesting beaches in Japan (B and C) and Australia (A), so their worldwide dispersal can be followed (Fig. 19.9). Populations in the region of the driftnet fishery in the North Pacific, and in the feeding grounds near Baja California, were predominantly Japanese stocks, with a minority of Australian stock. Consequently, females show fidelity to nesting sites, but not to feeding grounds. Similar studies have traced movement of endangered humpback whales (Baker & Palumbi 1996).

Y-specific probes allow male-specific dispersal and differentiation to be assessed in a parallel manner (Tucker & Lundrigan 1996). In humans, the use of mtDNA and Y-specific probes to estimate female and male dispersal, respectively, revealed that females disperse more effectively than males. This contrasts with the prevailing view that males spread their genes more effectively due to movements associated with warfare (Seielstad *et al.* 1998).

Detecting immigrants

Individual immigrants can be identified from multilocus genotypes using assignment tests

Dispersal of individuals can be identified from multilocus microsatellite genotypes (assignment tests) (Luikart & England 1999). Based on its

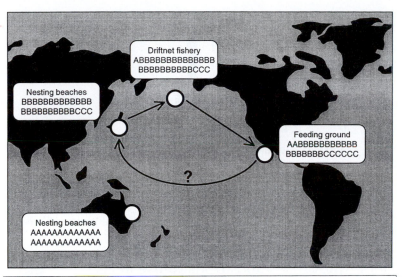

Fig. 19.9 Dispersal in loggerhead turtles based on mtDNA haplotypes (after Bowen *et al.* 1995). A, B and C are different mtDNA haplotypes.

genotype, an individual is assigned to the population with which it has the greatest similarity. If it is assigned to a population other than the one where it was collected, then it is likely to be an immigrant. This represents an advance over F_{ST}, which does not distinguish between current and historical patterns of dispersal. For example, if all individuals in geographic areas A and B have genotypes $A_1A_1B_1B_1C_1C_1D_1D_1$, and $A_2A_2B_2B_2C_2C_2D_2D_2$, respectively, then an individual in region B with the former genotype must be a migrant. An identical principle applies when populations differ in frequencies at several loci, but the computations are more complex. Assignment tests can also be used to detect hybridization and taxonomic relationship, as was done with the red and Algonquin wolves (Box 15.1).

Secondary contact between populations

Secondary contact between and genetic fusion of previously differentiated populations can be inferred when the distribution of pairwise sequence differences among individuals is bimodal (and other causes of this pattern can be excluded). For example, two distinct mtDNA haplogroups are present in each surveyed snow goose rookery in the Canadian Arctic and Russia (Fig. 19.10). Within any rookery, both mtDNA clades interbreed freely. The rookery sites occur in glaciated regions that were uninhabitable as recently as 5000–10 000 years ago. Current populations are huge, so this is not a recent drift effect. Thus, the rookeries have been established by migrants, presumably from two

> Secondary contact between populations gives a bimodal distribution of pairwise sequence differences among individuals

Fig. 19.10 Bimodal distribution of pairwise differences in mtDNA RFLPs for snow geese indicating secondary contact (after Avise 2000).

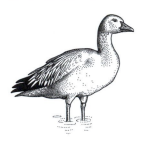

separate, diverged populations. Heterozygote advantage can be excluded as an explanation as it cannot operate on haploid mtDNA.

Identification of populations to use in recovery of endangered sub-species

Genetic markers can be used to identify the most closely related sub-species to use for crossing to recover a sub-species that has declined to a single individual

A sub-species that has declined to a single individual can only be recovered by crossing it to a related taxon. This was done unsuccessfully in the case of the dusky seaside sparrow. Subsequent genetic analyses revealed that the sub-species chosen to use in the cross (selected because of morphological similarity) was actually only distantly related to the dusky seaside sparrow. Other more closely related sub-species had been available (Avise 1996). In the parallel case of the Norfolk Island boobook owl, crosses of the one remaining female to a male from a related New Zealand sub-species has yielded 16 F_1 offspring. Subsequent mtDNA analyses confirmed that the population chosen for crossing was the most closely related one available (Example 15.2) and were concordant with morphological information.

Phylogeographic patterns across species

Past geological or climatic events may affect multiple diverse species in a similar manner

Phylogeographic patterns of sequence divergence across geographic regions are concordant for multiple species in a surprising number of cases (Avise 2000). For example, black sea bass, seaside sparrow, horseshoe crab, American oyster and tiger beetle in the southeastern USA all show distinctive mtDNA haplotypes in Gulf of Mexico, versus Atlantic coast, areas separated by the Florida peninsula (Avise 2000). These separations were not previously recognized, or predicted from current landforms. Such patterns seem to reflect separation of populations by major geological events, past climatic events, or a change in habitat resulting from climatic change. Many other cases of concordant phylogeographic patterns in distinct taxa have been found in the USA, including freshwater fish in east- versus west-flowing rivers in the southeast, and terrestrial and freshwater tetrapods between southeast and north-west. Similarly, four species of birds and a reptile display major genetic differences between the rainforest regions north and south of Cairns in northeastern Australia. While this region currently has essentially continuous rainforest habitat, the differentiation is presumed to reflect past rainforest contractions and expansions that led to long periods of isolation between the two areas (Joseph *et al.* 1995). Concordant patterns across distantly related species strengthen inferences that may be only weakly supported for an individual species.

Reintroduction and translocation

Sites for reintroductions and translocations

Reintroduction is a hazardous and expensive undertaking whose success is increased by selecting sites within the historical range of the species (Chapter 18). Characterization of an extinct population as belonging to an endangered species requiring reintroduction or translocation can suggest a suitable site (Box 19.2). Cooper *et al.* (1996) used DNA from subfossil bones to confirm that Laysan ducks recently existed on a Hawaiian island where they are now extinct. This island may therefore be a suitable site for re-establishment.

Potential reintroduction sites can be identified by PCR analyses on museum specimens collected from populations that are now extinct

Populations for reintroductions

Populations for re-stocking species should be those with the highest reproductive fitness in the wild habitat and the highest genetic diversity to optimize chances of survival. In the endangered topminnow fish, the population being used for re-stocking had lower allozyme variation and poorer fitness in the laboratory than an alternative population (Vrijenhoek 1994). This information led to the use of a more genetically diverse population for re-stocking, although analyses in another laboratory have cast doubts on some aspects of the story (Hedrick & Kalinowski 2000).

Choice among candidate populations for reintroduction can be made by identifying the population with the highest genetic diversity

The French Island population of koalas in Victoria, Australia has been used widely for introductions and translocations but had few founders and low genetic diversity (Chapter 16). This population is an unsuitable source for re-stocking. Other populations, with normal levels of genetic variation, should be used in the future.

A reintroduction program for the endangered shrub *Zieria prostrata* from a restricted area on the East Coast of Australia was abandoned following genetic analyses (Hogbin *et al.* 2000). An apparently unique plant, thought to have originated from an extinct population at a location distant from the remainder of the species, was destined to be the subject of a re-establishment program. However, it was found to be closely related to individuals from one of the extant populations, so the reintroduction plan was cancelled.

Reproduction, parentage, founder relationships and sexing

Genetic analyses can provide critical information on breeding systems, parentage, sex and founder relationships

Species with different forms of reproduction (asexual versus sexual, inbreeding versus outbreeding, etc.) require different management, and it is vital to distinguish them. Knowledge of parentage is critical to detect inbreeding, and to verify the accuracy of pedigrees used in genetic management. Correct assignment of sex is essential so that two individuals of the same sex are not paired and so that distorted sex-ratios can be recognized. Founder relationships are important in managing captive populations so that loss of genetic diversity and inbreeding can be minimized. Genetic marker analyses can provide much of this critical information.

Reproduction systems

Methods of reproduction and mating patterns can be resolved by typing mothers and offspring for multiple genetic loci

Plants have a diversity of mating systems from outbreeding to self-fertilization and clonal reproduction and some small plant populations may switch from outcrossing to selfing. Further, some species of fish, lizards and insects are parthenogenetic or self-fertilizing. As species with different mating systems typically require different management strategies for conservation purposes, it is crucial that the mating system for each threatened species be defined.

Breeding systems can be determined by genotyping mothers and offspring (Table 19.2). If all offspring contain the same genotype as the mother then reproduction is asexual (including ameiotic parthenogenesis). Conversely, if offspring contain only alleles present in the mother,

Table 19.2 | Determination of reproduction and mating systems using genetic markers

Breeding systems	Parent genotypes		Offspring genotypes
Asexual	AB	⇒	AB
Selfing	AB × AB	⇒	AA, AB, BB
Outbreeding	AB × CD	⇒	AC, AD, BC, BD
Mixed selfing and outcrossing			
	AB × AB	⇒	AA, AB, BB
	AB × CD	⇒	AC, AD, BC, BD heterozygote deficiency compared to outbreeding

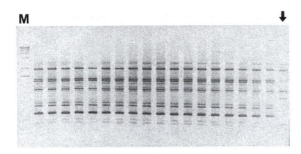

M ↓

Fig. 19.11 Clonal reproduction in the endangered Santa Cruz bush mallow (from Fritsch & Rieseberg 1996). RAPD analyses on 18 different plants from the NS(II) population (lanes 2–19) and one individual from the NS(I) population (arrow). Lane 1 is a DNA size marker (M). *All 18 bushes from the NS(II) population are identical (clones) and different from the NS(I) plant.*

but have a diversity of genotypes then they are the result of self-fertilization. Offspring containing alleles not found in the mother are the result of outcrossing.

All individuals in one of two populations of the endangered Santa Cruz bush mallow plant on Santa Cruz Island, California, were identical (indicating clonal reproduction) and different from individuals in the second population (Fig. 19.11). The endangered shrub *Haloragodendron lucasii* exists in a very restricted range in Sydney, Australia and comprises of only seven clones among 53 plants, based on allozyme and RAPD genotypes (Hogbin *et al.* 2000).

The amount of selfing in plants with mixed mating systems (some selfing and some outcrossing) can be estimated directly by typing maternal plants and their offspring (Hedrick 2000). Selfing of homozygous maternal plants results only in homozygous progeny, while outcrossing yields heterozygotes (H) at a rate dependent upon the combined frequency of alleles not found in the homozygote (q) (Table 19.3). Thus, the frequency of selfing (S) is

$$S = 1 - H/q \tag{19.3}$$

Heterozygous maternal plants can also be used to obtain estimates of selfing rates (Brown 1989; Hedrick 2000).

The level of inbreeding can be determined indirectly from deviations from Hardy–Weinberg equilibrium (Chapter 11). For example, $H_0/H_e = 0.68$ in endangered round-leaf honeysuckle plants from

In plants with mixed selfing and outcrossing, selfing rates can be determined directly by typing maternal parents and progeny using genetic markers

Selfing rates can be determined indirectly from the reduction in heterozygosity compared to Hardy–Weinberg expectations

Table 19.3 The proportion of progeny genotypes expected from a homozygous maternal genotype (A_1A_1) and a heterozygous maternal genotypes (A_1A_2) as a result of self-fertilization (S) and outcrossing (T). p and q are the frequencies of alleles A_1 and A_2 in the population

Maternal genotype	Frequency of matings	Progeny genotypes		
		A_1A_1	A_1A_2	A_2A_2
A_1A_1	S	S		
	T	Tp	Tq	
A_1A_2	S	¼ S	½ S	¼ S
	T	½ Tp	½ T	½ Tq

Source: Hedrick (2000).

Western Australia (Coates & Hamley 1999). Using Equation 11.7, the effective inbreeding coefficient

$$F_e = 1 - (H_o / H_e) = 1 - 0.68 = 0.32.$$

The selfing rate can be determined from the inbreeding coefficient. If S is the proportion of self-fertilized progeny in a partial selfer, then inbreeding coefficients of the parents F and progeny F' (before any selection), are related as follows (Barrett & Kohn 1991):

$$F' = S(1 + F) / 2$$

In the absence of inbreeding depression, equilibrium is reached when

$$F = S / (2 - S) \tag{19.4}$$

Consequently, with 40% selfing, the equilibrium inbreeding coefficient is $0.4 / (2 - 0.4) = 0.25$. When Equation 19.4 is rearranged, we obtain

$$S = 2F / (1 + F) \tag{19.5}$$

For round-leaf honeysuckle, the selfing rate is $S = 2 \times 0.32 / (1 + 0.32) = 0.48$.

Genetic markers such as allozymes have been used widely to estimate F and S. F is calculated from allele and genotype frequencies using Equation 11.7. The most commonly used model to estimate selfing and outcrossing is the mixed mating model (Barrett & Kohn 1991). It assumes that there are only two types of matings, self-fertilization and random mating. However, matings among related individuals also occur (**biparental inbreeding**, such as full-sib, half-sib or cousin matings). Consequently, the estimate of S is a measure of what the selfing rate would be, if all inbreeding was due to selfing.

Multilocus data provide more accurate estimates of true selfing rates. Further, in self-compatible plants, the difference between the mean of single locus estimates and the multilocus estimate provides an estimate of biparental inbreeding. For example, male-sterile individuals in seven populations of *Bidens* ssp. in Hawaii had average 'selfing' rates of 15%, and all of this must be due to biparental inbreeding (Sun & Ganders 1988). Similarly, the Pacific yew, the source of the anticancer compound taxol, is dioecious (separate sexes), but has an F of 47%. Again, all of this must be due to biparental inbreeding (El-Kassaby & Yanchuk 1994). Barrett & Kohn (1991) and Hedrick (2000) provide further details of methodology for estimating selfing and biparental inbreeding rates.

Parentage

Multiple DNA markers can be used to assign paternity and maternity

Information on parentage is essential to study the impact of inbreeding, to verify pedigrees used in genetic management of threatened species, and to determine the effective size of populations (Chapter 10). Often parentage cannot be determined from direct behavioural observations. For example, chimpanzee females copulate with many males during their fertile periods. Genetic marker information from mother,

Table 19.4 Parentage determinations in snow geese: genotypes at 14 nuclear RFLP loci for putative parents and goslings in a family of snow geese. Gosling 4 does not match its putative parents. Alleles that cannot be inherited from its putative parents are shown in bold and genotypes that cannot be derived from putative parents are underlined

	RFLP locus													
	A	B	C	D	E	F	G	H	I	J	K	L	M	N
Putative father	22	22	23	12	11	11	14	22	12	12	12	12	22	22
Putative mother	22	22	22	11	11	11	13	12	22	11	11	12	12	12
Gosling 1	22	22	22	12	11	11	11	12	12	11	12	11	12	12
Gosling 2	22	22	22	11	11	11	34	22	22	12	12	12	22	22
Gosling 3	22	22	22	12	11	11	13	22	12	11	11	22	22	22
Gosling 4	<u>23</u>	22	**11**	11	11	11	<u>**12**</u>	12	12	11	11	11	<u>11</u>	<u>11</u>

Source: Avise (1994).

offspring and putative fathers can be used to resolve these uncertainties (Fleischer 1996).

If a paternally derived allele in the offspring is not present in the suspected father, then that male can be excluded as a potential father (unless a new mutation has occurred). If many loci are used, positive paternity assignments can be made with high probabilities. DNA fingerprints and multilocus microsatellites provide the most suitable markers. Table 19.4 illustrates parentage determinations in snow geese, based on 14 nuclear RFLP loci. At several loci, the genotype of gosling 4 cannot be derived from those of its putative (candidate) parents by Mendelian inheritance. Possession of allele 3 at locus A excludes one or other putative parent as they are both 22 homozygotes. Loci M and N exclude the putative father as he lacks the 1 allele. C excludes both parents as gosling 4 carries alleles not present in either putative parent.

Paternity determinations using microsatellites in captive chimpanzees revealed that the dominant male in the colony was responsible for siring most, but not all, of the offspring (Houlden *et al.* 1997). Consequently, the need to move animals among zoos to minimize inbreeding and loss of genetic diversity is greater than if many males contributed to paternity, but it is less than if the dominant male fathered all offspring. Paternity analyses in wild chimpanzees surprisingly revealed that half of the offspring were sired during furtive matings with males from outside the group, despite fierce territorial defence (Gagneux *et al.* 1997). As turtles mate at sea, and swimming individuals are very difficult to identify, their mating pattern is impossible to observe directly. Allozyme analyses of loggerhead turtle clutches established that females mated with several males (Harry & Briscoe 1988). Further, more than two paternal microsatellite alleles were present in the progeny of a female (Bollmer *et al.* 1999).

Even in species where extensive behavioural observations have been made, genetic marker analyses have often revealed unexpected mating patterns. For example, splendid fairy wrens in Western Australia were reputed to have high rates of inbreeding, and no inbreeding depression (Ralls *et al.* 1986). Subsequent paternity analyses using allozymes revealed that 65% or more of progeny were fathered by males from outside the group (Rowley *et al.* 1993). Many birds with presumed monogamous mating systems have been shown to participate in extrapair copulations (see Fleischer 1996). Even in humans, genetic markers have revealed that 10% or more of children are not the offspring of their registered father (Dunbar 1998).

Pedigrees are used extensively in genetic management of captive populations, so it is important to verify their accuracy. DNA fingerprinting in the critically endangered Waldrapp ibis identified five of 33 offspring whose pedigrees were incorrect (Signer *et al.* 1994). The study also identified an additional unrelated founder, but indicated that three of the six previously known founders were probably siblings. There also appear to be errors in the Bali starling and Arabian oryx studbooks (Ashworth & Parkin 1992; Marshall *et al.* 1999), and genetic marker analyses have cast serious doubts about the accuracy of the Przewalski's horse pedigree (O. A. Ryder personal communication). More than one domestic horse appears to have contributed and parentage is questionable in other parts of the pedigree. Pedigree inaccuracies can be important in domestic animals. Thoroughbred horse registration in many countries requires that parentage be verified using genetic markers.

The above cases may reflect a wider problem with inaccuracies in the pedigrees of threatened species. This issue warrants further investigation, especially in species with small numbers of founders where pedigree inaccuracies may have serious consequences.

Determining founder relationships

Multilocus DNA markers can be used to delineate founder relationships

Small numbers of founders are frequently all that remain to initiate breeding programs of endangered species. Usually the relationships among founders are unknown. However, identifying related individuals is important for managing inbreeding and genetic diversity in the population. Genetic analyses using many loci (e.g. DNA fingerprinting or multiple microsatellite loci) can identify relationships in such cases. Studies in the California condor revealed three related groups of individuals amongst the 14 founders (Geyer at al. 1993). Similar studies have been conducted on Bali starling, Guam rails, Micronesian kingfishers, Mauritius pink pigeons and Arabian oryx (Ashworth & Parkin 1992; Haig *et al.* 1994, 1995; Mace *et al.* 1996; Marshall *et al.* 1999).

Sources of new founders

Where founder numbers are small, other potential founders can be examined, using genetic markers, to ensure that they belong to the correct species and are not affected by introgression

All potential founders should be used to establish captive breeding colonies. However, there may be uncertainties about the identity of some potential founders. These questions can be resolved using genetic

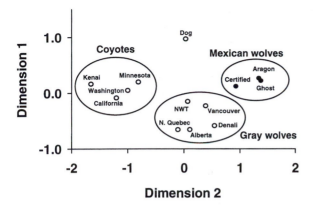

Fig. 19.12 Are uncertified populations 'pure' Mexican wolves? Multidimensional scaling of allele frequency data from 20 microsatellite loci typed on populations of Mexican wolves, coyotes, dogs and gray wolves (Hedrick *et al.* 1997). The Certified population is known to consist of 'pure' Mexican wolves, while the Aragon and Ghost Ranch populations were of questionable status. Different coyote and gray wolf populations are indicated by state or province. *The Aragon and Ghost Ranch populations cluster with Certified as a group distinct from the other canids, indicating that all are 'pure' Mexican wolves.*

analyses. For example, the Mexican wolf is extinct in the wild and the only Certified population was founded by only three or four animals. Two other populations existed, but it was unclear whether they had been subject to introgression from dogs, gray wolves, or coyotes. Molecular genetic analyses (based on allozymes, mtDNA, DNA finger-prints and particularly microsatellites) established that all three populations of Mexican wolves were similar, with no detectable introgression from dogs, gray wolves, or coyotes (Fig. 19.12). These three populations are now being combined. The study also determined that the Certified population had three, not four founders. In a similar manner, two potentially new founders for the US captive population of Speke's gazelle were shown to be unrelated to US animals (Butler *et al.* 1994). Since the US population was based on only four founders, these two animals have been added to the captive population.

Sexing of birds and mammals

Males and females of many bird species are morphologically indistinguishable. Birds must be sexed prior to pairing, as several cases of 'infertile' pairs in zoos have turned out to be two birds of the same sex.

Some mammals are also difficult to sex, especially cetaceans (whales and dolphins) and secretive species, as it may not be possible to sex individuals when collecting samples by skin biopsies, hair, etc. The sex of stored DNA samples may not be known.

Birds have ZZ male and ZW female sex-determination. Consequently, PCR primers for W chromosome specific sequences have been developed to distinguish males from females (Lambert & Millar 1995; Smith & Wayne 1996). W-specific fragments will amplify from the DNA of a ZW female, but not from a ZZ male (Fig. 19.13).

Molecular sexing is an important component in the program to recover the Norfolk Island boobook owl (Chapters 11 and 15). While the program had produced 12–13 individuals, of which seven were F_2, only two pairs were breeding. It was unclear whether this was due to hybrid sterility, unequal sex-ratio, or individuals of one sex being immature. As

Birds and mammals can be sexed using genetic markers on the heterogametic sex chromosome

Birds can be sexed using genetic markers on the W sex chromosome

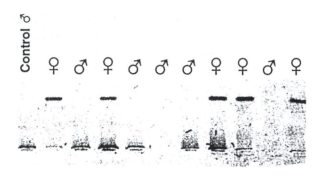

Fig. 19.13 Sexing the critically endangered Taita thrush using a W-specific probe (from Lens *et al.* 1998). PCR was used to amplify two loci, one on the W chromosome and one autosomal, using specific primers. DNA amplified for all 11 birds, showing that the PCR reactions had worked. Results after digestion with the restriction enzyme Hae III are shown; this digests the autosomal fragment, but not the W fragment, so a fragment is found for ZW females, but not for ZZ males.

females and males could not be distinguished by external morphology, a PCR-based technique was used to sex the birds (Double & Olsen 1997). The population was found to consist of six females and five males. A scarcity of mature males was the main factor slowing the recovery effort. The critically endangered black stilt in New Zealand (Millar *et al.* 1997) had declined to about 70 birds with only 12 breeding pairs. Molecular sexing was used to avoid single sex pairings in their recovery program. Molecular sexing in the critically endangered Taita thrush from Kenya has revealed a strongly distorted sex-ratio in one of three populations (only 10% females) (Fig. 19.13). Further, this study led to the identification of a morphological trait that can be used to sex individuals visually.

Since mammals typically have XX females and XY males, sex can be determined using molecular methods that detect Y chromosome specific loci. For example, Taberlet *et al.* (1997) sexed free-ranging Pyrenean brown bears from hair and faecal samples found in the field using a PCR amplification of a Y-specific locus (*SRY*). Similarly, molecular methods have been developed to sex cetacean skin biopsy samples using PCR amplification of X and Y chromosome specific loci (*SRX* and *SRY*) (Bérubé & Pasbøll 1996). This method has been applied to samples from humpback, fin, blue and minke whales, and narwhals and harbour porpoises.

> Mammals can be sexed using genetic markers on the Y chromosome

Disease

> Molecular methods provide rapid, reliable and highly sensitive means for detecting and investigating the biology of disease organisms, and delineating the source of new diseases

The disease status of animals is critical in identifying causes of population decline, and for checking candidates for translocation or reintroduction. PCR-based methods provide rapid, reliable and highly sensitive means for detecting disease organisms. For example, PCR has been used to study avian malaria in Hawaii, one of two diseases thought to have been major factors in the decline of Hawaiian birds. Higher-elevation habitats, considered safe from malaria-carrying mosquitoes, have been preserved for endangered forest birds. However, Cann *et al.* (1996) identified malaria in blood of birds from high-elevation habitats on Maui and Hawaii, indicating that these areas are not as safe as previously thought. Reservoirs of the disease were also found in introduced bird species in low-elevation habitats.

Gene trees based upon DNA sequences have been employed to determine the source of new diseases. HIV–1, one of the viruses that cause AIDS in humans, has been found to be most closely related to SIV from chimpanzees, while HIV–2 originated from sooty mangabeys (Sharp *et al.* 1996). Similarly, an epidemic causing high mortality in African lions in the Serengeti in 1994 was shown to be due to canine distemper, presumed to have switched species from local dogs (Roelke-Parker *et al.* 1996). Recommendations were made to vaccinate local dogs against distemper to minimize the risk of repeat epidemics in lions and, especially, in other rarer carnivores. Molecular genetic analyses have also been used to identify the source of introduced plant diseases in Australia and elsewhere (Gillings & Fahy 1994).

Diet

Diet is difficult to determine by direct observation in nocturnal and secretive species. Food items can be identified from faeces by using PCR with primers specific to suspected food items. This has been demonstrated in bears, where the plant *Photinia* was identified as a food item (Höss *et al.* 1992).

The role of predators in causing the decline of a threatened species has also been assessed using PCR-based amplification. Microsatellite typing on stomach contents of glaucous gulls in Alaska revealed that they were preying on emperor geese, but not on threatened spectacled eiders (Scribner & Bowman 1998). Since gull numbers have increased, gull predation appears to be a major factor in the decline in emperor geese numbers and their inability to recover. Gull removal has resulted in improved gosling survival.

> PCR with primers specific to suspected food items can be used to determine dietary items from gut contents or faeces

Summary

1. Molecular genetic analyses are invaluable in forensics and in resolving many aspects of species biology that are important in conservation.

2. Gene trees and coalescence methods have added greatly to the analytical methods available to infer population processes of interest in the life histories of threatened species.

3 Molecular genetic analyses have been used to determine population size, infer demographic history, detect population bottlenecks, measure effective population size, determine reproductive and mating systems, establish parentage, sex individuals, determine founder relationships, identify the source of new founders, measure

migration and gene flow, infer population structures, identify populations to use to alleviate inbreeding depression, detect introgression, identify sites and populations suitable for reintroduction, document disease status and the source of new diseases, and to identify dietary items.

FURTHER READING

Avise (1994) *Molecular Markers, Natural History and Evolution*. Has a lucid treatment of the use of molecular genetic techniques to understand species biology.

Avise (2000) *Phylogeography*. An excellent textbook on coalescence and phylogeography by the founder of the field.

Avise & Hamrick (1996) *Conservation Genetics*. Scientific reviews containing examples of the use of genetic markers to understand species biology.

Goldstein & Schlotterer (1999) *Microsatellites*. An edited volume devoted to microsatellite techniques, the marker of choice for many genetic analyses in conservation biology, and the information gained from such analyses.

Harvey *et al.* (1996) *New Uses for New Phylogenies*. A series of chapters by different authors on gene trees and coalescence. Advanced.

Hoelzel (1998) *Molecular Genetic Analysis*. An edited book with technical details and case studies on the use of molecular genetic methods to illuminate aspects of species biology.

Luikart & England (1999) A review of new methods for statistical analysis of microsatellite DNA data, along with list of relevant computer software.

Smith & Wayne (1996) *Molecular Genetic Approaches in Conservation*. This book contains much technical detail and many examples of the use of molecular genetic analyses to understand species biology.

Sunnucks (2000b) Recent review on the use of molecular genetic methods in population biology and conservation.

PROBLEMS

19.1 Coalescence time: What is the mean time to complete coalescence for four alleles in a population of $N_e = 50$? In a population of $N_e = 10$?

19.2 Bottleneck: What proportion of the autosomal genetic variation is expected to remain in the Isle Royale population of gray wolves, compared to the mainland wolves, if it was founded from (a) one female mated to a single male? (b) one female mated to four males? (c) two mated pairs? (d) five pairs? Explain the basis of your calculations.

19.3 Bottleneck: What proportion of the mainland mtDNA variation is expected in Isle Royale gray wolves with one, two or five female founders?

19.4 Bottleneck: If northern elephant seals declined to one male/10 females and remained at this size for seven generations (this is likely to exaggerate the duration of the bottleneck), what proportion of their initial nuclear heterozygosity would be retained? Can this bottleneck account for complete loss of allozyme genetic diversity?

19.5 Bottleneck: Model the decline in mtDNA genetic diversity in the nene to explain a drop in initial diversity from $H_0 = 0.80$ to $H_{75} = $

0.067 (Paxinos *et al.* in press). Find a population size that will explain this with constant size.

19.6 Reproduction systems: What are the methods of reproduction in the following cases?

(a) Mother A_1A_2, seven offspring A_1A_2

(b) Mother A_1A_2, offspring 5 A_1A_1, 13 A_1A_2, and 6 A_2A_2

(c) Mother A_1A_1, offspring A_1A_2 and A_1A_3

(d) Mother A_1A_1, offspring A_1A_2, A_1A_3, A_1A_4 and A_1A_5

(e) Mother A_1A_2, female offspring A_1A_3, A_2A_3, male offspring A_1 and A_2.

19.7 Reproduction systems: What are all the possible explanations for the Wollemi pine having no genetic diversity at several hundred loci?

19.8 Parentage determinations: Determine whether each of the goslings in the snow goose family shown below is compatible with their putative parents. Diploid genotypes at 14 nuclear RFLP loci are as follows (after Avise 1994). For example, the putative father has alleles 1 and 2 at locus A, 2 and 2 at locus B, etc.

	A	B	C	D	E	F	G	H	I	J	K	L	M	N
Putative father	12	22	24	11	11	11	11	12	11	11	11	12	11	12
Putative mother	22	22	12	11	22	11	12	12	22	11	11	11	22	12
Gosling 1	22	22	12	11	12	11	11	22	12	12	11	11	12	12
Gosling 2	22	22	24	11	12	11	12	11	12	11	11	11	22	11
Gosling 3	12	22	24	11	11	11	11	12	22	11	11	11	11	11
Gosling 4	23	22	22	11	11	11	22	11	12	11	11	11	11	22
Gosling 5	12	22	22	11	12	11	12	22	12	11	11	12	12	12

RFLP locus

Chapter 20

The broader context: population viability analysis (PVA)

Wild populations face threats from both deterministic factors (habitat loss, over-exploitation, pollution and introduced species) and stochastic events associated with small population size. Population viability analysis is used to assess the combined impacts of all these factors on extinction risk, and to evaluate alternative management options to recover species

Terms:

Demographic stochasticity, environmental stochasticity, genetic stochasticity, population viability analysis (PVA), sensitivity analysis

'It's a hard world out there': stylized scenario of the myriad risks faced by species in natural habitats.

What causes endangerment and extinction?

Genetic threats are only a part of the endangering processes faced by species in the wild. Consequently, it is important to place genetic concerns in the broader conservation context. This chapter provides a connection between conservation genetics and the broader field of conservation biology. It is concerned with assessing extinction risk due to all deterministic and stochastic threats. Further, it considers means for evaluating options for restoring threatened and endangered species.

Assessments of extinction risk are required so that populations can be categorized according to relative risk, and conservation priorities set. High risk species are accorded legal protection under endangered species legislation in most countries. Further, trade or movement of endangered species is restricted by countries that are signatories to the Convention on International Trade in Endangered Species (CITES). Until the 1990s, risk assessment was rather subjective, with listing of species as endangered being based largely on the persuasive powers of individuals. Recently, there has been an appreciation that designation of degree of endangerment must be based on objective, quantitative guidelines (Mace & Lande 1991; IUCN 1996). Objective and quantitative evaluation of risks faced by species can be provided through population viability analysis (PVA). In this chapter, we present an introduction to the field of population viability analysis; we discuss the factors important to population viability, how viability is assessed, and what has been learned using this approach.

Wild populations face a range of threats from deterministic and stochastic factors that may act, and interact, to drive populations to extinction.

> Population decline and extinction are due to a range of deterministic and stochastic factors, with genetic factors being only one of many components

Deterministic factors

Deterministic factors are those threats that have a consistent direction and relatively consistent magnitude. The deterministic factors that cause the decline and extinction of species are directly, or indirectly associated with human actions, namely:
- loss of habitat
- over-exploitation
- pollution
- introduced species
- cascades of extinction
- combinations of the above factors.

While habitat loss is the most important documented factor in endangerment and extinction, in most cases, several of the factors combine to drive species to extinction (WCMC 1992). Further, these deterministic factors reduce population sizes to the point where additional stochastic factors may become significant, and deliver the final blow.

> A large and increasing number of species have had their numbers reduced by deterministic factors associated directly or indirectly with human actions

Stochastic factors

Small populations face additional stochastic threats: demographic stochasticity, environmental stochasticity, catastrophes and genetic stochasticity

Stochastic factors are chance factors that come into play in small populations. They differ from deterministic ones in that they have large random components, with effects varying in direction and magnitude by chance. There are four forms of stochasticity relevant to extinction risk in small populations:

Demographic stochasticity

Birth and death rates and sex-ratios fluctuate naturally and with time (May 1973). This is due both to chance and to responses to external factors like weather, food availability, etc. (see 'Environmental stochasticity' below). The component of this variation that is independent of external factors and due simply to chance is demographic stochasticity. The smaller the population, the more likely it is to vary randomly in reproduction and survival rates and in sex-ratio. In very small populations, these may be the final cause of extinction. For example, the last six dusky seaside sparrows were all males (Avise & Nelson 1989).

Environmental stochasticity

Variation in birth and death rates is affected by variation in the environment due to fluctuations in rainfall, temperature, density of competitors and predators, food sources, etc. Environmental fluctuations are a regular feature of all natural environments. Some fluctuations are associated with climatic cycles, such as the *El Niño*–Southern Oscillation. Plant growth varies with rainfall and temperature. Thus, food supply for herbivores fluctuates and carnivore numbers track prey numbers. For example, birth and death rates follow climatic conditions in many species, including red kangaroos (Caughley & Gunn 1996). Cycles in lynx populations in Canada appear to be driven by the North Atlantic Oscillation, a meteorological fluctuation similar to *El Niño* (Stenseth *et al.* 1999). Environmental variation influences all individuals in the population in a similar way.

Catastrophes

Extreme environmental events such as cyclones, severe winters, fires, floods and disease epidemics have major impacts on many species, and may lead to declines and extinctions. For example, a hurricane caused a significant decline in population numbers of the endangered Puerto Rican parrot (Lacy *et al.* 1990). African lions in the Serengeti recently suffered significant mortality due to canine distemper (Roelke-Parker *et al.* 1996). Young (1994) listed 92 natural die-offs (with 70%–90% mortality) in large mammals due to starvation, severe winters, droughts and disease. An extreme catastrophe due to the impact of an extraterrestrial body led to a mass extinction 65 million years ago, including that of the dinosaurs (Raup 1991). Single catastrophes can affect populations, multiple populations, or entire ecological communities.

Genetic stochasticity

This encompasses inbreeding depression, loss of genetic variation and accumulation of new deleterious mutations. The magnitude of genetic stochasticity depends on mating system, population structure, numbers, and the severity of environmental effects (Chapters 2 and 10–13). Inbreeding depression is a stochastic factor as it occurs in small populations through unavoidable matings between relatives. However, it has predictably deleterious impacts on reproduction and survival. The impacts of genetic factors are dependent on effective population sizes, while demographic stochasticity is dependent on the census population size. The occurrence of environmental stochasticity is essentially independent of population size, but its impact is not.

Interactions of stochastic factors

The combined impacts of stochastic factors are more damaging than the sum of their individual effects. Human pressures typically lead to small population sizes. This promotes inbreeding and consequent reductions in birth and survival rates. In turn, this causes further reductions in population size, increased demographic instability and a downward cycle to extinction. These feedback loops are termed 'extinction vortices' (Fig. 20.1; Gilpin & Soulé 1986). For example, the greater prairie chicken population in Illinois initially declined due to habitat loss and fragmentation, but later decline involved genetic stochasticity in a feedback cycle (Westemeier *et al.* 1998). Genetic diversity was lost and the population became inbred resulting in reduced fertility and hatchability. The population size continued to decline despite habitat restoration, leading to further inbreeding depression and further declines in reproductive rate. The Illinois population only began to recover after unrelated birds introduced genetic diversity from other populations

> Stochastic factors operate in a feedback cycle termed the 'extinction vortex'

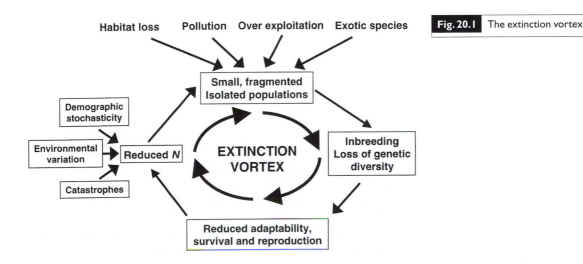

Fig. 20.1 The extinction vortex

(Fig. 12.10). Addressing the original cause of decline – habitat deterioration – was insufficient to recover the population.

Variation in population size due to demographic and environmental stochasticity and catastrophes reduces the effective population size and increases the rate of inbreeding

Demographic and environmental stochasticity and catastrophes increase fluctuations in population size. Consequently, they reduce the effective population size (Chapter 10) and thus make the impacts of inbreeding even more severe. For example, fluctuations in population size alone reduce the effective size of a bay checkerspot butterfly population in the USA to 25% of its mean population size (using data from Problem 20.1). It becomes inbred at four times the rate expected from its mean population size (assuming no immigration). Thus, demographic and environmental stochasticity and catastrophes interact with inbreeding. Their combined impacts reduce reproduction and survival more than expected from their individual effects, resulting in elevated extinction risk (van Noordwijk 1994; Tanaka 2000; B. Brook *et al.*, unpublished data).

Cumulative impacts

Extinction risk reflects the cumulative impacts, and interactions of all deterministic and stochastic factors

The total threat experienced by a population is the cumulative effects of deterministic factors, and demographic, environmental and genetic stochasticity, plus the occasional catastrophe. Consequently, actions to recover threatened species must not only address the original causes of decline (usually deterministic factors), but also cope with the additional stochastic threats. Identifying the most important factors determining extinction risk can help identify possible remedial action for threatened populations.

Predicting extinction probabilities: population viability analysis (PVA)

Population viability analysis is used to predict the probability of extinction due to the combined effects of deterministic and stochastic threats

Risk analyses for threatened species should be based on principles of population biology, involving demography, ecology and population genetics. The outcomes have a large stochastic element and involve probabilities rather than certainties. The process of combining these risk factors to project the future fate of populations is called population viability analysis (Fig. 20.2). PVA is defined as the process of evaluating the combined effects of threats faced by populations or species on their risks of extinction, or decline, and their chances of recovery within defined time frames.

This process arose out of the concept of minimum viable population size (Chapter 14). Shaffer (1981) and Gilpin & Soulé (1986) were largely responsible for developing the concept to combine deterministic risk factors with the stochastic ones.

PVAs are usually carried out by inputting, to a computer program, information on birth and survival rates and their variances, number of

Population Viability Analysis (PVA)

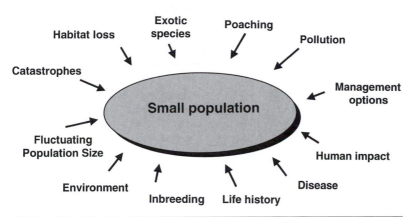

Population viability analysis (PVA) models the effects of different life history, environmental and threat factors on the population size and extinction risk of populations or species.

populations, population sizes, habitat capacities, frequencies and effects of threats (e.g. catastrophes, hunting, etc.), and other details about species life history (e.g. susceptibility to inbreeding depression, migration rates between populations, etc.) and then projecting forward in time (Fig. 20.3). The algorithms, formulae and concepts used in the computer simulations programs are based upon the accumulated knowledge of more than 100 years of research into population demography, ecology and genetics (where applicable). An example of the kind of input information required to run a PVA for the generic software package VORTEX (Miller & Lacy 1999) is given for the golden lion tamarin in Fig. 20.4.

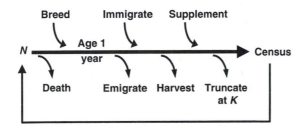

Fig. 20.3 Cycle of events in a typical PVA run as it progresses through generations (after Miller & Lacy 1999).

Many replicate runs (typically 500–1000) are conducted for a given set of input data, as individual population projections will produce different results as these are stochastic simulations. For example, the variability among replicate runs for the Capricorn silvereye (all using identical input data) is shown in Fig. 20.5. Results are usually summarized over all simulations. PVAs usually report population sizes, population growth

Replicate runs of PVA software using the same inputs give widely varying population trajectories due to stochastic variation

Fig. 20.4 Example of input information for a population viability analysis run using the VORTEX software package for the golden lion tamarin (after Ballou *et al.* 1998). This is only for one of several populations of this species. EV is the environmental variation for the parameter. Input variables are explained in Miller & Lacy (1999).

```
TAMARIN.OUT ***Output Filename
N ***Graphing Files?***
1000 ***Simulations
100 ***Years***
1 ***Reporting Interval***
0 ***Definition of Extinction***
1 ***Populations***
Y ***Inbreeding Depression?***
3.14 ***Lethal equivalents***
0.5 ***Prop. genetic load lethals***
N ***EV concordance repro – surv?***
4 ***Types Of Catastrophes***
M ***Monogamous, Polygynous, or
    Hermaphroditic***
4 ***Female Breeding Age***
4 ***Male Breeding Age***
16 ***Maximum Age***
0.5 ***Sex Ratio***
5 ***Max Litter Size (0 = N distribn) *****
N ***Density Dependent Breeding?***
75.7 ***breeding***
3.82 ***EV—Reproduction***
20.77 ***Population 1: % Litter Size 1***
57.94 ***Population 1: % Litter Size 2***
5.42 ***Population 1: % Litter Size 3***
15.21 ***Population 1: % Litter Size 4***
32.8 ***FMort age 0***
8.7 ***EV—FemaleMortality***
19.6 ***FMort age 1***
13.3 ***EV—FemaleMortality***
24.6 ***FMort age 2***
7.6 ***EV—FemaleMortality***
21.0 ***FMort age 3***
5.0 ***EV—FemaleMortality***
```

```
12.5 ***Adult Fmort***
6.7 ***EV—AdultFemaleMortality***
29.8 ***MMort age 0
7.0 ***EV—MaleMortality***
19.7 ***MMort age 1***
9.9 ***EV—MaleMortality***
23.9 ***MMort age 2***
5.0 ***EV—MaleMortality***
17.2 ***MMort age 3***
7.5 ***EV—MaleMortality***
16.0 ***Adult Mmort***
8.2 ***EV—AdultMaleMortality***
7.0 ***Prob. of Catastrophe 1***
1.0 ***Severity—Reproduction***
0.9 ***Severity—Survival***
1.0 ***Prob. of Catastrophe 2***
1.0 ***Severity—Reproduction***
0.5 ***Severity—Survival***
33.33 ***Probability Of Catastrophe 3***
1.0 ***Severity—Reproduction***
0.99 ***Severity—Survival***
5.0 ***Probability Of Catastrophe 4***
1.0 ***Severity—Reproduction***
0.95 ***Severity—Survival***
Y ***All Males Breeders?***
Y ***Start At Stable Age Distribution?***
350 ***Initial Population Size***
350 ***K***
0.0 ***EV—K***
N ***Trend In K?***
N ***Harvest?***
N ***Supplement?***
N ***AnotherSimulation?***
```

rate, and proportion of simulations extinct, and some report proportion of heterozygosity retained.

PVAs may be carried out using generic, off-the-shelf, software packages (such as GAPPS, RAMAS Metapop, RAMAS Stage, or VORTEX; Brook *et al.* 2000), or customized programs written for a specific species. The generic packages differ in their characteristics. All include demographic and environmental stochasticity. GAPPS and VORTEX are individual-based programs (i.e. they track the life of each individual in the population), while the RAMAS packages are matrix-based programs (that only track number of individuals). RAMAS Metapop and VORTEX are able to handle fragmented populations. Only GAPPS and VORTEX include genetic factors, but functions can be included in RAMAS Stage to include inbreeding effects.

Several hundred PVAs have been completed for threatened species (Lindenmayer & Possingham 1994; Menges 2000). The Conservation

> PVAs may be done by a variety of means including generic software packages, species-specific programs, or simple *r*-models

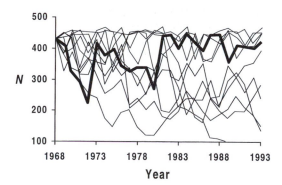

Fig. 20.5 Stochastic variability among replicate PVA runs in the projections for the Capricorn silvereye population from Heron Island in the Great Barrier Reef, Australia (from Brook & Kikkawa 1998). Input data are identical for all runs; the variability among runs results from the computer program using random number generators to mimic the demographic, environmental and catastrophic stochasticity natural to populations. How much variability is added by the random number generator depends on the population size, sampling theory, and the variance of rates provided by the input data. The bold line is the observed size of the population.

Breeding Specialist Group of IUCN alone has performed over 150 using VORTEX (Seal *et al.* 1998) and many have been done using the RAMAS packages (Akçakaya 2000). Many PVAs have also been done using customized software, including ones on matchstick banksia, northern spotted owl, Isle Royale gray wolf and red-cockaded woodpecker (Burgman *et al.* 1993; Boyce 1994; Vucetich *et al.* 1997; Letcher *et al.* 1998). Detailed case histories for several PVAs are given later in the chapter.

Limited life history data exist for most threatened species, so full population viability analyses may not be possible. A simplified version of PVA can be performed using stochastic r-models. These require only a time series of population size data to estimate the rate of population growth (r) and its variance. Simple stochastic simulations can predict the future population size trajectory and provide reasonable projections (see below). Example 20.1 illustrates a population trajectory in the bay checkerspot butterfly, the estimation of r and its variance and the projection from stochastic r-model simulations.

> A major limitation of PVA is that insufficient life history data exist for most species

---

| **Example 20.1** | Use of an r-model to project the future size of Bay checkerspot butterfly population in California (data from Foley 1994) |

The figure below shows the population size trajectory for a bay checkerspot butterfly populations from 1960 to 1986. There are two populations, so we will consider one here and leave the other for you to do as Problem 20.1.

The rate of population growth r, was obtained from the data as follows:

$$N_t = N_{t-1}\, e^r$$

Thus

$$N_t / N_{t-1} = e^r$$

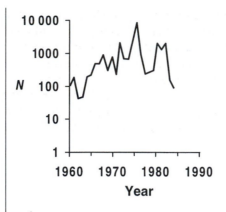

and

$$\ln (N_t/N_{t-1}) = r$$

For example, the numbers in the first two years were 90 and 175. From these, we obtain our first estimate of r, as follows:

$$r = \ln (175/90) = 0.665$$

In year 3, the numbers were 40, so for the year 2 to year 3 transition r is as follows:

$$r = \ln (40/175) = -1.476$$

A stationary population has $r = 0$, while positive r indicates a growing population and negative r a declining population. The mean r for this bay checkerspot butterfly population was 0.002 (essentially stationary) and its variance 1.456.

The stochastic projection for this population, obtained using r-model software, is shown in the figure below. Projections were done both to compare with the actual population trajectory for 1960–86, and to project forwards for an additional 25 years. Only three replicates are shown to avoid cluttering the figure.

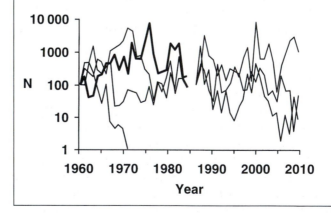

Even simpler methods may be used in predicting the future fate of populations when data are scarce. Some rely on surveying the opinions of experts. For example, Ralls & Starfield (1995) used methods from business management to evaluate the best strategy for management of endangered Hawaiian monk seals, where males on occasion mob and kill females. This led to the decision to remove males when the sex-ratio became distorted by excess males. The IUCN categorization system using criteria A–D also represents a simple means of predicting extinction risk (Chapter 1).

Genetics and PVA

Inbreeding depression is the only genetic threat that has been incorporated into PVAs. For this incorporation, we need to know:

- Susceptibility of the species to inbreeding depression. If not known, the median lethal equivalents (3.14) for captive mammals from Ralls *et al.* (1988) is typically used.
- What fitness components are affected by inbreeding.
- Is inbreeding depression linearly, or curvilinearly, related to F? Linearity is assumed for the default in VORTEX, while INMAT models a curvilinear (synergistic interaction) relationship.
- The genetic mechanism responsible for inbreeding depression, overdominance or dominance. This determines the extent of purging. Perhaps the best default is to assume that 50% of deleterious alleles are lethal and the rest are alleles of small effect, as occurs in fruit flies (Simmons & Crow 1977). This is possible in VORTEX, but not in other packages.
- The extent of isolation among fragments, i.e. the migration rates, as these affect the inbreeding coefficient.
- The breeding system (outbreeding versus selfing, monogamous versus polygamous versus hermaphrodite, etc.). This affects N_e.
- The relationship between catastrophes and inbreeding/genetic diversity. While the impacts of inbreeding are typically greater in stressful environments (Chapter 12), it is typically assumed in PVAs that there is no interaction between catastrophes and inbreeding.
- Population size.

Most PVAs ignore genetic issues, and are likely to underestimate extinction risk (Chapters 2, 12 and 16). Even when genetic factors are included (typically using VORTEX), inbreeding depression is normally only imposed on juvenile survival, even though it is clear that inbreeding depression affects reproduction, survival, mating ability, parental care and longevity (Chapter 12). It is possible to incorporate inbreeding depression for other components of fitness using GAPPS and INMAT, and with recent versions of VORTEX. The levels of inbreeding depression assumed are typically those from captive mammals, so impacts are underestimated as inbreeding depression is much greater in the wild than in captivity (Crnokrak & Roff 1999).

> PVAs show that inbreeding depression often increases the risk of extinction in threatened species

> PVAs typically do not encompass the full genetic impacts on population viability

All current PVA packages typically can not model all the details of a species breeding system and usually underestimate the impacts of variation in family sizes in reducing effective population sizes. For example, VORTEX can specify mating system (monogamy, polygamy, or hermaphrodite), variation in litter sizes and proportion of males participating in breeding. However, it assumes random mating within these constraints. From year to year, the probability of an individual having a given number of offspring is random within the constraints. In real populations individuals contributing above (or below) average numbers of offspring are likely to do this in successive years, i.e. the variance in family size is often underestimated in PVAs and N_e are higher than observed in real populations. Consequently, PVAs will often underestimate levels of inbreeding and inbreeding depression.

There is no contribution of loss of genetic diversity to fitness modelled, apart from that associated with inbreeding depression (i.e. evolutionary potential is ignored), although heterozygosity can be tracked using VORTEX. Further, new mutations are ignored in all PVAs.

Despite underestimating inbreeding impacts, PVAs have revealed that inbreeding depression substantially increases extinction risk for a range of species in single populations (Fig. 2.5 and Chapter 12). Further, it elevated extinction risk in two isolated black rhinoceros populations (Box 16.2). Genetic factors were important in the PVA on the Florida panther (see below). It predicted that the population was in danger of extinction within a short time and recommended action to alleviate inbreeding problems. Daniels *et al.* (2000) found important reductions in fitness in small populations using stochastic simulations for red-cockaded woodpeckers.

The main reason for small impacts of inbreeding depression is that short time frames are considered, or that the species has a long generation interval, so that there are few generations for inbreeding to accumulate (B. Brook *et al.*, unpublished data). Large populations are, not surprisingly, less susceptible than small populations to the impacts of inbreeding.

Insights into the causes of extinction from PVA

Demographic, environmental and genetic stochasticity reduce population growth and increase extinction risk

PVA is a tool that can be used to investigate the relative contributions of different factors, and to improve understanding of the causes of extinction. In this way, it complements results from simple analytical theory and from laboratory and field studies. The combination of these approaches is much more powerful than any one alone. Analytical theory involves simplistic models whose assumptions may be suspect. Simulations allow inclusion of more factors and greater reality. Laboratory studies involve real organisms and replication, but in simplified environments. Field studies involve the full complexity of real populations in real environments, but have limited replication and their results may apply only to a specific species in a specific environment.

The impacts of demographic, environmental and genetic stochasticity and catastrophes in reducing population growth and increasing extinction risk have been demonstrated in PVA simulations. The impacts can be evaluated by doing PVA simulations both with and without a factor and comparing the impacts on population growth and extinction risk. For example, we saw that inclusion, versus exclusion, of inbreeding depression increased extinction risk in models for a range of endangered species (Fig. 2.5 and Box 16.2).

The relationship between population size and extinction risk is predicted by theory and supported by extensive empirical data (Chapter 2). Extinction risk is greater in smaller than in otherwise equivalent larger populations of the same species. For example, Fig. 20.6 shows extinction probabilities of populations of Eld's deer with different carrying capacities. Extinction levels are highest in the smallest population and lowest in the largest, and increase with time. Similar relationships are evident in field data, including those on bighorn sheep (Fig. 2.5), on the relationships between island area and number of species (Terborgh & Winter 1980; Diamond 1984) and on extinctions in both National Parks and mountaintops in North America (Chapter 14).

Small populations have higher extinction risks than equivalent large populations of the same species

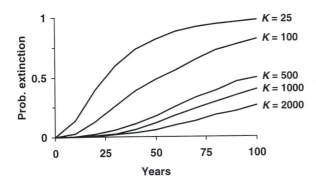

Fig. 20.6 Relationship between extinction risk and population size. Cumulative extinction risks of endangered Eld's deer (from Myanmar) over time in four populations of different sizes (based on data from Wemmer *et al.* 2000). Population sizes are limited by the carrying capacity of their environments (*K*). *Extinction risk is greater in smaller than in larger populations and increases with time.*

Demographic stochasticity substantially increases extinction risk in very small populations, but its impact becomes small once populations are above 50–100 individuals (Fig. 20.7). In the plant *Astrocaryum mexicanum*, extinction risk over 100 years due to demographic stochasticity is very high in populations of 10, but zero above population sizes of 50. A wide range of other evidence indicates that demographic stochasticity has minor impact in populations of over 100.

Demographic stochasticity increases extinction risk, but it has little impact in populations with sizes of greater than 100

Natural variation in climate and other environmental variables affect entire populations and may drive small populations to extinction. For example, Fig. 20.8 shows the fluctuations in population size due to environmental factors in both a large and a small population. The large population persists, but a similar amount of environmental stochasticity drives the smaller population to extinction. Environmental

Environmental stochasticity increases extinction risk at much larger population sizes than demographic stochasticity

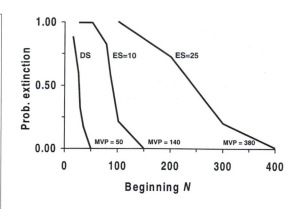

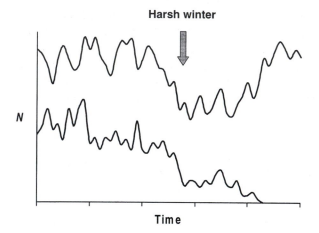

stochasticity has impacts over a much wider range of population sizes than demographic stochasticity (Fig. 20.7). For this plant, populations have to be above 140 before the extinction risks from environmental stochasticity over 100 years is restricted to 5%, while population of only size 50 are required with demographic stochasticity.

The impact of demographic and environmental stochasticity on population size is illustrated in Fig. 20.9. In populations beginning at size 200, environmental stochasticity markedly depresses population growth, compared to the deterministic case, while demographic stochasticity has no obvious effect.

This translates into differences in extinction risk (Fig. 20.7). Further, extinction risks are increased as the level of environmental variation increases. For example, in *Astrocaryum mexicanum*, the population size required to limit extinction probabilities to less than 5% over 100 years was 140 with low environmental variation (ES = 10) and 380 with high environmental variation (ES = 25) (Fig. 20.7).

Catastrophes, such as cyclones, severe winters, fires and disease epi-

Catastrophes increase extinction risk, with their impact depending upon their frequency and severity

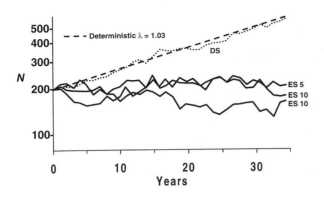

Fig. 20.9 Impact of environmental stochasticity (ES) and demographic stochasticity (DS) on population growth in the plant *Astrocaryum mexicanum* compared to deterministic growth (after Menges 1992). *With this initial size, environmental stochasticity depresses population growth, but demographic stochasticity does not.*

demics are more likely to drive smaller populations to extinction. Catastrophes are extreme forms of environmental variation, and their impact is similar in direction to that of environmental stochasticity (Soulé 1987). For example, a PVA on the Puerto Rican parrot (Box 20.1) identified catastrophes in the form of hurricanes as a major risk. Shortly after the PVA was completed, a hurricane hit the island and reduced the bird's population. The black-footed ferret was sent to extinction in the wild in 1987, primarily through a catastrophic canine distemper outbreak (Clark 1994).

| **Box 20.1** | **Population viability analysis for the Puerto Rican parrot** |

The endangered Puerto Rican parrot declined to 13–14 birds in the wild because of deforestation, poaching for the pet trade, predation and cyclones. A captive population was established by removing eggs from wild nests. At the time the PVA was done, the wild population had about 40 birds (Lacy *et al.* 1990). The PVA predicted a probability of extinction of over 30% over 100 years. The primary risk identified was from a catastrophe, especially in the form of hurricanes. The PVA recommended stockpiling of food for the parrots at the remote breeding centre, so that birds could be fed if a hurricane cut access roads. Since both the wild and the captive populations were on the island, it was recommended that a population be established elsewhere. The long-range plan called for the establishment of five independent wild parrot populations in Puerto Rico.

The recommendations were prescient! Soon after, the population suffered a serious set-back from a hurricane that devastated the forest habitat (Seal 1991). The stockpiled food allowed captive birds to be fed whilst the Centre was isolated and prevented their extinction. Careful genetic management was recommended for this small population as it is showing evidence of inbreeding depression (Brock & White 1992). The management plan has subsequently been criticized on the basis of the undesirability of fragmenting the population and on the disease risk posed by returning captive-bred birds to the wild (Wilson *et al.* 1994).

Species with low reproductive rates are generally more sensitive to stochastic factors than species with high reproductive rates

Immigration may 'rescue' populations and thus allow small populations to persist

The sensitivity of populations to demographic and genetic stochasticity is greatest in species with low reproductive rates, and least in species with high reproductive rates (Menges 1992; Mills & Smouse 1994). However, environmental fluctuations may have greater impacts on reproduction and survival in species with higher reproductive rates.

Many natural populations are fragmented, but maintain some migration among fragments. Populations that are too small to persist on their own may be 'rescued' by immigration from other small populations that are experiencing relatively independent fluctuations in population size. This occurs in the acorn woodpecker in the American southwest (Stacey & Taper 1992). A population with a carrying capacity of 52 was predicted to have a median persistence time of only 16 years (and a maximum of 48 years), although the real population had persisted for more than 70 years. When immigration was included in the model, persistence times increased; with five immigrants per generation, the probability of extinction over 1000 years dropped to zero. The real population was found to receive about 10 immigrants per year. In general, the 'rescue effect' of immigration will usually be even greater when inbreeding depression is included in models (Box 16.2; Richards 2000).

Recovering threatened populations

Population viability analysis is widely used as a management tool to compare options to recover species

A wide range of different procedures have been suggested to recover threatened populations, including legal restraints on exploitation, removing predators, improving habitat, reserving habitat, captive breeding, etc. PVA is frequently used to evaluate and compare these options. Typically, these commence with sensitivity analyses, followed by detailed PVAs that compare a range of specific management options.

Sensitivity analyses

Sensitivity analyses involve determining the relative impact of variation in parameters on extinction risk

Sensitivity analyses provide a highly useful tool in evaluating recovery programs for threatened species (Wisdom & Mills 1997; Mills & Lindberg 2000). These analyses involve varying input parameters by increments in either direction around the mean and evaluating their effects on extinction risk or population trajectories. In this way, the input parameters whose values most influence the output can be identified, i.e. is the outcome most sensitive to varying juvenile survival, or adult reproductive rate, or predation level, etc. Alternative management options can be compared, as can various causes of population decline. For example, sensitivity analyses identified first-year survival as the parameter whose variation had most impact on population growth rate in the greater prairie chicken (Wisdom & Mills 1997). Consequently, they recommended that management should focus on finding ways to improve nest success, brood survival and post-brood survival to one year of age.

Sensitivity analyses have altered our perceptions about the most important factors threatening cheetahs and loggerhead sea turtles. Predation on cheetah cubs by lions and hyenas had been viewed as the major threat to the cheetah's viability (Caro & Laurenson 1994). However, a sensitivity analysis revealed that populations were much more sensitive to adult than to juvenile survivorship (Crooks *et al.* 1998). In loggerhead turtles, many years of management focused on the seemingly obvious notion that increasing hatchling survival should reverse population decline. However, sensitivity analysis showed that the most efficient way to stop decline of the species was to reduce mortality of life stages that were being killed in shrimp nets (see Mills & Lindberg 2000).

Use of PVA in evaluating management options: case studies

The following gives a selection of case studies chosen to represent a diversity of PVA analyses where threats and management options differ.

Black-footed ferret

The ferret black-footed ferret once occupied an area of 40 million hectares, but its numbers were drastically reduced by control of prairie dogs (its prey) on agricultural lands. By the late 1970s, they were thought to be extinct (Seal *et al.* 1989; Clark 1994). In 1981, a small population of about 80 individuals was found in Wyoming, USA. Initial recovery efforts concentrated on maximizing the number of wild ferrets, and maximizing the number of prairie dog prey. An initial risk analysis identified stochastic factors (genetic, environmental and demographic stochasticity plus catastrophes) as potential problems. Several studies recommended captive breeding and reintroductions, but this was not implemented until after the catastrophic decline of the ferrets in 1985, due to bubonic plague among the prairie dogs and an epidemic of canine distemper in the ferrets. The initial program was bedevilled by bureaucratic and political problems. By 1986, only a handful of ferrets were left in the wild. All animals remaining in the wild were taken into captivity by 1987. This resulted in 18 individuals surviving to found the captive population.

A PVA in 1989 indicated that about 120 animals were required for a wild population to show greater than 95% probability of persisting for 100 years. Multiple independent populations were considered to provide the best insurance against overall loss of the species from chance extinctions (e.g. from disease in the ferrets, or their prey). There were additional serious genetic concerns about the population that this model did not include (i.e. loss of genetic diversity and inbreeding depression). The goals of the US Fish and Wildlife Service black-footed ferret recovery plan in 1987 were to increase the captive population to an effective size of 200 breeding adults by 1991, and to establish wild populations of 1500 adults in 10 or more populations by 2010 (a metapopulation).

The captive population has increased in size to about 300 adults and six wild populations have been established, but only two of the reintro-duced populations have been particularly successful so far (Chapter 18).

Florida panther

The Florida panther population in Florida, USA has dropped from 500 + at the turn of the century to fewer than 50 individuals by the later 1980s. Loss and fragmentation of habitat and unregulated killing were the main causes of decline. Causes of high mortality at that time include car kills, some illegal killing and possibly disease, and the population showed evidence of inbreeding depression (cryptorchidism, high fre-quency of sperm defects and kinked tail). A PVA on the Florida panther predicted that it would decline at 6%–10% per year in the wild and go extinct in 25–40 years due to inbreeding depression and demographic factors (Seal & Lacy 1989). Immediate extinction due to disease was a real risk. Recommendations to save the population from extinction were that (a) habitat be preserved, (b) a captive population be started using about 20 founders, followed subsequently by reintroductions, and (c) a male be transferred to an area that contained only females. Genetic research into the sub-population structure of the Florida popu-lation and its relationship to the rest of the species plus continuous monitoring and management of the wild population was also recom-mended.

Subsequently, genetic analyses revealed extremely low levels of genetic diversity in Florida panther compared to other panthers/ cougars. Further, a portion of the population was found to have hybri-dized with a South American sub-species (O'Brien et al. 1990). Subsequent genetic workshops resulted in a decision to augment this population with individuals from the Texas sub-species to overcome inbreeding depression (Hedrick 1995b). Eight females from Texas were introduced into the Florida panther population in 1995. Thirty-six intercross animals are known to have been produced, and 25 of these may still be surviving (Land & Lacy 2000). Current representation of Texas puma genes is 15%–29%. The F_1 hybrid kittens do not have cow-licks, or kinked tails and they appear more robust than 'pure' Florida panthers (Box 16.1). A subsequent PVA in 1999 concluded that the Florida panther no longer had a high risk of extinction (Maehr et al. 2001). Mortality rates due to collisions with cars were now lower, as cul-verts had been inserted under roads. Further, more extensive life history data indicated less threat than initial data.

Lord Howe Island woodhen

The Lord Howe Island woodhen population on the island of Lord Howe off the east coast of Australia declined to 20–30 individuals in the 1970s, because of combined impacts of past human exploitation and especially from predation and habitat destruction by introduced pigs. The woodhen recovered following extermination of pigs and a captive breeding and reintroduction program where 86 captive bred individu-als were released over four years (Chapter 18). A retrospective analysis of the Lord Howe Island woodhen recovery program indicated that both control of pigs and captive breeding and release were necessary to recover the population (B. W. Brook & R. Frankham unpublished data). Extinction probabilities over 100 years were 100% for no management, 44% for pig control alone, 99% for captive breeding of four years duration alone and 2% for the combination of pig control and captive breeding (the program actually implemented). The problem with pig control alone was that while it removed the main threatening process, it did not ensure that the population reached numbers high enough to avoid extinction from stochastic factors.

The woodhen now has a relatively stable population of about 200 on the island, and it has been downgraded from endangered to vulnerable and routine monitoring terminated. However, a prospective PVA on the woodhen concluded that the population is acutely sensitive to minor changes in mortality and fecundity, and to catastrophes due to exotic species, inbreeding or disease (Brook *et al.* 1997a). The establishment of a second, remote population on another island was recommended to minimize these risks, but this has not been implemented.

Chinook salmon

Chinook salmon in Oregon, USA have declined dramatically since early this century, due primarily to habitat degradation associated with siltation from road building and forestry. Ratner *et al.* (1997) conducted a PVA on the spring chinook population in the South Umpqua River that currently averages fewer than 300 spawners per year. Projected extinction risks over 100 and 200 years were very low, assuming no further habitat degradation. However, this conclusion was highly sensitive to uncertainty about density dependence. The projected extinction risk was 100% assuming continuing habitat degradation at a rate similar to that in the past.

Furbish's lousewort

This endangered herbaceous perennial plant was once thought to be extinct, but about 5000 individuals exist in 28 colonies along a 230-km stretch of a single river in Maine and New Brunswick in northeastern North America. The species is limited to periodically disturbed, north-facing riverbanks. It is an early successional hemiparasite that cannot invade disturbed riverbanks for at least three years, but is later crowded out by taller competitors, leading to regular rounds of colonization and population extinction. Thus, the species exists as a metapopulation. A PVA demonstrated that individual populations had 87% probabilities of extinction within 100 years, so that the survival of the species is critically dependent on the balance between colonization and extinction (Menges 1990). As extinctions currently exceed colonization, the long-term viability of this species is tenuous. Further, the long-term ability of the population to adapt is questionable as four populations of the species lack genetic diversity at 22 allozyme loci (Waller *et al.* 1987).

Matchstick banksia

The vulnerable matchstick banksia is a large shrub native to the southwestern part of Western Australia. There are about 340 plants confined to seven populations over a range of 60 km. The important factors affecting the dynamics of this species are variation in rainfall, the frequency of prescribed (controlled) fires and wildfires. Burgman & Lamont (1992) carried out a PVA incorporating demographic, environmental and genetic factors. Management options to maximize population size and to minimize the risk of extinction are different. The mean size is increased by a moderate frequency of prescribed fires at intervals of 11–25 years. However, this results in a risk of extinction of about 50% over 50 years, as intensive fires can destroy populations. The risk of extinction is minimized if the frequency of fires is kept as low as possible. However, this leads to a substantial decline in population size as recruitment occurs mainly after fires when the canopy-stored seed is released and existing plants are killed. If rainfall declines over the next 50 years due, say, to global climate change, the species has a low probability of persistence, even in the absence of prescribed fires. The only way to ensure a reasonable chance of persistence of the species is to intervene by watering seedlings whenever there is severe drought following a fire. Inbreeding depression has limited impact on this species over 50 years as it is long-lived (a mean generation time of 23 years). Predicted mean population sizes after 50 years were 171 without inbreeding depression and 161 with its effects included.

How useful are the predictions of PVA?

The PVA process may be more important to conservation than the PVA output

PVA often has its greatest value as a heuristic tool to assist planning for the recovery of threatened species, to allow iterative planning, to determine sensitivities and to compare recovery options, rather than in providing accurate predictions of extinction risk

The most important contributions of risk assessments using PVA do not necessarily come from the quantitative assessments of extinction risk themselves. Rather, the process of conducting a PVA involves:

* Summarizing information about the life history of the species
* Identifying all the threatening processes impacting upon it
* Assessing their likely importance
* Identifying potential recovery strategies and evaluating their relative impacts.

Thus, considerable benefits may be gained by the PVA process, even if the quantitative predictions are not particularly accurate. PVA provides a transparent planning process that should have internal consistency. Further, the recovery process can operate in an iterative manner. PVA projections can be updated as more information on the species is gathered.

A major benefit of PVA is that it typically involves meetings of all the experts on a species so that deficiencies in knowledge are identified and co-operation in recovery efforts is encouraged

A PVA is best conducted in a workshop environment, involving all the experts on a given threatened species. This approach is typically used by the CBSG. This process is highly beneficial as it focuses attention on what is, and is not, known about the species. Deficiencies in knowledge about the species are identified, often leading to the formulation of research proposals to remedy the deficiencies. Unpublished results and expert knowledge may become available for inclusion in the PVA. Endangered species conservation often involves individuals or groups with strongly divergent views and agencies with competing interests. Warring parties can be 'encouraged' to co-operate at workshops. Further, the PVA process increases the probability that funds for recovery programs or research will be made available.

How accurate are the predictions of PVA?

PVA packages are complex models akin to climate or economic models. Like those models, feedback is required between conception of the models, writing software and evaluation against real data, for improvement in predictive accuracy to occur. As PVA is a relatively new tool, its predictive powers have received only very limited evaluation, based on retrospective analyses utilizing well-studied species. The predictive accuracy of PVA is extremely important as serious inaccuracies may lead to inappropriate listing of species when they are not endangered, not listing truly endangered species, or inappropriate recovery options that impede rather than enhance recovery. Wide-ranging scepticism exists about the accuracy of PVA predictions, based on questions about insufficient data, ignoring threatening factors, adequacy of models, lack of empirical tests of predictive powers, etc. (see Caughley & Gunn 1996; Ludwig 1999). Further, evidence from PVA has been rejected in law courts (Talbot 1994).

> An evaluation of the predictive accuracy of PVA indicates that it provides reliable average predictions of the future fate of populations, but that predictions for individual populations may be uncertain

The predictive accuracy of PVA was evaluated in a retrospective study involving 21 species with records extending over at least 10 years. Models were parameterized using data from the first half of the records and used to predict the second half for which the real-world trajectory was known (Brook *et al.* 2000). Overall, the predictive accuracy was surprisingly good. Predicted probabilities of population decline (quasi-extinction risk) closely matched observed values (Fig. 20.10) and there were no significant biases. In general, predicted population size did not differ from those actually observed. Further, predictions from different software packages were highly correlated with each other and with predictions from simple stochastic *r*-models. A subsequent study of the predictive accuracy of stochastic *r*-models, based on retrospective studies on 195 populations, indicated that they had good predictive accuracy. Further, accuracy was consistently good for mammals, birds, reptiles, invertebrates and plants (B. Brook *et al.*, unpublished data).

The above PVA evaluation tested the average predictions over 21 populations. Since the fate of populations has large stochastic elements, predictions for individual populations may be quite uncertain. This

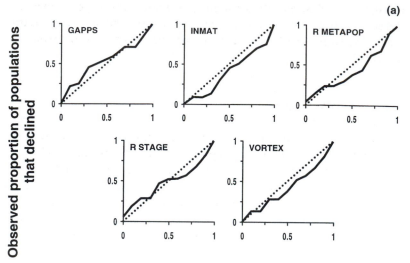

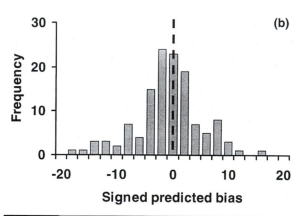

Fig. 20.10 Predictive accuracy of five PVA software packages (Brook et al. 2000). (a) Plot of predicted versus observed risks of population size decline in retrospective studies on 21 well-studied species. Data from the first half of each study were used to predict numbers in the second half. A perfect fit to reality lies on the 45° line. *Predictive accuracy was surprisingly good.* (b) Differences between projected and observed population size show no significant directional bias.

does not mean that they are not valuable. PVA predictions should be compared with daily weather forecasting, long-term weather forecasting and economic projections. These are all readily accepted by society, which also recognizes their less than perfect predictive abilities.

PVA therefore appears to be suitable for the conservation purposes for which it is being used, provided there are sufficient data. To be reliable, PVA models must adequately reflect important aspects of species biology. For example, the poorest projection in the above study was for the Soay sheep using INMAT. This package could not realistically model the over-compensatory density-dependent population cycle shown by the sheep (Chapman *et al.* 2001). Subjective assessment by humans is the main alternative to PVA, and this is notoriously inaccurate (Zeckhauser & Viscusi 1990).

Lessons learned

Shaffer *et al.* (2001) have provided an excellent overview of the lessons learned from PVA, but not acted upon: (a) the major limitation of PVA is lack of detailed population data, (b) there is a consensus that populations of less than a few thousand individuals are of questionable viability, but recovery goals for many threatened populations are less than this, and (c) there is no agreed and workable definition of population viability. In the sections below, we elaborate upon these issues.

Limitations of PVA

The PVA examples we have quoted are predominantly well-studied species with extensive data, i.e. the input parameters for PVA are reasonably accurate. This is rarely the case. For most threatened species, there is little information on numbers, even less on age-specific mortality and fecundity, and very rarely reliable estimates of variances for parameters. Often the primary cause(s) of species decline are unknown (Caughley & Gunn 1996). An accurate PVA requires sound data. However, PVAs may still have planning value, even if they are not particularly accurate, as we discussed above. In some cases, simple stochastic *r*-models can be used to project the population's fate. However, these do not usually lend themselves to evaluating management options, as sensitivity analyses are not possible.

> A major limitation of PVA is that there is usually limited information available on the biology of threatened species

We are surprisingly depauperate in our basic knowledge of the biology and ecology of endangered species. Consequently, long-term field studies need to be developed (Shaffer *et al.* 2001)

What is a viable population?

A viable population is one with a high probability of surviving for a long time. How high? How long? These are undefined quantities. However, 99% or 95% survival probability is most frequently used for the former, and time spans of 100 to 1000 years are normally considered for the latter (Shaffer 1981; Soulé 1987). IUCN (1996) defines lower-risk populations as having greater than a 90% probability of surviving for 100 years.

> There is no objective definition of a viable population

Shaffer (1981) defined a viable population as 'the smallest isolated population having a 99% chance of remaining extant for 1000 years despite the foreseeable effects of demographic, environmental and genetic stochasticity and natural catastrophes'. Soulé (1987) defined it as the 'minimum conditions for the long-term persistence and adaptation of species or populations in a given place'. By this, he meant the capacity of the group to maintain itself for the foreseeable future (usually centuries) with an agreed probability, say 95%.

These definitions all use years as their time frames. However, genetic concerns (inbreeding and loss of genetic diversity) accumulate over generations, rather than years. Demographic and ecological threats may also be more closely tied to generations than to years, as the major risks during lifetimes are typically associated with the reproductive transition from one generation to the next. PVAs on 30 species demonstrated that population viability scales to generations, rather than to chronological time (J. O'Grady *et al.*, unpublished data). Consequently, viable populations would more appropriately be defined in terms of persistence for a defined number of generations.

Minimum viable population sizes (MVP)

There is a consensus that the size required for a population to be viable in the long term is at least thousands to tens of thousands

As habitat and financial resources are limited, it is important to determine the minimum sizes required to maintain viable populations in the long term, and to determine their minimum habitat areas. MVP is the minimum number required for a population or species to be viable in the long term. PVA was originally devised to determine minimum viable population sizes and habitat areas for grizzly bears (Shaffer 1981).

Different estimates of the size required, based on a variety of theoretical arguments and on empirical data, are given in Table 20.1. Based on empirical evidence, Thomas (1990) suggested that 10 is far too small, 100 is usually inadequate, 1000 is adequate for species of normal variability in population sizes, while 10 000 should permit medium- to long-term persistence of birds and mammals that show strong fluctuations in population size. The required size is not universal, but depends on details of the biology and environment of the species.

Soulé (1987) also estimated that the size of populations required to attain a 95% expectation of persistence over several centuries would be in the low thousands. His estimates were based both on theory and on comparisons of population sizes of extinct and extant populations in US National Parks. Similarly, Belovsky (1987) inferred from extinction rates for cold-adapted mammals on mountaintops in southwestern USA over the last 8000 years that the required sizes were related to body size; 95% persistence for 100 years required populations of about 100 000 for mammals the size of shrews, while populations of around 400 were sufficient for animals the size of elephants, with intermediate-sized mammals lying between these values. The corresponding population sizes required for 95% persistence for 1000 years were 1 million and 5000, respectively. Species with higher variation in population size were predicted to require larger sizes and ones with low variation in population size needed smaller population sizes.

The importance of population size on probability of population survival is also demonstrated by the extensive data showing relationships

Table 20.1	Sizes required for long-term viability of populations to cope with different threats (see Chapter 14); variation refers to the propensity for population sizes to fluctuate.	
Threat	N_e	N
1. Loss of genetic diversity	500–5000	5000–50000
2. Mutational accumulation	1000	10000
3. Demographic stochasticity		10s – 100
4. Environmental stochasticity		1000+
5. Catastrophes		1000+
6. Combined empirical data (Thomas 1990)		
birds and mammals		
average variation		1000
high variation		10000
insects		
average variation		10000
high variation		100000

Source: Nunney & Campbell (1993); Thomas (1990).

between island area and number of species, indicating higher extinction rates on smaller islands (see Diamond 1984).

Minimum habitat area

In practice, the desired information for species conservation in nature may be the minimum habitat area required for a high probability of persistence for a long time. This information allows intelligent decisions to be made about the size of reserves and national parks. Minimum habitat area can be estimated from minimum viable population sizes and habitat requirements for the species. Example 20.2 illustrates the estimation of minimum habitat area for the golden lion tamarin; a minimum area of 24 km² is required for the tamarins to have a 90% chance of persistence for 100 years.

> Minimum habitat areas for long-term population persistence can be determined from MVP and the habitat required per individual for the species

Example 20.2	Minimum habitat area for golden lion tamarins

The minimum viable population size required for a 90% probability of persistence for 100 years in golden lion tamarins has been estimated as 175 tamarins, based on PVA analyses (J. J. O'Grady unpublished data). The minimum habitat area is estimated by multiplying this number by the habitat requirement per tamarin. The observed density of tamarins in Poço das Antas Biological Reserve in Brazil is one tamarin per 13.9 hectares (Ballou *et al.* 1998). Thus, the minimum habitat area (MHA) is

$$MHA = MVP \times \text{habitat requirement} = 175 \times 13.9 \text{ ha} = 2433 \text{ ha}$$
$$= 24.3 \text{ km}^2$$

The two existing reserves for golden lion tamarins encompass 79 km², about 50% of which is forested.

(The actual goal of the golden lion tamarin program is a 98% probability of persistence for 100 years, and a larger area is required for this; Ballou *et al.* 1998.)

Population sizes used to list and de-list threatened species are usually less than those recommended above

From the above it is clear that populations must have sizes at least in the order of a few thousand to be viable in the long term. Both the population size at the time species are recognized as threatened (listed), and the recovery targets under the USA Endangered Species Act are typically too small (Shaffer *et al.* 2001). The median size at listing is about 1000 individuals for animals and 100 for plants. Further, the median population size for a taxon to be considered recovered was about 1550.

A worrying implication of these numbers is that even the largest reserves (apart from the Arctic and Antarctic) are too small to maintain adequate population sizes for long-term survival of large herbivores and especially large carnivores (Shaffer 1987).

While major advances have been made in the science underlying conservation of threatened species, it is not always matched by appropriate action.

Summary

1. Wild populations face threats both from deterministic factors (habitat loss, over-exploitation, pollution and introduced species), and stochastic threats associated with small population size.

2. Small populations face threats due to demographic stochasticity, environmental stochasticity, catastrophes and genetic stochasticity. Genetic stochasticity encompasses inbreeding depression, loss of genetic variation and the accumulation of new deleterious mutations.

3. Extinction risk can be predicted using population viability analysis. Typically values of reproductive and survival parameters, population size, carrying capacity, along with information on environment and its variation, inbreeding depression, habitat quality and loss, etc., are input to computer packages and stochastic projections made.

4. Population viability analysis is widely used as a management tool to compare different options to recover a species.

5. Recovery of small threatened populations involves reversing both the original cause of decline and addressing stochastic threats.

FURTHER READING

Beissinger & McCullough (2001) *Population Viability Analysis.* Proceedings of a conference on PVA. See especially papers by Mills & Lindberg, Ralls *et al.*, and Shaffer *et al.*

Ecological Bulletin (2000) Special Issue on PVA. See especially papers by Akçakaya
& Sjögren-Gulve, Akçakaya, and Lacy.

Ferson & Burgman (2000) *Quantitative Methods in Conservation Biology*. A collection of reviews, many on risk assessment in conservation biology.

Soulé (1987) *Viable Populations for Conservation*. A comprehensive collection of
papers covering all major issues related to the viability of small populations.

Wilcove (1994) *The Condor's Shadow*. An enjoyable and informative book written
for a popular audience on the decline and recovery of wildlife in America.

PROBLEMS

20.1 Computing r and its variance: For a second population of Bay
checkerspot butterflies (data from Foley 1994), determine for each generation transition λ and r, and so calculate the mean r and the variance of r.

Year	N	Year	N	Year	N
1960	70	1970	820	1980	125
1961	350	1971	235	1981	316
1962	750	1972	1149	1982	109
1963	750	1973	370	1983	122
1964	1400	1974	177	1984	31
1965	2000	1975	317	1985	48
1966	1750	1976	1001	1986	18
1967	900	1977	190		
1968	576	1978	341		
1969	871	1979	135		

20.2 Management for recovery of endangered species: What action
would you suggest to recover the northern hairy-nosed wombat (see
Boxes 10.3 and 19.2)?

20.3 Management for recovery of endangered species: What action
would you suggest to recover a species of endangered *Partula* snail
from Tahiti? It is being predated by an introduced carnivorous snail.

20.4 Management for recovery of endangered species: What action
would you take to recover the Sumatran tiger? All tigers are threatened by habitat loss and harvesting for the Asian medicinal market.
The Sumatran tiger has six isolated populations in reserves, plus a few
other populations.

PRACTICAL EXERCISES: POPULATION VIABILITY ANALYSES
Population viability analyses can be carried out on any threatened
species where you can find adequate data. The following are suggestions. The VORTEX PVA package can be downloaded from the web free of
charge at:

http://www2.netcom.com/~rlacy/vortex.html

(Note: Input files for VORTEX have changed slightly with versions.)

1. Stochastic r-model: For the population of bay checkerspot butterflies described in Problem 20.1, use the mean r and variance of r to
project the population forward for 50 years using r-model software.

Run 50 replicates to evaluate the variance in outcomes. Begin runs with the average population size. Further, options that can be tried are (a) vary the starting population size and examine the extinction probability, (b) examine the fate of populations with positive, zero and negative r values, and (c) evaluate the effects of increasing and decreasing the variance of r.

2. Comparing management options using PVA: For the Lord Howe Island woodhen, compare the following options for recovery of the population when it was at a size of 20. (a) No action, (b) pig control alone (increase the carrying capacity from 20 to 200), and (c) captive breeding program with three pairs of founders (supplement the population with 30 individuals in each of years 1, 2 and 3), and (d) captive breeding plus pig control. Compare the probabilities of persistence with these scenarios. Information for input files is given in Brook *et al.* (1997b).

Take home messages from this book

1. The biological diversity of the planet is being rapidly depleted due to direct and indirect consequences of human activities (habitat destruction and fragmentation, over-exploitation, pollution and movement of species into new locations).

2. The major genetic concerns in conservation biology are inbreeding depression, loss of genetic diversity, genetic drift overriding natural selection, population fragmentation, genetic adaptation to captivity and taxonomic uncertainties.

3. Inbreeding and loss of genetic diversity are inevitable in all small closed populations.

4. Inbreeding has deleterious effects on reproduction and survival (inbreeding depression) in almost every species that has been adequately investigated.

5. Loss of genetic diversity reduces the ability of populations to adapt in response to environmental change (evolutionary potential). Quantitative genetic variation for reproductive fitness is the primary component of genetic diversity involved in adaptive changes.

6. Genetic factors generally contribute to extinction risk, sometimes having major impacts on persistence.

7. Ignoring genetic issues in the management of threatened species will often lead to sub-optimal management and in some cases to disastrous decisions.

8. The objective of genetic management is to preserve threatened species as dynamic entities capable of adapting to environmental change.

9. The first step in genetic management of a threatened species is to resolve any taxonomic uncertainties and to delineate any management units within species. Studies using genetic markers can typically aid in resolving these issues.

10. Genetic management of wild populations is in its infancy and is not generally adequate or optimal to ensure long-term viability (largely because genetic issues are often ignored).

11. The greatest unmet challenge in conservation genetics is to manage fragmented populations to minimize inbreeding depression and loss of genetic diversity. Translocations among isolated fragments or creation of corridors for migration are required to minimize extinction risks, but they are being implemented in very few cases. Concerns about possible outbreeding depression (often exaggerated) have discouraged translocations to address the impacts of population fragmentation.

12. Captive breeding provides a means for conserving species that are incapable of surviving in their natural habitats. Captive populations of threatened species are typically managed to retain 90% of their genetic diversity for 100 years, using minimization of kinship.

13. Genetic deterioration in captivity resulting from inbreeding depression, loss of genetic diversity and genetic adaptation to captivity, reduces the probability of successfully reintroducing species to the wild.

14. Population sizes of N_e much greater than 50 ($N > 500$) are required to avoid inbreeding depression and $N_e = 500\text{--}5000$ ($N = 5000\text{--}50\,000$) are required to retain evolutionary potential. Many wild and captive populations are too small to avoid inbreeding depression and loss of genetic diversity in the medium term.

15. Molecular genetic analyses contribute to conservation by aiding detection of illegal hunting and trade, and by providing essential information on unknown aspects of species biology.

16. Genetic factors represent only one component of extinction risk. Wild populations face threats from both deterministic factors (habitat loss, over-exploitation, introduced species and pollution) that contribute to population declines, and stochastic factors (demographic and environmental stochasticity, catastrophes and genetic stochasticity) that become increasingly important in small populations. Genetic factors typically interact with other factors.

17. The combined impacts of all 'non-genetic' and genetic threats faced by populations can be assessed using population viability analysis (PVA). PVA is also used to evaluate alternative management options to recover threatened species.

We trust that you have found this book informative, thought-provoking and interesting and that it will assist in your future conservation activities. The Earth's biodiversity is being lost at a frightening rate, and we must act now to conserve our life support system. We encourage you to participate in this wide-ranging activity, as an enormous task lies ahead.

Revision problems

R.1 IUCN categories: In what category would you place the Lord Howe Island woodhen? It has a stable population of about 200 and is restricted to Lord Howe Island (about 25 km²).

R.2 Allele frequencies: What are the Hardy–Weinberg expected genotype frequencies at a locus with three alleles A, B and C at frequencies of 0.1, 0.3 and 0.6?

AA	AB	BB	AC	BC	CC	Total

R.3 Linkage disequilibrium: Is the population with the following gametic frequencies in linkage equilibrium?

A_1B_1	A_1B_2	A_2B_1	A_2B_2
0.1	0.6	0.2	0.1

R.4 Heritability: What is the heritability of shell breadth in the snail *Arianta arbustorum* given the following data on 119 pairs of parents and their offspring (after Hartl & Clarke 1997)?

Number of families	Mean of parents (mm)	Offspring mean (mm)
22	16.25	17.73
31	18.75	19.15
48	21.25	20.73
11	23.75	22.84
4	26.25	23.75
3	28.75	25.42

(The covariance between mid-parent and offspring is 5.183, and the variances for offspring and mid-parents are 3.311 and 8.180.)

R.5 Mutation–selection equilibrium: What is the expected equilibrium frequency for the dominant D allele with a mutation rate of 4×10^{-6} and the following relative fitnesses?

DD	Dd	dd
0.8	0.8	1.0

R.6 Time taken to regenerate genetic diversity by mutation: How many generations would it take for a microsatellite allele that had been lost from euros on Barrow Island, Western Australia to regenerate its previous frequency of 0.25, given a mutation rate of 10^{-4} per gamete per generation?

R.7 Heterozygote advantage: What is the equilibrium frequency for the A allele, given the following survival values for the three genotypes (all genotypes have the same fertility)?

AA	Aa	aa
0.8	0.85	0.83

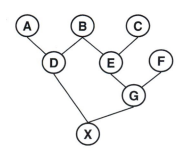

R.8 Loss of genetic diversity in small populations: How much of the original heterozygosity would have been retained over 150 years in an outbreeding population of *Diprotodon* (extinct, cow-sized marsupial) with an effective size of 20 and a generation length of 15 years?

R.9 Effective population size: What is the effective size of an insect population that fluctuates in size over three generations 100 000, 10 and 1000?

R.10 Inbreeding: What is the inbreeding coefficient for individual X in the pedigree in the margin?

R.11 Genetics of fragmented populations: What is F_{ST}?

R.12 Genetic distance: What is the genetic distance between a mainland and an island population with the following allele frequencies?

	A_1	A_2	A_3
Mainland population	0.2	0.3	0.5
Island population	0	0	1.0

R.13 Taxonomic uncertainties: Would you classify the two populations in Problem R.12 as separate species? Why?

R.14 Genetic management: How do you go about genetically managing a clonally reproducing plant species?

R.15 Genetic management: How are captive populations of threatened species managed using mean kinship?

R.16 Genetic management: How large should a captive population be for the endangered okapi to maintain 90% of heterozygosity for 100 years, if the generation length is 8 years?

Glossary

Additive: Locus where the heterozygote has a mean phenotype exactly intermediate between the two homozygotes. For example, if the mean enzyme levels for the genotypes FF FS and SS at the Adh locus are 100, 90 and 80 units of activity, then the locus is showing additive gene action. Also referred to as additivity.

Additive variance: That proportion of the genetic variation due to the average effects of alleles.

Allele: An alternative form of a gene locus, e.g. wild-type versus mutant, Fast versus Slow electrophoretic mobility, copies of a microsatellite locus with different numbers of repeats of the AC sequence.

Allelic diversity: A measure of genetic diversity within a population, computed as the average number of alleles per locus. For example, if the number of alleles at 6 loci are 1, 2, 3, 2, 1 and 1, then allelic diversity $= (1 + 2 + 3 + 2 + 1 + 1)/6 = 1.67$.

Allopatric: Populations, or species, whose geographical distributions do not overlap.

Allopolyploid: A species whose chromosomal complement derives from two (or more) separate species (compare **autopolyploid**), e.g. tobacco with 48 chromosomes is an allotetraploid derived from two diploid species, each with 24 chromosomes. Many plant species have evolved in this manner. A form of instantaneous speciation.

Allozygote: An individual that is homozygous for two alleles that are not recent copies of the same allele, i.e. not identical by descent. For example, the alleles may have the same electrophoretic mobility (or number of microsatellite repeats), but differ in DNA base sequence.

Allozymes: Alternative forms of a protein detected by electrophoresis that are due to alternative alleles at a single locus. Often referred to as **isozymes**.

Amino acid: The building blocks of a protein.

Amphidiploid: An allopolyploid species that shows chromosomal segregation as if it were a diploid, e.g. bread wheat has 42 chromosomes (an allohexaploid), but produces gametes with 21 chromosomes.

Amplified DNA: Many duplicated copies of a segment of DNA.

Associative overdominance: Heterozygote advantage due to linked loci that are exhibiting linkage disequilibrium. Heterozygote advantage due to a locus itself is referred to as intrinsic overdominance.

Assortive (assortative) mating: Preferential mating of individuals with similar phenotypes, e.g. by height.

Autopolyploid: A species derived by combining the two or more sets of chromosomes from the same species (compare **allopolyploid**).

Autoradiography: Detection of radioactively labelled molecules by their effects in exposing photographic film in the dark.

Autozygote: An individual that is homozygous for two alleles that are recent copies of the same allele and have identical (or near identical) DNA sequences. Having alleles that are identical by descent.

Average heterozygosity: A measure of genetic diversity within a population. Computed as the sum of proportion heterozygous at all loci / total number of loci sampled. For example, if the heterozygosities at 5 loci are 0, 0.10, 0.20, 0.05 and 0, then average heterozygosity $= (0 + 0.10 + 0.20 + 0.05 + 0)/5 = 0.07$.

Backcross: The cross of first generation progeny to one of the parent populations, or genotypes used to generate the F_1 progeny.

Balancing selection: Selection that maintains genetic variation in a population, encompassing heterozygote advantage (overdominance), frequency-dependent selection favouring rare genotypes, and forms of selection that vary over space or time in a way that favours some genotypes in some patch or season and others in other patches or seasons.

Binomial distribution: The distribution describing the number of occurrences of two (or more) events in a sample of size n, e.g. the number of heads and tails in 50 tosses of a coin.

Biodiversity: Biological diversity; the variety of ecosystems, species and populations within species and genetic variation within living organisms.

Biparental inbreeding: Inbreeding due to mating of relatives more remote than self (full-sibs, half-sibs, cousins, etc.).

Bottleneck: A sudden restriction in population size, used variously to refer to a population size bottleneck of one or a few generations, or to one of much longer duration.

Catastrophe: An extreme environmental fluctuation, due to a cyclone, drought, extremely cold winter, disease epidemic, etc. that has a devastating impact on a population.

CBSG: Conservation Breeding Specialist Group of the Species Survival Commission of IUCN.

Chloroplast DNA (cpDNA): Circular DNA molecules found in the chloroplasts of plants. They are usually maternally inherited.

Clade: A sub-group of organisms from among a larger group sharing common ancestry, not shared by the other organisms in the larger group.

Cline: Change in genetic composition of a population over a region of habitat, such as a latitudinal cline, or an altitudinal cline. For example, the frequency of alleles at the Adh locus in *Drosophila melanogaster* changes with latitude in both Australia and North America, while the frequency of glaucous leaves in several species of eucalypts changes with altitude in several mountains in the State of Tasmania in Australia. Clines may be due either to historical events (e.g. B blood group cline in humans) or to the balance between differential natural selection in different regions and migration between them.

Clone: Individuals with identical genotypes, e.g. cuttings deriving from a single plant, or several individual animals derived from a single animal by nuclear transplantation.

Coalesce: If two DNA sequence lineages converge at a common ancestral sequence, they are said to coalesce.

Coalescent theory: Investigations of the mathematical and statistical properties of genealogies (**gene trees**).

Coancestry: The coancestry to two individuals is the probability that two alleles, one from each individual, are identical by descent. Synonymous with **kinship**.

Coefficient of linkage disequilibrium (D): A measure of the non-random association of alleles at different loci. If the gametic types and frequencies are as follows:

$$A_1B_1 \quad A_1B_2 \quad A_2B_1 \quad A_2B_2$$
$$r \quad\quad s \quad\quad t \quad\quad u$$

then $D = ru - st$.

Co-dominance: The condition where the heterozygotes are distinguishable from homozygotes. For example, electrophoretically separated alleles at the Adh locus show a single band of fast mobility for the FF genotype, a single slow mobility band for the SS genotype, and a double-banded phenotype for the FS heterozygote (with one band corresponding to that in FF and another to that in SS).

Common ancestor: An individual that is an ancestor of both the mother and the father of a particular individual.

Conspecific: Belonging to the same species.

Convergent evolution: Evolution of similar phenotypes in distinct species subjected to similar environmental conditions, e.g. similar adaptations to marine environments in fish, marine mammals and reptiles.

cpDNA: See **chloroplast DNA**.

Critically endangered: A species with a very high probability of extinction within a short time, defined by IUCN as a 50% probability of extinction within 10 years, or three generations, whichever is longer.

Demographic stochasticity: Fluctuations in birth and death rates and sex-ratio due to chance alone. These may drive a small population to extinction through the chance fluctuations in very small populations. For example, 11 of the last 13 heath hens were, by chance, males.

Dioecious: Having separate sexes, especially applied to plants.

Directional selection: Selection in which the most extreme high (or low) individuals from a population are chosen as parents of the next generation. For example, animal breeders choose the most rapidly growing broiler chickens each generation, while swine are often selected for lowered fatness. Reproductive fitness is subjected to directional natural selection.

Disruptive selection: Selection of varying direction in different niches within the range of a species. For example, selection favoured melanic peppered moths in polluted areas of Britain, but non-melanic peppered forms in non-polluted areas.

DNA fingerprint: The 'bar code' produced by probing for minisatellites on the DNA of an individual. Also called variable number tandem repeats (VNTR).

Dominance: Deviation of heterozygote phenotype from the mean of homozygotes at a locus, say in the direction of the wild-type homozygote compared to the mutant homozygote.

Dominance variance: That proportion of the quantitative genetic variation due to the deviation of heterozygotes from the average effects of the two homozygotes.

Ecosystem services: Essential functions supplied free of charge by living organisms, including oxygen production from green plants, nutrient recycling, pest control and pollination of crop plants.

Ecotype: Populations within a plant species that are genetically adapted to different ecological conditions, often of soil and climate.

Effective number of alleles (n_e): The number of alleles that if equally frequent would result in the observed homozygosity. Computed as $n_e = 1/\Sigma p_i^2$, where p_i is the frequency of the ith allele. Less than the actual number of alleles, unless all alleles have the same frequencies.

Effective population size (N_e): The number of individuals that would result in the same inbreeding, or genetic drift if they behaved in the manner of an idealized population. These are respectively, the inbreeding and drift effective size.

Effectively neutral: The situation where the selective forces on an allele are so weak that it behaves as if it is not subject to natural selection. Occurs when the selection coefficient is less than about $1/(2N_e)$, where N_e is the effective population size.

Electrophoresis: A method for separating proteins or DNA fragments in a gel according to their net charges, shape and size.

Endangered: A species or population with a high probability of extinction within a short time, defined by IUCN as a 20% probability of extinction within 20 years, or 10 generations, whichever is longer.

Endemic: A population or species found in only one region or country; native to a region.

Environmental stochasticity: Natural fluctuations in environmental conditions, such as rainfall, food supply, competitors, winter temperatures, etc. These may drive a small population to extinction through chance fluctuations.

Epistasis: Interactions among gene loci in their effects on phenotype.

Epistatic variance: That proportion of the quantitative genetic variation due to the deviation of genotypic effects from the average effects of the constituent loci. Synonymous with **Interaction variance**.

ESU: See Evolutionarily significant unit.

Evolution: Change in the genetic composition of a population.

Evolutionary potential: The ability of a population to evolve to cope with environmental changes, such as those due to climate change or changed disease organisms. Usually equated with genetic diversity, as this is required for evolution to occur.

Evolutionarily significant units (ESU): Partially genetically differentiated populations that are considered to require management as separate units. ESUs have recently been defined as reciprocally monophyletic for mtDNA alleles and also significantly different in frequencies at nuclear loci.

Exon: Region of a functional locus that is transcribed and translated, e.g. that specifies amino acids in a protein.

Expected heterozygosity (H_e): The heterozygosity expected for a random mating population with the given allele frequencies according to the Hardy–Weinberg equilibrium. Calculated as $2pq$ for loci with two alleles, and $1 - \Sigma p_i^2$ for loci with any number of alleles. For example, if the allelic frequencies at a locus are 0.2 and 0.8, the expected heterozygosity is $2 \times 0.2 \times 0.8 = 0.32$.

Ex situ: Away from its normal habitat, such as an endangered species being conserved in captivity, an endangered plant being preserved in a seed store, or cryopreserved.

Extinction: Permanent disappearance of a population or species.

Extinction vortex: The likely interaction between human impacts, inbreeding, and demographic fluctuation in a downward spiral towards extinction. Typically habitat loss, introduced species and over-exploitation reduce the numbers of a species to where demographic instability and inbreeding lead to further declines in numbers that feedback into further declines towards extinction.

F: Wright's inbreeding coefficient. Fixation index.

F_{IS}: That proportion of the total inbreeding within a population due to inbreeding within sub-populations.

F_{IT}: The total inbreeding in a population, due to both inbreeding within sub-populations, and differentiation among sub-populations.

Fitness: Reproductive fitness, the number of fertile offspring surviving to reproductive age contributed by an individual.

Fixation: All individuals in a population being identically homozygous for a locus, e.g. all A_1A_1.

Fixation index: F_{ST}.

Forensics: Application of science to the law, including detection of illegal activities by scientific means. For example, DNA-based methods are being developed to test for tiger material in Asian medicines following PCR amplification.

Founder effect: Change in the genetic composition of a population due to origin from a small sample of individuals. A single generation bottleneck. Founder effects usually result in loss of genetic diversity, extinction of alleles, genetic drift and an increase in inbreeding.

Frequency-dependent selection: A form of natural selection where the relative fitnesses of genotypes vary with their frequencies. The form where genotypes have highest fitnesses when they are rarest retains genetic variation in the population, and is a form of balancing selection.

F statistics: Measures of total inbreeding in a population (F_{IT}), partitioned into that due to inbreeding within sub-populations (F_{IS}) and that due to differentiation among sub-populations (F_{ST}).

F_{ST}: The proportion of the total inbreeding in a population due to differentiation among sub-populations.

Full-sibs: Individuals sharing the same two parents. A full-sib mating is between a brother and a sister and is the most rapid form of inbreeding possible in species where self-mating is not possible.

Gene diversity: See **Expected heterozygosity**.

Gene dropping: Predicting the likely fate of alleles due to Mendelian segregation in small populations; usually done using many replicate computer simulations to predict the likely fate of ancestral alleles.

Gene genealogies: Trees showing the relationships between different copies of a single locus (**gene trees**).

Genetic distance: A measure of the genetic difference between allele frequencies in two populations, or species. The most commonly used form is **Nei's genetic distance**.

Genetic diversity: The extent of genetic variation in a population, or species, or across a group of species e.g. heterozygosity, or allelic diversity, or heritability.

Genetic drift: Changes in the genetic composition of a population due to random sampling in small populations. Results in loss of genetic diversity, random changes in allele frequencies, and diversification among replicate populations. Also referred to as **random genetic drift**.

Genetic load: The load of deleterious alleles in a population, some due to the balance between deleterious mutation and selection (mutation load) and some due to heterozygote advantage and other forms of balancing selection (balanced load).

Genetic stochasticity: Genetic effects in small populations due to inbreeding, loss of genetic diversity and mutational accumulation, that may drive a population or species to extinction.

Gene trees: Phylogenetic trees showing the relationships between different copies of a single locus (gene genealogies). The trees are usually devised on the basis of DNA sequences (e.g. for mtDNA).

Genome resource bank: The storage of genetic material for one or more species, including seed stores, cryopreserved gametes, embryos, or somatic cells, or a collection of DNA samples.

Genome uniqueness: The probability that an allele chosen at random from that individual is unique in the population (i.e. no other copies of the alleles exist).

Genotype $\times$ environment interaction: Differential performance of different genotypes in diverse environments. For example, many plants have populations (ecotypes) that grow and survive better in their home environment than when grown in other environments.

Haplotype: Allelic composition for several different loci on a chromosome, e.g. $A_1B_3C_2$.

Haplotype network: A diagram showing different haplotypes joined by lines to show relationships, typically with a line joining each haplotype differing by a single base in DNA sequence.

Hardy–Weinberg equilibrium: The equilibrium genotype frequencies achieved in a random mating population with no perturbing forces from mutation, migration, selection, or chance. If two alleles A_1 and A_2 have frequencies of p and q, the Hardy–Weinberg equilibrium frequencies for the A_1A_1, A_1A_2 and A_2A_2 genotypes are p^2, $2pq$ and q^2 respectively.

Harmonic mean: Reciprocal of the arithmetic mean of reciprocals $= n / \Sigma(1/X_i)$ The harmonic mean of effective population sizes in different generations describes the impact of population size fluctuations on the overall effective population size.

Hemizygous: Present in one copy, as for sex-linked loci in males.

Heritability (h^2): Proportion of the variation for a quantitative character due to genetic causes. The narrow sense heritability is the proportion of the variation due to additive genetic effects (variation in breeding value), while the broad sense heritability is the proportion due to total genetic effects. The heritability is specific to a particular population in a particular environment.

Hermaphrodite: An animal or plant with both sexes present in single individuals. Found in many plants and some animals, such as snails. Also known as monoecious.

Heterosis: Hybrid vigour. Superior performance of hybrid genotypes, usually indicating superiority to both parental genotypes. The converse of **inbreeding depression**.

Heterozygosity: The number of individuals heterozygous for a locus divided by total number of individuals sampled.

Heterozygote: An individual with two different alleles at a locus, e.g. A_1A_2.

Heterozygote advantage: A form of selection where the heterozygote has a higher fitness than the homozygotes. This results in active maintenance of genetic variation in very large populations. Also referred to as overdominance. One form of **balancing selection**.

Hitchhiking: Alleles at linked loci whose frequencies are changed due to selection at a nearby locus.

Homozygote: An individual with two copies of the same allele at a gene locus e.g. A_1A_1.

Idealized population: A conceptual random mating population with equal numbers of hermaphrodite individuals breeding in each generation, Poisson variation in family sizes (mean = variance = 2). Used as a standard to which other populations are equated when defining effective population sizes.

Identical by descent: Alleles that are identical copies of an allele present in a common ancestor.

Inbreeding: The mating of individuals related by descent, e.g. self-fertilization, brother $\times$ sister, or cousins matings.

Inbreeding coefficient (F): The most commonly used measure of the extent of inbreeding; the probability that two alleles at a locus in an individual are identical by descent. Ranges from 0 to 1.

Inbreeding depression: Reduction in reproduction, survival, or related characters due to inbreeding.

In situ conservation: Conservation of a species or population in its normal wild habitat.

Interaction variance: That proportion of the quantitative genetic variation due to the deviation of genotypic effects from the average effects of the constituent loci. Synonymous with **Epistatic variance**.

Introgression: Introduction of genetic material from another species or sub-species into a population. A threat to the genetic integrity to a range of canid, fish, plant, etc. species.

Intron: Region of a locus that is transcribed, but not translated.

Inversion: A chromosome aberration in which a region of chromosome has been turned through 180 degrees, such that gene order is changed, say from ABCDE to ADCBE. Results in 'suppression' of recombination, such that the combinations of alleles at different loci in the inversion are selected as a unit, rather than individually.

Isozymes: Alternative forms of a protein detected by electrophoresis. Often used interchangeably with **allozyme**, but isozymes may be due to protein differences specified by alleles at a single locus, or from different loci, while allozymes are differences due to alleles at a single locus.

IUCN: The World Conservation Union. The initials originally stood for the International Union for Conservation of Nature, later expanded to included 'and Nature Reserves', but the organization now refers to itself by the first mentioned name.

Kinship (k_{ij}): The kinship of two individuals is the probability that two alleles, one from each individual, are identical by descent. Synonymous with **coancestry**. Equivalent to the inbreeding coefficient of an offspring of the two individuals, if they had one.

Lethal: Inconsistent with survival, as in a recessive lethal allele that results in death when homozygous.

Lethal equivalents (B): A measure for comparing the extent of inbreeding depression in different populations. A group of detrimental alleles that would cause death if homozygous, e.g. one lethal allele, two alleles each with a 50% probability of causing death, etc. Determined as the slope of the regression of ln (survival) on the inbreeding coefficient F.

Lineage sorting: Random loss of genetic variants in different lineages deriving from a polymorphic common ancestral species (or population). Obscures patterns of phylogenetic relationship among populations, or species.

Linkage disequilibrium: Non-random association of alleles at different loci. Usually measured as the **coefficient of linkage disequilibrium** D.

Locus: A segment of DNA on a chromosome. The DNA may code for a gene product, or have a regulatory function, or it may be the DNA defined by a molecular method, e.g. microsatellite. Often called a gene locus.

Major histocompatibility complex (MHC): A large family of loci that play an important role in the vertebrate immune system and in fighting disease. These loci show extraordinarily high levels of genetic diversity.

Mean kinship (mk): The average kinship of an individual with all individuals in a population, including itself. Minimizing kinship is the current recommended method for genetically managing endangered species in captivity.

Meta-analysis: A statistical analysis that uses the combined information from several different studies, or several different species.

Metapopulation: A group of partially isolated populations of the same species that undergo local extinction and recolonizations.

MHC: See **major histocompatibility complex**.

Microsatellite: A locus with a short tandem repeat DNA sequence, such as the AC sequence repeated 10 times. Such repeats are found in many regions across the genome of most species. Microsatellites typically show variable number of repeats and high heterozygosities in populations. Consequently, they are highly informative genetic markers.

Minimum viable population size (MVP): The minimum size of population that will be viable in the long term, meaning a probability of extinction of say 1% in 1000 years, or 10% for 100 years. The initial sizes were derived from genetic considerations, but it rapidly became clear that demographic and environmental stochasticity and catastrophes must be considered as well.

Minisatellite: A region of DNA, usually in the 10s to 100s of bases in length that show variation in number of repeats. Also known as variable number tandem repeats (VNTR). When several such loci are probed they result in a DNA fingerprint that looks like a bar code.

Mitochondrial DNA (mtDNA): The circular DNA molecule contained within mitochondria. Usually maternally inherited.

Monomorphic: The presence of only one allele at a locus, generally taken to mean the most common allele is at a frequency of greater than 99%, or 95%. Lack of genetic diversity. Contrast with **polymorphic**.

Monophyletic: A group of species (or DNA sequences) that derive from the same common ancestral species (or DNA sequence). Converse is **polyphyletic**.

mtDNA: See **Mitochondrial DNA**.

Mutation: A sudden genetic change, i.e. parents lack the condition, but it appears in one or more offspring.

Mutation load: Deleterious mutations carried in a population. Homozygosity for such mutations is considered to be the main cause of inbreeding depression.

Mutational meltdown: The decline in reproductive rate and downward spiral towards extinction due to chance fixation of new mildly deleterious mutations in small populations. The process has two phases, the first where fitness drops, but populations are still able to more than replace themselves, and the second where the fitness is less than required for replacement and the population declines towards extinction; mutational meltdown strictly refers to the second phase.

Mutation–selection balance: The equilibrium due to the occurrence of deleterious mutations and the forces of natural selection removing them, resulting in low frequencies of deleterious mutations (**mutation load**).

MVP: See **Minimum viable population size**.

Natural selection: Mortality or differential reproduction due to natural environmental processes, as opposed to artificial selection due to human choice.

Nei's genetic distance (D_N): The most widely used measure of the genetic difference between allele frequencies in two populations, or species, devised by Masatoshi Nei. Calculated as the natural logarithm of **Nei's genetic similarity (I_N)**.

Nei's genetic similarity (I_N): The most widely used measure of the genetic similarity between allele frequencies in two populations, or species, devised by Masatoshi Nei.

Neutral mutation: A mutation that is equivalent in effects on reproductive fitness to the existing allele, such that its fate is determined by chance effects associated with population size (**random genetic drift**).

Non-synonymous substitution: A base substitution at a locus that results in a change in amino acid composition of a protein specified by the locus. Contrast with **synonymous substitution**.

Normal distribution: A symmetrical bell shaped distribution with a characteristic mean and variance as shown in the margin. 95% of values lie within 1.96 standard deviations of the mean. Many quantitative characters show approximately normal distributions. Also referred to as a Gaussian distribution.

Observed heterozygosity: The actual level of heterozygosity measured in a population, i.e. if there are two alleles at a locus, F and S, and a sample of individuals contain 60 FF, 30 FS and 10 SS, the observed heterozygosity is 30%. It is typically averaged across several loci, say 20–50 allozyme loci. Compare with **expected heterozygosity**.

Outbred: An individual whose parents are unrelated.

Outbreeding: Not inbreeding. A population that is not undergoing deliberate inbreeding. Approximately random mating.

Outbreeding depression: A reduction in reproductive fitness due to crossing of two populations (or sub-species, or species). The importance of outbreeding depression is a matter of controversy.

Overdominance: **Heterozygote advantage**; a form of selection where heterozygotes have a higher fitness than homozygotes, as found for sickle cell anaemia in malarial areas. This results in active maintenance of genetic variation in very large populations. A form of balancing selection.

Panmictic: Random mating.

Partial dominance: The condition where the heterozygote has a phenotype closer to one homozygote than the other, i.e. not completely dominant, additive, or completely recessive. For example, heterozygotes for most deleterious alleles are nearly, but not completely normal.

PCR: See **polymerase chain reaction**.

Pedigree: A chart specifying lines of descent and relationship of individuals.

Percentage of loci polymorphic (P): A measure of genetic diversity within a population, computed as (number of polymorphic loci / total number of loci sampled) $\times$ 100. For example if three loci are polymorphic, and seven are monomorphic,

$$P = (3/10) \times 100 = 30\%$$

Peripheral character: A character with limited relationship to reproductive fitness, e.g. bristle number in fruit flies, or tail length in rodents.

Phylogeography: The field of study concerned with the geographical distribution of genealogical lineages, especially within species. Typically DNA sequence trees are related to geographic origins of haplotypes.

Pleiotropy: The condition where an allele at a locus affects more than one character. For example, the *hal* allele in pigs results in sensitivity to halothane anaesthetic in homozygotes, as well as increased muscling, poorer meat quality and an increased risk of mortality when stressed.

Poisson distribution: A statistical distribution with variance equal to the mean. Used to predict the number of occurrences of rare events, such as the number of individuals carrying 0, 1, 2, etc. new mutations, or the distribution of families of sizes 0, 1, 2, 3, . . . assumed to occur in the idealized population. The probability of x occurrences $= m^x e^{-m} / x!$, where m is the mean and x takes the values 0, 1, 2, ... Similar to a binomial distribution when n is large and p (probability of an event occurring) is small.

Polyandry: A mating system in which females produce offspring from several males.

Polygamy: A mating system in which individuals mate with more than one of the opposite sex.

Polygene: More commonly referred to as a **quantitative trait locus**.

Polygyny: A mating system in which males mate with several females, e.g. harems.

Polymerase chain reaction (PCR): Method used to make replicate copies (amplify) of specific segments of DNA. The DNA is heated, primers (short segments of DNA flanking the segment of interest) added and the intervening DNA copied using thermostable *Taq* polymerase enzyme. Usually 30–40 cycles of amplification are performed in a thermocycler, each consisting of separation of complementary DNA strands, annealing of primers and extension at temperatures of 94 °C, 50–60 °C depending on primer sequences, and 72 °C, respectively.

Polymorphic: The presence of more than one allele at a locus, generally taken to mean the most common allele is at a frequency of less than 99%, or 95%. Existence of genetic diversity. Compare **monomorphic**.

Polyphyletic: A group of species (or DNA sequences) that derives from more than one ancestral species (or DNA sequence).

Population viability analysis (PVA): The process of predicting the fate of a population (including risk of extinction) due to the combined effects of all deterministic and stochastic threats faced by that population. Typically population size and structure, means and standard deviation of birth and death rates, plus risks and severity of catastrophes, levels of inbreeding depression, rate of habitat loss, levels of harvest, etc. are input into software packages and many replicates over several generations projected using Monte Carlo simulation. PVA is also used as a management tool to examine the impacts of different management options to recover threatened species.

Primer: A short nucleotide sequence that pairs with one strand of DNA and provides a free end at which DNA polymerase enzyme begins synthesis of a complementary segment of DNA.

Probe: DNA from a known locus used to hybridize with other DNA via complementary base pairing to identify similar sequences in the other DNA. The probe is usually radioactively labelled (e.g. with ^{32}P) so that fragments of DNA showing homology are detected using autoradiography.

Pseudogene: A non-functional copy of a locus. It may be related to a locus that codes for a protein, but this locus has mutations that make it non-functional, e.g. stop mutations part way through it.

Purging: Elimination of deleterious alleles from populations due to natural selection, especially that associated with populations subject to inbreeding.

PVA: See **Population viability analysis**.

Quantitative genetic variation: Genetic variation affecting a quantitative character, such as size, reproductive rate, behaviour or chemical composition. Presumed to be due to the cumulative effects at many loci (QTL). Also referred to as polygenic variation.

Quantitative trait locus (QTL): A locus affecting a quantitative character. Also referred to as polygene, but this term is going out of use.

QTL: See **Quantitative trait locus**.

Random genetic drift: Changes in the genetic composition of a population due to random sampling in small populations. Results in loss of genetic diversity, random changes in allele frequencies, and diversification among replicate populations. Frequently referred to as **genetic drift**.

Random mating: A pattern of mating where the chances of two genotypes, or phenotypes breeding is determined by their frequencies in the population; e.g. if AA and aa have frequencies of P and Q, respectively, the probability of the mating of AA females × aa males is PQ. Also known as random breeding.

Randomly amplified polymorphic DNA (RAPD): Genetic diversity detected following PCR amplification using random primers of DNA (usually 10 or more bases in length) to amplify random segments of DNA. Polymorphisms are detected as presence versus absence of bands and presence/absence is typically inherited as dominant/recessive.

RAPD: See **Randomly amplified polymorphic DNA**.

Realized heritability: The proportion of genetic variation due to additive genetic causes, estimated as the observed response to selection divided by the selection differential applied.

Reintroduction: Returning a species or population to part of its former range using individuals from captive populations.

Relative fitness: The fitness of a genotype, compared to another genotype, usually at the same locus; e.g. if survival rates of genotypes at a locus conferring warfarin resistance are 30%, 80% and 54% for RR RS and SS, then their relative fitnesses are $30/80 = 0.375$, $80/80 = 1$ and $54/80 = 0.68$, respectively.

Reproductive fitness: The number of fertile offspring surviving to reproductive age contributed by an individual. Characters that contribute to fitness include male fertility, female fecundity, parental care, offspring survival and offspring fertility. Often referred to as **fitness**.

Restriction enzyme: An enzyme that cuts DNA at points determined by specific DNA recognition sequences of various lengths, e.g. 4, 6 or 8 bases.

Restriction fragment length polymorphism (RFLP): This is genetic diversity detected by cutting DNA with restriction enzymes. These enzymes cut specific 4, 6 or 8 base sequences of DNA. If the sequence is mutated from the recognition sequence they do not cut, so the polymorphism is cut DNA versus not-cut DNA resulting in different sized fragments of DNA from different alleles.

RFLP: See **Restriction fragment length polymorphism**.

Selection coefficient (s): The difference in relative fitness between a genotype at a locus and the one with the highest fitness, e.g. if three genotypes A_1A_1, A_1A_2 and A_2A_2 have relative fitnesses of 1, 1 and 0.9, the selection coefficient for the A_2A_2 genotypes is $s = 1 - 0.9 = 0.1$.

Selection differential (S): A measure of the intensity of selection on a quantitative character – the difference in mean between the selected parents and the mean of the total population from which they derived. This takes positive or negative values according to the direction of selection.

Selective sweep: Action of natural selection driving a single allele to fixation, at the same time reducing genetic diversity at linked loci, or DNA bases (probably neutral to selection themselves), e.g. selection acting on one or a few bases in mtDNA resulting in fixation of a single mtDNA haplotype.

Selectively neutral: An allele whose fate is determined by chance sampling in a small population as the selective forces on it are weak in relation to the effects of chance, defined as $s < 1/2N_e$, i.e. both strictly neutral alleles and alleles subject to weak selection are selectively neutral in small populations.

Self-incompatibility: The inability of an individual (usually plant) to produce offspring following attempted self-fertilization. Many plant species have loci, typically with many alleles, that control self-incompatibility. It has probably evolved to avoid the deleterious effects of inbreeding.

Selfing: Self-fertilizing.

Self-sterility: See **Self-incompatibility**.

Sensitivity analysis: The set of analytical and simulation-based tools that evaluate how changes in specific life history attributes, habitat quality, predation, etc. affect population growth or extinction risk for a species. Typically life history attributes are varied and their relative impacts on population growth and extinction probability are evaluated.

Sex-linked: A locus found on the sex chromosomes (X in mammals, Z in birds and Lepidoptera), such that there is unequal transmission from the two sexes of parents to offspring of different sexes.

Sibling species: Two or more closely related species that are morphologically similar; e.g. the fruit fly species *Drosophila melanogaster* and *D. simulans* are essentially morphologically indistinguishable in females and can only be distinguished by male genitalia.

Silent substitution: A DNA base substitution that does not alter the amino acid composition of a polypeptide chain, such that it is probably not influenced by natural selection.

Single large or several small (SLOSS): The concept that compares the consequences of a single large population versus several small populations of equivalent total size, especially in terms of their extinction proneness.

Single nucleotide polymorphism (SNP): A position in the DNA of a species at which two or more alternative bases occur at appreciable frequency ($>1\%$).

SLOSS: See **Single large or several small**.

SNP: See **Single nucleotide polymorphism**.

Source–sink: A population structure where one population, the source, is permanent and supplies individuals to restart one or more transient populations (sinks).

Southern blot: Transfer of DNA from a gel to a membrane by blotting, originally with a wad of paper towels such that liquid is drawn from the gel through the membrane to the paper towel, with the DNA transferred at the same time from the gel to the membrane. Named after Ed Southern who invented the technique.

Speciation: The processes by which populations diverge and become reproductively isolated so that they develop into different species.

Species: Mayr defined species as 'groups of actually or potentially interbreeding natural populations which are reproductively isolated from other such groups' according to the **biological species concept**, i.e. there is potential or actual gene flow within, but not between species. Other definitions are used but are not always amenable to genetic interpretation.

Stabilizing selection: Selection favouring phenotypic intermediates at the expense of phenotypic extremes. Thought to occur on most quantitative characters (apart from fitness) in populations in stable environments.

Stable equilibrium: Allele frequency to which the population returns no matter in what direction the frequency is perturbed. Occurs with mutation–selection balance, heterozygote advantage, or other forms of balancing selection.

Stochastic: Having a chance element. Having variable outcomes described by a probability distribution, e.g. environmental and demographic stochasticity, genetic drift.

Supportive breeding: Regular augmentation of a wild population with individuals from a captive population maintained for that purpose.

Sympatric: Populations that share the same or overlapping geographical distributions.

Synonymous substitution: A base substitution at a locus that does not result in a change in amino acid composition of a protein specified by the locus. Thought to be neutral, or subject to weak selection. Contrast with **non-synonymous substitutions**.

Tandem repeats: Multiple copies of the same sequence lying one after another in a series, as in microsatellite repeats, or minisatellite repeats.

Taxa: Several populations belonging to a taxonomic unit, e.g. several species, or several sub-species, etc. Singular **taxon**.

Taxon: A taxonomic unit, such as a species, sub-species, genus, etc. Plural **taxa**.

Threatened: A population or species that has a finite risk of extinction within a relatively short time frame, say a greater than 10% risk of extinction within 100 years. Under the IUCN system the combination of critically endangered, endangered and vulnerable categories are threatened.

Transient polymorphism: The temporary state in which a locus is polymorphic, as when a favourable mutation rises in frequency towards eventual fixation, or neutral alleles drift in a population.

Translocation: The movement of an individual from one location to another as a result of human actions.

Transposons: Mobile genetic elements found in species from bacteria to mammals. Sequences of DNA that are able to move from one chromosomal location to another, often by replicating themselves. P elements in *Drosophila* are one well-studied example. Some have very similar structures to retroviruses, but do not exist outside the host cell. They are a major cause of mutations in *Drosophila* and probably all other species. Best understood as DNA parasites.

Trans-species polymorphism: An ancient polymorphism where related species share similar polymorphic alleles at a locus; e.g. these exist at MHC and self-incompatibility loci and are maintained by balancing selection.

Variance: The most commonly used measure of dispersion among quantitative measurements. The square of the standard deviation. The average of the squared deviation from the mean, computed as

$$V = \sum_{i}^{n} (X_i - \bar{X})^2 / (n - 1)$$

where X_i is the ith observation, $\bar{X}$ is the mean, and n is the total number of observations.

Vicariance: Separation of related populations or taxa, that previously had more-or-less continuous range, by an environmental event, such as rise of a mountain range, or break-up of a continent.

VNTR: Variable number tandem repeats; see **DNA fingerprint**.

Vulnerable: A species or population with a tangible risk of extinction within a moderate time, defined by IUCN as a 10% probability within 100 years.

Wahlund effect: Reduction in heterozygosity, compared to Hardy–Weinberg expectations, in a population split into partially isolated sub-populations. Named after its discoverer.

Answers to problems

Chapter 1

1.1 $\frac{1}{4} A_1 A_1 : \frac{1}{2} A_1 A_2 : \frac{1}{4} A_2 A_2$.

1.2 $1/16\ A_1A_1B_1B_1 : 1/8\ A_1A_1B_1B_2 : 1/16\ A_1A_1B_2B_2 : 1/8\ A_1A_2B_1B_1 :$
$1/4\ A_1A_2B_1B_2 : 1/8\ A_1A_2B_2B_2 : 1/16\ A_2A_2B_1B_1 : 1/8\ A_2A_2B_1B_2 : 1/16\ A_2A_2B_2B_2$.

1.3 The two loci are located on different chromosomes.

1.4

Complementary DNA	ATG AAA CCC TAA
Coding DNA strand	TAC TTT GGG ATT
mRNA	AUG AAA CCC UAA
tRNA anticodon	UAC UUU GGG AUU
Amino acids	met lys pro stop
	(note that the code is read from mRNA)

1.5 Expected numbers are 65 males and 65 females. $\chi^2 = 6.92$, df = 1, probability = 0.0085. Since the probability is less than 0.05, this represents a significant deviation from the 1:1 expectation.

1.6 Possible families: 4 females: 3 females and 1 male: 2 females and 2 males: 1 female and 3 males: and 4 males, with probabilities of 1/16: 1/4: 3/8: 1/4: 1/16, respectively.

1.7 The expected numbers are 90: 30: 30: 10, $\chi^2 = 7.778$, df = 3, probability = 0.051. Thus the observed numbers do not differ from the expectations.

1.8 Mean = 1.556 offspring and standard deviation = 1.13.

1.9 IUCN category Critically endangered under category D: number of mature individuals < 50 adults.

1.10 IUCN category Vulnerable under category A: numbers dropped by 90% in 30 years, or about 30% in 10 years.

1.11 IUCN category Extinct.

1.12 IUCN category Endangered; a decline of 5% per year, i.e. about 50% in 10 years.

Chapter 2

2.1 Inbreeding is the production of offspring from mating of individuals that are related by descent.

2.2 Inbreeding is of conservation concern because it leads to reduced reproductive rates and survival (inbreeding depression) in essentially all well-studied naturally outbreeding species and in many inbreeding species as well, i.e. it increases the risk of extinction.

2.3 The association between extinction rates and population size in bighorn sheep could be due to demographic stochasticity (fluctuations), environmental stochasticity, catastrophes, inbreeding depression, loss of genetic diversity or to combinations of these. Spread of disease from domestic sheep (this could be termed environmental stochasticity, or a catastrophe, depending upon severity) and inbreeding depression were favoured by the author.

Chapter 3

3.1 Genetic diversity is of importance in conservation biology as it is required for species to evolve to cope with environmental change. Further, loss of genetic diversity is associated with inbreeding and this reduces reproduction and survival rates.

3.2 Electrophoresis separates proteins according to their charge and molecular weight. Some DNA base differences result in different amino acids in proteins. Some amino acids are basic, some neutral and some acidic, so some of the amino acid differences result in charge differences that are detectable by electrophoresis.

3.3 Microsatellites are short tandem repeats in DNA that are often highly variable, e.g. $[AC]_{10}$ versus $[AC]_{12}$.

3.4 A restriction fragment length polymorphism. A DNA base difference is detected as the presence or absence of a sequence recognized by a restriction enzyme.

3.5 Random amplified polymorphic DNA. Short synthetic DNA primer sequences (often 10 bases in length) are used to prime DNA amplification. Polymorphisms are detected as the presence or absence of fragments.

3.6 Amplified fragment length polymorphism. Genomic DNA is cut with a restriction enzyme, specific DNA bases (adaptors) are added and the DNA is amplified using primers that are complementary to the adaptor sequences. Polymorphism is detected as presence or absence of DNA fragments.

3.7 A DNA fingerprint is a banding pattern similar to a bar code that is produced by cutting DNA with a restriction enzyme and probing with a variable number repeat sequence. These repeats are typically around 100 base pairs in length.

3.8 Microsatellites, RAPD and AFLP. Further, any locus for which primers can be designed (including mtDNA) can be amplified and typed by sequencing, SSCP, or by cutting with restriction enzymes.

3.9 Evolutionary potential depends on quantitative genetic variation for reproductive fitness characters.

3.10 Levels of genetic diversity for allozymes are significantly lower in vertebrates than in invertebrates or plants.

3.11 Endangered species on average have lower levels of genetic diversity than related non-endangered species.

Chapter 4

4.1 $p = 0.913$, $q = 0.087$.

4.2 The Hardy–Weinberg equilibrium expected frequencies are 0.8336, 0.1589 and 0.0076, and the expected numbers (expected frequencies $\times$ total numbers) are 474.3, 90.4 and 4.3. $\chi^2 = 0.137$, df $= 1$ ($3 - 1$ for total $- 1$ for using allele frequency), so probability is 0.71. Thus, the deviation from expectations is not significant.

4.3 $p_{85} = 0.193$, $p_{91} = 0.648$, $p_{93} = 0.023$, $p_{95} = 0.136$, and sum $= 1.0$.

4.4 Observed heterozygosity $= (13 + 2 + 12)/44 = 0.614$.

4.5 The expected frequencies of the six genotypes are as follows:

	91/91	91/95	91/97	95/95	95/97	97/97	Total
			Genotypes				
Expected frequency	p_{91}^2	$2p_{91}p_{95}$	$2p_{91}p_{97}$	p_{95}^2	$2p_{95}p_{97}$	p_{97}^2	1
	0.364^2	$2 \times 0.364 \times 0.352$	$2 \times 0.364 \times 0.284$	0.352^2	$2 \times 0.352 \times 0.284$	0.284^2	1
	0.1325	0.2563	0.2068	0.1239	0.1999	0.0807	1.0001
Expected number	5.83	11.28	9.10	5.45	8.80	3.55	44.01
Observed number	7	10	8	5	11	3	44

$\chi^2 = 1.185$, df $= 6 - 1 - 2 = 3$, probability $= 0.76$. Thus, the observed numbers do not differ significantly from Hardy–Weinberg expectations.

4.6 Genotype frequencies are given by the terms of $(p + q)^3$.

	FFF	FFS	FSS	SSS	Total
Expected frequency	0.6^3	$3 \times 0.6^2 \times 0.4$	$3 \times 0.6 \times 0.4^2$	0.4^3	1
	0.216	0.432	0.288	0.064	1

4.7 Expected frequency of AA $\times$ OO mating $= 2 \times f(\text{AA}) \times f(\text{OO}) = 2 \times 0.09 \times 0.36 = 0.0648$.

4.8

	MM	MN	NN	Total
Number	406	744	332	1482
Frequencies	0.274	0.502	0.224	1.0

Mating	Observed	Expected numbers		
MM $\times$ MM	58	$0.274^2 \times 741$	=	55.63
MM $\times$ MN	202	$2 \times 0.274 \times 0.502 \times 741$	=	203.85
MM $\times$ NN	88	$2 \times 0.274 \times 0.224 \times 741$	=	90.96
MN $\times$ MN	190	$0.502^2 \times 741$	=	186.73
MN $\times$ NN	162	$2 \times 0.502 \times 0.224 \times 741$	=	166.65
NN $\times$ NN	41	$0.224^2 \times 741$	=	37.18
Total	741		=	741.00

$\chi^2 = 0.794$, df $= 6 - 1 - 2 = 3$, probability $= 0.85$. Thus, the observed numbers do not differ significantly from those expected under random mating.

4.9 $n_e = 1/(0.73^2 + 0.27^2) = 1.65$.

4.10 $q^2 = 4/100 = 0.04$, thus, $q = \sqrt{0.04} = 0.20$.

4.11 $D = ru - st = 0.2 \times 0.1 - 0.5 \times 0.2 = -0.08$.

To obtain the gametic frequencies at equilibrium, we must first obtain the allele frequencies at the two loci. These are $p_{A1} = 0.5 + 0.2 = 0.7$, $q_{A2} = 0.3$, $p_{B1} = 0.4$, and $q_{B2} = 0.6$.

	A_1B_1	A_1B_2	A_2B_1	A_2B_2	Total
Equilibrium frequency	$p_{A1}p_{B1}$	$p_{A1}q_{B2}$	$q_{A2}p_{B1}$	$q_{A2}q_{B2}$	1
	0.7×0.4	0.7×0.6	0.3×0.4	0.3×0.6	1
	0.28	0.42	0.12	0.18	1

4.12 $D_{20} = D_0(1-c)^t = 0.2 \times (1-0.05)^{20} = 0.0717$.

Chapter 5

5.1 Parent mean = 19.971, offspring mean = 19.229, parent variance = 0.750, offspring variance = 1.288, covariance = 0.608.

5.2 Regression equation is offspring shell length = $3.03 + 0.811 \times$ parent shell length. Thus, the heritability of shell length is 0.811.

5.3 Offspring mean = 6.0, parent mean = 6.0, covariance = 5.6/6 = 0.933, parental variance = 28/6 = 4.667, and regression coefficient = 0.933/4.667 = 0.20. Thus the heritability is 0.20.

5.4 $h^2 = 2 \times 0.27 = 0.54$.

5.5
$$A_1A_1 \quad A_1A_2 \quad A_2A_2$$
$$a \qquad\quad a \qquad\quad -a$$

5.6 V_A will increase by 10%, while the heritability will increase by less than 10% as V_A is both the numerator and present in the denominator. V_D will increase by a factor of $(1.1)^2$, i.e. by 21%.

5.7 V_A will drop by 50%, h^2 will drop by less than 50% and V_D will drop by 75%.

5.8 $S = 8 - 10 = -2$.

5.9 $S = 490 - 450 = 40$ g. $R = Sh^2$. Thus, $R = 40 \times 0.35 = 14$ g.

5.10 $S = 9.96 - 9.42 = 0.54$ mm. Response $R = 0.54 \times 0.73 = 0.39$ mm.

Chapter 6

6.1 Divide all % survival values by 90 to obtain the following relative fitnesses:

$$A_1A_1 \quad A_1A_2 \qquad\qquad A_2A_2$$

1	$1 - hs$	$1 - s$
1	0.978	0.444

Thus, $s = 1 - 0.444 = 0.556$ and $hs = 1 - 0.978 = 0.022$.

6.2 $q_1 = 0.127$, $q_2 = 0.112$ and $q_3 = 0.101$.

6.3 $t = (1/q_t) - (1/q_0) = (1/0.001) - (1/0.17) = 994$ generations.

6.4

	Genotypes			
	AA	Aa	aa	Total
Genotype frequencies at fertilization	0.09	0.42	0.49	1.0
Relative fitnesses	1	1	0.9	
After selection	0.09	0.42	0.441	0.951
Adjust so total is 1	0.095	0.442	0.464	1.001

New frequency of $A = p_1 = [(2 \times 0.095) + 0.442]/2 = 0.316$
Change in frequency $\Delta p = p_1 - p_0 = 0.316 - 0.300 = 0.016$.

6.5

	Genotypes			
	AA	Aa	aa	Total
Genotype frequencies at fertilization	p^2	$2pq$	q^2	1.0
Relative fitnesses	1	$1 - s/2$	$1 - s$	
After selection	p^2	$2pq(1 - s/2)$	$q^2(1 - s)$	$1 - spq - sq^2$ $= 1 - sq$
Adjust so total is 1	$\dfrac{p^2}{1 - sq}$	$\dfrac{2pq(1 - s/2)}{1 - sq}$	$\dfrac{q^2(1 - s)}{1 - sq}$	

New frequency of A_2 (p_1)

$$p_1 = \frac{p^2 + pq(1 - s/2)}{1 - sq} = \frac{p^2 + pq - \frac{1}{2}spq}{1 - sq} = \frac{p - \frac{1}{2}spq}{1 - sq}$$

Change in frequency

$$\Delta p = p_1 - p_0 = \frac{p - \frac{1}{2}spq}{1 - sq} - p = \frac{p - \frac{1}{2}spq - p(1 - sq)}{1 - sq}$$

$$= \frac{p - p - \frac{1}{2}spq + spq}{1 - sq} = \frac{\frac{1}{2}spq}{1 - sq}$$

6.6 Use equations from Table 6.2 with $p = 0.1$, $q = 0.9$, $s = 0.1$ and $h = 0.02/0.1 = 0.2$

(a) $\Delta q = -\frac{1}{2}spq/[1 - sq] = -0.5 \times 0.1 \times 0.1 \times 0.9/[1 - 0.1 \times 0.9]$
$= -0.0090$

(b) $\Delta q = -spq^2/[1 - sq^2] = -0.1 \times 0.1 \times 0.9^2/[1 - 0.1 \times 0.9^2] = -0.016$

(c) $\Delta q = -sp^2q/[1 - s(1 - p^2)] = -0.1 \times 0.1^2 \times 0.9/[1 - 0.1(1 - 0.1^2)]$
$= -0.0018$

(d) $\Delta q = -spq[q + h(p - q)]/[1 - 2hspq - sq^2]$
$= -0.1 \times 0.1 \times 0.9[0.9 + 0.2(0.1 - 0.9)]/[1 - 2 \times 0.2 \times 0.1 \times 0.1 \times 0.9 - 0.1 \times 0.9^2] = -0.0073$

Chapter 7

7.1 The allele will increase in frequency by $up = 0.9 \times 10^{-4} = 0.00009$.

7.2 The equilibrium frequency is given by $q = u \,/\, (u + v) = 10^{-5}/(10^{-5} + 10^{-6}) = 0.909$.

7.3 $t = \dfrac{\ln p_0 - \ln p_t}{u} = \dfrac{\ln 1 - \ln 0.6}{4 \times 10^{-6}} = 127\,706$ generations.

7.4 $\hat{q} = \sqrt{u/s} = \sqrt{2 \times 10^{-5}/1} = 4.5 \times 10^{-3}$

Note that this is far lower than the observed frequency of 17%.

7.5 The mutation rate is estimated by rearranging Equation 7.4 and substituting, as follows:

$$u = sq^2 = 1 \times 0.17^2 = 0.0289$$

This is unrealistic as it is about 1000 times higher than typical mutation rates. Consequently, the chondrodystrophy allele is unlikely to be in mutation–selection equilibrium. The high frequency is probably due to the population bottleneck experienced by the California condor (see Chapter 8) where large chance changes in allele frequencies occurred; presumably the chondrodystrophy allele increased in frequency by chance, while many other deleterious alleles were probably lost.

7.6 $\Delta q = \Delta q_{\text{mutation}} + \Delta q_{\text{selection}} = up - \tfrac{1}{2}spq \,/(1 - sq) \sim up - \tfrac{1}{2}spq$

(It is reasonable to assume that the denominator of the selection term is approximately unity for a rare allele)

At equilibrium $\Delta q = up - \tfrac{1}{2}spq = 0$

$\therefore \tfrac{1}{2}spq = up$

so $\hat{q} = 2u/s$

7.7 The frequency of affected individuals (DD + Dd) is 10/94 000, so

$$q^2 + 2pq = 10/94\,000 = 1 - p^2$$

thus $p = 0.999947$, so $q = 5.3 \times 10^{-5}$

The relative fitness is 20%, so

$$1 - s = 0.2, \text{ and } s = 0.8.$$

The mutation–selection equilibrium for an autosomal dominant is:

$$\hat{q} = u/s$$

Thus the mutation rate u is

$$u = sq = 0.8 \times 5.3 \times 10^{-5} = 4.24 \times 10^{-5}$$

7.8 For loci with $s = 0.1$ and $u = 10^{-5}$, the equilibrium frequencies with different modes of inheritance are as follows:

Recessive autosomal	$\hat{q} = 10^{-2}$
Additive autosomal	$\hat{q} = 2 \times 10^{-4}$
Dominant autosomal	$\hat{q} = 10^{-5}/0.1 = 10^{-4}$
Sex-linked recessive	$\hat{q} = 3 \times 10^{-4}$
Haploid	$\hat{q} = 10^{-4}$

Thus, the equilibrium frequencies are usually greater for diploids than haploids (most mutations are recessive, or partial recessives), and greater for recessive than for dominants.

7.9 By rearranging Equation 7.5, we obtain:

$$m = \frac{q_1 - q_0}{q_m - q_0}$$

The data supplied are $q_0 = 0.000$ (African blacks), $q_m = 0.422$ (US Caucasians) and $q_1 = 0.045$ (US African Americans). Thus,

$$m = \frac{0.045 - 0}{0.422 - 0} = 0.11$$

Chapter 8

8.1 Probability that A_1 is absent in three offspring is the probability of three A_2A_2 offspring $= (\frac{1}{4})^3 = 1/64$.

8.2 The expected offspring are $\frac{1}{4} A_1A_1 : \frac{1}{4} A_1A_2 : \frac{1}{4} A_1A_3 : \frac{1}{4} A_2A_3$. Thus the probability that four individuals do not contain A_1 is the probability of four A_2A_3 offspring $= (\frac{1}{4})^4 = 1/256$. The probability that A_2 is absent from the four offspring $= (\frac{1}{2})^4 = 1/16$, and the probability that A_3 is absent in the four offspring is also $1/16$.

8.3 The probability that an individual does not contain A_2 is 0.9^2. (a) Thus, the probability that 12 individuals do not contain $A_2 = 0.9^{24} = 0.080$. (b) The probability that 100 individuals do not contain A_2 is $0.9^{200} = 7 \times 10^{-10}$. This is vastly lower than the answer to (a), i.e. the chance of losing an allele is strongly dependent on the population size.

8.4 The probability that an offspring does not have the A_1 allele is $\frac{1}{2}$, and the probability that n offspring do not have it is $(\frac{1}{2})^n$. To be 95% certain that the allele is retained, we set this equal to 0.05 and solve for n, i.e. $(\frac{1}{2})^n = 0.05$, so $n = \ln(0.05)/\ln(0.5) = 4.3$, i.e. about five individuals. The probability that the A_2 allele has a 95% chance of being retained also requires about five offspring following the same reasoning.

8.5 Proportion of heterozygosity lost is $1/(2N)$, so (a) $\frac{1}{2}$, (b) 0.1, (c) 0.036, (d) 0.007, (e) 0.0000017.

8.6 The probability that an allele with a frequency of q is lost following a single generation bottleneck is $(1 - q)^{2N}$. Thus, (a) $0.9^2 = 0.81$, (b) 0.656, (c) 2.66×10^{-5}, (d) 0.077.

Chapter 9

9.1 $H_e = 4N_e u / (4N_e u + 1) = 4 \times 20 \times 10^{-7} / (4 \times 20 \times 10^{-7} + 1) = 0.000008$

$$n_e = 4N_e u + 1 = 1.000008$$

9.2 $p_A = 0.802$ and $q_s = 0.198$, respectively. The observed and Hardy–Weinberg expected numbers are as follows:

	AA	AS	SS	Totals
Observed	400	249	5	654
Expected	420.7	207.7	25.6	654

The deviation from Hardy–Weinberg expectations in adults is significant ($\chi^2 = 25.8$, df $= 1$, probability < 0.0001). Thus, there is an excess of heterozygotes and a deficiency of homozygotes. The frequencies of the A and S alleles in infants are 0.814 and 0.186, respectively. The equivalent test for deviation from Hardy–Weinberg expectation in infants is non-significant ($\chi^2 = 0.14$, df $= 1$, probability $= 0.71$).

9.3 $s_1 = 0.01$ and $s_2 = 0.03$. Thus, the equilibrium frequency of A_2, q is

$$\hat{q} = s_1 / (s_1 + s_2) = 0.01 / (0.01 + 0.03) = 0.25$$

and the equilibrium frequency for A_1 is 0.75.

9.4

	RR	RS	SS
Survival	0.3	0.8	0.56
Relative fitness	0.375	1.0	0.70
	$1 - s_1$	1	$1 - s_2$

Thus, $s_1 = 0.625$ and $s_2 = 0.30$. Consequently, the equilibrium frequency for the R allele (p) is

$$\hat{p} = s_2 / (s_1 + s_2) = 0.30 / (0.625 + 0.30) = 0.324.$$

9.5 The selection coefficients s_1 and s_2 are 0.3 and 0.1. Thus, the equilibrium frequency q for the A_2 allele in all populations is

$$q = s_1 / (s_1 + s_2) = 0.3 / (0.3 + 0.1) = 0.75$$

(the initial frequencies are irrelevant).

9.6

	Genotypes			
	A_1A_1	A_1A_2	A_2A_2	Total
Frequencies at fertilization	p^2	$2pq$	q^2	1.0
Relative fitnesses	$1 - s_1$	1	$1 - s_2$	
After selection	$p^2(1 - s_1)$	$2pq$	$q^2(1 - s_2)$	$1 - s_1 p^2 - s_2 q^2$
Adjusted	$\dfrac{p^2(1 - s_1)}{1 - s_1 p^2 - s_2 q^2}$	$\dfrac{2pq}{1 - s_1 p^2 - s_2 q^2}$	$\dfrac{q^2(1 - s_2)}{1 - s_1 p^2 - s_2 q^2}$	1

$$\text{New frequency of } A_1 \, p_1 = \frac{p^2(1 - s_1) + pq}{1 - s_1 p^2 - s_2 q^2} = \frac{p - s_1 p^2}{1 - s_1 p^2 - s_2 q^2}$$

$$\Delta p = \frac{p - s_1 p^2}{1 - s_1 p^2 - s_2 q^2} - p = \frac{p - s_1 p^2 - p(1 - s_1 p^2 - s_2 q^2)}{1 - s_1 p^2 - s_2 q^2}$$

$$= \frac{p - s_1 p^2 - p + s_1 p^3 + s_2 pq^2}{1 - s_1 p^2 - s_2 q^2}$$

$$= \frac{pq(s_2 q - s_1 p)}{1 - s_1 p^2 - s_2 q^2}$$

At equilibrium, $\Delta p = 0$.

This occurs when $s_1 p = s_2 q$

Thus, the equilibrium frequency for A_2 is

$$\hat{q} = s_1 / (s_1 + s_2)$$

9.7 The relative fitnesses of the three pollen alleles are determined as follows:

Female parent	Pollen	Offspring		
		$S_1 S_2$	$S_1 S_3$	$S_2 S_3$
$1/3\ S_1 S_2$	S_3	—	$1/6\ S_1 S_2$	$1/6\ S_1 S_3$
$1/3\ S_1 S_3$	S_2	$1/6\ S_1 S_2$	—	$1/6\ S_2 S_3$
$1/3\ S_2 S_3$	S_1	$1/6\ S_1 S_2$	$1/6\ S_1 S_3$	—

This assumes that there is sufficient pollen to fertilize all plants. After reproduction, the three pollen alleles have made the same contributions to the progeny, $S_1 = S_2 = S_3 = 1/3$, so their fitnesses are:

$S_1 =$ freq. now / freq. before $= (1/3) / (1/6) = 2$

$S_2 = (1/3) / (1/3) = 1$

$S_3 = (1/3) / (1/2) = 2/3$

Consequently, their relative fitnesses (obtained by dividing by the highest fitness of 2) are $S_1 = 1$, $S_2 = 1/2$ and $S_3 = 1/3$. Thus, the rarest allele has the highest relative fitness and the most common the lowest fitness.

9.8 The relative fitnesses of the pollen alleles are determined as shown below:

Female parent	Pollen	Offspring					
		$S_1 S_2$	$S_1 S_3$	$S_2 S_3$	$S_1 S_4$	$S_2 S_4$	$S_3 S_4$
$1/3\ S_1 S_2$	$0.97\ S_3$		0.1618	0.1618			
	$0.03\ S_4$				0.0049	0.049	
$1/3\ S_1 S_3$	$0.97\ S_2$	0.1618		0.1618			
	$0.03\ S_4$				0.0049		0.049
$1/3\ S_2 S_3$	$0.97\ S_1$	0.1618	0.1618				
	$0.03\ S_4$					0.0049	0.049
Totals		0.3234	0.3234	0.3234	0.01	0.01	0.01

The relative frequencies of pollen that can fertilize $S_1 S_2$ are $0.33/0.34 = 0.97$ for S_3 and $0.01/0.34 = 0.03$ for S_4 (and similarly for the other female genotypes). The contributions of the four pollen alleles to the progeny are $0.3234\ S_1$, $0.3234\ S_2$, $0.3234\ S_3$ and $0.03\ S_4$. If we compare these contributions to their frequencies in the pollen to obtain their relative fitnesses, we obtain

$S_1 = 0.3234/0.33 = 0.98$
$S_2 = 0.3234/0.33 = 0.98$
$S_3 = 0.3234/0.33 = 0.98$
$S_4 = 0.03/0.01 = 3$
Thus the relative fitnesses of the four pollen alleles S_1, S_2, S_3 and S_4 are 0.33, 0.33, 0.33 and 1, respectively, i.e. the new S_4 allele has a much higher fitness than the existing alleles and will increase in frequency.

9.9 Selective neutrality occurs approximately when $s < 1/2N$, so an allele with a selection coefficient of 0.02 is effectively neutral when the population size is $0.02 < 1/2N$, so when $N < 2 \times 0.02$, i.e. when $N < 25$.

Chapter 10

10.1

(a) $H_t / H_0 = [1 - 1/(2N_e)]^t = [1 - 1/(2 \times 60)]^{100/20} = 0.959$.
(b) $H_t / H_0 = [1 - 1/(2 \times 10)]^5 = (19/20)^5 = 0.774$.

10.2

(a) $H_t/H_0 = 0.5 \sim e^{-t/2N_e}$, then take natural logarithms of both sides, yielding

$$\ln(0.5) = -t/2N_e$$

Thus,

$$t = -2 \ln(0.5) N_e = 1.39 N_e$$

(b) Set $e^{-t/2N_e} = 0.05$, and then take ln of both sides, and rearrange yielding

$$t = -2 \ln(0.05) N_e = 5.99 N_e$$

10.3 $\quad H_t / H_0 = \prod_{i=1}^{n} [1 - 1/(2N_i)]$

$$= [1 - 1/(2 \times 100)][(1 - 1/(2 \times 10)]$$
$$[1 - 1/(2 \times 100)][1 - 1/(2 \times 200)]$$
$$= 0.938$$

The second case is identical to the first, as the same terms enter the equation, but in a different order.

10.4 $H_{diploid} = 0$, $H_{allotetraploid} = 2pq = 0.18$.

10.5 $N_e = 4 N_{ef} N_{em} / (N_{ef} + N_{em}) = (4 \times 605 \times 6)/(605 + 6) = 23.8$. If the population had a 'normal' sex-ratio, $N_e = 605.7$, about 25 times higher.

10.6 $N_e = (4N - 2)/(V_k + 2)$. The mean family size $= (0 + 1 + 2 + 5)/4 = 2$, i.e a stable population. The variance in family size V_k is given as follows:

$$V_k = \frac{1}{n} \Sigma(k - \bar{k})^2 = [(0 - 2)^2 + (1 - 2)^2 + (2 - 2)^2 + (5 - 2)^2]/4 = 14/4 = 3.5$$

Note that there is a complete census of the population, so that n replaces $n - 1$ in the equation for the variance. Since there are four families, $N = 8$. Thus,

$$N_e = (4 \times 8 - 2)/(3.5 + 2) = 5.45.$$

This is only 68% of the population size of 8 potentially reproductive individuals.

10.7 $N_e = t / \Sigma(1/N_i) = 4 / \Sigma[(1/10) + (1/100) + (1/1000) + (1/250)] = 34.8$.

10.8 $N_e / N = 1 / (1 + F) = 1 / (1 + 0.18) = 0.85$.

10.9 The population size is not stable ($k > 1$ in both sexes), so we have to use Equation 10.5.

For females:

$$N_{ef} = (Nk - 1)/[k - 1 + (V_k / k)] = (80 \times 2.09 - 1)/[2.09 - 1 + (16.61 / 2.09)] = 18.4$$

Thus, for males

$$N_{em} = (Nk - 1)/[k - 1 + (V_k / k)] = (60 \times 2.46 - 1)/[2.46 - 1 + (22.5 / 2.46)] = 13.8$$

Finally, we combine these two estimates

$$N_e = 4 N_{ef} N_{em} / (N_{ef} + N_{em}) = (4 \times 18.4 \times 13.8) / (18.4 + 13.8) = 31.5$$

Thus the effective population size is about 23% of the actual population size.

10.10 $H_t / H_0 = 0.43 = e^{-t/2N_e} = e^{-17/2N_e}$

Take ln of both sides and rearranging yields

$$N_e = -17 / [2 \ln (0.43)] = 10$$

Chapter 11

11.1 $F = ¼$.

11.2 $F = 1 - [1 - 1/(2N_e)]^t = 1 - (1 - 1/10)^{10} = 0.65$.

11.3 $F = 1 - \prod_{i=1}^{t}[1 - 1/(2N_{ei})] = 1 - (1 - ¼)[1 - (1/200)](1 - ¼)[1 - (1/200)]$
$= 0.44$.

11.4 Using $p = 0.83$, $q = 0.17$, and $F = 0.5$, the expected genotype frequencies with selfing are:

$f(++) = p^2 + Fpq = 0.83^2 + 0.5 \times 0.83 \times 0.17 = 0.76$
$f(+/dw) = 2pq(1 - F) = 2 \times 0.83 \times 0.17 (1 - 0.5) = 0.14$
$f(dw/dw) = q^2 + Fpq = 0.17^2 + 0.5 \times 0.83 \times 0.17 = 0.10$

These sum to 1.0, as they should.

11.5 $q = 0.01$, so $p = 0.99$.
(a) Full-sib mating ($F = 0.25$), ratio $= 1 + [Fp / q]$
$= 1 + [(0.25 \times 0.99) / 0.01] = 25.75$.
(b) For first-cousin mating ($F = 1/16$), ratio $= 1 + [(0.99 / 16) / 0.01]$
$= 7.19$.

11.6 $F_t = ¼ (1 + 2 F_{t-1} + F_{t-2})$. Thus, the inbreeding coefficients for the first five generations of full-sib mating are 0.25, 0.375, 0.50, 0.594 and 0.672, respectively.

11.7 $2pq(1 - F) = 2 \times 0.4 \times 0.6 (1 - 0.47) = 0.254$.

11.8 $F_e = 1 - H_{Island} / H_{Mainland} = 1 - (0.36/0.792) = 0.545$.

11.9 $F_X = \Sigma(½)^n(1 + F_{ca})$. The paths are:

Path	n	F_{ca}	Contribution to F_X
IE**A**G**J**	5	0	$(½)^5$
IE**B**G**J**	5	0	$(½)^5$
IF**C**H**J**	5	0	$(½)^5$
IF**D**H**J**	5	0	$(½)^5$
			$F_X = 1/8$

11.10 $F_X = \Sigma(½)^n(1 + F_{ca})$. Parents L and M have G, C, A and B as common ancestors. The paths and their contributions to F are as follows:

Path	n	F_{ca}	Contribution to F_X
LIF**C**A**D**G**J**M	9	0	$(½)^9$
LI**G**D**B**EH**K**M	9	0	$(½)^9$
LI**G**D**B**E**J**M	8	0	$(½)^8$
LIF**C**G**J**M	7	0	$(½)^7$
LI**G**J**M	5	1/8	$(½)^5(1 + 1/8)$
			$F_X = 26/512 = 0.0508$

11.11 Individuals A, B, D, E, G and I are common ancestors causing relationships between parents I and L. The 11 paths of relationship, the number of paths joining parents through common ancestors (n), the inbreeding coefficients of common ancestors, and the contribution of each of the paths to the inbreeding coefficient F_X (rounded to four decimal places), are shown in the table. A, B and E are all assumed to be unrelated.

Individual I is the result of an inbred mating; there are three common ancestors of its parents F and G, A, B and D. The three paths to consider are

FC**A**DG, contributing $(½)^5$ to the inbreeding coefficient of I (F_I)

FC**B**DG, contributing $(½)^5$ to F_I, and

F**D**G, contributing $(½)^3$ to F_I

Thus, $F_I = (½)^5 + (½)^5 + (½)^3 = 3/16$.

Paths of relationship (common ancestors are bold)	n	F_{ca}	Contribution to F_X
IF**C**A**D**H**J**KL	9	0	$(½)^9$
IF**C**A**D**G**J**KL	9	0	$(½)^9$
IF**C**B**D**H**J**KL	9	0	$(½)^9$
IF**C**B**D**G**J**KL	9	0	$(½)^9$
IF**D**H**J**KL	7	0	$(½)^7$
IF**D**G**J**KL	7	0	$(½)^7$
I**G**D**H**J**KL	7	0	$(½)^7$
I**G**E**H**J**KL	7	0	$(½)^7$
I**G**J**KL	5	0	$(½)^5$
IKL	3	3/16	$(½)^3(1 + 3/16)$
IL	2	3/16	$(½)^2(1 + 3/16)$
			$F_X = 264/512 = 0.515625$

11.12 P(homozygosity for a rare recessive lethal at one locus)
$$= q^2(1 - F) + Fq \sim Fq = 0.5 \times 5 \times 10^{-4} = 2.5 \times 10^{-4}$$
P(not homozygous lethal at one locus) $= 1 - Fq = 1 - 2.5 \times 10^{-4}$
P(not homozygous lethal at 2000 loci) $= (1 - Fq)^{2000}$
$$= (1 - 2.5 \times 10^{-4})^{2000} = 0.61.$$
Thus, P(individual is homozygous lethal for at least one locus)
$$= 1 - 0.61 = 0.39.$$
Using a similar approach with random mating for 2000 loci,
P(individual homozygous for lethal for at least 1 locus) =
$1 - (1 - q^2)^{2000}$
$$= 5 \times 10^{-4}.$$

Chapter 12

12.1 $\Sigma 2pqdF$, i.e. number of loci polymorphic for deleterious alleles (Σ), heterozygosity for deleterious alleles ($2pq$), dominance of alleles (d), and inbreeding coefficient (F).

12.2 None, there are no heterozygotes and no hidden deleterious alleles.

12.3 Inbreeding depression $= 2pqdF$. $p = 0.9$, $q = 0.1$, and $F = 0.5$. To compute inbreeding depression (ID) we must compute d.

(a) $d = 89 - [(90 + 70) / 2] = 9$. Thus, $ID = 2 \times 0.9 \times 0.1 \times 9 \times 0.5 = 0.81$, i.e the population mean survival drops from 89.62 to 88.81 due to selfing at this locus (see Table 12.3 for formula to obtain means).

(b) $d = 90 - [(80 + 70)/2] = 15$. Thus, $ID = 2 \times 0.9 \times 0.1 \times 15 \times 0.5 = 1.35$

(c) $d = 80 - [(90 + 70)/2] = 0$. Thus, $ID = 0$.

12.4 $\delta = 1 - ($inbred fitness / outbred fitness$) = 1 - (0.45 / 0.75) = 0.4$ (i.e. a 40% reduction in survival due to inbreeding).

12.5 (a) Lethal equivalents per haploid genome $= B = 2.52$. (b) Lethal equivalents per diploid genome $= 2B = 2 \times 2.52 = 5.04$.

12.6 The information translates into the following equations:
Full-sibs: $\ln S_{FS} = a - BF = a - 1.57 \times 0.25 = a - 0.3925$.
Thus $S_{FS} = e^{a - 0.3925}$
Unrelated: $\ln S_U = a$
Thus $S_U = e^a$
The ratio of survival of full-sibs/unrelated $= e^{a - 0.3925}/e^a = e^{-0.3925} = 0.675$.
Thus, the survival of full-sibs is reduced by 32.5% compared to non-inbred individuals (the inbreeding depression).

12.7 One locus $ID = 2pqdF = 2 \times (1 - 5 \times 10^{-4}) \times 5 \times 10^{-4} \times 0.48 \times 0.5 \sim 2.4 \times 10^{-4}$.
Fitness due to inbreeding at 1 locus $= 1 - ID = 1 - 2.4 \times 10^{-4} = 0.99976$
Fitness due to inbreeding at 5000 loci $= 0.99976^{5000} = 0.30$
Total $ID = 1 - 0.30 = 0.70$.

Chapter 13

13.1 The impacts of fragmentation depend upon the details of gene flow among population fragments. If gene flow among the fragments is less than about one effective migrant per generation, then population fragments will become inbred and lose genetic diversity at an accelerated rate (compared to a single large population) and are likely to suffer elevated extinction rates.

13.2 $\sigma_q^2 = 0.015$.

13.3 $\sigma_q^2 = pq\,\{1 - [1 - 1/(2N_e)]^t\}$
(a) $\sigma_q^2 = 0.3 \times 0.7\,[1 - [1 - 1/(2 \times 50)]^{20} = 0.038$
(b) $\sigma_q^2 = 0.3 \times 0.7\,1 - [1 - 1/(2 \times 50)]^{100} = 0.133$

13.4 $F_{ST} = 1/(4N_e m + 1)$ (Equation 13.5), so
$N_e m = [1 / (F_{ST}) - 1]/4 = (1/0.2 - 1)/4 = 1$, i.e. one migrant per generation.

13.5 (a) $H_I = (0.5 + 0.2)/2 = 0.35$
$H_S = (2p_1 q_1 + 2p_2 q_2)/2 = (2 \times 0.5 \times 0.5 + 2 \times 0.5 \times 0.5)\,/2 = 0.5$
$H_T = 2pq$ (using combined allele frequencies) $= 2 \times 0.5 \times 0.5$
$= 0.5$

(b) $H_I = (0.5 + 0.32)/2 = 0.41$
$H_S = (2p_1 q_1 + 2p_2 q_2)/2 = (2 \times 0.5 \times 0.5 + 2 \times 0.8 \times 0.2)\,/2 = 0.41$
$H_T = 2pq$ (using combined allele frequencies) $= 2 \times 0.35 \times 0.65$
$= 0.455$

(c) $H_I = (0.5 + 0.13)/2 = 0.31$
$H_S = (2p_1 q_1 + 2p_2 q_2)/2 = (2 \times 0.5 \times 0.5 + 2 \times 0.2 \times 0.8)\,/2 = 0.41$
$H_T = 2pq$ (using combined allele frequencies) $= 2 \times 0.35 \times 0.65$
$= 0.455$

13.6 $F_{IS} = 1 - (H_I / H_S) = 1 - (0.052/0.074) = 0.30$
$F_{ST} = 1 - (H_S / H_T) = 1 - (0.074/0.098) = 0.24$
$F_{IT} = 1 - (H_I / H_T) = 1 - (0.052/0.098) = 0.47$
These statistics indicate that there is inbreeding within populations ($F_{IS} > 0$; probably as a result of selfing) and substantial differentiation among populations ($F_{ST} > 0$).

13.7 $H_I = (0.038 + 0.028 + 0.021) / 3 = 0.029$, and $H_S = (0.061 + 0.045 + 0.033) / 3 = 0.046$.
$F_{IS} = 1 - (H_I / H_S) = 1 - (0.029/0.046) = 0.37$
$F_{ST} = 1 - (H_S / H_T) = 1 - (0.046/0.053) = 0.13$
$F_{IT} = 1 - (H_I / H_T) = 1 - (0.029/0.053) = 0.45$

13.8 For the population of size 50, $F = 1 - [1 - 1 /(2N_e)]^t$
$= 1 - (99/100)^{30} = 0.26$
For populations of size 25, $F = 1 - (49/50)^{30} = 0.45$
For two pooled populations of size 25, $F = \frac{1}{4}\,(F_{N=25} + F_{N=25}) = 0.23$
(see Margan *et al.* 1998 equation 1)
Note that the inbreeding coefficient of the pooled populations is less than that of the single larger population.

Chapter 14

14.1 $N_e = V_A / 2\,V_m = V_A / (2 \times 3 \times 10^{-3}\,V_E) = 167\,h^2/(1 - h^2) = 29$.
14.2 Under these conditions, $V_m = 3 \times 10^{-4}\,V_E$, so $N_e = 294$.

14.3 Using Equation 10.1: $H_t/H_0 = [1 - 1/(2N_e)]^t \sim e^{-t/2N_e}$
and substituting $H_t/H_0 = 0.95$ and $t = 100$ years $/L$ generations

$$0.95 \sim e^{-100/2LN_e}$$

taking ln gives

$$\ln 0.95 = -100/2LN_e$$

Thus $N_e = -100/2L\ln(0.95) = 975/L$

14.4 $N_e = 475/L = 475/(1/3) = 1425$

14.5 $N_e = 475/L = 475/20 = 23.75$

14.6 From 14.3, the $N_e = 975/L$ is required to retain 95% of genetic diversity for 100 years, thus, for elephants

$$N_e = 975/26 = 37.5$$

and for deer mice $N_e = 975/(1/3) = 2925$.
To retain 90% of genetic diversity for 50 years, $H_t/H_0 = 0.90$ and $t = 50/L$

$$0.90 \sim e^{-50/2LN_e}$$

taking ln and rearranging yields

$$N_e = -50/2L\ln 0.90 = 237/L$$

Thus, for elephants $N_e = 237/26 = 9.1$, and for deer mice $N_e = 237 \times 3 = 711$.

14.7 The recovery goal of 2×150 wild populations and 1×150 captive populations will not cause immediate additional genetic problems of rapid inbreeding depression. If this results in an N_e of about $300 \times 0.1 + 150 \times .3 \sim 75$, then the rate of inbreeding per generation is only 0.0067. Further, the condor has a long generation interval, so the increase in inbreeding per year will be slow. However, this population size will not prevent slow deterioration in genetic diversity and slow build up of inbreeding.

Chapter 15

15.1 Taxonomic uncertainties may result in undiagnosed species being left to go extinct, undiagnosed species being hybridized to other species with deleterious consequences, or resources being wasted on populations belonging to common species, or conservation of hybrid populations that are not distinct species. Further, crosses of differentiated populations within species may result in outbreeding depression.

15.2 Two populations are sympatric if they occur in the same geographic location.

15.3 (a) Separate species as the distinct chromosome numbers indicate that they are not exchanging genes.
(b) They are not random mating, so they may be separate species. Information on additional loci would be desirable.

(c) As there are no alleles in common they are not exchanging genes, so they are likely to be separate species.

(d) Both populations share allele 1, so there may be gene flow. They probably belong to the same species, but more information is required to be certain as there is some degree of genetic differentiation.

15.4 Two populations are allopatric if they are not found in the same geographic location.

15.5 (a) Separate species as they have distinctly different chromosome numbers.

(b) There are insufficient grounds to classify Sumatran tigers as a separate species. The long isolation and the minor difference in mtDNA may be sufficient to classify them as a separate sub-species.

(c) Separate species, as they show extremely large genetic differences between the forms, well beyond the differences found for other 'good' species.

15.6 (a) $I_{xy} = \Sigma x_i y_i / \sqrt{\Sigma x_i^2 . \Sigma y_i^2} = (0.1^2 + 0.2^2 + 0.7^2) / \sqrt{(0.1^2 + 0.2^2 + 0.7^2)} = 1$

$$D = -\ln I_{xy} = -\ln (1) = 0$$

(b) $I_{xy} = 0, D = \infty$

(c) $I_{xy} = (0.5 \times 0 + 0.5 \times 0.7 + 0.3 \times 0) / \sqrt{(0.5^2 + 0.5^2 + 0)(0 + 0.7^2 + 0.3^2)} = 0.35 / 0.5385 = 0.65$

$$D = -\ln (0.65) = 0.43$$

15.7 (a) $I_{VG} = (0.023 \times 0.981 + 0.977 \times 0.019 + 0) / \sqrt{(0.023^2 + 0.977^2) \times (0.981^2 + 0.019^2)}$
$= 0.041126 / \sqrt{0.955058 \times 0.962722} = 0.043$

$$D = -\ln (0.043) = 3.15$$

(b) $I_{AG} = (0.019 \times 0.981 + 0.885 \times 0.019) / \sqrt{(0.019^2 + 0.885^2 + 0.096^2)(0.981^2 + 0.019^2)}$
$= 0.035454 / \sqrt{0.792802 \times 0.962722} = 0.0406$

$$D = -\ln (0.043) = 3.20$$

15.8 If the populations are called A, B and C, then A and B are classified as $\frac{-|-}{-|-}$ and so should be managed as a single unit.

1 Conversely, (A, B) versus C are classified as $\frac{+|+}{+|+}$ since they differ at microsatellite loci (reject genetic exchangeability for both recent and historical times frames) and for heritable characters likely to be of ecological significance (reject ecological exchangeability for both recent and historical times frames). Consequently, C should be managed as a separate unit from A–B.

15.9 $\frac{-|-}{+|+}$. There seem limited grounds for considering the two forms as other than part of a continuum. Allow gene flow between them. They may even represent one management unit with clinal variation.

Chapter 16

16.1 Introduce mainland individuals into the Barrow Island euro population, probably from the nearest mainland location to Barrow Island with euros. Females would probably have to be used as male aggression may make male introductions difficult.

16.2 Use the small population as it has a different genotype and so should alleviate inbreeding depression.

16.3 The best procedure would be to genotype all populations before deciding. If the population of concern and the large populations have the same genotypes, use the small population as it has more heterozygosity.

16.4 Introduce genetic material (e.g. pollen) from other populations. Since plants often show adaptive genetic differentiation, this should be done using nearby populations, but ones with distinct S locus alleles. Check the chromosomes to ensure all populations have the same ploidy before allowing any pollen flow.

16.5 Move individuals among the population fragments, such that Nm is greater than 1, i.e. move about 1–5 individuals among populations each generation on average.

16.6 Snail, as it is likely to have the lowest rate of gene flow.

16.7 The average growth rate and mature size of trees is likely to decline, as the harvest is removing the largest trees.

16.8 This species is an asexual clone. Management should aim to minimize demographic and environmental stochasticity and catastrophes by increasing the population size and having replicate populations in different locations.

Chapter 17

17.1 Captive populations deteriorate genetically due to inbreeding depression, loss of genetic diversity, mutational accumulation and genetic adaptation to captivity (that is deleterious when they are reintroduced to the wild).

17.2 $k_{GH} = 1/16$.

17.3 The most familiar way to complete this problem is to determine the inbreeding coefficient for a progeny X of Thelma and Rita if they could have one.

Path	Contribution to F_X
Thelma–**A**–H–Rita	1/16
Thelma–F–**A**–H–Rita	1/32
Thelma–F–**B**–H–Rita	1/32

$k_{Th-R} = F_X = 1/16 + 1/32 + 1/32 = 1/8$.

17.4 $k_{Th-Th} = \frac{1}{2}(1 + F_{Th}) = \frac{1}{2}(1 + \frac{1}{4}) = 5/8$.

17.5 mean $mk_{Ri} = \Sigma(k_{Ri-Th} + k_{Ri-L} + k_{Ri-Ri} + k_{Ri-Ro})/4$

$= (1/8 + 1/8 + 1/2 + 0)/4 = 6/(8 \times 4) = 3/16 = 0.1875$.

17.6 A 4-population group can be labelled as populations

1('genotype' AB), 2 (CD), 3 (EF) and 4 (GH). In the 1st generation, males move one group to the right, 1 to 2, 2 to 3, 3 to 4 and 4 to 1. Progeny in group 1 will have 'genotype' ABGH, 2 ABCD, 3 CDEF and 4 EFGH. In the 2nd generation males are moved two groups to the right, 1 to 3, 2 to 4, 3 to 1 and 4 to 2. Progeny in group 1 will have 'genotype' ABCDEFGH, 2 ABCDEFGH, 3 ABCDEFGH and 4 ABCDEFGH, i.e. all are now the same 'genotype' so avoidance of inbreeding is no longer possible in future generations.

17.7 Cloning is widely used in plant conservation, i.e. cuttings can be taken so that individual plants can be conserved, either by planting in the wild, or by taking them into botanical gardens. Tissue culture is another form of cloning that can be done with many plants. These forms of cloning can be used to rapidly increase population sizes without major costs to the individual. In mammals, only a few species that are closely related to domestic animals can be cloned using nuclear transplantation. Animal cloning is more difficult than plant cloning as a recipient mother is required; this must be of the same species, or a closely related species. The use of closely related species may lead to later behavioural problems, inappropriate learned skills, etc. We are not aware of birds having been cloned, but amphibians were the first animals to be cloned using nuclear transplantation. Currently, animal cloning is of little conservation value as so few species can be cloned. In the future, it may be used to increase the numbers of individuals of highly threatened species. However, it is likely to remain a high-cost venture that can be afforded in only a limited range of high profile species.

17.8 The options to manage recessive hairlessness in red ruffed lemurs are:
(a) ignore it
(b) remove affected individual from the gene pool
(c) remove potential carriers and affected individual from the gene pool
(d) remove affected individual from the gene pool and re-pair carriers that produce hairless offspring.
Given the allele frequency, about 1% of the progeny (q^2) will be hairless, so ignoring the condition or removing affected individual are both feasible options. If carriers were to be removed from the pedigree this would lead to removal of 18% of the individuals – this is too great a loss of individuals for an endangered species with only 125 individuals in captivity. If all potential carriers were to be removed, then much higher proportions of progeny would have to be removed. The final option minimizes the number of hairless offspring produced and removes only a few individuals from the breeding pool. When the population reaches higher numbers, it may become possible to eliminate the condition, especially if a molecular test for carriers was devised.

Chapter 18

18.1 Genetic adaptation to captive conditions results in improved reproductive fitness in captivity, but these adaptations are typically deleterious when captive populations are reintroduced into the wild.

18.2 Genetic adaptation to captivity depends upon the heritability of reproductive fitness in captivity (and thus on genetic diversity), upon selection in captivity (this depends upon the mortality rate and the difference in environment between captive and wild environments), upon the effective population size, upon the extent of migration into the population from wild populations and upon the generation length.

18.3 The genetic issues in reintroduction programs are:
  (a) genetic problems that arise during the decline of the wild population (inbreeding and loss of genetic diversity)
  (b) genetic deterioration in captivity due to inbreeding, loss of genetic diversity and genetic adaptations to captivity that reduce reproductive fitness in the wild environment
  (c) choice of reintroduction sites and the likely adaptation of the captive population to the sites
  (d) choice of individuals to reintroduce, including impact of reintroductions on the captive population, and impact of reintroductions on genetic diversity in the reintroduced population
  (e) inbreeding and reproductive fitness of the reintroduced population.

18.4 Removal of an individual with high mean kinship (and low H_e) will reduce mean kinship in the captive population and thus will increase heterozygosity (from Equation 17.5).

Chapter 19

19.1 Time for all alleles in a population to coalescence is approximately $4N_e [1 - (1/k)] = 3N_e$ generations, i.e. 150 generations for $N_e = 50$, and 30 generations for $N_e = 10$.

19.2 (a) ¾, (b) $N_e = 4 \times 1 \times 4/(4+1) = 3.2$, thus $H_1/H_0 = 1 - 1/(2 \times 3.2) = 0.84$, (c) 7/8, (d) 19/20.

19.3 (a) 0, (b) ½, (c) 4/5.

19.4 $N_e = 4 \times 1 \times 10/11 = 3.64$.
$H_t/H_0 \sim [1 - 1/(2 \times 3.64)]^7 = 0.36$ (approximate only). Thus, the bottleneck is insufficient to account for the complete lack of allozyme heterozygosity. The reason for the lack of allozyme variability is unknown. Presumably the population had been subjected to prior bottlenecks, due perhaps to disease epidemics.

19.5 mtDNA $H_{75}/H_0 = 0.067/0.80 = 0.084 = (1 - 1/N_{ef})^{75} \sim e^{-t/N_{ef}}$
$= e^{-75/N_{ef}}$

Taking ln and rearranging yields

$$N_{ef} = -75/\ln(0.084) = 30.$$

19.6 (a) Asexual / clonal.

(b) Compatible with selfing; only alleles present in the mother are found in the offspring and the ratio of genotypes fits selfing. However, data from further loci would be necessary to exclude outbreeding.

(c) Outcrossing; alleles not found in the mother are present in the offspring. Only one male (A_2A_3) is necessary to account for the offspring.

(d) Outbreeding; at least two males are necessary to account for the offspring (e.g. A_2A_3 and A_4A_5).

(e) Haplo-diploid; females diploid and males haploid. If only one locus of several showed this, it would indicate sex-linked inheritance.

19.7 The Wollemi pine may be asexually reproducing, or it could be a highly inbred homozygous population that is selfing, or even outcrossing. The former is the most likely explanation.

19.8 Offspring are compatible with putative parents for loci B, C, D, F, H, K, L and N. The following offspring are not compatible with the putative parents: locus A gosling 4, Locus E goslings 3 and 4, locus G gosling 4, locus I gosling 3, locus J gosling 1, locus M goslings 2, 3 and 4. Thus, goslings 1–4 do not belong to the putative parents, 2 father excluded, 3 and 4 father and mother excluded. Gosling 5 is the only one that belongs to the nest attendants.

Chapter 20

20.1 For the first time step from 1960 to 1961, $r = \ln(350/70) = 1.609$. For the full data set 1960–86, mean $r = -0.052$ and variance $(r) = 0.841$.

20.2 The major recommendations for the northern hairy-nosed wombat would be to preserve the habitat (remove cattle grazing – has been done) and attempt to increase the population size. To avoid catastrophes, establishment of another population is strongly recommended (e.g. Deniliquin where a population previously existed). Captive breeding has not been recommended as this species has not been bred in captivity. Research into captive breeding of the related southern hairy-nosed wombat is recommended.

20.3 The only immediate option is captive breeding, with populations maintained at several sites to avoid catastrophes. To reintroduce *Partula* into the wild would require extermination of the introduced carnivorous snail (improbable), or reintroduction to an island lacking the predatory snail. Reserve populations in captivity would still be required to avoid losing wild populations due the spread of the carnivorous snail.

20.4 With small overall populations and continued threats in the wild, reserve captive breeding populations are required (there are some captive animals). Management of the wild populations requires habitat preservation, control of poaching and genetic management to restore gene flow. Artificial insemination may be feasible to improve gene flow in this species. It may be possible to move females of this species, but it is likely to be difficult and costly.

Revision

R.1 Endangered as $N < 250$.

R.2

Expected	AA	AB	BB	AC	BC	CC	Total
frequencies	0.01	0.06	0.09	0.12	0.36	0.36	1

R.3 $D = -0.11$, so the population is not in linkage equilibrium, i.e. it is in linkage disequilibrium.

R.4 $h^2 = \text{Cov}_{OP}/V_P = 5.183/8.18 = 0.63$.

R.5 $\hat{q} = u/s = 4 \times 10^{-6}/0.2 = 2 \times 10^{-5}$.

R.6 $t = (\ln p_0 - \ln p_t)/u = (\ln 1 - \ln 0.75)/10^{-4} = 2877$ generations.

	AA	Aa	aa
Relative fitnesses	0.9412	1	0.9765
	$1 - s_1$	1	$1 - s_2$

$\hat{p} = s_2/(s_1 + s_2) = 0.0235/(0.0588 + 0.0235) = 0.29$.

R.8 $H_t/H_0 = 0.78$.

R.9 $N_e = 30$.

R.10 $F = 1/16$.

R.11 F_{ST} is a measure of the inbreeding due to differentiation in allele frequencies among populations. F_{ST} is inversely related to gene flow among populations, being 0 for undifferentiated populations, and 1 for completely differentiated populations.

R.12 $I_N = 0.5/\sqrt{(0.38 \times 1)} = 0.811$ and $D = 0.21$.

R.13 The populations are showing some reproductive isolation, but this is not surprising as they are allopatric and isolated by water. They probably belong to one species, but they may be subspecies. It would be preferable (obligatory) to have information on additional informative loci.

R.14 The first step would be to identify the clonal genotypes (these will often be in different populations) and then conserve the clones in the wild (and typically in captivity as well). In the wild the efforts should be to preserve habitat and to increase their population sizes.

R.15 From pedigrees, calculate kinship for all pairs of individuals in the population, and for all individuals with themselves. Calculate mean kinships for every individual. Choose individuals to reproduce based on minimizing mean kinship. Avoid mating between close relatives and those with very different mean kinships.

R.16 $N_e = 475/L = 475/8 = 59$.

References

(For a given author, single author papers are first, followed by papers with two authors, and finally papers with three or more authors in year order.)

Abplanalp, H. 1990. Inbreeding. Pp. 955–984 in R.D. Crawford, ed. *Poultry Breeding and Genetics*. Elsevier, Amsterdam, Netherlands.

Akçakaya, H.R. 2000. Population viability analyses with demographically and spatially structured models. *Ecol. Bull. 48*, 23–38.

Akçakaya, H.R. & P. Sjögren-Gulve. 2000. Population viability analyses in conservation planning: an overview. *Ecol. Bull. 48*, 9–21.

Allard, R.W. 1960. *Principles of Plant Breeding*. John Wiley & Sons, New York.

Allen, P.J., W. Amos, P.P. Pomeroy & S.D. Twiss. 1995. Microsatellite variation in grey seals *Halichoerus grypu* shows evidence of genetic differentiation between two British breeding colonies. *Mol. Ecol. 4*, 653–662.

Allendorf, F.W. 1986. Genetic drift and the loss of alleles versus heterozygosity. *Zoo Biol. 5*, 181–190.

Allendorf, F.W. & R.S. Waples. 1996. Conservation and genetics of salmonid fishes. Pp. 238–280 in J.C. Avise & J.L. Hamrick, eds. *Conservation Genetics: Case Histories from Nature*. Chapman & Hall, New York.

Allendorf, F.W., R.B. Harris & L.H. Metzgar. 1991. Estimation of effective population size of grizzly bears by computer simulation. Pp. 650–654 in *Proceedings of the Fourth International Congress of Systematic and Evolutionary Biology*.

Allison, A.C. 1956. The sickle-cell and hemoglobin C genes in some African populations. *Ann. Hum. Genet. 21*, 67–89.

Allison, A.C. 1961. Abnormal hemoglobin and erythrocyte enzyme-deficiency traits. Pp. 16–40 in G.A. Harrison, ed. *Genetical Variation in Human Populations*. Pergamon Press, New York.

Amos, B., C. Schlotter & D. Tautz. 1993. Social structure of pilot whales revealed by analytical DNA profiling. *Science 260*, 670–672.

Anonymous. 1996. Attwater's greater prairie chicken (*Tympanuchus cupido attwateri*). *Endang. Species Bulletin 21*(3), 31.

Ardern, S.L. & D.M. Lambert. 1997. Is the black robin in genetic peril? *Mol. Ecol. 6*, 21–28.

Arnold, M.L. & S.A. Hodges. 1995. Are natural hybrids fit or unfit relative to their parents? *Trends Ecol. Evol. 10*, 67–71.

Arnold, S.J. 1995. Monitoring quantitative genetic variation and evolution in captive populations. Pp. 295–317 in J.D. Ballou, M. Gilpin & T.J. Foose, eds. *Population Management for Survival and Recovery: Analytical Methods and Strategies in Small Population Conservation*. Columbia University Press, New York.

Ashworth, D. & D.T. Parkin. 1992. Captive breeding: can genetic fingerprinting help? Pp. 135–149 in H.D.M. Moore, W.V. Holt & G.M. Mace, eds. *Biotechnology and the Conservation of Genetic Diversity*. Clarendon Press, Oxford, UK.

Austin, C.R. & R.V. Short. 1984. *Reproduction in Mammals,* 2nd edn, vol. 4, *Reproductive Fitness*. Cambridge University Press, Cambridge, UK.

Australia Institute. 1997. Institute finds koalas contribute $1.1 billion to tourism. *Aust. Inst. Newsl.* No. 12 September (1977), 8–9.

Avise, J.C. 1994. *Molecular Markers, Natural History, and Evolution*. Chapman & Hall, New York.

Avise, J.C. 1996. Toward a regional conservation genetics perspective: phylogeography of faunas in the southeastern United States. Pp. 431–470 in J.C. Avise & J.L. Hamrick, eds. *Conservation Genetics: Case Histories from Nature*. Chapman & Hall, New York.

Avise, J.C. 2000. *Phylogeography: The History and Formation of Species*. Harvard University Press, Cambridge, MA.

Avise, J.C. & R.M. J. Ball. 1990. Principles of genealogical concordance in species concepts and biological taxonomy. *Oxford Surv. Evol. Biol. 7*, 45–67.

Avise, J.C. & J. L. Hamrick. (eds.) 1996. *Conservation Genetics: Case Histories from Nature*. Chapman & Hall, New York.

Avise, J.C. & G.C. Johns. 1999. Proposal for a standardized temporal scheme of biological classification for extant species. *Proc. Natl Acad. Sci. USA 96*, 7358–7363.

Avise, J.C. & W.S. Nelson. 1989. Molecular genetic relationships of the extinct dusky seaside sparrow. *Science 243*, 646–648.

Avise, J.C., J.M. Quattro & R.C. Vrijenhoek. 1992. Molecular clones within organismal clones: mitochondrial DNA phylogenies and the evolutionary histories of unisexual vertebrates. *Evol. Biol. 26*, 225–246.

Baker, C.S. & S.R. Palumbi. 1996. Population structure, molecular systematics, and forensic identification of whales and dolphins. Pp. 10–49 in J.C. Avise & J.L. Hamrick, eds. *Conservation Genetics: Case Histories from Nature*. Chapman & Hall, New York.

Baker, C.S., D.A. Gilbert, M.T. Weinrich, R. Lambertsen, J. Calambokidis, B. McArdle, G.K. Chambers & S.J. O'Brien. 1993. Population characteristics of DNA fingerprints in humpback whales (*Megaptera novaeangliae*). *J. Hered. 84*, 281–290.

Ballou, J.D. 1983. Calculating inbreeding coefficients from pedigrees. Pp. 509–520 in C.M. Schonewald-Cox, S.M. Chambers, B. MacBryde & L. Thomas, eds. *Genetics and Conservation: A Reference for Managing Wild Animal and Plant Populations*. Benjamin/Cummings, Menlo Park, CA.

Ballou, J.D. 1989. Inbreeding and outbreeding depression in the captive propagation of black-footed ferrets. Pp. 49–68 in U.S. Seal, E.T. Thorne, M.A. Bogan & S.H. Anderson, eds. *Conservation Biology and the Black-Footed Ferret*. Yale University Press, New Haven, CT.

Ballou, J.D. 1997. Effects of ancestral inbreeding on genetic load in mammalian populations. *J. Hered. 88*, 169–178.

Ballou, J.D. & T.J. Foose. 1996. Demographic and genetic management of captive populations. Pp. 263–283 in D.G. Kleiman, M.E. Allen, K.V. Thompson & S. Lumpkin, eds. *Wild Animals in Captivity: Principles and Techniques*. University of Chicago Press, Chicago, IL.

Ballou, J.D. & R.C. Lacy. 1995. Identifying genetically important individuals for management of genetic diversity in pedigreed populations. Pp. 76–111 in J.D. Ballou, M. Gilpin & T.J. Foose, eds. *Population Management for Survival and Recovery: Analytical Methods and Strategies in Small Population Conservation*. Columbia University Press, New York.

Ballou, J.D. & R. Oakleaf. 1989. Demographic and genetic captive-breeding recommendations for black-footed ferrets. Pp. 247–267 in U.S. Seal, E.T. Thorne, M.A. Bogan & S.H. Anderson, eds. *Conservation Biology and the Black-Footed Ferret*. Yale University Press, New Haven, CT.

Ballou, J.D. & K. Ralls. 1982. Inbreeding and juvenile mortality in small populations of ungulates: a detailed analysis. *Biol. Conserv. 24*, 239–272.

Ballou, J.D. & J. Seidensticker. 1987. The genetic and demographic characteristics of the 1983 captive population of Sumatran tigers (*Panthera tigris suma-*

trae). Pp. 329–347 in R.L. Tilson & U.S. Seal, eds. *Tigers of the World: The Biology, Biopolitics, Management, and Conservation of an Endangered Species*. Noyes Publications, Park Ridge, NJ.

Ballou, J.D., M. Gilpin & T.J. Foose. 1995. *Population Management for Survival and Recovery: Analytical Methods and Strategies in Small Population Conservation*. Columbia University Press, New York.

Ballou, J.D., R.C. Lacy, D. Kleiman, A. Rylands & S. Ellis. 1998. *Leontopithecus II: The Second Population and Habitat Viability Assessment for Lion Tamarins (*Leontopithecus*): Final Report*. Conservation Breeding Specialist Group (SSC/IUCN), Apple Valley, MN.

Barber, H.N. 1955. Adaptive gene substitution in Tasmanian eucalypts. I. *Evolution 9*, 1–14.

Barber, H.N. & W.D. Jackson. 1957. Natural selection in action in *Eucalyptus*. *Nature 179*, 1267–1269.

Barone, M.A., M.E. Roelke, J. Howard, J.L. Brown, A.E. Anderson & D.E. Wildt. 1994. Reproductive characteristics of male Florida panthers: comparative studies from Florida, Texas, Colorado, Latin America, and North American zoos. *J. Mammal. 75*, 150–162.

Barrett, S.C.H. & J.R. Kohn. 1991. Genetic and evolutionary consequences of small population size in plants: implications for conservation. Pp. 3–61 in D.A. Falk & K.E. Holsinger, eds. *Genetics and Conservation of Rare Plants*. Oxford University Press, New York.

Barrowclough, G.F. & R.J. Gutierrez. 1990. Genetic variation and differentiation in the spotted owl (*Strix occidentalis*). *Auk 107*, 737–744.

Barrowclough, G.F., R.J. Gutierrez & J.G. Groth. 1999. Phylogeography of spotted owl (*Strix occidentalis*) populations based on mitochondrial DNA sequences: gene flow, genetic structure, and a novel biogeographic pattern. *Evolution 53*, 919–931.

Bartley, D., M. Bagley, G. Gall & B. Bentley. 1992. Use of linkage disequilibrium data to estimate effective size of hatchery and natural fish populations. *Conserv. Biol. 6*, 365–375.

Beattie, A.J. 1995. Natural history at the cutting edge. *Ecol. Econ. 13*, 93–97.

Beck, B.B., L.G. Rapaport, M.R. Stanley Price & A.C. Wilson. 1994. Reintroduction of captive-born animals. Pp. 265–286 in P.J.S. Olney, G.M. Mace & A.T.C. Feistner, eds. *Creative Conservation: Interactive Management of Wild and Captive Animals*. Chapman & Hall, London.

Becker, W.A. 1984. *Manual of Quantitative Genetics*, 4th edn. Academic Enterprises, Pullman, Washington, DC.

Beheregaray, L.B., P. Sunnucks, D.L. Alpers, S.C. Banks & A.C. Taylor. 2000. A set of microsatellite loci for the hairy-nosed wombats (*Lasiorhinus krefftii* and *L. latifrons*). *Conserv. Genet. 1*, 89–92.

Behr, M.A., M.A. Wilson, W.P. Gill, H. Salamon, G.K. Schoolnik, S. Rane & P.M. Small. 1999. Comparative genomics of BCG vaccines by whole-genome DNA microarray. *Science 284*, 1520–1523.

Beilharz, R.G. 1982. The effect of inbreeding on reproduction in mice. *Anim. Prod. 34*, 49–54.

Beissinger, S.R. & D.R. McCullough. 2001. *Population Viability Analysis*. University of Chicago Press, Chicago, IL.

Belovsky, G.E. 1987. Extinction models and mammalian persistence. Pp. 35–57 in M.E. Soulé, ed. *Viable Populations for Conservation*. Cambridge University Press, Cambridge, UK.

Belyaev, D.K. 1979. Destabilising selection as a factor in domestication. *J. Hered. 70*, 301–308.

Benirschke, K. & A.T. Kumamoto. 1991. Mammalian cytogenetics and conservation of species. *J. Hered. 82*, 187–191.

Bensch, S., D. Hasselquist & T. von Schantz. 1994. Genetic similarity between parents predicts hatching failure: nonincestuous inbreeding in the great reed warbler? *Evolution 48*, 317–326.

Berger, J. 1990. Persistence of different sized populations: an empirical assessment of rapid extinctions in bighorn sheep. *Conserv. Biol. 4*, 91–98.

Berthold, P., A.J. Helbig, G. Mohr & U. Querner. 1992. Rapid microevolution of migratory behaviour in a wild bird species. *Nature 360*, 668–670.

Bérubé, M. & P. Pasbøll. 1996. Identification of sex in cetaceans by multiplexing with three ZFX and ZFY specific primers. *Mol. Ecol. 5*, 283–287.

Bever, J.D. & F. Felber. 1994. The theoretical population genetics of autopolyploids. *Oxford Surv. Evol. Biol. 8*, 185–217.

Bijlsma, R., J. Bundgaard & W.F. Van Putten. 1999. Environmental dependence of inbreeding depression and purging in *Drosophila melanogaster*. *J. Evol. Biol. 12*, 1125–1137.

Bijlsma, R., J. Bundgaard & A.C. Boerema. 2000. Does inbreeding affect the extinction risk of small populations? Predictions from *Drosophila*. *J. Evol. Biol. 13*, 502–514.

Billington, H.L. 1991. Effects of population size on genetic variation in a dioecious conifer. *Conserv. Biol. 5*, 115–119.

Bingaman-Lackey, L. 1999. *International Giraffe Studbook*. ISIS, Apple Valley, MN.

Birstein, V.J., P. Doukakis, B. Sorkin & R. DeSalle. 1998. Population aggregation analysis of three caviar-producing species of sturgeons and implications for the species identification of black caviar. *Conserv. Biol. 12*, 766–775.

Bishop, J.A. & L.M. Cook. 1975. Moths, melanism and clean air. *Scient. Am. 232*, 90–99.

Black, F.L. & P.W. Hedrick. 1997. Strong balancing selection at HLA loci: evidence from segregation in South Amerindian families. *Proc. Natl Acad. Sci. USA 94*, 12452–12456.

Black, J.M. 1995. The nene *Branta sandvicensis* recovery initiative: research against selection. *Ibis 137*, S153-S160.

Bohonak, A.J. 1999. Dispersal, gene flow and population structure. *Quart. Rev. Biol. 74*, 21–45.

Bollmer, J.L., M.E. Irwin, J.P. Rieder & P.G. Parker. 1999. Multiple paternity in loggerhead turtle clutches. *Copeia*, no. 2, 475–478.

Bonnell, M.L. & R.K. Selander. 1974. Elephant seals: genetic variation and near extinction. *Science 184*, 908–909.

Borlase, S.C., D.A. Loebel, R. Frankham, R.K. Nurthen, D.A. Briscoe & G.E. Daggard. 1993. Modelling problems in conservation genetics using captive *Drosophila* populations: consequences of equalization of family sizes. *Conserv. Biol. 7*, 122–131.

Botting, D. 1999. *Gerald Durrell: The Authorized Biography*. HarperCollins, New York.

Bouzat, J.L., H.A. Lewin & K.N. Paige. 1998. The ghost of genetic diversity past: historical DNA analysis of the greater prairie chicken. *Am. Natur. 152*, 1–6.

Bowdoin, J. & B. Williams. 1996. Conservation spotlight: the Attwater's prairie chicken. *Endang. Species Updates 13*, 12.

Bowen, B.W. & J.C. Avise. 1996. Conservation genetics of marine turtles. Pp. 190–237 in J.C. Avise & J.L. Hamrick, eds. *Conservation Genetics: Case Histories from Nature*. Chapman & Hall, New York.

Bowen, B.W., F.A. Abreu-Grobois, G.H. Balazs, N. Kamenzaki, C.J. Limpus & R.J.

Ferl. 1995. Trans-Pacific migrations of the loggerhead turtle (*Caretta caretta*) demonstrated with mitochondrial DNA markers. *Proc. Natl Acad. Sci. USA 92*, 3731–3734.

Bowles, M.L. & C.J. Whelan. 1994. *Restoration of Endangered Species: Conceptual Issues, Planning and Implementation*. Cambridge University Press, Cambridge, UK.

Bowman, J.C. & D.S. Falconer. 1960. Inbreeding depression and heterosis of litter size in mice. *Genet. Res. 1*, 262–274.

Boyce, M.S. 1994. Population viability analysis exemplified by models for the northern spotted owl. Pp. 3–18 in D.J. Fletcher & B.F.J. Manly, eds. *Statistics in Ecology and Environmental Monitoring*, vol. 2. University of Otago Press, Dunedin, New Zealand.

Boyd, L. & K.A. Houpt. 1994. *Przewalski's Horse: The History and Biology of an Endangered Species*. State University of New York Press, Albany, NY.

Bradshaw, A.D. 1991. Genostasis and the limits to evolution. *Phil. Trans. R. Soc. Lond. B 333*, 289–305.

Bradshaw, A.D. & T. McNeilly. 1981. *Evolution and Pollution*. Arnold, London.

Brewer, B.A., R.C. Lacy, M.L. Foster & G. Alaks. 1990. Inbreeding depression in insular and central populations of *Peromyscus* mice. *J. Hered. 81*, 257–266.

Briggs, D. & S.M. Walters. 1997. *Plant Variation and Evolution*, 3rd edn. Cambridge University Press, Cambridge, UK.

Briscoe, D.A. & N.N. Tait. 1995. Allozyme evidence for extensive and ancient radiations in Australian Onychophora. *J. Hered. 114*, 91–102.

Briscoe, D.A., J.M. Malpica, A. Robertson, G.J. Smith, R. Frankham, R.G. Banks & J.S.F. Barker. 1992. Rapid loss of genetic variation in large captive populations of *Drosophila* flies: implications for the genetic management of captive populations. *Conserv. Biol. 6*, 416–425.

Briton, J., R.K. Nurthen, D.A. Briscoe & R. Frankham. 1994. Modelling problems in conservation genetics using captive *Drosophila* populations: consequences of harems. *Biol. Conserv. 69*, 267–275.

Brock, M.K. & B.N. White. 1992. Application of DNA fingerprinting to the recovery program of the endangered Puerto Rican parrot. *Proc. Natl Acad. Sci. USA 89*, 11121–11125.

Brook, B.W. & J. Kikkawa. 1998. Examining threats faced by island birds: a population viability analysis on the Capricorn silvereye using long-term data. *J. Appl. Ecol. 35*, 491–503.

Brook, B.W., L. Lim, R. Harden & R. Frankham. 1997a. How secure is the Lord Howe Island woodhen? A population viability analysis using VORTEX. *Pacific Conserv. Biol. 3*, 125–133.

Brook, B.W., L. Lim, R. Harden & R. Frankham. 1997b. Does population viability analysis software predict the behaviour of real populations? A retrospective study on the Lord Howe Island woodhen *Tricholimnas sylvestris* (Sclater). *Biol. Conserv. 82*, 119–128.

Brook, B.W., J.J. O'Grady, A.P. Chapman, M.A. Burgman, H.R. Akçakaya & R. Frankham. 2000. Predictive accuracy of population viability analysis in conservation biology. *Nature 404*, 385–387.

Brookfield, J.F.Y. & P.M. Sharp. 1994. Neutralism and selectionism face up to DNA data. *Trends Genet. 10*, 109–111.

Brown, A.H.D. 1989. Genetic characterisation of plant mating systems. Pp. 145–162 in A.H.D. Brown, M.T. Clegg, A.L. Kahler & B.S. Weir, eds. *Plant Population Genetics, Breeding and Genetic Resources*. Sinauer, Sunderland, MA.

Brown, A.H.D. & A.G. Young. 2000. Genetic diversity in tetraploid populations of the endangered daisy *Rutidosis leptorrhynchoides* and implications for its conservation. *Heredity 85*, 122–129.

Brown, J.L. & E.R. Brown. 1998. Are inbred offspring less fit? Survival in a natural population of Mexican jays. *Behav. Ecol. 9*, 60–63.

Brown, S.M. & B.A. Houlden. 1999. Isolation and characterization of microsatellite markers in the black rhinoceros (*Diceros bicornis*). *Mol. Ecol. 8*, 1559–1561.

Bryant, E.H. & D.H. Reed. 1999. Fitness decline under relaxed selection in captive populations. *Conserv. Biol. 13*, 665–669.

Bryant, E.H., S.A. McCommas & L.M. Combs. 1986. The effect of an experimental bottleneck upon quantitative genetic variation in the housefly. *Genetics 114*, 1191–1211.

Bryant, E.H., L.M. Meffert & S.A. McCommas. 1990. Fitness rebound in serially bottlenecked populations of the housefly. *Am. Natur. 136*, 542–549.

Bryant, E.H., V.L. Backus, M.E. Clark & D.H. Reed. 1999. Experimental tests of captive breeding for endangered species. *Conserv. Biol. 13*, 1487–1496.

Burdon, J.J. 1987. *Diseases and Plant Population Biology*. Cambridge University Press, Cambridge, UK.

Burgman, M.A. & B.B. Lamont. 1992. A stochastic model for the viability of *Banksia cuneata* populations: environmental, demographic and genetic effects. *J. Appl. Ecol. 29*, 719–727.

Burgman, M.A. & D.B. Lindenmayer. 1998. *Conservation Biology for the Australian Environment*. Surrey Beatty & Sons, Chipping Norton, NSW, Australia.

Burgman, M.A., S. Ferguson & H.R. Akçakaya. 1993. *Risk Assessment in Conservation Biology*. Chapman & Hall, London.

Buri, P. 1956. Gene frequency in small populations of mutant *Drosophila*. *Evolution 10*, 367–402.

Burton, R.S., P.D. Rawson & S. Edmands. 1999. Genetic architecture of physiological phenotypes: empirical evidence for coadapted gene complexes. *Am. Sci. 39*, 451–462.

Bush, G.L. 1975. Modes of animal speciation. *Ann. Rev. Ecol. Syst. 6*, 339–364.

Bush, G.L., R.W. Neck & G.B. Kitto. 1976. Screwworm eradication: inadvertent selection for noncompetitive ecotypes during mass rearing. *Science 193*, 491–493.

Butler, D. & D. Merton. 1992. *The Black Robin: Saving the World's Most Endangered Bird*. Oxford University Press, Auckland, New Zealand.

Butler, M.A., A.R. Templeton & B. Read. 1994. DNA fingerprinting in Speke's gazelle: a test for genetic distinctness, and the correlation between relatedness and similarity. *Mol. Ecol. 3*, 355–361.

Buza, L., A. Young & P. Thrall. 2000. Genetic erosion, inbreeding and reduced fitness in fragmented populations of the endangered tetraploid pea *Swainsonia recta*. *Biol. Conserv. 93*, 177–186.

Byers, D.L. & T.R. Meagher. 1999. Mate availability in small populations of plant species with homomorphic sporophytic self-incompatibility. *Heredity 68*, 353–359.

Caballero, A. 1994. Developments in the prediction of effective population size. *Heredity 73*, 657–679.

Calero, C., O. Ibanez, M. Mayol & J.A. Rosello. 1998. Random amplified polymorphic DNA (RAPD) markers detect a single phenotype in *Lysimachia minoricensis* J.J. Rodr. (Primulaceae), a wild extinct plant. *Mol. Ecol. 8*, 2133–2136.

Cann, R.L., R.A. Feldman, L. Agullana & L.A. Freed. 1996. A PCR approach to detection of malaria in Hawaiian birds. Pp. 202–213 in T.B. Smith & R.K. Wayne, eds. *Molecular Genetic Approaches in Conservation*. Oxford University Press, New York.

Caro, T.M. & M.K. Laurenson. 1994. Ecological and genetic factors in conservation: a cautionary tale. *Science 263*, 485–486.

Carrington, M., G.W. Nelson, M.P. Martin, T. Kissner, D. Vlahov, J.J. Goegert, R. Kaslow, S. Buchbinder, K. Hoots & S.J. O'Brien. 1999. HLA and HIV–1: heterozygote advantage and *B*35-Cw*04* disadvantage. *Science 283*, 1748–1752.

Caughley, G. & A. Gunn. 1996. *Conservation Biology in Theory and Practice.* Blackwell Scientific, Cambridge, MA.

Chan, S.H., T. Tan, A. Kamarudin, G.B. Wee & V.S. Rajan. 1979. HLA and sexually transmitted disease in prostitutes. *Br. J. Venereal Dis. 55*, 207–210.

Channell, R. & M.V. Lomollno. 2000. Dynamic biogeography and conservation of endangered species. *Nature 403*, 84–86.

Chapman, A.P., B.W. Brook, T.H. Clutton-Brock, B.T. Grenfell & R. Frankham. 2001. Population viability analyses on a cycling population: a cautionary tale. *Biol. Conserv. 97*, 61–69.

Charlesworth, B. 1998. The effect of synergistic epistasis on the inbreeding load. *Genet. Res. 71*, 85–89.

Charlesworth, B. & D. Charlesworth. 1999. The genetic basis of inbreeding depression. *Genet. Res. 74*, 329–340.

Charlesworth, B. & K.A. Hughes. 2000. The maintenance of genetic variation in life-history traits. Pp. 369–392 in R.S. Singh & C. Krimbas, eds. *Evolutionary Genetics from Molecules to Morphology.* Cambridge University Press, Cambridge, UK.

Charlesworth, D. & P. Awadalla. 1998. Flowering plant self-incompatibility: the molecular population genetics of *Brassica* S-loci. *Heredity 81*, 1–9.

Charlesworth, D. & B. Charlesworth. 1987. Inbreeding depression and its evolutionary consequences. *Ann. Rev. Ecol. Syst. 18*, 237–268.

Charlesworth, D., M.T. Morgan & B. Charlesworth. 1993. Mutation accumulation in finite outbreeding and inbreeding populations. *Genet. Res. 61*, 39–56.

Chen, X. 1993. Comparison of inbreeding and outbreeding in hemaphroditic *Arianta arbustorum* (L.) (land snail). *Heredity 71*, 456–461.

Cheverud, J., E. Routman, C. Jaquish, S. Tardif, G. Peterson, N. Belfiore & L. Forman. 1994. Quantitative and molecular genetic variation in captive cotton-top tamarins (*Saguinus oedipus*). *Conserv. Biol. 8*, 95–105.

Ciofi, C. & M.W. Bruford. 1998. Isolation and characterization of microsatellite loci in the Komodo dragon *Varanus komodoensis. Mol. Ecol. 7*, 134–136.

Claridge, M.F., H.A. Dawah & M.R. Wilson. 1997. *Species: The Units of Biodiversity.* Chapman & Hall, London.

Clark, T.W. 1994. Restoration of the endangered black-footed ferret: a twenty-year overview. Pp. 272–297 in M.L. Bowles & C. J. Whelan, eds. *Restoration of Endangered Species: Conceptual Issues, Planning and Implementation.* Cambridge University Press, Cambridge, UK.

Clark, T.W., R.P. Reading & A.L. Clarke. 1994. *Endangered Species Recovery: Finding the Lessons, Improving the Process.* Island Press, Washington, DC.

Clarke, B.C. 1969. The evidence for apostatic selection. *Heredity 124*, 347–352.

Clarke, G.M. 1995. Relationships between developmental stability and fitness: applications for conservation biology. *Conserv. Biol. 9*, 18–24.

Clausen, J., D.D. Keck & W.M. Hiesey. 1940. Experimental studies on the nature of Species. I. Effect of varied environments on Western North American Plants. *Carnegie Institute of Washington Publications No. 520.* Carnegie Institute, Washington, DC.

Coates, D.J. & V.L. Hamley. 1999. Genetic divergence and the mating system in the endangered and geographically restricted species *Lambertia orbifolia* Gardner (Proteaceae). *Heredity 83*, 418–427.

Cody, M.L. & J.M. Overton. 1996. Short-term evolution of reduced dispersal in island plant populations. *J. Ecol. 84*, 53–61.

Coltman, D.W., W.D. Bowne & J.M. Wright. 1998. Birth weight and neonatal survival of harbour seal pups are positively correlated with genetic variation measured by microsatellites. *Proc. R. Soc. Lond. B 265*, 803–809.

Coltman, D.W., J.G. Pilkington, J.A. Smith & J.M. Pemberton. 1999. Parasite-mediated selection against inbred Soay sheep in a free-living island population. *Evolution 53*, 1259–1267.

Conway, W.G. 1986. The practical difficulties and financial implications of endangered species breeding programmes. *Int. Zoo Yb. 24/25*, 210–219.

Cook, L.M. 1965. Inheritance of shell size in the snail *Arianta arbustorum*. *Evolution 19*, 86–94.

Cooper, A., J. Rhymer, H.F. James, S.L. Olson, C. E. McIntosh, M.D. Sorenson & R.C. Fleischer. 1996. Ancient DNA and island endemics. *Nature 381*, 484.

Cooper, S.J.B., C.M. Bull & M.G. Gardner. 1997. Characterization of microsatellite loci from the socially monogamous lizard *Tiliqua rugosa* using a PCR-based isolation technique. *Mol. Ecol. 6*, 793–795.

Costanza, R., R. d'Arge, R. de Groot, S. Farber, M. Grasso, B. Hannon, K. Limburg, S. Naeem, R.V. O'Neill, J. Paruelo, R.G. Raskin, P. Sutton & M. van den Belt. 1997. The value of the world's ecosystem services and natural capital. *Nature 387*, 253–260.

Cott, H.B. 1940. *Adaptive Coloration in Animals*. Methuen, London.

Coulson, T.N., J.M. Pemberton, S.D. Albon, M. Beaumont, T.C. Marshall, J. Slate, F.E. Guinness & T.H. Clutton-Brock. 1998. Microsatellites reveal heterosis in red deer. *Proc. R. Soc. Lond. B 265*, 489–495.

Coyne, J.A. & H.A. Orr. 1989. Patterns of speciation in *Drosophila*. *Evolution 43*, 362–381.

Cracraft, J. 1997. Species concepts in systematics and conservation biology: an ornithological viewpoint. Pp. 325–339 in M.F. Claridge, H.A. Dawah & M.R. Wilson, eds. *Species: The Units of Biodiversity*. Chapman & Hall, London.

Cracraft, J., J. Feinstein, J. Vaughn & K. Helm-Bychowski. 1998. Sorting out tigers (*Panthera tigris*): mitochondrial sequences, nuclear inserts, systematics, and conservation genetics. *Anim. Conserv. 1*, 139–150.

Craig, J.L. 1994. Meta-populations: is management as flexible as nature? Pp. 50–66 in P.J.S. Olney, G.M. Mace & A.T.C. Feistner, eds. *Creative Conservation: Interactive Management of Wild and Captive Animals*. Chapman & Hall, London.

Crandall, K.A., O.R.P. Bininda-Edmonds, G.M. Mace & R.K. Wayne. 2000. Considering evolutionary processes in conservation biology: an alternative to 'evolutionarily significant units'. *Trends Ecol. Evol. 15*, 290–295.

Crnokrak, P. & D.A. Roff. 1999. Inbreeding depression in the wild. *Heredity 83*, 260–270.

Crooks, K.R., M.A. Sanjayan & D.F. Doak. 1998. New insights into cheetah conservation through demographic modelling. *Conserv. Biol. 12*, 889–895.

Crow, J.F. & M. Kimura. 1970. *An Introduction to Population Genetics Theory*. Harper & Row, New York.

Crozier, R.H. 1997. Preserving the information content of species: genetic diversity, phylogeny, and conservation worth. *Ann. Rev. Ecol. Syst. 28*, 243–268.

Culver, M., W.E. Johnson, J. Pecon-Slattery & S.J. O'Brien. 2000. Genomic ancestry of the American puma (*Puma concolor*). *J. Hered. 91*, 186–197.

Daily, G.C. 1999. Developing a scientific basis for managing Earth's life support systems. *Conserv. Ecol. 3*, 14 [online] URL http://www.consecol.orf/vol3/iss2/art14.

Daniels, S.J. & J.R. Walters. 2000. Inbreeding depression and its effects on natal dispersal in red-cockaded woodpeckers. *Condor 102*, 482–491.

Daniels, S.J., J.A. Priddy & J.R. Walters. 2000. Inbreeding in small populations of red-cockaded woodpeckers: analyses using a spatially-explicit simulation model. Pp. 129–147 in A.G. Young & G.M. Clarke, eds. *Genetics, Demography and Viability of Fragmented Populations*. Cambridge University Press, Cambridge, UK.

Darwin, C. 1876. *The Effects of Cross and Self-Fertilization in the Vegetable Kingdom*. John Murray, London.

Daszak, P., A.A. Cunningham & A.D. Hyatt. 2000. Emerging infectious diseases of wildlife: threats to biodiversity and human health. *Science 287*, 443–449.

Daugherty, C.H., A. Cree, J.M. Hay & M.B. Thompson. 1990. Neglected taxonomy and continuing extinctions of tuatara (*Sphenodon*). *Nature 347*, 177–179.

David, P. 1998. Heterozygosity–fitness correlations: new perspectives on old problems. *Heredity 80*, 531–537.

Davis, J. (ed.) 1992. *The Wildlands Project*, Wild Earth Special Issue. Cenozoice Society Inc., Canton, NY.

Dayanandan, S., J. Dole, K. Bawa & R. Kesseli. 1999. Population structure delineated with microsatellite markers in fragmented populations of a tropical tree, *Carapa guianensis* (Meliaceae). *Mol. Ecol. 8*, 1585–1592.

De Bois, H., A.A. Dhondt & B. Van Puijenbroek. 1990. Effects of inbreeding on juvenile survival of the okapi *Okapi johnstoni* in captivity. *Biol. Conserv. 54*, 147–155.

de la Peña, M., S.F. Elena & A. Moya. 2000. Effects of deleterious mutation accumulation on the fitness of RNA bacteriophage MS2. *Evolution 54*, 686–691.

Demauro, M.M. 1993. Relationship of breeding system to rarity in the lakeside daisy (*Hymenoxys acaulis* var. *glabra*). *Conserv. Biol. 7*, 542–550.

Demauro, M.M. 1994. Development and implementation of a recovery program for the federally threatened lakeside daisy (*Hymenoxys acaulis* var. *glabra*). Pp. 298–321 in M.L. Bowles & C.J. Whelan, eds. *Restoring of Endangered Species: Conceptual Issues, Planning and Implementation*. Cambridge University Press, Cambridge, UK.

Dhondt, A.A. & E. Mattysen. 1993. Conservation biology of birds: can we bridge the gap between head and heart? *Trends Ecol. Evol. 8*, 160–161.

Diamond, J.M. 1984. 'Normal' extinctions of isolated populations. Pp. 191–246 in M. H. Nitecki, ed. *Extinctions*. University of Chicago Press, Chicago, IL..

Diamond, J. 1991. *The Third Chimpanzee*. Radius, London.

Diamond, J. 1997. *Guns, Germs and Steel*. W.W. Norton & Co., New York.

Diamond, J. & J.I. Rotter. 1987. Observing the founder effect in human evolution. *Nature 329*, 105–106.

Dietz, J.M., A.J. Baker & J.D. Ballou. 2000. Demographic evidence of inbreeding depression in wild golden lion tamarins. Pp. 203–211 in A.G. Young & G.M. Clarke, eds. *Genetics, Demography and Viability of Fragmented Populations*. Cambridge University Press, Cambridge, UK.

Dinerstein, E. & G.F. McCracken. 1990. Endangered greater one-horned rhinoceros carry high levels of genetic variation. *Conserv. Biol. 4*, 417–422.

Dizon, A., G. Lento, S. Baker, P. Parsboll, F. Capriano & R. Reeves. 2000. *Molecular Genetic Identification of Whales, Dolphins, and Porpoises: Proceedings of a Workshop on the Forensic Use of Molecular Techniques to Identify Wildlife Products in the Marketplace*. NOAA Technical Memorandum NMFS. US Department of Commerce, Washington, DC.

Dobson, A.P. 1999. Introduction: Genetics and conservation biology. Pp.

xiii–xviii in L.F. Landweber & A.P. Dobson, eds. *Genetics and the Extinction of Species*. Princeton University Press, Princeton, NJ.

Dobson, A.P., G.M. Mace, J. Poole & R.A. Brett. 1992. Conservation biology: the ecology and genetics of endangered species. Pp. 405–430 in R.J. Berry, T.J. Crawford & G.M. Hewitt, eds. *Genes in Ecology*. Blackwell, Oxford, UK.

Dobzhansky, T., F.J. Ayala, G.L. Stebbins & J.W. Valentine. 1977. *Evolution*. W.H. Freeman, San Francisco, CA.

Double, M. & P. Olsen. 1997. Simplified polymerase chain reaction (PCR)-based sexing assists conservation of an endangered owl, Norfolk Island boobook *Ninox novaeseelandiae undulata*. *Bird Conserv. Int. 7*, 283–286.

Drake, J.W., B. Charlesworth, D. Charlesworth & J.F. Crow. 1998. Rates of spontaneous mutation. *Genetics 148*, 1667–1686.

Duda, T.F.J. & S.R. Palumbi. 1999. Molecular genetics of ecological diversification: duplication and rapid evolution of toxin genes of the venomous gastropod *Conus*. *Proc. Natl Acad. Sci. USA 96*, 6820–6823.

Dudash, M.R. 1990. Relative fitness of selfed and outcrossed progeny in a self-compatible, protandrous species, *Sabatia angularis* L. (Gentianaceae): a comparison of three environments. *Evolution 44*, 1129–1139.

Dudash, M.R. & C.B. Fenster. 2000. Inbreeding and outbreeding depression in fragmented populations. Pp. 35–53 in A.G. Young & G.M. Clarke, eds. *Genetics, Demography and Viability of Fragmented Populations*. Cambridge University Press, Cambridge, UK.

Dudley, J.W. 1977. 76 generations of selection for oil and protein percentage in maize. Pp. 459–473 in E. Pollak, O. Kempthorne & T.B. Bailey, eds. *Proceedings of the First International Conference on Quantitative Genetics*. Iowa State University Press, Ames, IA.

Dunbar, R. 1998. Your cheatin' heart. *New Scient.* (21 November), 29–32.

Durrell, G. 1990. *The Ark's Anniversary*. Collins, London.

East, E.M. 1916. Studies on size inheritance in *Nicotiana*. *Genetics 1*, 164–176.

Edwards, S.V. & P.W. Hedrick. 1998. Evolution and ecology of MHC molecules: from genomics to sexual selection. *Trends Ecol. Evol. 13*, 305–311.

Ehrlich, P.R. & A.H. Ehrlich. 1981. *Extinction: The Causes and Consequences of the Disappearance of Species*. Ballantine Books, New York.

Eldridge, M.D.B. 1991. Chromosomal rearrangements and speciation in rock wallabies, *Petrogale*. PhD thesis, Macquarie University, Sydney, NSW, Australia.

Eldridge, M.D.B. & R.L. Close. 1992. Taxonomy of rock-wallabies, *Petrogale* (Marsupialia: Macropodidae). I. A revision of the eastern *Petrogale* with a description of three new species. *Aust. J. Zool. 40*, 605–625.

Eldridge, M.D.B. & R.L. Close. 1993. Radiation of chromosome shuffles. *Curr. Opin. Genet. and Devel. 3*, 15–22.

Eldridge, M.D.B., J.M. King, A.K. Loupis, P.B.S. Spencer, A.C. Taylor, L.C. Pope & G.P. Hall. 1999. Unprecedented low levels of genetic variation and inbreeding depression in an island population of the black-footed rock-wallaby. *Conserv. Biol. 13*, 531–541.

Elgar, M.A. & D. Clode. 2001. Inbreeding and extinction in island populations: a cautionary tale. *Conserv. Biol. 15*, 284–286.

El-Kassaby, Y.A. & A.D. Yanchuk. 1994. Genetic diversity, differentiation, and inbreeding in Pacific yew from British Columbia. *J. Hered. 85*, 112–117.

Ellstrand, N.C. & J. Antonovics. 1985. Experimental studies of the evolutionary significance of sexual reproduction. II. A test of the density-dependent selection hypothesis. *Evolution 39*, 657–666.

Ellstrand, N.C., H.C. Prentice & J.F. Hancock. 1999. Gene flow and introgression from domesticated plants into their wild relatives. *Ann. Rev. Ecol. Syst. 30*, 539–563.

Emerson, B.C. & G.P. Wallis. 1994. Species status and population genetic structure of the flightless chafer beetles *Prodontria modesta* and *P. bicolorata* (Coleoptera; Scarabaeidae) from South Island, New Zealand. *Mol. Ecol. 3*, 339–345.

Endler, J.A. 1986. *Natural Selection in the Wild*. Princeton University Press, Princeton, NJ.

England, P.R. 1997. Conservation genetics of population bottlenecks. PhD thesis, Macquarie University, Sydney, NSW, Australia.

England, P.R., D.A. Briscoe & R. Frankham. 1996. Microsatellite polymorphisms in a wild population of *Drosophila melanogaster*. *Genet. Res. 67*, 285–290.

Evans, P.G.H. 1987. Electrophoretic variability of gene products. Pp. 105–162 in F. Cooke & P.A. Buckley, eds. *Avian Genetics: A Population and Ecological Approach*. Academic Press, London.

Eyre-Walker, A. & P.D. Keightley. 1999. High genomic deleterious mutation rates in hominids. *Nature 397*, 344–347.

Falconer, D.S. 1977. Some results of the Edinburgh selection experiments with mice. Pp. 101–115 in E. Pollak, O. Kempthorne & T.B. Bailey, eds. *Proceedings of the First International Conference on Quantitative Genetics*. Iowa State University Press, Ames, IA.

Falconer, D.S. & T.F.C. Mackay. 1996. *Introduction to Quantitative Genetics,* 4th edn. Longman, Harlow, UK.

Falk, D.A. & K.E. Holsinger. 1991. *Genetics and Conservation of Rare Plants*. Oxford University Press, New York.

Falk, D.A., C.I. Millar & M. Olwell. 1996. *Restoring Diversity: Strategies for Reintroduction of Endangered Plants*. Island Press, Washington, DC.

Fenner, F. & F.N. Ratcliffe. 1965. *Myxomatosis*. Cambridge University Press, Cambridge, UK.

Ferson, S. & M.A. Burgman. 2000. *Quantitative Methods in Conservation Biology*. Springer-Verlag, New York.

Fiedler, P.L. & P.M. Karieva. 1998. *Conservation Biology for the Coming Decade*, 2nd edn. Chapman & Hall, New York.

Findlay, C.S. & F. Cooke. 1983. Genetic and environmental components of clutch size variance in a wild population of lesser snow geese (*Anser caerulescens caerulescens*). *Evolution 37*, 724–734.

Finnegan, D.J. 1989. Eukaryotic transposable elements and genome evolution. *Trends Genet. 5*, 103–107.

Fischer, M. & D. Matthies. 1998. Effects of population size on performance in the rare plant *Gentianella germanica*. *J. Ecol. 86*, 195–204.

Fitzsimmons, N.N., S.W. Buskirk & M.H. Smith. 1995. Population history, genetic variability, and horn growth in bighorn sheep. *Conserv. Biol. 9*, 314–323.

Fleischer, R.C. 1996. Application of molecular methods to the assessment of genetic mating systems in vertebrates. Pp. 133–161 in J.D. Ferraris & S. Palumbi, eds. *Molecular Zoology: Advances, Strategies, and Protocols*. Wiley–Liss, New York.

Fleischer, R.C., C.L. Tarr & T.K. Pratt. 1994. Genetic structure and mating system in the palila, an endangered Hawaiian honeycreeper, as assessed by DNA fingerprinting. *Mol. Ecol. 3*, 383–392.

Foley, P. 1994. Predicting extinction times from environmental stochasticity and carrying capacity. *Conserv. Biol. 8*, 124–137.

Foose, T.J. 1986. Riders of the last ark: the role of captive breeding in conservation strategies. Pp. 141–165 in L. Kaufman & K. Mallory, eds. *The Last Extinction.* MIT Press, Cambridge, MA.

Foose, T.J. 1991. Viable population strategies for reintroduction programmes. Pp. 165–172 in J.H.W. Gipps, ed. *Beyond Captive Breeding: Re-Introducing Endangered Mammals to the Wild*, vol. 62. Zoological Society of London, Oxford, UK.

Foose, T.J., L. de Boer, U.S. Seal & R. Lande. 1995. Conservation management strategies based on viable populations. Pp. 273–294 in J. D. Ballou, M. Gilpin & T. J. Foose, eds. *Population Management for Survival and Recovery: Analytical Methods and Strategies in Small Population Conservation.* Columbia University Press, New York.

Forbes, S.H. & J.T. Hogg. 1999. Assessing population structure at high levels of differentiation: microsatellite comparisons of bighorn sheep and large carnivores. *Anim. Conserv. 2*, 223–233.

Fowler, K. & M.C. Whitlock. 1999. The variance in inbreeding depression and the recovery of fitness in bottlenecked populations. *Proc. R. Soc. Lond. B 266*, 2061–2066.

Frankel, O.H. 1970. Variation, the essence of life. *Proc. Linn. Soc. NSW 95*, 158–169.

Frankel, O.H. 1974. Genetic conservation: our evolutionary responsibility. *Genetics 78*, 53–65.

Frankel, O.H. & M.E. Soulé (eds.) 1981. *Conservation and Evolution.* Cambridge University Press, Cambridge, UK.

Frankel, O.H., A.H.D. Brown & J. Burdon. 1995. *The Conservation of Plant Biodiversity.* Cambridge University Press, Cambridge, UK.

Frankham, R. 1980. The founder effect and response to artificial selection in *Drosophila.* Pp. 87–90 in A. Robertson, ed. *Selection Experiments in Laboratory and Domestic Animals.* Commonwealth Agricultural Bureaux, Farnham Royal, UK.

Frankham, R. 1983. Origin of genetic variation in selection lines. Pp. 1–18 in *Proceedings of the 32nd Annual Breeders' Roundtable.*

Frankham, R. 1990a. Are responses to artificial selection for reproductive fitness traits consistently asymmetrical? *Genet. Res. 56*, 35–42.

Frankham, R. 1990b. Contribution of novel sources of genetic variation to selection response. *Proc. 4th World Congr. Genet. Appl. Livestock Prod. 13*, 185–194.

Frankham, R. 1995a. Conservation genetics. *Ann. Rev. Genet. 29*, 305–327.

Frankham, R. 1995b. Inbreeding and extinction: a threshold effect. *Conserv. Biol. 9*, 792–799.

Frankham, R. 1995c. Effective population size / adult population size ratios in wildlife: a review. *Genet. Res. 66*, 95–107.

Frankham, R. 1995d. Genetic management of captive populations for reintroduction. Pp. 31–34 in M. Serena, ed. *Reintroduction Biology of Australian and New Zealand Fauna.* Surrey Beatty & Sons, Chipping Norton, NSW, Australia.

Frankham, R. 1996. Relationship of genetic variation to population size in wildlife. *Conserv. Biol. 10*, 1500–1508.

Frankham, R. 1997. Do island populations have lower genetic variation than mainland populations? *Heredity 78*, 311–327.

Frankham, R. 1998. Inbreeding and extinction: island populations. *Conserv. Biol. 12*, 665–675.

Frankham, R. 1999. Quantitative genetics in conservation biology. *Genet. Res. 74*, 237–244.

Frankham, R. 2000a. Modeling problems in conservation genetics using laboratory animals. Pp. 259–273 in S. Ferson & M. Burgman, eds. *Quantitative Methods in Conservation Biology.* Springer-Verlag, New York.

Frankham, R. 2000b. Genetics and conservation: Commentary on Elgar & Clode. *Aust. Biol. 13(3)*, 45–54.

Frankham, R. 2001. Inbreeding and extinction in island populations: reply to Elgar and Clode. *Conserv. Biol. 15*, 287–289.

Frankham, R. & I.R. Franklin. 1998. Response to Lynch and Lande. *Anim. Conserv. 1*, 73.

Frankham, R. & D.A. Loebel. 1992. Modelling problems in conservation genetics using captive *Drosophila* populations: rapid genetic adaptation to captivity. *Zoo Biol. 11*, 333–342.

Frankham, R. & K. Ralls. 1998. Conservation biology: inbreeding leads to extinction. *Nature 392*, 441–442.

Frankham, R. & K.E. Weber. 2000. Nature of quantitative genetic variation. Pp. 351–368 in R.S. Singh & C.B. Krimbas, eds. *Evolutionary Genetics: From Molecules to Morphology*. Cambridge University Press, Cambridge, UK.

Frankham, R., H. Hemmer, O.A. Ryder, E.G. Cothran, M.E. Soulé, N.D. Murray & M. Snyder. 1986. Selection in captive populations. *Zoo Biol. 5*, 127–138.

Frankham, R., K. Lees, M.E. Montgomery, P.R. England, E. Lowe & D.A. Briscoe. 1999. Do population size bottlenecks reduce evolutionary potential? *Anim. Conserv. 2*, 255–260.

Frankham, R., H. Manning, S.H. Margan & D.A. Briscoe. 2000. Does equalisation of family sizes reduce genetic adaptation to captivity? *Anim. Conserv. 4*, 357–363.

Frankham, R., D.M. Gilligan, D. Morris & D.A. Briscoe. 2001. Inbreeding and extinction: effects of purging. *Conserv. Genet. 2*, 279–284.

Franklin, I.R. 1980. Evolutionary change in small populations. Pp. 135–150 in M.E. Soulé & B.A. Wilcox, eds. *Conservation Biology: An Evolutionary–Ecological Perspective*. Sinauer, Sunderland, MA.

Franklin, I.R. & R. Frankham. 1998. How large must populations be to retain evolutionary potential. *Anim. Conserv. 1*, 69–71.

Fritsch, P. & L.H. Rieseberg. 1996. The use of random amplified polymorphic DNA (RAPD) in conservation genetics. Pp. 54–73 in T.B. Smith & R.K. Wayne, eds. *Molecular Approaches in Conservation*. Oxford University Press, New York.

Fuerst, P.A. & T. Maruyama. 1986. Considerations on the conservation of alleles and of genic heterozygosity in small managed populations. *Zoo Biol. 5*, 171–179.

Futuyma, D.J. 1979. *Evolutionary Biology*. Sinauer, Sunderland, MA.

Futuyma, D.J. 1998. *Evolutionary Biology*, 3rd edn. Sinauer, Sunderland, MA.

Fyfe, R.W. 1978. Reintroducing endangered birds to the wild: a review. Pp. 323–329 in S. A. Temple, ed. *Endangered Birds: Management Techniques for Preserving Threatened Species*. University of Wisconsin Press, Madison, WI.

Gagneux, P., D.S. Woodruff & C. Boesch. 1997. Furtive mating in female chimpanzees. *Nature 387*, 358–359.

Garcia-Dorado, A., C. Lopez-Fanjul & A. Caballero. 1999. Properties of spontaneous mutations affecting quantitative traits. *Genet. Res. 74*, 341–350.

Garrett, L. 1994. *The Coming Plague: Newly Emerging Diseases in a World out of Balance*. Virago Press, London.

Gentry, A.H. 1986. Endemism in tropical versus temperate plant communities. Pp. 153–181 in M.E. Soulé, ed. *Conservation Biology: The Science of Scarcity and Diversity*. Sinauer, Sunderland, MA.

Georghiou, G.P. 1986. The magnitude of the resistance problem. Pp. 14–43 in *Pesticide Resistance: Strategies and Tactics for Management*. National Academy Press, Washington, DC.

Georgiadis, N., L. Bishof, A. Templeton, J. Patton, W. Karesh & D. Western. 1994. Structure and history of African elephant populations. I. Eastern and Southern Africa. *J. Hered. 85*, 100–104.

Geyer, C. J., O.A. Ryder, L.G. Chemnick & E.A. Thompson. 1993. Analysis of relatedness in the California condor, from DNA fingerprints. *Mol. Biol. Evol. 10*, 571–589.

Gilbert, D.A., C. Packer, A.E. Pusey, J.C. Stephens & S.J. O'Brien. 1991. Analytical DNA fingerprinting in lions: parentage, genetic diversity and kinship. *J. Hered. 82*, 378–386.

Gillespie, J.H. 1991. *The Causes of Molecular Evolution*. Oxford University Press, New York.

Gilligan, D.M. 2001. Conservation genetics and long term survival: testing models using *Drosophila*. PhD thesis, Macquarie University, Sydney, NSW, Australia.

Gilligan, D.M., L.M. Woodworth, M.E. Montgomery, D.A. Briscoe & R. Frankham. 1997. Is mutation accumulation a threat to the survival of endangered populations? *Conserv. Biol. 11*, 1235–1241.

Gilligan, D.M., L.M. Woodworth, M.E. Montgomery, R.K. Nurthen, D.A. Briscoe & R. Frankham. 2000. Can fluctuating asymmetry be used to detect inbreeding and loss of genetic diversity in endangered populations? *Anim. Conserv. 3*, 97–104.

Gillings, M.R. & P. Fahy. 1994. Genomic fingerprinting: towards a unified view of the *Pseudomonas solanacearum* species complex. Pp. 95–112 in A.C. Hayward & G.L. Hartman, eds. *Bacterial Wilt: The Disease and its Causative Agent*, Pseudomonas solanacearum. CAB International, Wallingford, UK.

Gilpin, M. 1991. The genetic effective size of a metapopulation. *Biol. J. Linn. Soc. 42*, 165–176.

Gilpin, M.E. & M.E. Soulé. 1986. Minimum viable populations: processes of species extinction. Pp. 19–34 in Soulé, M.E., ed. *Conservation Biology: The Science of Scarcity and Diversity*. Sinauer, Sunderland, MA.

Ginsberg, J. 1993. Can we build an ark? *Trends Ecol. Evol. 8*, 4–6.

Gipps, J.H.W. (ed.) 1991. *Beyond Captive Breeding: Re-Introducing Endangered Mammals into the Wild*, vol. 62. Symposia of the Zoological Society of London, Oxford, UK.

Glenn, T.C., W. Stephan & M.J. Braun. 1999. Effects of a population bottleneck on whooping crane mitochondrial DNA variation. *Conserv. Biol. 13*, 1097–1107.

Goldberg, T.L. 1997. Inferring the geographic origins of 'refugee' chimpanzees in Uganda from mitochondrial DNA sequences. *Conserv. Biol. 11*, 1441–1446.

Goldstein, D.B. & C. Schlotterer. 1999. *Microsatellites: Evolution and Applications*. Oxford University Press, Oxford, UK.

Gorman, M. 1999. Oryx go back to the brink. *Nature 398*, 190.

Gottelli, D., C. Sillero-Zubiri, G.D. Appelbaum, M.S. Roy, D.J. Girman, J. Garcia-Moreno, E.A. Ostrander & R.K. Wayne. 1994. Molecular genetics of the most endangered canid: the Ethiopian wolf *Canis simensis*. *Mol. Ecol. 3*, 301–312.

Grant, B.R. & P.R. Grant. 1989. *Evolutionary Dynamics of a Natural Population: The Large Cactus Finch of the Galapagos*. University of Chicago Press, Chicago, IL.

Grant, B.S. 1999. Fine tuning the peppered moth paradigm. *Evolution 53*, 980–984.

Grant, P.R. & B.R. Grant. 1992. Demography and the genetically effective size of two populations of Darwin's finches. *Ecology 73*, 766–784.

Grant, P.R. & B.R. Grant. 1995. Predicting microevolutionary responses to directional selection on heritable variation. *Evolution 49*, 241–251.

Grant, P.R. & R.B. Grant. 2000. Quantitative genetic variation in populations of Darwin's finches. Pp. 3–40 in T.A. Mousseau, B. Sinervo & J. Endler, eds. *Adaptive Genetic Variation in the Wild*. Oxford University Press, New York.

Grant, V. 1981. *Plant Speciation*, 2nd edn. Columbia University Press, New York.

Grativol, A.D., J.D. Ballou & R.C. Fleischer. 2001. Microsatellite variation within and among recently fragmented populations of the golden lion tamarin (*Leontopithecus rosalia*). *Conserv. Genet. 2*, 1–9.

Greaves, J.H., R. Redfern, P.B. Ayres & J.E. Gill. 1977. Warfarin resistance: a balance polymorphism. *Genet. Res. 30*, 257–263.

Groombridge, J.J., C.G. Jones, M.W. Bruford & R.A. Nichols. 2000. 'Ghost' alleles of the Mauritius kestrel. *Nature 403*, 616.

Groves, C.P., C. Westwood & B.T. Shea. 1992. Unfinished business: Mahalanobis and a clockwork orang. *J. Hum. Evol. 22*, 327–340.

Guerrant, E.O.J. 1996. Designing populations: demographic, genetic and horticultural dimensions. Pp. 171–207 in D.A. Falk, C.I. Millar & M. Olwell, eds. *Restoring Diversity: Strategies for Reintroduction of Endangered Plants*. Island Press, Washington, DC.

Haig, S.M. & J.C. Avise. 1996. Avian conservation genetics. Pp. 160–189 in J.C. Avise & J.L. Hamrick, eds. *Conservation Genetics: Case Histories from Nature*. Chapman & Hall, New York.

Haig, S.M., J.D. Ballou & S.R. Derrickson. 1990. Management option for preserving genetic diversity: reintroduction of Guam rails to the wild. *Conserv. Biol. 4*, 290–300.

Haig, S.M., J.R. Belthoff & D.H. Allen. 1993. Population viability analysis for a small population of red-cockaded woodpeckers and evaluation of enhancement strategies. *Conserv. Biol. 7*, 289–301.

Haig, S.M., J.D. Ballou & N.J. Casna. 1994. Identification of kin structure among Guam rail founders: a comparison of pedigrees and DNA profiles. *Mol. Ecol. 3*, 109–119.

Haig, S.M., J.D. Ballou & N.J. Casna. 1995. Genetic identification of kin in Micronesian kingfishers. *J. Hered. 86*, 423–431.

Haig, S.M., R.S. Wagner, E.D. Forsman & T.D. Mullins. 2001. Geographic variation and genetic structure in spotted owls. *Conserv. Genet. 2*, 25–40.

Hairston, N.G.J., W. Lampert, C.E. Caceres, C.L. Holtmeier, L.J. Weider, U. Gaedke, J.M. Fischer, J.A. Fox & D.M. Post. 1999. Rapid evolution revealed by dormant eggs. *Nature 401*, 446.

Haldane, J.B.S. 1924. A mathematical theory of natural and artificial selection. Part I. *Trans. Cambridge Phil. Soc. 23*, 10–41.

Haldane, J.B.S. & S.D. Jayakar. 1963. Polymorphism due to selection of varying direction. *J. Genet. 58*, 237–242.

Halley, J. & A.R. Hoelzel. 1996. Simulation models of bottleneck events in natural populations. Pp. 347–364 in T.B. Smith & R.K. Wayne, eds. *Molecular Genetic Approaches in Conservation*. Oxford University Press, New York.

Hamer, T.E., E.D. Forsman, A.D. Fuchs & M.L. Walter. 1994. Hybridization between barred and spotted owls. *Auk 111*, 487–492.

Hamrick, J.L. & M.J.W. Godt. 1989. Allozyme diversity in plant species. Pp. 43–63 in A.H.D. Brown, M.T. Clegg, A.L. Kahler & B.S. Weir, eds. *Plant Population Genetics, Breeding, and Genetic Resources*. Sinauer, Sunderland, MA.

Hamrick, J.L. & M.J.W. Godt. 1996. Conservation genetics of endemic plant species. Pp. 281–304 in J.C. Avise & J.L. Hamrick, eds. *Conservation Genetics: Case Histories from Nature*. Chapman & Hall, New York.

Hanski, I.A. & M.E. Gilpin. 1997. *Metapopulation Biology: Ecology, Genetics and Evolution*. Academic Press, Orlando, FL.

Harris, H., D.A. Hopkinson & Y.H. Edwards. 1977. Polymorphism and the subunit structure of enzymes: a contribution to the neutralist–selectionist controversy. *Proc. Natl Acad. Sci. USA 74*, 698–701.

Harry, J.L. & D.A. Briscoe. 1988. Multiple paternity in the loggerhead turtle (*Caretta caretta*). *J. Hered. 79*, 96–99.

Hartl, D.L. & A.G. Clark. 1997. *Principles of Population Genetics*, 3rd edn. Sinauer, Sunderland, MA.

Hartl, G.B. & Z. Pucek. 1994. Genetic depletion in the European bison (*Bison bonasus*) and the significance of electrophoretic heterozygosity for conservation. *Conserv. Biol. 8*, 167–174.

Harvey, P.H., A.J. Leigh Brown, J. Maynard Smith & S. Nee. 1996. *New Uses for New Phylogenies*. Oxford University Press, Oxford, UK.

Hastings, A. & S. Harrison. 1994. Metapopulation dynamics and genetics. *Ann. Rev. Ecol. Syst. 25*, 167–188.

Hayasaka, K., T. Gojobori & S. Horai. 1988. Molecular phylogeny and evolution of primate mitochondrial DNA. *Mol. Biol. Evol. 5*, 626–644.

Hebard, F.V. 1994. Inheritance of leaf and stem morphology traits in crosses of Chinese and American chestnut. *J. Hered. 85*, 440–446.

Hedrick, P.W. 1983. *Genetics of Populations*. Science Books International, Boston, MA.

Hedrick, P.W. 1987. Genetic bottlenecks. *Science 237*, 963.

Hedrick, P.W. 1992. Genetic conservation in captive populations and endangered species. Pp. 45–68 in S.K. Jain & L.W. Botsford, eds. *Applied Population Biology*. Kluwer, Dordrecht, Netherlands.

Hedrick, P.W. 1994. Purging inbreeding depression and the probability of extinction: full-sib mating. *Heredity 73*, 363–372.

Hedrick, P.W. 1995a. Elephant seals and the estimation of a population bottleneck. *J. Hered. 86*, 232–235.

Hedrick, P.W. 1995b. Gene flow and genetic restoration: the Florida panther as a case study. *Conserv. Biol. 9*, 996–1007.

Hedrick, P.W. 1996. Bottleneck(s) or metapopulation in cheetahs. *Conserv. Biol. 10*, 897–899.

Hedrick, P.W. 2000. *Genetics of Populations*, 2nd edn. Jones & Bartlett, Sudbury, MA.

Hedrick, P.W. & S.T. Kalinowski. 2000. Inbreeding depression in conservation biology. *Ann. Rev. Ecol. Syst. 31*, 139–162.

Hedrick, P.W. & T.J. Kim. 2000. Genetics of complex polymorphisms: parasites and maintenance of MHC variation. Pp. 204–234 in R.S. Singh & C.K. Krimbas, eds. *Evolutionary Genetics from Molecules to Morphology*. Cambridge University Press, Cambridge, UK.

Hedrick, P.W. & P.S. Miller. 1992. Conservation genetics: techniques and fundamentals. *Ecol. Applic. 2*, 30–46.

Hedrick, P.W. & J.D. Parker. 1997. Evolutionary genetics of haplo-diploid organisms and X-linked chromosomes. *Ann. Rev. Ecol. Syst. 28*, 55–83.

Hedrick, P.W. & O. Savolainen. 1996. Molecular and adaptive variation: a perspective for endangered plants. Pp. 99–102 in J. Maschinski, H.D. Hammond & L. Holter, eds. *Southwest Rare and Endangered Plants: Proceeding of the Second Conference*. US Department of Agriculture, Forest Service, Rocky Mountain Forest and Range Experiment Station, Fort Collins, CO.

Hedrick, P.W., W. Klitz, W.P. Robinson, M.K. Kuhner & G. Thomson. 1991. Population genetics of HLA. Pp. 248–271 in R.K. Selander, A.G. Clark & T.S. Whittam, eds. *Evolution at the Molecular Level*. Sinauer, Sunderland, MA.

Hedrick, P.W., R.C. Lacy, F.W. Allendorf & M.E. Soulé. 1995. Directions in conservation biology: comments on Caughley. *Conserv. Biol. 10*, 1312–1320.

Hedrick, P.W., P.S. Miller, E. Geffen & R. Wayne. 1997. Genetic evaluation of the three Mexican wolf lineages. *Zoo Biol. 16*, 47–69.

Helenurm, K. 1998. Outplanting and differential source population success in *Lupinus guadalupensis*. *Conserv. Biol. 12*, 118–127.

Herbert, G., L.A. Lyons, S.J. O'Brien & S. Easteal. 1999. Patterns of primate evolution and phylogeny inferred from multiple loci in the nuclear genome. P. 24 in *Proceedings of the Seventh Annual Conference of the Society for Molecular Biology and Evolution*, Brisbane, Qld, Australia.

Heschel, M.S. & K.N. Paige. 1995. Inbreeding depression, environmental stress, and population size variation in scarlet gilia (*Ipomopsis aggregata*). *Conserv. Biol. 9*, 126–133.

Hey, J. 1999. The neutralist, the fly and the selectionists. *Trends Ecol. Evol. 14*, 35–38.

Hill, W.G. 1981. Estimation of effective population size from data on linkage disequilibrium. *Genet. Res. 38*, 209–216.

Hill, W.G. 1982. Predictions of response to artificial selection from new mutations. *Genet. Res. 40*, 255–278.

Hillis, D.M., C. Moritz & B.K. Mable. 1996. *Molecular Systematics*, 2nd edn. Sinauer, Sunderland, MA.

Hindar, K., N. Ryman & F. Utter. 1991. Genetic effects of cultured fish on natural fish populations. *Can. J. Fish. Aq. Sci. 48*, 945–957.

Hodskins, L.G. (ed.) 1997. *AZA Annual Report on Conservation and Science 1996–1997*, vol. 1. American Zoo and Aquarium Association, Silver Spring, MD.

Hoelzel, A.R. (ed.) 1998. *Molecular Genetic Analysis: A Practical Approach*, 2nd edn. Oxford University Press, Oxford, UK.

Hoelzel, A.R., J. Halley, S.J. O'Brien, C. Campagna, T. Arnbom, B. Le Boef, K. Ralls & G.A. Dover. 1993. Elephant seal genetic variation and the use of simulation models to investigate historical population genetics. *J. Hered. 84*, 443–449.

Hoffmann, A.A. & P.A. Parsons. 1991. *Evolutionary Genetics and Environmental Stress*. Oxford University Press, Oxford, UK.

Hoffmann, A.A. & P.A. Parsons. 1997. *Extreme Environmental Change and Evolution*. Cambridge University Press, Cambridge, UK.

Hogbin, P.M., R. Peakall & M.A. Sydes. 2000. Achieving practical outcomes from genetic studies of rare Australian plants. *Aust. J. Bot. 48*, 375–382.

Hohenboken, W.D., Y. Kochera & P.S. Dawson. 1991. Variability among families of *Tribolium castaneum* in inbreeding depression for fitness traits. *J. Anim. Breed. Genet. 108*, 446–454.

Holden, C. 2000. DNA test to thwart tiger trade. *Science 287*, 963.

Höss, M., M. Kohn, S. Pääbo, F. Knauer & W. Schroder. 1992. Excrement analysis by PCR. *Nature 359*, 199.

Houlden, B.A., P.R. England, A.C. Taylor, W.D. Greville & W.B. Sherwin. 1996. Low genetic variability of the koala *Phascolarctos cinereus* in southeastern Australia. *Mol. Ecol. 5*, 269–281.

Houlden, B.A., L. Woodworth & K. Humphreys. 1997. Captive breeding, paternity determination and genetic variation in chimpanzees (*Pan troglodytes*) in the Australasian region. *Primates 38*, 341–347.

Houlden, B.A., B.H. Costello, D. Sharkely, E.V. Fowler, A. Melzer, W. Ellis, F. Carrick, P.R. Baverstock & M.S. Elphinstone. 1998. Phylogeographic differentiation in the mitochondrial control region in the koala, *Phascolarctos cinereus* (Goldfuss 1817). *Mol. Ecol. 8*, 999–1011.

Houle, D., B. Morikawa & M. Lynch. 1996. Comparing mutational variabilities. *Genetics 143*, 1467–1483.

Howard, D.J. & S.H. Berlocher 1998. *Endless Forms: Species and Speciation*. Oxford University Press, New York.

Huenneke, L.F. 1991. Ecological implications of genetic variation in plant populations. Pp. 30–44 in D.A. Falk & K.E. Holsinger, eds. *Genetics and Conservation of Rare Plants*. Oxford University Press, New York.

Huey, R.B., G.W. Gilchrist, M.L. Carlson, D. Berrigan & L. Serra. 2000. Rapid evolution of a geographic cline in size in an introduced fly. *Science 287*, 308–309.

Hughes, A.L. & M. Yeager. 1998. Natural selection at major histocompatibility complex loci of vertebrates. *Ann. Rev. Genet. 32*, 415–435.

Hughes, L. 2000. Biological consequences of global warming: is the signal already apparent? *Trends Ecol. Evol. 15*, 56–61.

Hurst, L.D. & J.R. Peck. 1996. Recent advances in understanding of the evolution and maintenance of sex. *Trends Ecol. Evol. 11*, 46–52.

Husband, B.C. & D.W. Schemske. 1996. Evolution of the magnitude and timing of inbreeding depression in plants. *Evolution 50*, 54–70.

Husband, B.C. & D.W. Schemske. 1997. The effect of inbreeding in diploid and tetraploid populations of *Epilobium angustifolium* (Onagraceae): implications for the genetic basis of inbreeding depression. *Evolution 51*, 737–746.

Huttley, G.A., M.W. Smith, M. Carrington & S.J. O'Brien. 1999. A scan for linkage disequilibrium across the human genome. *Genetics 152*, 1711–1722.

Hutton, J. & B. Dixon. 2000. *Endangered Species, Threatened Convention: The Past, Present and Future of CITES*. Earthscan Publications, London.

IUCN. 1987. *The IUCN Policy Statement on Captive Breeding*. IUCN, Gland, Switzerland.

IUCN. 1996. *1996 IUCN Red List of Threatened Animals*. IUCN, Gland, Switzerland.

IUCN. 1997. *Red List of Threatened Plants*. IUCN, Gland, Switzerland.

Jaenike, J.R. 1973. A steady state model of genetic polymorphism on islands. *Am. Natur. 107*, 793–795.

James, F. 1995. The status of the red-cockaded woodpecker in 1990 and the prospect for recovery. Pp. 439–451 in D.L. Kulhavy, R.G. Hooper & R. Costa, eds. *Red-Cockaded Woodpecker: Recovery, Ecology and Management*. Center for Applied Studies, Stephen F. Austin State University, Nacogdoches, TX.

Jewell, P.A. 1976. Selection for reproductive success. Pp. 71–109 in C.R. Austin & R.V. Short, eds. *Reproduction in Mammals*, vol. 6, *The Evolution of Reproduction*. Cambridge University Press, Cambridge, UK.

Jiménez, J.A., K.A. Hughes, G. Alaks, L. Graham & R.C. Lacy. 1994. An experimental study of inbreeding depression in a natural habitat. *Science 266*, 271–273.

Johns, G.C. & J.C. Avise. 1998. A comparative summary of genetic distances in the vertebrates from the mitochondrial cytochrome *b* gene. *Mol. Biol. Evol. 15*, 1481–1490.

Johnson, M.S. & J.R.G. Turner. 1979. Absence of dosage compensation for a sex-linked enzyme in butterflies (*Heliconius*). *Heredity 43*, 71–77.

Johnston, L.A. & R.C. Lacy. 1995. Genome resource banking for species conservation: selection of sperm donors. *Cryobiology 32*, 68–77.

Johnston, P.G., R.J. Davey & J.H. Seebeck. 1984. Chromosome homologies in *Potorous tridactylus* and *P. longipes* (Marsupialia: Macropodidae) based on G-banding patterns. *Aust. J. Zool. 32*, 319–324.

Jones, D.A. & D.A. Wilkins. 1971. *Variation and Adaptation in Plant Species*. Heinemann, London.

Jones, L.P., R. Frankham & J.S.F. Barker. 1968. The effects of population size and selection intensity in selection for a quantitative character in *Drosophila*. II. Long-term response to selection. *Genet. Res. 12*, 249–266.

Joseph, L., C. Moritz & A. Hugall. 1995. Molecular data support vicariance as a source of diversity in rainforests. *Proc. R. Soc. Lond. B 260*, 177–182.

Kalinowski, S.T., P.W. Hedrick & P.S. Miller. 1999. No inbreeding depression observed in Mexican and red wolf captive programs. *Conserv. Biol. 13*, 1371–1377.

Karieva, P.M., J.G. Kingslover & R.B. Huey. 1993. *Biotic Interactions and Climate Change*. Sinauer, Sunderland, MA.

Kärkkäinen, K., V. Koski & O. Savolainen. 1996. Geographical variation in the inbreeding depression of Scots pine. *Evolution 50*, 111–119.

Keightley, P.D. 1996. Nature of deleterious load in *Drosophila*. *Genetics 144*, 1993–1999.

Kettlewell, H.B.D. 1958. A survey of the frequencies of *Biston betularia* (L.) (Lep.) and its melanic forms in Great Britain. *Heredity 12*, 551–572.

Kettlewell, H.B.D. 1973. *The Evolution of Melanism*. Clarendon Press, Oxford, UK.

Kimura, M. 1983. *The Neutral Theory of Molecular Evolution*. Cambridge University Press, Cambridge, UK.

King, H.D. 1939. Life processes in gray Norway rats during fourteen years in captivity. *Am. Anat. Mem. 17*, 1–77.

Kinnaird, M.F. & T.G. O'Brien. 1991. Viable populations for an endangered forest primate, the Tana River crested mangabey (*Cercocebus galeritus galeritus*). *Conserv. Biol. 5*, 203–213.

Kleiman, D.G., B.B. Beck, J.M. Dietz & L.A. Dietz. 1991. Cost of a re-introduction and criteria for success: accounting and accountability in the golden lion tamarin conservation program. Pp. 125–142 in J.H.W. Gipps, ed. *Beyond Captive Breeding: Re-Introducing Endangered Mammals to the Wild*. Clarendon Press, Oxford, UK.

Kleiman, D.G., M.R. Stanley Price & B.B. Beck. 1994. Criteria for reintroductions. Pp. 287–303 in P.J.S. Olney, G.M. Mace & A.T.C. Feistner, eds. *Creative Conservation: Interactive Management of Wild and Captive Animals*. Chapman & Hall, London.

Kleiman, D.G., M.E. Allen, K.V. Thompson & S. Lumpkin (eds.) 1996. *Wild Mammals in Captivity: Principles and Techniques*. University of Chicago Press, Chicago, IL.

Klein, J., A. Sato, S. Nagl & C. O'hUigin. 1998. Molecular trans-species polymorphism. *Ann. Rev. Ecol. Syst. 29*, 1–21.

Knapp, E.E. & A.R. Dyer. 1998. When do genetic considerations require special approaches to ecological restoration? Pp. 345–363 in P.L. Fiedler & P.M. Karieva, eds. *Conservation Biology for the Coming Decade*, 2nd edn. Chapman & Hall, New York.

Koenig, W.D., D. Van Vuren & P.N. Hooge. 1996. Detectability, philopatry, and the distribution of dispersal distances in vertebrates. *Trends Ecol. Evol. 11*, 514–517.

Komdeur, J. 1996. Breeding of the Seychelles magpie robin *Copsychus sechellarum* and implications for its conservation. *Ibis 138*, 485–491.

Komdeur, J., A. Kappe & L. van de Zande. 1998. Influence of population isolation on genetic variation and demography in Seychelles warblers: a field experiment. *Anim. Conserv. 1*, 203–212.

Kondrashov, A.S. & D. Houle. 1994. Genotype–environment interactions and the estimation of the genomic mutation rate in *Drosophila melanogaster*. *Proc. R. Soc. Lond. B 258*, 221–227.

Kosuda, K. 1972. Synergistic effects of inbreeding on viability in *Drosophila virilis*. *Genetics 72*, 461–468.

Kozol, A.J., J.F.A. Traniello & S.M. Williams. 1994. Genetic variation in the endangered burying beetle *Nicrophorus americanus* (Coleoptera: Silphidae). *Ann. Ent. Soc. Am. 87*, 928–935.

Kreitman, M. 1983. Nucleotide polymorphism at the alcohol dehydrogenase locus of *Drosophila melanogaster*. *Nature 304*, 412–417.

Kreitman, M. 1996. The neutral theory is dead. Long live the neutral theory. *BioEssays 18*, 678–683.

Kreitman, M. & H. Akashi. 1995. Molecular evidence for natural selection. *Ann. Rev. Ecol. Syst. 26*, 403–422.

Kulhavy, D.L., R.G. Hooper & R. Costa. 1995. *Red-Cockaded Woodpecker: Recovery, Ecology and Management*. Center for Applied Studies, Stephen F. Austin State University, Nacogdoches, TX.

Lacy, R.C. 1987. Loss of genetic diversity from managed populations: interacting effects of drift, mutation, immigration, selection, and population subdivision. *Conserv. Biol. 1*, 143–158.

Lacy, R.C. 1997. Importance of genetic variation to the viability of mammalian populations. *J. Mammal. 78*, 320–335.

Lacy, R.C. 1998. Partitioning additive, dominance, epistatic and maternal effects on reproductive performance in crosses between subspecies of *Peromyscus polionotes*. Pp. 88 in J. Sved, ed. *45th Annual Meeting of the Genetics Society of Australia Inc.* Genetics Society of Australia Inc., Sydney.

Lacy, R.C. & J.D. Ballou. 1998. Effectiveness of selection in reducing the genetic load in populations of *Peromyscus polionotus* during generations of inbreeding. *Evolution 52*, 900–909.

Lacy, R.C., N.R. Flesness & U.S. Seal. 1990. *Puerto Rican Parrot Population Viability Analysis*. Captive Breeding Specialist Group, Species Survival Commission, IUCN, Apple Valley, MN.

Lacy, R.C., G. Alaks & A. Walsh. 1996. Hierarchical analysis of inbreeding depression in *Peromyscus polionotus*. *Evolution 50*, 2187–2200.

Lacy, R.C., J.D. Ballou & J.P. Pollak. 2000. *PM2000*. Chicago Zoological Society, Chicago, IL.

Laerm, J., J.C. Avise, J.C. Patton & R.A. Lansman. 1982. Genetic determination of the status of an endangered species of pocket gopher in Georgia. *J. Wildl. Manag. 46*, 513–518.

Lahaye, W.S., R.J. Gutierrez & H.R. Akçakaya. 1994. Spotted owl metapopulation dynamics in Southern California. *J. Anim. Ecol. 63*, 775–785.

Laikre, L. & N. Ryman. 1991. Inbreeding depression in a captive wolf (*Canis lupus*) population. *Conserv. Biol. 5*, 33–40.

Laikre, L., R. Andren, H.O. Larsson & N. Ryman. 1996. Inbreeding depression in brown bear, *Ursus arctos*. *Biol. Conserv. 76*, 69–72.

Laikre, L., N. Ryman & N.G. Lundh. 1997. Estimating inbreeding in a small, wild muskox *Ovibos moschatus* population and its possible effects on population reproduction. *Biol. Conserv. 79*, 197–204.

Lambert, D.M. & C.D. Millar. 1995. DNA science and conservation. *Pacific Conserv. Biol. 2*, 21–38.

Lamotte, M. 1959. Polymorphism of natural populations of *Cepaea nemoralis*. *Cold Spring Harbor Symp. Quant. Biol. 24*, 65–84.

Land, D.E. & R.C. Lacy. 2000. Introgression level achieved through Florida panther genetic restoration. *Endang. Species Updates 17*, 99–103.

Lande, R. 1988. Genetics and demography in biological conservation. *Science 241*, 1455–1460.

Lande, R. 1995a. Mutation and conservation. *Conserv. Biol. 9*, 782–791.

Lande, R. 1995b. Breeding plans for small populations based on the dynamics of quantitative genetic variance. Pp. 318–340 in J.D. Ballou, M. Gilpin & T.J. Foose, eds. *Population Management for Survival and Recovery: Analytical Methods and Strategies in Small Population Conservation.* Columbia University Press, New York.

Lande, R. & G.F. Barrowclough. 1987. Effective population size, genetic variation, and their use in population management. Pp. 87–123 in M.E. Soulé, ed. *Viable Populations for Conservation.* Cambridge University Press, Cambridge, UK.

Lande, R. & D.W. Schemske. 1985. The evolution of self-fertilization and inbreeding depression in plants. I. Genetic models. *Evolution 39*, 24–40.

Landweber, L.F. & A.P. Dobson. (eds.) 1999. *Genetics and the Extinction of Species: DNA and the Conservation of Biodiversity.* Princeton University Press, Princeton, NJ.

Lanza, R.P., B.L. Draper & P. Damiani. 2000. Cloning Noah's ark. *Scient. Am. 87*(5), 84–89.

Latter, B.D.H. 1998. Mutant alleles of small effect are primarily responsible for the loss of fitness with slow inbreeding in *Drosophila melanogaster. Genetics 148*, 1143–1158.

Latter, B.D.H. & J.A. Sved. 1994. A reevaluation of data from competitive tests shows high levels of heterosis in *Drosophila melanogaster. Genetics 137*, 509–511.

Latter, B.D.H., J.C. Mulley, D. Reid & L. Pascoe. 1995. Reduced genetic load revealed by slow inbreeding in *Drosophila melanogaster. Genetics 139*, 287–297.

Lawton, J.H. & R.M. May. (eds.) 1995. *Extinction Rates.* Oxford University Press, Oxford, UK.

Leakey, R. & R. Lewin. 1995. *The Sixth Extinction: Biodiversity and its Survival.* Phoenix, London.

Leberg, P.L. 1990a. Influence of genetic variability on population growth: implications for conservation. *J. Fish Biol. 37 (suppl. A)*, 193–195.

Leberg, P.L. 1990b. Genetic considerations in the design of introduction programs. Pp. 609–619 in *Transactions of the 55th North American Wildlife and Natural Resources Conference.*

Leberg, P.L. 1996. Applications of allozyme electrophoresis in conservation biology. Pp. 87–103 in T.B. Smith & R.K. Wayne, eds. *Molecular Genetic Approaches in Conservation.* Oxford University Press, New York.

Leberg, P.L., P.W. Stangel, H.O. Hillstead, R.L. Marchinton & M.H. Smith. 1994. Genetic structure of reintroduced wild turkey and white-tailed deer populations. *J. Wildl. Manag. 58*, 698–711.

Ledig, F.T. & M.T. Conkle. 1983. Gene diversity and genetic structure in a narrow endemic, Torrey pine (*Pinus torreyana* Parry ex Carr). *Evolution 37*, 79–85.

Legge, J.T., R. Roush, R. DeSalle, A.P. Vogler & B. May. 1996. Genetic criteria for establishing evolutionarily significant units in Cryan's buckmoth. *Conserv. Biol. 10*, 85–98.

Lens, L., P. Galbusera, T. Brooks, E. Waiyaki & T. Schenck. 1998. Highly skewed sex ratios in the critically endangered Taita thrush as revealed by CHD genes. *Biodiver. Conserv. 7*, 869–873.

Lerner, I.M. 1954. *Genetic Homeostasis.* Oliver & Boyd, Edinburgh, UK.

Les, D.H., J.A. Reinhartz & E.J. Esselman. 1991. Genetic consequences of rarity in *Aster furcatus* (Asteraceae), a threatened, self-incompatible plant. *Evolution 45*, 1641–1650.

Lesica, P., R.F. Leary, F.W. Allendorf & D.E. Bilderback. 1988. Lack of genetic diversity within and among populations of an endangered plant *Howellia aquaticus*. *Conserv. Biol. 2*, 275–282.

Letcher, B.H., J.A. Priddy, J.A. Walters & L.B. Crowder. 1998. An individual-based, spatially-explicit simulation model of the population dynamics of the endangered red-cockaded woodpecker, *Piciodes borealis*. *Biol. Conserv. 86*, 1–14.

Lewis, W.H. (ed.) 1980. *Polyploidy: Biological Relevance*. Plenum Press, New York.

Lewontin, R.C. 1974. *The Genetic Basis of Evolutionary Change*. Columbia University Press, New York.

Lewontin, R.C. & L.C. Birch. 1966. Hybridization as a source of variation for adaptation to new environments. *Evolution 20*, 315–336.

Li, C.C. 1955. *Population Genetics*. University of Chicago Press, Chicago, IL.

Li, C.C. 1976. *First Course in Population Genetics*. Boxwood Press, Pacific Grove, CA.

Li, W.-H. & Graur, D. 1991. *Fundamentals of Molecular Evolution*. Sinauer, Sunderland, MA.

Lindenmayer, D.B. & H.A. Nix. 1993. Ecological principles for the design of wildlife corridors. *Conserv. Biol. 7*, 627–630.

Lindenmayer, D.B. & H.P. Possingham. 1994. *The Risk of Extinction: Ranking Management Options for Leadbeater's Possum using Population Viability Analysis*. Center for Resource and Environmental Studies, Australian National University, Canberra, ACT, Australia.

Little, R.M., T.M. Crowe & W.S. Grant. 1993. Does hunting affect demography and genetic structure of the greywing francolin *Francolinus africanus*? *Biodiver. Conserv. 2*, 567–585.

Liu, F., L. Zhgang & D. Charlesworth. 1998. Genetic diversity in *Leavenworthia* populations with different inbreeding levels. *Proc. R. Soc. Lond. B 265*, 293–301.

Lively, C.M. & M.F. Dybdahl. 2000. Parasite adaptation to locally common host genotypes. *Nature 405*, 679–681.

Lively, C.M., C. Craddock & R.C. Vrijenhoek. 1990. Red Queen hypothesis supported by parasitism in sexual and clonal fish. *Nature 344*, 864–866.

Loeschcke, V., J. Tomiuk & S.K. Jain. (eds.) 1994. *Conservation Genetics*. Birkhäuser, Basel, Switzerland.

Longmire, J.L., G.F. Gee, C.L. Hardenkopf & G.A. Mark. 1992. Establishing paternity in whooping cranes (*Grus americana*) by DNA analysis. *Auk 109*, 522–529.

Loope, L.L. & A.C. Medeiros. 1994. Impacts of biological invasions on the management and recovery of rare plants in Haleakala National Park, Mau, Hawaiian Islands. Pp. 143–158 in M.L. Bowles & C.J. Whelan, eds. *Restoration of Endangered Species: Conceptual Issues, Planning and Implementation*. Cambridge University Press, Cambridge, UK.

Lopez, M.A. & C. Lopez-Fanjul. 1993. Spontaneous mutation for a quantitative trait in *Drosophila melanogaster*. II. Distribution of mutant effects on the trait and fitness. *Genet. Res. 61*, 117–126.

Lopez-Fanjul, C. & A. Villaverde. 1989. Inbreeding increases genetic variance for viability in *Drosophila melanogaster*. *Evolution 43*, 1800–1804.

Ludwig, D. 1999. Is it meaningful to estimate probability of extinction? *Ecology 80*, 298–310.

Luikart, G. & J. Cornuet. 1998. Empirical evaluation of a test for identifying recently bottlenecked populations from allele frequency data. *Conserv. Biol. 12*, 228–237.

Luikart, G. & P.R. England. 1999. Statistical analysis of microsatellite DNA data. *Trends Ecol. Evol. 14*, 253–256.

Lynch, A.J.J., R.W. Barnes, J. Cambecedes & R.E. Vaillancourt. 1998. Genetic evidence that *Lomatia tasmanica* (Proteaceae) is an ancient clone. *Aust. J. Bot. 46*, 25–33.

Lynch, M. 1991. The genetic interpretation of inbreeding depression and out-breeding depression. *Evolution 45*, 622–629.

Lynch, M. 1996. A quantitative–genetic perspective on conservation issues. Pp. 471–501 in J.C. Avise & J.L. Hamrick, eds. *Conservation Genetics: Case Histories from Nature*. Chapman & Hall, New York.

Lynch, M. & B. Walsh. 1998. *Genetics and Analysis of Quantitative Traits*. Sinauer, Sunderland, MA.

Lynch, M., J. Conery & R. Bürger. 1995. Mutational meltdowns in sexual populations. *Evolution 49*, 1067–1080.

Lynch, M., J. Blanchard, D. Houle, T. Kibota, S. Schultz, L. Vassilieva & J. Willis. 1999. Perspective: spontaneous deleterious mutation. *Evolution 53*, 645–663.

MacCluer, J.W., J.L. VandeBerg, B. Read & O.A. Ryder. 1986. Pedigree analysis by computer simulation. *Zoo Biol. 5*, 147–160.

Mace, G.M. 1986. Genetic management of small populations. *Int. Zoo Yb. 24/25*, 167–174.

Mace, G.M. & R. Lande. 1991. Assessing extinction threats: towards a reevaluation of IUCN threatened species categories. *Conserv. Biol. 5*, 148–157.

Mace, G.M., T.B. Smith, M.W. Bruford & R.K. Wayne. 1996. An overview of the issues. Pp. 1–21 in T.B. Smith & R.K. Wayne, eds. *Molecular Genetic Approaches in Conservation*. Oxford University Press, New York.

Mackay, T.F.C. 1989. Mutation and the origin of quantitative variation. Pp. 113–119 in W.G. Hill & T.F.C. Mackay, eds. *Evolution and Animal Breeding: Reviews on Molecular and Quantitative Approaches in Honour of Alan Robertson*. CAB International, Wallingford, UK.

Mackay, T.F.C., J.D. Fry, R.F. Lyman & S.V. Nuzhdin. 1994. Polygenic mutation in *Drosophila melanogaster*: estimates from response to selection of inbred strains. *Genetics 136*, 937–951.

Madsen, T., B. Stille & R. Shine. 1996. Inbreeding depression in an isolated population of adders *Vipera berus. Biol. Conserv. 75*, 113–118.

Madsen, T., R. Shine, M. Olsson & H. Wittzell. 1999. Restoration of an inbred adder population. *Nature 402*, 34–35.

Maehr, D.S., R.C. Lacy, E.D. Land, O.L. Bass & T.S. Hoctor. 2001. A reassessment of Florida panther viability analysis and recovery efforts from multiple perspectives. In S.R. Beissinger & D.R. McCullough, eds. *Population Viability Analysis*. University of Chicago Press, Chicago, IL.

Magin, C.D., T.H. Johnson, B. Groombridge, M. Jenkins & H. Smith. 1994. Species extinctions, endangerment and captive breeding. Pp. 3–31 in P.J.S. Olney, G.M. Mace & A.T.C. Feistner, eds. *Creative Conservation: Interactive Management of Wild and Captive Animals*. Chapman & Hall, London.

Majerus, M.E.N. 1998. *Melanism: Evolution in Action*. Oxford University Press, Oxford, UK.

Maki, M. & S. Horie. 1999. Random amplified polymorphic DNA (RAPD) markers reveal less genetic variation in the endangered plant *Cerastium fischerianum* var. *molle* than in the widespread conspecific *C. fischerianum* var. *fishcerianum* (Caryophyllaceae). *Mol. Ecol. 8*, 145–150.

Maki, M., M. Masuda & K. Inoue. 1996. Genetic diversity and hierarchal population structure of a rare autotetraploid plant, *Aster kantoensis* (Asteraceae). *Am. J. Bot. 83*, 296–303.

Malecot, G. 1969. *The Mathematics of Heredity*. W.H. Freeman, San Francisco, CA.

Manly, B.F.J. 1985. *The Statistics of Natural Selection on Animal Populations*. Chapman & Hall, London.

Margan, S.H., R.K. Nurthen, M.E. Montgomery, L.M. Woodworth, D.A. Briscoe &

R. Frankham. 1998. Single large or several small? Population fragmentation in the captive management of endangered species. *Zoo Biol. 17*, 467–480.

Marker, L. & S.J. O'Brien. 1989. Captive breeding of the cheetah (*Acinonyx jubatus*) in North American zoos (1871–1986). *Zoo Biol. 8*, 3–16.

Marshall, D.R. & A.H.D. Brown. 1975. Optimum sampling strategies in genetic conservation. Pp. 53–80 in O.H. Frankel & J.G. Hawkes, eds. *Crop Genetic Resources for Today and Tomorrow*. Cambridge University Press, Cambridge, UK.

Marshall, T.C. & J.A. Spalton. 2000. Simultaneous inbreeding and outbreeding depression in reintroduced Arabian oryx. *Anim. Conserv. 3*, 241–248.

Marshall, T.C., P. Sunnucks, J.A. Spalton, A. Greth & J.M. Pemberton. 1999. Use of genetic data for conservation management: the case of the Arabian oryx. *Anim. Conserv. 2*, 269–278.

Martins, P.S. & S.K. Jain. 1979. Role of genetic variation in the colonizing ability of rose clover (*Trifolium hirtum* ALL.). *Am. Natur. 114*, 591–595.

Mather, K. 1973. *Genetical Structure of Populations*. Chapman & Hall, London.

Maughan, P.J., M.A.S. Maroof & G.R. Buss. 1995. Microsatellite and amplified length polymorphisms in cultivated and wild soybean. *Genome 38*, 715–723.

May, R.M. 1973. *Stability and Complexity in Model Ecosystems*. Princeton University Press, Princeton, NJ.

May, R.M. 1995. The cheetah controversy. *Nature 374*, 309–310.

Mayden, R.L. 1997. A hierarchy of species concepts: the denouncement in the saga of the species problem. Pp. 381–424 in M.F. Claridge, H.A. Dawah & M.R. Wilson, eds. *Species: The Units of Biodiversity*. Chapman & Hall, London.

Mayr, E. 1963. *Animal Species and Evolution*. Harvard University Press, Cambridge, MA.

McCauley, D.E. & M.J. Wade. 1981. The population effects of inbreeding in *Tribolium. Heredity 46*, 59–67.

McCullough, D.R. 1996. *Metapopulatons and Wildlife Conservation*. Island Press, Washington, DC.

McCullough, D.R., J.K. Fischer & J.D. Ballou. 1996. From bottleneck to metapopulation: recovery of the Tule elk in California. Pp. 375–403 in D.R. McCullough, ed. *Metapopulations and Wildlife Conservation*. Island Press, Washington, DC.

McIntosh, N. 1999. Hawaii's endangered humpback whales. *Endang. Species Updates 16*, 60–63.

McKenzie, J.A. 1996. *Ecological and Evolutionary Aspects of Insecticide Resistance*. Academic Press and R.G. Lands Co., Austin, TX.

McKenzie, J.A. & P. Batterham. 1994. The genetic, molecular and phenotypic consequences of selection for insecticide resistance. *Trends Ecol. Evol. 9*, 166–169.

McKusick, V.A. 1969. *Human Genetics*, 2nd edn. Prentice-Hall, Englewood Cliffs, NJ.

McNeely, J.A., K.R. Miller, W.V. Reid, R.A. Mittermeier & T.B. Werner. 1990. *Conserving the World's Biological Diversity*. IUCN, World Resources Institute, Conservation International, WWF-US and the World Bank, Washington, DC.

McNeill, W.H. 1976. *Plagues and Peoples*. Anchor Press, Garden City, NY.

Meagher, S. 1999. Genetic diversity and *Capillaria hepatica* (Nematoda) prevalence in Michigan deer mouse populations. *Evolution 53*, 1318–1324.

Meagher, S., D.J. Penn & W.K. Potts. 2000. Male–male competition magnifies inbreeding depression in wild house mice. *Proc. Natl Acad. Sci. USA 97*, 3324–3329.

Meffe, G.K. & C.R. Carroll. 1997. *Principles of Conservation Biology*, 2nd edn. Sinauer, Sunderland, MA.

Mejdell, C.M., O. Lie, H. Solbu, E.F. Arnet & R.L. Spooner. 1994. Association of major histocompatability complex antigens (*BoLA-A*) with AI bull progeny test results for mastitis, ketosis and fertility in Norwegian cattle. *Anim. Genet.* 25, 99–104.

Menges, E. 1990. Population viability analysis for an endangered plant. *Conserv. Biol.* 4, 52–61.

Menges, E.S. 1991. Seed germination percentage increases with population size in a fragmented prairie species. *Conserv. Biol.* 5, 158–164.

Menges, E.S. 1992. Stochastic modeling of extinction in plant populations. Pp. 253–275 in P.L. Fiedler & S.K. Jain, eds. *Conservation Biology: The Theory and Practice of Nature Conservation Preservation and Management*. Chapman & Hall, New York.

Menges, E.S. 2000. Population viability analyses in plants: challenges and opportunities. *Trends Ecol. Evol.* 15, 51–56.

Merila, J. & B.C. Sheldon. 2000. Lifetime reproductive success and heritability in nature. *Am. Natur.* 155, 301–310.

Mesta, R. 1999. Final rule to remove the American peregrine falcon from the federal list of endangered and threatened wildlife, and to remove the similarity of appearance provision for free-ranging peregrines in the continental United States. *Federal Register* 64(164), 46541–46558.

Miklos, G.L.G. & R.M. Rubin. 1996. The role of genome project in determining gene function: insights from organisms. *Cell* 86, 521–529.

Millar, C.D., C.E.M. Reed, J.L. Halverson & D.M. Lambert. 1997. Captive management and molecular sexing of endangered avian species: an application to the black stilt *Himantopus novaezelandiae* and hybrids. *Biol. Conserv.* 82, 81–86.

Millar, J.G. 1999. Proposed rule to remove the bald eagle in the lower 48 states from the list of endangered and threatened wildlife. *Federal Register* 64(128), 36453–36464.

Millar, J.S. & R.M. Zammuto. 1983. Life histories of mammals: an analysis of life tables. *Ecology* 64, 631–635.

Miller, P.M. & R.C. Lacy. 1999. *VORTEX: A Stochastic Simulation of the Extinction Process. Version 8 User's Manual*. Conservation Breeding Specialist Group (SSC/IUCN), Apple Valley, MN.

Mills, L.S. & F.W. Allendorf. 1996. The one-migrant-per-generation rule in conservation and management. *Conserv. Biol.* 10, 1509–1518.

Mills, L.S. & M.S. Lindberg. 2001. Sensitivity analysis to evaluate the consequences of conservation action. In S.R. Beissinger & D.R. McCullough, eds. *Population Viability Analysis*. University of Chicago Press, Chicago, IL.

Mills, L.S. & P.E. Smouse. 1994. Demographic consequences of inbreeding in remnant populations. *Am. Natur.* 144, 412–431.

Milne, H. & F.W. Robertson. 1965. Polymorphism in egg albumen and behaviour in eider ducks. *Nature* 205, 367–369.

Miyamoto, M.M., M.W. Allard & J.A. Moreno. 1994. Conservation genetics of the plain pigeon (*Columba inornata*) in Puerto Rico. *Auk* 111, 910–916.

Montalvo, A.M. & N.C. Ellstrand. 2000. Transplantation of the subshrub *Lotus scoparius*: testing the home-site advantage hypothesis. *Conserv. Biol.* 14, 1034–1045.

Montgomery, M.E., J.D. Ballou, R.K. Nurthen, P.R. England, D.A. Briscoe & R. Frankham. 1997. Minimizing kinship in captive breeding programs. *Zoo Biol.* 16, 377–389.

Montgomery, M.E., L.M. Woodworth, R.K. Nurthen, D.M. Gilligan, D.A. Briscoe & R. Frankham. 2000. Relationships between population size and genetic diversity: Comparisons of experimental results with theoretical predictions. *Conserv. Genet. 1*, 33–43.

Morin, P.A., J. Wallis, J.J. Moore & D.S. Woodruff. 1994. Paternity exclusion in a community of wild chimpanzees using hypervariable simple sequence repeats. *Mol. Ecol. 3*, 469–478.

Moritz, C. 1995. Uses of molecular phylogenies for conservation. *Phil. Trans. R. Soc. Lond. B 349*, 113–118.

Moritz, C., J. Worthington Wilmer, L. Pope, W.B. Sherwin, A.C. Taylor & C.J. Limpus. 1996. Applications of genetics to the conservation and management of Australian fauna: four case studies from Queensland. Pp. 442–456 in T.B. Smith & R.K. Wayne, eds. *Molecular Genetic Approaches to Conservation*. Oxford University Press, New York.

Morris, C.A. 1998. Genetics of disease resistance in *Bos taurus* cattle. *AGRI 23*, 1–11.

Morton, N.E., J.F. Crow & H.J. Muller. 1956. An estimate of the mutational damage in man from data on consanguineous marriages. *Proc. Natl Acad. Sci. USA 42*, 855–863.

Mourant, A.E., A.C. Kopéc & K. Domaniewsha-Sobczak. 1976. *The Distribution of the Human Blood Groups and Other Polymorphisms*. Oxford University Press, London.

Mousseau, T.A. & D.A. Roff. 1987. Natural selection and the heritability of fitness components. *Heredity 59*, 181–197.

Mousseau, T.A., B. Sinervo & J.A. Endler. 2000. *Adaptive Genetic Variation in the Wild*. Oxford University Press, New York.

Muir, C.C., B.M.F. Galdikas & A.T. Beckenbach. 1998. Is there sufficient evidence to elevate the orangutan of Borneo and Sumatra to separate species? *J. Mol. Evol. 46*, 378–381.

Mundy, N.I., C.S. Winchell, T. Burr & D.S. Woodruff. 1997. Microsatellite variation and microevolution in the critically endangered San Clemente Island loggerhead shrike (*Lanius lucovicianus mearnsi*). *Proc. R. Soc. Lond. B 264*, 869–875.

Murawski, D.A., I.A.U.N. Gunatilleke & K.S. Bawa. 1994. The effects of selective logging on inbreeding in *Shorea megistophylla* (Dipterocarpaceae) from Sri Lanka. *Conserv. Biol. 8*, 997–1002.

Murray, J. & B. Clarke. 1968. Inheritance of shell size in *Partula*. *Heredity 23*, 189–198.

Myers, N. 1979. *The Sinking Ark: A New Look at the Problem of Disappearing Species*. Pergamon Press, New York.

Nei, M. 1975. *Molecular Population Genetics and Evolution*. North-Holland Publishing Co., Amsterdam, Netherlands.

Nei, M. 1987. *Molecular Evolutionary Genetics*. Columbia University Press, New York.

Nei, M. 1996. Phylogenetic analysis in molecular evolutionary genetics. *Ann. Rev. Genet. 30*, 371–403.

Nei, M. & A.L. Hughes. 1991. Polymorphism and evolution of the major histocompatibility complex in mammals. Pp. 222–247 in R.K. Selander, A.G. Clark & T.S. Whittham, eds. *Evolution at the Molecular Level*. Sinauer, Sunderland, MA.

Nei, M. & S. Kumar. 2000. *Molecular Evolution and Phylogenetics*. Oxford University Press, New York.

Nei, M. & N. Takezaki. 1994. Estimation of genetic distances and phylogenetic trees from DNA analysis. *Proc. 5th World Congr. Genet. Appl. Livestock Prod. 21,* 405–412.

Neigel, J.E. 1996. Estimation of effective population size and migration parameters from genetic data. Pp. 329–346 in T.B. Smith & R.K. Wayne, eds. *Molecular Genetic Approaches in Conservation.* Oxford University Press, New York.

Nelson, M. 1995. Rediscovery of the Palo Verdes blue butterfly. *Endang. Species Bulletin 19*(6), 3.

Nesje, M., K.H. Roed, D.A. Bell, P. Lindberg & J.T. Lifjeld. 2000. Microsatellite analysis of population structure and genetic variability in peregrine falcons (*Falco peregrinus*). *Anim. Conserv. 3,* 267–275.

Nevo, E., A. Bieles & R. Ben-Shlomo. 1984. The evolutionary significance of genetic diversity: ecological, demographic and life history correlates. Pp. 13–213 in G.S. Mani, ed. *Evolutionary Dynamics of Genetic Diversity.* Springer-Verlag, Berlin, Germany.

Newman, A., M. Bush, D.E. Wildt, D. Van Dam, M.T. Frankenhuis, L. Simmons, L. Phillips & S.J. O'Brien. 1985. Biochemical genetic variation in eight endangered or threatened felid species. *J. Mammal. 66,* 256–267.

Newman, D.K. 1995. Importance of genetics on survival of small populations: genetic drift, inbreeding, and migration. PhD thesis, University of Montana, Missoula, MT.

Newman, D. & D. Pilson. 1997. Increased probability of extinction due to decreased genetic effective population size: experimental populations of *Clarkia pulchella. Evolution 51,* 354–362.

Newmark, W.D. 1995. Extinction of mammal populations in western North American national parks. *Conserv. Biol. 9,* 512–526.

Nicholas, F.W. 1987. *Veterinary Genetics.* Clarendon Press, Oxford, UK.

Nielsen, E.E., M.M. Hansen & V. Loeschcke. 1999. Genetic variation in time and space: microsatellite analysis of extinct and extant populations of Atlantic salmon. *Evolution 53,* 261–268.

Norman, J., P. Olsen & L. Christidis. 1998. Molecular genetics confirms taxonomic affinities of the endangered Norfolk Island boobook *Ninox novaeseelandiae undulata. Biol. Conserv. 86,* 33–36.

NPWS. 1998. *Wollemi Pine (*Wollemi nobilis*) Recovery Plan.* NSW National Parks and Wildlife Service, Hurstville, NSW, Australia.

Nunney, L. 1999. The effective size of a hierarchically structured population. *Evolution 53,* 1–10.

Nunney, L. & K.A. Campbell. 1993. Assessing minimum viable population size: demography meets population genetics. *Trends Ecol. Evol. 8,* 234–239.

Nusser, J.A., R.M. Goto, D.B. Ledig, R.C. Fleischer & M.M. Miller. 1996. RAPD analysis reveals low genetic variability in the endangered light-footed clapper rail. *Mol. Ecol. 5,* 463–472.

O'Brien, S.J. 1994. Genetic and phylogenetic analyses of endangered species. *Ann. Rev. Genet. 28,* 467–489.

O'Brien, S.J. & J.F. Evermann. 1988. Interactive influence of infectious disease and genetic diversity in natural populations. *Trends Ecol. Evol. 3,* 254–259.

O'Brien, S.J. & E. Mayr. 1991. Bureaucratic mischief: recognizing endangered species and subspecies. *Science 251,* 1187–1188.

O'Brien, S.J., M.E. Roelke, N. Yuhki, K.W. Richards, W.E. Johnson, W.L. Franklin, A.E. Anderson, O.L.J. Bass, R.C. Belden & J.S. Martenson. 1990. Genetic introgression within the Florida panther *Felis concolor coryi. Natl Geogr. Res. 6,* 485–494.

O'Brien, S.J., J.S. Martenson, S. Miththapala, D. Janczewski, J. Pecon-Slattery, W.

Johnson, D.A. Gilbert, M. Roelke, C. Packer, M. Bush & D.E. Wildt. 1996. Conservation genetics of the Felidae. Pp. 50–74 in J.C. Avise & J.L. Hamrick, eds. *Conservation Genetics: Case Histories from Nature.* Chapman & Hall, New York.

Oedekoven, K. 1980. The vanishing forest. *Envir. Policy and Law 6,* 184–185.

Ohta, T. 1992. The near neutral theory of molecular evolution. *Ann. Rev. Ecol. Syst. 23,* 263–286.

Ohta, T. 1996. The current significance and standing of neutral and near neutral theories. *BioEssays 18,* 673–677.

Olney, P.J.S., G.M. Mace & A.T.C. Feistner. (eds.) 1994. *Creative Conservation: Interactive Management of Wild and Captive Animals.* Chapman & Hall, London.

Oostermeijer, J. G. B. 2000. Population viability analysis of the rare *Gentiana pneumonanthe*; the importance of genetics, demography and reproductive biology. Pp. 313–334 in A.G. Young & G.M. Clarke, eds. *Genetics, Demography and Viability of Fragmented Populations.* Cambridge University Press, Cambridge, UK.

O'Ryan, C., J.R.B. Flamand & E.H. Harley. 1994. Mitochondrial DNA variation in black rhinoceros (*Diceros bicornis*): conservation management implications. *Conserv. Biol. 8,* 495–500.

O'Ryan, C., E.H. Harley, M.W. Bruford, M. Beaumont, R.K. Wayne & M.I. Cherry. 1998. Microsatellite analysis of genetic diversity in fragmented South African buffalo populations. *Anim. Conserv. 1,* 85–94.

Osborne, W.A. & J.A. Norman. 1991. Conservation genetics of corroboree frogs, *Pseudophryne corroboree* Moore (Anura: Myobatrachidae): population subdivision and genetic divergence. *Aust. J. Zool. 39,* 285–297.

Paetkau, D. & C. Strobeck. 1994. Microsatellite analysis of genetic variation in black bear populations. *Mol. Ecol. 3,* 489–495.

Paetkau, D., W. Calvert, I. Stirling & C. Strobeck. 1995. Microsatellite analysis of population structure in Canadian polar bears. *Mol. Ecol. 4,* 347–354.

Pain, S. 1998. Jungle survivor: Vietnam's unique rhinos are facing extinction. *New Scient.* (20 June), 25.

Palacios, C. & F. González-Candelas. 1997. Analysis of population genetic structure and variability using RAPD markers in the endemic and endangered *Limonium dufourii* (Plumbaginaceae). *Mol. Ecol. 6,* 1107–1121.

Pannell, J.R. & B. Charlesworth. 1999. Neutral genetic diversity in a metapopulation with recurrent local extinction and recolonization. *Evolution 53,* 664–676.

Parham, P. & T. Ohta. 1996. Population biology of antigen presentation by MHC class I molecules. *Science 272,* 67–79.

Patenaude, N.J., J.S. Quinn, P. Beland, M. Kingsley & B.N. White. 1994. Genetic variation of the St. Lawrence beluga whale population assessed by DNA fingerprinting. *Mol. Ecol. 3,* 375–381.

Paxinos, E., C. McIntosh, K. Ralls & R. Fleischer. 1997. A noninvasive method for distinguishing among canid species: amplification and enzyme restriction of DNA from dung. *Mol. Ecol. 6,* 483–486.

Paxinos, E.E., H.F. James, S.L. Olson & R.C. Fleischer. in press. Prehistoric decline of genetic diversity in a Hawaiian goose (*Branta sandvicensis*) population revealed by analysis of subfossil DNA.

Peacock, M.M. 1997. Determining natal dispersal patterns in a population of North American pikas (*Ochotona princeps*) using direct mark–resight and indirect genetic methods. *Behav. Ecol. 8,* 340–350.

Pearce, F. 1999. Counting down. *New Scient.* (2 October), 20–21.

Penn, D.J. & W.K. Potts. 1999. The evolution of mating preference and major histocompatibility complex genes. *Am. Natur. 153*, 145–164.

Polans, N.O. & R.W. Allard. 1989. An experimental evaluation of the recovery potential of ryegrass populations from genetic stress resulting from restriction of population size. *Evolution 43*, 1320–1324.

Potts, W.K., C.J. Manning & E.K. Wakeland. 1994. The role of infectious disease, inbreeding and mating preference in maintaining MHC genetic diversity: an experimental test. *Phil. Trans. R. Soc. Lond. B 346*, 369–378.

Powers, D.A., T. Lauerman, D. Crawford & L. DiMichele. 1991. Genetic mechanisms for adapting to a changing environment. *Ann. Rev. Genet. 25*, 629–659.

Primack, R.B. 1998. *Essentials of Conservation Biology*, 2nd edn. Sinauer, Sunderland, MA.

Primmer, C.R., A.P. Móller & H. Ellegren. 1996. A wide-range survey of cross-species microsatellite amplification in birds. *Mol. Ecol. 5*, 365–378.

Princée, F.P.G. 1995. Overcoming the constraints of social structure and incomplete pedigree data through low-intensity genetic management. Pp. 124–154 in J.D. Ballou, M. Gilpin & T.J. Foose, eds. *Population Management for Survival and Recovery: Analytical Methods and Strategies in Small Population Conservation.* Columbia University Press, New York.

Prober, S.M., L.H. Spindler & A.H.D. Brown. 1998. Conservation of the grassy white box woodlands: effects of remnant population size on genetic diversity in the allotetraploid herb *Microseris lanceolate. Conserv. Biol. 12*, 1279–1290.

Prosser, M.R., H.L. Gibbs & P.J. Weatherhead. 1999. Microgeographic population genetic structure in the northern water snake *Nerodia sipedon sipedon* detected using microsatellite DNA loci. *Mol. Ecol. 8*, 329–333.

Prout, T. 2000. How well does opposing selection maintain variation? Pp. 157–181 in R.S. Singh & C.B. Krimbas, eds. *Evolutionary Genetics: From Molecules to Man.* Cambridge University Press, Cambridge, UK.

Quammen, D. 1996. *The Song of the Dodo: Island Biogeography in an Age of Extinction.* Hutchinson, London.

Ralls, K. & J. Ballou. 1983. Extinction: lessons from zoos. Pp. 164–184 in C.M. Schonewald-Cox, S.M. Chambers, B. MacBryde & L. Thomas, eds. *Genetics and Conservation: A Reference for Managing Wild Animal and Plant Populations.* Benjamin/Cummings, Menlo Park, CA.

Ralls, K. & A.M. Starfield. 1995. Choosing a management strategy: two structured decision-making methods for evaluating the predictions of stochastic simulation models. *Conserv. Biol. 9*, 175–181.

Ralls, K., P.H. Harvey & A.M. Lyles. 1986. Inbreeding in natural populations of birds and mammals. Pp. 35–56 in M.E. Soulé, ed. *Conservation Biology: The Science of Scarcity and Diversity.* Sinauer, Sunderland, MA.

Ralls, K., J.D. Ballou & A. Templeton. 1988. Estimates of lethal equivalents and the cost of inbreeding in mammals. *Conserv. Biol. 2*, 185–193.

Ralls, K., D.P. Demaster & J.A. Estes. 1996. Developing a criterion for delisting the southern sea otter under the US Endangered Species Act. *Conserv. Biol. 10*, 1528–1537.

Ralls, K., J.D. Ballou, B.A. Rideout & R. Frankham. 2000. Genetic management of chondrodystrophy in the California condor. *Anim. Conserv. 3*, 145–153.

Ramsey, J. & D.W. Schemske. 1998. Pathways, mechanisms, and rates of polyploid formation in flowering plants. *Ann. Rev. Ecol. Syst. 29*, 467–501.

Ratner, S., R. Lande & B.R. Roper. 1997. Population viability analysis of spring chinook salmon in the South Umpqua River, Oregon. *Conserv. Biol. 11*, 879–889.

Raup, D.M. 1991. *Extinction: Bad Genes or Bad Luck?* W.W. Norton, New York.

Rave, E.H., R.C. Fleischer, F. Duvall & J.M. Black. 1994. Genetic analyses through DNA fingerprinting of captive populations of Hawaiian geese. *Conserv. Biol. 8*, 744–751.

Reed, D.H. & E.H. Bryant. 2000. Experimental test of minimum viable population size. *Anim. Conserv. 3*, 7–14.

Reed, D.H. & R. Frankham. 2001. How closely correlated are molecular and quantitative measures of genetic diversity: a meta-analysis. *Evolution 55*, 1095–1103.

Reed, J.Z., D.J. Tollit, P.M. Thompson & W. Amos. 1997. Molecular scatology: the use of molecular genetic analysis to assign species, sex and individual identity to seal faeces. *Mol. Ecol. 6*, 225–234.

Reeve, H.K., D.F. Westneat, W.A. Noon, P.W. Sherman & C.F. Aquadro. 1990. DNA 'fingerprinting' reveals high level of inbreeding in colonies of the eusocial naked mole-rat. *Proc. Natl Acad. Sci. USA 87*, 2496–2500.

Rhymer, J.M. & D. Simberloff. 1996. Extinction by hybridization and introgression. *Ann. Rev. Ecol. Syst. 27*, 83–109.

Richards, A.J. 1997. *Plant Breeding Systems*, 2nd edn. Chapman & Hall, London.

Richards, C.M. 2000. Inbreeding depression and genetic rescue in a plant metapopulation. *Am. Natur. 155*, 383–394.

Richman, A.D. & J.R. Kohn. 1996. Learning from rejection: the evolutionary biology of single-locus incompatibility. *Trends Ecol. Evol. 11*, 497–502.

Richter, J. 1996. New friends for the Kirtland's warbler. *Endang. Species Bulletin 21*(3), 12.

Rieseberg, L.H. 1991. Hybridization in rare plants: insights from case studies in *Cercocarpus* and *Helianthus*. Pp. 171–181 in D.A. Falk & K.E. Holsinger, eds. *Genetics and Conservation of Rare Plants*. Oxford University Press, New York.

Rieseberg, L.H. & S.M. Swensen. 1996. Conservation genetics of endangered island plants. Pp. 305–334 in J.C. Avise & J.L. Hamrick, eds. *Conservation Genetics: Case Histories from Nature*. Chapman & Hall, New York.

Roberts, R.C. 1966. The limits to artificial selection for body weight in the mouse. I. The limits attained in earlier experiment. *Genet. Res. 8*, 347–360.

Robertson, A. 1952. The effect of inbreeding on the variation due to recessive genes. *Genetics 37*, 189–207.

Robertson, A. 1956. The effect of selection against extreme deviants based on deviation or on homozygosis. *J. Genet. 54*, 236–248.

Robertson, A. 1960. A theory of limits in artificial selection. *Proc. R. Soc. Lond. B 153*, 234–249.

Robertson, A. 1962. Selection for heterozygotes in small populations. *Genetics 47*, 1291–1300.

Robichaux, R.H., E.A. Friar & D.W. Mount. 1997. Molecular genetic consequences of a population bottleneck associated with reintroduction of the Mauna Kea silversword (*Argyroxiphium sandwicense* ssp. *sandwicense* [Asteraceae]). *Conserv. Biol. 11*, 1140–1146.

Rodríguez-Trelles, F. & M.A. Rodríguez. 1998. Rapid micro-evolution and loss of chromosomal diversity in *Drosophila* in response to climate warming. *Evol. Ecol. 12*, 829–838.

Roelke, M.E., J. Martenson & S.J. O'Brien. 1993. The consequences of demographic reduction and genetic depletion in the endangered Florida panther. *Curr. Biol. 3*, 340–350.

Roelke-Parker, M.E., L. Munson, C. Packer, R. Kock, S. Cleaveland, M. Carpenter, S.J. O'Brien, A. Pospischil, R. Hofmann-Lehmann, H. Lutz, G.L.M. Mwamengele, M.N. Mgasa, G.A. Machange, B.A. Summers & M.J.G. Appel. 1996. A canine distemper virus epidemic in Serengeti lions (*Panthera leo*). *Nature 379*, 441–445.

Roff, D.A. 1997. *Evolutionary Quantitative Genetics*. Chapman & Hall, New York.

Roff, D.A. & T. A. Mousseau. 1987. Quantitative genetics and fitness: lessons from *Drosophila*. *Heredity 58*, 103–118.

Roldan, E.R.S., J. Cassinello, T. Abaigar & M. Gomendio. 1997. Inbreeding, fluctuating asymmetry, and ejaculate quality in an endangered ungulate. *Proc. R. Soc. Lond. B 265*, 243–248.

Rossetto, M., P.K. Weaver & K.W. Dixon. 1995. Use of RAPD analysis in devising conservation strategies for the rare and endangered *Grevillea scapigera* (Protaceae). *Mol. Ecol. 4*, 321–329.

Rossetto, M., G. Jezierski, S.J. Hopper & K.W. Dixon. 1999. Conservation genetics and clonality in two critically endangered eucalypts from the highly endemic south-western Australian flora. *Biol. Conserv. 88*, 321–331.

Rowley, I., E. Russell & M. Brooker. 1993. Inbreeding in birds. Pp. 304–328 in N.W. Thornhill, ed. *The Natural History of Inbreeding and Outbreeding: Theoretical and Empirical Perspectives*. University of Chicago Press, Chicago, IL.

Rumball, W., I.R. Franklin, R. Frankham & B.L. Sheldon. 1994. Decline in heterozygosity under full-sib and double first-cousin inbreeding in *Drosophila melanogaster*. *Genetics 136*, 1039–1049.

Rundle, H.D., L. Nagel, J. Wenrick Boughman & D. Schluter. 2000. Natural selection and parallel speciation in sympatric stickleback. *Science 287*, 306–308.

Russell, W.C. 1999. *The 1999 Black-Footed Ferret Studbook*. University of Wyoming, Laramie, WY.

Russell, W.C., E.T. Thorne, R. Oakleaf & J.D. Ballou. 1994. The genetic basis of black-footed ferret reintroduction. *Conserv. Biol. 8*, 263–266.

Ruwende, C., S.C. Khoo, R.W. Snow, S.N.R. Yates, D. Kwaitkowski, S. Gupta, P. Warn, C.E.M. Allsopp, S.C. Gilbert, N. Peschu, C.I. Newbold, B.M. Greenwood, K. Marsh & A.V.S. Hill. 1995. Natural selection of hemi- and heterozygotes for G6PGD deficiency in Africa by resistance to severe malaria. *Nature 376*, 246–249.

Ryder, O.A. 1988. Founder effects and endangered species. *Nature 331*, 396.

Ryder, O.A. & R.C. Fleischer. 1996. Genetic research and its applications in zoos. Pp. 255–262 in D.G. Kleiman, M.E. Allen, K.V. Thompson & S. Lumpkin, eds. *Wild Mammals in Captivity: Principles and Techniques*. University of Chicago Press, Chicago, IL.

Ryder, O.A., A.T. Kumamoto, B.S. Durrant & K. Benirschke. 1989. Chromosomal divergence and reproductive isolation in dik-diks. Pp. 208–255 in D. Otte & J.A. Endler, eds. *Speciation and its Consequences*. Sinauer, Sunderland, MA.

Ryder, O.A., A. McLaren, S. Brenner, Y.-P. Zhang & K. Benirschke. 2000. DNA banks for endangered animal species. *Science 288*, 275–277.

Ryman, N., R. Baccus, C. Reuterwall & M.H. Smith. 1981. Effective population size, generation interval, and potential loss of genetic variability in game species under different hunting regimes. *Oikos 36*, 257–266.

Ryman, N., F. Utter & K. Hindar. 1995. Introgression, supportive breeding, and genetic conservation. Pp. 341–365 in J.D. Ballou, M. Gilpin & T.J. Foose, eds. *Population Management for Survival and Recovery: Analytical Methods and Strategies in Small Population Conservation*. Columbia University Press, New York.

Saccheri, I.J., P.M. Brakefield & R.A. Nichols. 1996. Severe inbreeding depression and rapid fitness rebound in the butterfly *Bicyclus anynana* (Satyridae). *Evolution 50*, 2000–2013.

Saccheri, I., M. Kuussaari, M. Kankare, P. Vikman, W. Fortelius & I. Hanski. 1998. Inbreeding and extinction in a butterfly metapopulation. *Nature 392*, 491–494.

Saccheri, I.J., I.J. Wilson, R.A. Nichols, M.W. Bruford & P.M. Brakefield. 1999. Inbreeding of bottlenecked butterfly populations: estimation using the likelihood of changes in marker allele frequencies. *Genetics 151*, 1053–1063.

Sampson, J.F., B.G. Collins & D.J. Coates. 1994. Mixed mating in *Banksia brownii* Baxter Ex R Br (Proteaceae). *Aust. J. Bot. 42*, 103–111.

Satta, Y., C. O'Huigin, N. Takahata & J. Klein. 1994. Intensity of natural selection at the major histocompatibility complex loci. *Proc. Natl Acad. Sci. USA 91*, 7184–7188.

Schemske, D.W. 2000. Understanding the origin of species. *Evolution 54*, 1069–1073.

Schonewald-Cox, C.M., S.M. Chambers, B. MacBryde & W.L. Thomas. 1983. *Genetics and Conservation: A Reference for Managing Wild Animal and Plant Populations.* Benjamin/Cummings, Menlo Park, CA.

Schulman, F.Y., R.J. Montali, M. Bush, S.B. Citino *et al.* 1993. Dubin–Johnson-like syndrome in golden lion tamarins. *Vet. Pathol. 30*, 491–498.

Schwartz, M.K., D.A. Tallmon & G. Luikart. 1998. Review of DNA-based census and effective population size estimators. *Anim. Conserv. 1*, 293–299.

Scobie, P. 1997. *SPARKS 1.42 (Single Population Animal Records Keeping System).* International Species Information System, St. Paul, MN.

Scribner, K.T. & T.D. Bowman. 1998. Microsatellites identify depredated waterfowl remains from glaucous gull stomachs. *Mol. Ecol. 7*, 1401–1405.

Seal, U.S. 1991. Life after extinction. Pp. 39–55 in J.H.W. Gipps, ed. *Beyond Captive Breeding: Re-Introducing Endangered Mammals to the Wild*, vol. 62. Zoological Society of London, Oxford, UK.

Seal, U.S. 1992. *Aruba Island Rattlesnake (Crotalus durissus unicolor): International Symposium and Workshop on the Conservation and Research of the Aruba Island Rattlesnake: Population and Habitat Viability Assessment.* Aruba Department of Agriculture Husbandry and Fisheries, Captive Breeding Specialist Group (CBSG/SSC/IUCN), American Association of Zoological Parks and Aquariums, Apple Valley, MN.

Seal, U.S. & R.C. Lacy. 1989. *Florida panther Felis concolor conyi Viability Analysis and Species Survival Plan.* Conservation Breeding Specialist Group (SSC/IUCN), Apple Valley, MN.

Seal, U.S., E.T. Thorne, M.A. Bogan & S.H. Anderson. 1989. *Conservation Biology and the Black-Footed Ferret.* Yale University Press, New Haven, CT.

Seal, U., F. Westley, O. Byers & G. Ness. 1998. Bringing people into population and habitat viability analyses. *Endang. Species Updates 15*, 111–113.

Seddon, J.M. & P.R. Baverstock. 1998. Variation on islands: major histocompatibility complex (*Mhc*) polymorphism in populations of the Australian bush rat. *Mol. Ecol. 8*, 2071–2079.

Seebeck, J.H. & P.G. Johnson. 1980. *Potorous longipes* (Marsupialia: Macropodidae): a new species from Eastern Victoria. *Aust. J. Zool. 28*, 119–134.

Seielstad, M.T., E. Minch & L.L. Cavalli-Sforza. 1998. Genetic evidence for a higher female migration rate in humans. *Nature Genetics 20*, 278–280.

Selander, R.K. 1970. Behavior and genetic variation in natural populations. *Am. Zool. 10*, 53–66.

Serena, M. (ed.) 1995. *Reintroduction Biology of Australian and New Zealand Fauna.* Surrey Beatty & Sons, Chipping Norton, NSW, Australia.

Seymour, A.M., M.E. Montgomery, B.H. Costello, S. Ihle, G. Johnsson, B. St. John, D. Taggart & B.A. Houlden. 2001. High effective inbreeding coefficients correlate with morphological abnormalities in populations of South Australian koalas (*Phascolarctos cinereus*). *Anim. Conserv. 4*, 211–219.

Sgrò, C.M. & A.A. Hoffmann. 1998. Effects of stress combinations on the expression of additive genetic variation for fecundity in *Drosophila melanogaster*. *Genet. Res. 72*, 13–18.

Shabalina, S.A., L.Y. Yampolsky & A.S. Kondrashov. 1997. Rapid decline in fitness in panmictic populations of *Drosophila melanogaster* maintained under relaxed natural selection. *Proc. Natl Acad. Sci. USA 94*, 13034–13039.

Shaffer, M.K. 1981. Minimum viable populations size for species conservation. *Bioscience 31*, 131–134.

Shaffer, M. 1987. Minimum viable populations: coping with uncertainty. Pp. 69–86 in M.E. Soulé, ed. *Viable Populations for Conservation*. Cambridge University Press, Cambridge, UK.

Shaffer, M., L. Hood, W.J. Snape III & I. Latkis. 2001. Population viability analysis and conservation policy. In S.R. Beissinger & D.M. McCullough, eds. *Population Viability Analysis*. University of Chicago Press, Chicago, IL.

Sharp, P.M., D.L. Robertson & B.H. Hahn. 1996. Cross-species transmission and recombination of 'AIDS' viruses. Pp. 134–152 in P.H. Harvey, A.J. Leigh Brown, J. Maynard Smith & S. Nee, eds. *New Uses for New Phylogenies*. Oxford University Press, Oxford, UK.

Sherwin, W.S. & P.R. Brown. 1990. Problems in the estimation of the effective size of a population of the eastern barred bandicoot (*Perameles gunii*) at Hamilton, Victoria. Pp. 367–373 in J.H. Seebeck, P.R. Brown, R.L. Wallis & C.M. Kemper, eds. *Bandicoots and Bilbies*. Surrey Beatty & Sons, Chipping Norton, NSW, Australia.

Sherwin, W.B., N.D. Murray, J.A. Marshall Graves & P.R. Brown. 1991. Measurement of genetic variation in endangered populations: bandicoots (Marsupialia: Peramelidae) as an example. *Conserv. Biol. 5*, 103–108.

Sherwin, W.B., P. Timms, J. Wilcken & B. Houlden. 2000. Analysis and conservation implications of koala genetics. *Conserv. Biol. 14*, 639–649.

Shields, W.M. 1983. Genetic considerations in the management of the wolf and other large vertebrates: an alternative view. Pp. 90–92 in L.N. Carbyn, ed. *Wolves in Canada and Alaska: Their Status, Biology and Management*. Canadian Wildlife Service Report Series no. 45, Canadian Wildlife Service, Ottawa, Canada.

Signer, E.N., C.R. Schmidt & A.J. Jeffreys. 1994. DNA variability and parentage testing in captive Waldrapp ibises. *Mol. Ecol. 3*, 291–300.

Simmons, M.J. & J.F. Crow. 1977. Mutations affecting fitness in *Drosophila* populations. *Ann. Rev. Genet. 11*, 47–78.

Simmons, M.J. & J.F. Crow. 1983. The mutation load in *Drosophila*. Pp. 1–35 in M. Ashburner, H.L. Carson & J.N. Thompson Jr., eds. *The Genetics and Biology of Drosophila*, vol. 3c. Academic Press, London.

Simpson, G.G. 1961. *Principles of Animal Taxonomy*. Columbia University Press, New York.

Sinclair, A.R.E. 1996. Mammal populations: fluctuation, regulation, life history and their implications for conservation. Pp. 127–154 in R.B. Floyd, A.W. Sheppard & P.J. De Barro, eds. *Frontiers of Population Ecology*. CSIRO Publishing, Melbourne, VIC, Australia.

Singer, M.C., C.D. Thomas & C. Permesan. 1993. Rapid human-induced evolution of insect–host associations. *Nature 366*, 681–683.

Singh, N., S. Agrawal & A.K. Rastogi. 1997. Infectious diseases and immunity: special reference to major histocompatibility complex. *Emerg. Infect. Dis. 3*, 41–49.

Singh, R.S. & C. Krimbas. (eds.) 2000. *Evolutionary Genetics: From Molecules to Morphology*. Cambridge University Press, Cambridge, UK.

Slade, R.W., C. Moritz, A.R. Hoelzel & H.R. Burton. 1998. Molecular population genetics of the southern elephant seal *Mirounga leonina*. *Genetics 149*, 1945–1957.

Slate, J., L.E.B. Kruuk, T.C. Marshall, J.M. Pemberton & T.H. Clutton-Brock. 2000. Inbreeding depression influences lifetime breeding success in a wild population of red deer (*Cervus elaphus*). *Proc. R. Soc. Lond. B 267*, 1–6.

Slatkin, M. 1995. A measure of population subdivision based on microsatellite allele frequencies. *Genetics 139*, 457–462.

Slatkin, M. & W.P. Maddison. 1989. A cladistic measure of gene flow inferred from the phylogenies of alleles. *Genetics 123*, 603–613.

Sloane, M.A., P. Sunnucks, D. Alpers, L.B. Beheregaray & A.C. Taylor. 2000. Highly reliable genetic identification of individual northern hairy-nosed wombats from single remotely collected hairs: a feasible censusing method. *Mol. Ecol. 9*, 1233–1240.

Small, M.P., T.D. Beacham, R.E. Withler & R.J. Nelson. 1998. Discriminating coho salmon (*Oncorhynchus kisutch*) populations within the Fraser River, British Columbia, using microsatellite DNA markers. *Mol. Ecol. 7*, 141–155.

Smil, V. 1999. How many billions to go? The peaking of the population growth rate deserves wider recognition. *Nature 401*, 429.

Smith, H.G. 1993. Heritability of tarsus length in cross-fostered broods of the European starling (*Sturnus vulgaris*). *Heredity 71*, 318–322.

Smith, T.B. & R.K. Wayne. (eds.) 1996. *Molecular Genetic Approaches in Conservation*. Oxford University Press, New York.

Smith, T.B., L.A. Freed, J.K. Lepson & J.H. Carothers. 1995. Evolutionary consequences of extinctions in populations of a Hawaiian honeycreeper. *Conserv. Biol. 9*, 107–113.

Soulé, M.E. 1980. Thresholds for survival: maintaining fitness and evolutionary potential. Pp. 151–169 in M.E. Soulé & B.A. Wilcox, eds. *Conservation Biology: An Evolutionary–Ecological Perspective*. Sinauer, Sunderland, MA.

Soulé, M.E. 1985. What is conservation biology? *Bioscience 35*, 727–734.

Soulé, M.E. (ed.) 1987. *Viable Populations for Conservation*. Cambridge University Press, Cambridge, UK.

Soulé, M.E. & R. Frankham. 2000. Sir Otto Frankel: memories and tributes. *Conserv. Biol. 14*, 582–583.

Soulé, M.E. & D. Simberloff. 1986. What do genetics and ecology tell us about the design of nature reserves? *Biol. Conserv. 35*, 19–40.

Soulé, M.E. & B.A. Wilcox. (eds.) 1980. *Conservation Biology: An Evolutionary–Ecological Perspective*. Sinauer, Sunderland, MA.

Soulé, M.E., M. Gilpin, W. Conway & T. Foose. 1986. The millenium ark: how long a voyage, how many staterooms, how many passengers? *Zoo Biol. 5*, 101–113.

Spielman, D. & R. Frankham. 1992. Modelling problems in conservation genetics using captive *Drosophila* populations: improvement in reproductive fitness due to immigration of one individual into small partially inbred populations. *Zoo Biol. 11*, 343–351.

Spiess, E.B. 1989. *Genes in Populations*, 2nd edn. John Wiley & Sons, New York.

Srikwan, S. & D.S. Woodruff. 2000. Monitoring genetic erosion in mammal populations following tropical forest fragmentation. Pp. 149–172 in A.G. Young & G.M. Clarke, eds. *Genetics, Demography and Viability of Fragmented Populations*. Cambridge University Press, Cambridge, UK.

Stacey, P.B. & M. Taper. 1992. Environmental variation and the persistence of small populations. *Ecological Applications 2*, 18–29.

Stangel, P.W., M.R. Lennartz & M.H. Smith. 1992. Genetic variation and population structure of red-cockaded woodpeckers. *Conserv. Biol. 6*, 283–292.

Stanley Price, M.R. 1989. *Animal Re-Introductions: The Arabian Oryx in Oman*. Cambridge University Press, Cambridge, UK.

Stear, M.J., K. Bairden, S.C. Bishop, J. Buitkamp, J.L. Duncan, G. Gettinby, Q.A. McKellar, M. Park, J.J. Parkins, S.W. Reid, S. Strain & M. Murray. 1997. The genetic basis of resistance to *Ostertagia circumcincta* in lambs. *Vet. J. 154*, 111–119.

Steinberg, E.K. & C.E. Jordan. 1998. Using molecular genetics to learn about ecology of threatened species: the allure and the illusion of measuring genetic structure in natural populations. Pp. 440–460 in P.L. Fiedler & P.M. Karieva, eds. *Conservation Biology: For the Coming Decade*, 2nd edn. Chapman & Hall, New York.

Stenseth, N.C., K.-S. Chan, H. Tong, R. Boonstra, S. Boutin, C. J. Krebs, E. Post, M. O'Donoghue, N.G. Yoccoz, M.C. Forshhammer & J.W. Hurrell. 1999. Common dynamic structure of Canada lynx populations within three climatic zones. *Science 285*, 1071–1073.

Storfer, A. 1996. Quantitative genetics: a promising approach for the assessment of genetic variation in endangered species. *Trends Ecol. Evol. 11*, 343–348.

Strickberger, M.W. 1985. *Genetics*, 3rd edn. Macmillan, New York.

Strickberger, M.W. 1996. *Evolution*, 2nd edn. Jones & Bartlett, Sudbury, MA.

Stukely, M.J.C. & C.E. Crane. 1994. Genetically based resistance of *Eucalyptus marginata* to *Phytophthora cinamomi*. *Phytopathology 84*, 650–656.

Sukumar, R., U. Ramakrishnan & J.A. Santosh. 1998. Impact of poaching on an Asian elephant population in Periyar, southern India: a model of demography and tusk harvest. *Anim. Conserv. 1*, 281–291.

Sun, M. 1996. The allopolyploid origin of *Spiranthes hongkongensis* (Orchidaceae). *Am. J. Bot. 83*, 252–260.

Sun, M. & F.R. Ganders. 1988. Mixed mating systems in Hawaiian *Bidens* (Asteraceae). *Evolution 42*, 516–527.

Sunnucks, P. 2000a. Conservation myths. *Nature Australia*, Summer 1999–2000, 5–6.

Sunnucks, P. 2000b. Efficient markers for population biology. *Trends Ecol. Evol. 15*, 199–203.

Sunnucks, P. & N. Tait. 2001. Velvet worms: tales of the unexpected. *Nature Australia 27(1)*, 60–69.

Taberlet, P., J.J. Camarra, S. Griffin, E. Uhres, O. Hanotte, L.P. Waits, C. Dubois-Paganon, T. Burke & J. Bouvert. 1997. Noninvasive genetic tracking of the endangered Pyrenean brown bear population. *Mol. Ecol. 6*, 869–876.

Talbot, J. 1994. Record of hearing #10151. Land and Environment Court of New South Wales.

Tanaka, Y. 2000. Theoretical properties of extinction by inbreeding depression under stochastic environments. Pp. 274–290 in S. Ferson & M. Burgman, eds. *Quantitative Methods in Conservation Biology*. Springer-Verlag, New York.

Tanton, J.H. 1994. End of the migration epoch? *The Social Contract IV(3)*, 162–176.

Taracha, E.L.N., B.M. Goddeeris, A.J. Teale, S.J. Kemp & W.I. Morrison. 1995. Parasite strain specificity of bovine cytotoxis T cell response to *Theileria parva* is determined primarily by immunodominance. *J. Immunol.* 155, 4854–4860.

Tarr, C.L. & R.C. Fleischer. 1999. Population boundaries and genetic diversity in the endangered Mariana crow (*Corvus kubaryi*). *Mol. Ecol.* 8, 941–949.

Tarr, C.L., S. Conant & R.C. Fleischer. 1998. Founder events and variation at microsatellite loci in an insular passerine bird, the Laysan finch (*Telespiza cantans*). *Mol. Ecol.* 7, 729–731.

Taylor, A.C., W.B. Sherwin & R.K. Wayne. 1994. Genetic variation of microsatellite loci in a bottlenecked species: the northern hairy-nosed wombat *Lasiorhinus krefftii*. *Mol. Ecol.* 3, 277–290.

Taylor, A.C., A. Horsup, C.N. Johnson, P. Sunnucks & W.B. Sherwin. 1997. Relatedness structure detected by microsatellite analysis and attempted pedigree reconstruction in an endangered marsupial, the northern hairy-nosed wombat *Lasiorhinus krefftii*. *Mol. Ecol.* 6, 9–19.

Templeton, A.R. 1986. Coadaptation and outbreeding depression. Pp. 105–116 in M.E. Soulé, ed. *Conservation Biology: The Science of Scarcity and Diversity*. Sinauer, Sunderland, MA.

Templeton, A.R. 1998. Nested clade analyses of phylogeographic data: testing hypotheses about gene flow and population history. *Mol. Ecol.* 7, 381–397.

Templeton, A.R. & B. Read. 1984. Factors eliminating inbreeding depression in a captive herd of Speke's gazelle. *Zoo Biol.* 3, 177–200.

Templeton, A.R. & B. Read. 1994. Inbreeding: one word, several meanings, much confusion. Pp. 91–105 in V. Loeschcke, J. Tomiuk & S.K. Jain, eds. *Conservation Genetics*. Birkhäuser, Basel, Switzerland.

Terborgh, J. & B. Winter. 1980. Some causes of extinction. Pp. 119–134 in M.E. Soulé & B.A. Wilcox, eds. *Conservation Biology: An Ecological–Evolutionary Perspective*. Sinauer, Sunderland, MA.

Thomas, A. 1995. Genotypic inference with the Gibbs sampler. Pp. 261–270 in J.D. Ballou, M. Gilpin & T.J. Foose, eds. *Population Management for Survival and Recovery: Analytical Methods and Strategies in Small Population Conservation*. Columbia University Press, New York.

Thomas, C.D. 1990. What do real populations tell us about minimum viable population sizes? *Conserv. Biol.* 4, 324–327.

Thomas, D.A. & H.N. Barber. 1974. Studies on leaf characteristics of a cline of *Eucalyptus urnigera* from Mount Wellington, Tasmania. I. Water repellency and the freezing of leaves. *Aust. J. Biol. Sci.* 22, 501–512.

Thompson, J.N. 1998. Rapid evolution as an ecological process. *Trends Ecol. Evol.* 13, 329–332.

Thornhill, N.W. (ed.) 1993. *The Natural History of Inbreeding and Outbreeding: Theoretical and Empirical Perspectives*. University of Chicago Press, Chicago, IL.

Thurz, M.R., H.C. Thomas, B.M. Greenwood & A.V.S. Hill. 1997. Heterozygote advantage for HLA class-II type in hepatitis B virus infection. *Nature Genetics* 17, 11–12.

Tongue, S. 1999. Species safety nets. *Lifewatch*, Summer 1999, 12–14.

Touchell, D.H. & K.W. Dixon. 1993. Cryopreservation of seed of Western Australian native species. *Biodiver. Conserv.* 2, 594–602.

Travis, S.E., J. Maschinski & P. Kleim. 1996. An analysis of genetic variation in *Astragalus cremnophylax* var. *cremnophylax*, a critically endangered plant, using AFLP markers. *Mol. Ecol.* 5, 735–745.

Tucker, P.K. & B.L. Lundrigan. 1996. The utility of paternally inherited nuclear genes in conservation genetics. Pp. 74–86 in T.B. Smith & R.K. Wayne, eds. *Molecular Genetic Approaches in Conservation*. Oxford University Press, New York.

Tudge, C. 1991. *Last Animals at the Zoo: How Mass Extinctions can be Stopped*. Island Press, Washington, DC.

Tudge, C. 1995. Captive audiences for future conservation. *New Scient.* (28 January), 51–52.

Turcek, F.J. 1951. Effect of introductions on two game populations in Czechoslovakia. *J. Wildl. Manag. 15*, 113–114.

Van Dierendonck, M.C. & M.F. Wallis de Vries. 1996. Ungulate reintroductions: experiences with the takhi or Przewalski Horse (*Equus ferus przewalskii*) in Mongolia. *Conserv. Biol. 10*, 728–740.

van Noordwijk, A.J. 1994. The interaction of inbreeding depression and environmental stochasticity in the risk of extinction of small populations. Pp. 131–146 in V. Loeschcke, J. Tomiuk & S.K. Jain, eds. *Conservation Genetics*. Birkhäuser, Basel, Switzerland.

van Treuren, R., R. Bijlsma, N.J. Ourborg & W. van Delden. 1993. The significance of genetic erosion in the process of extinction. IV. Inbreeding depression and heterosis effects caused by selfing and outcrossing in *Scabiosa columbaria*. *Evolution 47*, 1669–1680.

Van Valen, L. 1973. A new evolutionary law. *Evol. Theory 1*, 1–30.

Varvio, S., R. Chakraborty & M. Nei. 1986. Genetic variation in subdivided populations and conservation genetics. *Heredity 57*, 189–198.

Vila, C., P. Savolainen, J.E. Maldonado, I.R. Amorim, J.E. Rice, R.L. Honeycutt, K.A. Crandall, J. Lundeberg & R.K. Wayne. 1997. Multiple and ancient origins of the domestic dog. *Science 276*, 1687–1689.

Vincek, V., C. O'Huiguin, Y. Satta, N. Takahata, P.T. Boag, P.R. Grant, B.R. Grant & J. Klein. 1997. How large was the founding population of Darwin's finches? *Proc. R. Soc. Lond. B 264*, 111–118.

Volf, J. 1999. *Pedigree Book of the Przewalski's Horse* (Equus przewalskii). Prague Zoo, Prague, Czech Republic.

Vollestad, L.A., K. Hindar & A.P. Moller. 1999. A meta-analysis of fluctuating asymmetry in relation to heterozygosity. *Heredity 83*, 206–218.

Vrijenhoek, R.C. 1994. Genetic diversity and fitness in small populations. Pp. 37–53 in V. Loeschcke, J. Tomiuk & S.K. Jain, eds. *Conservation Genetics*. Birkhäuser, Basel, Switzerland.

Vrijenhoek, R.C., E. Pfeiler & J. Wetherington. 1992. Balancing selection in a desert stream-dwelling fish, *Peociliopsis monacha*. *Evolution 46*, 1642–1657.

Vucetich, J.A. & T.A. Waite. 2000. Is one migrant per generation sufficient for the genetic management of fluctuating populations? *Anim. Conserv. 3*, 261–266.

Vucetich, J.A., R.O. Peterson & T.A. Waite. 1997. Effect of social structure and prey dynamics on extinction risk in gray wolves. *Conserv. Biol. 11*, 957–965.

Wallace, B. 1963. The elimination of an autosomal lethal from an experimental population of *Drosophila melanogaster*. *Am. Natur. 97*, 65–66.

Waller, D.M., D.M. O'Malley & S.C. Gawler. 1987. Genetic variation in the extreme endemic *Pedicularis furbishiae* (Scrophulariaceae). *Conserv. Biol. 1*, 335–340.

Walter, H.S. 1990. Small viable population: the red-tailed hawk of Socorro Island. *Conserv. Biol. 4*, 441–443.

Wang, D.G., J.B. Fam, C.J. Siao, A. Berno, P. Young, R. Sapolsky, G. Ghandour, N.

Perkins, E. Winchester, J. Spencer, L. Knuglyak, L. Stein, L. Hsie, T. Topaloglou, E. Hubbell, E. Robinson, M. Mittman, M.S. Morris, K. Shen, D. Kibum, J. Rioux, C. Nusbaum, S. Rozen, T.J. Hudson, R. Lipschutz, M. Chee & E.S. Lander. 1998. Large-scale identification, mapping and genotyping of single-nucleotide polymorphisms in the human genome. *Science 280*, 1077–1082.

Wang, J. & A. Caballero. 1999. Developments in predicting the effective size of subdivided populations. *Heredity 82*, 212–226.

Ward, R.D., D.O.F. Skibinski & M. Woodwark. 1992. Protein heterozygosity, protein structure, and taxonomic differentiation. *Evol. Biol. 26*, 73–159.

Waser, N.M. 1993. Population structure, optimal outbreeding, and assortative mating in angiosperms. Pp. 173–199 in N.W. Thornhill, ed. *The Natural History of Inbreeding and Outbreeding: Theoretical and Empirical Perspectives*. University of Chicago Press, Chicago, IL.

Wayne, R.K. 1996. Conservation genetics in the Canidae. Pp. 75–118 in J.C. Avise & J.L. Hamrick, eds. *Conservation Genetics: Case Histories from Nature*. Chapman & Hall, New York.

Wayne, R.K., N. Lehman, D. Girman, P.J.P. Gogan, D.A. Gilbert, K. Hansen, R.O. Peterson, U.S. Seal, A. Eisenhawker, L.D. Mech & R.J. Krumenaker. 1991. Conservation genetics of the endangered Isle Royale gray wolf. *Conserv. Biol. 5*, 41–51.

Wayne, R.K., M.W. Bruford, D. Girman, W.E.R. Rebholz, P. Sunnucks & A.C. Taylor. 1994. Molecular genetics of endangered species. Pp. 92–117 in P.J.S. Olney, G.M. Mace & A.T.C. Feistner, eds. *Creative Conservation: Interactive Management of Wild and Captive Animals*. Chapman & Hall, London.

WCMC. 1992. *Global Biodiversity: Status of the Earth's Living Resources*. Chapman & Hall, London.

Weber, K.E. 1996. Large genetic change at small fitness cost in large populations of *Drosophila melanogaster* selected for wind tunnel flight: rethinking fitness surfaces. *Genetics 144*, 205–213.

Weber, K.E. & L.T. Diggins. 1990. Increased selection response in larger populations. II. Selection for ethanol vapor resistance in *Drosophila melanogaster*, at two population sizes. *Genetics 125*, 585–597.

Weigensberg, I. & D.A. Roff. 1996. Natural heritabilities: can they be reliably estimated in the laboratory? *Evolution 50*, 2149–2157.

Wemmer, C., A. Thau, S.T. Khaing, S. Montfort, T. Allendorf, J. Ballou & S. Ellis. 2000. *Thamin Population and Habitat Viability Assessment*. Conservation Breeding Specialist Group (SSC/IUCN), Apple Valley, MN.

Wendel, J.F. & R.G. Percy. 1990. Allozymic diversity and introgression in the Galapagos Islands endemic *Gossypium darwinii* and its relationship to continental *G. barbadense*. *Biochem. Syst. Ecol. 18*, 517–528.

Westemeier, R.L., J.D. Brawn, S.A. Simpson, T.L. Esker, R.W. Jansen, J.W. Walk, E.L. Kershner, J.L. Bouzat & K.N. Paige. 1998. Tracking the long-term decline and recovery of an isolated population. *Science 282*, 1695–1698.

White, M.J.D. 1978. *Modes of Speciation*. W.H. Freeman, San Francisco, CA.

Whitfield, J. 1998. A saola poses for the camera. *Nature 396*, 410.

Whitfield, P., P.D. Moore & B. Cox. 1987. *The Atlas of the Living World*. Weidenfeld & Nicolson, London.

Whitlock, M.C. & K. Fowler. 1999. The change in genetic and environmental variance with inbreeding in *Drosophila melanogaster*. *Genetics 152*, 345–353.

Wilcken, J. 2001. The cost of inbreeding revisited: inbreeding, longevity and sex-ratio. MSc thesis, Macquarie University, Sydney, NSW, Australia.

Wilcove, D.S. 1994. *The Condor's Shadow: The Loss and Recovery of Wildlife in America.* W.H. Freeman, New York.

Wilcove, D.S., M. McMillan & K.C. Winston. 1993. What exactly is an endangered species: an analysis of the endangered species list, 1985–1991. *Conserv. Biol. 7*, 87–93.

Wildt, D.E. 1996. Male reproduction: assessment, management, and control of fertility. Pp. 429–450 in D.G. Kleiman, M.E. Allen, K.V. Thompson & S. Lumpkin, eds. *Wild Mammals in Captivity: Principles and Techniques.* University of Chicago Press, Chicago, IL.

Wilson, E.O. 1975. *Sociobiology: The New Synthesis.* Harvard University Press, Cambridge, MA.

Wilson, E.O. & W.H. Bossert. 1971. *A Primer of Population Biology.* Sinauer, Stamford, CT.

Wilson, M.H., C.B. Kepler, N.F.R. Snyder, S.R. Derrickson, F.J. Dein, J.W. Wiley, J. M. J. Wunderle, A.E. Lugo, D.L. Graham & W.D. Toone. 1994. Puerto Rican parrots and potential limitations of the metapopulation approach to species conservation. *Conserv. Biol. 8*, 114–123.

Wilson, P.J., S. Grewal, I.D. Lawford, J.N.M. Heal, A.G. Granacki, D. Pennick, M.T. Theberges, D.R. Voigt, W. Waddell, R.E. Chambers, P.C. Paquet, G. Goulet, D. Cluff & B.N. White. 2000. DNA profiles of the eastern Canadian wolf and the red wolf provide evidence for a common evolutionary history independent of the gray wolf. *Can. J. Zool. 78*, 2156–2166.

Wisdom, M.J. & L.S. Mills. 1997. Sensitivity analysis to guide population recovery: prairie chickens as an example. *J. Wildl. Manag. 61*, 302–312.

Wolf, C.M., B. Griffith, C. Reed & S.A. Temple. 1996. Avian and mammalian translocations: update and reanalysis of 1987 survey data. *Conserv. Biol. 10*, 1142–1154.

Woodford, J. 2000. *The Wollemi Pine: The Incredible Discovery of a Living Fossil from the Age of the Dinosaurs.* Text Publishing, Melbourne, Vic, Australia.

Woodworth, L.M. 1996. Population size in captive breeding programs. PhD thesis, Macquarie University, Sydney, NSW, Australia.

Woodworth, L.M., M.E. Montgomery, R.K. Nurthen, D.A. Briscoe & R. Frankham. 1994. Modelling problems in conservation genetics using *Drosophila*: consequences of fluctuating population sizes. *Mol. Ecol. 3*, 393–399.

Worthington-Wilmer, J., C. Mortiz, I. Hall & J. Toop. 1994. Extreme population structuring in the threatened ghost bat, *Macroderma gigas*: evidence from mitochondrial DNA. *Proc. R. Soc. Lond. B. 257*, 193–198.

Wright, S. 1931. Evolution in Mendelian populations. *Genetics 16*, 97–159.

Wright, S. 1940. Breeding structure of populations in relation to speciation. *Am. Natur. 74*, 232–248.

Wright, S. 1968. *Evolution and the Genetics of Populations*, vol. 1, *Genetic and Biometric Foundations.* University of Chicago Press, Chicago, IL.

Wright, S. 1969. *Evolution and the Genetics of Populations*, vol. 2, *The Theory of Gene Frequencies.* University of Chicago Press, Chicago, IL.

Wright, S. 1977. *Evolution and the Genetics of Populations*, vol. 3, *Experimental Results and Evolutionary Deductions.* University of Chicago Press, Chicago, IL.

Wright, S. 1978. *Evolution and the Genetics of Populations*, vol. 4, *Variability within and among Natural Populations.* University of Chicago Press, Chicago, IL.

Xu, X. & U. Arnason. 1996. The mitochondrial DNA molecule of Sumatran orangutan and a molecular proposal for two (Bornean and Sumatran) species of orangutan. *J. Mol. Evol. 43*, 431–437.

Young, A.G. & G.M. Clarke. (eds.) 2000. *Genetics, Demography and Viability of Fragmented Populations*. Cambridge University Press, Cambridge, UK.

Young, A.G. & B.G. Murray. 2000. Genetic bottlenecks and dysgenic gene flow into re-established populations of the grassland daisy *Rutidosis leptorrynchoides*. *Aust. J. Bot. 48*, 409–416.

Young, A.G., A.H.D. Brown, B.G. Murray, P.H. Thrall & C.H. Miller. 2000. Genetic erosion, restricted mating and reduced viability in fragmented populations of the endangered grassland herb *Rutidosis leptorrhynchoides*. Pp. 335–359 in A.G. Young & G.M. Clarke, eds. *Genetics, Demography and Viability of Fragmented Populations*. Cambridge University Press, Cambridge, UK.

Young, T.P. 1994. Natural die-offs of large mammals: implications for conservation. *Conserv. Biol. 8*, 410–418.

Zeckhauser, R.J. & W.K. Viscusi. 1990. Risk within reason. *Science 248*, 559–564.

Zegers, G. 2000. Genetic variability and resistance to infectious disease with particular emphasis on the major histocompatibility complex in the valley pocket gopher. PhD thesis, University of California, Santa Cruz, CA.

Zhi, L., W. B. Karesh, D.N. Janczewski, H. Frazier-Taylor, D. Sajuthi, F. Gombek, M. Andau, J. S. Martenson & S.J. O'Brien. 1996. Genomic differentiation among natural populations of orangutan (*Pongo pygmaeus*). *Curr. Biol. 6*, 1326–1336.

Zhou, K., S. Ellis, S. Leatherwood, M. Bruford & U. Seal. 1994. *Baiji Population and Habitat Viability Assessment*. Conservation Breeding Specialist Group (SSC/IUCN), Apple Valley, MN.

Index